Olympics: The India Story

Boria Majumdar
Nalin Mehta

Harper Sport
An Imprint of HarperCollins*Publishers*

First published in hardback in India by
HarperCollins *Publishers* in 2008

Published in paperback in 2012 by Harper Sport
An imprint of HarperCollins *Publishers*
Building 10, Tower A, 4th Floor, DLF Cyber City, Phase II,
Gurugram Haryana – 122002, India
www.harpercollins.co.in

2 4 6 8 10 9 7 5 3

P-ISBN: 978-93-5029-338-6
E-ISBN: 978-93-5029-509-0

Typeset in 10.5/13 American Garamond
Jojy Philip New Delhi - 15

Printed and bound at
MicroPrints India, New Delhi

Olympics: The India Story

Boria Majumdar is Senior Research Fellow at University of Central Lancashire and Adjunct Professor, Monash University, Australia. He was Fellow of the International Olympic Museum in Lausanne in 2005 and has taught courses on the Olympic Games and Olympism at the Universities of Chicago and Toronto. He will be covering the London Olympic Games for Times Now Television.

Nalin Mehta is Visiting Senior Research Fellow at the Asia Research Institute and Institute of South Asian Studies, National University of Singapore. He was Fellow of the International Olympic Museum in Lausanne in 2007. Mehta's books include the award-winning *India on Television* and, with Boria Majumdar, the best-selling *Sellotape Legacy: Delhi and the Commonwealth Games*.

Praise for the Book

'... pioneering and long awaited book ... replete with little known, lively and telling details presented in an enchanting manner ... [It] by virtue of its depth, dimension and erudition opens up fresh debates and numerous areas of research—besides being a delightful read' – *Hindustan Times*

'... this book is a triumph of Olympic proportions for both authors and the publisher and is worthy of a gold medal on its own' – *The New Indian Express*

'[This book]... is of great importance to Indian sport ... This work may well set the tone for more serious writing on Indian sport and what makes it so special. It is a relief to note that there are writers who can think beyond medals, but also about the stories of sportspersons' – *The Indian Express*

'Meticulous research and scholarly presentation of facts and figures laced with an emotional tinge are the essential ingredients of this excellent work ... The authors deserve to be complimented for taking upon themselves the onerous task of piecing together information from diverse sources ... Replete with information and anecdotes supported by statistics, this endeavour by the two authors fulfils the need for an authentic document about the history and growth of Olympism in India' – *The Hindu*

'... the first detailed history of India's Olympic experience. This is the first time that documented history has been used to tell the India Olympic story, one of sordid, self-serving politics, egos, power equations and regionalism ... it is a valuable addition to contemporary knowledge' – *India Today*

'... Majumdar and Mehta will give sports historians much to cheer about. There is no doubt that they have combed the archives with rigour ... As an academic work and a splendid primer for further research, the book is a triumph' – *Mint*

'This book by two well-known Indian sport historians is a comprehensive documentation of India's experiences in the Olympics and also explores the complex role that regional and national identities play in it' – *The Deccan Herald*

'... adds up to a well-produced holistic account of India at the Games' – *Business Standard*

'The authors have aptly summed up a few of the ills that trouble our Olympians ... A readable account which should wake up every Indian with some interest in sport' – *The Tribune*

'A well-researched effort, the book brings out some astounding details of Indian sport, its origins, the politics, passion and sacrifices' – *DNA*

'The authors, for a change, do not flog the hackneyed theory of India's failure stemming from a lack of sporting culture and because the nation is burdened with a corrupt, sporting bureaucracy. The book sees the story from a historical and cultural perspective which has so far evaded the eye of the nation's sporting cognoscenti: that both these perspectives are important in understanding India's tryst with the Olympics ... Majumdar and Mehta place their arguments well' – *Tehelka*

'... the Games to India have been about more than just sporting glory. Nationalism, factionalism, corruption India's Olympic efforts have had it all. Majumdar and Mehta's narrative is as much about the Olympics' place in India as it is about India's place in the Olympics ... The content alone earns the book its place on any sports fan's bookshelf' – *Business World*

'Majumdar and Mehta seize upon one of the most unlikely members of the "Olympic Family", as insiders like to call it, to reveal a complex and culturally specific organization that simultaneously mirrors, parallels, contradicts and defies other developments in the polity at any given time ... Majumdar and Mehta ... focus more at the meta-level and, tellingly, begin and end with early and postmodern versions of the struggle for control over Indian sport. In between those chapters they range through India's hockey success and failures; trace the complex rise of other sports; see sport at the centre of non-aligned movement strategy for both Nehru and Indira Gandhi; slot the rise of the media via radio and television as key components in the story; and see modern Indian Olympism struggling against media-savvy sports, especially cricket ... the spread is excellent, the information marvellous, the interpretation satisfying ... This book will be well-cited and, more importantly, will spring a lot more studies to give us even more insight than we have now' – *Biblio: A Review of Books*

For John MacAloon and Bruce Kidd—the two people who inducted me into Olympic Studies

—Boria Majumdar

For my late grandfather who came out of retirement to help organize the 1982 Asiad and gave me my first memory of Appu

—Nalin Mehta

Contents

Preface to the Second Edition

The Tricolour since Beijing: Indian Sport, Olympism and Nationalism

When Sir Dorabji Tata organized the first modern meet of Indian athletes with an eye on the 1920 Antwerp Olympic Games, he found that despite running barefoot, their performance compared 'well with the times done in Europe or elsewhere'. Suitably impressed, Tata personally financed three of the best runners for Antwerp, a move that in his own words 'fired the ambition of the nationalist element in the city'.[1] Eighty-nine years after that wind-swept day in Pune, when Tata first dreamt of an individual Olympic gold for India, shooting prodigy Abhinav Bindra finally found the Holy Grail in the 2008 Beijing Games. As the Indian tricolour was hoisted in Beijing, the poise and pride on the bespectacled shooter's visage spoke to a billion Indians, becoming a leitmotif of gung-ho chest thumping in media commentaries and nationalist iconography. In a country undergoing a media revolution like no other—India now has about 700 satellite TV networks, more than 300 of which broadcast news—the Beijing victory created an unprecedented national frenzy.[2] In a country of a billion, and a competitive media industry looking for new heroes and new stories, the lone gold medal was justification enough to spark off celebrations worthy of topping the medals tally.

This book was written and first published in India just before the 2008 Beijing Games and the Indian performance necessitated a suitable Afterword. It was added in the updated version published by Routledge in the Beijing aftermath in April 2009. With London just months away and promising to be a defining moment in the history of India's Olympic sport, a further revised and updated edition was a necessity. Here it is.

For Indian sport, Beijing and the years that followed proved to be a watershed. Beijing 2008 was much more than a sporting spectacle not just because India's performance was its best ever at the Games but also because it heralded the promise of a new beginning for Indian sports. Bindra was not an aberration. His performance was followed by near-podium finishes in badminton, tennis and archery and the gains have been consolidated since, written about at length in the chapter on Indian sport later on in the book. Just when it was turning out to be a tale of so near yet so far in China, Vijender Kumar (bronze in boxing, 75 kg) and Sushil Kumar (bronze in wrestling, 66 kg freestyle) ensured that the Indian tricolour went up twice more at Beijing. Their achievements, analysed for hours on television, turned them into national celebrities overnight. If the media catharsis that followed was any indication, for the first time, Olympic sports, apart from hockey, was at the centre stage of what could be termed as the national consciousness.

It was an indication that decades of ill treatment and neglect, which had reduced Olympic sport to a footnote in India, might just change. At a time when the country was reeling under the impact of serial blasts in Gujarat and Karnataka, the medal successes helped emphasize the point that across contexts and timeframes an Olympic gold can catapult sport to the forefront of a nation's imagination. Three major themes emerged in the discourse that followed: renewed media focus on Olympism as a nationalist playing field, the promise of a new Indian Olympic culture and the fear that without systemic change in Indian sporting structures, this would be yet another false dawn.

For the first time in Indian Olympic history, the media appropriated these accomplishments in a manner associated commonly with cricket. All of a sudden, Bindra was flooded with sponsorship offers that had long since been reserved for over-pampered cricket stars alone. A poll on Times Now, India's most popular English TV news channel, revealed that the national religion of cricket had slid in the popularity charts. According to the survey, 53 per cent of sports fans in Chennai and 44 per cent in Kolkata were glued to the Olympics. In contrast, 41 per cent of sports fans in Chennai and 29 per cent in Kolkata watched the Indian cricket team in action against the Sri Lankans. In Mumbai, an amazing 64 per cent of the fans interviewed were unaware of the cricket series between India and Sri Lanka.[3]

The medal haul—by Indian standards—it seemed, had suddenly woken up the country to the significance of the Olympics as an event that Indians could win at as well.

The medal winners seemed to satisfy a national yearning and in the process made a statement about the significance of sport in an era of escalating political turmoil. Olympic success, the victories demonstrated, held the promise of uniting Indians across the country. With some of India's greatest sporting achievements at the Olympics coming at a time when the nation was seeking answers to sudden terror attacks, their impact was all the more visible. In the days before the Olympic Games, most Indians were grappling with the political crisis at hand and were hardly concerned about what the small contingent of 56 could achieve in Beijing. So much so that Suresh Kalmadi, then President of the Indian Olympic Association (IOA) and now facing serious charges for alleged misappropriation of CWG 2010 funds, had issued a statement asking sports fans not to expect miracles from the athletes. Set against this backdrop of gloom and limited expectations, India's successes shone even brighter.

The success of the three Beijing winners was as much a testament to their own skills as it was a metaphor for the larger story of India. They had arguably shattered the grand narrative of failure that has characterized Indian sport just as the emergence of the IT industry in the 1990s signified the end of the 'Hindu rate of growth' that defined the economy since the 1950s. Just as a Narayan Murthy or an Azim Premji—founders of the IT giants Infosys and Wipro—created the self-belief for Indian business to act as a global player after decades of isolationism and the license-permit raj, so did the Beijing victories usher in a new era of self-confidence in sport. As John MacAloon argues, the Olympics are a 'crucible of symbolic force' into which the world pours its energies and a stage upon which, every four years, it plays 'out its hopes and its terrors'.[4] For every Indian, that terror always came in the form of a question: A billion people and no gold medal. Why? Beijing provided that answer, and hence the nationalist frenzy that ensued.

The annals of Indian sports writing have been full of complaints about sporting failures for far too long. Analysts have blamed the system, they have blamed the politicians who run it, they have even questioned Indian genetics. Every four years, it has become a collective national ritual to blame everyone else when found wanting in the global mirror of the Olympics, only to move on and repeat the same catharsis four years later. The Beijing athletes showed that it is possible to succeed in spite of the system. The BJP's late General Secretary and former Cabinet minister Pramod Mahajan once said only half-jokingly that the Indian IT and beauty industries rose to great heights only because the government did not realize their presence until they had already made a mark.

Abhinav Bindra's success too followed a similar template, at least with respect to the national sporting superstructure. Born with the luxury of affluence and an indoor shooting range in his backyard, he emerged as a child prodigy, only to taste initial defeat at Sydney and Athens. He could as easily have given up, blamed the system and have been content with his World Championship and Commonwealth Games medals. But he persevered. His was a victory born out of the pain of loss and an iron will to succeed. Here at last was India's answer to those who point to the success of Surinam's Anthony Nesty or that of the Ethiopian runners, for that matter. It is indeed possible to succeed without access to government-sponsored sporting facilities. This is not to argue against creating efficient systems—that would be a terrible folly—but in sports there are moments when all it boils down to is self-belief.

Did Beijing mark the arrival of a national Olympic culture? The three medals won at Beijing were certainly the catalyst to help correct years of frustration at India's poor sporting performances. With various state governments setting up academies to promote boxing, wrestling and shooting, India looked poised to have an Olympic sporting culture of its own, a belief further consolidated by India's performances at the 2010 Commonwealth Games and the subsequent Asian Games at Guangzhou.

Beijing was no flash-in-the-pan success. Bindra, for instance, was only part of a phalanx of world-class Indian shooters that have emerged in the past decade. Beijing was his moment but each member of the

Indian shooting team was capable of winning a medal. Similarly, Vijender Kumar was part of a boxing team where his compatriot Akhil, and not him, was tipped for a medal in the run-up to the Games. His defeat of the reigning world champion, Russian Sergei Vodapoyanov, in the 54 kg pre-quarterfinal round turned him into a national hero before he crashed out in the quarter finals, just like his 19-year old roommate Jitender Kumar, who fought valiantly despite ten stitches on his chin. This is the terrifying beauty of sport, its unpredictability. This is why we watch it—because it showcases all that is glorious and tragic about human nature, all that is uncertain and indescribable. The key for the future is to invest in having enough people at the top echelon of any sport, for one to click when the moment comes.

What now of the future? There are many in India who look longingly across the border at China's awe-inspiring sporting machine. The Chinese too built their success by focusing on key sports initially —gymnastics, table tennis, badminton and athletics. India, however, cannot hope to replicate the Chinese model blindly. The organization of Indian sport is far too complicated and far too political to allow for a uni-linear approach like the Chinese or the East Europeans before them.[5] Like Indian democracy, Indian sport too has evolved its own unique model, distinct from everyone else.

When Kapil Dev's unfancied team won the cricket World Cup in 1983, no one could have predicted that the surprise victory, coinciding with the television revolution, would ignite deeper processes that would ultimately turn India into the spiritual and financial heart of the global game. Successes at Beijing, Delhi and Gunagzhou have created opportunities that if harnessed well could well usher in a new era in Indian sport. As Bindra grabbed gold and the boxers charged through the early rounds, for the first time, a national television audience, led on by a cheerleading media focused on Olympic sports.

The fact that the entire boxing team had emerged from the small north-Indian town of Bhiwani with few facilities or that Sushil Kumar had trained in Delhi's Chatrasal stadium with rotting wresting mats and twenty other wrestlers as room-mates provided too irresistible a story of human triumph against all odds. The hype was such that even the Haryana chief minister turned up at Vijender's house to watch his semifinal bout. It was a televised photo opportunity for the politician but also an event that led government officials to build a new paved road overnight to show their boss that developmental schemes were working. Similarly, the Delhi chief minister immediately announced a huge cash award for Sushil Kumar on his return to India.

When K.D. Jadhav won India's last wrestling medal at the Helsinki Olympics in 1952 the celebrations at home were extremely muted, restricted to the sports pages of newspapers unlike the mega hype around Sushil Kumar and the new phalanx of Indian boxers. To compound Jadhav's agony, the political class gave the victorious hockey team of 1952 a tumultuous welcome in ceremonies across the country while he had to make do with a localized cavalcade of a hundred bullock carts from his native village. In 1952, hockey was a potent symbol of Indian nationalism and Jadhav despite winning independent India's first individual Olympic medal was left to ultimately die in poverty. He was forced to sell off his wife's jewels to build a modest cottage and won a posthumous Arjuna award only in 2001. In sharp contrast, governmental coffers opened up for the Kumars after Beijing. Even more so, in a nation starved of sporting glory, the intense media focus on the Beijing and Guangzhou battlers turned them into new nationalist heroes. Clearly, the registers of iconicity have changed in the intervening years, with individual success becoming an important barometer of nationalist triumph.

What explains the change? Let us be clear: this is not necessarily about some newly found love or understanding of sports. There is a marked disconnect between the hype about a resurgent India that the Beijing, Delhi and the Guangzhou boys supposedly represent and the reality. On the morning Sushil Kumar won the bronze medal, most media outlets carried online stories saying he had 'crashed out' of the Olympics. There was an even an undertone that he had somehow wasted his first round bye. Few, at least on television or in the immediate internet discourse, remembered the repechage rule until the Jat from Najafgarh pleasantly shocked the nation with his marathon string of victories to clinch bronze.

Television helped in the creation of a national public focused on boxing, a process that has gained in momentum since with Indian boxers regularly winning at the world stage. A caveat, however, is in order here. While celebrating their achievements, it is important to remember that the boxers have emerged from a town which goes sometimes for days without electricity, where the rains have made it impossible to drive a car faster than 5 km/hour on most roads and where most people had to rely on inverters to watch the home boys win. In such a setting, sport has emerged as a way out for many. The real success of Bhiwani lies in the rock-solid confidence of the new generation of athletes and a nascent public-private partnership which has allowed them to transcend a system used to mediocrity. They have not been content to merely repeat the past and this is the new Indian spirit that needs to be celebrated.

Like K.D. Jadhav sixty years ago, virtually every winning athlete from Bhiwani in the past—at the Commonwealth Games, the Asiad and the SAF Games—has been welcomed home by celebratory motorcades of locals, except that they were rarely noticed by the mainstream press. Perhaps, the next time this will change, with a more concerted national focus on sport—an approach where the likes of Akhil Kumar who did not win are not forgotten.

In an atmosphere of relative optimism, a note of caution is necessary. India's sporting system needs an overhaul and the years since Beijing have created a possibility for such a change to come about. However, unless the government, sports administrators, the IOA, and, finally, the corporates come forward to embrace Olympic sport, Beijing 2008 will remain an aberration. Private efforts such as the Mittal Champions Trust and Olympic Gold Quest must contribute more towards Indian sport. Tough questions need to be asked. What happened, for instance, to the Indian Army's celebrated Mission Olympics and why couldn't it be integrated with the larger national effort?

While India celebrates Bhiwani for what it has done to place boxing on the national map, it is time to replicate such achievements across the country. With boxing being a television-friendly sport and with 24-hour television channels multiplying almost daily, the media would surely embrace boxing if properly marketed and managed. With such a systemic overhaul, India can expect more medals in boxing in the 2012 Games and Vijender's bronze will then have the significance of being more than an Olympic medal in the overall sporting context.

If India fails to take advantage of the fertile condition created by

Beijing and its aftermath, its lasting legacy will have been confined to sports history books by the end of London 2012.

To finish off with an interesting story: A senior journalist had asked Abhinav on his return to India: 'Is this Abhinav's gold or India's gold?' Abhinav, epitome of political correctness, was quick to suggest that it was India's without question. India has a real chance of winning medals in at least six disciplines at London, and if that happens, it will certainly be India's gold for all time. However, if London 2012 doesn't go to plan, Abhinav's gold will forever remain his, a moment of individual brilliance lost amidst countless failures since independence.

ENDNOTES

1. Nalin Mehta, 'Smile, Sir Dorabji', *The Indian Express*, 12 August 2008.
2. For the astonishing expansion of Indian satellite television see Nalin Mehta, *India on Television: How Satellite News Channels Changes the Way We Think and Act* (New Delhi: Harper Collins, 2008). For the massive expansion of the Indian newspaper industry and its 'mass-ification' see Robin Jeffrey, *India's Newspaper Revolution: Capitalism, Politics and the Indian Language Press* (New Delhi: Oxford University Press, 2003, 2nd ed.)
3. Boria Majumdar, 'Seize this moment', *The Times of India*, 25 August 2008.
4. Quoted in Nalin Mehta, 'Smile, Sir Dorabji', *The Indian Express*, 12 August 2008.
5. For the Chinese model of sporting success see, for instance, Fan Hong, Duncan Mackay, Karen Christensen (eds), *China Gold: China's Quest for Olympic and Global Glory* (Great Barrington, M.A.: Berkshire, 2008).
6. On current form, India can realistically expect medals in shooting, tennis, boxing, archery, badminton and wrestling.

Acknowledgements

We would like to thank the staff of the IOC Olympic Studies Center at Lausanne, Switzerland, for unlimited access to the IOC archives. We are grateful especially to Nuria Puig, Philleppe Blanchard, Ruth Beck Perrenoud and Patricia Eckert for accommodating our requests at extremely short notice. Former President Juan Antonio Samaranch was kind enough to give us time, which helped clarify several doubts. Randhir Singh, Secretary General of the IOA has been a constant source of support. Yaduraj Singh and Shiv Kumar Sharma at the IOA helped us with unlimited access to the archive and Rajesh Tomar helped us with details whenever we were in need of clarification.

We are also indebted to the staff of the International Olympic Academy in Olympia, Greece; Wayne Wilson, Director of the Amateur Athletic Federation, Los Angeles; the National Library in Kolkata; the National Archives and Teen Murti Library in Delhi. Our research assistants Sabyasachi Mallick and Tupur Chattopadhyay have done a fabulous job chasing leads at short notice.

Milkha Singh, Leander Paes, P.K. Banerjee, P.T. Usha, Manavjit Singh, Rajyavardhan Rathore and Gulu Ezekiel were always willing to share their experiences and tell us more. Karl Lennartz, President of the Association of Olympic Historians, was a great help when we met him in Beijing. His, we are certain, remains the best personal collection on Olympism in the world.

A special thanks to Prof. John Macaloon, colleague at the University of Chicago, for pointing us to the IOC archive at Lausanne. Without his initiative this research would not have happened.

We greatly appreciate the support of our publisher, and friend, V.K. Karthika. Not only had Karthika encouraged us to do the first edition in 2008 but when asked if she'd be interested in an updated revised edition on the eve of London, she was every bit as keen as was Shantanu. We appreciate their help at every step.

Finally, we are most grateful to our families for standing by at moments of difficulty and supporting all our endeavours.

Nitika and Sharmistha remain our biggest inspiration and also our most severe critics. For the many nights of reading they have put in, taking time off their own work, we will always remain indebted.

BORIA MAJUMDAR
London,
April 2012

NALIN MEHTA
Singapore,
April 2012

Prologue

'History consists of the corpus of ascertainable facts. The facts are available to the historian in documents, inscriptions and so on, like fish on the monger's slab. The historian collects them, takes them home, and cooks and serves them in whatever style appeals to him.' So writes E.H. Carr in *What is History*? Carr goes on to define history as 'an unending dialogue between the past and the present'; for him the chief function of the historian 'is to master and understand the past as a key to understand the present.' That key, though, is of use only if there is a lock it can fit into, secrets it can prise open, lost stories it can resurrect.

At a time when historians around the world are increasingly recognizing global stories of Olympism as crucial to understand the working of societies, there has been no detailed history of India's Olympic experience. This is a glaring anomaly for a country that became the first colonized nation to join the Olympic movement, one that dazzled the world with its early hockey wins and one whose Olympic history contains within its folds hitherto unknown chapters of the development of Indian nationalism and identity. So far, however, historians of Indian sport, or more specifically historians of Olympism, have met an insurmountable barrier as they sought to decipher the Indian story. To unlock the past and to achieve what Carr has outlined above, the historian needs to have at his or her disposal the best and most authentic of sources, that is, letters, artefacts, photographs, correspondence and private papers containing information on the history of the Games in India, from its inception in the early 20th century. Yet, until now, little material of this kind has been available in the public domain. All that we have had so far are memoirs of a few hockey players—Dhyan Chand, Aslam Sher Khan—and books written on the achievements of some rare Indians on the Olympic stage by sports writers.[1] By themselves, these are invaluable, but they are not enough to piece together a comprehensive and complete history.

In that sense, this monograph is unique because it is built on an as yet virgin archive of Indian history. For the first time we had unlimited access to the hitherto inaccessible 'official' archive of the International Olympic Committee at the IOC museum in Lausanne, Switzerland, an archive that contains virtually every piece of correspondence ever exchanged between Indian sports, administrators and the IOC, alongside much more. As such, it was like hoping to find Alladin's lamp and finding not just the magic lamp, but Alladin's cave as well. The treasure trove of material we uncovered in the vaults of the IOC forms the nuts and bolts of the story that we have pieced together.

Some things are destined to happen. This monograph was one such. Neither of us started our academic careers as historians of Olympism or the Olympic movement. Yet, in our view, this monograph has come together with consummate ease; not because we have some special expertise, but because the material we found locked up in the archives was in part self-explanatory. Ticking away in the air-conditioned chambers of the Olympic museum, exciting but forgotten moments of Indian sport leapt up at us from the dusty files. Filed away with Swiss precision, all they needed was meticulous analysis. The material was so complete, we are confident that this is not only the first, but also the most eclectic history of India's Olympic encounter. How it came together is in itself a lesson in the vagaries of history writing, the beauty of the chance encounter that leads to vital clues and the element of good luck that all historians sometimes need to uncover the right trail.

On the IOC's Trail: Discovering the Archive

The book is entirely the product of a decision in the mid-1990s by the International Olympic Committee to set up a public archive for scholars, in the guise of the Olympic Studies Center at Lausanne, Switzerland. It was a rare gesture for an institution of this nature. The IOC has also taken the initiative to encourage scholars from around the world to make use of the resource. Funding scholars to dig into this fascinating archive, the IOC has tried to live up to the declared ideals of the centre, to 'preserve and disseminate the collective memory of the Olympic movement and to coordinate and promote research, teaching and publications about Olympism'. Yet, no Indian scholar had ever dug into the centre's resources before. This is not surprising since the IOC's fellowship programme is of rather recent vintage and not too well known outside sport history departments in the West where Olympic studies is now among the fastest growing disciplines. For us, it boiled down to a fortuitous, chance suggestion to apply for the fellowship. I was teaching at the University of Chicago in early 2004 when John Macaloon, one of the leading scholars of Olympism, suggested that I apply for the fellowship. It tickled my curiosity, as it would add to the cricket and football stories that I had retold in print over the years.

As fellows of the museum, with total access to the archive it has been a matter of great satisfaction personally to be able to document this story. We are extremely confident that as more Indian scholars find their way to this unique archive in the future, our efforts will be revised and subsequently improved upon.

Lausanne: The Thrill of Discovery

By the banks of Lake Geneva, the IOC Museum makes a wonderfully picturesque setting. It is post-card Switzerland: the Alps all around, rural France across the lake and the pristine mountainous air. Could it be possible that this building, Juan Antonio Samaranch's last gift to the IOC before he quit office, situated so far from the dusty playing fields of India, contained the real answers to the riddles that plague India's Olympic story? Why did Indian hockey rise the way it did? Why did it collapse equally suddenly? Why does India not win Olympic medals? What indeed does India's Olympic progression tell us about the nature of Indian society and politics and the manner in which these have evolved?

Soon after my formal introduction to the staff of the Studies Center in December 2004, I casually inquired into what the archive contained on India. Much had not been written on the subject: except the occasional tribute to our rare Olympic achievers or the scathing critiques following dismal outings at various Games, literature on India at the Olympics is minimal. The answer I got from the museum staff was startling. I was told there was hardly anything that would be of significance to an Indian historian in what is the world's largest repository of Olympic records. It was a reality check, and for the first two weeks I was left with nothing to do but read the voluminous tomes of the IOC's Executive Council minutes through the years. The Indian presence in these records was limited to saying a mere 'yes' or 'no' every two or three years. With my search looking like a wild goose chase, I had almost given up by the end of the second week. I had gone to uncover India's Olympic history but there seemed no such thing in the records. Feeling deflated, I was preparing to use the remaining time on my fellowship as an opportunity to explore Switzerland.

Then, like so often in academic research, pure chance brought us the vital clue that we needed. Nuria Puig, a very senior IOC employee, casually mentioned over coffee in the first-floor restaurant that I should read some of the letters exchanged between the IOC's successive presidents and the heads of the Indian Olympic Association (IOA), for they made fascinating reading. After two weeks of being told that there was absolutely no specific material on India, after two weeks of sympathetic glances from the IOC's librarians, this casual remark was like raindrops after a long drought. This was the precisely the kind of thing I was looking for and hadn't found. Nuria hadn't even finished her sentence before I dragged her off to the library to show me some of the letters. What opened up before me was a virtual treasure: an entire cabinet full of files containing memos, letters and documents exchanged between the IOC and Indian sports administrators over the last 75 years. There were thousands of these documents and god knows how many more cabinets inside. I was suddenly aware that here, right in front of me, was the material which would help us piece together the story of India's Olympic encounter. The librarians had not pointed these out to me simply because this correspondence had been filed away as part of normal bureaucratic procedure. No one had ever asked for an Indian collection, so a dossier had never been created.

Reading some of the material over the next three weeks, I realized that it was impossible for me to finish researching the entire collection in the time I had at Lausanne. Going back was an option, and I have gone back on numerous occasions since, but what a project of this size desperately needed was a collaborator, a co-author who would finish researching the archive and help piece the story together.

It was then that I happened to bump into Nalin Mehta on a sunny Melbourne afternoon while on a fellowship at La Trobe University. He was just finishing his research on the impact of satellite television on the Indian polity and was, as luck would have it, in the process of applying for a fellowship to visit Lausanne to study the role played by the army in the development of Indian sport. It was a fortuitous meeting and the synergy took little time to develop. Once Nalin too won the IOC fellowship and finished scouring the archive, it was only a matter of time before we started writing.

It is essential to declare at the outset that two fundamental motives inspired our decision to move ahead with the project. The first was the determination to contribute to the growing corpus of research in Olympic history, a discipline much developed in recent years. The second was to understand the Olympic story against the backdrop of what was happening inside a colony fighting for independence and then in a young, independent nation trying to establish its post-colonial identity in the world. This motivation has subsequently emerged as the central theme of the book. The thread running through the entire book is the politicized nature of India's Olympic encounter. The Indian Olympic story, the book demonstrates, is also a story of Indian politics, of power equations, regionalism and the failed commercialism of Olympic sports vis-à-vis cricket.

A History of India's Olympic Encounter: A Political Story

In his justly celebrated essay on the dynamics of the Balinese notion of cock-fighting, anthropologist Clifford Geertz famously noted: 'The Balinese cockfight is—or more exactly, deliberately is made to be—a simulation of the social matrix, the involved system of crosscutting, overlapping, highly corporate groups—villages, kin groups, irrigation societies, temple congregations, "castes"—in which its devotees live. And as prestige, the necessity to affirm it, defend it, celebrate it, justify it, and just plain bask in it…is perhaps the central driving force in the society.'[2] By transposing the terms 'cockfight' with hockey or cricket and 'Bali' with India, one may in essence capture the significance of sport in the subcontinent. India's cricket, hockey and football teams represent India; and not Bengal, Maharashtra or Tamil Nadu. Sport is perhaps the most visible site for the playing out of the erotic passions of nationhood, where being Indian matters more than anything else. This has become marked in recent years with the passionate display of the tricolour during international sports tournaments.[3] If only for a few weeks every year, Indian sports fans, from home and the diaspora, celebrate the cardinal truth of being 'Indian'. For a country obsessed with history and transformed by its well-spread post-colonial diaspora, the need to find a common barometer of 'Indian-ness' may seem unlikely, even unnecessary. But look beneath the surface and the central role of sport in fashioning a common national identity is difficult to doubt.

Indians across the country, it is known, learn varied versions of their history in school textbooks. While for school kids in the east it is Subhas Chandra Bose who led the nation to freedom; in pockets of the west dominated by lower caste groupings it may be Ambedkar or Phule; in the north Indian heartland it is Gandhi. Modern textbooks of political history in Bihar even extol Lalu Prasad Yadav as a social reformer, while Mayawati may peer out of certain textbooks in Uttar Pradesh. India's plural education system is the playing field for as many political 'histories' as there are claimants and political masters. In stark contrast to this peculiar situation, most discussions of 'Indian' hockey/cricket and issues governing their fortunes are still relatively uniform and are mentioned almost daily in the national/local media. The intersecting vectors of politics and commerce continually influence sport in India but there is no doubt that sport itself is intrinsically linked to ideas of identity, of self and of nationalism.

Yet, in the vast literature on Indian history, sport, one of the most important cultural practices of the 20th and 21st centuries, finds little mention. The reason behind this absence, not only in the Indian context but worldwide more generally, scholars like Dipesh Chakrabarty have pointed out, are varied and complex. For Chakrabarty, the contours of the (British) social history or 'history from below' movement, which influenced much of the writing of Indian social history and into which sports scholars wanted to be integrated, had certain built-in intellectual priorities. Sporting events, he argues, were seen as less important than strikes or some other act of overt class conflict or class resistance.[4] Chakrabarty is thus of the opinion that even though the defenders of sports history in the 1970s and 1980s perceived it as central to the business of social history, it 'never quite became a mainstream subject to historians who saw themselves as engaged in that trade'.[5]

If we advance Chakrabarty's argument to the present, it can be argued that historians can hardly attempt to understand the workings of contemporary Indian societies without bringing sport or cinema into their ambit. Cricket, it is widely acknowledged today, is the single most important realm for the articulation of Indian nationalism. It is for this reason that cricket often obscures the importance of other sports, pushing them to the backburner in studies attempting to understand contemporary India's sporting contours. However, as this book will demonstrate, a study of India's Olympic encounter not only enriches our understanding of the present, it also enhances the comprehension of our nationalist past by introducing nuances that conventional historical narratives have tended to gloss over.

It is important to reiterate that the story of Indian cricket cannot pass as the story of Indian sport. Cricket in contemporary India is imbued with a frenzied sense of hyper-nationalistic jingoism and is certainly one of the strongest of contemporary Indian allegiances. It is also true that nothing beyond international cricket or a hyper commercialized spectacle like the Indian Premier League matters in India. Regional domestic competitions like the Ranji and Duleep trophies are almost in disarray, with no fan loyalty whatsoever, deflating the argument that India is a cricket-crazy country. If only India had done well in Olympic sports, as was the case with hockey until the 1960s, the popularity and commercial currency of international cricket would surely be under threat. Yet, stories of failure on the Olympic stage, often for reasons unconnected to sport, help us understand post-colonial India better, an attempt that lies at the very heart of this effort.

To wrap up, when we formally proposed to our publishers, that we wanted to document this hitherto untold story, their initial reaction was one of surprise. 'How long can it be? One chapter? How much can there be to the story of India at the Olympics?' they asked. Did it even merit a book? Clearly, they were converted to the cause. We now leave it to our readers to make up their minds on the matter.

Boria Majumdar

1

Games of Self-Respect
A Colony at the Olympics

> There are so many communities, so many different religions, so many languages and dialects, so many different customs and ideals, that it is almost impossible to select a national team.
>
> — Sir Dorabji Tata, IOA president, 1929[1]

India was the first colonized Asian nation to take part in the Olympic Games. Its embrace of the Olympic movement, while still a British colony, was no mere coincidence. It was intricately linked to the forces of nationalism, the politics of self-respect and indeed the inculcation of what has been called the British 'Games Ethic' among Indian elites. Colonial India's early Olympic encounter was born out of a complex interplay of all three factors and it forms a crucial missing link in the story of Indian nationhood. Historians now widely recognize the important role played by sport in the creation of identities and social imaginaries. Indeed it is now widely recognized that Japan, the only Asian country with a longer Olympic history than India's, embraced Olympism partly because of a deep-rooted desire to showcase Japanese modernity after the Meiji Restoration and to take on the 'West' on equal terms. Olympism became so important for modern Japanese identity that when Tokyo bid for the 1940 Games, it went so far as to tie its candidature to the celebrations of the '2,600th anniversary of the Japanese empire', pulling out all stops in an aggressive diplomatic campaign that split European nations down the middle.[2] Tokyo's emotional gambit, combined with some smart cultural hardsell, succeeded when Mussolini withdrew Rome's bid. Though the 1940

Games never took place, the politics of the 1940 Games provide a fascinating study of just how central sport can become for nationalistic identity-making.[3] In this context, in India, a number of historians have finely documented how the imperial game of cricket became an arena for colonial Indians to fight for political recognition.[4] Yet, despite its great importance, cricket never gave 'India'—the nation—any significant international triumph until well after independence. It was in Indian hockey, and in the Olympic Games, that the nationalist aspirations of colonial India found full expression. This chapter draws out the pre-history of how this came to be so, of why colonial India embraced the Olympics, and why the still nascent and obscure Games started by a French aristocrat in 1896 became so important for the creation of a nascent Indian identity.

The history of Indian sport can only be understood in light of the fact that sport was always inculcated as a crucial binding factor in the British empire. Forged in the 19th century by traders, military officers, missionaries and proponents of 'muscular Christianity', the sporting bond was not only maintained and extended by governing circles, but carefully cultivated among a selective section of the population through informal forms of exchange rather than authoritative imposition. Sport became a source of considerable cultural power, conveying through its different forms a moral and behavioural code—the Games Ethic—to connect and unite the far-flung British territories in Asia, Africa, the Caribbean, North America, Oceania, and of course, the British Isles. The introduction of all organized Western sport in India, from hockey to cricket to soccer, can all be traced to this idea. It took until 1920 for India to participate in the Olympic Games and no formal institutional mechanism for supporting Olympic sport was established in the subcontinent until the early 1920s. But by the mid-1920s, driven by nationalist enterprise and princely patronage, India's Olympic structure was well in place.

The Indian Olympic Association (IOA) as we know it today was formed in 1927[5] and a strong Indian contingent participated in the Amsterdam Games of 1928, winning India her first gold medal in hockey in the very first year of official participation. A precursor to the IOA had been formed in 1923 with the same name and it had served the Olympic cause for three years until 1926 before being shut down. At a time when nationalist sentiment in India was gaining pace, the Olympics were the only international arena where Indian-ness could be projected on the sporting field. India's participation in the Olympics, from the 1920s, was an important watershed for the politics of colonialism. Indians went to participate in the Olympics on equal terms with the British, at a time when the colony was not even invited to the first British Empire Games (1930) (later Commonwealth Games) in Canada.[6] Apart from Bermuda, British Guyana and Newfoundland, only the white settler dominions of Australia, South Africa and New Zealand were invited to the first Empire Games. The organizers even paid for the costs of athletes from the white settler dominions. The exclusion of non-white athletes from big colonies, despite India's success at the Olympic Games, meant that the Empire Games were fraught with tension.[7] The decision to prohibit India from competing at the first British Empire Games ignited angry demonstrations from both the pro-British aristocracy and the nationalist middle classes.[8] In fact, it has been argued that it was partly the chance to participate in the Games that persuaded Prime Minister Nehru to keep India in the Commonwealth. The Games helped provide an arena for nationalist ambition and anti-colonial sentiment and while they extended imperial cultural power, they also offered an opportunity for the once subordinate and colonized to 'beat the master at his own game'. This was now true for the African, Asian and Caribbean Commonwealth as it already was for the white settler dominions such as Australia, Canada and New Zealand.

This chapter documents the origins of Olympism in India and what it meant for India, for the British empire and for the global Olympic movement. As a movement led by nationalist elites and princes, the early story of Indian Olympism is also the story of a global league of upper-class elites, connected through patronage networks in Europe, who passionately pushed the Olympic ideal. Until the 1920s, the Olympics were largely a Euro-centric enterprise, but India's embrace of Olympism in the 1920s was also simultaneously accompanied by a powerful push for diffusing the Olympic ideal in Latin America and South-East Asia. As this chapter will show, in all three cases, the same strategy was followed: the use of the global network of the YMCA and the co-option of local elites with enough private resources and

European contacts to liaise with the Olympic movement's centre. In that sense, the origins of Olympic sport in India that this chapter documents is a missing piece in the global story of Olympism. In a Europe divided by war, the IOC pushed this expansion as a strategy for survival and in India the ideal was appropriated by elite nationalists as a new avenue for self-respect, modernity and identity politics in the sporting arena. Olympism came to India as part of the processes of globalization, decades before the term itself became fashionable. But once it was initiated, it was appropriated by and became inseparable from the forces of nationalism to begin with, and the centrifugal regional tendencies thereafter.

'100 Yards Round a Bend' to Antwerp: Peasants on the Athletics Track

To Sir Dorab Tata goes the credit of starting systematic Olympic activity on Indian soil in 1920. Son of the pioneering nationalist steel baron Jamsetji Tata, Dorabji was intimately involved in fulfilling his father's idea of creating an indigenous and modern steel industry in India. He is widely credited with the establishment of the Tata Steel Company in Jamsetpur (now Jamshedpur) that became India's largest private enterprise of the time. Simultaneously, in the great tradition of Parsi philanthropists in colonial India, some of his most valuable contributions came as a benefactor for sport, culture and education.[9] Before taking an interest in Olympism, Sir Dorabji had already played a key role in the establishment of school and college cricket in Mumbai in the 1880s. Until the 1890s, the structure of cricket in Mumbai educational institutions was 'crude and indefinite'. It was under Sir Dorabji's initiative that the move to form the Bombay High School Athletic Association gathered momentum. Determined to eliminate differences of caste and creed on the sporting field, he wished to unite local clubs and inculcate notions of 'fair play' among young boys. At first, the success of the scheme seemed doubtful as there was a question mark over whether European schools would join such a union.

However, with the elite Cathedral School joining hands with Sir Dorabji, the Association came into existence in 1893 and initiated the famous Harris Shield tournament in 1896. It is now the oldest surviving inter-school cricket tournament in India and has served as a nursery for many Indian cricketers, most prominently Sachin Tendulkar and Vinod Kambli. It was in a Harris Shield game that Tendulkar first hit the headlines when he shared a world record partnership of 664 with Kambli. The Association also propelled the formation of cricket clubs in each school and ensured the appointment of coaches, which served the dual purpose of providing employment to veteran cricketers while also promoting the game.

A principal obstacle that Sir Dorabji and his men faced was the paucity of playgrounds in late 19th and early 20th century Bombay (now Mumbai). To redress this, a games fee was levied in most high schools, but in order to safeguard the interests of poorer students, those from modest backgrounds were exempted. With aristocratic and upper-class patronage coming their way, many schools revoked the levy in course of time.[10]

Sir Dorabji was largely educated in England and his interest in sport was a product of his Western upbringing, which exposed him to the period ideology of athleticism and the 'Games Ethic'. The Games Ethic saw sport as a form of moral education and it was central to the ideology of English education at the time, in public schools and in universities. It was the key to the socialization in metropolitan Britain of future administrators and conquerors of the Empire.[11] This concept of sport as an element of cultural power may also be set in the wider context of a strong theoretical literature emanating largely from the work of Antonio Gramsci, whose analysis of hegemony shifted the Marxist analytical emphasis from the economic base to the cultural superstructure. Gramsci showed how even severe deprivation could not easily shake the belief of the masses in values shared with the ruling groups and conditioned by cultural attitudes formed in the superstructure. In that sense, sport was central to the British imperial setting as a powerful but largely informal social institution that could create shared beliefs and attitudes between the rulers and the ruled while at the same time enhancing the social distance between them. Such was its power as a cultural edifice that Cecil Headlam could write of cricket in 1902:

> First the hunter, the missionary, and the merchant, next the soldier and the politician, and then the cricketer—that is the history of British colonisation...The hunter may exterminate deserving species, the

> missionary may cause quarrels, the soldier may hector, the politician blunder—but cricket unites, as in India, the rulers and the ruled. It also provides a moral training, an education in pluck, and nerve, and self restraint, far more valuable to the character of the ordinary native than the mere learning by heart of Shakespeare or an essay of Macaulay which is reckoned education in India.[12]

This was the underlying philosophy behind the colonial policy of most sports. Of course, 'it is wise to appreciate that there was no culturally monolithic response to attempts to utilize sport as an imperial bond... the nature of interpretation, assimilation and adaptation and the extent of resistance and rejection' varied.[13] But there is no doubt that the appropriated virtues of athleticism, as taught in the British public school, were in turn reformulated by the educated colonial middle classes and subsequently imposed upon the masses. In Sir Dorabji's words:

> Having been educated in my youth in England I had shared in nearly every kind of English Athletics and acquired a great love for them. On my return to India I conceived the idea of introducing a love for such things there. I helped set up with the support of English friends, as General Secretary, a High School Athletic Association amongst numerous schools of Bombay, in the first place for cricket, and then for Athletic Sports Meetings which embraced nearly all the events which form part of the Inter-University contests every year in London.[14]

Adopting a game also meant adopting the entire paraphernalia of modernity that went with it. It didn't just mean playing a foreign game, it also meant adopting European clothes, European rules and European notions of order and 'fair play'.

Sport became the playing field where tradition and modernity met, clashed, and fused. A good example here is that of the Deccan Gymkhana. After the successful start of the Harris Shield, the idea was modified in Poona (now Pune) with the creation of the Gymkhana. The committee which ran the Gymkhana was not conversant with the details of managing such athletic meets on European lines and wanted to develop their sports programme more in line with established Indian traditions. Sir Dorabji, who was nominated the president of the Gymkhana, played a central role in the fusion of foreign and indigenous cultures that ensued. At the first athletic meet the Gymkhana organized, Dorabji found that the competitors were 'all boys of the peasant class working in the fields and living off poor fare...'[15] Naturally they had no idea of European rules or modern training of any kind. On attending a meeting of the Gymkhana, Sir Dorabji found that they were proposing to run their 100-yard heats round a bend without strings. This was because their sports ground was very small and the track was part of a rough unrolled grass field. To the peasants, running was running, but now it had to be undertaken under standardized and controlled conditions. In Sir Dorabji's letters on the subject, preserved at the International Olympic Museum, the one thing that strikes the reader most palpably is his sense of wonder at this clash of peasant and Western cultures in the races at the Deccan Gymkhana.[16]

Other popular events included the long distance race of about 25 miles, rightly designated the Marathon. The peasants who participated were used to running barefoot on hard macadamized or dirt roads. Despite their lack of training and primitive conditions, the first three or four men ran the distance in fair time. As Sir Dorabji observed, their time 'would compare well with the times done in Europe or elsewhere'.[17] In 1919, some of their times were close to the times clocked in the Olympics. Suitably impressed, the Tata scion decided to send three of the runners, even at his own expense, to the Antwerp Games of 1920. This was the birth of India's Olympic encounter and nationalist sentiment was at its core. As Dorabji Tata described his motives in a personal letter to the IOC president, Count Baillet Latour, in 1929:

> I therefore offered to arrange for the sending of three of the best runners to Antwerp to run the Olympic Marathon at the next meeting, when I hoped that with proper training and food under English trainers and coaches they might do credit to India. This proposal fired the ambition of the *nationalist element* in that city to try and send a complete Olympic team.[18]

But the peasant athletes had little idea of what was required to participate in the Olympics nor of the standard of performance essential to qualify for any of the events. For instance, a key member of the Gymkhana, when asked what time he thought was standard for a 100-yard race replied that it could be anything 'from half a minute to a minute'. He was 'astounded' when told that it was not a matter of minutes but rather of tenths of seconds.

Despite their naivety on the rules of modern sport, Deccan Gymkhana members were all fired by a strong nationalist imagination to send a team to the Olympics and started raising subscriptions to finance a team to Antwerp and set up an Indian Olympic Association. It seems that despite the enthusiasm of the organizers, public money at this early stage was not too forthcoming. This meant that India's first tryst with international sport came to be financed largely by a combination of money from Tata, sundry princes, public collections—these increased substantially in later years—and interestingly, the Government of India. Apart from Tata's own correspondence, a report published in the *Statesman* substantiates this point. The secretary of the Bombay branch of the proposed Indian Olympic Association sent the editor of the daily a letter appealing for support. The letter mentioned that a batch of six amateur athletes had been selected by a committee presided over by H.G. Weber and were soon to set sail for Antwerp by the steamer *Mantua* under the supervision of Dr A.H. Fyzee, India's national tennis champion. The cost of the adventure was estimated at Rs 35,000 rupees of which only Rs 18,000 had been collected so far. Of this, the Government of India contributed Rs 6,000, apart from helping to secure a passage for the touring party. The great cricketer, the *jamsaheb* of Nawanagar, Ranji, was expected to represent the country at the Olympic Council in Belgium and he too had assured the team all possible assistance. The *Statesman* report ended with an appeal to the public to contribute to India's Olympic cause. Contributions were to be sent to the secretary of the Indian Olympic Association located at Pragmahal in Bombay.[19] The public response, though, was lukewarm. In the end, Sir Dorab personally bore a great deal of the expenditure, apart from taking a keen personal interest in selecting the participants.[20] In return for his munificence, he was asked to become president of the proposed Indian Olympic Association and head the Indian cause at the meeting of the International Olympic Committee in Europe.

India's hurriedly put together Olympic contingent hardly created an impression at Antwerp and, by extension, in India. A good barometer of this is the fact that the Olympic Games barely merited a mention in Indian newspapers. If it did, it was only in the nature of one-line news briefs. Sample this one-line update, probably inserted by a sub-editor at *Amrita Bazar Patrika* published from Calcutta (now Kolkata): 'In catch-as-catch-can wrestling (featherweight) at the Olympic Games, Bernard (Britain) best Shimpe (British India) in 19 seconds.'[21] Little else is known about the men who represented India at Antwerp but one thing is certain: the Indian athletes did not do well and did not catch the nationalist imagination as their backers had hoped. As is clear from the preceding paragraphs, the six or seven athletes who traveled to Europe had little idea about modern sport. Moreover, as Dorabji Tata recounts, there was plenty of discord among them, leading to a series of unpleasant incidents.[22] Tata, who was not in good health, only visited Antwerp briefly to meet his colleagues at the International Olympic Committee. On account of an ailing health, he did not find time to witness the Games or meet the Indian contingent. India's first appearance at the Olympics in Antwerp ended in sporting failure but the very fact that the athletes reached there was an achievement. At least, the journey had begun.

'India' Goes to Paris

Not overtly concerned with the failure at Antwerp, India once again entered a team at the Paris Games of 1924 and this time the nine-man contingent was better organized. If the contingent for the Antwerp Games was more the result of a locally driven initiative, spearheaded by Tata and his experiences at the Deccan Gymkhana, by this time a truly national effort had developed.

The team for Antwerp had been selected largely by Tata after seeing some local runners in Poona. Now, for Paris, the Indian team was selected after rigorous screening of athletes at what was called an 'Olympic Games' in Delhi. These were the first 'national' congregation of Indian athletes in any organized form. In the words of A.G. Noehren, leader of the Madras (now Chennai) YMCA and secretary of the newly-established Indian Olympic Association, the Delhi 'Olympic Games' were a

> unique contribution made to the country...and it is fair to state that these have been far more successful, have created a wider interest throughout the country and has produced more permanent results than any of us dared to hope for.[23]

In 1920, the money had largely come from Tata, the princes and the government. Back then it was largely an initiative driven from Pune and Bombay. But by 1924, the funding poured in from diverse regions across the country. The subscription drive undertaken to finance the Games and the trips of the selected members to Paris was a success. A detailed breakdown of public funding for the Games shows the marked progress of the Olympic idea in the public mind by 1924. The Punjab Olympic Committee took the lead, contributing Rs 1,114, 'which represented contributions made by Punjab school boys through 47 schools'. Punjab, in total, contributed Rs 2,500. UP, Bihar, Orissa and Madras contributed Rs 2,000 each while Central Provinces contributed Rs 1,500. Calcutta too contributed Rs 4,000 towards the fund.[24] From the north to the west to the south, the Olympic ideal seemed to be catching the public imagination.

Besides, as before, the princes were also approached and the Maharaja of Patiala, the nation's leading sports patron, contributed enough to fund the participation of the Patiala long jumper Dalip Singh. The army too was sounded out to contribute to the passage of its representative and the government was called upon to put in a sum of Rs 5,000. [25]

That Olympic sports were gaining currency in India is evident from the manifold increase in press coverage between 1920 and 1924. Newspapers across the country carried news of multiple regional 'Olympic Trials' and the 'Olympic Games' at Delhi were reported thus:

> The All India Olympic meeting to be held at the Roshanara Club, Delhi on February 8–9 promises to be a unique event in the history of sports in India. Reservations have already been booked for the Indian team, which will proceed to France on the steamer 'Lancashire' ex-Colombo on 29 May. The team will be accompanied by a professional coach who will continue to train the players on steamer deck and in France for a month before the Olympic begins.[26]

The detailed programme of the meet and the timings of all the events featured prominently in the dailies and provincial successes at the meet were greeted with considerable cheer in the regions. For instance, the fact that Bengali athletes made the finals in nine events was reported at length in the province and much was made of the fact that Bengal had beaten Madras, which had six final qualifications and Punjab, which had made it to the final of five events. The two stars from Bengal, T.J. Pitt and J.S. Hall, were both eventually selected to travel to Paris. The overwhelming popularity of this meet, and the regional pride it evoked, is borne out by the following report in Calcutta's *Amrita Bazar Patrika*:

> The weather condition was excellent and spectators numbered several thousands. Viceroy and Lady Reading were present. In four events—hurdles, one mile, long jump and three miles, provincial and Indian records were beaten, although the world records have not been touched. Bengal was first in the composition of India's Olympic team having won three places...At a meeting of the All India Olympic Committee held after the meet it was decided to send these men to Paris as the money is available—
>
> 1. Dalip Singh of Patiala for Long Jump
> 2. Lakshmanan of Madras (Hurdles)
> 3. M.R. Hinge of Bombay (Marathon)
> 4. T.K. Pitt of Bengal (100 and 440 Yards)
> 5. J. S. Hall of Bengal (220 Yards)
> 6. Sepoy Pala Singh of UP (Three Miles)
> 7. J. C Heathcote (Madras), High Jump
> 8. M.V. Venkatramaswamy (Madras), One Mile.[27]

Patiala in the west, Madras in the south, Bombay and Bengal: already the regional composition of the Paris team was beginning to represent the disparate regions of India. H.C. Buck of the YMCA College of Physical Education in Madras, an American who had pioneered athletics coaching in India, escorted the athletes. Though the Indians did not win medals, they acquitted themselves better than at Antwerp, with two of them—T.K Pitt in the 400 metres and Dalip Singh in the broad jump—performing well.[28]

The organized planning for the Indian participation at the Paris Games was driven by the formation of a permanent All India Olympic Association. Sir Dorabji Tata was invited to assume the presidency of the new body[29] but it did not survive for more than three years. In 1927, another body, the Indian Olympic Association, was formed and it continues to administer Indian sport till the present day. Once again,

Dorabji Tata was the president and A.G. Noehren the secretary. It was the new IOA that led India's preparations for the 1928 Olympiad in Amsterdam where India had her first taste of Olympic success.

'A Continent as Big as Europe': The YMCA, India and the Global Olympic Movement

To make sense of how the Olympic ideal progressed in India through the 1920s, it is imperative to see it in the context of global trends about Olympism in the same period and the 'Olympic explosion' that took place in another under-developed region, Latin America. In both regions, the Young Men's Christian Association (YMCA) played a pivotal role in stimulating Olympism. The Olympic movement needed a vehicle of organization in every new country it targeted. The YMCA, a global body with finely organized national tentacles in many under-developed countries, provided a ready option. As we shall see, Dorabji Tata's association with both bodies proved a pivotal fulcrum.

The Latin American 'Olympic explosion' in the 1920s, as Cesar Torres calls it, was largely possible because of a partnership between the IOC and the YMCA. According to Torres' masterful study, the 'explosion' occurred due to a confluence of three factors: 'Latin American sporting cultures at the end of the First World War; an appreciation of De Coubertin's new strategies of globalization developed during the war; and a recognition of the crucial role that an alliance between the IOC and the Young Men's Christian Association (YMCA)...'[30]

During the First World War, De Coubertin was gravely concerned that the Games might be exterminated by the tumultuous political conditions created by the continuing violence. This anxiety made it essential to seek newer pastures for his Olympic ideology and he began to see this expansion as the key to the survival of the Olympic Games. The emphasis was to spread the Olympic gospel to areas unaffected by the war. If he could globalize Olympic affairs, De Coubertin thought, he would ensure that if not in Europe the Games would at least continue in other corners of the world. He was simultaneously growing more and more anxious about the potential of the Inter-Allied Games being organized in the US. These Games, designated as the 'Military Olympics', were being planned in collaboration with the YMCA. Nervous about its bearing on the Olympic endeavour, De Coubertin, as Torres mentions, wrote to Elwood S. Brown, the international director of the YMCA on 25 January 1919, objecting against the 'action of the YMCA in deciding to hold Olympics in France in 1919'. Brown immediately wrote back allaying De Coubertin's fears, declaring that the Inter-Allied Games 'is not a rival of the Olympic Games in any sense'.[31] His assurance had a comforting effect on De Coubertin and this started a long association between the two that lasted several years and transformed the fundamental nature of the Olympic movement.

It was at Brown's insistence that De Coubertin agreed to utilize the wide reach of the YMCA to spread the message of Olympism across Latin America. Stressing the role of the YMCA, Brown declared:

> a most unusual opportunity now existed to give a great impulse to physical training throughout the world, to develop backward areas along the lines of Olympic ideas and ideals, and to contribute definitely to the extension of your Committee's influence.[32]

Assured of De Coubertin's support, Brown officially presented his proposal to the IOC at Antwerp in August 1920. It is of great importance that Sir Dorabji Tata, representing British India, was present in this session and followed the entire deliberation with keen interest. The proposal stressed the idea that the YMCA and the IOC had similar goals and drew attention to the YMCA's global structure. All its branches played key roles in promoting physical education and 'manly sporting activity' and its organizational strength, Brown noted, was expected to add manifold to the IOC's global potency.

The YMCA had already held regional games like the Far Eastern Games in 1913 that helped in stimulating popularity of Olympic sports across the world. IOC recognition, Brown insisted and De Coubertin concurred, would impart legitimacy to these efforts and this was the primary reason why the IOC unanimously accepted the scheme proposed by Brown. 'With the partnership fully endorsed and Brown named South American *charge-de mission*, the IOC and the YMCA embarked on the first project the YMCA had in store, the 1922 Latin American Games.'[33]

Dorabji Tata had already learnt his lessons at Antwerp and soon after his return to India insisted on enlisting the support of Dr A.G. Noehren of the Madras YMCA for India's Olympic cause. It was no accident that the selection trials in Delhi for the 1924 team were conducted under the expert supervision of H.C. Buck, staff of the Madras YMCA College of Physical Education.[34]

On the IOC's part, it did everything possible to encourage British India to join the Olympic family. The YMCA presence did much to boost the IOC's confidence and even though there was no permanent Indian Olympic institution in 1920 or 1924, the IOC allowed the Indian delegation to participate in the Games as part of its vision to globalize the movement. While Tata acted as a bridge, the IOC was also independently in touch with the Indian YMCA. There is evidence for this in a letter from Dr J. Henry Gray, national physical director for the YMCA for India, Burma and Ceylon to Count Baillet Latour on 28 December 1928. The letter was primarily meant to update the IOC president on the progress of Olympism in India. To start with, Dr Gray thanked the IOC president for sending him back issues of the 'International Olympic Bulletin' and also for including him in the IOC's mailing list. He then suggested that Olympic organization in India had begun on a positive note in 1922 and the power behind this, as in Latin America, was the YMCA.[35]

Though the involvement of the YMCA had lost its sheen with the resignation of Dr Noehren in 1927, YMCA cadres were still carrying on the bulk of the work in the provinces to promote Olympic sports and were instrumental in maintaining the fabric of the provincial sports organizations. In a country the size of India, this was no small matter. As Tata noted:

> India is such a vast continent, as big as Europe without Russia. When I went to Calcutta to see the Olympic Games last month, for the eight days that I was away from Bombay five of those were spent in the train.[36]

The YMCA's early role in the Indian Olympic movement cannot be emphasized enough. Its national network provided a lifeline for those who wanted to set up a national sporting movement.

'Impossible to Select a National Representative': The 'Nation' in the Games

The YMCA provided a vital crutch in the early years and nobody knew better than Tata that the Olympic movement in India was still in its infancy. Central to the challenge was the problem of creating a national consciousness in a land divided along the multiple axes of region, caste and language. Writing in 1929, a year after India had won its first hockey gold in Amsterdam, Tata acknowledged:

> ... India is not yet ripe for the International Olympic Games. The love of such things is not ingrained here. There are so many communities, so many religions, so many languages and dialects, so many different customs and ideals, that it is almost impossible to select a national representative that would meet all requirements.[37]

There were two other major problems: the lack of stadiums and the relatively small size of a leisured class that could patronize sport as a watching public. As Tata noted at the end of his tenure as the head of the Indian Olympic movement, the foremost necessity was to have permanent stadiums, which would allow the organization of the Games in at least two of the provinces. He had already approached the provincial municipalities and the government for funds to implement his projects of stadium building but nothing had come out of such overtures. Local stadiums were an urgent necessity because it would be impossible for the poor to travel long distances. Dorabji also stressed the point that the leisured class in India was much smaller than in Europe and the majority of Indians had little leisure time to devote to sports, making the progress of Olympic sports increasingly difficult. Finally, each province had its own indigenous pastime and people did not take much interest in other events.[38]

It may be mentioned here that Dorab Tata was not alone in pressing for the building of stadiums in India. In Bengal too, the Raja of Santosh, Sir Manmatha Nath Roy Chowdhury, emphasized a similar need for a permanent venue for sport in the 1920s:

> Speaking for Bengal, I may say, without any fear of contradiction, that a sports stadium in Calcutta is the need of the moment. Sport in Bengal will receive a serious check if we fail to provide at the psychological moment a central home for sports. Besides, in a city like Calcutta where the huge sporting crowds always cause anxiety to the police and people alike, the problem of providing accommodation for spectators can no longer be ignored...We must have a sports stadium, which could accommodate in its auditorium no less than 60,000 people.[39]

Be that as it may, the Tata–Noehren combination successfully created the Indian Olympic Association in 1927. However, within months of its establishment, the organization entered troubled waters with both leaders resigning on personal grounds. Noehren resigned because he was leaving India permanently for England while Tata gave up the presidency for reasons of ill-health. In a letter to the IOC president, Count Baillet Latour, on 21 February 1927, he outlined his reasons in detail:

> I have sent in my resignation as President of the All India Olympic Committee and I also wish to resign from the international Olympic Committee. I feel that with my advancing age and infirmities I can no longer devote the time and energy necessary for the position. It is with very great regret that I feel compelled to resign...It has not been decided who the new President or Secretary will be.[40]

In view of his vision for the promotion of Olympic sport in India, it was not surprising that the IOC accepted Sir Dorab Tata's resignation with considerable reluctance.[41]

Patiala and the Rest: The Princes and the Politics of Colonial Sport

The issue of picking successors for Dorab Tata and A.G. Noehren had become politicized from the start. At the heart of it was the battle between the Indian princes for control over Indian sport which was seen as an avenue for social mobility. In this context, there is no more celebrated example of the importance of sport for many princes than that of Ranji. It is now well documented that Ranji, a disinherited prince, won back his crown of Nawanagar largely because of the social capital he had gained as a cricketing icon in England.[42] By the time Tata resigned from the presidency of the IOA, the Olympic movement too had become a prize catch for the princes to fight over. In fact, in his very first letter acknowledging Tata's resignation, the IOC president noted that the name of the prince of Kapurthala had been suggested to him as a possible successor.[43] The debate over succession raged on at several levels: at one level it was about which prince would now get to establish control as a patron; at another level it was about whether the issue was solely a domestic one with the IOA unilaterally empowered to nominate a successor; and thirdly it was about whether the IOC, which had helped India all along, could justifiably interfere in the succession dispute.

With the princely spheres of influence in cricket and football already well demarcated[44] and with Olympic sport gaining in prominence, it wasn't surprising that the succession dispute became a battle royale between several Indian princes with an interest in sport. Key players were soon split along lines of allegiance and each player tried to make a case for his candidate being the most suitable replacement. Of all the qualities sighted as essential in the successor, the one common denominator was that the candidate had to have the personal means and influence to visit Europe frequently. This was considered crucial to keep a tab on international developments, liaise with the IOC, learn of its plans and programmes and having thus imbibed new ideas implement them back home. Sir Dorabji Tata repeatedly emphasized in all his correspondence with the IOC, that a regular presence in Europe was a necessary precondition.[45] This pointed towards two things. First, the global Olympic movement at this stage was still a league of gentlemanly elites from various countries. Second, though the movement rode on nationalist emotions within India, it was still top-driven and controlled by moneyed and political elites. The days of democratization of the movement were still in the future and many would argue that this is a process that, at least in India, is still far from completion, as the subsequent chapters highlight.

Reacting to the IOC's suggestion that the Maharaja of Kapurthala, a frequent visitor to Europe, be nominated his successor, Tata in a handwritten letter to the president from Geneva on 16 June 1927 stated that the Indian Olympic Association had already requested 'His Highness the Maharaja of Burdwan' to assume the presidency. Burdwan had not yet said yes and Tata appeared apprehensive about his candidacy:

> The Maharaja I know has been the local President for the Presidency of Bengal, but I am not aware that he has taken any personal interest in the working of the All India Olympic Association. I do not know with whom the nomination of the President for All India rests, with your committee or the Indian committee. I imagine that they will be a little jealous of their privileges and claim the right to nominate their own President.[46]

In a clear indicator of the battle for control among Indian princes, he admitted that his own presidency so far had created a lot of discord in India from a rival section, which wanted Ranji, the great princely icon of Indian sport, to lead the Olympic movement. That crisis had only been averted because Tata, himself good friends with Ranji, heartily acquiesced with the suggestion only to be told by the Jam sahib of Nawanagar that he did not want anything to do with the IOA at that stage.[47]

Tata personally was in favour of the Maharaja of Kapurthala, who, he thought, was better qualified to represent India at the IOC. 'Kapurthala is every year in Europe and unlike me or Burdwan can be present at all European functions.' Because he travelled to India every winter after his European vacation was over, he was also in a position to closely monitor the day-to-day activities of the Indian Association.[48]

As the names of Kapurthala, the Jam of Nawanagar and Burdwan were doing the rounds, the powerful Maharaja of Patiala, already a key figure in Indian cricket, threw his hat in the ring. It can be surmised that Patiala's coming into the fray was the principal reason behind Ranji's backing off. This was because Patiala had been Ranji's strongest source of financial support at times of crisis. In fact, the connection between Ranji and Patiala was very well known in Indian sporting circles. Ranji had played for Patiala's team in 1898–99 and had been his ADC in the years before he won the crown of Nawanagar. While touring Bengal in 1899, Ranji and Patiala had been accorded a royal reception, the Calcutta Town Hall spending the huge sum of Rs 3,000 on the occasion.[49]

Patiala's interest in Olympic affairs fundamentally transformed equations in India. By September 1927, Tata was informing his friend Count Baillet Latour that the Maharaja of Kapurthala had already declined the presidency of the IOA. Burdwan too had decided to withdraw his candidature, clearing the turf for Patiala.[50] The dispute lingered, and by early 1928 Tata had developed serious doubts about the suitability of princes who themselves were not sportsmen, heading sporting organizations. In a letter to the count, he suggested that though the maharajas were keen on shooting, hunting, polo and other sporting activities, they had little knowledge of track and field events and not all of them were frequent visitors to Europe. He emphasized that the only reason he had backed Kapurthala so far was because Kapurthala visited Europe regularly. However, he had since then realized that the Maharaja had little knowledge of Olympic sports and would hardly be of any practical assistance to the IOC's cause. In Tata's words:

> The same applies to the Maharaja of Burdwan who has declined the Presidentship... It is going to be very difficult to find a prominent man in India who takes interest in running, jumping and this type of sport who can spare the time to come to Europe every year...I think that if the Maharaja Jam Saheb of Nawanagar could be persuaded to accept the appointment he would be the most suitable man as he is a good general all round sportsman.'[51]

Worried about the leadership vacuum, in October 1927, the IOA once again requested Tata to reconsider his resignation. His refusal to do so meant that by the end of 1927, Patiala was the lone candidate left in the race for the presidency. As he had so often done in cricket with his affluence, he successfully outmanoeuvred the others and posited himself as the saviour of the Olympic cause in India. Soon after assuming charge, he took the perfect diplomatic step in appointing Dorab Tata as honorary life president of the IOA in recognition of his efforts to promote Olympism in India.

The Patiala Era

Aside from Ranji, if there was one Indian prince who was genuinely interested in sport for its own sake, it was Maharaja Bhupinder Singh of Patiala. He first became interested in Olympic matters in 1923 when a Patiala athlete, Dalip Singh, failed to make it to the Indian Olympic team to Paris. As Anthony De Mello writes:

> His failure was, apparently, because he had been unavoidably prevented from attending the trials, which had recently been held at Lahore. Dalip Singh appealed for help to the Ruler of Patiala, who not only helped the young man to get his rightful place in the team, but also ordered the formation of the Patiala State Olympic Association. [52]

It was this incident that aroused Bhupinder Singh's interest in Olympic matters and 'already he was rehearsing for the role he was soon to play'.[53]

Soon after taking charge as president of the Indian Olympic Association, Bhupinder faced the difficult task of sending a team to the Amsterdam Games of 1928. With virtually no official funds available for the purpose, the task was an onerous one. It was as a result of his labours that India managed to send seven athletes and 15 hockey players to Amsterdam. As De Mello asserts, 'Without the efforts of Bhupinder Singh it is more than likely that our hockey wizards would not then, nor for many years to come, have had the opportunity so completely to baffle the game's experts from the rest of the world'.[54] He goes on to suggest that the 'self-imposed task of sending our Olympic team to Amsterdam was only one of many such undertaken by Bhupinder Singh. He was instrumental in sending teams to the Far Eastern Games in Tokyo (1929), the Olympic Games at Los Angeles (1932), the Western Asiatic Games at Delhi (1934), the Empire Games (Exhibition) of 1936 and also the Olympiad at Berlin in the same year'.[55]

But Patiala's rise as the pre-eminent patron of Indian Olympism created serious resentment, not only among the other princes but also among the power players in the Indian Olympic structure. Efforts to discredit him and prevent him from appointing Punjab's G.D. Sondhi as India's delegate in the IOC continued. With the influence of Tata and the YMCA gradually decreasing, Sondhi, educationist and secretary of the Punjab Olympic Association, emerged as Patiala's man at this early stage of India's Olympic encounter. As early as 30 March 1931, Patiala urged the IOC president to allow Sondhi to stand in for Sir Dorabji at the IOC session in Los Angeles in case he was unable to attend. As he argued, Indian representation in the IOC session was crucial because 'India is becoming more and more conscious of the importance of its position in international sport and we wish for as full a representation as possible on the international sports bodies'. India's success at hockey had strengthened its case for greater representation at the highest decision-making body of the Olympics and Patiala pushed further, asking for a permanent place for Sondhi at the international Olympic table:

> By winning an international event like hockey in the first year of its entrance into international competition, India has a good claim to have two members in charge of her affairs at the IOC...[56]

The IOC's subsequent acceptance of Sondhi as the official Indian representative gave the formal seal to Patiala's dominance in India's Olympic affairs.

The one body that was most miffed at the rise of Patiala was the YMCA, which had played such an important role in the movement so far. Using his proximity to Count Baillet Latour, the IOC president, Henry Gray, national director of the YMCA for India, Burma and Ceylon, sent the IOC a scathing critique of India's Olympic affairs on 28 December 1928. He lamented that Olympic organization was sagging nationwide and ascribed the loss of steam directly to Patiala's ascent. Gray argued that the new leadership was not 'representative' and that control had passed to a very small group, chiefly three men in north India representing the Punjab and the army. He minced no words: 'This leadership does not have the confidence of the entire country, is not familiar with conditions nor acquainted with the leaders in the other parts of the empire'. He felt that this was because most local provincial committees had lost their voting rights after failing to pay their dues to the national body. Gray specifically criticized the management of the team to Amsterdam, where Patiala had played a central role. He argued that the 'masses continued to remain uninvolved in Olympic activity across the country' and went on to suggest that unless immediately checked, the 'top control of the movement will be secured by a semi-interested small group of people who do not represent the country as a whole'. Even the remedies he suggested were clearly directed at challenging the monopoly established by Patiala over India's Olympic affairs: that a 'really worthy' successor be appointed to fill the vacancy left by Tata at the IOC and the restoration of the active leadership of the YMCA as the 'best qualified body in India' to lead the Olympic cause.[57]

That nothing resulted from any of these complaints was because of the affluence and influence of the house of Patiala and the paucity of funds from other sources to promote Olympic sports in the country as a whole. Funding continued to be a crucial concern even for Sondhi, Patiala's own envoy. As he wrote to the IOC president on 1 May 1935:

> It costs me a great deal of money to attend the Olympic Games, which I regard as a work of national importance and national credit. I am therefore asking if it would be at all possible for you to write to Lord Willingdon, the Viceroy and Governor General of India, who is also the Patron of the IOA, to request him to recognize the attendance of the

> Indian representative on the IOC as a national service and to get me some monetary help from the Government for attending the Games.[58]

While Patiala was thus consolidating his position at the helm of the Indian Olympic Association, the IOC president repeatedly asked Dorab Tata to reconsider his resignation from the International Olympic Committee. Tata's stature was such that the Maharaja of Patiala could not but support this suggestion on being asked. As Count Baillet Latour mentioned:

> ... after a year of troubles and inquiries, he (Patiala) wires to me that you are the only possible man. What else can I do than to say to you: Please come back, we all welcome you. What else can you do than to answer: I am coming back. Please do so.[59]

But Tata, by now 70 years old, steadfastly refused, citing his old age and ill-health.[60] By stepping aside, he left the field open for Patiala's complete dominance over the Indian Olympic firmament, a dominance that continued over the next few decades even after independence, as the subsequent chapters will show.

It can be suggested that Patiala, as he had done in cricket, had used his trusted weapon—patronage—to gain control of Olympic matters in India. He had not only funded Indian teams to various international meets but had also built a grand stadium in Amritsar to promote track and field competitions. Patronage worked well because at the time of his assumption of the office of president, the IOA was in a sorry financial state. Most provinces were in arrears in their contributions, some of them for a period of over two years. Rs 10,000 was all that was available to the IOA for sending the team to Amsterdam. Immediately before submitting his resignation, the YMCA's Noehren drew attention to the difficulties confronting the IOA:

> It must be obvious that the whole success of India's participation rests on a financial basis and that the IOA will be powerless to send even a small team abroad, unless all Provinces pay up their outstanding obligations and that this revenue be further supplemented by private donations.[61]

The fact that Patiala could sideline the YMCA so effectively in taking over Indian Olympism, despite the sterling role played by that organization in laying the early seeds of the Olympic idea in India and despite its influence with the IOC, is a measure of his success. The opposition, however, refused to give up the fight, borne out by the tumultuous story of India's Olympic encounter all through the 1930s, a thread we pick up in the next chapter.

CONCLUSION

In his much acclaimed biography of Pierre De Coubertin, John J. Macaloon writes:

> But in the final reckoning, his [De Coubertin's] eyes remained too focused by the period in which he had forged an identity and the Olympics had been reborn, the 1880s and 1890s. He failed to see that the games had become not something different from, but something much more than, what he had intended. From a small public novelty of the belle époque, an athletic competition wrapped in a prepotent historical conceit and adorned with verdant social claims, the games had been transformed in four decades [by the 1920s] into a crucible of symbolic force into which the world poured its energies and a stage upon which, every four years, it played out its hopes and its terrors.[62]

A small part of this transformation was also enacted in India, which by the late 1920s had entered the Olympic family in earnest and where, as in other parts of the world, control of Olympic matters resulted in fascinating battles of intrigue and power play that defined and transformed established contours of the domestic political landscape. The uncovering of the story of India's encounter with Olympism demonstrates beyond doubt that globalized sport was a potent reality in the early 20th century, from which colonial India benefited significantly. Acceptance of this truth will ensure that Indian historians bring our tryst with Olympism into their ambit of study to better understand the colonial past and dig deeper for the roots of popular culture at home and abroad.

This chapter has aimed to document the early history of Olympism in India and in doing so has attempted to demonstrate the already globalized nature of the colonial Indian elite. These men, educated in the West and inspired by the gospels of internationalism, helped to dramatically alter a narrow national outlook. Sir Dorabji J. Tata was one such. Following him, the Olympic torch passed into the hands of the Maharaja of Patiala and his trusted lieutenant G.D. Sondhi. Control of Olympic sport was, among other things, a time tested way of establishing 'manly' credentials. As Rosalind O' Hanlon has argued, manly qualities:

> ...were displayed in very direct and physical ways: in the splendour of men's physiques, the dazzle of equipage, the grim efficiency of their weapons and the magnificence of their fighting animals. Here, allies, troops, patrons, and rivals continually weighed and judged, challenged and affirmed each other's possession of the manly qualities and competence deemed essential in the successful ruler, ally, military commander and warrior.[63]

Having already fashioned a stranglehold over cricket by the late 1920s, control over the nation's expanding Olympic horizon allowed Patiala to establish himself as the patriarch of India's sporting world. His monopoly was challenged on occasions but such confrontations, more often than not, proved feeble retorts rather than strong rebuffs. Yet, such attempts continued through the 1930s and 1940s and are as much a part of India's Olympic encounter as the eight gold medals India won at hockey between 1928 and 1956. To these concealed and often profoundly intriguing side stories we turn in the following chapter.

2

'Everyone Wants a Bite of the Cherry'

The Struggle for Control of Olympic Sports in India

Soon after its formation, the IOA became a battleground for various regional factions. This contest for control in the early decades of its existence cannot be understood in isolation. Rather, it was part of the larger story of establishing hegemony over the Indian sporting scenario, which included dominance over two of the nation's foremost passions, cricket and football. By the late 1930s, Bengal's dominance over football and Bombay's dominance over cricket was relatively secure, a feature that did much to shape the fortunes of Olympic sports in India.[1] Having ceded ground to the west and east over cricket and football respectively, the north led by the house of Patiala, and its trusted lieutenant G.D. Sondhi, was determined to establish a stranglehold over India's Olympic affairs. At a time when British recognition and support proved to be pivotal in shaping the development of Indian football in the 1930s,[2] Patiala was determined to enlist the support of the IOC in determining the future of Olympic sports in India. This explains the detailed updates sent by Sondhi to De Coubertin on the successful staging of the first Western Asiatic Games in Delhi in 1934.[3]

Just as the issue of control over the IOA had become contested by the early 1930s, the formation of the All India Football Association (AIFA) had triggered a bitter struggle between Bengal and the other Indian states for the control of soccer. This struggle, which intensified in 1930–36, was replicated in the realms of swimming, cycling, hockey and other Olympic sports, making the Indian sporting horizon of the 1930s a contested domain. Such discord between the regions continued into the 1960s and in part explains India's poor performance at international sporting contests after independence in 1947.

Common to these power tussles is the fact that principal actors remain unchanged across sports. For example, while Patiala was a leading patron of cricket and the IOA, Pankaj Gupta led Bengal's challenge in cricket, football and hockey. With each sports administrator having multiple designations and responsibilities,[4] it was not uncommon to see the contest over football or cricket spreading to hockey or swimming and the other way round. Gupta, who had lost control over cricket to Bombay in the 1920s, got his own back in football in the 1930s. For Sondhi, on the other hand, control over the IOA was crucial to contend with the challenge posed by Bengal. The common denominator in all these skirmishes was a desperate effort to solicit the support of the international controlling body, making these encounters fascinating mini-battles of intrigue and power play. In each sport, as rival factions battled each other, support from the controlling international body provided legitimacy and so each faction lobbied hard for international recognition. In such a scenario, the IOC emerged as a sort of a neutral referee, whose patronage was pivotal in realizing the ambitions of regional sport satraps.

This chapter outlines some of the earliest skirmishes over Olympic sport in India to show that administrative and regional infighting has been a constant feature of Indian sport from the very beginning. These scuffles, highlighting the deep-rooted divides across regions, draw attention to the fragmented nature of the emerging Indian nation in the 1930s and 1940s and prove that beyond the oft-cited reasons of lack of infrastructure or failed commercialization, there are other deeper causes for India's pathetic record in the Olympic Games for nearly a century.

'Special' Punjab: Patiala and the Humouring of the IOC

Even before G.D. Sondhi had replaced Sir Dorab Tata as India's representative on the IOC, he emphasized to the IOC president the 'special' work the Punjab Olympic Association was doing to promote Olympic sports in India. Writing to the IOC in 1931, he suggested that the Punjab Olympic Association was engaged in a series of tasks, which were to be performed by individual national sporting associations. For instance, it single-handedly tried to promote swimming, volleyball, hockey, basketball and wrestling in the province, not waiting for the state associations to contribute to such efforts. In the same letter, he stressed the fact that most other Indian provinces were doing hardly anything to promote Olympic sports and weren't organized enough to contribute to the promotion of the Olympic ideal. Bengal, he suggested, was the only other province that had some 'good organization'. 'What we need is governmental support...If the government could sanction money to enable me to visit the headquarters of the backward provinces much more in the way of encouraging sports and athletics activity could be achieved.'[5]

Sondhi sent De Coubertin a chain of letters between January and May 1934, all aimed at impressing upon him the vigour with which Olympic ideals were being pursued in India. For instance, the first letter emphasized that it would be a cause of satisfaction for the founder of the Olympic movement to note that his 'great example in founding the world international brotherhood of sport is being imitated on a small scale in the East'. Sondhi was referring to the Western Asiatic Games Federation, which was founded in 1933 and which organized the first Western Asiatic Games in New Delhi in March 1934. The Maharaja of Patiala as president of the IOA and the Viceroy of India offered support to the initiative, which eventually brought together India, Afghanistan, Ceylon and Palestine for a two-day sporting carnival. The letter ended with the request for a message of good wishes for the event from De Coubertin, 'our revered founder of the modern Olympic Games'.[6]The story of the Western Asiatic Games is recounted in detail in Chapter 7 but for now, it is pertinent to note that in letter after letter, Sondhi's principle aim was clear: to win over De Coubertin and establish himself and Patiala as the keepers of the Olympic flame in India.

He once again wrote to De Coubertin, then honorary life president of the IOC, at the conclusion of the Western Asiatic Games. This letter was more in the form of a report detailing the successful organization of the Games in New Delhi.[7] In yet another letter written in end May 1934, Sondhi sent De Coubertin the constitution of the Games declaring, 'At a meeting of the Western Asiatic Games Federation it was decided to adopt the enclosed constitution of the Federation after submitting it to you for your kind opinion. It was felt that the opinion of the founder of the International Olympic Committee should be obtained before making our constitution final. I shall be most thankful if you can find time to go through it and honor us with your remarks'.[8]

These efforts by Sondhi were clearly aimed at keeping the IOC in good humour, knowing full well that the IOC's support would prove crucial in shaping the fortunes of the IOA in the first decade of its existence. The IOC's involvement in IOA activities led by Patiala and Sondhi was decisive in impressing upon rivals that the IOA was the only internationally recognized governing body for Olympic sports in India.

The Polluted Pool: The Early Struggles Over Swimming

The IOC's patronage was crucial in tipping the scales in the factional fights that engulfed various Olympic sports in India during the 1930s. A good case in point is the struggle over swimming in this period. That India's pools had become muddied was first evident when Fédération Internationale de Natation (FINA) in its meeting on 8–9 May 1935 decided to cancel the affiliation of the IOA for non-payment of dues. Going a step further, FINA in a startling move recognized the National Swimming Association (NSA) based in Calcutta as the official governing body for swimming in India.[9] The problem was that NSA was simply a small Calcutta body with virtually no standing outside the city. It had cleverly managed to lobby support with FINA but its recognition as the official Indian swimming body was a clear illustration of the challenges faced by early sports administrators as they tried to put in place global systems of governance. Until then, Indian swimming had been controlled by the IOA and on hearing the news in June 1935, a distressed Sondhi immediately turned to the IOC for arbitration. He wrote to the president of the IOC, complaining that FINA's act was prejudiced and arbitrary. What was most surprising was that FINA had granted affiliation to a body which did not represent more than a handful of clubs in Calcutta. As Sondhi informed the IOC: 'From inquiries I find that this association does not control swimming even in the whole town of Calcutta, leave alone the whole of the Bengal province, and the country. The F.I.N.A. should before accepting the affiliation of such a one-town Association, have satisfied itself that it really controlled swimming all over the country'.[10]

So how did this small Calcutta body succeed in convincing FINA of its all-India credentials? It is instructive that NSA won FINA's favour through systematic lobbying to discredit the IOA. Its officials, on their own accord, wrote to FINA seeking to find out if the IOA had defaulted in paying its membership dues. On hearing that it had, the NSA volunteered on its own accord to pay the outstanding amount. It fraudulently communicated to FINA that it was doing so on the IOA's behalf, because the body had sanctioned the recognition of the NSA as the governing body for swimming in India. Quite insidiously, NSA officials simultaneously wrote to the IOA, expressing their willingness to bail the body out of financial distress. They indicated that the payments being made to FINA were a gesture of goodwill, never once mentioning that they wanted to replace the IOA as the central administrative body for swimming in the country. When Sondhi discovered the intrigue, he was livid:

> .... it seems to me, reading between the lines, that the National Swimming Association is playing a double game, on the one side with F.I.N.A. paying the arrears of the Indian Olympic Association and getting affiliated in its own name; and on the other side writing to the Indian Olympic Association to imply that the arrears have been paid and settled on behalf of the Indian Olympic Association. Apart from everything else then, the very double-dealing of the National Swimming Association should disqualify them from ever representing India. Besides, there is the established point that the National Swimming Association consists of a few swimming clubs of Calcutta and no more.[11]

In sharp contrast, the IOA enjoyed the affiliation of 'all the important provinces of India'.[12] Having expressed his angst, Sondhi urged the IOC president to intervene on behalf of the IOA and request FINA to hold off on granting affiliation to the NSA before a probe was conducted on whether the association could claim to represent the whole country. He also suggested that FINA should give the IOA an opportunity to pay off its arrears or set up an association representative of Indian swimming. If it did so 'it will have earned the gratitude not only of the Indian Olympic Association, but also of the vast majority of swimmers in the country'.[13]

He was confident that swimmers or swimming associations from other parts of the country would refuse to accept the hegemony of the NSA and would be unwilling to join a local body operating out of Calcutta. Having garnered support in western India and strengthened by the growing proximity the IOC, Sondhi denounced the authority of the NSA, arguing that it deceitfully claimed to represent a host of swimming associations of the country. Having done so, the IOA proceeded to challenge the authority of FINA itself by asking the IOC for a series of clarifications: was there any rule of the IOC that a country participating in a particular game in the Olympic Games must be affiliated to the international federation controlling that particular game? Was there a rule of the IOC which prevented a country from taking part in any game or sport in the Olympic Games, if its dues to the appropriate international federation were not settled?[14] Sondhi was looking for a way to regain control, and if a loophole could help him circumvent FINA's authority, he wanted to find it. Simultaneously, the IOA did make an effort to strike a compromise, suggesting that FINA, if it wanted, could empower the IOA to set up a regulatory body for swimming in India.[15]

Support from the IOC was one prong of the battle. The second challenge was to garner support within India. Accordingly, continuing its offensive against the NSA, the IOA issued a circular to state Olympic Associations urging them to unite in opposition to the rebel body. The circular emphasized that the IOA wasn't averse to setting up a governing body for swimming, which would include representation from associations across the country. Significantly, the circular also declared that the IOA was in correspondence with the IOC and expected to receive official sanction for its proposals. IOA officials clearly saw the IOC's support as their ultimate trump card in this struggle for domestic control.

With Sondhi pressing hard for IOC intervention, the NSA launched its own public relations offensive with the Olympic czars in Lausanne. That it was determined to spite the IOA was evident on 16 September 1935 when the joint secretary of the NSA wrote to the president of the IOC. The letter was more of an exploratory probe, aimed at trying to dig up more information about the financial crisis afflicting the IOA and to find out if the crisis had embittered its relations with the IOC. However, the effort to malign the IOA was couched in the benevolent idiom of trying to facilitate the participation of the Indian swimming team at the Berlin Olympic Games. This, the NSA emphasized, wasn't possible with an impecunious IOA at the helm of Indian swimming. But the real rub lay in the wording:

> It is being rumored here that the Indian Olympic Association has failed to meet its financial obligations to your organization and has in all probability lost their affiliation as a result thereof. The Federation Internationale de Natation Amateur has recently been pleased to accept our affiliation with them, subject to the confirmation of certain statements by us and we are vitally interested in the matter as we are making an earnest endeavor to enter a team of Indian swimmers for the forthcoming Olympiad in Berlin.[16]

Expressing its determination to promote swimming in India, the NSA asked the IOC president for a series of clarifications. Most of these were designed to find out more about the relationship between the IOA and the IOC and in the process discredit the IOA in the eyes of the parent institution. Even as it enquired if the IOA had defaulted in paying its dues to the IOC, most other clarifications indicated that the NSA was aware of the failure of the IOA to pay up and was using 'non-payment' as an opportunity to strike back. It asked the IOC 'whether the Indian Olympic Association has failed to meet its obligations and thereby forfeited its status? How should entries from India be forwarded to the IOC under such circumstances?' Also, whether entries for the swimming events at the Berlin Games could be forwarded directly to the IOC by 'our Association which is the National Governing Body for Swimming in India' recognized by FINA?[17] In effect, the NSA was not just content with winning control over swimming from the IOA. It wanted to finish off the IOA altogether.

The Hatkhola Club and 'Unfair Treatment': Bengal vs the IOA

The battle for hegemony over swimming continued for the next year and a half, with both sides trading charges and trying to enlist the support of the IOC and FINA. The impact of the tussle was felt nationally with clubs from both ends of the Indian heartland divided in loyalty. Piqued club authorities questioned the viability of the tussle and whether it was doing any good to the cause of swimming in the country. The tussle ignited a trail of fascinating letters between some of these clubs and Olympic officials in Lausanne. For instance, in March 1938, the hands of the NSA were strengthened when Calcutta's wonderfully named Hatkhola Club (established in 1920 and literally meaning 'all embracing' or 'one that welcomes all'), expressed anger at the 'high handed attitude' of the IOA.[18] The Hathkola Club is significant because it represented a significant stream of elite opinion in Calcutta. Its president, Sir Hari Sanker Paul, was the Mayor of the city and now its secretary wrote to the secretary of the IOC to complain that the domineering attitude of the IOA was affecting the country's swimmers, sportsmen and women who were unwarranted casualties in the power rivalry.[19] It questioned if there was a way by which the IOA and the NSA could bury the hatchet and co-exist peacefully. It also suggested that there was a precedent in the way the All India Football Association led by Bengal ended a similar standoff against football bodies from the other provinces by helping the formation of the All India Football Federation in 1937. These steps revitalized and revolutionized Indian football and the way it was organized in the country. A similar solution, it was suggested, was possible if the obdurate IOA was willing to recognize the NSA and willing to treat it as a body eager to alter the miserable plight of Indian swimming. In case the face-off hardened, Indian swimming, it was lamented, would become the greatest casualty. As a Calcutta club, Hatkhola's loyalty was firmly with the NSA, as is evident from the following letter to the secretary to the IOC:

> In 1934, NSA of Calcutta applied to the F.I.N.A. for affiliation for the control of swimming in India and in 1936 at Berlin, the F.I.N.A. finally accepted the affiliation of the NSA. As the IOA is the forwarding agent (of swimmers) for the international contests, the NSA applied for affiliation to the IOA. I am sorry to inform you that their application has

> been rejected and the IOA on their own accord are going to hold the All India swimming trial on 28th and 29th May 1938 for selection of Indian swimmers for the 2nd Western Asiatic Games to be held in Palestine in June 1938, without the help of the NSA.[20]

It wasn't just a question of which organization was more competent. Regional identity was a crucial marker in this battle. Hatkhola opposed the IOA because it believed that the IOA was vindictive towards Bengal; a point that its avid correspondent to the IOC emphasized by citing the 'unfair' treatment meted out to the Bengal Amateur Swimming Association. Though the Association consisted of some of the most eminent gentry from Calcutta and represented the interests of most swimmers and swimming associations of the province, the IOA had refused to recognize it. Interestingly, the unfair treatment meted out to Bengali swimming associations did not end at the pool. It also extended to athletic clubs, as is evident from the bitter experience of the Hatkhola Club:

> Our club has both sections, swimming as well as athletics. Last year my boys joined the aquatic sports not registered with the Bengal Olympic Association (BOA). This year we applied for registration for our two walking competitions to the BOA and they informed us over phone that our club as well as the competitors would not be registered as our swimmers have joined the unregistered sporting body.[21]

The Hatkhola cause gathered strength because it had touched the sympathetic chord of unfair treatment to sportspersons. This was evident when the IOC wrote back saying that the club's recommendation of setting up a separate governing body for each sport would be considered seriously. Encouraged by the IOC response, the club sent another letter demanding a series of clarifications, which were similar in nature to those asked for by the NSA a couple of years earlier:

1. Does the Bengal Olympic Association have the authority to refuse registration of a club and its competitors because they have aligned themselves with the NSA, which has been recognized by FINA as the governing body for swimming in India?
2. Is the affiliation of the NSA of India with FINA final and is it the only body which could select Indian swimmers for international contests?

3. Has the Indian Olympic Association any power to hold All India swimming trials for the second Western Asiatic Games after the NSA has been accepted by FINA?
4. Who has the authority to select Indian swimmers for the second Western Asiatic Games, the IOA or the NSA?[22]

The battle had reached an impasse and on the eve of the second Western Asiatic Games the two organizations—the national Olympic body and the 'national' swimming body—reached a temporary truce in the interests of Indian sport. In fact, it was a wise move on the part of the IOA to extend an olive branch to the NSA. The NSA on its part agreed that some of its policies needed to be altered to bring other provincial associations into the ambit of Indian swimming. However, the NSA also suggested that as it had already affiliated itself with FINA, there was no reason why the IOA shouldn't recognize it as the sole arbiter of swimming in the country.

The NSA claim could have been sounder if it had been able to claim any achievement on the international stage beyond electing office bearers and writing letters to other provincial associations demanding recognition. The IOA, on the other hand, could point to solid achievements. It had organized a series of international sporting contests at home and arranged the sending of Indian sides to multiple Olympiads. It still enjoyed the support of the largest number of sports bodies in the country, including a good number within Bengal.

To Compete or Not to Compete: Two Indians and the IOC

As the waves gradually receded in the pools, the IOA found itself confronting another crisis—a stormier one, perhaps, with Pankaj Gupta, the legendary Bengali sports administrator, taking on Sondhi for his alleged assertions against Indian participation in the forthcoming 1940 Tokyo Olympic Games.[23]

Sondhi, it was revealed later, had suggested in certain quarters that India should not participate in the Games unless she was prepared to mount a strong challenge for the medals. Winning, Sondhi asserted, was very important, for it was the only way a nation was honoured on the Olympic stage. Gupta perceived this plea for improvement as a tirade against the Olympic movement and suggested to the IOC president that Sondhi be admonished for his insolent remarks. As secretary of the Bengal Hockey Federation, he informed the IOC that such statements by Sondhi, the national and international face of the IOA, were a cause for major embarrassment in the country and also dampened the spirits of Indian sportspersons training for the Games. The emerging Bengali sports media offered support to Gupta in his attempt to malign Sondhi and advocated a more vital role for Bengal in steering Olympic affairs in India.[24]

Reacting to Gupta's remarks, the IOC president, Count Baillet Latour, returned the original letter to Sondhi and asked him to respond to the allegations. Sondhi, stung by the unfair criticism, responded to each accusation in detail, clarifying the position of the IOA in the process. He sent Gupta a detailed response on 16 June 1939 and followed it up with a reply to the IOC the next day, firmly cementing his position as the rightful face of Olympism in India.[25]

His response to Gupta was firm and was full of quotes from the Olympic oath to prove his point. He cited the oath on multiple occasions to drive home his perspective. For example, the oath declares, 'We swear that we will take part in the Olympic Games in loyal competition respecting the regulations which govern them and desirous of participating in them in the true spirit of sportsmanship for the honour of our country and for the glory of sport'. Sondhi emphasized the words, 'honour of the country' and suggested that these words represented the central tenet of the oath. 'It is not a truism that no one can glorify sport who does not bring honor to his country.'[26] He went on to affirm that while the IOC selected its members for the qualities it deemed essential to make them worthy members of the committee, it also expected its members to take the lead 'even at the risk of advocating unpopular views'. He stressed that there were instances when non-participation in an Olympiad was essential to be better prepared for the next:[27]

> The International Olympic Committee is more vitally concerned in preaching the high ideals of real sportsmanship and in raising the general physical health of the peoples of countries than in merely taking part in the Games. Participation in the Games is important, but only because it tends to draw pointed attention to the necessity of physical

> improvement, and because it brings the youth of various nations together and provides opportunities for international understanding. It would be quite in order for a member of the International Olympic Committee to advise his country to refrain from taking part in some particular event at the Olympic Games so that the country may husband its resources for improving sports generally and thus reach a higher standard in the next Olympic Games.[28]

Citing the above refrain in the Olympic oath, he suggested that there was nothing unfair or offensive in his actions in trying to urge sports bodies to raise the bar before participating in the Games. He declared that while it wasn't essential to win on all occasions, a person could win if he was well trained and capable of giving a worthy account of himself. 'Mere taking part is not enough...you will admit that if success in the Olympic Games brings public renown, a consistent and continuous poor showing is likely to do the reverse.'[29]

That Sondhi was firmly in the saddle was apparent from his confident reply to the IOC president on 17 June 1939 in which he thanked Count Baillet Latour for sending him Gupta's letter and for his assessment that it was a vain attempt to malign Sondhi before the IOC. That he had an upper hand in the conflict was evident when he declared, 'I do not mind even adding that, but for my hard endeavors for over ten years there would hardly have been an Indian Olympic Association.'[30]

In the same letter, he challenged Gupta's authority and claimed that Gupta had sent the complaint in his personal capacity and it did not have the support of the President of the Bengal Hockey Association (BHA). 'Mr. P. Gupta had written to you in his capacity as Secretary of the Bengal Hockey Association. A reference to the President of the Bengal Hockey Association, however, has elicited the fact that Mr. Gupta was not at all asked by the Hockey Association to write to you on this subject. It was entirely on his own that he chose to make wrong use of his position as secretary of the BHA.'[31]

He also tried to explain to the IOC president the circumstances which had provoked the vitriolic attack against him. Disappointed with India's consistently poor showing at the Games since Antwerp in 1924, Sondhi had suggested that India shouldn't waste money in sending teams which were incapable of winning laurels for the country. Just making up the numbers did not justify the huge expenditure involved, more so in a situation when there was not much money for sports in the country anyway. Instead, he suggested that India should make optimal use of the limited resources at hand and send a competitive team to Helsinki in 1944. The money saved from not sending a team to Tokyo could be utilized for performance enhancement by employing first-class coaches, an improvement that he hoped to showcase at multiple international forums prior to the Helsinki games in 1944.[32] 'I have never written against taking part in the Olympic Games, and as you very well know, I have tried very hard to get Hockey included in the Olympic programme, so that we could play a worthy part in the Games. A good deal of the agitation is due to people who think that their chances of going abroad as managers of the Indian Teams have been lessened by my advocating abstention from the athletics section of the Games.'[33]

The concluding lines marked a direct attack against Gupta, who had already served as the manager of the Indian Olympic contingents in 1932 and 1936. This controversy did not continue for long as the Tokyo and Helsinki Games were cancelled with the outbreak of World War II. Even after the war, however, the IOA had little respite, with the focus shifting to the velodrome in the 1950s, when yet another sporting federation, the National Cyclists' Federation of India, rose up in rebellion.

When the Spokes Came Off: Fighting Over Cycling

Nothing epitomizes the early battles between Indian sport administrators better than the case of Indian cycling in the 1950s. Cycling was a sport at which Indians had shown much promise in the early years. The first Indian cyclist of distinction was Janki Das, who participated in the British Empire Games at Sydney (Australia) in 1938, with Swami Jagan Nath accompanying him as his manager.[34] The Cycling Federation of India was formed a year later and in 1940 it was affiliated with the Union Cyclists Internationale (UCI).[35] The inevitable then happened. A rival body came up when Sohrab H. Bhoot of Bombay formed the National Cyclists' Federation of India (NCFI).[36] Bhoot had been part of the original team of Dorab Tata that founded the Indian Olympic movement and in 1948 he managed to merge both organizations under the banner of the

NCFI.[37] The crisis, it appeared, had been resolved, and in the early years a relatively stable NCFI consistently sent Indian teams to international competitions. Indian cycling teams participated in the 1948 London Olympics and the World Cycling Championships at Amsterdam in 1946 and Brussels in 1949.[38]

It is not surprising, therefore, that cycling was one of the sports included in the first Asian Games held at the National Stadium in New Delhi in 1951.[39] Bhoot used the opportunity to formally constitute the Asian Cycling Federation with himself as its founder president. It is pertinent to note, though, that a number of Indian cyclists performed with distinction at the first Asiad:

1.	R.K. Mehra	:	Silver Medal in 4000 m Team Pursuit
2.	Madan Mohan	:	Silver Medal in 4000 m Team Pursuit
3.	Lhanguard	:	Silver Medal in 4000 m Team Pursuit
4.	Gudev Singh	:	Silver Medal in 4000 m Team Pursuit
5.	N.C. Bysack	:	Bronze Medal in 1000 m Time Trial
6.	Sanwas Shah	:	4th Position in 120 Miles Road Race

The Asiad, however, did not prove to be the kick-off for Indian cycling that it could have been. Through the 1950s Indian cyclists continued to participate in various international championships and road races[40] without much success. The real story of cycling unfolded off the tracks and it was a story that explained much about the failure of Indian sport.

By the early 1950s, Bhoot was not only the president of NCFI, but astonishingly also its chairman, honorary secretary and honorary treasurer. No doubt he had many talents but none of them related to running a cycling federation. 'The attraction of running a sport federation it seems lay in the chance to become the arbiter of foreign tours.' Complaints flooded in about the 'dubious methods' being used by the talented Mr Bhoot in 'collecting money from Cyclists and Cycling Associations for promised trips abroad'.[41] In 1953, he led an Indian cycling team to Romania that failed miserably: one cyclist was scratched from the sprint event, another finished last in his heat and a third fell off his cycle while negotiating a bend. *The Times of India* had no doubts about who was to blame. In an acerbic analysis, its correspondent mused that the 'enterprising and resourceful' Bhoot (who was untraceable for a few days after the disaster) must have been busy writing a textbook for his 'proprietary organization'. He then twisted the blade in, noting that Bhoot's musings could only be titled: 'How to Make Cycling Pay in Six Easy Lessons'.[42]

The reports were not without substance. In 1955, Bhoot took another team of cyclists to participate in the World Festival of Youth in Warsaw and the World Cycling Championship at Rome and Milan. Poland's High Committee of Culture issued first-class air tickets for the cyclists and also arranged for free board and lodging. Yet, they were 'required' to pay Rs 6,000 each to the enterprising Bhoot before their departure from Bombay. This was a huge sum in 1955. The ten 'chosen' cyclists finally arrived in London on 27 May. Strangely, half of them were sent back the very next day 'as they had no more money'. The others were forced to find work to fund the rest of their trip. According to an IOA note to the IOC, the Indian cyclists did find work at the R. Woolfe Rubber Factory at Uxbridge in London. Adrift in a foreign land, the team members were forced to pay a further sum of £40 each to Bhoot. Only then they could travel onward for the races.[43]

Worse was to come in Warsaw. By then, the cyclists were so angry at Bhoot's 'disgraceful behaviour' that they refused to take part in the races.[44] An unperturbed Bhoot simply exited Warsaw, leaving the team to its own devices. The Poles had already paid for first-class air tickets, which never reached the cyclists. Now the Polish Cyclists' Federation stepped in to bale out the stranded Indians by paying for tickets to Vienna and back home.[45]

The Warsaw incident was not an isolated case. In the same year, the chairman of the Warsaw–Berlin–Prague Road Race informed the IOA that all competitors taking part in the race had been given valuable gifts by the organizers. In the case of the Indian cyclists, however, the gifts had been 'appropriated' by Bhoot and all protests 'had been of no avail'.[46] The IOA's Bhalindra Singh was unambiguous in his judgment: 'Mr Bhoot conducted himself in a similar manner regarding the small sums of money given to the competitors in the Road Race as pocket money.'[47]

Not surprisingly, Indian cyclists were so angry that Bhoot was actually 'beaten up' during the Second Youth Sports Games of 1955.

The aggrieved cyclists might have got their own back in that sordid incident but the cause of Indian cycling had been hurt immeasurably by now. As Raja Bhalindra Singh noted, the team, selected not on the basis of 'cycling ability, but of their financial position', was an extremely weak one and brought no credit to itself in the Peace Race, and did not even enter for the Second Youth Sports Games.[48]

While on this trip, the Indian team also travelled to Italy, and once again a 'regular fight' broke out between the cyclists and Bhoot at a Milan hotel. Things got so bad that the police had to be called in and the headlines in the Italian press said it all. Sample some of these: 'Strange story of Indian cycling team'; 'Milan hotel proprietor calls in police'; 'Indian cyclists stranded'; 'Manager vanishes with money'; 'Disgraceful scene in Milan'.[49] It couldn't have been worse for India. No wonder the cyclists had failed to realize the promise they had shown in the first Asiad.

With Indian cycling turning into an international scandal, the IOA unanimously resolved to disaffiliate the NCFI. The problem was that the NCFI was still recognized by cycling's international body, UCI. The IOC's influence as an arbiter thus became crucial and the stand-off led to a seven-year battle between the IOA and the NCFI to curry the Olympic body's favour.

Bhoot was not one to take the NCFI's disaffiliation lying down. It was now his turn to complain to the IOC, and he mounted a vociferous defence arguing that the cycling federation had been victimized due to 'frivolous and false complaints' from some 'rebel' cyclists.[50] Appealing to the IOC executive committee in September 1956, he wanted nothing less than the NCFI's full reinstatement as the governing body for cycling in India:

> I was attempting till the last minute to settle the affairs with our National Olympic Committee who have acted unjustly and unconstitutionally to disaffiliate this federation from membership...The IOA should not have interfered into the day to day affairs of this federation. Instead it wrongly took up the cause of the rebels on the basis of frivolous complaints just to spite the representative of this federation on the IOA who has from time to time pointed out the irregularities of the IOA who manage their affairs in complete ignorance of the principles of the Olympic charter.'[51]

The IOA by now was encouraging the 'rebel' cyclists—the ones who had risen up against Bhoot—to form a parallel body for cycling in India and promising to recognize it as the central governing body for the sport in the country.

Bhoot now took his lobbying to a new level, meeting the IOC president, Avery Brundage, at London's Dorchester Hotel in July 1955. His principal concern was to find out if the IOA could encourage the formation of a parallel body for cycling in India. He knew that parallel sport bodies were a complete anathema to the IOC, and the gambit seemed to work. As he noted, 'Mr. Brundage kindly gave me his decision and followed it up with a letter from Chicago dated 27 July 1955 outlining the duties and powers of a National Olympic Committee. The president of the IOA willfully ignored the directions of Mr Brundage and continued to interfere in the affairs of this Federation on the plea that the IOA had a right to look into and guide the destiny of a national sports federation'.[52]

Bhoot's line of argument before the IOC is particularly instructive. It harked again to the familiar theme of regional rivalries that was by now a staple of warring Indian sporting factions. Bhoot's target was Patiala himself and in a telling critique he outlined the nature of the prince's complete control of Indian sport. As he put it to the IOC:

> You Gentlemen are well aware of the scandalous and unconstitutional affairs of the IOA...The present President who is an ex-Maharaja of a small Indian state is holding the position uninterrupted for the last 18 years, more for political reasons than sports. A very autocratic President, who never allows a member to discuss pros and cons of the items on the agenda, forces his views against the right thinking majority members including myself.[53]

Bhoot was attempting to be the lone voice to oppose Patiala's dominance in Indian sport. Himself under a thick cloud of corruption, he rounded off his tirade with a threat to expose the 'corruption' at the IOA if the IOC did not restore the authority of the NCF. He even raised the spectre of India failing to compete in the Melbourne Games of 1956 if Patiala's stranglehold remained:

> The affairs of the IOA are at present in an awfully bad mess with hardly any funds at their disposal and always depending on the benevolence of the Government of India who have a great say in matters relating to sports in

> India...Over and above this the IOA has to give a satisfactory explanation to the IOC to their different queries, which they are now attempting to patch up in a highly perfunctory way, without any attempt to make any substantial change in the constitution...I request the President Mr. Brundage to direct the IOA to reinstate the NCF immediately into IOA fold and help us to send an Indian cycling team to Melbourne specially as this federation has some very good class of road riders. If the IOA refuses to reinstate this federation in spite of your directives a lot of scandal will come to light and may be the Indian Olympic team will not be accepted by the organizing committee of the Melbourne Games.[54]

Bhoot's own reputation was far from clean but his offensive, it seems, succeeded in safeguarding his control over the NCFI. This then was the story of Indian sport officialdom: each faction trying to claim the moral high ground, lobbying for international recognition, and hoping to keep its own hold intact, while the game continued to suffer.

The dispute was finally settled six years later in 1962 when the IOA finally agreed to a truce with the selection of Abhijit Sen of Sen Raleigh Cycles as president of the National Cyclists Federation of India (NCFI).[55] Subsequently, the federation with its newly elected office bearers was granted recognition by the government of India. Soon after the ice was broken, an Indian cycling team consisting of Lalbir Singh, Sucha Singh, Amar Singh, Amar Singh Sokhi and Chetan Singh Hari with R.K. Mehra as manager-cum-coach participated in the 1964 Tokyo Olympics. The team, which had no experience of the 45-degree track used in the Tokyo Games, failed to put up a creditable performance. The failure at Tokyo had an adverse impact on the fortunes of the sport and no Indian team was allowed to participate in international contests till the Bangkok Asian Games of 1970. At Bangkok, a team of nine cyclists participated with reasonable success, and that performance cleared the way for subsequent Indian cycling teams to take part in international competitions. In 1966, the NCFI changed its nomenclature to the Cycling Federation of India (CFI), by which name it is still known today.[56]

Conclusion

As mentioned at the start of this chapter, the state of India's Olympic affairs—in this case the relationship between the IOA and the federations at the helm of individual sports spread across the country—was hardly stable in the 1930s and 1940s. Accordingly, the history of India's Olympic movement can only be analyzed if observed alongside the unpleasant political reality of regionalism dominating the Indian political and cultural scene, which dictated the evolving relationship between the sports associations located in the different provinces. Another constant factor that needs to be taken into account in studying the early years of turmoil is the role played by the IOC. In other words, when pressed by rival associations from across the country, the IOA led by Sondhi and later the Maharaja of Patiala unfailingly attempted to invoke IOC support to retain control.

The object of this chapter has been to demonstrate the importance of studying the multiple day-to-day skirmishes across Olympic sports to understand the fractured nature of Olympism in India, which in turn explains India's miserable performance at the Games. It also attempts to show that this history was always full of nuances, the scopes of which went beyond the sports pitch. The story of Olympism in India makes sense when the narrative is read alongside the realities of domestic politics and also the equations governing the country's other major sports, cricket and soccer.

Interestingly, the growing conflict over the control of Olympic sports in the 1930s and 1940s did enough to create the impetus necessary for the growth of Olympism in India. The IOA, seeing a chance to profit from the financial frailty of the sports federations, did its best to consolidate its stranglehold over Indian Olympic affairs. That it was successful is evident from the non-participation of Indian cyclists in international competitions in the years of struggle between the IOA and the CFI.

Using its financial potency, the IOA consolidated its relationship with the IOC. This was repeatedly borne out with the IOC refusing to be drawn into India's 'internal disputes' and suggesting that decisions about India's participation in the Olympic Games could only be taken by the IOA. Also, the continuing dominance of the House of Patiala at the IOA, which is partially true even today, draws attention to how these princely houses restructured their domains of influence after independence in 1947.

While bitter regional conflict dominated the all-India scene, the consistent success of the Indian hockey team on the Olympic stage in 1928–56 proved that it was possible for a sport to rise above such rivalries. The monopoly over international hockey was the oxygen that sustained the Olympic movement in India in its early years, making India's Olympic encounter far more vivacious and attractive. To these glory years we turn in the next chapter.

3

The Golden Years
'We Climb the Victory Stand'

India claims to be the foremost in many things in the world. The world admits that she is foremost in hockey.

—A. M. Hayman, President, Indian Hockey Federation, 1932[1]

Hockey, more than any other game, is etched in the Indian psyche. It is hockey that brings out the magic and mystery, the poetry and prose in Indian sport.

—Rajdeep Sardesai, 1992[2]

'We Were Made Heroes'

One of the world's oldest sports, hockey predates the ancient Olympic Games by a little more than 1,200 years. However, the modern game of field hockey (as distinct from ice hockey) evolved in the British Isles in the middle of the 19th century. The British helped spread hockey globally, promoting it in parts of the empire as part of the civilizing process, and subsequently its popularity became especially visible in the Indian subcontinent by the early 20th century. In colonial India, especially in the early decades of the 20th century, hockey was as popular as cricket and football, the country's other passions. Even school and college magazines of the period are replete with descriptions of hockey matches, and they specifically draw attention to India's spectacular performance in the Olympics.[3]

In India, organized hockey started in Calcutta in 1885 when the first hockey clubs were formed. Within a decade the great tournaments that were to become the breeding grounds of the national team had been established. The Beighton Cup in Calcutta and the Aga Khan Tournament in Bombay were both set up in 1895. Having established itself in the east and west of the country, hockey moved north to the Punjab, first to the Army cantonments and then it made its way into the Punjab University Sports tournament in 1903. In the same year, Lahore started its famous Hot Weather Tournament.[4] These tournaments were to be the lifeline of Indian hockey all through its golden age. Writing of the Beighton Cup in 1952, the great Dhyan Chand, who cut his hockey teeth first in the Army, and then with the Jhansi Heroes observed:

> In 1933, the Jhansi Heroes decided to participate in the Beighton Cup hockey tournament. My life's ambition was to win the Beighton Cup, as I had always regarded this competition as the blue riband of Indian hockey. In my opinion it is perhaps the best organized hockey event in the country. Calcutta is indeed lucky that it has at least three or four first class hockey grounds on the maidan, and this is a great advantage to run a tournament on schedule. Instituted in 1895, this tournament has had a non-stop run. World Wars I and II did not affect the tournament. Threats of Japanese bombs and actual bombings in Calcutta while the hockey season was on also did not prevent the tournament from being held. That being said, it is sad to think that the tournament had to yield to the communal frenzy, which gripped the nation in 1946–47.[5]

Like the Bombay Pentangular in cricket, these tournaments helped in popularizing the game beyond the confines of Army cantonments. The first attempts at forming a national association took place in Calcutta in 1907–08.[6] The political chaos that engulfed Bengal after its partition in 1905, however, put paid to these efforts. The move was revived in the 1920s when C.E. Newham, president of the Punjab Hockey Federation, started a campaign to create a central organization to govern Indian hockey. This second attempt at establishing a nodal organization also ended in failure and it was not until November 1925 that a governing body for hockey was established.

The princely state of Gwalior was the new centre. Writing in 1959, this is how A.S. De Mello described the formation of the Indian Hockey Federation (IHF):

> In 1924, at the request of the now defunct Western India Hockey Association, Lieutenant Colonel Luard, who was then President of the

> Gwalior Sports Association, addressed all hockey associations, clubs and individuals interested in the game and invited them to a meeting in Gwalior. This meeting, which took place on November 7th, 1925, resulted in the official formation of the Indian Hockey Federation.[7]

At the inaugural meeting of the federation, Gwalior, Bengal, Punjab, Sind, Rajputana, Western India, Punjab University and the Army Sports Control Board were represented. For the first two years, Gwalior was treated as the headquarters, subsequently it moved to Delhi in 1927.[8]

The formation of the IHF was a landmark event because it enabled international exposure for Indian players for the first time. Soon after its formation the IHF organized India's first international tour, the trip to New Zealand in 1926. The Indian team immediately made its mark and their wizardry proved to be a commercial success as well. The New Zealand Hockey Federation made a profit of GBP 300 after paying the Indians a healthy sum of GBP 500. The Indians ended the tour with 18 victories in 21 matches, and just one defeat. They scored a total of 192 goals, conceding 24, at an average of 9.31 goals per match. Astonishingly, the Indians registered a double-digit score in as many as nine games.[9]

It was on this tour that Dhyan Chand established himself as the premier star of Indian hockey. For him, an enlisted sepoy in the Army and a man not born into privilege, like some of his counterparts, the opportunity to represent India was an unexpected windfall. His outright delight is beautifully portrayed in his autobiography:

> It was a great day for me when my Commanding Officer called me and said: 'Boy, you are to go to New Zealand.' I was dumbfounded, and did not know what to reply. All I did was to click my heels snappily, give as smart a salute as I possibly could, and beat a hasty retreat. Once out of sight of the officer, I ran like a hare to reach my barracks and communicated the good news to my fellow soldiers. And what a reception they gave me! I lost no time in getting prepared for the trip. I was not a rich man, my earnings as a *sepoy* being only a few rupees a month. My parents were not rich either. All thoughts of outfitting and equipping myself in the proper manner for an overseas tour of this nature had to be given up for want of sufficient resources. I clothed myself as inexpensively as possible, and my main personal outfit was my military kit...As soldiers, particularly those belonging to the Other Ranks (read lower ranks), it

> was a great experience for us. Prior to this tour we could never conceive of being feted and entertained at private houses and public functions in such a glorious and enjoyable manner. We were made heroes, and on my part, if I may put it quite modestly, I proved myself a great success and left behind a great impression.[10]

Riding on this success and encouraged by the colonial British government's support, the IHF applied for and subsequently obtained global affiliation in 1927. This was crucial to India's participation at the Amsterdam Games in 1928. It was in Amsterdam that India started its uninterrupted reign over the world of hockey for the next two decades.

'Can I See My Trousers in the Sun': The Beginning

Men's hockey first appeared at the 1908 Olympic Games in London. It reappeared in Antwerp in 1920, returning to stay from the 1928 Amsterdam Games onwards. Women's hockey waited much longer, finally debuting in 1980. Between 1928 and 1956, India won six straight Olympic gold medals and 24 consecutive matches, a record likely to stand for the foreseeable future. Indians have won two more gold medals since, in 1964 and 1980. In fact, it was at India's insistence that hockey was reinstated at Amsterdam after being dropped from the program of the eighth Olympiad in Paris in 1924.

Anthony S. De Mello—from whose autobiographical essay we have borrowed the sub-title of this chapter—writes that before leaving for Amsterdam, India's hockey players, were 'confident that they would not disgrace themselves'.[11] At the same time they did not approach the Games with any fantastic hopes. Jaipal Singh, who had a first-class degree from his native Ranchi and was then a student at Balliol College, Oxford, was appointed captain of the team. A Munda tribal from Chhotanagpur, the forested plateau of undivided Bihar, Jaipal is a fascinating character in Indian history whose influence in later years extended far beyond the hockey field. As Ramachandra Guha writes, he later became the *marang gomke*, or 'great leader' of the tribals of Chhotanagpur and in the Constituent Assembly 'he came to represent tribals not just of his native plateau, but all of India'. It was his interventions in the Constituent Assembly that ultimately led to the reservation of seats for tribals in government jobs and in legislative bodies after independence.[12] Sent to Oxford by missionaries, Jaipal successfully led a team comprising of Indians studying at British universities to Belgium and Spain and earned a reputation as a great hockey player in the UK, as is evident from the numerous profiles published in *World Hockey* magazine. When the team for Amsterdam was announced it included Jaipal, S. M. Yusef and the Nawab of Pataudi Senior, who were already in Britain. Thirteen players sailed from Bombay, nine of them Anglo-Indians, to lead India's challenge at the 1928 Olympics.[13] However, before sailing for London, there was a last-minute alarm when it was revealed that because of insufficient funds only 11 of the 13 selected players could undertake the tour. The shortfall, contemporary reports revealed, was Rs 15,000. That it was a crisis was evident when the federation announced that in case sufficient funds weren't garnered, Shaukat Ali of Bengal and R.A. Norris of the Central Provinces would not accompany the team. In the end, it was largely owing to the munificence of the sports-loving public of Bengal, who organized public collections to make up the funding shortfall, that the two players were able to make the trip.[14]

While he became known in later life as a prominent Parliamentarian and Adivasi leader, Jaipal described his hockey career in the UK in his memoirs thus:

> The effect of the tours of Indian students I conducted every year with the help of Aga Khan, 'Kanji' Baroda, Patiala, Bhopal and other Indian royalty was the formation of the Indian Hockey Federation...India decided to send a team to the Amsterdam Olympiad in 1928. I was still at Oxford a probationer for the Indian Civil Service...As after 1926 I could not play for the University team, I played for the Wimbledon Hockey Club...As at Oxford I continued to receive publicity in the London press.[15]

In a clear reflection of how haphazardly that first Olympic team was put together, and also of the times, he goes on to narrate the strange manner in which he was appointed captain of the Indian team:

> One early evening two Britishers, Colonel Bruce Turnbull and Major Ricketts, both of the Indian army, called at the Church Imperial Club. Turnbull was Secretary of the Army Sports Board in India and Ricketts was his lieutenant. I stood them drinks. They told me the Indian hockey

> team was coming the following week on its way to Amsterdam. 'We want you to captain the team.' I agreed but told them I would have to get leave from the India Office for absence during term time. I did not get leave! I decided to defy the ruling and face the consequences.[16]

Jaipal met his team when their boat docked at Tilbury on 30 March 1928. Having lived in England for a few years by now, he was unimpressed by what he saw as their rustic 'untidy dress and crude demeanor'. The team was put up in a pension at South Kensington and Jaipal invited them a couple of times to the well-known Veeraswamy's restaurant on Regent Street. 'It was expensive to feed them. The Indian dishes were Hyderabadi but not cheap.' Soon after arrival the players started addressing Jaipal as 'skipper' though he was yet to accept the offer formally. In the first few practice sessions, Shaukat Ali and Dhyan Chand caught Jaipal's attention. Shaukat represented Calcutta Customs and could play in any position. Dhyan Chand, a Lance Naik in the Indian Army, had made his name in New Zealand, scoring the bulk of the goals for the Indian Army team in 1926. Dhyan Chand, Jaipal states:

> ...was humble. He had only one pair of trousers. I took him to Austin Reed on Regent Street. We went downstairs. Trousers galore were shown. 'Can I take them upstairs and see them in the sun?' That finished me. I told Shaukat the story. 'What else do you expect of a Lance Naik?' he laughed.[17]

The Indians played a series of matches in London against leading club sides and haphazardly put together national teams like the Anglo Irish. Dhyan Chand scored in almost every game. India's last engagement in England was at the Folkstone Easter Festival where they beat the English national team 4–0 and a team calling itself the Rossalians 18–0. Following these victories, the British and French press in unison suggested that the Indians were favourites for the hockey gold in Amsterdam.[18] And they weren't wrong.

'The World's Best Centre-Forward': Amsterdam 1928

At Amsterdam the onus was on the hockey team to lead the Indian challenge. The athletes, Chawan in the 10,000 metres, Hamid in the 400 metres hurdles and Murphy in the 800 metres, had failed to qualify for the second round. In hockey, India played its first match against Austria winning 6–0, an encounter reported in detail at home. Already, Dhyan Chand was being described as the 'world's greatest centre forward'. As the *Statesman* put it:

> The Indian Hockey team has successfully surmounted the first obstacle towards the prize for which they journeyed to Europe. India defeated Austria 6–0 with the world's greatest center forward Dhyan Chand giving another masterly exhibition. He scored all 3 goals in the first half. After the interval Dhyan Chand scored the fourth goal. The fifth was obtained by Shaukat Ali while Gately secured the last goal...[19]

Dhyan Chand eventually scored 14 of India's 29 goals in Amsterdam.

The very next day, the *Statesman* published another detailed report on India's 9–0 win over Belgium. The space allotted to the report was nearly double compared to the first, an indication of the growing popularity of the team back home:

> All India followed up their brilliant victory over Austria by defeating Belgium 9–0. The point about today's victory was it proved India can pile up goals even if Dhyan Chand does not think it necessary to improve his goal average. In his skilful manner he worked out scoring possibilities yet tapped the ball either to Feroze Khan or Marthins. Seaman, whose clever stick work on left wing has been the feature of the tour, bewildered Belgium's goalkeeper twice. Allen in India's goal did not have much to do. Jaipal Singh was brilliant and Penniger did all that was required of him with polish...[20]

Subsequently, the Indians beat Denmark and Switzerland to set up a title clash with hosts Holland on 26 May 1928.

When the Indians trounced Holland 3–0 in the final, the press back home went wild. The *Statesmen* had an entire report titled 'How India Won Honors' and went on to suggest that 40,000 people went into raptures over the brilliant exhibition of hockey displayed by the Indians in the final. It reported that despite having to reconstruct their side in the absence of Feroze Khan, who had broken his collarbone in the clash against Denmark, and Shaukat Ali, who was down with the flu, India won comprehensively.[21] Interestingly, the report does not mention the absence of captain Jaipal Singh who had, for personal reasons, walked out of the team before the semi-final. This is one of the most enduring mysteries of the tour and perhaps the first known political controversy within the national hockey team. Jaipal too is remarkably silent about this discord in his memoirs, one that had raised doubts over who had actually captained the final victory—Jaipal or Penniger. Jaipal left the Olympic team on the eve of the semi-final and did not take part in the final either. He refused to discuss the issue ever again in public and until new evidence emerges, the mystery of why he walked out of that first Indian Olympic team will remain unsolved.[22]

Coming back to the victory, the *Statesman* report quoted earlier also hit upon another intriguing aspect of those years of Indian dominance at the Olympics: 'It is no empty title, for the critics are of the opinion that even if England had been competing in the Games, honors would have gone to India, though possibly not with the record of not conceding a goal remaining intact'.[23] The colony had won in Europe but the colonizer was absent. In fact, there was a rumour in Olympic circles that England had initially entered a team for the Olympic hockey competition at Amsterdam. According to this rumour, after the 4–0 drubbing they received at the Folkestone festival at the hands of the Indians, the English were scared of losing on an international stage to their 'colony' and withdrew from the event. This belief was wide-spread enough for Dhyan Chand to refer to it is his recollections:

> I reiterate that this is mere hearsay (that England dropped out of the Amsterdam Games fearing the Indians), although we fondly hoped that at least in future Olympics we would have the honor of meeting Great Britain and showing them how good or bad we were. It is my regret that this hope was never realized so long as I participated in Olympic events.[24]

The English team did not participate in the Olympics until 1948, by which time India was an independent nation.[25] When India beat England 4–0 in the 1948 Games, it unleashed great celebrations in the newly independent nation and the win contributed to national self-confidence and self-belief.[26]

It was in Amsterdam that the legend of Indian hockey was created. Even the Dutch papers praised the team with generosity; 'So agile are the Indians that they could run the full length of the hockey field, juggling a wooden ball on the flat end of the hockey stick'.[27]

England may not have participated but soon after the win, the Viceroy, Lord Irwin, sent a telegram to the team manager B. Rosser: 'Please convey to Jaipal Singh and all members of his team my heartiest congratulations on their magnificent victory. All India has followed the triumphal progress throughout the tour and rejoice in the crowning achievement'.[28] This telegram, which mentions Jaipal as captain, laid the captaincy debate to rest.

India scored 29 goals in Amsterdam, without conceding even one, and averaged more than five goals per match. Interestingly, the Olympic hockey competition was played in May, while the actual Olympiad, including the opening ceremony and other events, took place two months later in July. As a result, the victorious Indian team did not have the good fortune of enjoying the Olympic atmosphere, the rituals of the opening ceremony and the subsequent ambience of the Olympic village.

In London, the victory became a source of great nationalist celebration for the Indian community. Indian women organized a tea party in the team's honour and presented them with turbans. Interestingly, as Jaipal pointed out, 'The Anglo Indians never wore them!'[29] They were also entertained to lunch at Veeraswamy's by Dr Paranjpe, a member of the Indian Council. And when the team reached Bombay, it was welcomed by a huge throng of adoring fans. Mole Station overflowed with a wildly cheering crowd trying to get a glimpse of the new heroes. In the audience was Dr G.V. Deshmukh, the Mayor of Maharashtra, who was there to accord the team a civic reception, and a representative of the Governor of Mumbai, who sent a congratulatory message.[30]

Jaipal, who had broken his term at Oxford without leave to play in the Games, paid a personal price for the victory. He returned to Oxford after the festivities were over, only to be confronted with angry dons. As he put it:

> I was told that as I had broken term I would have to stay for one more year. Captaining India to world championship was no prize for the British. I resigned from the ICS and refused to pay back 350 pounds. I was not put in gaol.[31]

Jaipal's resignation from the ICS after that first hockey win led him away from sport to a different arena: he gradually moved into politics and became the leader of the Adibasi Mahasabha in 1938. The man who had looked in derision at Dhyan Chand for his rustic manners now became the champion of India's tribals. He held the view that the tribals were 'the original inhabitants' of the subcontinent—hence the term 'adibasi' or 'adivasi'. As Ramachandra Guha has pointed out, Jaipal went on become the greatest defender of tribal rights in the Constitutional Assembly and his interventions were erudite as well as spirited, as for instance when he opposed the prohibition of alcohol which had been inserted as a Directive Principle. Alcohol, he said, was part of the daily and ritual life of the tribals of India and he denounced the ideas of prohibition as an interference:

> ...with the religious rights of the most ancient people in the country... it would be impossible for paddy to be transplanted if the Santhal does not get rice beer. These ill clad men...have to work knee-deep in water throughout the day, drenching rain and in mud. What is it in the rice beer that keeps them alive? I wish the medical authorities in this country would carry out research in their laboratories to find out what it is that the rice beer contains, of which the Adibasis need so much and which keeps them [protected] against all manner of diseases.[32]

Jaipal's hockey adventure led to his premature departure from the ICS but the ICS's loss was independent India's gain. It was Jaipal who initiated the demand for a separate tribal state of Jharkhand, which was ultimately carved out of Bihar in 2001.

Loans of Glory: En Route to Los Angeles, 1932

Global economic depression, starting from the Wall Street crash in 1928, meant that India, Japan and the United States were the only entrants competing for hockey honours at the Los Angeles Olympiad in 1932. However, that does not take away from the fact that the Indians were far superior to any of their contemporaries. With a view to defending the title won at Amsterdam, the IHF tried to pick the best team possible for the 1932 Games and organized an inter-provincial trial in Calcutta in March 1932. Only Dhyan Chand was an automatic choice. Based on performance at the trials, the appointed representatives of the provinces affiliated to the federation picked the rest of the national team led by Lal Shah Bokhari. G.D. Sondhi was appointed manager and Pankaj Gupta the non-playing captain and assistant manager of the touring side.

The effects of the depression were also felt in India and the IHF found it exceedingly difficult to raise funds to undertake the tour. In the end, money came from a diverse range of sources: contributions from Viceroy Lord Willingdon, the Governors of the provinces, a few of the princely families, public collections by the nation's sporting public and proceeds from exhibition football and hockey matches played in Calcutta, Bhopal, Bombay, Madras, Bangalore, Singapore and Colombo. Even this was not enough to cover all the expenses but at least the team was able to leave Indian shores.[33]

Picking the team was the easy part but sending it overseas was a huge financial challenge. To cope with the financial shortfall, the federation took a loan of Rs 7,500. It organized exhibition matches for the national team at Colombo, Madras, Bombay, Delhi and Lahore on the team's homeward journey and hoped that proceeds from these matches would wipe out the debt entirely. A sports goods dealer from Sialkot, Uberoi and Co. chipped in by supplying the players with hockey sticks and balls. The sticks, it is evident from players' memoirs, were the very best available globally.

Despite the challenges, the IHF was reluctant to forgo the opportunity of international glory. A measure of the obstacles faced in sending the team is borne out by the reminiscences of Pankaj Gupta:

> Before the Los Angeles Games, I, in my capacity as Hony Secretary of the Indian Hockey Federation and Mr. A.M. Hayman, the President, had more than our share of headaches. First there was the question of finance and secondly it was debatable whether it was worthwhile sending a team to play against such weak opposition as that provided by the USA and Japan. Several meetings were held and the IHF took a bold decision, prompted by the fact that if India did not take part the event might be deleted from the Games and possibly not revived...I am glad that we, in the larger interest of international glory, decided to send our team.[34]

In the same article, he emphasized Bengal's contribution in promoting hockey in India and declared, 'it might be news to many that most of the money at the earlier stages of India's participation in Olympic hockey came from Bengal. I must not be misunderstood when I refer to Bengal, which I have not done from any parochial angle but public memory is always short and history and tradition should not be forgotten.'[35] He went on to state that in his opinion the best Indian team ever produced was the 1932 Olympic team, which played on consecutive days despite having to undertake overland third-class travel on the Continent to meet expenses.[36]

India's newly picked team played its first pre-Olympic tour match at Bhopal on 15 May against a team from Aligarh University. The national team won easily, scoring five goals each on either side of half time. On 16 May they played the Bhopal team, beating them 8–2. While at Bhopal the team was accorded royal treatment as guests of the Nawab. Prince Rahid-uz-Zafar Khan, who made a contribution of Rs 1,000 towards the tour fund, organized a reception in their honour. At the time of the visit, the Nawab of Bhopal was away on official work and sent the team the following message:

> I extend a most hearty welcome to the members of the Olympic Hockey Team on their visit to Bhopal and my keenest regret is my absence from my state on this occasion. But my inability to show you and your team hospitality in person will not diminish the cordiality, which my state will offer you on my behalf, or the sincerity of my good wishes for the success of your mission. Our Indian team represents the true spirit of sportsmanship in India and carries with it the good wishes of all people. We are confident that all of you will...keep the flag flying in all the countries you include in your tour. Your sporting achievements will... add further glory to the fair name of India and enhance its reputation among the nations of the West...[37]

This message is indicative enough of the respect accorded to the players by the Nawab. For players like Dhyan Chand and Roop Singh, men from underprivileged and humble backgrounds, the game was a means to social respectability. Like in football and cricket, princely patronage played a crucial role.

The communal riots in Bombay, though, cast a deep shadow on the team when it moved to Bombay for three matches between 19 and 21 May. Attendance at these games was affected by the riots and from here the players moved on to Bangalore, Madras and then Colombo. Travelling around the country, raising money for their

Olympic journey, the guiding principle for these players was the idea of 'national self-respect'. As skipper Lal Shah Bokhari put it in a message issued in Madras: 'I can assure my countrymen that we will bring respect to India and we will maintain our tradition as World's Champion Hockey playing nation'.[38]

The money-raising drive did not end in India. En route to Los Angeles, the team played exhibition games at every port at which they docked. The only aim was to raise the money to wipe out their loans. Everywhere, their exhilarating stick work left dazzled onlookers in its wake. Watching them play in Ceylon, for instance, the Governor declared in awe, 'Is it really over? I feel I have been watching your team play for only five minutes'.[39] From Colombo the team set sail for Singapore on board the steamship Haruna Maru. The final destination of the pre-Olympics tour was Japan where the Indians beat an unofficial Japanese team by 11 goals on 20 June. Having won hearts in Tokyo, the Indians proceeded to defend their crown at Los Angeles.

Their arrival in America was greeted with much fanfare, with Indians settled in California coming out in large numbers to fete the team. The citizens' forum of San Francisco organized a civic reception in honour of the Japanese, Philippine and Indian Olympic athletes when the boat carrying the Indian team stopped in San Francisco for two days on 6 July 1932. At the reception the Mayor presented a key of the city to each delegation. Finally, after a 42-day voyage, the Indians arrived in Los Angeles. Once settled, they were all praise for the Olympic village and the training facilities at the University of California. What especially impressed the Indians was the wholesome food on offer in the Olympic village.[40] Local newspaper reports in the US mentioned that while the Indians indulged in light exercise, the US and Japanese teams practised all day long to improve their skills.[41]

Indians in America: The Real Action

The first Indians in action at the Los Angeles games were the sprinters M. Sutton and R. Vernieux. Both athletes performed well and were successful in making it to the British Empire team picked to face the Americans after the Olympics. This was the first occasion when Indian athletes made it to the Empire team.[42] While the Indians acquitted themselves well in athletics, in swimming N.C. Mallick lost out in the 400 metres freestyle competition, coming fourth in his heat. However, his timing was considerably better than what he had clocked at home, a remarkable achievement in a short span of time.

In hockey, India's preparations did not go to plan with Hammond and Jaffer down with muscle strain and Lal Shah, the captain, badly hurt following an injury in practice. Penniger joined the injured list on 2 August when he suffered a hit on his eyebrow which required requiring stitches. Finally, a day before the first encounter against Japan, India's goalkeeper R.J. Allen, who had distinguished himself at Amsterdam by not conceding a single goal, suffered a strained muscle that forced him out of the contest. Hind, the reserve goalkeeper, replaced him.[43]

11–1

In the opening match of the hockey competition at Los Angeles, the Indians overwhelmed the Japanese by 11 goals to one. If contemporary reports are anything to go by, India's clinical display mesmerized the Japanese, who had no answer to the deft stick work and ball control exhibited by the Indians. Dhyan Chand scored four goals while Roop Singh and Gurmit Singh scored three goals each. Carr scored the final goal for India after a brilliant solo run. Match reports mentioned that the Indians would have fared better but for the soft turf to which they were still not accustomed.[44]

Having beaten the Japanese by a convincing margin, it seemed inevitable that the Indians would retain the gold they had won at Amsterdam. Their confidence was evident when they decided to make a series of changes to the team in the match against the US to ensure that all 15 players in the squad played a hand in the victory. Olympic rules necessitated that a player had to play a part in the competition to be entitled to a medal.[45]

24–1

This was how the match against the US, which saw the Indians make a mockery of the Americans by beating them 24–1, was reported back home:

> India has retained the world hockey championship. Today, before a crowd that sat amazed at the skill of the Indians, the US suffered a defeat by 24 goals to 1. It was greatly expected that India would win easily but not even her most optimistic admirers thought goals would come at the rate of one in every two minutes. The Americans worked hard but the game was a revelation to them. Amazingly clever stick work of the Indians, the perfect understanding between forwards, the manner in which half backs came up to support and strengthen each attack, the flick passes of both forwards and halves—all these were new to the Americans who often were so spell bound by these tactics that they could only stand and gape at their nimble opponents. Roop Singh scored 12 goals and Dhyan Chand 7, Gurmit Singh scored 3 and Jaffer and Penniger 1 each.[46]

In the immediate aftermath of the victory there were spectacular scenes of jubilation when India's flag fluttered at the summit of the stadium and the band played the national anthem of British India. Newspapers across the world paid tribute to the incalculable superiority of the Indians and surprisingly did not express astonishment at the magnitude of the score, which was an international record. Rather, newspapers in the US expressed satisfaction that the US was able to score a lone goal against the mighty Indians.[47] The US captain's comment that for most of the game 'they were chasing shadows' aptly summed up the nature of the encounter. Finally, a special broadcast was arranged to comment on India's incomparable prowess in hockey and pay tribute to the Indian team's exceptional conduct and widespread popularity.[48]

The Viceroy, who had helped in raising funds for the team, sent a congratulatory message as well: 'I am delighted and proud to learn of the splendid victory of our hockey team. Please give all members of the side my warm congratulations upon retaining World's Championship'.[49] The director of the Olympic Village wrote the following message to Pankaj Gupta: 'The Indian team being in the village longer than any of the others became part of the family. On behalf of all my associates and myself here I want to thank you, and through you the entire Indian delegation, for the splendid cooperation you gave us in the operation of the village'.[50]

Not surprisingly, after the final, the Indian community in Los Angeles went berserk. Many contributed generously to raise a pool of $400 needed to enable the Indians to travel around the country exhibiting their skill. The post-Olympic tour lasted for almost a month.[51]

'He Is an Angel'

India started her post-Olympic tour at Philadelphia with a rematch against the United States on 20 August. This time around the final score was a wee bit respectable for the United States, with the Indians winning 20–1. The visit to Philadelphia was followed by a return visit to California before the Indians embarked upon a tour of Europe. Again financial considerations were paramount here. When in Los Angeles, the advantages of returning via Europe were considered by the Indian delegation. Pankaj Gupta was determined to make this happen and did a great deal to obtain quotations for rail and steamer fares. When it came to know about the Indian intention to travel through Europe, the German Hockey Association invited the Indians to play a certain number of Games in the continent. The Indians accepted the offer as it did not involve a substantially higher expenditure than if they returned via Japan.[52]

The Indian Olympic team played nine matches in Europe on their way back and won each one of them—despite Europe being a logistical nightmare, as reported by the president of the IHF:

> Every member of our party enjoyed the tour immensely, notwithstanding the strenuous travel we had to undertake. To play the match at Budapest on 15 September, we had to travel by bus from Vienna to that city and back, a distance of 500 kilometers. We left Vienna at 10.30 am, arrived at Budapest at 5 pm., played at once, and returned to Vienna at 2 am the following morning.[53]

The Indians received their warmest reception in Amsterdam. People at the Dutch capital were jubilant to have the team back in the city. Old acquaintances like Leming, attaché to the Indian team four years earlier, organized a civic reception for the Indians in which the players were presented with the local mascot—a monkey.[54]

Contemporary reports make it clear that Dhyan Chand was an idol in the hockey world of Europe. Germany held him dear, calling their best hockey player 'the German Dhyan Chand.' At Prague a young lady insisted after the match on kissing India's hockey wizard, a demand that made him extremely uncomfortable. 'He is an angel,' she declared before kissing him. In Germany the Indians met the German national team in Munich and beat them 6–0. After the match, the Indian contingent presented a stick signed by the entire squad to their hosts at the German Hockey Federation.[55]

In all, the Indian team played 28 matches on tour and scored a total of 263 goals.

The Problem of the Rupee

Neither the Olympic title nor the spectacular display put up on numerous occasions across the world was enough to solve the financial crisis that plagued Indian hockey. At the start of the tour, the team was short of the estimated expenditure by Rs 8,000–10,000. The contributions received as a result of matches played at various places on the way to Los Angeles had made up a large part of this deficit. However, expenses in America were way in excess of the estimate and transport charges for excess baggage throughout the tour weighed heavily on the touring party. Added to this was the extra expenditure incurred in Europe to play a series of exhibition matches in several European countries. As the IHF president put it: 'We all took too much luggage with us. This involved us in avoidable expenditure in transport charges. This is a matter that should receive careful attention in subsequent tours'.[56]

Tour expenses were met from the special fund and by drawing upon the few thousands from the main account of the federation. The final debt stood at a substantial Rs 12,000. The team was forced to issue a plea to sports fans and sporting clubs back home to come forward and make a donation to the tour fund.

Interestingly, the managers of the team were determined to get the accounts of the tour fund audited at the earliest instance and were also keen to publish a summary of the receipts and expenditures incurred to ensure transparency.[57] Whether this was eventually done is not known.

The 'National' Game: What Was Special about Hockey?

Why was India so good at hockey in those early years? Commenting on the Indian success at Amsterdam, A.B. Rosser, the manager, declared in his report, 'The success of the Indian team was due to positional play, combination of forwards with halves, likewise of halves with backs, the tackle back, quick movement and first time passes, deft stick work both in attack and defence, frequent use of hand to stop the ball and the feint to baffle the defence'.[58] From this description it is evident that the Indians were sound in the basics and adept at tactics and strategy.

The managers of the 1932 Indian touring team further developed Rosser's analogies. They argued that because the grounds in India were hard, it allowed the Indians to develop a fast game. Also, the Indians were supple of wrist, making possible the dribble. They played in light footwear, which enabled quickness of movement. Swami Jagannath, a player, organizer and subsequently a professional hockey umpire, offered a similar explanation. 'The chief factors which contribute to the success of the Indians in the field of hockey are the extensive plots of land available as playing fields, heavy rainfall over only a short period of the year giving generally dry and hard grounds, the light physique of the people and the supple movements of their bodies.'[59] The comparatively low cost of practice was another reason behind India's supremacy in world hockey.

Writing in the 1960s, C.D. Parthasarathy argued that it was only when a series of rule changes were introduced and a series of amendments passed that India's superiority was challenged. For example, the introduction of free hit for 'bully' made skill secondary. Also, the new penalty corner rule introduced in the 1950s made goal scoring easier, rendering ineffective the natural Indian flair with the ball. Gradually, crisp, sharp, short passes and the dribble, a feature of India's play, gave way to long and powerful hits and first-time passes. Soon, power counted more than precision and the Indians lost out, unable to counter the innovative techniques of the Europeans.[60]

However, none of these explanations convincingly clarifies the reasons for India's early superiority or the subsequent decline in Indian hockey. For, even after the rule changes were introduced, the Indians won silver at Rome in 1960 and gold at Tokyo in 1964.

Rather, it can be suggested that the most striking feature of the successful Indian tours in 1928 and 1932 was the absence of divisions among players or officials on lines of class, caste or economic privilege.

In 1932, the entire touring party with the exception of G.D. Sondhi stayed together at the Olympic village. This also included the president of the IHF, A.M. Hayman. In his review of the tour, Hayman singled out this sense of camaraderie and fellow feeling among the players and officials as the central factor that contributed to India's continuing dominance in world hockey. He ended his report with the words:

> I have been with the Olympic team throughout the tour. I lived with the players at the Olympic village at Los Angeles. I entered into all their frolic and fun. I have never lived with better companions. At all times and in all places everyone of them behaved as a true sportsman and gentleman.[61]

It was this feeling of camaraderie among players that held the Indian team together during their amazing run of six consecutive Olympic gold medals in 1928–56 and partly explains why India could do it in hockey but was unable to scale similar heights in cricket or football in the 1930s–40s.

It is perhaps worth suggesting that the camaraderie was a product of the players' backgrounds and professions. Unlike in cricket, where the princes always held the upper hand because the players were dependant on them for patronage, in hockey the players were mostly professionals in other fields, with an innate sense of discipline governing their lives. Hockey players who weren't part of the Army were professionals employed by institutions like the Railways and on most occasions had graduate degrees.

A study of the class composition and professions of the players of the 1932 Indian Olympic team helps substantiate this point. While the captain Lal Shah Bokhari was a member of the Punjab Provincial Service, goalkeeper Richard Allen James worked for the Port Commissioners in Calcutta. Eric Penniger, who captained the team in the absence of Jaipal Singh at Amsterdam, worked for the North Western Railway, as did his second-in-command Arthur Charles Hind. Others employed by the Railways included Carlyle Tapsell (Bengal Nagpur Railway), William Sullivan (Central India Railway) and Richard John Carr (East India Railway). Dhyan Chand, as mentioned earlier, was a Lance Naik in the Army while Roop Singh, Muhammed Jaffer, Aslam Bagga, Masud Minhas and Gurmit Singh were either in college or had just finished their bachelor's degrees from well-known institutions like Chief's College or Islamia College in Lahore.[62] In hockey, there were none like Lala Amarnath or Mushtaq Ali who could rise to prominence because the Maharaja of Patiala and the Nawab of Bhopal accorded them patronage.

In sharp contrast to the rosy picture painted by the hockey team, the Indian cricket team which toured England in 1932 was a divided house. The sharply divided nature of the team is portrayed in *Twenty-Two Yards to Freedom: A Social History of Indian Cricket:*

> The team that was initially united under Patiala's leadership was deeply divided by the end. Soon after the tour was over, Vizzy donated a pavilion to the newly built Ferozeshah Kotla Stadium in Delhi, naming it after Lord Willingdon. These efforts to curry favour with the Viceroy were successful, and though Patiala was elected chancellor of the Chamber of Princes in 1933, his influence over Indian cricket was on the wane.[63]

Mihir Bose also draws attention to this deep-seated internal discord in his seminal work on the history of Indian cricket:

> Willingdon's hostility to Patiala had coincided with the waning of the latter's cricket power. He had been the kingmaker of the 1932 tour, but in the winter of 1933–34 he was pushed to the sidelines. The emergency Board of Control meeting in Delhi on 1 May 1933 showed that the associations, which had once survived because of his generosity were now turning against him.'[64]

That the scenario had not improved is evident from a letter written by Mushtaq Ali to his mentor C.K. Nayudu when on tour in England in 1946. Written on 1 August 1946 from the Carlton Hotel in Taunton, the letter goes thus:

> ...Now Sir I must tell you something from this end, how Indian cricket is and how we are doing in this country. In my humble opinion this tour is worse than 1936, the same old trouble: no team work at all. Every member of the team is for himself. No one cares for the country at all. Amarnath is the cause of all these things. Pataudi is a changed man... and is very much against the Indian players. C.S. Nayudu plays in the team not as a bowler but as a fielder only...Whenever a county player is set for a big score you will find the Indian captain back in the pavilion. As a captain he is worse than a school boy...I am very much fed up with him as are the other members of the team. Believe me Sir, the second Test match was ours after such a nice start. We collapsed because he sent

> in Abdul Hafeez at No 3 instead of going in himself...I think Merchant is a much better captain than this fellow.[65]

In football too the picture was similar, evident from the tremendous infighting between provincial football organizations in the run-up to the formation of the All India Football Federation in 1937. It started when the Indian Football Association (IFA) based in Calcutta, unhappy with its role as a regional institution, aimed to govern the development of football in the whole country, posing as the governing body for soccer in India. It was as a mark of protest against such intentions of the IFA that other state associations for soccer formed the All India Football Association (AIFA) in September 1935. The formation of the latter led to a battle for supremacy between the Indian states, Bengal on the one hand and the western and northern states on the other. Unfortunately for Indian football, players too were drawn into this conflict and were forced to take sides. When the Chinese Olympic team visited the country for a series of charity games before the Berlin Olympiad of 1936, there was a huge dispute over the venues and also over the players picked to represent India against the Chinese team. That there was an overwhelming majority of Bengali players in the team did not go down well with soccer players from northern and western India.

In fact, it was only when the representative of the Army Sports Control Board, a key player in the whole controversy, decided to bring about a compromise between the provinces by taking the initiative to form AIFF that the conflict came to an end. Eventually, the Army was forced to issue a circular to all the soccer associations of the country declaring that a conference would be held at Simla (now Shimla) in May 1937 where AIFF would finally come into existence. While this solution was not something Bengal desired, it was the best result under the circumstances. Bengal was in no position to alienate the Army Sports Control Board, whose support was key to the survival of IFA. It tried its best to postpone the formation of AIFF to September but the Army Sports Board held firm. In a personal letter sent to the Maharaja of Santosh, the president of IFA, the representative of the Army Sports Control Board declared his intention to go ahead with the formation of AIFF at Simla in May 1937, solving the crisis that had plagued the fortunes of soccer in India for almost a decade.[66]

In hockey, there were no early administrative and political divides, like in the other two games. The players, unsullied by administrative wrangles, played as one unit. The hockey team rose to national prominence for its performances on the international stage as a 'national' team. It was this nationalist link that bound it in the early years. While the politics of nationalism operated in both cricket and soccer,[67] neither of these two games produced triumphs for the 'national' team. The great 1911 victory of the Calcutta-based Mohun Bagan Club over the British East York Regiment is seen by a number of historians as not just a sporting but also a nationalist milestone that spurred on the Swadeshi movement.[68] By the 1930s, the noted literary figure Sajani Kanta Das had noted that three things personified Bengali colonial identity: Mohun Bagan, Subhash Chandra Bose and New Theatres.[69] Yet soccer's triumphs were not the triumphs of a 'national' team in the way that hockey's was and soccer remained enmeshed in regional rivalries between Bengal and other rival provinces until much later.

In sharp contrast, the astonishing success rate of Indian hockey in the late colonial and early post-colonial period, when it won six successive gold medals at the Olympics between 1928 and 1956, turned that game into a symbol of nationalist sentiment as a whole. So much so that when the IOC toyed with the idea of dropping hockey as an event in the 1952 Helsinki Olympics, India offered to host the event separately in New Delhi. The success of the Indian hockey teams in beating Western teams demonstrated to the nationalists that Indians could compete on equal terms with the West. The success of the Indian hockey teams was such that after independence the ministry of sport, not surprisingly, chose hockey as the official 'national game' of India.

Onwards to Berlin

Beyond a shadow of doubt, India had established itself as the world's foremost hockey playing nation by 1932. At the same time, there's little doubt that the absence of leading European and Australasian nations at Los Angeles had diluted the impact of the Indian triumph. In fact, their absence transformed India's title defence at Berlin in

1936 into something far more significant than a quest for another Olympic gold. That the Indians were in no mood to relinquish their hold on the world title was evident when on its second tour to New Zealand in 1935 the team stunned the world by winning all the 48 games played. The Indians scored a record 584 goals and conceded just 40. It was indication enough that India was ready to take on Europe at Berlin. What made the Indian dream run at the Nazi Olympiad especially momentous was that for the first time in history the legendary Dhyan Chand was named captain, an appointment that hinted at the decisive collapse of the privilege barrier in hockey. To Berlin we travel in the next chapter.

4

Hitler's Games
Captain Dhyan Chand and Indian Nationalism in the Third Reich

Nowadays I hear of the princely comforts provided for national teams traveling overseas, and the fuss players raise if they happen to miss even a cup of tea! When we used to travel, the name of our country and the game were the only two things that mattered.

—Dhyan Chand on India's title defence at the 1936 Berlin Olympic Games[1]

'Will India Lose Under My Charge?' Dhyan Chand's Delhi Dilemma

Despite having comprehensively beaten the world in 1928 and 1932, India's supremacy in field hockey was still in doubt on the eve of the Berlin Games in 1936. This was because all of Europe had stayed away from the 1932 hockey competition at Los Angeles on account of the Great Depression and also because European hockey had improved by quite a few notches in the interim. Accordingly, trying to defend the title at Berlin in 1936 was the biggest challenge Indian hockey had ever faced. That India was ready for it was evident when the Indian team won all 48 matches on its tour of New Zealand in 1935.[2]

But it's the nature of sport that even the greatest of champions can have an off-day. There was a big flutter when the Indian Olympic team, picked after the inter-province trials at Calcutta in January–February 1936, lost 1–4 to a Delhi Hockey XI on 16 June at the Mori Gate ground. This was unprecedented and the shock defeat started dark murmurs. Touring international cricket sides would in later years learn to attribute their defeats in the Indian capital to the mysterious malady called 'Delhi belly'. Dhyan Chand, the newly appointed captain of the national team, did not, of course, use the same excuse but his bewilderment and shock were there for all to see. In his autobiography, published 16 years later, he beautifully described the after-effect of this wake-up call:

> My experiences thus far had been to win matches and not lose them. I remember that in 1932, after our return from the Olympic tour, we beat Delhi by 12 goals to nil. I never recognized Delhi as a big hockey playing center, but on this day they were right on top of us and completely outplayed us. The news of this defeat created adverse opinions about us, and while we were touring other centers before we finally sailed from Mumbai, this particular defeat kept worrying me. For the first time I was captaining the Olympic team; will India lose the title under my charge?[3]

Later generations would justifiably remember Dhyan Chand as a wizard who could do no wrong. But his musings after the Delhi defeat revealed the eternal truth of all sport: even the greatest of legends are only human. By now Dhyan Chand was worried about his legacy and suffered from moments of self-doubt. In the run-up to the Berlin Games, Dhyan Chand's anxieties were particularly pertinent, for his appointment as captain was mired in controversy. Despite being the best player, Dhyan Chand's claims for captaincy had been circumvented in 1932 on account of what was seen as his inferior social status. A lowly soldier in the Army, he had been passed up as captain earlier despite being the best player in the team and its talisman. By 1936 the sheer weight of his exploits and his towering presence on the field forced a rethink. But Dhyan Chand was only too conscious of the new responsibility and the tremendous burden on him at a time when social divides still largely governed public life. One small slip, and the knives would be out for him. As he noted, 'I was bypassed in 1932 possibly because of my academic handicaps and so-called social position in life. I was still an ordinary soldier, holding a minor rank.'[4] Palwankar Baloo, the great Dalit cricketer at the turn of the 20th century, whose social origins initially denied him entry into the Hindu Gymkhana in Bombay, would have sympathized. Baloo overcame high-caste derision to become one of the Hindu

Gymkhana's greatest stars in the Bombay Pentangular but was never made captain. It wasn't until 1923 that his brother Palwankar Vithal broke the captaincy barrier in cricket.[5] In Dhyan Chand's case, class barriers had been the biggest obstacle and the fact that he was finally given the captaincy placed him under enormous pressure at Berlin.

To the Führer: An Indian in Berlin

Of all the Olympics before the world wars, none is better documented on film than the Berlin Games. This can partly be attributed to advances in film technology but a major reason lies in the propaganda value of the Games for Adolf Hitler, who had ridden on the Weimar Republic's post-Versailles discontent and humiliation to achieve power through the Berlin putsch of 1933.[6] Berlin won the bid for the 1936 Games long before Hitler and the Nazis came to power[7] but for a leader who had just openly repudiated the Treaty of Versailles, the Olympics became an occasion to promote Nazi ideology.[8] Joseph Goebbels, the Reich minister for popular enlightenment and propaganda, played a big part in convincing Hitler of the publicity value of the Games and film-maker Leni Reifenstahl, a favourite of Hitler's, was commissioned to film them. Her film *Olympia* originated many of the techniques now commonplace to the filming of sports.[9]

The video archives of the International Olympic Museum contain reams of footage of the Games that captured them in every dimension—both on and off the field. In the IOC videos, Hitler and Nazi officials feature as prominently as the athletes themselves; Wehrmacht soldiers and disciplined rows of volunteers form the backdrop to what German officials wanted to be remembered as the greatest Games ever. Hitler removed signs stating 'Jews not wanted' and similar slogans from main tourist attractions. Simultaneously, Berlin was 'cleaned up', the ministry of interior authorizing the chief of Berlin Police to arrest all gypsies and keep them in a special camp.[10] All in all, the German government was believed to have spent the then astronomical sum of about $30 million on an event that was meant to showcase the master Aryan race, as Hitler believed the Germans to be, as also to package the progressive and united face of Germany for a global audience.[11]

It was to these Games that Dhyan Chand's hockey players and the rest of the Indian athletes, still a part of the British empire, now headed. Interestingly, when the Indians, twice Olympic champions, set sail from Bombay on what was perhaps the mission of their lives, there was scarcely anybody around to see the team off. As recounted by one of the team members:

> Only the Bombay Customs players, Aslam, Feroze Khan, Jagat Singh and Brewin were with us, so were Behram Doctor and S.K. Mukherjee. The pier was crowded but none took notice of us world champions! Those of us who had been on tour before found this a new experience and not a pleasant one.[12]

The first part of the journey was rough due to turbulent seas and all the players, except C. Tapsell, E.J.C. Cullen and Assistant Manager Pankaj Gupta, were seasick. While most of them recovered in a few days, Joe Phillips and Babu Nimal from Bombay repeatedly requested the team management to send them back. By now the team was worried about this lack of practice. The *Statesman* correspondent accompanying the hockey players noted that they were used to practising on the deck but the rough seas precluded that possibility until the fifth day of the voyage when they played hockey for an hour.[13]

In fact, only when the boat docked at Aden were the Indians able to practice full throttle. In Aden, the Indians had four hours on shore and kept themselves busy. The seriousness with which the hockey players were approaching their title defence was apparent from the fact that even on this small break in their voyage all they wanted to do was play. Soon after arrival the visitors went looking for a hockey ground and found the regimental training field of the 5/14 Punjab Regiment, which was then stationed at Aden. Members of the regiment, who had no prior knowledge of the arrival of the Indian Olympic team, were puzzled but elated at suddenly seeing their countrymen. This episode was documented by one of the players in his diary:

> We left the boat with hockey sticks in hope that some hockey field or a plot of ground might be available where we could stretch our limbs. We asked the bus driver to take us to a hockey ground and he took us to a sandy plot of land, level but full of pieces of bricks, which we afterwards found to be the regimental ground.[14]

Once the nets were put up, the Indians asked the officer present if the ground could be used for practice. An unnamed Indian player later recounted to a newspaper reporter that at first, 'He hesitated but as soon as he discovered we were the All-India team and that Dhyan Chand was with us...he allowed us to play.'[15] The name of Dhyan Chand worked like a charm and once the regiment learnt of the team's arrival the bugle was sounded; in five minutes the entire battalion came out of its barracks to watch the players. It was a surprise gift for them and many of the subedars and privates who knew Dhyan Chand were pleased to see him in Aden. They felt embarrassed because the Indians had come without prior notice and hastily tried to put together a civic reception for the world champions.

During their brief stay at Aden, the Indian hockey players also found time to watch a game of football and were amazed at the high standard and popularity of the sport. As an Indian player recalled: 'A football match was being played on an adjoining ground and there were large crowds watching the game. I was surprised to see football popular in a desert and was more surprised to see the Arabs and Somalis play barefeet...The scouts from Calcutta instead of going to Quetta, Rangoon and Bangalore would be well advised to come to Aden. I found four players good enough for any Calcutta team. Their dribbling and ball control were revelations to me.'[16]

Getting Göring and Goebbels' Autograph: In the Heart of the Third Reich

For the Indian team, surviving as it was on a budget, the journey to Berlin was not the most comfortable. Having docked in Marseilles late on the night of 10 July, the Indians were to catch a connecting train to Paris en route to Berlin, but they missed the connection. As Dhyan Chand explained: 'Dock workers there were on strike, and the passengers were put to great difficulty in getting their baggage through. It took us time to unload our luggage ourselves and get it through the Customs and other formalities, and the result was that we missed our train to Paris. We were lodged in an ordinary hotel in Marseilles for the night'. [17] It was only on the morning of 11 July that the Indians boarded a train for Paris. In Paris, as in Aden, not many were aware of their arrival and the players spent a quiet day, undisturbed by the city's sports media. For some of them 'this was fame with a vengeance'.[18] In sharp contrast to the luxuries afforded to many modern sportsmen, this team of Olympic champions arranged its own travel at the lowest cost. Dhyan Chand's recollection of this journey was written in words that leap out of the mists of the past to stab at the heart. As he put it in his usual nonchalant way: 'We took a night train to Berlin. It was a job even to secure the third class seats provided to us. The night was cold and there was no sleeping accommodation. Cheerfully we forgot all these comforts. We were on a mission for our country'.[19]

The Indians finally landed in Berlin on 13 July and were accorded a splendid welcome at Berlin station. They may not have received a send-off worthy of the Olympic champions in Bombay but in a Berlin striving hard to put its best step forward, they were received as heroes. Dr Diem, chairman of the organizing committee of the Berlin Olympiad, welcomed the Indians, his speech being relayed through a microphone to a large waiting crowd. In a reminder of the fact that they were playing on behalf of the British Indian empire, 'God Save the King' was played, and a band escorted the Indians to a bus, which drove through the streets of Berlin to the city hall, where the Mayor of Berlin welcomed the Indians according to established Olympic tradition. Each member of the team was presented with an album containing pictures of Berlin, and Dhyan Chand received a medal:[20] his celebrity status had preceded him.

By all accounts, the Third Reich pulled out all stops in welcoming the Indians. Here, in the heart of Britain's greatest adversary, they were not just colonial subjects but honoured guests. After the welcome ceremony, the Indians were motored to the Olympic village 20 miles from the city. At the entrance to the village, the commandant in charge of security received the team. 'God Save the King' was played once again and the Union Jack with the star of India was hoisted next to the village gate. Eleven nations had already arrived and later the band members escorted the Indians to their cottage at the further end of the village. Unlike in 1932, when the team was quartered four men to a cottage, at Berlin the team stayed in one barrack containing 11 rooms and a common room.[21] This was five-star treatment by any standards. Dhyan Chand wrote:

> The cottage had 20 beds, a telephone and a refrigerator. Everything was kept spick and span, and every minute detail of our comforts had been attended to. Two stewards were there to look after us. One was Otto, an old-seasoned sailor who had visited India several times and spoke English well. The other was named Schmidt, and he spoke English haltingly. [22]

In a reflection of the importance accorded to the Olympiad by the top brass of the Third Reich, the Games Village was often visited by top dignitaries. Hermann Göring, whose Air Force just four years later was to launch the London Blitz, and Joseph Goebbels, who had designed much of the propaganda around the Games, took personal interest. A bemused Dhyan Chand noted, 'One day while we were in the dining hall, who should walk in but the burly Hermann Goering, clad in his military attire! We were after him in a trice to get his autograph. Later some of us obtained Dr. Goebbels' autograph.'[23] The Indians, it is evident from contemporary reports, were impressed with the arrangements and there was no grouse except on the question of distance.

But there was a hockey title to be defended. The day after they arrived in Berlin, the Indians went out to check the venue for the hockey competition. An unnamed player noticed the differences between the facilities at Los Angeles and Berlin: 'The Olympic stadium here is a bit smaller than the American one. There is one advantage here—all the stadiums are located on one big plot of ground, whereas in America, barring the swimming and the main stadium, the others are quite apart.'[24]The Indians also had to adjust to the weather. Writing to his family back home, an Indian player mentioned that the climate in Berlin was chilly and on days it rained consistently. A military officer had been appointed as the attaché of the Indian team and they were being well looked after. This was essential as the city was far away and the team was feeling a bit out of sorts because of the distance.[25]

'The Shock of Defeat': They Could be Beaten

Dhyan Chand's team had begun its tour preparations with a shock defeat to a local team in Delhi. Now in the first warm-up game on German soil, the team lost again. The Indians suffered a shock defeat against a German XI, losing 1–4. The Delhi defeat could have been dismissed as a one-off, but it had already planted the seeds of doubt in Dhyan Chand's mind. This German blitzkrieg in Berlin was more serious and it served as a perfect wake-up call. The Indians now knew that they were not invincible and the Europeans had caught up. It retrospect, it served Dhyan Chand well because it led to a complete reappraisal of team strategy. Sixteen years later, the proud Indian captain wrote:

> As long as I live, I shall never forget this match or get over the shock of defeat which still rankles in me. Hitler's Germany had made great strides in their game...The result of the play shocked us so much that we could not sleep that night. Some of us even did not have our dinner. At night Pankaj Gupta, Jaffar and myself went into a conference, in which Jagannath also joined. We were unanimous that a substitute be obtained in place of Masood. That same night Gupta rushed to Berlin and sent a cable to Kunwar Sir Jagdish Prasad, president of the IHF, asking him to send Dara, failing whom Frank Wells or Eric Henderson, and also Pinniger. We decided that if Pinniger was not available, Cullen of Madras should be posted as center-half and not Masood. This we did until Dara arrived just a day before we played France in the semi-finals.'[26]

Dara was a Lance Naik stationed at Jhelum and was familiar as an inside forward with Dhyan Chand's play.[27] Money was short but such was the urgency that the federation tried to arrange Dara's passage by air so that he could reach Berlin before the Olympic matches began on 2 August. Despite the best efforts of the IHF, Dara had to wait in Karachi for nine days before he managed a seat in an aircraft. He left by Imperial Airways, entrained at Brindisi, reached Rome, rested there for a day and finally reached Berlin by air to play in the semi-final against France the next day. This was still considered quick work and the team thanked the federation for this admirable handling of Dara's last-minute inclusion.[28]

The psychological impact of that early defeat was enormous and it set off a great deal of criticism. The *Statesman*, which had a correspondent covering the hockey team's travails, now devoted an entire special report titled 'Why SOS Cable was sent to India'. The dispatch from Berlin began with the following post-mortem:

> Friends in India must have been startled by the cable which Professor Jagannath sent to the Indian Hockey Federation's President suggesting that Pinniger and an inside right should be sent to Berlin by air. Why this was thought necessary was explained to me by Mr Gupta, the

> assistant manager. It was felt that the team had no regular inside right and when they met at Bombay, Dhyan Chand at once suggested to the manager that Frank Wells should have been included in the team as Wells had proved a good partner to him in New Zealand. At Bombay, it was felt that with Emmett as inside right the team might shape up well.[29]

That the Indians were aware of the onerous nature of the task at hand was borne out when Professor Jagannath declared in an interview that the standard of European hockey had improved considerably in the four years between 1932 and 1936. In the same interview, he sounded optimistic about India's chances of defending the title they had won at Amsterdam in 1928 and defended easily at Los Angeles in 1932. 'Our Indian team is a good blend of youth and experience and we shall do our best to maintain the high standard of Indian hockey. Dhyan Chand and R.J. Allen, center forward and goalkeeper, are the only members of the 1928 team, who have retained their places this year, but many of the others now with us were members of the 1932 team, which visited Europe after the Los Angeles Games.'[30]

After the shock defeat in the first practice game, the Indians started playing every day but were still dissatisfied with some of their combinations. They went through rigorous physical drills in the morning and in the afternoon divided themselves into two sides to practice match situations for more than an hour. By now the players had settled down and the thinking was that there was no cause for alarm, with six practice games still to be played. Interestingly, these practice games were not played in front of spectators. They were played on private grounds and the media wasn't permitted to cover these matches. The teams were allowed to make as many changes as they liked and none of the matches had an official status. In the second practice game, the Indians were back on song and won comfortably. This performance was a major confidence booster, as evident from the following recollection, 'Cullen played a very good game at center half and Jaffer was tried at inside right, where he was a success. If nobody arrives from India, I think Jaffer will be our inside right and Cullen centre half.'[31]

That the locals too were warming up to the Indians once they started winning was evident after the practice game in Stettin, which the Indians won 5–1. Interestingly, Dhyan Chand refereed the game. The visit to Stettin, 100 miles from Berlin, reminded many in the team of their visit to New Zealand when swarms of autograph hunters never let the players out of sight. There were also a series of formal and informal functions organized by the locals to make the visitors feel at home.[32]

The shock defeat in the first practice game had prompted the team management to institute strict codes of discipline. As M.N. Masood writes, 'It was also decided that every member should go to bed at ten in the evening. However, Mr Jagannath, Mr Gupta, Dhyan Chand and Gurcharan Singh went to see Menaka's dancing the fourth day after this decision, and Mr Jagannath went again the following evening, returning at two in the morning.'[33] Newspaper archives and contemporary reports of the period give no clue about the identity of the intriguing Ms Menaka but it's clear that it wasn't just all work for the Indians in Berlin; they were also having a good time. As Masood noted, 'the senior members seldom went to bed at the fixed hour, and as the days passed, no restriction in regard to bed hours appeared to bind anyone until abruptly the following notice was seen on 28th July: "It has been observed that the members of the hockey team are not keeping regular hours. In the interest of sound training and physical fitness, it is essential to observe regularity in meals, physical training and rest..."'[34]

For many of India's competitors in beating Dhyan Chand's team would have been the greatest challenge. And it seemed that they would stop at nothing to make this possible. A controversy suddenly arose about the amateur status of the players and a question was raised with hockey's international administrators about how India's supposedly amateur players could stay away from work for so long to play hockey. Of course, every other participating country could have been asked the same question. Dhyan Chand narrated this distraction thus:

> While we were in Berlin, a point was raised before the International Hockey Federation (FIH) that the Indian team was not composed of all amateurs. They posed the question: How could a player be away from his country and place of work for more than five months at a stretch if he is an amateur? Were the players being reimbursed for the pecuniary losses they were supposed to suffer? They gave the example of our

> 1935 six-month tour of New Zealand. We succeeded in convincing the authorities that the players were on leave with or without pay, and that the IHF did not reimburse us in any way except meeting our normal expenses. According to my information, Mr G.D. Sondhi was responsible for convincing the FIH gods about the *bona fides* of our players.[35]

The inimitable Mr Sondhi had worked his charm again.

'Marriage Procession of Rich Hindu Gentleman': The Refusal to Salute Hitler

The Berlin Olympics were declared open on 1 August 1936. M.N. Masood, a member of the team, has left a minute-by-minute description of the opening ceremony that provides fascinating reading. It was nothing less than a grand spectacle of Hitler's 'thousand-year Reich'. The Wermacht, as we have already noted, was fully mobilized in setting up the support infrastructure and the competitors were transported to the venue in Army trucks. The Indians, with Dhyan Chand carrying the flag, were by far the most colourfully dressed of the contingents on show. As Masood noted, 'With our golden "kullahs" and light blue turbans, our contingent appeared as members of a marriage procession of some rich Hindu gentleman, rather than competitors in the Olympic Games'.[36] But this was no ordinary 'marriage procession'—its members were about to make a huge political statement by becoming one of the only two contingents who refused to salute Adolf Hitler.

The opening ceremony of the Berlin Olympics was one of the great set-pieces of the Nazi era. As the giant Zeppelin, the Hindenberg, circled majestically over the stadium, Hitler and his Minister of Interior arrived amid great fanfare to inspect a military guard of honour. M.N. Masood noted the fervour that the Führer generated:

> When the Führer neared the Stadium, a multitude of young boys who were watching the proceedings from outside, saw their idol approaching towards them. With one great cry, they shouted 'Heil, Hitler!' and broke the silence of the Maifield.[37]

In four years, that war cry would reverberate around the world but the lightening Panzer blitzkriegs and the horrors of the holocaust were still in the future. For the moment, at least some Indians were impressed by this disciplined spectacle of the resurgent Third Reich. As 'the hundred thousand Germans in the Stadium stood to their feet and sang with one voice' the two German national hymns, 'Deutschland' and 'Horst Wessel-Lied', Masood writes that it 'made a strange impression' upon the Indian contingent and 'not an eye was left dry'.

> India rose before our imagination...somehow the spring of our national feelings was touched, and the unity and solidarity of the people in the Stadium made us look with shame and regret at our poverty, destitution and discord.[38]

But nationalist aspiration was not the same thing as sympathy for the Nazi cause. What Masood does not mention in his elaborate description is the serious controversy the Indians created at the opening ceremony by not offering the raised-arm salute to Hitler during the march past. The Indians were the only contingent, apart from the Americans, to not perform the raised-arm salute as a mark of respect for the German Chancellor.

Loyalist newspapers like the *Statesman* focused more attention on the defiant US contingent, simply mentioning the Indian refusal to salute in passing. This was partly because of the dark cloud that hung over American participation in the days before the Games and the threat of boycott by some US athletes—Jewish athletes Milton Green and Norman Canners true to their word. The high-profile American contingent, remained uncertain whether its participation might be interpreted as support for the Nazi regime and its anti-Semitic policies, had barely made it to Berlin after a narrowly won vote orchestrated by sport administrator and future IOC President Avery Brundage.[39] But their contingent refused to dip its flag or 'doff its headgear' when passing the podium, eliciting 'a certain amount of whistling from a section of the crowd'.[40]The Berlin Games was ultimately to be remembered for the exploits of the African-American athlete Jesse Owens whose triumph disproved Nazi theories of Aryan dominance. For most journalists, the Americans were the story of the Games but the Indian decision not to salute Hitler was a grand gesture of defiance, totally in sync with the tenets of the dominant stream of Indian nationalism and the Congress Party. This perhaps is why loyalist newspapers in India chose not to play it up. The Calcutta *Statesman*, reporting on the ceremony, chose to place its coverage of the Indian defiance on its political pages, as opposed to the sports pages where all Olympic news normally figured.[41]

It is significant that G.D. Sondhi, one of the officials accompanying the Indian contingent, was deeply influenced by Nehruvian ideas. In the late 1940s, inspired by Nehru's internationalist ideals and the dream of pan-Asian unity, he was to single-handedly evolve and create the framework for the Asian Games (see Chapter 7). At a time when Britain was courting Hitler with its policy of appeasement—just two years later the prime minister, Neville Chamberlain, was to triumphantly declare 'peace for our times' after the Munich conference—the Indian decision not to salute the Führer, it seems, stemmed ideologically from the anti-Nazi posture taken by the Congress under Gandhi and Nehru. From the 1920s, the Congress had repeatedly expressed opposition to Britain in the event of a European war but regarded Fascism and Nazism as a form of Western imperialism.

In 1936, the same year as the Indians were marching in Berlin, Nehru told the Lucknow session of the Congress that 'Capitalism in its difficulties took to Fascism', and 'fascism and imperialism... stood out as the two faces of the now decaying capitalism'.[42] It was as impossible for India to support Britain's new opponents as it was to support Britain. From 1938 onwards, Gandhi began pointedly opposing Hitler in the pages of *Harijan*—at one point even sending him a letter to desist from violence.[43] In 1939, the Congress in its session at Tripuri resolved to 'keep aloof from both imperialism and fascism'.[44]

There is no evidence in contemporary sources to show any direct linkages between the Congress and the athletes' decision to not salute Hitler in Berlin. But the fact remains that it was a political act, breathtaking in its audacity, in direct opposition to most other contingents at the Games, including the British. Managers like Sondhi cannot but have been influenced by nationalist sentiment as articulated by the Congress leadership. The 'marriage procession' carried a bite.

It is significant that by the time the Games began, Indian fans at home were also fully geared for action. This is borne out by the increased sales of Phillips radio sets. The company had arranged for special coverage from Berlin, which was advertised thus:

> At a time like this news cannot travel quickly enough and it is with great interest that we are able to report that special arrangements have been

> made for broadcast commentaries from the Berlin stadium...The world organization of Philips Radio with their two broadcasting stations are concentrating their resources for the benefit of Indian listeners. They have obtained information concerning these broadcasts and special plans have been made for reception of commentaries and eyewitness accounts from Berlin. Philips dealers in India's leading cities will be able to supply details of the programmes and the times when transmission will take place...We would advise those readers without all wave sets or with obsolete models to go to a Philips dealer and hear the latest Philips all waves sets specially designed for reception in India...[45]

To flag off the special broadcasts, Philips had organized a talk titled 'All About the Olympiad, Berlin 1936' by Biren Roy, India's representative at the World Municipal Congress in Berlin, on 31 July 1936. The talk was broadcast between 9.05 p.m. and 9.24 p.m.[46] This was among the first radio programmes in India at a time when the medium was just making inroads. Although the first Indian radio stations—opened by the privately owned Indian Broadcasting Company in 1927—had been commercial ventures, they had failed and were taken over by a reluctant colonial regime in 1930. Radio became a government department and the state assumed a monopoly over all broadcasting.[47] The nomenclature of All India Radio was adopted in 1936 and the Olympic programme with Biren Roy was a major highlight.

'Not an Indian to Uphold the Name': The Failure in Other Sports

By the time the hockey team started its title defence, most Indian athletes had already fallen by the wayside. While Rahim could not make it to the final round of the shotput competition, Raonak Singh who competed in the 10,000 metres was a long way last from the start and dropped out at the end of 5,000 metres. Singh caused much amusement among the spectators because despite running last almost throughout, he retired at the end of 15 laps. G.P. Bhalla too failed to make it to the final of the 800 metres. He also finished last in the first heat of the 5,000 metres. In wrestling, the Indians, Rashid in the welter weight and Rasul in the middle weight, were eliminated in the first round.[48]

India's poor showing was the subject of much scornful reporting back home. The correspondent for the *Statesman* was scathing: 'There is the same old story to tell about Indian athletes and wrestlers at Olympic Games—failure and more failure. A wonderful country is ours, with a population of over 350 million and some of the finest specimens of manhood in the world. But our great country, with its vast resources, its princely patrons of sport and its wonderful climate cannot produce a single winner in the greatest of athletic festivals. Running, Walking, Swimming, Wrestling, Boxing, Rowing—the manliest of sports and not an Indian to uphold the name of his country'.[49] He went on to suggest that the Indians will have learnt a lesson from the failure at Berlin and will seriously settle down to think about the next Games at Tokyo in 1940. Winning the hockey title only isn't enough. 'Why should not India produce a winner in the marathon race in 1940?'[50]

It is, however, naïve to blame the athletes for India's disastrous showing in Berlin. The team management was equally to blame. One of India's wrestlers, Karim, would have surely put up a creditable performance had he been allowed to fight in his own weight category. Instead, when he reached Berlin, instructions came from Sondhi that Karim must decrease his weight to appear in the welter weight class, with the result that for about 15 days his coach kept him in such strict training that he lost a good many pounds and became much weaker.

Despite Sondhi's efforts, Karim could not get down to the desired class and one day before the actual competition he was told that he would have to compete in his usual weight category. He was too weak to perform and was knocked out in the first round.[51]

More shame awaited the Indians in the marathon. Swami finished 37th in 3 hours 11 minutes 47 4/10 seconds. By the end of the race he was so exhausted that he had to be removed to hospital where he needed to recuperate for the next two days.[52]

One interesting sidelight of the Indian performance at the Berlin Games was the exhibition of traditional Indian games on the Olympic stage. A party of 24 athletes from the Hanuman Vyayamprasarak Mandoli, Amroti, had sailed for Berlin on 9 July by the *Conte Verde* to exhibit Indian games and exercises. Interestingly, the team was composed of Harijans, Brahmins and Mohammedans. Its organizers wanted to display an India that had overcome caste and religious divides and the participants from diverse social strata were chosen with deliberate care. Their exhibition at Berlin is a fascinating but forgotten interlude in the interplay between Indian nationalism and Olympism.[53]

'Past His Best Days': The Carping Critics and Dhyan Chand's Title Defence

Hungary, 4–0

In a marked improvement from Los Angeles, 14 nations entered the Olympic hockey competition at Berlin. They were divided into three groups, which were as follows: Group I – India, USA, Yugoslavia, Czechoslovakia, Hungary; Group II – Germany, Afghanistan, Denmark, Japan; Group III – Holland, France, Belgium, Switzerland and Spain. It was announced that members of each group would play each other in a league format and India was slotted to open its campaign against the United States on 2 August.

However, with only four days to go for the Games, Czechoslovakia and Yugoslavia withdrew from the competition. As both of these teams were in India's group, the organizers had to redo the groupings yet again. Afghanistan was moved to Group I, and Spain was moved from Group III to Group II. According to the new format the winners of Group I were slotted to play the runners-up of Group III and the winners of Group II were due to play the winners of Group III in the semi-finals.[54] Even this grouping had to be changed when on the eve of the competition the Spaniards withdrew, citing political reasons. Eventually the Indians were left with USA, Japan and Hungary in Group I.

They started their campaign well, defeating Hungary 4–0. The Indians scored twice in each half. Roop Singh scored three goals and Mahmood Jaffer, playing in an unaccustomed position, got the remaining one. Though the win looked convincing on paper, the match demonstrated that the standard of hockey in Europe was much advanced. It was reported in the press back home that while the Indians were better than their opponents, their superiority was not as marked as on previous visits to Europe:[55]

> Most disappointing was the revelation that Dhyan Chand, undoubtedly the world's greatest center forward, is past his best days. He showed much skill with the stick and excellent judgment in combining with his brother but much of his wizardry has disappeared. He is now no better than any forward on the side. Indeed it is doubtful whether Roop Singh, his younger brother, is not now the cleverer player.[56]

The correspondent went on to lament that India's display, startling enough for those seeing the team for the first time, was disappointing to the many who knew that India had many dozens of hockey players of international class. He concluded saying, 'The 1936 side is considered weaker than the side that played several matches in Germany in 1932 and cannot be compared to the 1928 side, which won the Olympic tournament at Amsterdam.'[57]

From local reports on the game, it is evident that the only players who stood out were Roop Singh in the forward line and Tapsell at right back. The relatively mediocre performance of the Indians was partly ascribed to the poor weather conditions. It was a second-session match and kick-off was at 6 p.m. local time. In fact, the game started 'under a canopy of clouds and a cold icy wind was blowing across the ground'. Within five minutes of the start it began to rain heavily and continued to pour till half-time. Accordingly, the ground was very heavy and with thick grass on the field it was impossible to play quality hockey. The local papers were full of praise for the Hungarian goalkeeper who, it was argued, saved his team from a bigger defeat.[58]

Yet another match report, however, mentioned that the Indians had the game in their hands throughout. All through the match, the play was confined to the Hungarian 25-yard line. Allen, the Indian goalkeeper, did not touch the ball once. Only twice in each half did the Hungarians cross the Indian goal line.[59]

USA, 7–0

The Indians followed up the victory against Hungary by defeating the Americans 7–0. Roop Singh, Dhyan Chand and Jaffer each scored two goals while Cullen scored one. In this match the Indians did not play their strongest side and rested three of their key players for the more strenuous engagements to follow.

Even a 7–0 verdict failed to convince the scribes back home. The *Statesman* argued, 'The fact remains, however, that at Los Angeles four years ago India defeated USA by more than 20 goals scoring when and how they liked. The US have improved since then but their improvement does not represent the difference between 1932 and 1936, which goes to confirm that Indian hockey has gone back in four years and that the present team is by no means as strong as the two previous Olympic teams'.[60]

The Indian team management also conceded that the US had made considerable strides in the four years since Los Angeles. This was especially noteworthy because the Americans had been playing hockey for only five years and there were only 10 professional clubs in the US.[61]

Even Dara's arrival to reinforce the team did not evoke enthusiasm. It was suggested that he could only have a minor influence and it was foolish to think that he would be the difference between victory and defeat.[62]

Japan, 9–0

Journalists covering the Games also thought India's hockey team was a victim of its own past exploits. Despite the huge margins of victory, journalists already foresaw a tough contest with Germany for Dhyan Chand's team. The negative tone of the reporting did not abate even as the Indians beat Japan 9–0 to top Group I. 'Germany has made tremendous strides and if the Indians are to win they will want to play even better than they did today, when they gave their best display up to date. Further they will need the same dry weather conditions as prevailed today. A record crowd of 16,000 including the Gaekwad and Maharani of Baroda watched the match.'[63] The video archives of the IOC contain fascinating pictures of the Indian princely entourage among the sea of German spectators, resplendent in saris and jewels.[64]

At the end of the group stage, the *Statesman* predicted:

> Here's a prophecy! We shall win the Olympic hockey championship again. If we are beaten, it will be by Germany, who have improved a hundred percent since we last met them. And if Germany win, it will be a lesson to India that she deserves, India has not improved a hundred percent—not on this team's showing. Perhaps it is because she has not

> sent her best team this time. This is the impression I have gained from conversations I have had with Professor Jagannath, manager of the team and Mr. Gupta, the popular assistant manager.[65]

France, 10–0

It was only when the Indians trounced the French 10–0 in the semi-final that the tenor of reporting improved. The *Statesman* correspondent, for example, mentioned in his match report that the Indian display, which was their best until then, aroused great enthusiasm among the fans. 'The Indians have become firm favourites for the championship. Germany, who will meet them in the final, have not the same speed and skill.'[66] The local German press too, overtly critical of the Indians to start with and predicting a German gold in hockey, appeared restrained after the Indians trounced the French. This was reported in India with much glee. 'The forwards who had never before combined so effectively played sparkling hockey and German newspapers, who were ruthlessly criticizing the Indians stating they had little chance of winning, at once changed their views and commented in glowing terms on India's victory against the French.'[67]

Barefoot Dhyan Chand and those 'Flickering Sticks': The Hat-trick

Against all expectations of a resurgent German team challenging the Indians, Dhyan Chand and his team crushed Germany 8–1 to win their third consecutive Olympic Gold. Forced to swallow their dire predictions, the sports writers once again wrote flowery paeans of praise. The title defence was narrated in great detail and was along expected lines. Three sub-headings in the *Statesman* summed up the mood of the match report: India's Triumph, Science Scores Over Force, and Dhyan Chand in Form.[68]

The match report left little doubt about India's overwhelming supremacy: 'In the second half science triumphed over force and the skill of Indian forwards, assisted by a hardworking trio of halves brought goal after goal. The vast crowd rose as one man as the Indians made raid after raid, completely outwitting the home defence with their speed and stickwork and their uncanny accuracy of shooting.

Goal after Goal was scored to the bewilderment of the German side and though they played with their greatest pluck and gameness and managed to score once, they were a well beaten team.'[69] It was in this game that Dhyan Chand truly came into his own in the Berlin Olympics. He had discarded his stockings and spiked shoes and wore rubber sole shoes, which increased his speed manifold. That he was at his best is borne out by the handsome scoreline of 8–1. Dhyan Chand himself scored six goals.

The German papers, which until now had been predicting a German gold, were full of praise for the Indians after the final. A correspondent for the *Morning Post* argued that Berlin would remember the Indian hockey team for long. 'These players, it is said, glided over turf as if it is a skating rink and their flickering sticks had the Japanese, normally so agile, mesmerized.' The reporter went on to conclude, 'Nature seems to have endowed Indians with a special aptitude for hockey'.[70] The legend of Indian hockey and the game's special affinity with the 'Orient' was embellished further. It is a tenet of Indian sporting folklore that Hitler personally met Dhyan Chand and offered him an officer's commission in the Wermacht if only he would play for Germany. This story is almost certainly apocryphal because none of the contemporary sources mention this incident and neither does Dhyan Chand in his autobiography.

Soon after the victory, the Viceroy congratulated the team on its record-breaking performance. Interestingly, the German Consul General from India sent the following message to Sir Jagdish Prasad, president of the IHF, 'Please accept my heartiest congratulations on India's hockey team's remarkable performance at the Berlin Olympic Games. World's best team won the final'.[71] Georg Evers, president of the Deutsch Hockey Bund and the International Hockey Federation, congratulated Dhyan Chand on his team's triumph: 'You and your boys have done wonderfully to foster the game of hockey in our country. I hope that you will return to Indian with good impressions and with the same feeling of friendship to the German hockey players as we feel towards you...Tell them how much we all admired the skill and artful performance of the perfect hockey they have shown us'.[72]

On their way back from Berlin, the Indian team stopped over in London. Lore has it that they met Douglas Jardine, already a star for his role in cricket's Bodyline controversy. It was reported in the press back home that Jardine stopped his car and posed for a picture with Dhyan Chand and Roop Singh. The team sailed back to India in the streamer *Strathmore*. Travelling with the team was the Nawab of Pataudi, the Maharajkumar of Vizianagaram and the Governors of Bombay, Madras and Mysore.

Extremely disappointing, however, was the way the team was welcomed in India on its return. Just as it received no public send-off when embarking for Berlin, there was no public homecoming on their victorious return. Masood describes the event thus:

> Bombay received us at the Ballard Pier with only two of its representatives —Mr. Behram Doctor of the Bombay Hockey Association and Mr. Mukherjee of the Bombay Olympic Association. At the railway stations in Germany, we had to be escorted by cordons of volunteers for fear of being squeezed in by enthusiasts...while in India, the land of our birth, we were welcomed by only two of her sons...Rain came in big drops as we were landing as a benevolent gesture of welcome from the heavens, and also showing the citizens of Bombay the state of our feelings of being neglected.[73]

Modern Indian hockey players, neglected and forgotten in the passions over cricket, would have empathized. While the reception, or rather the lack of it, accorded to the team on 29 September was shocking, the federation led by the president deserved praise for the way in which it helped prepare the team for Berlin. As in the previous Olympics, the IHF was severely constrained for funds. In April 1936, the federation had a little more than Rs 6,600 left in its coffers. It needed Rs 40,000 to send the team to Berlin. Its financial troubles were compounded when the inter-provincial trials at Calcutta did not yield much by way of gate sales. Despite this, by the end of May, the federation had raised Rs 35,000 by way of contributions from princes, private individuals and several provincial hockey associations. The Nizam of Hyderabad contributed Rs 5,000 and the Gaekwad of Baroda £ 200.[74] The president and office-bearers of the association also made personal contributions to make the trip possible. In fact, even when it was known that the federation would incur an additional expense of Rs 1,700 in sending Dara to reinforce the team, it did not flinch.

Conclusion

The 1936 Olympic campaign finally put to rest the question mark against India's hockey supremacy. India had won all its matches in style, scoring 38 goals in the process and conceding only one. Dhyan Chand, once discriminated against for his inferior social status, had consolidated his position as the darling of the Western world. A statue of his was erected in Vienna. Another statue erected later in Delhi's National Stadium remains the only sculpture dedicated to a hockey player in independent India. His six goals against the Germans in the final were no less an achievement than Jesse Owen's four gold medals in track and field. As Gulu Ezekiel wrote, 'While on the track Jesse Owens exploded the many myths of Aryan superiority, which the Nazi forces had carefully propounded, on the hockey field Dhyan Chand created magic.'[75] It was not without reason that the government of India issued a postage stamp in his honour and conferred on him one of India's highest civilian distinctions, the Padma Bhushan, in 1956.

After Berlin 1936, there was little doubt that the Indians would once again start their title defence as favourites in Tokyo four years later. Tokyo had won the vote to stage the Games of the Twelfth Olympiad by a margin of 36–27 against Helsinki, a product of careful and calculated exertion of political influence on the members of the IOC. Eventually, however, the outbreak of World War II meant there would be no Olympic Games until 1948 in London. There, the Indian hockey players presented their countrymen with a befitting independence gift—yet another Olympic hockey gold, which was made sweeter by a 4–0 victory over England. To this dream run we turn in the next chapter.

5

The 'National' Game
Hockey in the Life of Independent India

(Sport is) a most pervasive and enduring theme in the history of British imperialism. The central feature of its power is the subconscious influence it has exerted in both colonial and post colonial conditions.

—Brian Stoddart[1]

When Nehru met me during the opening ceremony of the Bhakra Canal, he asked me, 'Are you playing hockey? Do you play every day? Are your other colleagues also playing seriously? Are they all well and happy?' He had asked me so many questions in one breath that all I could answer was 'Yes, sir.'

—Balbir Singh Senior[2]

For a newly independent India, the London Olympic Games of 1948 was more than a mere sporting event. The event offered an opportunity for assertion and was a stage for a young nation to cement for itself a place in the world parliament of successful sporting nations. It was also a platform for an infant Indian nation-state to compete with its former master and give vent to years of frustration and discontent.

The Indian hockey team satisfied this national yearning, in the process winning for itself its fourth straight Olympic gold, having already won top honours at Amsterdam in 1928, Los Angeles in 1932 and Berlin in 1936. The golden journey did not stop in 1948 but continued until 1964 with a brief silver interlude in 1960, when India had to cede top spot to arch rivals Pakistan.

When the Indian hockey team won gold at the London Olympic hockey stadium in 1948, defeating the English 4–0 in the final, much more than an Olympic victory was scripted. It was a newly independent nation's declaration against the forces of colonialism, retribution for humiliation meted out by the English for almost 200 years and finally a statement to the world about the significance of 'sport' in an era of de-colonization. Hockey, the victory demonstrated, held the promise of being the new opiate of the masses.

Without exaggeration, it was a mirror in which communities were beginning to see themselves. It was at once a source of exhilaration, pride and national bonding. The sport, for many in the country, offered a substitute to religion as a source of emotive attachment and spiritual passion, and for many, since it was among the earliest of memorable post-independence experiences, it infiltrated memory, shaped enthusiasms and served fantasies.

Though claims of hockey as the 'national' game of the country originated as far back as the turn of the century and gathered momentum after wins at Amsterdam, Los Angeles and Berlin, it was not until London that hockey's supremacy was assured. Before 1948, both cricket and soccer enjoyed a similar popularity, and the question of which of these two would capture the Indian sporting heart in the immediate post-independence context was still unanswered.

Also, at the time when the Indian hockey team was contesting for honours in London, the nation's borders were set alight by the first war with neighbours Pakistan, the 'unfinished agenda' of Partition which was to lead to further wars in 1965, 1971 and continual tension since. Therefore, in the months before London, the Indians back home were firmly focused on the political crisis at hand and were hardly able to fathom the true scale of the nation's achievement on the Olympic stage. Compared to the Games of 1928, 1932 and 1936, London 1948 offered a fundamentally different challenge for Indian hockey. More so, because the players, for the first time, weren't representing British India but were playing for their motherland. This was the first time the Indians were playing for the new tricolour and against the British, under whose imperial flag they had participated in previous Games. The significance of this transformation is best borne out by the legendary Dhyan Chand. Writing in his autobiography, he declared: 'I envy the 1948 Indian Olympic team to whom fell that honour (of meeting and defeating the English on the Olympic stage). How I wish I had at least been present to witness the historic occasion. But, like most of you, I was fated to be thousands of miles away at home listening to the radio and reading press reports.'[3]

Also contributing to the significance of London 1948 was the prospect of the first India–Pakistan encounter. For India and Pakistan, it was natural that the political arena should shift to the sporting field, providing symbolic battlegrounds for national supremacy. As George Orwell put it: 'Serious sport has nothing to do with fair play. It is bound up with hatred, jealousy, boastfulness, and disregard for all the rules'.[4] Nationalistic sport, as is well known, is the most serious of all sport.

That partition had altered the relationship between players who had once played together for India is evident from the following recollection by Balbir Singh Senior, India's star performer at the London Games: 'It was at the London Olympics that Pakistan made their first appearance. The Indian and Pakistani teams were billeted at different places. We first met at Wembley Stadium during the ceremonial opening of the games. Niaz Khan, A.I.S. Dara, Shah Rukh, Mehmood and Aziz saw us, but I was surprised to see that our old friends were deliberately keeping a distance from us. The openness of old was gone.'[5]

Interestingly, this extreme communalization and politicization of sport was not unique to India–Pakistan or India–England, nor was it a state of affairs peculiar to the East. English imperialism, it is sometimes overlooked, was local before it was global. In sport, the resonances have been loud and long-lasting. Jeremy Black wrote in *The British Seaborne Empire*: 'Naval power was important in the attempts by the English Crown to enforce imperial pretensions in the British Isles'.[6] England's first imperial territories were Ireland, Scotland and Wales. And England's local empire has produced sporting ripples across, and beneath, the surface of its relationship with the Irish, Scots and Welsh on modern sports fields.

Rugby football, for example, serves as an occidental political barometer. For all the intensity of the rivalry between the Celtic nations, England, for them, is the nation to defeat, and if possible, humble. Sport, as in the subcontinent, has helped sustain local resentments, insecurities and inferiorities. Nowhere is this residual animosity towards England as a nation more aggressively expressed than at Murrayfield, the national Scottish rugby stadium, and in the passionate rendering of the now official anthem of the Scottish Rugby Union, 'The Flower of Scotland'—a lament for lost nationhood.

This chapter, using contemporary reports and eyewitness accounts, attempts to recreate Indian hockey's golden run in 1948–64, also focusing on how and why the Indian team was unexpectedly humbled by Pakistan in 1960. In doing so, it seeks to highlight the challenges confronting Indian hockey in an era dominated by concerns over agricultural development and industrialization in the country. It was an era when sport, understandably, took a backseat in the list of governmental priorities, making the golden run all the more spectacular. Finally, it turns its attention to Moscow 1980, the last occasion when India had the honour of hearing the national anthem play at the Olympics. Despite the anti-Communist boycott, which had taken some of the sheen off the Moscow Games, India's gold medal winning effort will always constitute an important chapter in the story of the nation's Olympic encounter.

Victorious in England: London, 1948

In comparison to other competing nations, the Indian hockey team arrived in London fairly late, on 14 July 1948. The late arrival was occasioned by the fact that they had been engaged in a special training camp in Bombay, honing their skills for the tough challenge that awaited them in London.[7] As part of the preparation, they played a series of practice games against leading domestic sides, matches that served as ideal training before the actual contest.

Dhyan Chand had retired and so had many of the stalwarts from Berlin. This was in many ways a new Indian team. It had many of the strengths of its predecessors but also some frailties, which meant that its success could not be taken for granted. In the first of these matches, the Indian Olympic side defeated the Best of Bombay 2–0 while in the second encounter the Indians trounced a formidable Bombay XI 5–1. For the Indians, the star of the show was the vice-captain, K.D. Singh Babu. Writing about him, the hockey correspondent of the *Times of India* declared, 'It is tempting to write that Babu is as elusive as Dhyan Chand, India's Olympic wizard, but that would be an exaggeration. I am content to say that India is lucky to have such a brilliant forward in the team. If Babu could convince himself to part with the ball a little often, he would be a complete answer to any selector's prayer'.[8]

This victory was followed up by a win against an Anglo-Indian team at Madras, the margin of victory being a comfortable four goals to two. Interestingly, in this match the Anglo Indians led the Indian Olympic team 1–0 at half time. However, in the last 10 minutes of the game, 'the Olympic side monopolized the play and registered three more goals, the goal getters being Glacken, Babu and Latif'.[9] In the final preparatory match, the Indians got the better of a South Indian XI by four goals to one. Once again the Indians after being down 0–1 at half-time staged a brilliant recovery to win the contest comfortably in the end.[10]

That the Indians did not leave anything to chance is evident from an interaction between the secretary of the Indian Gymkhana in London and Pankaj Gupta, the manager of the Indian Olympic team. Even before the Indians had reached London, Gupta, with the help of the secretary of the gymkhana, had reserved the No. 1 cricket ground of the gymkhana at Osterley as the practice ground for the Indian team. The significance of this effort was recorded by the *Times of India*: 'Anybody who has knowledge of London and the Indian Gymkhana will realize that the No. 1 cricket ground at Osterley is a very good ground for hockey practice. (Here) the Indian hockey team will find everything laid on for them for their practice before the Olympic Games.'[11]

Despite efforts at professionalism by the Indian team management, the selection of the team wasn't free of the vices of regionalism. This explains the surprise omission of Leslie Woodcock, who was a strong contender for a berth, and Permual, the brilliant Maharashtrian left-back who had played very well in the trials.[12]

The Indians flew to London by Air India's *Mogul Princess* on 13 July 1948 and were received at the London airport by the chef de mission of the Indian contingent, Moinul Haq. Soon after, they were taken to their designated quarters at a camp in Richmond, some miles from London, where they were thrilled to know that Indian food had been arranged for them. The *Times of India* reported the satisfactory mood in the Indian camp thus, 'The Indians have been getting not only

Indian food in all its courses, but in plenty. The waiters are all Indian and most of them come from Bengal. In the dining hall typical India prevails—everything is Indian; the usual talking and shouting and heaps of food, chapattis, dal, vegetable curry, meat curry, Indian sweets and so on and so forth and at the end of a long meal each boy gets a bottle of milk. What a contrast to the experience of previous Indian teams that had visited foreign countries on similar mission(s)'.[13]

It must be mentioned, however, that the Indians weren't allowed to stay at the Richmond camp for the entire duration of their stay. A few days before the competition began, they were asked to move to an empty school in the north-west London suburb of Pinner. The Richmond camp, it was noted, was emptied to accommodate athletes from the advanced Western nations. In an attempt to conceal such discriminatory treatment, the organizers declared, 'Many of the men moving out are feeling bitter but they should not. The position was explained to them when they came. Most of the accommodation was booked long in advance by countries whose teams are arriving only a week or so before the games begin'. The Indian officials mounted a protest against such discriminatory treatment, which in turn contributed to hardening the determination of the Indian hockey team.[14]

Indian 'Sunshine' in London: The Great Post-Colonial Showdown

With Czechoslovakia, Poland and Hungary failing to submit their team entries to the Olympic Games Organizing Committee on time, a revised Olympic hockey itinerary was drawn up, with the participating teams divided into three pools. India was drawn in Pool A with Spain, Austria and Argentina. Great Britain was drawn in Pool B with Afghanistan, Switzerland and United States. Pool C constituted of Pakistan, Holland, France, Belgium and Denmark.[15]

India started her campaign against Austria, winning comfortably by a margin of eight goals. Despite the big margin, the quality of play wasn't of the highest standard expected from the Indians. This was remedied in the next encounter against Argentina. Despite a relatively softer turf compared to the match against the Austrians, the Indian forwards put on an exemplary display, defeating the Argentines by nine goals.[16] This was followed by a hard fought two-goal victory against Spain, which propelled India to the semi-finals. While India was due to play the Dutch in the semi-finals, Pakistan had qualified from the other half of the draw and was to play the hosts, Great Britain. Even before the semi-finals were played, there was talk of a possible India–Pakistan final. Bruce Hamilton writing for the *Times of India* declared on 8 August that experts who had seen the teams in action in London had forecast an India–Pakistan final. He went on to suggest that India and Pakistan were the two outstanding teams of the competition not only because of their high scoring and margins of victory but also for their superior individual skills. 'No other team can match them for the spectacular way they carry the ball down the wings, dodging opponents and flicking it from one to another or seizing every chance they get in the scoring area.'[17]

However, he went on to sound a note of caution, suggesting that the unpredictability of the weather could ruin the chances of an India–Pakistan final because the European teams were far better equipped to handle the heavy turf in comparison with teams from the subcontinent. 'But there is one factor to be remembered—London's unpredictable weather. This weekend has been wet and miserable and the forecast is for continued unsettled weather. This may be decisive in tipping the scales in favour of Great Britain—at present the strongest challenger the Indian and Pakistani teams have.'[18]

His analysis was based on India's lacklustre performance against Spain. Playing in wet muddy conditions, the Indians had found that their stick work lacked the gloss it had on dry turf in earlier games. Especially for those without long stud boots, the soft turf made it impossible to control the ball. Most of them slipped on the wet ground and in the process their lightning speed of attack suffered.

Speaking of the Europeans, Hamilton mentioned that the wet conditions had not affected their game as much as it had the men from the subcontinent. 'A heavier combination, relying more on team work than individual play and familiar with wet grounds, Great Britain may find that these conditions will suit them well.'[19]

That he was right was evident when the British outclassed the Pakistanis in their semi-final, booking a date with India in the final. India, on the other hand, played a scratchy game to beat the Dutch.

The match report published in the *Times of India* was skeptical of India's chances in the final. 'India will meet Great Britain in the Olympic Hockey final on August 12 and unless the Indian players cut out their soft fancy stuff and adopt direct methods, India may find it difficult to retain the title...These two matches (semi-finals) proved two things clearly. First, English and Continental hockey has improved immensely and their game is based on entirely different strategy and technique. Second, Indians and Pakistanis must learn to play in heavy boots, which give a better foothold on heavy turf.'[20] The report concluded with words of caution for the Indians on the eve of the final. 'Finally, another thing was proved: namely, that to play against Britain a team must have sufficient vigour and stamina to last till the end. In today's match India's players were flat in the last ten minutes...'[21]

The stage was now set for a dream final: the defending champions from newly independent India taking on their former imperial masters who had avoided playing Olympic hockey as long as India remained a colony. That the Indians were aware of the symbolic significance of the challenge at hand was evident from a report filed by Alex Valentine in the *Times of India* of 12 August. He declared that the Indians had decided not to play any further practice matches but had started a two-day 'armchair strategy' session in preparation for the final. 'The chief factor in Thursday's final, readily recognized by both sides, will be the weather. The Indians want hot sunshine for the next two days, the Britons want rain, or at least no heat.' That the weather had already tilted the balance in favour of the British was borne out when the groundsman in charge of the pitch declared in jest, 'A heat wave between now and the final will not leave the pitch much harder than what it is now'.[22]

When it poured on the eve of the final on 11 August, most of the Indian players decided to take the field in studded boots instead of playing barefoot. Also, they were aware of the extra sporting connotations of the contest, a fact evident from the following statement by Balbir Singh Sr: 'Britain had been Olympic hockey champions in the 1908 Games at London and in the 1920 Games at Antwerp. Once India made their entry in the 1928 Games at Amsterdam, they decided not to play. Britain never played an India XI as long as they remained our rulers. The 1948 Olympic hockey final was the first meeting between Britain and India'.[23]

The Indians were embroiled in yet another controversy when the organizers decided to hold the third place play-off between Holland and Pakistan before the final. The Indians perceived this as a deliberate attempt to favour the British. The ground, already soft because of rain, would be further damaged by the play-off, seriously impacting the skilled play of the Indians. A.C. Chatterjee, manager of the Indian team, summed up the discontent in the Indian camp: 'This in itself is enough to cut our chances by at least fifty percent, but instead of giving the finalists the advantage of the best possible ground under the conditions, the organizers have allowed the comparatively unimportant third place match to go on first. I shudder to think what the ground will look like when we take the field.'[24]

Anthony S. De Mello, commenting on the improved performances of the Europeans in London, declared, 'It seems to me that it is not at all too much to suggest that India's example of polish and skill at hockey in earlier years had inspired these other countries to play the game better and better. If this is so—and I am sure that it is—it means that India, despite the brevity of her international sporting career, has had something of real value to give to the rest of the world'.[25]

Despite the odds stacked firmly against them in the final, the Indians won the battle in style, defeating the British 4–0. The overwhelming Indian superiority was borne out by the match report by Alex Valentine in the *Times of India*:

> India won the 1948 Olympic Hockey Championship in decisive fashion at the Wembley Stadium tonight, defeating Great Britain by four goals to nil. India's superiority was never in dispute. Despite the heavy, muddy turf and the light rain, which fell for considerable time during the game, the Indians outclassed the British team with their superb ball control, accurate passing and intelligent positional play. Long before half time it was evident that India should win comfortably. If England had had any other goalkeeper but Brodie, India might have doubled their score...(By the middle of the second half) Britain had resigned to the fact that they had lost the game. But they were determined not to lose it by a greater margin. Whatever energies they had left they put into their defence. As the minutes dragged to the closing whistle, it was apparent the Indians were not going to get through the wall of

> British defenders. Full time came with yet another Indian attack on the British goal—and the match closed as it had opened. Only now the Indians were four ahead.[26]

This British defeat, achieved on British soil, unleashed some of the wildest celebrations Indian hockey has ever known. To give a cricketing analogy, most Indians today remember the delightful Indian invasion at Lord's after the victory at the 1983 World Cup. The images of those celebrations, beamed live on television, are now etched forever in India's public memory. There were no live cameras to record the landmark hockey win in London for posterity but contemporary press reports note that the few thousand Indian spectators present were delirious. Amidst spectacular scenes of jubilation, the Indian high commissioner, V.K. Krishna Menon, ran on to the ground to join the celebrations. Reviled by Western—especially American—diplomats, even the stern Menon—'the devil incarnate', 'Mephistopheles in a Saville Row suite', 'the old snake charmer'—who was to later 'bore' the United Nations with his marathon seven-and-a-half hour speech on Kashmir—let his hair down that day. As reminisced by Balbir Singh Sr:

> After the victory, V.K. Krishna Menon, free India's first high commissioner in London, came running to congratulate us. He joined us for a group photograph. Later, he also gave an official reception at India House, where a big gathering of sports lovers was present. The Olympics over, we went to the European mainland and visited France, Czechoslovakia and Switzerland. This brief tour, a fortnight in duration, was more of a goodwill nature, and earned India a great deal of fame. None of us had visited Europe before, and we were thrilled by the sights we saw.[27]

On their return to India, a red carpet welcome was given to the team. The victory celebrations continued for several days and climaxed in Delhi where the President Rajendra Prasad and Prime Minister Jawaharlal Nehru attended an exhibition match involving the Olympic team in a jam-packed National Stadium.[28] The victorious team of 1952 was to receive a similar grand welcome but in terms of its significance, the London hockey victory would not get a worthy rival until the national hysteria that overtook India when Ajit Wadekar's cricketers beat England in England in 1971. This was the true measure of what the hockey players had achieved a year after independence. The legacy of colonialism clearly mattered deeply.

If sport is in fact a metaphor (and in some cases a metonym) for war, then hockey had proved to be India's most trusted weapon in the troubled years after partition. In the complex post-independence context, prowess in sport wasn't enough. Accomplishments had to be demonstrated in contests against the colonizers, which would mark a symbolic victory against the erstwhile colonial state and satisfy the insatiable national thrust for equality and revenge. To substantiate the point: even when India won gold medals in field hockey in the Olympic Games in 1928–36, hockey could never outrank cricket or soccer in colonial India. This is because Britain refused to participate in Olympic hockey contests in these years, knowing that the Indians were favourites to win the gold. This is especially interesting because Britain had won the Olympic gold in field hockey in 1904 and 1920, the only years when hockey was played before 1928 and years when India did not participate. Absence of competitions against the colonizer, it can be argued, had relegated hockey in the Indian sporting hierarchy. When the Indians had finally trounced the British in 1948, winning the Olympic gold medal in the process, there was no disputing the fact that hockey had consolidated its position as India's national sport.

India Goes to Finland: Helsinki 1952

At Helsinki, the competition wasn't stiff enough to challenge the Indians. However, the internal discussions that marked Indian sport were gradually becoming apparent in hockey too. Even as the Olympic team was being finalized on 13 June 1952, power-hungry administrators were engaged in mini-battles of intrigue to push their 'favourites' into the team at the last minute. The Uttar Pradesh and West Bengal associations were seeking the inclusion of an additional player and unhealthy parochialism was evident in their choices. As the *Times of India* reported, 'The effort to push Malhotra back into the team, who was originally selected and then dropped in favour of Jaswant and Gurung, smacked of provincialism'.[29]

Even more worrisome was what followed. Telegrams were sent from Bombay to all the affiliated associations, requesting their consent to the inclusion of Malhotra from Uttar Pradesh as an additional half.

The telegram mentioned that Captain Digvijay Singh Babu and coaches Habul Mukherjee and Harbail Singh had stressed the need for Malhotra, especially in the event of an India–Pakistan final. 'The latter portion of the plea struck several associations as very odd. They failed to understand how a player could be indispensable only for one game and could not be required for others.'[30]

With Uttar Pradesh making a case for Malhotra, Bengal wasn't to be left behind. Soon after the first telegram had been sent from Bombay, a second telegram was sent from Calcutta. The contents of this telegram make fascinating reading: 'As there are five halves already in the team the eighteenth player should be a forward and Bengal would be prepared to pay the expenses of C S Gurung, if selected'.[31] Anticipating criticism, the telegram added that Gurung should be selected not because he was from Bengal but because he had performed well throughout the season. The *Times of India* made the following comment: 'The state of affairs is very illuminating and depressing, as these attempts to wangle in players come just on the eve of the team's departure. It may be mentioned that in 1948 also a similar selection of some Bengal players at a late hour had been allowed on the same condition—expenses borne by the Bengal Association'.[32]

An interesting feature of Indian hockey at this time, evident from attempts to thrust players into the national team by agreeing to pay for their passage, was the poor financial state of the sport. The financial crisis was aggravated when the government decided to further reduce the subsidy offered to the nation's premier Olympic sport. The financial condition of the Indian Olympic Association too was dire and it wasn't sure if it had the funds to send all, or even most, of the selected Indian athletes to Helsinki. This was evident from a circular issued by the IOA to the secretaries of the affiliated national federations in which it declared many athletes to be 'doubtful starters' owing to a lack of funds. The circular also declared that the financial condition was alarming and added that the government of India had reduced its grant-in-aid from Rs 1,00,000 to Rs 70,000. State governments too weren't as forthcoming as in 1948 and some had removed sport from their immediate radar in favour of other, more pressing concerns. As the *Times of India* reported, 'This has resulted in a large gap between expected income and anticipated expenditure'.[33]

Despite hardship, the IOA finally managed to send the hockey team to Copenhagen, allowing them to acclimatize to the Scandinavian weather. Finally, the Indians started their title defence, defeating the Austrians 4–0. The performance, however, was at best scratchy and it was widely reported that the Indians had lost the edge which had won them four consecutive Olympic gold medals. 'The Champions won, as they were expected to, but they found the Austrians no easy obstacle on a pitch rendered slippery by rain.'[34] The sense of unease within the Indian camp was epitomized by the statements of Pankaj Gupta on the eve of the semi-final against the British. 'I want you boys to play your normal game; first-time clearances, short-passing and nippy thrusts. You know it too well, that's your natural style. No showmanship, mind you.'[35]

In their semi-final against the British, the Indians were a transformed side. This is how Balbir Singh Sr, who scored a hat-trick, his second in Olympic hockey, described the performance against Britain: 'We were a completely changed lot in the semi-final against Britain. We moved swiftly and smoothly and scythed their defence with copy-book moves...It was an accident that I got that goal. But I scored two more before the interval to get my second hat-trick in Olympic hockey—my first was in my maiden appearance in the London Olympics. Britain reduced the margin (1–3), but that was all they could do. India had reached the final'.[36]

Even after a better Indian showing in the semi-final, the final against Holland was expected to be a close affair. This was because of two reasons. First, the rains had made the ground wet and slippery, conditions that were expected to favour the Dutch more than the Indians. Second, the Indians looked to be over reliant on Balbir Singh Sr, a point repeatedly emphasized by the *Times of India*: 'The Indians need to visit the practice grounds regularly to remedy defects in their forward line, for it is too much to expect Punjab's twenty-eight-year-old centre forward Balbir Singh to initiate and execute all his side's attacks'.[37]

These predictions weren't accurate as the Indians retained the title fairly convincingly, defeating Holland 6–1 in the final. Balbir Singh Sr was once again the star, scoring his third Olympic hat-trick in style and scoring 9 out of the 13 Indian goals at Helsinki. In his own words, 'I was in my element that day and scored five of my team's six goals. The match gave me another hat-trick, my third in Olympic hockey. Holland got a consolation goal, but overall it was a one-sided final'.[38]

On arriving home in India, the team was accorded a royal reception in the capital. If anything, the number of functions far exceeded those in 1948 and the celebrations continued for nearly a month. At the official function in Delhi, the Olympic team played a match against a Rest of India XI in a packed stadium. Present in the audience were President Rajendra Prasad and Prime Minister Nehru.

That the players were overwhelmed by the response in India is evident from the recollections of Balbir Singh:

> The train in which we traveled was literally mobbed by enthusiastic hockey fans. People surged around our compartment and waited for our *darshan*. When we emerged from the train, they almost crushed us with bear hugs and shows of affection. We endured it all with a smile. The four Punjab Police players—Dharam, Udham, Raghbir and I—were taken in open jeeps in a huge procession in Jalandhar. Thousands of people lined the streets and cheered us from treetops and housetops. We were showered with small gifts, baskets of fruit and sweets and garlands—these constituted the people's simple way of showing their gratefulness.[39]

Balbir Singh had emerged a worthy successor to the mantle that Dhyan Chand had left behind.

Winning by a 'Short Whisker': Melbourne 1956

The Indian dominance was to continue in Melbourne where India was to win its sixth consecutive gold medal. But already those in charge of Indian hockey were worried about the warning signs that emerged in the Games. As Pankaj Gupta noted soon after the win:

> Yes, India maintained her supremacy in world hockey at Melbourne by a short whisker and this, I say, must make us pause. We can no longer take anything for granted. The standard of world hockey has improved and other nations like Holland, England, Germany and Pakistan have caught up with India in technique as well as in standard. Complacency must give way to genuine concern. We have an unparalleled wealth of hockey talent, which I regretfully consider, is not being fully exploited.[40]

As is evident from the above words, the Indians were aware that Melbourne 1956 was a far tougher assignment compared to Helsinki 1952. This may have prompted them to appoint Balbir Singh Sr, the nation's leading star, as captain. Under him, now an Olympic veteran and twice gold-medal winner, India started in style, humbling the Afghans 14–0 in their opening engagement at Melbourne Olympic Park. Strangely, even this high margin of victory failed to satisfy the Indian scribes covering the tournament. Following the victory, the *Hindu* reported, 'It was one way traffic throughout but if we were represented by our 1932 or 1936 teams, we may have registered a cricket score.'[41] This comment also brings to the fore the kind of aura around Dhyan Chand and his teammates and demonstrates the pressure the Indian team was under, to stand up to its glorious past.

The high margin of victory was, however, soured by an injury to Balbir Singh, who broke a finger and was out of action for the next few games. With India heavily reliant on his outstanding scoring abilities, this was looked upon as a major blow to its chances of retaining the gold.[42] But even without Balbir in their ranks, the Indians bulldozed their way past the US 16–0[43] and beat Singapore 6–0. The match against Singapore, however, brought out some of the weaknesses that were to hamper India's chances in the semi-final against Germany. Without Balbir in the team and with the Singaporeans resorting to ultra-defensive tactics, the Indians found it extremely hard to score. Not until the 23rd minute of the game were the Indians able to break the deadlock, a first for Indian hockey in the Olympics.[44] Though the Indians were all over their opponents in the second half and ended the group with the total tally of 36 goals in favour with none against, critics were sceptical of India's chances in the semi-final against Germany, a chain of thought best summed up by Pankaj Gupta:

> I happened to be at Melbourne, where there were occasions when I felt most uneasy at watching our hockey team in action. Our earlier matches against Afghanistan, USA and Singapore were no criterion but our main hurdles were Germany in the semi-final and Pakistan in the final. Our victories over Germany and Pakistan were both lucky and unimpressive.[45]

That India's victory against Germany hadn't done much to silence critics is apparent from the critical tone of the report in the *Hindu:*

> The stock of hockey in the Indian sub-continent went down at the main stadium of the MCC cricket ground today when both India, reigning Olympic champions since 1928, and Pakistan qualified for the final beating Germany 1–0 and Great Britain 3–2 respectively. India's

> nine-man selection committee must seriously consider their next step in selecting India's national team in future. Never before in India's Olympic history has any nation provided such stiff opposition to India. Something has gone wrong somewhere, otherwise how we could win by the narrowest margin in the game in which we had been world beaters is difficult to appreciate...[46]

'Victory Casts Its Own Spell': The First India–Pakistan Face-off

That the final in Melbourne was India's first meeting against Pakistan on the Olympic stage was weighing on the minds of players from both teams. The Indians were under intense pressure on the eve of the final, a state of affairs palpable in the reminiscences of Balbir Singh Sr:

> I could not sleep that night (on the eve of the final), and after tossing about restlessly for a while, I went out for a stroll. It was quite late in the night when someone called out my name. Turning, I saw Ashwini Kumar, his face creased with worry. Ashwini put his arm around my shoulder and guided me to my room. He talked cheerfully, gave me a tablet, made me lie down, and sat next to me.[47]

The tension was greater for the Indians because they had more to lose than Pakistan had to gain. For Pakistan, a silver medal would be a triumph, whereas for India anything but gold would be a disappointment. This explains the unrivalled scenes of jubilation following India's narrow 1–0 victory in the final. The celebrations were more in relief than anything else. India, despite all criticism, had managed to retain her crown. As Balbir Singh Sr said:

> Victory casts its own spell; every nation rejoices in it, and we were no exception. There were the usual rounds of celebrations and hugging and kissing among players and officials. We were feted and felicitated and hunted down for autographs. I had been through this remarkable experience at London and Helsinki. But Melbourne was different. Our supporters, hundreds of them Australians and New Zealanders, were flushed with the thrill that India had beaten Pakistan in the Olympic final. Several hundred of enthusiastic friends we made on our 1955 New Zealand tour met us again in Melbourne. They were among our most vociferous fans...That day when I led my team out to the victory rostrum, I swelled with pride. Sharing the rostrum on either side of me were the captains of Pakistan and Germany, the silver and the bronze

> medal winners. The crowd cheered us. It was a thrilling experience to acknowledge their applause. The National Anthem sounded sweet, and the tricolour, fluttering proudly in the stiff breeze, looked a grand sight.[48]

The celebrations, however, failed to conceal the fact that in Melbourne the Indians had lost more than they had gained. It was visible to all that India's supremacy was now a thing of the past and unless the Indians improved their game by a few notches, it was only a matter of time before they were humbled by the Pakistanis or the Europeans led by the Germans and the Dutch.

Pankaj Gupta tried to sum up the grim situation:

> I am going to stick my neck right out by saying that morally we lost the final against Pakistan whom we managed to beat by one goal thanks to a penalty conversion by Gentle. It was an even game up to a point but then Pakistan were all over us. Even before Gentle had scored the all important goal, shortly before the interval, Pakistan were awarded a penalty bully and according to my interpretation of the rules it should have been a goal but fortunately for us the Australian umpire ignored the infringement by Amir Kumar and we breathed again. If they had been a goal up things might have been a lot different.[49]

In another article Gupta attempted to explain the reasons behind the decline:

> The supremacy of a country in any game depends a lot on those who play the game, those who manage it and those who govern the country. We have indeed players of a caliber who can still hold their own in the international arena despite the fact that other nations have lately emerged as opponents truly worthy of our steel... We have a great responsibility on our shoulders and we must see that the game does not suffer because of parochial interest, personal sentiment or administrative interference at Governmental level... *We have wonderful players and if the right team and right skipper and manager are chosen there is no reason why we should not continue to remain world champions for a long time.*[50]

His last statement summed up the dangers that were eating into the foundations of Indian hockey. The words 'right skipper and right manager' smacked of the very provincialism that was corrupting Indian hockey and it was time the game was given a reality check. Rome 1960 was the occasion when this finally happened.

'Debacle': Rome 1960

From the very start, India's campaign at Rome appeared jinxed. Almost all its victories were by narrow margins and on more than a couple of occasions it was plain lucky. Though the Indians started well, winning the opening match 10–0 against Denmark, the performance was far from satisfactory. Following this victory, the *Hindu* reported that the Indian forwards were yet to show thrust or combination and if Prithpal Singh had not given them a three-goal lead within the first 15 minutes, things might have been difficult, although Denmark was no match for India.[51] In the quarter-final against Australia, India won by the narrowest of margins, 1–0, the winning goal scored at the last minute of the second extra period. Throughout the match the Indians missed easy openings and as recorded by Pankaj Gupta, 'This match does not reflect credit to the world champions and I consider it a providential escape in this match'.[52] Against New Zealand and Holland too the Indians were scratchy and only Bhola among the forwards and Prithpal by virtue of his penalty corner conversion did justice to their pre-tournament billing.

Against Holland, for the first time in Olympic history, the Indians were down a goal for most of the first half. The match was in fact tied one apiece until the last seven minutes, when the Indians scored three quick goals. To Holland's credit, they had the better of the exchanges in the initial minutes and defended stubbornly in the beginning of the second half when the Indians went on an all-out attack.[53] Even in the semi-final against Britain, the Indians were seen defending for most of the first half and when the British stepped up the pressure at the start of the second half, looking for the equalizer, it was only goalkeeper Laxman's brilliance that saved India the blushes. He saved four strikes from Mayes and Hindle and with Prithpal Singh playing a great game at the back, India scraped through to the final.[54]

In the final, India could never assume ascendancy, as was expected from the world champions. In front of the biggest crowd ever assembled for a hockey match, one which was telecast throughout Western Europe via the Euro vision link up, the Pakistanis had the best of a final which never reached the expected high standards because of the poor ground conditions. Both sides were under intense pressure to win and the Indians lost the plot more than the Pakistanis, losing their Olympic title in the process. At the interval, Pakistan was up by a goal, scored by Naseer in the eleventh minute of the match. Even when the Indians pressed for the equalizer towards the close of play, they failed to create any significant opening. With five minutes to go, the Pakistanis resorted to time-wasting tactics by hitting the ball out of play at every opportunity. The fairly large Indian section of the crowd jeered such conduct but it enabled Pakistan to hold on to their important one-goal lead.[55]

As soon as the match ended, the Pakistanis went berserk. Their players were seen running right across the pitch, embracing and shaking hands with each other and the Pakistani fans celebrated way into the night. It was the first time in Olympic history that the Indian hockey team had been pushed to number two on the podium and Pakistan cherished its moment of glory.

As we have seen, the signs of India's impending decline had been evident since the early 1950s. Through it all, India was still winning. This defeat, that too at the hands of Pakistan, meant that Rome was seen as nothing short of a 'debacle' in the annals of Indian hockey.[56] The pages of IOC's official magazine during this period are full of heart-rending post-mortems and prescriptions for the regaining of lost glory. Two things stand out in this collective chest-beating after the defeat: one, blame was heaped upon the political rivalries of regional sporting satraps, which were supposed to have damaged Indian hockey and two, the debate between 'robust' (European style) and 'skilful' (Indian) hockey.[57] By the 1980s, most contemporary commentators would date the decline of Indian hockey to the rise of astro-turf and the Indian failure to adapt to a more physically demanding form of the game. The records indicate, however, that this debate between the 'Indian' and 'the Western' form of the game far predated astro-turf. Thus S.M. Sait emphatically declared in 1962 that 'we have to concede that that our standard of hockey has deteriorated'. In his view, the Indians had erred in adopting foreign tactics:

> It is very strange that our players instead of continuing to play the old type of scientific and skilful hockey have made the mistake to take up hard-hitting type of hockey which was almost alien to us. It was a delight in the past to watch our forwards indulge in quick short passing and skilful

> dribbling... Now what we saw in Rome was a different picture altogether. Our players were trying to outdo our opponents in hard hitting and individual thrusts. It is needless to say that we failed miserably.[58]

It is telling that what Western commentators had long recorded as typical examples of 'magical' Indian stick work was seen by Indian commentators as 'scientific' hockey. Now it was felt that India's players were losing out in a bid to imitate the Western players.

But perhaps the deeper malaise was that of provincial rivalry, on which blame was attributed by all who worked closely with Indian hockey after the 1950s. No one explained this better than Charanjit Rai, who in a prescient article in *Indian Olympic News* noted that the loudest voices of recrimination after the Rome defeat came not from former players but from 'those who had never achieved this distinction' and held positions of power at the state and national level in hockey's administrative structure.[59] In an early precursor of Dhanraj Pillai's famous lament in the early years of the 21st century against the czars of Indian hockey, Rai argued that the players would be affected 'unless treated fairly and sympathetically' off the field. Not mincing words about the politics of player selection that had already begun to haunt the game, Rai argued that the only way to regain the title at Tokyo was to 'select the team purely on merit...Even when ten players have been selected purely on merit and one position has been filled in with an undeserving player, this injustice has an adverse effect on the other ten. They may not express their resentment but subconsciously it finds it outlet adversely affecting their performance on the field'.[60] Rai's analysis carried hints of 'injustices' done and 'undeserving' players wrongly promoted. Whatever the truth of this assertion, the fact that such talk was already becoming part of the public discourse about hockey is significant. He had touched upon the malaise that was creeping into Indian hockey and one that continues to haunt it to the present day.

'Sweet Revenge': Tokyo 1964

The defeat to Pakistan had a deep impact on Indian hockey and the next four years were spent in plotting how to regain the title. As the Indians were about to embark on their journey of revenge, the sports media back home was optimistic about its chances of wresting the crown back from Pakistan at Tokyo. At the same time, scribes suggested that if the team did manage to win, it would have performed a much greater task compared to the stalwarts of the golden age of Indian hockey. This was because in the 1930s and 1940s India had the best players in every position and there was hardly any serious competition to post a significant challenge to its supremacy. However, by the 1950s, hockey had established firm roots in Europe and also South East Asia and there was no question of an easy victory for either India or Pakistan.[61]

As far as preparations were concerned, the Indians did their best before Tokyo. The players came together for an intensive training session at a pre-Olympic camp and also toured New Zealand and Malaysia as part of their Olympic planning. Also, there didn't appear to be any major dissensions within the team, and regionalism had not yet afflicted the Olympic preparations in the way it had in the lead-up to London, Helsinki or Melbourne.

However, India did have her task cut out at Tokyo partly because some of its own players had helped train the Europeans and South East Asians. Former Indian greats like Penniger, Cullen, Gentle, Kishen Lal and Carr had accepted professional assignments in nations across the world. With the Indian diaspora gradually spreading its wings, many Indians who could have donned India colours had gone abroad to strengthen the teams of countries they settled in.[62] Finally, the Indians had also somewhat modified their earlier style of play and had resorted to power hockey, depending more on short corner and long corner conversions than field goals, allowing the Europeans the opportunity to catch up.

That the gap had indeed narrowed was evident in the first match itself when the Indians struggled to beat Belgium in a hard fought encounter.[63] Things were even more difficult in the second engagement against Germany as the Indians struggled to hold the Germans to a 1–1 draw. They were shocked when the Germans took the lead in the 20th minute and it appeared at one point that the match was beyond India. Finally, they managed to save the day via a penalty corner conversion by Prithipal Singh. Things barely improved in the match against Spain: the Indians were once again held to a one-all draw. The Indian scribes were acutely disappointed at the performance, manifest from the match report in the *Hindu*: 'Gone are the days when hockey fans all over the world were only concerned with the margins of India's victory. Today it has become a matter of survival and at the moment India is finding it difficult even to qualify for the semi-final...India is now occupying the third place in Pool B with Germany and Spain taking the first two places respectively. While Germany has five points, Spain and India have four each with Spain having the better goal average'.[64]

Another factor that hadn't endeared the Indians to experts was their rough approach. Willic, a former German star, summed up the rising discontent against the Indian style of play:

> I have never known India playing the man instead of the ball and at this rate nobody will have any respect for India. What is more, the entire ground of Indian officials were mum and blind over this. You taught us and the world how to play, but now it is you who have forgotten how to play. From a player's point of view and now as a coach I appeal to you to put an end to this state of affairs.[65]

Eventually, India managed to scrape through to the semi-final with a 2–1 win against Holland. T.D. Parthasarathy in his match report drew attention to what could have been a real tragedy:

> Making the semi-final grade was a real ordeal for India who had to thank providence that it managed to beat the Netherlands by the odd goal in three...India was lucky to win because after Netherlands had leveled matters, the latter all but got the lead. The goal was, however, disallowed...In the 20th minute the Dutchmen forced a short corner and following a melee in front of India's goal, the Netherlands inside left Van Hooft took everybody by surprise by scoring. This created a sensation among the Netherlands followers. The Dutch players threw their sticks up in the air in jubilation, but to the surprise of all, including many in the Indian camp the British umpire Kendrick Eaves disallowed the goal for offside. The decision came as a rude shock to the Netherlands, who seemed unable to recover from this.[66]

In the semi-final against Australia, the Indians fared better, winning the contest 3–1 and as Parthasarathy said, 'All said and done the victory was well deserved, and fighting back to the wall, the Indian team did a grand job'.[67]

'Really Extraordinary': The Roman Revenge

If hockey has any gods then they could not have scripted a better final line-up than India vs Pakistan. Here was a wounded champion striving to regain its lost title from the challenger. The off-field rivalry between the nations added an extra needle to the contest. In less than a year, both countries would be at war over the Rann of Kutch and the tensions were already building. In modern terms, the only thing comparable to the emotionalism of this final is the incredibly tense India–Pakistan game in the cricket World Cup of 1999 at the height of the Kargil war. In 1964, the war was still months away but hockey pride had to be restored. This was 'war minus the shooting'. Finally, India re-established its supremacy in world hockey by defeating Pakistan 1–0. Rene G. Frank, the secretary general of International Hockey Federation, has left a moving description of this final and the emotions that moved both teams:

> The India–Pakistan final which was played in a highly-charged emotional atmosphere was really extraordinary. It was one of the best and probably the best of the matches which I have had opportunity to attend. Two fine teams of appreciably equal strength were each doing their utmost to win...
>
> If India finally proved a winner by a narrow margin, this was because in my personal opinion its players seemed to me to be inspired with a greater will than their opponents to carry off this victory which enabled them to regain the title of Olympic Champion which they had always held and which was wrested from them for the first time in 1960 by Pakistan.[68]

The performance of Indian goal-keeper Laxman stood out in the match. Most observers agreed that the result might have been different had it not been for his athletic defending.

The celebrations matched the occasion. The victory was followed by 'indescribable scenes of joy (which lasted) for many minutes'.[69] That it meant much to a troubled India, ravaged by a war against China in 1962, is evident in the way the press back home and wrote about the victory. 'Eleven gallant men will import eleven pieces of gold into India next week and they will be allowed through the customs with smiles and congratulations. We never expected it to be an easy job but we worked for it most sincerely...We started shakily but as the tournament progressed we have gained strength and courage and we made it.'[70] The golden glow of this victory was felt around the country. A paan shop in Delhi distributed soft drinks for free soon after the Indians regained the gold. A taxi driver, when interviewed, suggested that he had been waiting for this moment for four years and a number of college students declared that the victory would encourage many in the capital to take to hockey. The prime minister, Lal Bahadur Shastri and President Radhakrishnan expressed delight and sent congratulatory cables to captain Charanjit Singh. The news of India's victory was conveyed to Shastri when he was addressing a public meeting at Khatauli village in UP. He immediately reacted by giving his audience the news of the nation's triumph in Tokyo.[71]

It should be mentioned here that the huge crowd present in Tokyo for the final was a model sporting audience. To start with, the average spectator did not take sides. Before the start of the game, Pakistani flags were distributed free in the students' gallery. Though they were briefed to support Pakistan, they mistakenly started shouting 'Indo, Indo'. When they realized that they were waving Pakistani flags, they started rooting for Pakistan.[72]

Tokyo 1964, it can be suggested, was one of Indian hockey's finest achievements. It was only after 16 years, in Moscow in 1980, that the Indians once again managed to finish ahead of the field. In the interim, though they won the World Cup at Kuala Lumpur in 1975, at the Olympics India's performance witnessed a sharp decline. At Montreal in 1976, it finished a dismal seventh. Inside the country too, hockey had been thrown into turmoil by the start of the 1970s, a story we recount in the next chapter.

While some critics rubbish India's victory at Moscow, pointing to a depleted field, there's little doubt that an Olympic gold medal winning performance will always rank as an important chapter in India's sport's history.

THE 'RED' GOLD: MOSCOW 1980

Given the absence of several leading hockey nations of the world, many tend to undermine the value of India's gold medal winning performance at Moscow. While there is some value in such arguments because nations like Pakistan, Holland and Germany stayed away because of the boycott, there's little doubt that an Olympic gold will always remain special. Athletes who won honours at Moscow 1980 and Los Angeles 1984 can hardly be discredited by citing the boycott.

India had prepared well for Moscow. To ensure it was well acclimatized, the team had been sent ahead of the remainder of the contingent. This allowed the players time to get used to the polygrass surface being used for the first and only time in Olympic history.[73] In fact, there was quite a controversy over the use of polygrass because there was a powerful lobby advocating the use of astro-turf, a group led by the influential president of the International Hockey Federation, Rene Frank. Rumours floating in Moscow made it evident that the ageing IHF chief had insisted at one stage that the Moscow tournament should be played only on astro-turf. However, the Russians, who could tackle the boycott so successfully and so ruthlessly, were not to be browbeaten. They made known to Frank that they could afford to run the Olympics minus the hockey tournament. As mentioned by the director of India's National Institute of Sport, R.L. Anand, 'Rene Frank got the message and gave in on the issue of the surface'.[74]

India started the contest well, crushing the lowly ranked Tanzanians 18–0. K. Datta, covering the tournament for the *Times of India*, declared in his match report, 'The score line seems to have been taken out a page from the history of Indian hockey. The matches were one sided then. It was also overwhelmingly one sided today at the Dynamo Stadium when our men opened the campaign in the 22nd Olympics'.[75]

Balbir Singh Sr, who was in the audience, was happy at the way the Indians performed and said it was refreshing to see Indian players strike rich form and score a huge haul of goals in their very first tie, though against feeble opposition.[76]

The Indians were brought back to earth in their very next encounter against the Poles, managing a last-second equalizer to score a 2–2 draw. 'To say that Fernandes's goal in India's last gasp effort came as a great relief would be the understatement of the Olympic year.'[77] It is of interest that the Indians were left fuming at the end of this match against some of the umpiring decisions that went against them. They were extremely critical of Dutch umpire Bob Davidson and blamed their inability to convert penalty corners on him.

However, as the *Times of India* reported, a very thin line divides a clean hit from a cut. It depended on what the umpire thought about it and 'it is better if our players get used to European umpiring rather than quibble about it. Most important they should be reminded of the old adage that it never pays to challenge the umpire or behave peevishly.'[78]

Against Spain, in the following match, India snatched a last-minute equalizer to stay afloat in the competition. The Indians were once again upset with some of the umpiring decisions, though the manager of the team, Dayanand, ruled out any possibility of lodging a formal complaint with the organizers. What was good to see in the match against Spain was the Indians' superior physical ability. As the *Times of India* reported, 'This Indian team in Moscow may not be the best to be sent out for an Olympic campaign, but it is fighting fit'.[79]

India followed up the draw against Spain with a 13–0 victory over Cuba that ensured that a win against the Russians in the last group tie would propel them into the final.[80]

Against the Soviets, the Indians displayed real pluck and skill and won a close contest 4–2. For a change, the umpiring worked in India's favour and often the Russians were left ruing their misfortune. The outstanding Indian star was Mohammed Shahid, who played an excellent match as game maker, setting up multiple openings for the forwards.[81] It was his form that gave the Indians hope for the final against Spain, whose penalty corner conversion record was much better than the Indians.

'They Do All Sorts of Things with Stick and Ball': Gold at Last

India tasted gold in Moscow after 16 years, beating Spain 4–3. K. Datta in the *Times of India* described the final thus: 'An Olympic hockey gold medal at last. But India should have won it by a more convincing margin. They played as they should have played till they led three-nil with twenty minutes to go. Then the defence began letting them down and when the end came the lead had thinned down to the barest minimum'.[82] Congratulating the Indians on the victory, Horst Wein, the German coach of the Spanish team, said that the gold medal would help India return to the pole position in world hockey. According to him, the young team was the best India had sent to the Olympics for some time. It was quick and its players fit. Its ability to swiftly counterattack and keep fighting until the end was something the European teams had to take note of.[83]

Elated at the victory, Prime Minister Indira Gandhi, Union Education Minister B. Shankaranand and Chief Minister of Maharashtra A.R. Antulay sent congratulatory messages to the winning team.[84] The locals too were delighted at the way the Indians had performed and Russian kids who had not seen a field hockey game before were mesmerized by the skill and artistry on display. Even before the final, Leonia Kondrashov, 12, was so taken by the Indians that he suggested that if he had his way he would straightway award the gold medal to them. 'The game looks so nice when the Indians play it. They do all sorts of pretty things with stick and ball.'[85]

The doubters, however, remained. Rene Frank, president of FIH, who had so movingly described the great Indian victory at Tokyo in 1964, now felt that the Moscow win was nothing but a flash in the pan. In an interview given to K. Datta for the *Times of India*, he stated that over time the standard of Indian hockey had gone down while the Europeans had improved considerably. This had resulted in a leveling of standards. 'The Europeans first learnt the finer points from Indian hockey and then evolved tactics of their own. Indian hockey has evolved no new tactics. It is stagnant. It likes to live on old prestige... The organization of Indian hockey also is not what it should be.'[86]

Vasudevan Bhaskaran, the coach of the Indian team at Moscow, was however of a different opinion and suggested that there was no reason to underrate India's achievement in Moscow. He had high praise for the newcomers, 14 of whom were playing in their first Olympics, and said he hadn't seen a more gifted player in India than Mohammed Shahid, who was naturally endowed with physical attributes that made for a talented inside forward. 'For years India should be able to depend on this versatile star,' he said.[87]

Back home, the hockey fraternity looked upon the victory as having heralded a renaissance in Indian hockey and there was hope all around that the golden run could be sustained. That such hope was unfounded was evident when the Indians were once again pushed to the fifth spot at Los Angeles in 1984. Also, the infighting that had corrupted the edifice of Indian hockey continued unabated, resulting in a string of poor Olympic performances between 1984 and 2004.

It is the story of this infighting which, more than anything else, orchestrated the decline in India's national sport and this is what we discuss in the next chapter.

6

'The Fall of Rome'
The Decline of Indian Hockey

The future of Indian Hockey is indeed gloomy and the average Indian expects us to do everything possible to see that Indian Hockey is once again supreme in the world.

—Pankaj Gupta, honorary secretary, IOA, 1962[1]

Not only did artificial turf replace real sod, but also plastic balls replaced leather ones. A slow, analytical game gave way to one of nonstop, true-hop action. For India it was like starting over with all nations even in field hockey.

—Steve Ruskin, *Sports Illustrated*, 1996[2]

I helped India win the last Asian Games Gold in 1998 as a captain and what do I see on my return? Seven players instantly sacked from the side. It can only happen in this godforsaken country.

—Dhanraj Pillay, 2007[3]

In contrast to the upbeat nature of hockey in colonial and early post-colonial India,[4] the period since the late 1970s presents a rather dismal picture. As early as 1976, *World Hockey* magazine in an article analyzing this decline decided to define it with the pathos-ridden headline, 'The Fall of Rome'.[5] India performed miserably in the Olympics and the Champions' Trophy in the 1980s and 1990s. In the eight-nation tournament in Holland in August 2005, the Indian hockey team finished a dismal seventh.[6] It was only in the 2007 Asia Cup that Indian hockey demonstrated possibilities of a resurgence, winning the competition by defeating arch-rivals Korea 7–2 in the final.[7]

That this was a mirage became clear when India, for the first time in history, failed to qualify for the Olympics, losing out 0–2 to Great Britain in the finals of the Olympic qualifying match at Santiago, Chile on 9 March 2008. This was its second consecutive loss to Britain in the tournament, having lost 2–3 at the group stage. Indian hockey had come full circle. The contest, which started at 3.30 a.m. India time on Monday 10 March, was shown live back home. Hopes of a last-minute resurgence were snuffed out in first 15 minutes of the encounter, with the Indians conceding two goals.

From the very first minute, the Indians seemed to be under pressure. Prabhjot Singh hardly looked the world's leading forward we claimed he was, Ramchandra Raghunath hardly the penalty corner specialist who could help us forget Jugraj Singh's accident and Dilip Tirkey, the captain, was a shadow of his former self, having lost the skill and the punch that had once made him one of the best defenders in the world.

India's performance was such that even if it had won, the victory wouldn't have done much to contest the fact that since the late 1970s hockey has languished (bronze medals in Mexico in 1968 and Munich in 1972, a World Championship win in Malaysia in 1975 and gold in Moscow in 1980 notwithstanding) and it is hardly comparable in popularity to cricket, which has gained in reputation since. With cricket reigning as the national passion, mass spectatorship in hockey in contemporary India is a rarity. Often, it is less than five per cent of the spectator base for cricket in the country.

Hockey's failure to retain its earlier glory has been the primary reason for the game's decline. The IOA and the IHF blame the corporate world and the media for stepmotherly treatment, but poor marketing strategies, internal politicking and the myopic views of the officials who run these institutions are also accountable for the decline the sport.

Further, hockey continues to be regarded as a male domain, a taboo for respectable middle-class women. Nothing illustrated this better than the venal sport administrator in the 2007 Shahrukh Khan starrer *Chak De India* who unfeelingly told Kabir Khan, angling for a job as the coach of the women's national team (Shahrukh's character in the film): 'Bhaiyya, these are Indian women. How will those who wield the chakla and belan wield the hockey stick?' In contrast to other

Asian nations such as China and Korea, women hockey players in India (despite having achieved considerable success in recent times) mostly try their hand at the game without hope of earning a livelihood from it. In fact, despite the tremendous success of *Chak De*, and the cult following of its fictional women's hockey team, the film did not quite see a 'mass exodus of SRK's female fans from the theatres to the Astro-turf'.[8] In a reflection of the institutional challenges to women's hockey, no more than 22 women turned up for the trials for Mumbai's team for the nationals in 2008. This, despite the fact that the current Mumbai team features as its second goalkeeper Nisha Nair, more famous for her role as the Jharkhand hockey player Soi Moi in *Chak De*.

Hockey associations continue to stagnate and financial crisis is a permanent companion of the women's game. Leading stars are hardly ever given due recognition, and the jobs on offer are never higher than the clerical grade. It is commonplace to see noted women hockey players languishing in penury after retirement, only to be rescued from such a plight by welfare organizations and sports enthusiasts. Under such circumstances, women are often forced to give up hockey, if they take i up at all.[9]

Sadly, the IOA and the IHF have both contributed to this plight. Most of the measures taken to develop hockey date back to the colonial period; in post-independence India, neither the IOA nor the IHF have made any serious attempts to match the commercial success of cricket. Such apathy has contributed to converting hockey, metaphorically speaking, into a low-end vocation in contemporary India. While the glamour of cricket has turned it into an aspirational sport, fully in tune with the consumer ethic of a globalizing society, hockey has stagnated. In the past two decades, cricket has steadily expanded its catchment area, attracting talented players from classes and areas not traditionally associated with the game—'middle and urbanized India'.[10] Hockey, on the other hand, despite its traditionally larger base, has languished.

Administrative lethargy is a central reason for this decline. This is best evident from the lack of protest on the part of the IHF when field hockey was moved from grass to astro-turf in the mid-1970s. The year astro-turf was adopted in 1975, India was a top hockey nation, having just won the World Cup in Malaysia. But astro-turf decisively changed the balance. It is instructive that Germany won the first international tournament ever played on the artificial surface. *World Hockey* magazine detected the meaning of that victory immediately, interpreting it as a sign of Europe bouncing back in 'the see-saw battle between Europe and Asia at the head of the world rankings'.[11] Being the only sport where the Indians could flex their muscles on the Olympic stage, the IHF and the IOA's lack of initiative to pre-empt the shift is revealing.

While this move to artificial turf seriously impacted India's fortunes, it is not the only reason for the sad plight of Indian hockey. Pakistan, a nation economically worse off than India and one which has far fewer artificial turfs, has done particularly well in recent times, even winning the eight-nation unofficial world championships at Amstelveen in August 2005. If Pakistan can, why can't India? Or for that matter, if India could win despite even greater systemic hurdles in the colonial period, then why not now?

This chapter aims to use the sudden decline of Indian hockey as an entry point to comment on the functioning of the IHF and the IOA since the 1970s. The story of sports administration in 1970s India, it will transpire, was but a small part of a far more important story of regional assertion, of the contest for supremacy between lobbies associated with the north and the south of India.[12] It is an irony that the Indian hockey team, has often blamed its plight on the poor administration of the sport.[13] The recent recourse to a government ruling passed in 1975, which specifies that no official can stay at the helm of a sport for more than two terms,[14] marks the completion of a cycle of administrative anarchy that started three decades ago when the country's hockey federation was fractured down the middle between the north and south factions.

The chapter is based on the premise that a full history of India's Olympic sporting experience must be framed within the broader themes of South Asian history and should not be restricted to the history of Olympism in general or Indian hockey in particular. It is part of the growing academic concern to locate sport within the broader socio-economic processes that have shaped colonial and post-colonial societies in South Asia. Throughout this history, hockey is used as the prism/metaphor to analyze the working of sports administrators in India. Studying this will help us understand the complexities of modern Indian society, while bringing to light the role played by sport in creating and moulding such complexities. It will be evident from this study that hockey was, and remains, a cultural form adopted by Indians to fulfill social, political and economic aspirations and imperatives.

The prime intention here is also to assess how hockey has defined and continues to define sporting relations in India, to delineate the inter-relationship between those who support, promote, play and view the game, to comment on the nature of Indian sports administration and finally to emphasize that a study of Indian hockey in the 1970s goes beyond the playing field and shifts focus to the push and pulls of competitive regionalism in a seemingly united, independent nation state.

When It All Went Wrong: Astro-turf and the 'North-South' Divide

The politics of regional identity had emerged as a powerful factor in south India by the late 1960s. The foremost instance is the success of the Dravida Munnetra Kazhagam (DMK) in Tamil Nadu in the general elections of 1967. The DMK grew out of the Dravidian movement started by E.V. Ramaswamy or 'Periyar' who was a lifelong 'fervent opponent of the Northern domination of Indian politics, culture and religion'.[15] Its roots lay in the linguistic nationalisms that had been an issue right from the debates in the Constituent Assembly and threatened to tear apart the country in the language agitations of the 1950s—most notably in Andhra Pradesh after Potty Srimalu's fast-unto-death. Linguistic nationalism was arguably only a sub-set of cultural nationalism. While the politics of Tamil Nadu, Andhra Pradesh and Kerala were distinctly different, the subliminal strains running through much of the power play in these states was fuelled by much larger ideological battles that defined what can be called a north–south divide.

Yet, when it came to sport, and in the case of the country's leading Olympic sport, hockey, the south was still subservient to the stranglehold exerted by the north. As a result, southern sports administrators were determined to challenge the well-entrenched northern supremacy even if that damaged 'national interest' in the long run. In the fight with the north for the control of Indian hockey, the southern bloc led by M.A.M. Ramaswamy enlisted the support of the FIH in the early 1970s.[16] Evidence in the IOC's archives proves beyond doubt that the Ramaswamy faction won control and retained it despite severe opposition, only because of the legitimacy bestowed upon it by the international federation. This alliance pre-empted the possibilities of a strong Indian protest when the shift to artificial turf was proposed in the mid-1970s. As a close ally of the International Hockey Federation and its president Rene Frank, Ramaswamy, having assumed presidency of the Indian federation, had little choice but to offer tacit consent to the move to astro-turf.[17] A fight for supremacy between the north and south blocs, this chapter will demonstrate, was at the root of the Indian apathy, central to the subsequent decline of India's leading Olympic sport. It follows that more than the shift to astro-turf, it was regional power play that resulted in the disappearance of hockey from its position of centrality in the Indian sporting landscape.

'Where Cows are Sacred and Fake Grass an Anathema': The Mysterious Shift to Artificial Turf

The shift to artificial turf was a chance development. It was during a visit to Montreal in 1973, the venue of the 1976 summer Olympics, that the president of the FIH and other leading administrators realized the impossibility of organizing the Olympic hockey competition. Not one of the grounds picked as possible venues for the proposed competition was up to the mark. Further, it was apparent that the organizers weren't capable of making the grounds fit for play in the fickle Canadian climate. There wasn't adequate time between the end of winter and the start of the summer games for the pitches to be readied.[18]

In this situation, Montreal's Mayor, Drapeau and the vice-president of the Montreal Olympics Organizing Committee came up with the idea of using an artificial turf pitch in place of the traditional grass surface for the competition. This, it was suggested, would enable the

Olympic tournament to go on without hindrance. 'To show what could be done and to allow the FIH to judge whether such a surface was really suitable, a demonstration of hockey was laid on in Toronto in a stadium which normally was used for American football.'[19]

The trial was successful and the people present in Toronto were profoundly impressed with the success of the experiment. The outcome was that the FIH, based on a highly favourable recommendation from its president, consented in a few months' time to allow the Montreal Olympic hockey tournament to be played on artificial turf instead of grass. Soon after the FIH had given its consent, an astro-turf constructed by the Monsanto company was sampled by some of the best European talent. A match was organized by the French Hockey Federation near Paris, followed by a magnificent dinner in honour of past international players. Most present were impressed with the turf and consented to the shift. Interestingly, Asia, the traditional home of hockey, was not represented at these meetings.

A grand premier on artificial turf took place in Montreal on 19 July, when an eight-nation Olympic preparatory tournament opened on what was later to be used as the surface for the Olympic Games. India pulled out of this tournament at the last minute and was not able to experience first-hand the realities of playing on artificial turf. The Europeans, on the other hand, loved it. As reported by the *World Hockey* magazine:

> As soon as the first few matches had taken place, it was abundantly clear that playing hockey on artificial surface of this type produced enormous benefits... artificial grass permits easier ball control and this in itself helps to reduce the number of infringements of the rules—which means less whistle and fewer stoppages. The game thus becomes easier to follow, as well as being a faster spectacle and much more interesting from a spectator point of view.[20]

The scribe went on to state that yet another great advantage of playing on artificial turf was the large number of games that could be completed on one day on the same pitch, given that maintenance was simple and inexpensive. He also declared that playing on an artificial surface greatly reduced the chances of injury to players compared to the experience of playing on a conventional turf pitch. 'Despite the high initial cost, there is bound to be a considerable increase in the construction of artificial surfaces for hockey pitches. Here is a fundamental advance, which can only be to the benefit of our sport. Without any doubt the increased attraction for players and spectators opens up vast new horizons.'[21]

From the 1976 Montreal Olympic Games onwards, field hockey has been played exclusively on artificial turf. This was possible because India, where 'cows are sacred and fake grass an anathema'[22]—as one foreign scribe argued—did not raise even a feeble voice of protest. Whatever little protest was voiced came from the 'north' lobby, which had been ousted from power by the 'south' faction led by M.A.M. Ramaswamy. Having succeeded in gaining control of the IHF with full support from the FIH, Ramaswamy was in no mood to oppose the move to astro-turf even if it spelt doom for India. Statements like 'Astro-turf is a very costly affair', made by the Indian star Ajit Pal Singh, fell on deaf ears. As Singh, a veteran of three Olympics (1968, 1972 and 1976) argued: India, as late as 1996 could afford no more than 12 astro-turf fields, in sharp contrast to countries like Holland which had many more.[23]

Yet, the IHF lent its full support to the FIH in consolidating the shift. Like the dog that did not bark in *The Hound of the Baskervilles*, allowing Sherlock Holmes to unearth the truth, for the historian, the Indian Federation's support for astro-turf is a telling clue to the politics that defined it.

'Considerable Trouble Between the North and the South': Hockey's Tragedy

Things had been going reasonably well for Indian hockey until 1973 when Ashwini Kumar, president of the Indian Hockey Federation, was forced to step down from his post due to burgeoning opposition against him. His resignation was followed by a long spell of anarchy within the ranks of the IHF and conflict between the north and south blocs as the Punjabi P.N. Sahni and the Madras–based M.A.M. Ramaswamy engaged in a bitter struggle for the presidency.[24] As Rene Frank of the FIH described it: '...the fight started in 1973/74 by some sports leaders of the North, having close links with the Sikh community, in order to avoid that the hockey leadership should go to the South.'[25] While Sahni had the backing of Kumar, Ramaswamy, an extremely influential Madras businessman, had the backing of some in the Central government in Delhi.

The feud turned murky when the group led by Sahni made every effort to stall Ramaswamy's assumption of the IHF presidency, so much so that the government had to appoint a reputed Supreme Court judge to oversee the hockey federation's elections.[26] With the dispute at its height in 1974, the IOA cancelled the affiliation of the IHF and took over the administration of hockey in the country. This decision by the IOA is commented upon in a confidential letter written by Raja Bhalindra Singh, then president of the IOA, to Rene Frank, president of the FIH. In his letter, Raja Bhalindra Singh expressed deep resentment over the actions of the Ramaswamy faction in taking the IOA to court, alleged unwarranted interference by the government, and suggested that such actions might have prevented the IOA from selecting a team for the forthcoming Teheran Asian Games: 'This, you will agree, was a very cruel blow to our efforts in sending a representative team and went a long way in demoralizing the selected team, which, at the moment is under training'.[27] He went on to suggest that the IOA had been able to obtain a temporary injunction from the High Court against the restraint imposed by the lower judiciary on team selection.

In the time-honoured tradition of Indian officialdom, Bhalindra Singh appealed to the IOC to intervene in his favour to 'nip the evil in the bud' and to pre-empt governmental intervention while hockey was suffering.[28] With the IOA appealing to the IOC for help, Ramaswamy enlisted the support of the FIH. Significantly, he seems to have argued that as a south Indian he was a victim of a northern conspiracy. It was an argument that appealed to Frank and he was to consistently back Ramaswamy thereafter.[29]

A year after participating in the Asian Games at Teheran, the Indian hockey team, still under the stewardship of the IOA, won the World Cup for the first and only time in its history at Kuala Lumpur under the coaching of Balbir Singh Jr. So bad was the administrative situation by now that the coaching camp before the tournament and the tour itself had to be funded by the Punjab government in the absence of funding from a dysfunctional IHF.[30] This had some unforeseen consequences. The camp, as Balbir Singh wrote:

> ...was held on the campus of Punjab University, Chandigarh. A newly constructed girls' hostel was given as the residence for the trainees. This being in front of another girls' hostel across the road, some girls started making courtesy calls at our visitors' lounge. This was discouraged by having the front gate locked, and advising the girls to watch the players in action on the field. That prompted the players to give their best during practice sessions to impress the girls.[31]

On such vagaries is sporting success scripted!

Internal squabbling within the IHF temporarily seemed to come to an end in 1975, when Ramaswamy won an acrimonious election against Sahni and was duly recognized as president. But the angry losers would not back off. There were numerous affiliated units that were opposed to the move and therefore refused to participate in the activities of the IHF.[32] IOA chief Bhalindra Singh, a natural votary of the north lobby, did not stop here and went on to write another letter to the president of the FIH, Rene Frank. In his letter, he drew attention to the gross anomalies that accompanied the election of Ramaswamy to the IHF presidency and pointed out that besides these there were other 'specific anomalies, which went against the existing constitution of the Indian Hockey Federation.' For instance, the IHF constitution only allowed those personnel to hold portfolios who represented a body that was affiliated to or was an associate of the IHF. Yet, it had selected Prithpal Singh as the chairman of the selection committee when he did not represent any IHF affiliate. Singh wanted the IOA to retain control of Indian hockey for a little longer while the dispute with Ramaswamy was sorted out:

> I find that as we near 15th August 1975, the attitude of Mr. Ramaswamy is hardening towards an amicable settlement, perhaps, purely on the ground that the adherent membership of the IOA, would, in any case, expire on 15th August 1975, whereafter he could make a direct appeal to the International Hockey Federation for recognition. You will agree that such a psychological approach is possible on the part of Mr. Ramaswamy and I thought it best to bring this to your notice at this very stage.[33]

Even Pakistan threw its hat into the ring in trying to exploit the volatile situation in India. In a letter to the IOC president, Lord Killanin, the Pakistan Hockey Federation urged the IOC to institute a commission of inquiry into the affairs of Indian hockey so that an example was set 'for other countries in Asia who may be tempted to follow the example of India' and openly defy IOC rules prescribed in the Olympic charter.[34]

Aware of the brewing discord and confident of support from the FIH, Ramaswamy promptly announced his intention to bring under one roof all those affiliated units and individuals who had stayed away from the meeting that elected him president. The meeting was held, strangely enough, under the auspices of the ministry of education in New Delhi.[35] The IOA also approached the newly elected president with a request that in the interest of cordiality and to ensure that a sense of confidence prevailed among all the affiliated units of the IHF, he should take action to give, as far as possible, equitable representation to the affiliated members.[36] Nothing was done to fulfill the promise, and for some time the IHF continued to function as a preserve of individuals from the south. In all this the FIH's support for Ramaswamy was crucial. In 1978, for instance, Bhalindra Singh forwarded to the IOC a dossier of Rene Frank's latest correspondence with the north Indian faction, sarcastically noting: 'You can see from this whether Mr. Frank is determined to view this controversy from a very narrow angle, and will probably in the last analysis throw his weight with the Indian Hockey Federation rather than National Olympic Committee'.[37]

The fight between the IOA and the IHF flared up again in mid-1977 on the eve of the meeting of the IOA general assembly. At a meeting on 2 July 1977, members of the IOA general council expressed dissatisfaction with the working of the IHF and it was 'desired that the IOA must make concerted moves to remedy the situation and if necessary place the entire situation before the Government'.[38] As a follow-up, Air Chief Marshall O.P. Mehra, who had succeeded Raja Bhalindra Singh as the president of the IOA in 1975, wrote to Ramaswamy on 19 July 1977, inviting him to a meeting in August that year to address the growing ill-will.[39] Ramaswamy wrote back, informing Mehra that he was out of the country in August but would meet the IOA president in early September 1977. A tentative meeting was set up for 3 September but it never materialized.

Not surprisingly, the IOA executive council, which met on 24 September 1977, expressed deep resentment at the conduct of the

IHF and its president. In a letter dated 6 October 1977 and addressed to M. Dayanand, secretary of the IHF, Air Vice Marshall C.L. Mehra, secretary general of the IOA, alleged that the president of the IHF, despite having been in Delhi for meetings with officials of the ministry of education, had preferred not to get in touch with the president of the IOA. Accordingly, the IOA had reached the conclusion that the IHF was not interested in arriving at an amicable solution. In another letter addressed to Ramaswamy on 11 October 1977, the IOA congratulated him on his work in securing the rights to host the 1982 World Cup in India and assured him that the resources of the IOA were at all times at his disposal. The flurry of letter-writing did not abate and in another confidential letter written on 7 November 1977, the IOA repeated its long-standing request for a meeting. Finally, on 23 December 1977, the secretary of the IOA in a personal note to the president of the IHF almost pleaded for his intervention:

> As you may be aware, the IOA General Assembly meeting will be held in New Delhi on 14 January 1978 at 1400 hours. You will recollect that in the last General Assembly meeting held in July 1977, members of the IOA had raised certain issues connected with the workings of the Indian Hockey Federation...Given that the meeting between yourself and the IOA has not materialised in spite of efforts made in that direction and given that the IOA General Assembly may raise issues relating to hockey, we request you to kindly attend this meeting along with your Secretary so that first hand clarifications can be given to all points raised. This will also avoid any decisions being taken by the IOA in your absence. You will agree that this is in the best interests of the IOA and the IHF.[40]

In the absence of any effort on the part of the IHF and its president to attend the meeting of 14 January 1978, and given that the IHF had done little in the interim to address the concerns raised against its functioning, the IOA had no option but to suspend the functioning of the IHF. The concerns against the IHF arose out of the following issues:

1. The IHF had not paid its dues to the IOA, amounting to approximately Rs 45,000. Some of the amounts, it was observed, had been outstanding for years. It was noted by the IOA general council that its president had made personal efforts to get the IHF to clear its dues and had convened a host of meetings with

the treasurer and secretary of the IHF. And even when the IHF conceded to having defaulted, no action was taken to repay the outstanding dues.

2. Non-implementation of the ruling announced by the IOA that each state or affiliated member should be represented by 'one unit only'. This resolution had been adopted to prevent the mushrooming of dissident groups and had been implemented by all other national federations/associations. The IHF's refusal to accede to the ruling was perceived as creating a dangerous precedent for other national federations.
3. Non-implementation of the assurance given by the president of the IHF, M.A.M. Ramaswamy, to give equitable representation to those associations/individuals absent when he was elected president.
4. The acceptance of interference from a member of the government in the selection of the Indian hockey team and in the management of the day-to-day affairs of the federation.[41]

Of these concerns, the fourth and final one had deep roots and went back to instances of interference by Union Minister for Works and Housing Sikandar Bakht. Only a week before the meeting of the IOA general assembly, Bakht had attended the probables camp at Patiala and made statements contesting the rights and jurisdiction of the IOA. First, he had unilaterally foiled attempts to reinstate the three dissident hockey stars, Surjit Singh, Virender Singh and Baldev Singh, declaring that 'discipline in sports was essential and there must be respectful distance between players and selectors'.[42] When asked if his stand amounted to interference in the affairs of the IOA, Bakht was abrasive in declaring that the 'Government had every right to ensure that public funds were not misused by any sports body. In Socialist countries sports were totally run by the government and there was no objection to it'.[43]

Governmental interference, of course, was complete anathema to the IOC, for which amateurism was an article of faith. This had been emphasized most emphatically by the IOC president Lord Killanin on his visit to India in December 1977.[44] Speaking to the media, Killanin had declared that if any instance of willing submission by a national federation to government or outside dictates was brought before an international federation recognized by the IOC, that national federation could be suspended by the international federation concerned. He reiterated that the IOC had the right to authorize a national Olympic committee to run the affairs of a national federation in which dispute existed and which was adversely affecting the interest of the sportsmen concerned.[45]

The IOA's resentment towards Bakht becomes evident from a confidential letter written by Raja Bhalindra Singh to the president of the International Olympic Committee:

> Unfortunately a minister of government who has no direct connection with sports has been using his official position to interfere in the affairs of the Indian Hockey Federation, and has gone so far as to influence the selection of the national team. This has been resented and has attracted a lot of adverse public criticism both in Parliament and outside. The official government stand, that of the Ministry of Education and Sports, is one of unhappiness. However, the minister continues to interfere and the President of the IHF, whose own position is not too secure, continues to flout all norms of behaviour by seeking help from this extra constitutional authority, and in a most authoritarian way flout both the autonomy of his Federation as well as the spirit of the constitution of the National Olympic Committee. He refused to listen to the National Olympic Committee and has not even cared to be present in the various meetings convened to set matters right.[46]

Despite having suspended the IHF at its meeting of 14 January, the president of the IOA once again invited the president of the IHF to a meeting to resolve differences in a letter dated 17 January 1978.[47] The IHF responded by dragging the IOA to court and obtained an injunction contesting the disqualification.[48] Why did Ramaswamy not take the opportunity to talk to the opposition? He explained his reasons for not attending the proposed meeting with the IOA in a personal letter to Rene Frank. While it is intriguing to wonder why reasons were cited to the FIH and not to the IOA, the reasons themselves seem no less dubious. The three reasons cited by Ramaswamy were as follows:

1. The 14th of January was Pongal Day—one of the most important feast days for us in South India and I had to respect my revered father's wishes and participate in the religious ceremonies at home.

2. As Chairman and Senior Steward of the Madras Race Club, I had to be present at the Race Course to officiate the running of the South India derby.
3. The first circular and second circular convening the IOA meeting did not include any item on hockey affairs.[49]

He went on to state that sport in India was under the direct control of the union government and Prime Minister Morarji Desai had given Sikandar Bakht complete charge of hockey. He also assured the international federation president that in the battle against the IOA, the IHF was assured of Bakht's support.

The letter ended with the assertion that the resolution suspending the IHF was illegal and the Madras High Court, on 18 January 1978, had already granted a temporary injunction against the suspension.[50] He followed this letter with another long memo addressed to the president of the IOA on 31 January 1978 and declared that unless the IOA withdrew the order of suspension, any meeting between the two organizations would prove futile.[51]

In the corridors of international sporting officialdom, the conflict was couched in north–south terms. Certainly, this was how Rene Frank saw it when he joined hands with the IHF. Supporting his claims in a memo to the IOC president on 27 February 1978, Frank suggested that the opposition lobby, which had failed to check Ramaswamy's ascendancy to the presidency of the IHF, was using the instance of action taken against three Punjabi players to resume the tussle. As he put it: 'It must be noted that players involved are most probably all Punjabis, three of them belonging to a team of which Kumar is the chief'.[52] He went on to argue that as far as the suspension of the IHF by the IOA was concerned, 'we fully disapprove it. It must also be noted that all the people involved belong to the North'.[53] He concluded with the assertion that Ramaswamy, who was a member of his council, was an eminent personality in south India, was the director of a number of companies and had helped his association financially since becoming president.[54]

When he learnt of Frank's pro-Ramaswamy lobbying with the IOC, the IOA's Air Chief Marshal Mehra went to great lengths to try and explain the reasons behind the IOA's actions. He repeatedly argued that had it been the intention of the IOA to take over the functioning of the IHF, it would not have allowed Ramaswamy to go ahead with the planning of the India–Pakistan hockey series later in the year and would not have permitted the IHF to run a conditioning camp for the World Cup to be played in Argentina.[55]

Things came to a head when Frank's confidential letters to the IOC president found their way into various Indian newspapers in June 1978.[56] Nor surprisingly, Frank's analysis of the infighting as a symptom of the north–south divide provoked a hostile reaction in the national media.[57] A good example of the outrage it caused is the analysis of veteran sportswriter Bobby Talyarkhan. He argued that Frank had overstepped his limits in declaring 'that the real trouble is between the north and the south of India'. Talyarkhan, who had earlier supported the IHF against the IOA and had been against the IOA takeover of the functioning of the IHF during the 1975 World Cup, now pointed out:

> Frank has gone so far as to mention the Sikhs as an entity and I assert this is none of his business. By stating what he has done Rene Frank is merely adding fuel to fire...Frank has no business to go into any details calculated to turn India's hockey control into a burning cauldron... India's sport has enough internal squabbles for a foreigner to step in and add to the troubles.'[58]

Simultaneously, Frank's allegations were also perceived as a serious slur on the reputation of the IOA. Upset at the press leaks, on 24 June 1978 Air Chief Marshal Mehra wrote a sharp rejoinder to Frank, specifically refuting the allegations of a north-India bias on the IOA's part.

> ...the subject of North and South relations in India is a very sensitive one and if some of your friends in India have informed you that it provides a background to the present imbroglio in Indian Hockey, it is not true.... Raja Bhalindra Singh [Mehra's predecessor as IOA President] is a widely respected sports administrator in the country and uptil today no one has ever blamed him for any parochial feeling. Then again Mr. Ashwini Kumar when he left the Indian Hockey Federation, had more than a majority in the House.[59]

Mehra insisted that 'a paid employee' of the IHF had leaked the Frank letters containing the north–south references to the press. This, he argued, was a sure sign that Indian hockey was 'not in safe hands' and that 'a number of undesirable people' had found their way into it.[60]

Mehra did not stop there. On 30 June, he complained to the IOC president. Again he argued that the issue of 'north–south relations' was a rather sensitive one and it was unethical on Frank's part to comment on such matters. He reminded Killanin of a letter he had sent on 27 March, which mentioned that Frank had 'hurt our national sentiments by giving a political slant to the dispute by referring to personal interests and North versus the rest of India as factor'.[61] He also drew attention to Frank's silence over a similar tussle in Pakistan, arguing that the Pakistani government's takeover of the nation's hockey affairs by disbanding the hockey federation had far more serious consequences for the international sporting fraternity. In the four-cornered fight over Indian hockey, Mehra was hoping that the IOC would exert pressure and rein in Frank so as to balance the scales in the infighting between the IOA and the IHF.[62]

Whether the north–south divide was genuine, or whether it was merely a convenient platform to mask simple old-fashioned lust for power is a moot point. While the administrators argued and jostled, the game continued to suffer. The immutable fact is that vicious infighting was true of almost all Indian sports, and was always seen as an example of India's regional differences by international officials. Writing to Rene Frank in 1978, Lord Killanin noted:

> Over my Olympic years, we have had considerable trouble between the North and the South and there was some opposition even to the election of Mr. Kumar, who is an excellent man, because both he and Bhalindra Singh come from the North....
>
> Your federation is not the only one which has had trouble in India of a fairly similar nature...[63]

If Indian sport were to have an epitaph, this would be it.

'Conflict Has So Far Defied Solution': The Indian Sports Landscape

Instances of regional conflict were hardly new to Indian sport. In colonial conditions, for example, British recognition and support had proved pivotal in shaping the development of Indian soccer in the 1930s and 1940s. Just as in the case of hockey, Bengali dominance over soccer was unquestioned until the 1920s. However, this state of affairs underwent a transformation from the close of the decade. At the root of this transformation lay the changes in the status of the sport in the rest of the country, when other provinces averse to soccer gave up their earlier repugnance and emerged conscious patrons of the sport. This in turn marked the onset of a phase of crisis in Indian soccer that was to culminate the formation of the All India Football Federation in 1937. In this phase, Bengali soccer patrons led by the Maharaja of Santosh continually drew upon British support, considered key to retaining their supremacy over the control of soccer in India.[64]

About the time when the hockey scene in India imploded, a number of other sports were also in turmoil. Multiple organizations were claiming control of wrestling, shooting, athletics and volleyball, complicating the Indian sporting landscape like never before. Ashwini Kumar highlighted the complex situation in a letter to Lord Killanin on 6 August 1977.

Kumar reported that there were three parallel federations trying to gain control of wrestling affairs in India. Even more unfortunate was the fact that some members of the National Olympic Committee had thrown their weight behind one of the factions 'and queered the pitch as far as sorting out the differences between the contending parties are concerned...The only solution lies in the majority of the wrestling organizers merging to form a body under an agreed President'.[65]

The situation in volleyball had been equally volatile between 1974 and 1977 but as Kumar argued, 'all of the warring factions have showed keenness to come to an understanding and have promised that they will most probably join hands sometime in the beginning of September. If this happens, it will be a great day for Indian volleyball, a game in which India has a lot of talent, but which has been moribund for the last three years'.[66]

Two parallel bodies had also sprung up in athletics, both claiming to control the fate of Indian track and field. Again it fell upon Raja Bhalindra Singh to arbitrate the dispute and impress upon members that strong measures needed to be taken to stop this increasing tendency on the part of recalcitrant members to form parallel bodies. Finally, in August 1977, Bhalindra Singh was successful in bringing peace amongst the athletic fraternity, with the factions agreeing to come together under the tutelage of a common president.

The fourth dispute referred to by Kumar in his letter to Lord Killanin centred on the National Rifle Association of India:

> The national body which looks after this sport unfortunately consists of a large number of individual members who do not represent any sporting fraternity, club or state association. This is against the rules and regulations of the Olympic charter. Most of these individual members are local businessmen from Delhi who have 'bought' a seat on the national body. They refuse to resign and have not allowed any shooting activity in this country for the last couple of years. Recently, all the genuine workers and enthusiasts of the game got together and passed a resolution of no-confidence in the parent body and have informed the NOC that they will no longer be a part of the National Rifle Association of India. This conflict has so far defied a solution.[67]

Kumar was writing about shooting but he could have been outlining the status of virtually any sports body in India.

To solve these disputes the IOA proposed the following addition to its constitution in August 1977:

> In order to avoid a situation where due to conflicts/divergence of views in National federations, individuals/institutions take recourse to a court of law for an arbitration judgment, it has been decided that some kind of machinery should be established within the Indian Olympic Association, the NOC of India and its affiliated units, which would give the former organization (Indian Olympic Association) some kind of authority to solve the conflicts and disputes in the National Federations. In pursuance of this, it has been agreed that a rule be incorporated in the constitution of the Indian Olympic Association stating that all National Federations and their affiliated units will submit disputes/conflicts within their organization to the Indian Olympic Association for settlement. The IOA will take note of all the details submitted and give a decision in the matter expeditiously within a stipulated time frame. The National Federations will not submit their disputes and conflicts to a court of law. A similar provision will be incorporated by the National Federations in their respective constitutions stating that, 'no National Federation or its affiliated unit will take their disputes/conflicts to a court of law. All disputes/conflicts will be submitted to the IOA for settlement. The IOA, after examining all the details, will give their final decision in the matter which will be binding on all concerned.'[68]

More than 30 years later, Indian sport continues to remain hostage to the politicking of its administrators. The reasons may be debatable—

competitive regionalism or power politics—but infighting is now a permanent feature of all Indian sports, much more than the promotion of the various games themselves. This has had a disastrous impact on the development of competitive sport in the country. Coming back to hockey, the last word on this belongs to the mercurial Dhanraj Pillay. If anyone has carried the flickering flame of Indian hockey in recent years, it is he; if anyone has symbolized the tragedy of Indian hockey in recent years, it is he. It is, therefore, instructive to hear him speak on Indian officialdom:

> What I am saying is that the IHF just does not care. For them, the post and the aura of being IHF president are more important than anything else. Their ego is on a high such as you can never imagine. But we also have our egos. Don't you feel players like us have done something for the nation to take notice?[69]

Pillay, of course, has had numerous public run-ins with hockey officials but his anguish is genuine and deep-seated and in it lies the real tragedy of Indian sport, not just of Indian hockey. And it can be surmised that the sacking of K.P.S. Gill by the IOA after IHF Secretary Jyothikumaran was caught on tape accepting a bribe is certainly not the last tragedy that we have seen in Indian hockey after its failure to qualify for the Beijing Olympiad.

THE SPORTS–POLITICS VORTEX

The similarity between instances of politicization of sports, though located in completely different conditions and timeframes, are difficult to miss. While in the case of soccer, Bengali sports patrons had sought to enlist British support, in the case of hockey almost half a century later the IOA and the IHF tried to garner international support—from the IOC and the International Hockey Federation (FIH). Such attempts to internationalize internal rifts have adversely affected India's international standing, although this has hardly been recorded in India's political history.

In post-independence, hockey was one sport where the nation had a resounding global presence. However, with the rise of regionalism at the national level, concurrent with the move to astro-turf, India's dominance soon gave way to subjection. And despite signs of resurgence in the last two years, culminating in the brilliant demolition of France

8–1 to qualify for the London Olympics, doubts persist over India's ability to compete with the best European and Australian talent. Failure to qualify for the Champions Trophy and a string of unexpected defeats like in the hands of Malaysia at the 2010 Asian Games have raised a number of questions over the current team's ability to compete at the highest level. While Michael Nobbs has brought about a sea change in the team's mentality, London 2012 will be his ultimate test.

For India, historically, hockey has been a vehicle to express both national and regional achievement and ambition, but in quite different ways. This chapter has expanded the political analysis of hockey in arguing that even at periods when performances were at a low ebb (1970–90), the sport was a site to settle regional discord. This was an uneasy phase, with the unwilling intervention of the central government in sport, evident from its apathy over checking Sikandar Bakht's intrusion into the affairs of the IOA. Such apathy was part of the general official neglect of sport. With the government continuing to view sport as entertainment and leisure until the early 1970s, there were no incentives for bureaucrats or politicians to perceive a sporting portfolio as special. This had its roots in the government's difficulty to understand the political significance of sport and it changed only partly during the organization of the 1982 Asian Games, when the Indian state put its full weight behind the popular appeal of sport.

Even today, the dynamics of how sport and contemporary Indian society influence each other seldom finds mention in histories of modern India. Suffice it to say that sport has globally become crucial to modern human existence, having made itself indispensable to a world infested by terror. Sport and politics in any country are inextricably linked, and India is no exception. The sooner Indian social science recognizes this reality, the better. This will help provide a more nuanced understanding of the complexities of modern India.

7

'The Big Brother of Asia'

Nehruvian India, Sports Diplomacy and a New Order

You have certainly made New Delhi the capital of Asia.
—Anthony De Mello to Jawaharlal Nehru after first Asian Games, 1951.[1]

At the IOC museum in the sleepy Swiss town of Lausanne, the waters of the picturesque Lake Geneva wash up on the doorstep. On the other side of the Lake's glistening waters one can see France—it seems to be in touching distance—and all around are mountains, of the kind made famous by Yash Chopra films and Swiss tourism postcards. Lausanne is the quintessential Swiss town: there is the famous medieval Gothic cathedral, the modern shopping arcades built around it and, of course, the lovely villas. Almost everything is within walking distance; Lausanne is self-contained, almost still in its calmness, content with its serenity and the artistic grandeur of nature as far as the eye can see.

It also as far as one can imagine from the wheat-growing fields of Sansarpur, the crowded training grounds of Mumbai or the bustling dust bowls of Jhansi where India's Olympic dreams were first nurtured. The IOC museum is now the buzzing headquarters of the global Olympic movement but it staggers the mind to imagine that this town houses the headquarters of a movement that now has more member-states than the United Nations;[2] it fed on globalization decades before the term became fashionable.

In many ways, Switzerland is the headquarters of internationalism—a casual walk around Geneva with its rows of UN offices and the famous banks is enough to confirm that—but the internationalism of the Olympic movement is of a different order. The Swiss tradition of banking, the presence of UN bodies, the NGOs, the Red Cross—are all rooted in the Swiss tradition of neutrality. The Olympic movement too draws from that legacy but it is fundamentally based on the power of an idea, an idea that has meant different things to different people. At the turn of the 19th century, when Baron De Coubertin dreamt up the idea of the modern Olympic Games, it was a Euro-centric enterprise that later developed a life of its own. In a world where European powers held sway over most of the globe, the notion of a brotherhood of sportsmen ignited minds, most strikingly in the colonies. We have already seen how the ideas of the aristocrat from France struck a chord with leading members of the Indian elite like Sir Dorabji Tata and G.D. Sondhi, who sowed the first seeds of the movement in India. The great Indian successes at hockey cemented the dream further and gradually disseminated the notion of the Olympics as a global showcase of national pride. In the colonies, the Olympics came to symbolize something deeper than a simple test of athletic skills. It was about identity and equality as much as it was about westernization and about modernity. From China to India, the Olympic movement in the early years in most parts of Asia was led by a coalition of elite gentry and proselytizing officials of the YMCA, supported by imperial officials who saw the Games as a means of ushering in modernity, as defined by the standards of the time.

Participation was one thing, but what if the Games themselves could be brought to Asia? As early as 1913, the first miniature 'Olympics' came to be organized in Asia, early prototypes of what later became the Asian Games. The first prototype was the short-lived Far-Eastern Championship Games, largely an exercise limited to Japan, China and the Philippines. The second was the even more short-lived Western Asiatic Games, largely an exercise by India in concert with its immediate neighbours. Finally came the modern Asian Games, in tandem with the process of decolonization. All these events owed allegiance to the Olympic movement. They were mini-Olympics, sanctioned and coordinated in collaboration with the IOC to spread the Olympic ideal but they took on a deeper meaning in Asia. They were linked to the larger ebbs and flows of global and regional politics, with the newly emerging countries of Asia jostling for identity and space. Sport and the Asian Games became a medium for this struggle.

India is central to this story. The Olympic movement had so caught the imagination of sports administrators in India that they played a pioneering role in building the Asian Games movement. It was an Indian initiative that created the modern Asian Games, and the first Games were held in Delhi. It was also intrinsically linked to the larger Indian self-image of being a major Asian power and the Nehruvian idea of India's centrality in a new global order. Through the years of the freedom struggle, a belief in the inherent unity of Asian countries—'a common identity stemming from a shared aspiration of their peoples for political independence from the West and rooted in their cultural and religious similarities'[3]—had been an article of faith among nationalist Indians. By the 19th century, figures like Keshab Chandra Sen and Swami Vivekanand had become important proponents of Asianism. After World War I, Rabindranath Tagore became one of the first major exponents of the idea that Asia, the continent of 'eternal light', was united by what he saw as a common spiritual bond.[4] The theme of Asian unity had emerged most prominently in Japan after its victory over Russia in 1905. The cries of 'Asia for Asiatics' that emerged from Japan[5] and the notion of a united Asia fighting against Western imperialism struck a chord among Indian nationalists, soon becoming a central tenet of Indian nationalism.[6] As Nehru put it:

> Our struggle was but a part of a far wider struggle for freedom; the forces that moved us were moving millions of people all over the world and driving them to action. All Asia stirs from the Mediterranean to the Far East, from the Islamic West to the Buddhist East...[7]

By the 1920s, Gandhi, C.R. Das, Srinavasa Iyengar and M.A. Ansari had mooted the idea of an Asian federation to promote the cause of freedom in 'Eastern countries'. The Congress Working Committee even passed a resolution, initiated by S. Satyamurthi in 1928, to take steps to form a Pan-Asiatic federation.[8] Central to the Indian conception of a united and rejuvenated Asia was the theme of Indian political leadership. As Satyamurthi told the Congress Working Committee in Calcutta in 1928, he saw 'nothing less for the future of India than that she should be the leader of a renascent Asia'.[9] To Indian nationalists like the Congress Mayor of Calcutta, speaking at the same Congress session, a united India was to be nothing less than the 'leader of an Asiatic Zollverein'.[10] The intellectual foundations of these ideas were later to become the well-springs of Nehru's much-hyped engagement with China in the first years after independence— the halcyon days of Hindi-Chini *bhai-bhai*—followed by the spirit of Bandung in 1955 when New Delhi sought to become the natural leader, not just of a newly emerging Asia but also of Africa.

A number of scholars have focused attention on the legacy of the internationalist vein in Indian nationalism, its implications for the foreign policy of independent India and ultimately how this vision floundered in the face of global realpolitik. The Asian Games of 1951 are a missing link in this story, are a forgotten chapter in independent India's early steps towards Asian prominence.

The Indian initiative for the Asian Games was more than just about sport. The Games were deeply tied to the ideals, hopes and aspirations of Nehruvian India. They are also a useful prism to understand the struggle for Asian leadership that unfolded thereafter. By 1962, the Chinese invasion was to painfully shatter some of these dreams, but there was another forgotten battle that unfolded in that year. This was a silent battle between India and Sukarno's Indonesia, which increasingly sought to assume leadership of the developing world. A conflict between Indian and local officials at the 1962 Jakarta Asiad led to Indonesia's suspension from the IOC. Sukarno, who had been central to the Bandung initiative, responded with the now largely forgotten Games of the New Emerging Forces (GANEFO). GANEFO, he declared, was directly linked to the spirit of Bandung,[11] and to his ideas of a 'new world of the brotherhood of man', which he had outlined at the UN General Assembly in 1960.[12] GANEFO was nothing less than a bid for the leadership of the developing world; sport was the conduit. This chapter will uncover some of the layers of the deeper story of the Asian Games, its links with Olympism, and the competitive politics of the newly independent nations of Asia that unfolded through the Asian Games.

'The Oriental Olympiad': The Far Eastern Asian Games

The first off-shoot of the Olympics in Asia was the Far-Eastern Asian Championship Games (FECG) that lasted from 1913 to 1934. They have been variously described as the 'first regional sports event ever to unite Asian athletes under the banner of Asian games'[13] and the 'first Oriental Olympic Games'.[14] But the Far Eastern Games were not a truly Asian event, as we understand Asia today. They were restricted almost entirely to Philippines, Japan and China. India was the first country outside the East Asian troika to take part but that was as late as 1930 and only once. Indonesia was the second, taking part in the 1934 Games.[15] Of the 10 occasions on which these Games took place, four were staged in Manila, three in Shanghai and three in Japan.[16] As the first assemblage of an international sporting competition in Asia, it was an important marker and a precursor of what was to come but as the name implies, the Far Eastern Games was just that: about the Far East. Fan Hong, in her study, has emphasized the 'Asian' nature of the FECG[17] but part of the problem is the definition of Asia itself. The answers to the question of what constitutes Asia constantly shift as one moves from countries in West Asia to Japan. Even today a term like 'Asian' in the street language of Australia, for instance, stands as short-hand for Chinese or East Asian, while in London, the same term connotes people of South Asian descent. 'Asia' itself is a constructed identity. The political idea of Asia has undergone many manifestations, slowly emerging to its present form.

The FECG was defined by three main factors: the role of the YMCA as an agent of change; colonial politics and the forces of modernity and change as they clashed with tradition; and the larger struggle for self-assertion between Japan and China that increasingly came to dominate the Games until they folded up.[18] As in India and Latin America, the YMCA played a crucial role in inculcating modern Western sport in China, Japan and the Philippines. It started what was later regarded as the first national sporting event in China in 1910. It was here that the meaning of sport as an agent of modernity emerged most starkly in the form of the athlete Sun Baoqing. A high jumper, he performed poorly in the initial stage because his traditional long pigtail kept knocking off the bars. One evening, an angry Sun chopped off the pigtail—central to his identity under Manchu law—and won the high jump championship the next day. As Fan Hong points out, his 'action was more than a symbolic gesture: for men, the body became an icon of modernity, reconstruction and rehabilitation'.[19]

Accordingly, when C.H. Robertson of the Tianjin YMCA and Elwood S. Brown acting for the Philippines YMCA put together the first Far Eastern Asian Games, at the heart of the model of this new 'Asian' Olympiad was the notion of spreading 'Western morality and masculinity among the weaker Oriental people'.[20] For the politically subordinated Chinese athletes though, competing at the first Games with the still colonized Filipinos was about nationalist assertion and inserting themselves into 'the struggle that modernity posed for all the world's nation-states'.[21]

From the very beginning and De Coubertin was in the picture, and the YMCA and the IOC marched in tandem. Brown even wrote to the founder of Olympism reporting that the objective of his initiative was to train 'oriental' athletes to participate in the Olympics. The nomenclature itself left no scope for ambiguity. The first Far Eastern Games were named the Far Eastern Olympiad. But De Coubertin's insistence on saving the word 'Olympic' only for the original championship meant the Far Eastern Olympiad changed names to become the Far Eastern Championship Games from 1915 onwards.[22]

There was an attempt to expand the scope of FECG by inviting India to the fifth Games at Shanghai in 1921 but the huge distance and heavy costs put paid to the hopes. Thailand, Java, Malaya and Ceylon did not participate in Shanghai for precisely the same reason and the story was repeated in every subsequent instance of the FECG. There were also disagreements over who should or should not participate and the FECG remained confined to the original three nations.[23] We have seen the great lengths to which the founders of India's Olympic movement went to ensure Indian participation at the Olympics. The East Asian equivalent of it was just not as enticing or important in their view, at least at that stage. Moreover, the idea that Asia could emerge as a power bloc on its own, one that could redefine world politics, had still not gained the currency that it would gain later in the halcyon days of non-alignment and the Bandung Conference. That would come later, as the nationalist movements of Asia gathered pace and in the early years of decolonization. It is no accident that the first truly pan-Asian Games were organized in Delhi in the first flush of Indian independence and aggressively promoted as the harbinger of a new age.

The FECG collapsed under the weight of the Sino-Japanese political rivalry. George Orwell was referring to Western sporting rivalries when he first wrote the lines 'war minus the shooting' to describe modern sport but he would have been right to describe Sino-Japanese sporting contests in the same words. From 1923 onwards, Japan dominated the Games and each defeat was like a knife prick at Chinese notions of honour and self-respect. As one contemporary Chinese account noted:

> The Republic of China, with three thousand years civilization...was defeated, sent away crying, by a small nation of three islands! This is not only a shame—it is pathetic!...If we still have hot blood...Wake up, the healthy athletes of the Republic. Use your blood and freshness and move forward to take back your position on the international sports stage.[24]

The sporting rivalry mirrored the intense political gulf between the two countries and the Japanese invasion of Manchuria in 1931, followed by the installation of the puppet Manzhuoguo regime, brought things to a head. Japan demanded the inclusion of Manzhuoguo as an independent state in the FECG, which the Chinese delegates absolutely refused. For them, Manchuria was an integral part of Chinese territory, a festering symbol of Chinese humiliation. On 21 May 1934, the dispute forced the dissolution of the FECG itself after China protested against what it called a Japanese–Philippines conspiracy to push the proposal through.[25] Japan, in concert with the Philippines, then tried to set up a new event called the Oriental Championship Games. It was to be hosted in Tokyo in 1938, and Manzhuoguo was to participate, but the gathering clouds of World War II ensured that the new championship never took place.[26]

Dress Rehearsal at Delhi: The Western Asiatic Games

The closure of the Far Eastern Games was closely followed by a similar experiment by Indian sports administrators: the Western Asiatic Games (WAG). It was a mirror image of the Far Eastern Games, except that it replicated the model with West Asian countries and India's immediate neighbours. As the constitution of the organizing body made clear, it was to consist of the countries 'East of the Suez and West of Singapore'.[27] If the Far Easterners could have their own games, so would the West Asians. As Indian officials clarified in an official note to the IOC, the Far East was too far for the rest of the Asian countries and 'in too disturbed a condition'.[28]

The moving force behind the Games was G.D. Sondhi, Patiala's man, who by this time virtually controlled the Indian Olympic movement. A former hockey player for Trinity College, Cambridge, and a cross-country runner for Punjab University,[29] Sondhi was the son of a renowned barrister in Jalandhar and would later become the first Indian principal of Government College, Lahore.[30] As described in the first chapter, Sondhi was the prime mover in the Punjab Olympic Association and with Patiala's support, took over the mantle of Indian Olympism in the late 1920s.

The Western Asiatic Games were organized by Sondhi in 1934 soon after he became a full member of the IOC. Like the FECG, the WAG was clearly meant to be a mini-Olympic in the region. As has been mentioned in Chapter 2, Sondhi explained to De Coubertin:

> I hope it will give you great pleasure to learn that your great example in founding the world international brotherhood of sport is being imitated on a small scale in the East.[31]

Notwithstanding this grandiose description, only three nations took part in WAG, besides India. Afghanistan, Ceylon and Palestine were the only other contestants.

The same problems that plagued the FECG plagued the WAG. India had invited every country between the Suez and Singapore. As Sondhi informed De Coubertin, the problems of distance, economic depression and more significantly, 'absence of sports interest' proved a dampener. There just weren't enough organized sports bodies in West Asia to take part and those that existed did not have enough money. There is little documented data to piece together the WAG story but the Sondhi letters preserved at the IOC Museum at Lausanne indicate that the Indian organizers found it too difficult to generate political support in the countries of the region. Sondhi, for instance, tried hard for Persia's participation but failed. But there is no doubt that he saw this event as a mini-Olympics, repeatedly asking De Coubertin—'our revered founder of the modern Olympic games'—for inspirational messages. [32] It is not known what exactly De Coubertin wrote back but he did send a 'kind message of good will' that was duly read out at the opening ceremony.[33] It can be surmised that De Coubertin could not but be overjoyed at this Punjabi from Lahore planting in the dusty plains of New Delhi a sapling from the original Olympic tree.

The event itself was primarily sponsored by the Maharaja of Patiala, with some support from the Viceroy in terms of infrastructure.[34] The participants were hosted at Delhi's Irwin amphitheatre where they took on each other in hockey and athletics. The only two other events—swimming and diving—were hosted in Patiala in the absence of suitable facilities in New Delhi.[35] By all accounts the Games—the first multilateral international sports event in India—went off well and the member countries agreed to host the next event in Palestine in 1938.[36] The Dutch East Indies and Persia joined the Federation as well but the approach of World War II and the political troubles in Palestine meant that these hopes never fructified. [37] The Western Asiatic Games died in the city of its birth—New Delhi.

'Delhi: Capital of Asia'
The First Asiad and Nehruvian India

The first two Asian attempts at imitating the Olympics in the region ended with World War II. They also suffered from being specific only to their immediate regions and not being pan-Asian. The end of the war and the process of decolonization thereafter provided the opportunity for a truly pan-Asian Olympic-type event. India played a pivotal role in stitching together the new Asian Games. As Indian administrators went about creating the Asian Games Federation and the first Delhi Asiad of 1951, they were also driven by the idea of a resurgent independent India and Nehru's notion of a new world order: decolonized states, led by India, marching forward to take their rightful place. At the heart of the story of the Delhi Asiad was a desire for newly independent India to be noticed, the moment of arrival signified by an international event of Olympian proportions. The symbolism of Delhi being at the centre of a new Asian federation was central to this vision, perfectly in tune with the internationalist ideals of Nehruvian India. Sport was to be a binding force in this new alignment of emerging nations. Writing in 1959, Anthony De Mello, the main organizer of the 1951 Asiad, recounted the opening ceremony in words that merit repetition:

> What was the greatest moment in Indian sport?...there was never an occasion to beat that of March 4th, 1951. On that historic day for the sport of India—indeed for the sport of Asia, even the world—the first Asian Games were opened...It was Asia marching ever nearer to the great Olympic ideal of 'Citius, Altius, Fortius'—faster, higher, stronger....
>
> *India—the 'Big Brother of Asia'*—had given the lead in this the finest sporting venture of the Orient.[38]

Just four years after independence, with hundreds of thousands of Partition refugees still camping in the environs of Delhi, India's capital put together the first truly pan-Asian sporting event. It was a time of hope, of idealism. Energetic Punjabi refugees had already begun changing the face of Delhi and of much of north India. Just two months earlier, India, with a new constitution, had turned a republic; C. Rajagopalachari had just replaced Lord Mountbatten as Governor General; Britain's decision to quit had just begun a domino effect in colonies across Asia and Africa; and Nehru was at the height of his powers. It is not too difficult to see why an Indian watching the parade of nations marching under the shadow of the majestic ramparts of Delhi's Purana Qila, the Old Fort, would begin fancying his country as the new 'Big Brother' of Asia. As De Mello put it: 'The Games had been, at once, the beginning of one era and the end of another'.[39]

The birth of the Asian Games is a fascinating interplay of the progress of Indian nationalism and the country's ambitions of leadership in the post-colonial world. The idea of the Games itself was born at the Asian Relations conference held in Delhi on the eve of Indian independence in 1947. Attended by 21 countries and officially organized by the Indian Council of World Affairs,[40] this conclave of Asian countries had been put together by the personal efforts of prime minister-designate Jawaharlal Nehru as he tried to forge an Asian coalition. Nehru had personally raised the funds for this conference. In February 1947, for instance, he wrote to the King of Nepal for assistance; King Tribhuvana responded immediately with a donation of Rs 10,000.[41] Nehru was clear about his idea of Asianism. As he told delegates in his welcoming speech:

> For too long we of Asia have been petitioners in Western courts and chancellories. That story must now belong to the past. We stand on our own feet and co-operate with all others who are prepared to co-operate with us. We do not intend to be the play things of others.[42]

Mahatma Gandhi, Sarojini Naidu and Nehru, all spoke at the conference about Asia being a distinct entity, with a special message of enlightenment.[43] With their words setting the backdrop, it was at this conclave that G.D. Sondhi, who had organized the Western Asiatic Games, conceived the idea of an Asian Games Federation. He immediately wrote to the Maharaja of Patiala that they could take advantage of the presence of high-profile international delegates at the conference to build contacts and to sell the idea. Patiala agreed and Sondhi then circulated a note explaining the objectives of the proposed federation to many of the delegates. 'Most of them expressed their approval, and some of them were very enthusiastic.'[44]

Nehru himself was supportive of the move. Sondhi took the prime minister-designate in confidence and it was Nehru's suggestion to change the name from the Asiatic Games, as originally proposed, to the Asian Games.[45] The conference itself gave birth to the Asian Relations Organization that survived until 1955.[46] The Asian Relations Organization was to be the kind of pan-Asian federation that the Congress nationalists had always hoped to lead. The failures were to come later. If there was to be a political federation, then what better way to showcase its unity than through a pan-Asian Games.

'The Miracle' Games and the Problem of 'Asian Unity': Idealism and Reality

With the idea of the Asian Games approved, the gap between idealism and reality hit home. The first problem was domestic. Many in the IOA itself were loath to accept the responsibility of hosting an ambitious event of this nature. The IOA formally said yes at its annual meeting in Lucknow in 1948 but 'did not take any further action on the matter'.[47] There is no mention in the archival records of the IOA and the IOC about why the proposal was not taken forward, considering it had the backing of its president, the Maharaja of Patiala; its secretary, Sondhi; and no less a person than Nehru. But we can surmise that the problem was infighting within the IOA of the kind that has been detailed in previous chapters. The clue lies in the fact that Sondhi and Patiala decided to bypass the IOA and modified their plan for the first Asian Games. The IOA's approval was essential if the Asian Games were to be an international competition featuring various games.

Faced with opposition within the IOA, Sondhi shrunk his proposal and decided to host just an Asian athletic meet. Such a meet only needed approval from the Amateur Athletic Federation of India (AAFI). Sondhi himself headed this body and not only did the AAFI give permission in February 1948, it also gave its president, Sondhi, 'full powers and every encouragement to go ahead with his plans'.[48] In a further sign of the magnitude of the problems within the IOA, the Maharaja of Patiala agreed, on Sondhi's request, to head the organizing body.[49] Here was the IOA president, the all-powerful Patiala whose money and clout virtually controlled Indian sport, unable to get his own body to organize the Asian Games and now agreeing to bypass it via his protégé's Athletic Federation. The first Asiad was now to be the first Asian Athletic Championship.

Invitations to other Asian countries went out in July 1948. But now the organizers ran into their second problem. This was the gap between the rhetoric of Asian solidarity and the practical difficulties in achieving such an ideal. In July 1948, most of the countries that had been approached were busy preparing for the London Olympics, also to be held that year. It was one thing to talk of Asian solidarity at the Asian Relations Conference, quite another to give up the Olympics for it. As an IOA note later explained, the response to the invitations was, to say the least, 'rather disappointing'.[50]

But the persistent Sondhi would not give up. He flew to London for the Olympics and used the gathering of international sports officials to try his luck again. On 8 August 1948, Sondhi managed to convene a meeting of most of the Asian representatives at the Mount Royal Hotel. He invited all the Asian teams in London, and senior officials representing the still-undivided Korea, China, Philippines, Burma and Ceylon made it for the meeting. Singapore, Lebanon, Pakistan, Afghanistan, Iran, Iraq and Syria stayed away.[51] It was a clear reflection of the political divides within Asia.

The managers at the Mount Royal meeting agreed to form the Asian Games Federation. They also agreed to award Delhi the first Asian Games, originally scheduled for 1950, as well as an invitation athletics meet in February 1949. But there were more snags to come.

The invitation meet never materialized, 'on account of various causes, internal and external, and invitations were reluctantly withdrawn'.[52]

What did materialize was another international conclave in Delhi to give final form to the Asian Games Federation. The London meeting had resulted in an agreement for such a body. Now its constitution had to be drawn up and the agreements had to be signed. Ever persistent, Sondhi wrote again to the national Olympic committees of Asia, apart from those who had said yes in London. When many did not reply, he personally contacted their embassies and delegations in Delhi and some promised to nominate representatives. Eight countries eventually made it for the Delhi conclave on 12–13 February 1949 that finally gave birth to the Asian Games. Philippines and Burma sent sports officials; Pakistan, Ceylon, Indonesia, Afghanistan, Nepal and Siam sent diplomatic nominees from their respective embassies and high commissions. Iran too had agreed by now, but its representative was unable to attend.[53] They agreed on a constitution and signed.[54] Finally, the Games, to be held every four years, were to be a reality. Despite the hurdles so far, the meeting itself was seen by many in Delhi as yet another example of its growing clout in the post-colonial world. As Anthony De Mello, who later headed the organization of the Delhi Asiad, noted 10 years later:

> Looking back on it, and seeing it in the shadow of the great sporting event which was soon to follow, it may seem a matter of little importance. But the fact that these countries were prepared to come to us for so important a meeting was extremely gratifying; India if anyone had ever doubted it, was certainly now established in the eyes of the sporting world. More—she was now proving herself to be a focal point of interest and activity.[55]

In a sense, the initial disappointments that the Indians faced in putting together the Asian Games Federation also reflected the larger problems inherent in the idea of Asianism itself. Many of these had surfaced at Nehru's Asian Relations Conference as well. As India pushed the idea of a pan-Asian brotherhood, delegates from Burma, Ceylon and Malaya expressed their fear that British imperialism might be replaced by economic and demographic aggression by India and China. In 1949, the first prime minister of Ceylon, D.S. Senanayake, made this concern explicit, saying that there was 'an undercurrent of apprehension regarding the possibility of Indian expansion involving Ceylon'.[56]

As T.A. Keenleyside noted, constant talk of Indian leadership in South Asia and South-East Asia did not help. The fear of an Indian hegemony 'manifested itself in harsh immigration and citizenship restrictions against Indians in Burma and Ceylon after independence, and in periodic anti-India demonstrations in Nepal in the 1950s and 60s'.[57] The smaller nations were uncomfortable with a powerful India while the bigger ones, like China and Indonesia, were unhappy with its leadership pretensions. All these underlying tensions manifested themselves at the Asian Relations Conference.

New Delhi, however, saw things differently. Writing in 1951, Congressman Mohanlal Gautam was still optimistic, hailing the Conference as having 'rediscovered the unity of Asian peoples and [having] laid the foundation for closer union in the future in defence of themselves and in promoting world peace'.[58] But neutral scholars in retrospect could see that side by side with the idealistic talk, the Asian Relations Conference also reflected the inherent problems with the pan-Asian idea. It was marred by:

> the unrepresentative nature of many delegations, by Sino-Indian rivalry for leadership, and by the permanent unpreparedness of many states to support the idea of a permanent Asian organization.
>
> As a result the Asian Relations Organization that emerged out of the conference never proved effective and was finally abandoned in 1955.[59]

Unlike many other Indian nationalists, Nehru read the signs early. More than anyone else he knew the practical difficulties involved and he was beginning to get sceptical about the Asian Relations Organization long before it folded up but his early leaning towards the pre-independence idea of India as a leader of Asia remained. As late as March 1949, just a few months before the constitution of the AGF was drawn up in Delhi, Nehru told a conference in Indonesia that 'there was a certain looking in the direction of India' and a feeling that she would 'possibly play a fairly important part in bringing Asian countries together'.[60] More than anything else, it was this sentiment that spurred on Sondhi and his band as they strove to put together the first Asiad, the larger ideology of Nehruvian India driving the creation of the first pan-Asian games. Quite appropriately, it was Nehru who coined the Asian Games motto: 'Play the Game in the Spirit of the Game'.[61]

Many of the problems that plagued this wider attempt at Asian political unity also plagued the early planning for the Asian Games: the problem of contact between various countries, wide differences in perception and struggles over leadership. Not surprisingly, Anthony De Mello later wrote about the experience of organizing the first Delhi Asiad as one that had turned him into a 'firm believer in miracles'.[62]

'Divine Providence': Cricket Money, the Asian Olympiad and Bandung's Missing Link

It was one thing for Nehru and the Congress to support the Asian Games, quite another to pay for it. India had just gone through the largest and bloodiest forced migration in history. Partition had created an estimated 20 million refugees—about a million came to Delhi alone—and crores were being spent on their rehabilitation all over north India. Entire new cities were springing up as the refugees began building their lives afresh and an independent government that Churchill had claimed would 'descend into chaos' had to be run. Tricky negotiations were on to incorporate the 565 princely states of India and in the middle of it all, a war was being fought in Kashmir. With tribal raiders from Pakistan knocking on the outskirts of Srinagar, the 161 Infantry Brigade had just been air-lifted to its defence. The ceasefire would not come until 1949.

While the two armies were shooting at each other, the Pakistanis were demanding the Rs 55 crore that had been promised to them from the coffers of the Reserve Bank of India at the time of Partition. A reluctant Nehru and Sardar Vallabhbhai Patel, the Home Minister, agreed to give Pakistan its share of the treasury only after Gandhi fasted in protest, but newly independent India was left with a depleting exchequer and problems on many fronts.[63] The rioting only stopped after Gandhi's assassination in 1948 and the communal balance was still razor-thin.

Nehru had supported the Asiad but as he strove to enforce control in what was already a poor country, now facing a mass refugee problem, there was little left over for the Asian Games. The government, in fact, gave no aid at all. The Asian Games was to be India's showcase for the world, but unlike the second Asiad of 1982, the first one was mounted purely through non-governmental money.

The Asiad did have the full patronage of the establishment, prime minister downwards, but that did not mean money. As the organizers scrambled to arrange the funding, the Games were first postponed from February 1950, the originally planned date, to November 1950; and then finally to March 1951. Later chroniclers would wax eloquent about how it was until then the 'greatest carnival of international sport ever held in India' but few knew how close it came to being abandoned altogether.[64] Invitations had already been sent out in 1949 but Delhi just wasn't equipped. 'There was no stadium in Delhi, no cinder track, no equipment, no funds…'[65] So bad was the situation that the gallant Sondhi who had taken the idea forward purely by his own initiative, now decided to quit in helplessness. Sondhi resigned from the directorship of the First Asiad on 13 April 1950 and it seemed at the time that his decision also signified the end of the dream.[66]

What happened next comes from the memoirs of the man who stepped into the breach: Anthony De Mello, a founder member and then president of the Board of Control for Cricket in India. De Mello faced a gargantuan task. As he recounted nine years later, 'It was unprecedented in Olympic and Asiad history that a major sports meet would be staged without Government aid of any sort.' As a comparative yardstick, the Philippines government spent £1,00,000 on the second Asiad in 1954 at Manila; the Japanese government built a new stadium in Tokyo for the third Asiad in 1956 and gave a grant-in-aid of £3,00,000; and the British built a new swimming pool along with a government grant of £6,00,000 for the British empire and Commonwealth Games at Cardiff in 1958.[67] The Delhi organizers had no such help.

What De Mello had, though, was influence; his own and that of the establishment. An Anglo-Indian born in Karachi, he had been educated at Cambridge and from the 1920s onwards had become one of the big movers and shakers of Indian sport. In the late 1920s, he was central to the formation of the Board of Control for Cricket in India, becoming its founding secretary. He also founded Bombay's now iconic Cricket Club of India (CCI) in 1933[68] and just before taking over the Asiad job he had set up the National Sports Club of India (NSCI) in the same city. If anyone in India could organize an event from scratch, it was Anthony De Mello. De Mello did two things as soon as he took charge. To solve the money crunch, he got his own NSCI to provide a loan of Rs 1 lakh for the Asiad.[69] This was in addition to the funds he arranged from the CCI.[70] This served as the seed money for the Games. Such are the ironies of history that the first Asiad was largely financed by money from two Bombay clubs: one focused only on cricket, which has never featured in the Games till date.

De Mello's second and more interesting move was to form an organizing committee consisting of some of India's most influential personalities. The government may not have had the funds to spend on sport, but many in it believed in the Asiad. A way would be found. This is partly why De Mello took up the job in the first place:

> It was a challenge to Indian sportsmen—and, seeing in this light, I accepted the now vacant directorship. Not without some temerity, I may say, but I was greatly helped by the knowledge that many influential people and sporting bodies throughout India were ready to do what they could to lighten the task.[71]

The composition of De Mello's 18-member organizing committee in this context is revealing. Headed by the Maharaja of Patiala, this committee consisted of five senior Indian Civil Service officers, four royals, the Chief of Army Staff, a major general, industrialist Naval Kishore Tata and influential builder Sir Sobha Singh.

The first result of bringing such a group of men together came when Gen K.M. Cariappa, the Army chief, immediately agreed to solve the problem of building a new Asiad village by lending two Army buildings near the proposed stadium. As De Mello put it, '"influence"—if you like to call it that—brought us the Asiad village for the 1,000 athletes, managers and officials'.[72] The only other direct governmental support, besides intellectual patronage, came in the form of exemption of duties on the sports goods of contestants, 'half-price' railway tickets for their travel and cars for transportation.[73]

Nehru's government may not have had the money but many of its top officials and local notables shared a common vision. In the massive IOA documentation of the first Asiad, nowhere did we come across any note of bitterness about the lack of governmental funding. In fact, the overarching sense in the records is one of excitement, of the anticipation of what the Asiad would do for India's standing and a general consensus that it had widespread support from all sections in

India. Even Sondhi, who quit the Asiad Organizing Committee because of the huge odds, wrote sympathetically later about how Asia was 'by and large…a poor continent' and how it was understandable that it did not have the resources to spend on sport. Sondhi was clear that the Asian Games should not go 'beyond our means and objectives', and deprive 'thousands, if not millions' in the quest for nationalistic glory. Speaking at a seminar in the Philippines in 1961, the man who more than anyone else created the concept of the Asian Games, cautioned against incurring 'heavy financial burdens' in the search for prestige at the Asian Games.[74] This was in some ways the true measure of Nehruvian India. The Asian Games, so crucial to Indian aspirations and so tied into the Nehruvian vision, were not put together by Nehru's government. They were created by a loose coalition of sports administrators, elites and government officials—all contributing what they could—in the service of a common ideal. Sample this note that De Mello wrote to Nehru on the successful conclusion of the Games:

> *The magic is yours (of our Supreme Captain) and I did my humble bit to make that magic work and be seen by Asia.*
>
> *You have certainly made New Delhi the Capital of Asia.* The Young Athletes of Asia have now all returned to their homes and countries. They were magnetized by your interest in them in their village… [75]

To be seen by all Asia, to take the lead and to build a new India at all costs: here was a man who had been forced to borrow Rs 1 lakh from his own club and who in his own words had gone through numerous 'conferences of war'[76] scrounging for the money for Nehru's glory, dedicating it all to the old nationalist dream of making Delhi the new Asian colossus. This was the essence of Nehruvian India in the 1950s—hope, new aspirations and the spirit of service had still not been extinguished by the disappointments that were to come later.

The Asiad, De Mello later recounted, convinced him of the power of 'miracles' and made him a firm believer in the 'guidance and guardianship of Divine Providence'.[77] When he took over, he had barely a year to organize the Asiad and with his influential committee, he 'bulldozed' and 'prayed by turns'.[78] He flew to England, where a string of hectic negotiations followed. British contractors and engineers were persuaded to complete the construction of the new National Stadium and a new swimming pool within the 300 days or so that were left for the Games. Lillywhites, an English sports goods dealer, agreed to set aside for Delhi a proportion of the most modern track and field equipment it had been preparing for the Helsinki Olympics of 1952. Another British firm, which supplied 'such things' to Windsor Castle and Eton agreed to send the filtration plant for the swimming pool in time.[79]

How was all this done? Again, we come back to that one word that keeps cropping up in De Mello's memoirs: influence. In building the new National Stadium, De Mello had immense support from Rajkumari Amrit Kaur of Kapurthala, then serving as the health minister. The detailed proposals and coloured drawings of the planned National Stadium were shown to Nehru himself, who 'appreciated them' but refused to accept the plan to name it after himself. De Mello had wanted to name his new Asiad arena the Nehru Stadium. On Nehru's suggestion, the name was changed to the National Stadium.[80]

Despite the widespread support, the core team itself was small and ad hoc. De Mello had only two others working for him full-time—a railway official who had taken time off for the project and his wife who doubled as stenographer, typist, accountant and clerk.[81] The sports editor of the *Tribune* was roped in for help, initially on a part-time basis. Later, on a request from Patiala, he joined full-time, with support from his newspaper's trustees.[82] The Asiad team eventually moved into the military buildings provided by General Cariappa and when they were ready, they invited Rajendra Prasad, President of India, to be the patron-in-chief. Nehru and his deputy prime minister, Vallabhbhai Patel, became the official patrons of the Games.[83]

Nehru himself performed the opening ceremony of the spanking new National Stadium, in the presence of 30,000 cheering spectators. In the spirit of the time, the IOA's official newsletter saw no irony in noting later that the stadium, funded by NSCI money, 'was a gift of the National Sports Club of India to the nation'.[84] Built around the Bhavnagar stand of the old Irwin stadium, it was completed within 300 working days 'to serve the nation' in the Asiad.[85] Over 40,000 cubic yards of earth were excavated to form a sunken arena and to raise embankments. The embankments were then covered with some seven miles of concrete stepped paving to provide seating arrangements for 30,000 spectators. It made for a picturesque sight;

the brand new stadium, with its new six-lane cinder running track, its new 450-metre concrete cycling track, its new Olympic standard swimming pool and club house, all in the backdrop of the majestic ruins of the Purana Qila.[86]

When the 600 contestants of the 11 participating countries finally marched into the new stadium, bursting with 40,000 cheering spectators, for the opening ceremony on 4 March 1951, many of those present read a great deal of symbolism into the event.[87] President Rajendra Prasad, the old nationalist, told the assembled audience that the Asian Games would only 'promote the realization of understanding and friendship' and 'cement the ties between the peoples of Asia'.[88] The chief organizer felt the Games had done even more:

> I believe that no event outside the field of sport has done more to further Asian unity than the Games at New Delhi...These Games, drawing together widely differing races and people from a great continent, were a perfect example of the power for good contained in sporting contests and the part it can play in making the world a finer place for our children and theirs to come.[89]

How valid were these sentiments? On the plus side, Afghanistan, Burma, Ceylon, Indonesia, Iran, Japan, Malaya, Philippines, Singapore and Thailand participated. On the negative side, Pakistan refused to attend. Vietnam was absent because of Indian's refusal to accept its government. Syria and Iraq stayed away as well. The politics that plagued the Asian Relations Organization played out at the Asian Games as well.[90]

Yet the Asian Games marked a new beginning in many ways. The Chinese, for instance, did not participate but in a little known footnote of history, the People's Republic sent 10 special observers as goodwill ambassadors. Crucially, they were the first official Chinese representatives to visit India after independence, and their presence was given due importance in Delhi, with the prime minister receiving them for breakfast at his own residence.[91]

Philippines and Japan were technically still in a state of war, their governments still not having signed a peace agreement. Their teams were deliberately assigned quarters adjacent to each other in the Games village. 'By the end of the Games they had reached such a state of intimacy that cameras were being exchanged for guitars and kimonos for bush shirts and moss shirts.'[92] In fact, Japan, still reeling from World War II and the atom bombs at Nagasaki and Hiroshima, only just made it to the Games. If the Games had not been postponed, the Japanese delegation would not have been able to participate. But it came first in the medals tally, with 11 golds in a total medal haul of 32, India following closely with 27 medals, 10 of them gold.[93] Two of the Indian golds came from the spikes of Lavy Pinto, the Bombay athlete, who became the fastest man in Asia, winning the men's 100m and 200m races.[94]

The overwhelming sentiment at the Games was one of a new start and of hope. Little wonder then that Rabindranath Tagore, that great exponent of Asian-ness, was quoted at the closing ceremony:

> Thou has made me known to friends
> Whom I knew not;
> Thou has given me seats in homes
> Not my own;
> Thou has brought the distant near
> And made a brother of the stranger.[95]

The bonhomie on display at the Asian Games lifted a great deal of the gloom that had engulfed proponents of Asian-ness after the fissures that became apparent at the Asian Relations Conference of 1947. As one scholar summarized it, 'The [Asian Relations] conference marked the apex of Asian solidarity and the beginning of its decline'.[96] By 1950, Nehru himself had been disillusioned enough by the fruitless quest for pan-Asian solidarity to firmly assert that Asia was not a political entity and that all Asian conferences were useless.[97] Yet, a year later, standing in Delhi's new stadium, with Countess Edwina Mountbatten beside him—she had flown in especially for the event[98]—watching the multi-nation parade, Nehru's inaugural address once again reflected the hope that typified his brand of internationalism:

> [The Games] bring together the youth of many countries and thus help, to some extent, in promoting international friendship and cooperation. In these days when dark clouds of conflict hover over us, we must seize the opportunity to promote understanding and cooperation among nations.[99]

He was speaking in a city, 'all' of which was 'caught up in the wonderful spirit which prevailed' at the Games. Connaught Place, the main shopping arcade, was 'gaily decked up' in the flags of all the competing nations for 'eight wonderful days of sport'.[100] Nehru, who was so closely involved in the Games, could not but have been untouched by the optimism of the time. The man who just a year before the Asian Games had dismissed all Asian conferences as 'useless' would four years later play a crucial role in the Bandung Asia–Africa conference with Indonesia and Burma, working together with China to project the emergence of Asia and Africa as an independent force in the world. Although it failed much of its promise in later years, Bandung was an important milestone in Indian foreign policy, the precursor even of what was to become the non-aligned movement. A number of scholars have drawn a direct link between Nehru's Asian Relations Conference and Bandung.[101] The narrative that we have pieced together in this chapter shows that the Asian Games of 1951 was the missing link in this story. The 1951 Asiad is a forgotten episode in the story of independent India. It was, however, a crucial marker of new India and its self-image as it set about carving a new identity for itself.

The Storming of an Embassy: GANEFO and the Fight for Asian Leadership

The Asian Games was organized, and continues to be organized, under the larger umbrella of the International Olympic Committee. They are Asia's mini-Olympics and as in the story of the Olympics itself, the Asiad is the playground of international power play and diplomatic one-upmanship. If the Delhi Asiad was about India staking a claim to Asian leadership, the fourth Asian Games at Jakarta in 1962, followed by Sukarno's revolt against the IOC with his Games of the Newly Emerging Forces (GANEFO) in 1963, were about Indonesia laying claim to that legacy. The story of GANEFO is the story of Sukarno's efforts to do a Nehru and become the pre-eminent leader of the post-colonial countries of Asia and Africa. India was central to this fascinating interlude in the global Olympic movement. When Indonesia failed to allow Taiwanese and Israeli athletes to take part in Jakarta, it was Indian officials who took on Sukarno's regime and the resultant confrontation led to Indonesia's expulsion from the IOC. Sukarno, with Chinese support, responded with the creation of

GANEFO, explicitly linking it to his global leadership aims. Again, it was Indian officials who lobbied the hardest against him at the IOC. China, which had just humiliated India in the border war of 1962, played a crucial role in funding and supporting Sukarno. Seven years after the bonhomie of Bandung, the Asian Games became the arena for the fight for Asian leadership, India and Indonesia being the protagonists and China the silent mover in the backdrop.

Indonesia's bid to host the fourth Asian Games was indelibly linked to Sukarno's politics. Ever since independence, he had turned athletic performance and sport into outlets for a new Indonesian nationalism. For instance, sports like korfball and *kasti*, which were considered part of the Dutch colonial inheritance, were abolished from physical education programmes at all school levels and indigenous Indonesian sports like the martial art form *pencak silat* were revived.[102] Sukarno saw sport as a 'summing up of many revolutions in one generation' and insisted that the main motive for Indonesia's hosting of the Asiad was its 'self-confidence' and 'physical and mental strength' because of its colonial past.[103] The problem was that by the early 1960s, the Indonesian economy, much like the Indian economy in 1951, was in too weak a shape to invest in a sporting event like the Asiad. Inflation had reached 600 per cent per annum and there was a heavy burden from the Dutch period, government debt having reached a figure as high as $1.1 billion.

But it would take more than a financial crisis to stop a leader hoping to use the Asiad to strengthen his position among the newly emerging countries of Asia and Africa. He banked on communist support, asking the Soviet Union to loan him $12.5 million to build the required infrastructure.[104] Sukarno was taking advantage of the Soviet need to build allies in the Cold War and was also relying on a great deal of Chinese support. As we shall see, the alignments within the Sino-Russian bloc would play a crucial role in the politics that unfolded at the Asian Games and at GANEFO.

Jakarta was refurbished like never before for the Asiad. The money that poured in was used to build, among other things, a brand new sports complex, Gelora Bung Karno; the city's 'first modern international hotel', Hotel Indonesia; a big national monument; the first modern shopping centre with an escalator, the 'Sarinah'; and a new highway bypass.[105] The gleaming new Jakarta was to be Sukarno's show window to the world.

The problem arose over Israeli and Taiwanese athletes. Both countries were recognized by the IOC—the People's Republic of China did not become an official member of the IOC until 1979—but not by Indonesia. Both Israel and Taiwan were also recognized by the Asian Games Federation (AGF) under whose aegis the games were organized every four years. Indonesia could not refuse them entry openly, so it resorted to subterfuge. Athletes from these countries were invited but their packets containing identity cards, it turned out, were full of blank cards instead![106] Considerable intrigue surrounded the participation of these two countries even before the Games started. There was talk that the participant identity cards could be used as substitutes for official visas and they may be given over on entry at the Jakarta airport. Israel, for instance, had already cabled the Indonesians to keep their cards ready and a plane was on stand-by to fly to Jakarta as soon as assent was received. As things turned out, the identity cards were never sent and things came to a head on 21 August 1962 when a Taiwanese official was returned from the Jakarta airport. His plane was not even allowed to land and it seemed that Indonesia had finally drawn the line with this refusal.[107]

It was at this point that India took an aggressive stance. On 24 August, the day the Games were scheduled to start, G.D. Sondhi, representing India at the Asian Games Federation Congress, also being held in Jakarta, objected strongly to the Indonesian action. Arguing that the exclusion of athletes based on politics was against the Asian Games charter, he proposed that the status of Asiad be withdrawn from the Games. Sondhi wanted Jakarta to be punished by taking away the mantle of the Asian Games and turning the Games into 'merely an international athletic and sports meeting'. The assembled delegates agreed to his first point but there were obvious practical difficulties in accepting the second. Athletes from 18 countries had already arrived in Jakarta and the Congress ended that session by allowing the opening ceremony to go on, along with a request to Sukarno to allow the Taiwanese and Israelis even at this late stage.[108]

The Games duly opened later that day but the political question continued to haunt the event. Sondhi would not let go and continued to press his point about the withdrawal of Asiad status at successive meetings of the AGF executive committee on 27–29 August. On 30 August, when the Indonesians officially informed the AGF that President Sukarno had refused to budge, Sondhi once again moved a resolution to 'declare the Games in progress an Asian Games, not the Fourth Asian Games'.[109] The persistence he had shown in pushing through the idea of the Delhi Asiad was once again in evidence here in Jakarta.

Sondhi's constant badgering led to a political reaction. Representatives of a political party known as the Popular National Front called on Sondhi to register their protest. It was now a full-blown diplomatic crisis. As the official IOA report into the events of that August in Jakarta put it, Sondhi's proposals were received in Indonesia as:

> tantamount to an insult to the President of Indonesia who had declared the Fourth Asian Games Open. Djakarta newspapers took up the cry and the atmosphere became charged with excitement. The matter passed out of the realm of sport. National aggrandizement...became blatant. It got the better of sport.[110]

With political temperatures rising, the Indonesian foreign minister intervened, inviting Sondhi for a luncheon meeting to work out a compromise. The two came up with a bureaucratic solution familiar to even the most lay observer of Indian governance: the gambit of an enquiry committee. Sondhi agreed to withdraw his resolution on the withdrawal of Asiad status while the minister agreed to facilitate the formation of an enquiry committee to probe the exclusion of Israel and Taiwan.[111]

The crisis, it seemed, had ended. Both sides, however, had underestimated the powerful sentiment unleashed by Sondhi's proposals. The compromise was just the lull before the storm. On the morning of 3 September, the Indian embassy in Jakarta was 'stormed' by an irate mob. Half an hour later, by 10.30 a.m., another mob gathered outside Sondhi's hotel. They were in search of the Indian who wanted to withdraw Asiad status from the Games in their city. They searched the hotel room by room for the hapless Mr Sondhi who, fortunately, had left just a short while earlier. With Jakarta now unsafe, Sondhi flew out of the city that very evening and returned to India. Before leaving he wrote a letter to the AGF withdrawing his resolution, pending an enquiry, as was agreed. But it proved too little, too late.

Sukarno, it seems, saw the Indian action as an affront to the spirit of Bandung. That very evening he held a meeting at Merdeka Palace with his state minister and sports minister to discuss the fallout of the public demonstrations. The meeting ended with Sukarno firmly declaring his resolve to break out of the Asian Games format and create his own Games of the New Emerging Forces (GANEFO). The Indonesian President linked this directly with the 'spirit of Bandung' and what he saw as Indian backstabbing:

> If it is the view and attitude of the majority of the AGF, which is the representative of the 13 nations that signed the convention of Asia–Africa Bandung Conference, that the Asian Games does not truly reflect the true spirit of Bandung, then we must stage a new Asian Games, which does truly represent the spirit of Bandung. Right now, we stage a new games among the New Emerging forces at once, as soon as possible, yes, in 1963.[112]

This was the first articulation of the GANEFO idea. An Indian protest had given Sukarno the chance to build a new platform to project himself as the new hero of the developing world, much as Nehru had done until now. It was no coincidence that as soon as the idea was released to the press, the People's Republic of China, which would invade India just a month later in October 1962, was the first to accord official approval and support.

The drama was still to unfold in Jakarta. The day after the declaration of GANEFO and Sondhi's enforced escape from the city, India was playing in the football finals. But anti-Indian passions were so high that the Indian team was treated virtually like an enemy nation. As the official Indian report put it:

> Unfortunately, it was worse than the worst for when we...looked like winning a very large section of the crowd of a hundred thousand persistently booed the team. Not satisfied, it continued to boo when the Victory Ceremony to present the Gold medals to our team was performed. The National Anthem was drowned in the booing.[113]

Ironically, India's greatest success in international football was eclipsed by what was until then the greatest crisis to engulf India–Indonesia diplomatic relations. The booing continued even at the closing ceremony when the Indian team entered the stadium for the march past.[114]

Reading the evidence more than 50 years after those tense days in Jakarta, it seems that the protests were not entirely spontaneous. Certainly the Indians did not think so. The IOA official report was clear that the violence was orchestrated because:

> a powerful political party stepped in with an obviously fantastic declaration that any move to change the name of the Games would be treated as an insult to the President of Indonesia and an affront to the dignity of the State. The decision of a sporting matter...was wrested from the body which should control Sport Indonesia. It passed into the hands of a political party.[115]

Sukarno saw a political opportunity in the Indian opposition and seized the initiative.

India Versus Indonesia: IOC, GANEFO and Asian Power Play

The IOC responded quickly to the Indonesian decision not to include Taiwan and Israel. On 7 February 1963, the IOC indefinitely suspended Indonesia. The news was greeted with great glee in the Tel Aviv and Taiwanese press[116] but India's role in this move was crucial. This was the first time in its history that the Lausanne-based IOC had sacked a member. Sondhi played a big hand in this decision. In the mythology of the IOC, devoted as it is to the notion of amateurism, political interference is the one notion that is more of an anathema than any other. Accordingly, soon after his return to Delhi, Sondhi, also a member of the IOC, got busy writing to the president, Avery Brundage, explaining the 'governmental' designs in the incidents at Jakarta. As he put it:

> ... it is clear that the Government of Indonesia—under strong pressure from the local Chinese and the Communist Government of China—was determined not to invite the Taiwanese teams. Pressure from Arab states was likewise responsible for non-issuance of Identity cards to Israel...
>
> All show of welcoming Taiwan and Israel representatives, prior to the Games was an elaborate hoax. The Government of Indonesia was determined *not to* invite these countries.[117]

It is no coincidence that Sondhi was among the four members of the IOC executive board who ultimately took the decision to suspend Indonesia.[118] An angry Sukarno saw this as a humiliation and instructed the Indonesian Olympic Association to resign immediately. The Indonesian sport minister denounced the Olympic Games as an 'imperial tool' while announcing his President's intentions to organize his own kind of Olympiad.[119]

Ironically, what Indonesia saw as imperialism was led by Indian officials. In fact, the Indians were so put off by the events at Jakarta that they now upped their demands. By January 1963, the IOA was demanding nothing less than a full apology from Indonesia for 'misbehaviour with the Indian National Anthem' and threatening the return of all medals won by Indian athletes at Jakarta.[120] Indian sports officials also began to lobby global opinion in other sports bodies apart from the IOC. For instance, in September 1962, delegates at a meeting of the International Amateur Athletic Federation were convinced by the Indian representative to ask Indonesia for an apology to India and to Sondhi.[121] India may not have been a powerful force as a sporting nation but its sports administrators did seem to have influence beyond its performance on the playing field.

As the Indians lobbied opinion against Sukarno, he got busy with his new GANEFO. It may have been started as a result of a spat with Sondhi but GANEFO was also a product of a particular time in Indonesia's political history. Rusli Lutan and Fan Hong have noted that Indonesia, still striving to create a post-Dutch identity, was at the time engaged in a revolution to obtain West Arian from the Dutch, while simultaneously confronting Malaysia. As Sr Soebandrio, the state minister of Indonesia, told the Indonesian athletes at the Games:

> Indonesia is now struggling to finish its revolution...GANEFO aims to finish mankind's revolution to achieve a new world order which will be full of fairness, prosperity, safety and peace, and free from exploitation and suppression.[122]

Sukarno saw in the Games an opportunity to become the leader of the 'New Emerging Forces'—all those countries struggling for a New World Order—but his biggest ally was Beijing. The Chinese prime minister, Zhou Enlai, wrote to him expressing full cooperation and delegations of specially deputed Chinese experts began arriving in Indonesia to put the Games together. The PRC, which was excluded from the Olympic movement, saw GANEFO as an opportunity to gain global legitimacy. Maoist China pulled out all the stops 'to persuade Asian and African countries to join the games.' In addition, the PRC gifted the Indonesians with $18 million to organize GANEFO.[123]

The rhetoric of GANEFO made it explicit that the Games would be based on the 'spirit of Bandung' but it was also a direct challenge to India and the Olympic movement. As many as 42 countries took part in the first Games at Jakarta that began on 10 November 1963. Most of the participating countries did not send official teams for fear of being barred from the Olympics. Despite this, at the time GANEFO did seem like a major challenger to the Olympic movement. The Indians were the most vocal in their opposition and made common cause with the IOC. In letter after letter to the IOC which faced its biggest potential crisis since its formation, Indian officials rammed home their opposition to GANEFO and took a hard line against what they saw as 'political influence' by Sukarno.[124] The ill feeling generated by the unpleasantness at Jakarta was a driving force but also at the heart of their efforts was a sense that a successful GANEFO would leave India powerless in Asian sport. As an editorial in the official IOA newsletter summed up:

> The agitation against him [G.D. Sondhi]...ended in disgraceful violence, with thousands of Indonesians raiding the Indian Embassy.
>
> The whole move behind this appears to be to form an Afro-Asian Sports body, in which India, who gave Asia the present Games, will have no say.[125]

Just as the Indians were scared of losing their hegemony in Asian sports management, the IOC was worried about the prospect of a rival body. When Cambodia hosted a mini-'Asian' GANEFO in 1966, 37 countries participated. Again the PRC underwrote the event by building a brand new stadium. Beijing had successfully turned sport into a tool of influence. As a worried IOC president, Avery Brundage, noted, the PRC was using the Games to strengthen its diplomatic linkages across Asia and Africa, giving, for instance, Congo Brazzaville a $20 million loan for sporting activity.[126] The IOC's immediate priority was to avoid a split engineered by Beijing.

The IOC need not have worried. The GANEFO initiative died a natural death with Sukarno's relinquishing of power in 1966. The new Suharto regime was not interested in pursuing sport diplomacy at a time when the Indonesian economy was in grave crisis. Moreover, Chinese and Indonesian diplomatic relations first cooled off and then were broken. GANEFO lost its primary sponsor. Cairo was to host GANEFO II in 1966 but with the Chinese and the Indonesians not interested any more, the lack of financial resources meant that GANEFO died a natural death.[127]

Conclusion

Thus ended the battle for Asian supremacy between India and Indonesia. If the first Asiad in Delhi had sounded the drumbeats of the Indian bid for Asian leadership, the fourth Asiad in Jakarta represented in microcosm the challenges it faced from Indonesia. Just seven years after Nehru and Sukarno jointly declared their bid for Asian-African unity in the Indonesian town of Bandung, an Indonesian crowd sacked the Indian embassy, forced the Indian sports representative to flee Jakarta and booed not just the Indian football team but also the Indian national anthem. The Indian response was to get Indonesia suspended from the IOC and Sukarno responded with what was then the greatest breakaway challenge the IOC had ever faced. GANEFO threatened to overturn the Olympic movement. Indian and IOC officials had the most to lose if GANEFO succeeded: India, its Asian hegemony, and the IOC, its global control over international sport.

In the end, GANEFO was a vehicle for Indonesian and Chinese self-expression and the means to advance the political aims of both nations. Communist China used GANEFO to gain greater legitimacy while Indonesia used it to further its aim of becoming the star of the Third World. GANEFO was always dependent on these two countries and when their partnership collapsed the movement collapsed with it. It remains a perfect example of the interplay between politics and sport.

8

Appu on Television
The 1982 Asiad and the Creation of a New Indian Public

The IX Asian Games marked the start of a new era in Indian sport-consciousness. Thanks to the television explosion, which occurred simultaneously with the Games…

—Rajiv Gandhi, prime minister of India, 1985[1]

The IX Asian Games of 1982 could well be called the 'Indira Gandhi' Games.

—Buta Singh, chairman and chief coordinator, 1982 Asiad[2]

Appu and the End of the 'Rip Van Winkle Slumber': TV, Advertising and the Consumer Economy

Rarely has a sporting event so fundamentally transformed a country as the 1982 Delhi Asian Games transformed India. Most global sports events change the physical infrastructure of the cities they are held in, with positive or negative consequences in the long term. In the West Indies, for instance, the IMF says that the massive construction for the disastrous 2007 Cricket World Cup unleashed such consequences that the Caribbean islands will take years to recover.[3] Similarly, the large-scale housing built for the 2000 Sydney Olympics shot up real-estate prices in Australia's largest city to unprecedented levels after the Games and they have never gone down since.[4]

Like any other host city of an international sporting event, Delhi too had its share of new infrastructure for the Asian Games—new flyovers, new hotels, new buildings—that significantly changed the dynamics of the city. The Delhi Asiad also changed India because it marked the creation of a national television network for the first time. When Indira Gandhi swept back to power in 1980, she saw the Asian Games as a stage for the government to showcase a shining India to itself and to the world. Television was to be the tool. Appu, the tubby elephant mascot of the Games, was also symbolic of the advancing, prosperous nation-state, but taking Appu to the drawing rooms of its citizens required a unified national service along with an enhanced level of technology to facilitate it. While the expansion of television in the mid-1980s was the result of a confluence of factors—the creation of an indigenous satellite capability, the availability of low-cost transmitters, the coming together of various policies initiated in the 1970s—it was the Asiad that provided the trigger.

Much like the 1951 Asian Games, the 1982 Asian Games were also intrinsically linked to the internal and external politics of the ruling elite. The difference was that unlike Nehru, Indira Gandhi's government directly took over the entire event and its organization. One offshoot of this direct control was the impact on Doordarshan and Indian television. As the host, India had to provide live telecast facilities to other participating countries. When an embarrassed government realized how backward its own facilities were, it started an overhaul unprecedented in the annals of television history. At a time when even Sri Lanka had colour television, it wouldn't look good for Indira's India to be beaming the Games in black and white, as was the norm until then. So the creation of a national service was also accompanied with the introduction of colour television. The overhaul of Indian television and the creation of a televised national service was to unleash far-reaching changes in Indian society.

In May 1982, just months before the Asian Games, an article in *India Today* magazine noted that Indian broadcasting had remained in a 'Rip Van Winkle slumber'.[5] Though Indian television had started in 1959, it remained an experiment restricted to just the national capital until as late as 1972.[6] Despite adopting an economic model of development that relied entirely on a centralized technocratic system of allocation, Nehruvian India failed to make the most of radio and television for these purposes in the early years after independence. Of course, the spread of broadcasting would not necessarily have guaranteed developmental gains or greater national integration, as later efforts proved, but this was in sharp contrast to the prevailing ideology and other economies of the time that the nationalist elite admired. The Soviet Union, for instance, put far greater emphasis on the use of the media for furthering its goals; China founded the Shanghai TV University in 1960 to put TV sets in every classroom of the Shanghai region; Indonesia was entirely covered by radio signals from more than 20 stations by the late 1930s; the Dutch East Indies by 1942 had a highly developed pluralist tradition of radio broadcasting with indigenous stations spread throughout the main urban centres.[7] In sharp contrast, India had lost the opportunity to extend the tentacles of television throughout the country in the first three decades of independence.

The Asian Games became the catalyst to change all that. After independence, Indian television had been tightly controlled by the state for two reasons: it was envisaged as a modern tool for development and a medium for welding the nation together. Broadcasting was seen as a powerful tool of political and cultural control; a unique portal, in a Foucauldian sense, for entering the homes of its citizens daily with the audio-visual message of its idea of India, conflated often with the idea of the ruling party.[8] Doordarshan was the state's own theatre, an arena where the 'nation' and the 'state' were omnipresent, an organic whole, existing in perpetuity and the centre of all activity. Classically Nehruvian in its intellectual pedigree, this was, however, an un-Nehruvian policy in the sense that Nehru himself never saw any use for broadcasting in this fashion. The state's attitude towards broadcasting during his premiership in the early years of independence was to dismiss it as a luxury for the affluent; after all, electricity had to come before television. It was not Nehru, but his daughter Indira Gandhi and grandson Rajiv Gandhi who drove the use of television as a mass medium to further the state's political and economic objectives.[9] Television was consciously turned into a mass medium in the 1980s as a political/developmental strategy, kickstarted partly by the need to package it as India's show window on the international stage during the 1982 Asian Games in New Delhi.

The development of a national television network after the Asiad created a national market for advertisers for the first time. It was a development which augmented the creation of a new 'consumer class' and this formed the basis for a new notion of collectivity expressed as 'the middle class'.[10] There are deep linkages between the expansion of television, the growth of Indian advertising and the creation of a new consumer economy centred on the middle classes. Advertising is the herald of capitalism and its expansion in India is intrinsically linked with the spread of television. Advertising was looked upon with suspicion in the rhetoric of the newly independent Indian state until well into the mid-1980s even though it was allowed on All India Radio in 1967 and on Doordarshan from 1976.[11] Yet, the volumes of advertising remained negligible until the creation of the national network after the 1982 Asiad gave advertisers access to a truly national market of consumers.

Television has been central to the fortunes of Indian advertising and it expanded exponentially in the 1980s, hand-in-hand with the setting up of Doordarshan's national television service. Television advertising played a crucial role in the creation of a consumerist ethic and the Indian middle class. Television advertising rose by an astonishing 31 times between 1980–81 and 1990–91, from Rs 80.8 million to Rs 2,538.5 million. Total advertising on all media in this period, 1981–89, rose by five times.[12] By 1992, India had 34 million television sets; it was the centre of a large television economy that provided the bedrock for the satellite television revolution of the 1990s that was to turn it into the third largest television market in the world, home to the largest number of satellite networks.[13]

None of this would have been possible without the turning point of 1982. This was the true legacy of the 1982 Asian Games. And like the 1951 Games, these Games fell under the rubric of the Olympic movement.

The 'Indira Gandhi' Games: The Politics of the 1982 Asiad

'The IX Asian Games of 1982 could well be called the "Indira Gandhi Games" for it was her foresight, inspiration, dynamism and drive that rescued the Games from what could well have been oblivion, to a successful staging that is unanimously regarded as the greatest ever Asiad.'[14]

So wrote Buta Singh, the chairman of the Asiad organizing committee and a minister in Indira Gandhi's government.[15] As sycophancy goes, this was well in tune with the flavour of the times—every government achievement was linked directly to the leader. It was the kind of statement that Congress leaders are prone to make, every great success being attributed in fawning prose to the ruling scion of the Gandhi family. Moreover, Buta Singh was writing in the official report of the Asian Games, published a year after Indira's assassination and at a time when her son Rajiv Gandhi had just attained power in the greatest mandate in Indian history, greater even than his grandfather, Nehru's. Buta Singh himself was a cabinet minister and could not but have recounted the official version of the Asiad in this manner.

Yet, on this occasion, his uninhibited praise for Indira Gandhi was not entirely without cause. More than anything else, the 1982 Asiad was an Indira Gandhi show. Quite unlike her father, who patronized the 1951 Games but stopped short of direct government intervention or financing, the 1982 Games were entirely run by her government. It was a grand festival of India, designed for a global audience, and choreographed by a prime minister who was desperate to regain international legitimacy. Indira Gandhi had just returned to power after a stunning victory in 1980 but the opprobrium of the 1975–77 Emergency remained. Indeed, on trip after foreign trip, she strained to regain her pre-Emergency international image, on one occasion telling reporters in London, 'I hope you will stop calling me the Empress of India now'.[16] It is no coincidence that a full eight months in 1982 were also devoted to a Festival of India in the United Kingdom, featuring everything from the 'high and classical to the earthy and folky'. It was promoted and partly funded by the Government of India and Mrs Gandhi visited the UK during the Festival, emerging as the 'star of the show', a welcome change from the image of an 'ogress' that had plagued her after the Emergency.[17] Not surprisingly, similar Festivals of India followed in the US, the USSR and France. As Ramachandra Guha has noted, 'Mrs Gandhi was deeply concerned about the battering her image had taken in the West. Now that she had returned to power via the ballot box, she was determined to repair the damage'.[18] At such a time, what better occasion to showcase the new India, and the new Indira, than the

Asian Games. This is why the 1982 Games became so important for the prime minister, the Asiad and the Olympic movement playing a big part in her international resurrection.

It is impossible to separate the politics of Indira Gandhi from the story of the 1982 Asian Games. Indeed, there is evidence to suggest that India wanted to use the Asiad to make a bid for the Olympics. As early as 1981, Raja Bhalindra Singh, the president of the IOA, wrote to the IOC's Juan Antonio Samaranch putting on record India's desire to host the 1992 Olympics Games. As he explained, with the staging of the Asiad, 'New Delhi would have the required sports infrastructure as well as the organizational capability to handle a "sports festival" of the type of the Olympic Games'.[19] Indira Gandhi played a pivotal role in the Indian desire to use the Asiad as a springboard to host the Olympics. In fact, the archives of the IOC are full of cordial personal dispatches between Samaranch and the prime minister's office through 1980–84, exchanges that are testimony to the importance that Indira Gandhi placed on her equation with the IOC.[20]

Soon after the 1982 Games, at the 86th Session of the IOC held in Delhi, Samaranch was to confer on Indira Gandhi the rare honour of the Golden Olympic Order—rare because she was only the seventh person, the first Asian and the first woman to receive it.[21] Samaranch, whose visit to India was treated like a state visit by the Indian government, publicly announced that by supporting the Asiad and the Olympic movement, Indira was only emulating Nehru, 'following closely in her father's footsteps, not only being the Prime Minister of India, but also by her attitude toward sport'. For a leader who after the Emergency had faced the strongest criticism from her father's international friends about betraying his legacy—indeed Ramachandra Guha has even speculated that it was this personal criticism that may have been pivotal in her decision to ultimately revoke the Emergency[22]—these words would have been sweet music as she tried to repair her international standing. The prestige of holding an Olympic event would put the icing on the cake. Indeed, Samaranch virtually endorsed Mrs Gandhi's desire in Delhi, going so far as to equate her with the nation itself in an eulogy that would have made Debakant Barooah—the man who first coined the term 'India is Indira, and Indira is India'—proud. Sample these words from Samaranch:

> Her {Indira Gandhi's} devotion to and interest in, the organization of the Ninth Asian Games greatly contributed to its brilliant success. India has shown that it's capable of successfully organising the most important sports event in the world—the Olympic Games...
>
> Mrs Gandhi has continuously fought for the broadest cooperation, friendship and understanding, between peoples, and for the peace of the nations no less, since she has been elected the chairperson of the Non-Aligned Summit.[23]

Her international standing was as important to Indira as it had been to Nehru. Olympic diplomacy played as big a part in this as her diplomacy within the non-aligned movement and the Commonwealth.

It hadn't always been like this. It is instructive that Mrs Gandhi's aggressive wooing of the IOC only began when she returned to power in 1980. In fact, in 1974, a year before she imposed the Emergency, her government had tried to impose such direct control over India's sports bodies that for a while a direct confrontation between her regime and the IOC looked inevitable. The bone of contention was a diktat to Indian sports bodies by the ministry of education and welfare in April 1974 to get their affairs in order. Presaging the Emergency, the circular cited as its justification 'the growing criticism in Parliament, Press and otherwise, of the low standard of sports and games in the country and the manner in which these are organized'. The ministry made it clear that henceforth governmental aid would only be given to sports bodies that fulfilled stringent criteria: no person could hold office in such bodies for more than six years at the most, annual accounts would have to be audited, coaches would only be appointed with prior approval of the All India Council of Sports.[24] The ministerial fiat was in line with Mrs Gandhi's notions of statist intervention and the role of sports in her worldview. Two years later, at the height of the Emergency, she was to make this clear in a stern message to Indian athletes participating in the Montreal Olympics:

> As an old civilization, India has its own sports and traditions of building strength and stamina. Some epic figures like Bhim and Hanuman symbolize these qualities. But it is high time we also look to contemporary sports and strained every nerve to attain international standards. Nothing worthwhile is achieved without singleness of purpose, dedication and continuous effort...This is what our young men and women must do

> in order to improve their performance and bring a good name to our beloved country.[25]

True to its word, the government acted quickly. O.P. Mehra, who had retired as air chief marshal, was appointed president of the IOA in 1976 as the government's nominee, and the powers-that-be refused permission to Indian members to attend IOC meetings.[26] For the IOC, an organization which prides itself on amateurism and keeping away from governmental intervention, the ministry's guidelines and the threat of a funding squeeze were like a red rag to a bull. Indeed, it violated Article 8 of the IOC charter which calls for complete absence of government interference in sport. Sure enough, IOA officials wasted no time in complaining to the IOC about the ministerial diktat, asking for succour. Through 1974 and 1975, the IOA continued to resist governmental moves to dilute its autonomy, blaming governmental agencies instead for the poor state of facilities for sport.[27] The declaration of the Emergency on 26 June 1975 further complicated matters. At a time when Mrs Gandhi's political opponents were being arrested across the country, IOA officials saw the ministerial intervention as 'only the thin end of the wedge' and were so filled with 'fear and apprehension' that they were even loath to put down all details of their interaction with government nominees on paper. Raja Bhalindra Singh rushed to Montreal in 1976 to apprise the IOC chief of the latest developments because as an IOA official noted, 'certain aspects of the matter are highly confidential and need personal discussion'.[28]

In a sign of the times, except for one instance during the Emergency, IOA officials themselves did not take the risk of complaining against Mrs Gandhi, lest the letters be intercepted. Instead they cleverly got their friends from other countries to take up their cause. And so the IOC was flooded by indignant missives from places as far apart as Nairobi and Lahore, all complaining about the Indian government's high-handedness, and demanding IOC intervention at the highest levels. Note, for instance, this missive by four concerned gentlemen from Nairobi to the IOC president:

> ... if no action is taken by you immediately this disease is going to spread in all the Asian and African Countries and will finish the accepted principles of the Olympic movement in these countries.....

> The Indian people are helpless and could not send this letter to you *owing to the declaration of Emergency in the Country as every letter is censored before it leaves the country.*[29]

The letter urged the IOC to disaffiliate India immediately if the government did not back off, as 'a lesson to others'. There is evidence to suggest that these were not just some well-meaning Kenyans writing on their own accord to the IOC and that the hard-hitting letter was sent at the initiative of Indian sports officials. The fact that the letter was accompanied by a copy of the original and confidential government missive to the IOA and other sports bodies implies that it must have been smuggled out of India to the sympathetic Kenyans.

The IOC archives also contain another fascinating anonymous letter from Pakistan. It was, in word and spirit, almost a copy of the Kenyan plea, and posted just five days later from Lahore. Five years ago, in 1971, Indian forces had dismembered Pakistan in a humiliating feat of arms that helped create Bangladesh but this letter took up cudgels on behalf of Indian sportsmen who it claimed were being oppressed by a government hiding 'behind an iron curtain'.[30] It too contained the same plea—the same complaints about the Emergency and the same call for urgent action:

> It is all the more important that immediate action and enquirs is [sic] made so that an example is set for other countries in Asia who may be tempted to follow the example of India if the open defiance of IOC rules is not curbed and nipped in the bud.[31]

Our anonymous Lahore correspondent(s) may not have enjoyed the same refined typist and proof-reader as the Kenyans, but the message was the same. And this letter too was accompanied by a photocopy of the Indian government's confidential circular that started the confrontation. IOA officials clearly knew how to get around the censors to get their message out. At a time when the freedom of the press was severely curtailed in India, this was nothing less than IOA adopting Russian style *samizdat*, or the techniques of the anti-Soviet underground, to circulate its messages to the outer world. The Emergency and the international condemnations of it further strengthened the moral legitimacy of Indian sport officials as they portrayed themselves as the victims of an anti-democratic regime.

This wasn't just a bureaucratic battle being fought on the side in the corridors of global sport officialdom. What gave it urgency was the fact that the Asian Games Federation awarded New Delhi the IX Asian Games in 1976. There isn't sufficient material in the IOC archives to piece together the government's response to the publicity battle that was being fought against it at the IOC. The official report of the Delhi Games was to note later, that at one stage, 'there was a real possibility that the IX Asiad would not be held in Delhi at all.' The report claimed that this was because of the change of government in Delhi. Indira Gandhi lost the general election in a landslide after revoking the Emergency in 1977 and the writers of the official Asiad report in 1985 implied that the new Janata government that ruled India between 1977 and 1980 was disinterested and 'delayed progress' in preparing for the Delhi Games. But the claim must be seen in light of the fact that in 1980 Indian sports officials, who had locked horns with her during the Emergency, believed that nothing was worse for the Games than Indira Gandhi's surprise return to power. In fact, the IOA had used the freedom of the Janata regime to remove the officials appointed by government diktat, like the former air chief marshal. In a sign of the changing times, a BJP member of Parliament, V.K. Malhotra, was appointed the president of the IX Asian Games committee. So it was not surprising that as late as April 1980, Ashwini Kumar, the secretary of the Asiad Organising Committee and an IOC member, wrote to the IOC chief about his apprehensions about Indira Gandhi:

> As you know there has been a new Government elected at the Centre in India. Some years back, you will remember Government tried to dominate the sports scene, and came down heavily on those members of the National Olympic Committee who were for autonomy in sports...
>
> A similar situation seems to be brewing up again...[we fear] the [National Olympic] Committee [would] become a handmaiden of the new Junta...I don't think the new Committee will find favour with the powers that be, and some of the old members like Air Chief Marshal (Retd.) Mehra may again be on their old game, and intrigue with some of the ruling Parliamentarians and Government functionaries, to reduce the power and prestige of the National Olympic Committee.[32]

Talking specifically about the Asian Games, the letter painted a dark picture, pointing out how close the Games were to being abandoned altogether:

> ...in the organization of these Games, Government was putting up many hurdles. A stage may even arise that all of us may throw up our hands in despair and call quits from the 1982 Asian Games.[33]

But the pessimistic Ashwini Kumar had not reckoned with Indira Gandhi's desire to use the Asian Games as a vehicle for her own politics and diplomacy. Soon after taking power, Mrs Gandhi's government took over control of the Asiad. In September 1980, her cabinet brought all the implementing agencies under one command—the Asian Games Special Organising Committee (AGSOC). Unlike Nehru's government in 1951, state funding was generously given without delay and the Asiad was turned into a massive state venture, just the way Sukarno had done with the Jakarta Games in 1962. The Union Cabinet approved the budget for the Games and the AGSOC was mandated to function on its behalf. As Buta Singh noted: 'The delegation of such powers by the Cabinet was in itself an indication of the tremendous importance attached by the Government of India, to the IX Asian Games... It [would] enable Government to take decisions without time-consuming circulation of proposals to various Ministries/ Departments for their considered view and approval.'[34] Command of the AGSOC was given to Buta Singh, himself a government minister, and its secretariat was headed by an IAS man, S.S. Gill.[35] The full scale of the governmental intervention is evident from the composition of the AGSOC. Apart from sports officials, it consisted of as many as 33 members of Parliament, six Central government ministers and a couple of chief ministers. In addition it boasted as many as 11 secretaries in the government of India, several joint secretaries; representatives from the department of revenue (customs) and the vice-chairman of the Delhi Development Authority. This was complemented by the army chief, the naval chief, the air chief, the vice chief of army staff, the Delhi police commissioner; and the director generals of the National Cadet Corps, the Central Reserve Police Force, the Border Security Force, Doordarshan and All India Radio. Completing the list of heavyweights were the chairmen of various governmental bodies: Air India, Indian Airlines, the Delhi Transport Corporation, ITDC, Hindustan Aeronautical Limited, Steel Authority of India, Trade Fair Authority of India, the Railways Board, Indian Oil Corporation and many such.[36] The full might of the government was put behind the event. It was a far cry from Anthony De Mello and his small core team of just two full-time members in 1951.

The Asiad also became the blooding ground of Rajiv Gandhi in the power structures of Delhi. Content with his airline pilot job, he had never shown an interest in politics until the untimely death of his brother Sanjay Gandhi in a plane crash in 1980. A reluctant Rajiv only entered politics because, as he put it, 'mummy must be helped somehow' and after winning the Lok Sabha by-election from Amethi in 1981,[37] the 1982 Asiad proved to be his first leadership experience in a political context. Rajiv was only one of the 33 members of Parliament who were part of the Special Organising Committee of the Games but as the son of the prime minister he had a moral and unofficial authority that far outstripped the others'. Indeed, the official report of the Asiad makes special mention of Rajiv's 'drive, zeal and initiative' which were mainly responsible for the 'outstanding success of the IX Asian Games.' The ever-pliant Buta Singh was as transparent in praising Rajiv's contributions, as he was when praising Indira:

> In the run-up to the Games, Prime Minister Rajiv Gandhi who was at the time a Member of Parliament, inspired the members of the AGSOC-project engineers and workers, to what seemed to be impossible deadlines while completing the stadia, fly-overs and organizational arrangements for the IX Asian Games. It was his thrust, leadership, dynamism and follow-up action that inspired and produced the near miraculous success that the IX Asian Games achieved in staging the biggest Asiad in the limited time frame of 22 months.[38]

Undoubtedly, Buta Singh's own political ambitions and the sycophancy around the Gandhi family partly explained the high praise. But to cynically dismiss Indira and Rajiv Gandhi's role in the 1982 Asiad purely because of the ecstatic accolades by their partisan followers would be to miss the wood for the trees. The 1982 Asiad was as important for Indira Gandhi's politics as the 1951 event had been for Nehru's, except that their reasons were not entirely the same.

The denouement of the 1982 Games came in 1985 when under Rajiv's government V.C. Shukla, another minister, and by now the president of the IOA, formally bid for the 1992 Olympic Games on behalf of Delhi, committing himself to a guarantee deposit of $100,000.[39] It was a bid that stemmed from the success of the 1982

Games but it was never followed up energetically, partly because by 1987, Rajiv was engulfed in crisis after crisis—Punjab, Assam, Sri Lanka, Bofors, Ram-Janmabhoomi, Shah Bano—but also partly because he did not seem to have too much faith in Shukla.[40]

'Stop the Export of Bread': The 'Super Asiad' and Delhi's Makeover

Like Jakarta in 1962, Delhi's skyline too changed due to the 1982 Asiad, but on a larger scale. The event that the Games' organizers called the 'Super Asiad'[41] was to fundamentally change the infrastructure of Delhi. The most obvious manifestation of the changes were the new stadia, referred to by their creators as the 'temples of Indian sport'.[42] They were borrowing their terminology from Nehru's memorable description of the great new dams of the 1960s—the oft-repeated quote on how these constituted the new 'temples of modern India'. Certainly the organizers of the Asian Games thought they were doing no less for Indian sport. Five new stadiums were constructed in two years: the Jawaharlal Nehru stadium, with a seating capacity of 75,000; the Indraprastha Indoor Stadium with a seating capacity of 25,000, and the third largest dome in the world, the Velodrome; the Talkatora Swimming Stadium; and the Tughlakabad Shooting Range.[43]

Delhi also got seven new flyovers, four equipped with high-mast lighting. Most accounts of the period give prominence to the flyovers, particularly since some of them were unnecessary at the time. But this was not all. The organizers also widened 290 km of roads; re-designed 50 intersections; and developed 19 areas within the city. Anticipating tourists and visitors, two new hotels were built—Kanishka and Ashok Yatri Niwas—with 3,500 rooms. The international airport got brand new arrival and departure lounges. At a time when getting a telephone connection was a privilege, the telecom department laid 12,000 new lines, putting 150 km of cables between the stadia and the hotels. No wonder the official Asiad report described the hectic preparations as 'Asiad Fever':

> For two years preceding the Games, Delhi throbbed with the cacophony of gyrating cement mixers, that kept rhythm round the clock with giant pile-drivers and massive earth movers, as Project Engineers, workers,

> planners and architects, went all out to meet the deadline—June 1982! If the pace was frantic—the dedication was total.[44]

Some of the changes were subliminal. For instance, all the five units of the Indraprastha power station, for the first time, were provided air pollution control equipment. More than four lakh trees were planted and all archaeological monuments spruced up. [45]Special attention was paid to the monuments near the stadia and those near the other venues and the athletes village. In the athlete's village itself, the wall of Siri Fort—Allaudin Khilji's 13th century capital—was restored, and monuments like the Tofewala Gombad were renovated and flood-lit. Shahjahan's Red Fort too got a 'lusty scrub'.[46]Unauthorized hoardings across the city were removed and new fogging equipment was introduced as an anti-malaria measure.[47]

The organizers were certainly not implementing these measures for altruistic reasons. Their main purpose was to put Delhi's best foot forward for international visitors and at times the lengths they went to were ridiculous. For instance, they wanted to portray a city blooming with flowers. And since November, the month of the Games, is generally a poor month for flowers in Delhi, they flew in the requisite flowers from Bangalore. After detailed discussions with horticulturists, Delhi's municipal gardeners were ordered not to water the city's bougainvilleas to ensure their flowering in November.[48]

Delhi's power distribution also got a shot in the arm. An additional 60 megawatts of power were made available for the Games—about one-tenth of the city's total requirement at that time of the year. This was ensured by augmenting Delhi's own power stations at Indraprastha and Badarpur with supplies from outside. To ensure better distribution, more transformers and 15 sub-stations were installed. Unforeseen hitches came in the way. The organizers discovered that the phone system was so poor that communication between the power sub-stations and their control rooms often went awry. So they invested in a special wireless VHF system that was imported from abroad. To ensure that the events were not disrupted due to voltage fluctuations that were common in the city, special giant transformers were brought in from Kerala and Bombay, on specially built railway wagons. All this infrastructure remained after the Games.[49] Additionally, Delhites began getting an extra 15 million gallons of water a day after the completion of the Ganga-Yamuna link.[50] All of this was done in less than two years. When it was over and the organizers sat down to take stock, Buta Singh was to marvel at the perpetual question that came up: 'Was it or was it not madness, to have tried to build A, train up B, etc. within the constricted time-frame'.[51]

The organization was not without its glitches. For instance, the taraflex, the synthetic surface to be installed at the volleyball court in the Indraprastha indoor stadium, got delayed. The ship only arrived from France in the Bombay docks by mid-September 1982, by which time the trials of the new stadia had already begun in Delhi. The volleyball nationals were due at the stadium on 19 September as a way of trying out the new surface. Except that the surface was lying rolled up in a ship called the *Amethyst* outside the Bombay harbour. 'In the congested Bombay port, there was not a chance of the ship getting a berth.'[52]

Just a few years earlier, V.S. Naipaul had dedicated an entire essay to the horrors of babudom at the Bombay port, painting in stark detail the madness of bureaucracy that faced the new traveller with baggage. But this was not some foreign tourist coming home to see the land of his forefathers. Nothing less than the honour of the country was at stake here and the power of government can never be underestimated. After frantic phone calls to the chairman of the Bombay Port Trust, the *Amethyst* was taken off the waiting list and the taraflex bundles unloaded by the midnight of 17 September. That same morning they were flown into Delhi by a special Indian Airlines airbus and the material was laid in the stadium for the matches, due to begin in a few hours. Officials worked through the night to position the rolls so that the public could watch the volleyball nationals. In a government notorious for poor delivery systems, this was proof that if those at thc highest level wanted to get something done, it would be done.

Another such example is the hilarious story of how far-off Madhya Pradesh was spared some power-cuts due to the Asiad. It seems that the organizers wanted a particular type of teak-wood for the volleyball and badminton courts at the Indraprastha stadium. This was located in Madhya Pradesh. But then they realized that continuous power cuts in the state would delay the sawing of the teak logs and thus delay their being sent to Delhi. So, in time-honoured fashion, a phone call was made from Delhi to the chairman of the Madhya Pradesh electricity board. The compilers of the official report chose not to see any humour in the situation, dryly pointing out:

> ... the power cut was lifted in respect of this particular lot of teak logs, and it was only as a result of this, that the supplies were received in time.[53]

It is not clear which part of Madhya Pradesh the teak logs were sourced from, or if the residents knew that they were beneficiaries of the Asian Games but it is certain they suffered no power cuts during the time it took to cut the logs. Surely this was a first in the history of international sport: residents of a far-off town getting uninterrupted power supply so that the host city could receive its building materials in time.

There were other serious problems such as the faulty design of the Talkatora swimming stadium. Originally conceived as an arena with a roof and air-conditioning, it was realized too late that it would no longer be possible to construct the roof. So it was left roofless, the organizers having to construct 'additional works to give the top portion of the structure a look of completion...Similarly, at the last minute, the heating system of the Swimming Pool and the Diving Pool, because it was open, had to be enlarged considerably, to maintain the temperature of the pool'.[54]

The 1951 Asiad had played host to just 489 athletes from 11 countries. The 1982 Asiad played host to as many as 5,000 athletes, 3,000 technical officials and another 2,000 overseas guests.[55] For these guests, a special Asiad Village was built in the vicinity of the Siri Fort. With 850 dwelling units spread over 135 acres, its centrepiece was a dining hall with a capacity of 1,800. In the manner of Indian bureaucrats, the compilers of the official report of the Games have left behind delicious statistics of what it took to feed the denizens of the village. On a daily basis, it meant 20,000 eggs, 10,000 litres of milk and 10,000 slices of bread for breakfast. Each meal needed 1,250 chickens, 2,500 kg meat and fish, 500 cauliflowers, 400 kg cabbage and 500 kg carrots. The residents also consumed 10,000 apples, 10,000 bananas, 10,000 oranges and 10,000 cups of ice-cream daily.[56] The cuisines were Indian, Continental and Chinese. How much of this material actually went to the athletes is not known. But the meticulous accounting was another triumph of the record-keeping abilities of the ubiquitous Indian clerk.

Table 8.1
Menu for Asiad Village

Lunches	*Dinner*
1. Fruit Juices	1. Fruit Juices
Assorted Salads	Asparagus Soup
Fried Fish Tartare Sauce Fried Potatoes Carrots Vichy	Assorted Salads Fish Belle Meuniere
Mutton Roganjosh Plain Pulao Dal Makkhani Paneer Kofta Curry Bhindi Masala	Fish Belle Meuniere Pommes Hongroise
Chilly Fried Chicken Vegetable Fried Noodles	Cauliflower A L'ANGLAISE
Chapati—Nan Yoghurt Paneer Kofta Yoghurt Nan Papad Achar Chutney	Murgh Palak Yellow Rice
Cheese Platter Vegetable Fried Rice Fried Mushrooms Bamboo Shoots	Chilly Fried Pork
Fresh Fruits Assorted Ice Creams Coconut Barfi Tea—Coffee	Cheese Platter Trifle Pudding Tea—Coffee
2. Fruit Juices	2. Fruit Juices
Assorted Salads	Mulligatawny Soup
Chicken Chasseur	Assorted Salads

Lunches	*Dinner*
Potatoes Maitre D'hotel French Beans in Butter	
Masala Fried Fish Vegetable Pulao Matar Paneer Yellow Dal Nan/Paratha Yoghurt	Fish D'Antin PommesDauphinoise Vegetables in Cream
Prawns with Garlic Sauce Vegetable fried rice Bamboo Shoot and Beans Sprouts Yoghurt Papad-Achar-Chutney	Bhuna Beef Vegetables Pulao Dal Lobia Fried Bhindi
Cheese Platter Fried Rice with Ham and Beans Sprout	Fried Chicken with Pineapple
Fresh Fruits	Cheese Platter
Assorted Ice Creams Rasmalai	Eclairs
Tea—Coffee	Tea—Coffee

In an illustration of how serious the government was about feeding its guests in the Indian spirit of hospitality, it took steps to increase the capacity of bread-making and to remove glitches in the movement of milk and milk products, not only in Delhi, but also outside the city. Milk cooperatives in Gujarat were alerted far in advance of the Games for the supply of milk. Our favourite story is about the decision to impose 'controls' on the export of bread from Delhi to other areas, which could result in shortages during the Games.[57] The rest of India could eat roti, the foreign athletes had to get their bread.

The stamp of Indira Gandhi was unmistakable. In the run-up to the Games, she personally visited every single stadium, dined at the Games Village and personally monitored virtually every aspect.[58] The army and the NCC were specially tasked with the ceremonial functions of the opening and closing ceremonies. This included a nationwide effort to showcase the diverse cultures of India in the form of dance and song performances and the director general of the NCC, Narendra

Singh, recalls that Indira Gandhi personally summoned him and asked him to take charge.[59] All state chief ministers were ordered to support the cultural programmes in conjunction with the NCC and the army's formation commanders received special orders to coordinate the event. Rajiv Gandhi brought in sitar maestro Ravi Shankar to compose the music for the Asian Games hymn at the opening ceremony and its English translation was recited by the other great icon of modern India, Amitabh Bachchan.[60]

What is an event in India without elephants? For the Asiad, whose mascot itself was the tubby baby elephant, Appu, the government specially brought in elephants from Kerala for the opening ceremony. Transported by train, the heaviest of them weighed 5,000 kg. The youngest, three-year-old Pushpa, weighed in at 750 kg.[61] The last word perhaps belonged to Sepp Blatter, then the Secretary General of the International Football Federation, FIFA. While congratulating the organizing committee, he noted: 'There is very little I could say towards their improvement'.[62]

Appu on INSAT: The Transformation of Indian Television

Six months before the Asiad, in May 1982, *India Today* carried as its cover story a review of Indian television. The headline—'The Tedium is the Message'—left the magazine's readers in no doubt about its views on the industry. It began with its authors imagining the state of television two years into the future. In light of what was to happen after the Asiad, it deserves to be quoted in full:

> 1984: It is a television boom the like of which India has never seen. From the slopes of the Malabar Hills in Bombay, to lush green pastures near Meerut and the sprouting urban jungle of New Delhi's Defence Colony, the fashionable New Alipore area of Calcutta and the trusted old Anna Salai Road of Madras, it is the same old spectacle of thousands of TV aerials sticking up in haughty silhouette.
>
> The Indian channels are humming with cascading electromagnetic waves—some skimming along the earth, others ricocheting back from the two Bharatiya pies-in-the-sky hovering 26,000 km above the ground. Giant microwave towers have been set around the nation like stiff giants.

> The TV commercial section never had it so good. The three daily Chitrahars, with three 10 minute slots on sale, are each fetching Rs. 2,000 per second.[63]

Then the authors return to reality, arguing that this futuristic 'scenario is comic, conjectural, satirical, emphasizing the dark side of the millennium'. In their view, the 'bumbledom of Doordarshan' had so far only confirmed the 'idiocy of its originators'; it had not 'merely standardised mediocrity but institutionalized it', mired as it was in a governmental 'Rip Van Winkle slumber'. But the article was written because the authors had noted that Indian television now stood on the brink of what they called 'the 'Great Leap Forward', 'the biggest ever in Indian broadcasting'.[64] They described the massive overhaul that Doordarshan was going through as it sought to create a nationwide network ahead of the Asian Games.

In order to understand the pivotal role of the Asiad in creating such a network, it is necessary to recount a short history of the medium in India. The next section outlines the contours of this story before returning to the Asiad and what it meant.

58 TV Sets: The Nehruvian Legacy

Independent India's experience with television during 17 years of Jawaharlal Nehru's stewardship was negligible. Although India did not inherit any television apparatus from the British on 15 August 1947, it did inherit a broadcasting structure in the form of All India Radio, with 14 radio stations, a developed bureaucracy and a colonial state's mechanism for official censorship.[65] Independent India followed the colonial practice of keeping broadcasting a preserve of the state, which fitted the larger Nehruvian idea of keeping the 'commanding heights' of the economy under state control. Except that, in this period, far from being a 'commanding height', broadcasting was barely a molehill.

The first television broadcasts were put together by All India Radio in September 1959. They were watched by 'teleclubs' organized around the 21 gifted television sets that were installed within a 25-km radius in Delhi.[66] UNESCO chipped in with a gift of 50 television sets and the Ford Foundation helped fund the first formal educational telecasts for 250 schools around Delhi on selected days of the week.[67] The initial broadcasts reveal the motivations of the programmers and their controllers: they were restricted to four subjects—road sense, food adulteration, care of public property and manners.[68] It took another six years for a daily one-hour service to appear. This began in 1965 with help from the West German government and transmissions consisted of news bulletins in Hindi and agricultural programmes for farmers.[69] Television continued to be run as an ad hoc division of All India Radio until 1976. Hemmed in by bureaucracy, and with no incentive for talent, programming, in the words of one observer, often ranged from the 'staid to the downright ridiculous'. Bhaskar Ghose recalls seeing a song being telecast with only one image occupying the screen: a record playing on a gramophone.[70] Of course there were some exceptions but more than anything else it was this image of a visual gramophone—'radio with pictures'—that typified television programming in its early years.

India's television encounter of the 1960s remained a developmental exercise and a curiosity restricted only to a few bureaucrats, politicians and select localities in Delhi. For the rest of India, television simply did not exist. The lone transmission from Delhi operated on a weak signal and the state simply did not allow any infrastructure for the development of the industry. When Nehru died in 1964 the country had a grand total of 58 licensed TV sets.[71] None of this reflects planned social intervention through broadcasting, and certainly no concern for entertainment. Nehru saw no reason for the commercial development of broadcasting and the disliked advertising, as his writings before independence reflect:

> With all its splendid manifestations and real achievements, we have created a civilization which has something counterfeit about it. We eat ersatz food produced with the help of ersatz fertilizers; we indulge in ersatz emotions, and our human relations seldom go below the superficial plane. The advertiser is one of the symbols of our age with his continuous and raucous attempts to delude us and dull our powers of perception and induce us to buy unnecessary and even harmful products.[72]

The first Indian television factory opened in 1969 in Kanpur and, in an indication of the minuscule size of the existing market, produced 1,250 sets in its first year of manufacture.[73] Broadcasting had largely been ignored and 10 years after independence fewer than one in five Indian villages, where 85 per cent of the population lived, had a radio.[74] Private commercial broadcasting, and advertising, was illegal because broadcasting was expected to serve the state's objectives—yet the state's planners, Nehru's influential circle at the Planning Commission, did not follow this strategy with any zeal. Not surprisingly, in a scathing report in 1966, the Chanda Committee blamed the poor state of television on a mindset that saw television as 'an expensive luxury intended for the entertainment of the affluent society' and one that could wait until the fulfillment of the larger blueprint for economic development.[75] It is clear that on the highway of Nehruvian planning broadcasting was a distant outpost, far from the main route but considered strategic enough to warrant a permanent guard. The state's busload of goodies, and it was a large busload, mostly bypassed it but stopped by occasionally with the promise of a regular fixture when the roads were better connected and streetlights had been put up.

Indira, 'the televisionary': The Lead-up to the Asiad

Television had been restricted to the Delhi area until as late as 1972 when a TV transmitter was set up in Bombay, followed by strategic transmitters in the border cities of Amritsar and Srinagar in 1973.[76] This was still nowhere near a national presence and the first semblance of a symbolic India-wide network emerged only in the first year of the Emergency, with the setting up of new stations in Lucknow, Madras and Calcutta in 1975. With severe censorship imposed upon the print media, the Indira Gandhi government saw broadcasting as a crucial tool to direct public opinion.[77]

For a variety of reasons, Indira Gandhi understood the potential of television as a mass medium far more than any of her political contemporaries. In this context, Sevanti Ninan has noted an old joke about India's first three prime ministers: 'Nehru was a visionary, Lal Bahadur Shastri a revisionary and Indira Gandhi a televisionary'.[78] Indira Gandhi kick-started the process that turned television into a mass-medium. One reason for this was her faith in development communication, goaded on by the visionary scientist Vikram Sarabhai.

The Emergency was also the high point of experiments like SITE which sought to use the power of satellites and television for rural education.[79] However, as one critic wrote just after the Emergency, 'Mrs. Gandhi didn't give it [television] much importance...until she discovered what a powerful weapon it could be both for offence and defence'.[80] Mrs. Gandhi's policies bear this out. As she turned Nehru's lofty but flawed ideal of centralized planning[81] into dogma, inserting 'socialism' into the constitution and unleashing a new brand of populist politics to successfully break the power of the Congress hierarchy, Mrs Gandhi saw the potential for using television as the state's visual messenger. In essence, this was based on what has been called the hypodermic needle model, so dear to Soviet-style planners.[82] Television was to be the syringe that would deliver the required medicine into society, the assumption being that it would be accepted unquestioningly by every host. Of course, communication studies from the 1970s onwards have shown that television reception works in much more complex ways and that different people interpret the same messages differently based on their individual circumstances.[83]

At the height of the Emergency in 1976, three important things happened: television was separated from All India Radio and put under a new entity called Doordarshan, though it remained under the control of the ministry of information and broadcasting; the government reduced excise duties on television sets, which encouraged local manufacture; and for the first time, advertising was allowed on television. All three measures spurred the expansion of television. The creation of Doordarshan meant the recognition of television as a separate medium from radio and the easing of duties led to a spurt in the production of television sets. From just one company producing 1,250 sets in 1969, India had progressed to 40 companies making a quarter of a million by 1977.[84] All of these measures would come together in the lead-up to the Asiad when television was truly pushed into a giant leap forward.

To 'Muster a National Will': The Asiad and the Idiot Box

Television became a mass medium in India only during the 1980s. Three factors contributed to this: the creation of a national network of transmitters linked with satellite technology; Doordarshan's commercialization and resultant focus on entertainment; and economic reforms that made television sets cheaper. The turning point for television was 1982. The New Delhi Asian Games are widely held to have been the trigger that unleashed its potential and the decisive leap was possible because a number of policies that had been initiated in the 1970s came to fruition at the crucial moment. The Asian Games was a stage for the government to showcase a shining India to itself and to the world and television was the medium. Appu, the elephant mascot of the Games, was also symbolic of the advancing, prosperous nation-state, but taking Appu to the drawing rooms of its citizens required a unified national service along with an enhanced level of technology to facilitate it. This capacity had to be created if India had to look good internationally and the Asian Games, therefore, became the catalyst for sprucing up television and stitching for it a brand new suit.

The first direct result of the Asian Games was the introduction of colour television and the creation of a 'national' service. As the host country, it was up to India to provide a live telecast of the Games to other participating countries and Doordarshan's technical backwardness was painfully brought home. Doordarshan still operated in black and white and Vasant Sathe, minister for information and broadcasting, discovered to his horror that even tiny Sri Lanka had colour television. Many of the broadcasting organizations from the participating countries demanded colour feeds, and it would not do to appear backward. Despite stout resistance from the prime minister's scientific advisors, who cited the traditional argument about India not being able to afford the luxury, the decision was taken to convert to colour transmission.[85]

The most significant milestone of 1982, though, was the introduction of what later came to be known as the National Programme, joining together previously unconnected television centres. Within the dominant ideology of the state, television had always been seen as an agent for political and cultural control but the development of the indigenous satellite programme in 1982, for the first time, provided a viable instrument to realize this vision. The launch of INSAT-1A, and later INSAT-1B, allowed the creation of the National Programme which was envisaged as a tool for uniting people and for developing an awareness of the 'oneness of India'. The satellite system allowed a massive expansion of television through a gradual build-up of low power transmitters that could pick up television signals bounced off satellites. It freed Doordarshan from the complexity of starting a new programme production facility every time it set up a relay transmitter and it meant that every transmitter in the country could pick up the television signal from the centre in Delhi.

Symbolically, the 'national' colour transmissions and the National Programme commenced on Independence Day in 1982.[86] The National Programme included news bulletins in Hindi and English along with current affairs programmes that were meant to take the nation-state, in all its splendour, directly to viewers. For the first time, all of India would see the same image at the same time and the Asian Games could be transmitted to every home across the country in glorious colour. The catalyst for the National Programme was the Asian Games and the official motivation behind it is revealing. It was aimed as much at the domestic audience as it was at the foreign. According to the government's Asian Games Report, the main thrust of the TV programmes was:

> To reassure the public, domestic and foreign, that the Games would take place on schedule...To stimulate interest and *muster a National will, behind Asiad 82, and make the people realize that as hosts, both our national honour and prestige was involved.*[87]

To muster the 'national will' so dear to Indira Gandhi's government, for the first time in India, the Asian Games programming was telecast live to 41 stations nationwide. Of these, 27 were connected directly to Delhi via the indigenous satellite INSAT-1A [88] This is not to suggest that the unified National Programme would not have fructified without the Asiad. It is true, however, that the Games gave an almost war-like urgency to the effort that would otherwise have taken much longer. For instance, Doordarshan set up an Asian Games cell in early 1981. Its task was to provide comprehensive coverage of the Games to the Indian audience as well as to foreign TV organizations, either through direct relay via satellite or through recorded programming. It was upon its recommendations that the government leased a television transponder from INTELSAT that enabled the live coverage.[89] No wonder the Asiad organizers boasted:

> The Asian Games brought about more changes in the TV technology in India, than at any time since its inception. The smooth and excellent changeover to colour technology, during the Asian Games will always be a remarkable feat by Doordarshan, as also their contribution towards the generating of sports consciousness among the people, throughout the length and breadth of India.[90]

Part of the changes was the introduction of new equipment, new technology and new training to Doordarshan's staffers. As Bhaskar Ghose, who later headed Doordarshan, noted: 'Equipment poured in; squads of programme executives and engineers were sent for training and Doordarshan entered the age of modern television.'[91]

This was not without hiccups. For instance, the special underwater cameras necessary for the coverage of swimming events never arrived. Doordarshan's producers, who had no prior training in sport coverage, had no choice but to innovate. Bhaskar Ghose, in his memoirs, recounts an incident in this regard that was to become a part of Doordarshan lore. A producer from Calcutta, Ananya Bannerjee, was in charge of the swimming coverage and all she had was a normal camera. So she laid a set of rails along the swimming pool on which a camera trolley could be pulled as the swimmers raced each other. It was the only way the swimming event could be covered but the sight of the rusty rail tracks alongside Delhi's brand new swimming pool was ugly and Vasant Sathe was furious. According to Ghose, he ordered that the rails be removed immediately. The feisty Ms Bannerjee stood her ground. 'I put them there,' she retorted, 'and they will stay there'. A nonplussed Sathe relented and though Ananya was later taken to task by her terrified superiors, her trolley on rails stayed and the coverage, it seems, 'was pretty good'.[92] With such improvisation and typical jugaad was the Asian Games covered. What the historian cannot afford to miss from this incident is the unusual similarity it bears with the technique used by Leni Reifenstahl in shooting *Olympia* during the 1936 Berlin Olympiad. Whether or not Ananya had seen or read about *Olympia*, the similarities lead us to surmise that she was well aware of the techniques used almost fifty years earlier.

The preparations for the Asiad gave Delhi's television czars the technology to create the National Programme, thus starting a new era in Indian television. Not surprisingly, the reception of this programming never quite had the impact that was intended and varied greatly across regions. The state controlled television but it was also a cultural arena where ideas circulated, often with unintended consequences.[93] The National Programme created, for instance, a great deal of regional resentment in non-Hindi-speaking areas. Between 8.30 p.m. and 11 p.m. daily, all regional stations had to perforce link up to the National Programme from Delhi but the problem was that this programming was largely in Hindi. Bhaskar Ghose cites how the chief secretary of Tamil Nadu accused him of dividing the country and the chief minister of Karnataka sarcastically thanked him for reducing the load-shedding in his state as 'all television sets were switched off after 8.30 p.m. as soon as the National Programme started'.[94] As Table 8.2 shows, until then the limitations of technology had meant that the existing Doordarshan centres outside Delhi enjoyed virtual autonomy and freedom in local programming. They were government stations, but virtually independent of each other. Technology now allowed Delhi to take control and become predominant with its Hindi and English programming.

Table 8.2
Doordarshan Today

JULLUNDUR-AMRITSAR
8-02 p.m, Punjabi lok geet 6.15 Jhil mil tare 6.45 Kudrat de sab bande 7.00 5th World Cup Hockey 7.30 Assin tussin 8.00 News 8.20 Aur bhi gham hain zamane mein (Part VIII) 9.00 'Majama' skit 10.00 Caravan
DELHI
2 p.m. Direct telecast of the 5th World Cup Hockey Tournament at Bombay 6 p.m. News in brief 6.02 Children's programme 6.15 Nazrulgaan: Aparajita Ghosh 6.30 Nagar Nagarik 7 Krishi darshan 7.30 Pradeshikchitrahaar 8 Samachar 8.20 Aur bhi gham hai zamane mein — a serial play 8.50 A film on Martin Luther King 9.20 Apne hi desh mein 9.45 News 10.05 Patrika.
SRINAGAR
7 p.m. Butraat: Death anniversary of Lal Bahadur Shastri 7.30 Chhakri Ruff: Kashmiri folk music 7.45 Badhte qadam 7.15 Naqsho naghma 8.55 Khel aur khilari 9.25 Ab kya hai: a serial feature in Urdu.

From 1982, the expansion of the television network became a key governmental priority. Doordarshan's budget, for instance, swelled from Rs 5 crore in 1980–81 to Rs 14 crore in 1982–83.[95] The expansion drive thereafter continued like a juggernaut. To cite one example, between July and October 1984, practically one transmitter a day was commissioned.[96] India had only 18 TV transmitters in 1980. By 1985 this number had increased to 172 and more than 500 transmitters were functioning by the end of the decade.[97] The planned penetration was accompanied by an expansion of viewership as well. India had a little over 2 million TV sets in 1982. It had taken two decades to reach that figure but it is from the Asiad onwards that we see the makings of a mass medium. By 1986, 3 million TV sets were being produced in India, including 7 lakh colour sets[98] and by 1992, 34 million Indians owned TV sets.[99] By the end of the decade, television had turned into a mass medium with a nationwide penetration.

This process was also helped by a broader attempt within the government to undo the failures of the 'licence-permit raj' and Indira Gandhi's pro-business policy turn between 1980 and 1984. As part of this change, duties on import of colour television sets had been reduced in 1982 and those on electronic imports were also relaxed. The bureaucratic state was not dismantled but steel and cement prices were decontrolled, manufactured imports were liberalized and controls on entry and expansion by national firms in certain sectors were eased. This was an early phase of economic liberalization. Mrs Gandhi's critics characterized it as a 'rightwards' turn while her advisers called it 'pragmatic'.[100]

Rajiv Gandhi tried to make an explicit break with the past in 1985 with the open enunciation of a new economic policy and the first liberalizing budget of this early phase of opening up. The 1985 budget included measures for liberalization of import restrictions, especially in electronics.[101] This made television sets cheaper and, spurred on by the increasing penetration of Doordarshan's transmitters, sales shot up.

Television's exponential expansion in the 1980s was also fuelled by, and synonymous with, its commercialization. Until the late 1970s, television was an enterprise of, by, and for the socialist state but advertising became capitalism's Trojan horse into this system. Entertainment programming was introduced in tandem with national programming in the early 1980s and it rode on the back of two related developments: the advent of commercials and the out-sourcing of programmes to independent producers. The creation of a 'national' network became a magnet for advertisers because it opened up the possibility of constructing a 'national' market. It changed the very nature of Doordarshan and fuelled the massive expansion of television in the 1980s. It is significant that advertising before the Asiad initially had little immediate impact. In its first year, 1976–77, Doordarshan made less than one per cent of its annual budget from advertising.[102] The reason for this initial lukewarm response by private industry lay in the limited reach of Doordarshan at the time. Television penetration was very low and because there was no unified 'national' broadcast, there was no 'national' market for advertisers to target. The handful of TV stations that existed were not connected to each other. In the absence of powerful transmitters and satellite technology, each local station produced its own programming, predominantly in its own regional language, and practically functioned as an autonomous government unit. The Asiad and national programming changed all that.

Encouraged by the phenomenal success of *Hum Log*, which also became a vehicle for turning its sponsor Nestle's Maggi noodles into a highly successful brand, a number of companies rushed in to sponsor a slew of popular television serials—*Buniyaad*, *Ramayan*, *Mahabharat*, *Khandan*, *Nukkad* and *Chanakya*—as telecast fees and commercial

Fig. 8.1: Doordarshan Gross Advertising Revenues (Rs million)[105]

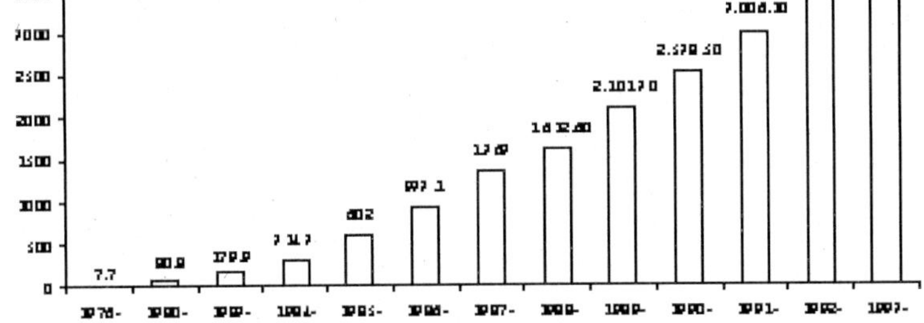

airtime rates got higher and higher.[103] A look at Doordarshan's advertising revenue from 1977 to 1994 in Fig. 8.1 illustrates the fast pace of advertising growth. Between 1980–81 and 1990–91, the revenue increased a whopping 31 times, from Rs 80.8 million to Rs 2.53 billion. At the start of the decade this had seemed an unlikely possibility. Doordarshan's revenue of Rs 7.7 million in its first year, 1976–77, had been less than one per cent of its annual budget. By 1990, Doordarshan's advertising revenue constituted about 70 per cent of its annual expenditure.[104]

The focus of this advertising was on 'exploding new middle classes'; television, in the eyes of the advertisers, enabled their transformation into consumers. One of the classic studies of Indian advertising, William Mazarella's *Shoveling Smoke*, documents how advertisers and marketers certainly saw television as the one crucial factor that led to the creation of a new, consuming middle class in the 1980s, as opposed to traditional notions of saving and hoarding money. In the words of one marketer, the new commodity images on television opened up for millions 'whole new worlds which they never knew existed'.[106] Mohammad Khan, who in a four-decade career in advertising, set up three cutting edge advertising agencies— Rediffusion, Contract and Enterprise—argues that television induced 'a 180 degree change in consumer attitudes'. As he put it:

> The biggest turning point has been commercial television. We used to live in a culture that saved money, stashed it underground or invested in gold. Anything that gave you pleasure was considered immoral. TV showed us the world and opened the floodgates for consumerism.[107]

This perception, in turn, fuelled television advertising and by the end of the 1980s, Doordarshan was hooked on to its new cash cow. Television programming became increasingly focused on the middle classes and yet Doordarshan always had to balance its newly emerging commercial ethic within a public discourse that repeatedly emphasized the need for programmes harnessed to the modernist project of national development.[108] Doordarshan's entire strategy was focused on co-opting upwardly mobile classes who were 'captured' simultaneously as a market for consumer goods advertised by sponsors of programming and as an audience for nationalist serials.[109] Television heralded a new era of consumerism.

The power of the medium is such that it unleashed deep and unanticipated processes within Indian society. The televised portrayal of *Ramayan* (1987–90) is a case in point. India's greatest epic now adapted for the small screen on the brand new national network would never have had the kind of impact it eventually did if it had been telecast in the old days of unconnected TV stations working in splendid isolation. It was commissioned by the same S.S. Gill who, by a quirk of fate, was in charge of the Asiad secretariat in 1982 and by now was information and broadcasting secretary. Gill emphasized that the epic encapsulated pan-Indian, and indeed, universal values[110] but it was criticized for being perceived in the context of the rightward shift of the Rajiv Gandhi regime in the same period, exemplified by the central government's role in allowing the Babri Masjid's locks to be opened. *Ramayan* fed on religious fervour and quickly turned into '*Ramayan* fever'. Contemporary press reports detailed instances of mass devotion and empty streets when the series aired on Sunday mornings:

> In many homes the watching of *Ramayana* has become a religious ritual and the television set...is garlanded, decorated with sandalwood paste and vermillion, and conch shells are blown.[111]

There is now a substantial literature establishing the crucial role Doordarshan's *Ramayan* played in fashioning the setting for the Hindutva revival in the mid-1980s which centred around the Ram Janmabhoomi–Babri Masjid dispute. As Arvind Rajagopal points out:

> Drawing on myth and devotionalism to portray a golden age of tradition that was yet ahead of the modern era in statecraft and warfare, the show which ran from January 1987 to September 1990 adroitly made appeals to diverse social groups, under a symbolic rubric that could be tied to the banner of Hindu assertion...If inhibition and prohibition earlier joined to limit religion's use for systematic political mobilization, what was offered now was an extra charge in bringing together previously separated realms.[112]

While it is impossible to establish any direct link between the series and the politics of the period, television certainly reshaped the context in which politics was conceived, enacted and understood. *Ramayan* symbolized the central role television had come to occupy as a cultural and political actor in Indian society by the late 1980s. By the end of the 1980s, it had become a nation-wide phenomenon and was embedded in popular culture.

The fervour around Doordarshan's *Ramayan* illustrated that at a deeper level, when television arrives in a society, it alters the societal matrix. For instance, writing of the social impact of television when it first arrived in Canada, Robin Jeffrey recounts:

> Our habits changed. At first, before our family had a television, we started dropping in on friends at the starting times of popular programs. Then, when we had a television set, we went out much less and stayed up later at night. Sports, election nights and momentous events kept us around the set like thirsty animals around a waterhole.[113]

The exact nature of television's influence on societies has been debated ever since Marshall McLuhan argued that new technology itself was a 'revolutionizing agent',[114] coining his now famous aphorism: 'The medium is the message'. Insisting that every new technology, by itself—from the wheel and the alphabet to the telegraph and television—had changed social relations and mental attitudes,[115] McLuhan understood new media like television 'not just [as] mechanical gimmicks for creating illusions of the world', but as containing 'new languages and unique powers of expression'[116]:

> The new media are not ways of relating us to the old 'real' world; they are the real world and they reshape what remains of the old world at will...The effects of new media in our sensory lives are similar to the effects of new poetry. They change not our thoughts but the structure of the world.[117]

In the Indian case, Doordarshan's *Ramayan* was only the outward manifestation of the deep subliminal changes that the national television network, created in part due to the Asiad, had begun to effect within the societal framework.

Writing in 1985, Prime Minister Rajiv Gandhi emphasized the long-term impact of television and the Asiad on Indian sport:

> The IX Asian Games marked the start of a new era in Indian sport-consciousness. Thanks to the television explosion, which occurred simultaneously with the Games, the entire nation participated in them, and the eyes of the young and not so young were riveted on the stadiums and tracks in Delhi.[118]

Rajiv was right except in one detail. The impact of the 'television explosion' went far beyond the realm of sport. The Asiad, in fact, was pivotal in creating a new televisual Indian public—television augmenting the creation of new notions of identity, consumerism, culture and nationalism.

Conclusion

The 1982 Asiad was a landmark in Indian history on various registers. It became Indira Gandhi's vehicle for rehabilitating her global image, battered black and blue by the Emergency. Juan Antonio Samaranch's award of the Olympic Order of Gold to the Indian prime minister in 1983 marked the culmination of a systematic engagement between Mrs Gandhi's government and the IOC after a sustained war of attrition between her and Indian sports administrators during the years of the Emergency. The Games were as important in India's global branding as they were in the government's domestic positioning. The Asiad became the government's vehicle to propagate nationalism and led to a concerted nationwide effort to project India as a modern nation on the world stage. It also irrevocably changed Delhi's skyline, with the construction of large-scale new infrastructure and the improvement of existing facilities.

But by far the greatest legacy of the 1982 Asiad was the creation of the nationwide television network. Created to showcase India and the Games for distant lands, but equally to bind the nation into one community focused on this one event, the television network irrevocably changed India. A nationwide network may have been created anyway had the Asian Games not been held in India but there is no doubt that the Games proved to be a major catalyst. The government was forced to pursue television as a priority and policies initiated in the 1970s all came together as the Asiad provided the spark and an immediate urgency. Television policy encapsulated the state itself and the television set was envisaged as the nation-state's daily messenger into citizen's homes. A national service was created in 1982 precisely to project this. The Asiad was a landmark in the creation of a new 'visual' public. The daily ritual of Indians everywhere watching the same programming at the same time was meant to reinforce the centrality of the nation-state. Its impact, of course, differed widely but the creation of mass television in India is the true legacy of the Games. The advent of television as a major factor in Indian society was to have a far-reaching impact on Indian sport and it is to this that we turn in the next chapter.

9

When Olympic Sports Lost Out
Cricket, Television and Globalization in India

One of the greatest tragedies of our hockey is that its most glorious phase preceded the era of live television in India.

—Shekhar Gupta, 2002[1]

Television makes cricket bigger than the sport and the time that each cricket player gets on the screen is more than even what Shahrukh Khan enjoys on a 70mm multiplex.

—Sundeep Misra[2]

Café 20: Aaj Tak Bhangra, Cricket and a Hunger Strike

The twenty-fourth day of September 2007 began as just another day on Aaj Tak, India's most popular Hindi satellite news channel. The first news bulletin of the day opened with the headlines of the hour but when the camera cut to the news anchor, viewers saw a sight they had never seen before. Instead of the usual serious looking news anchor, dressed in a tie and suit, and sitting in the usual news studio, the camera cut to a new special studio with the tagline Café 20 prominently displayed in the background. Eight of Aaj Tak's most prominent news anchors were sprawled out at four separate tables in a café-like setting and they were all wearing the Indian cricket team's blue uniform. It was the morning of the India–Pakistan final in the Twenty–Twenty Cricket World Cup in South Africa and India's biggest news channel had decided to focus on the build-up to the game, to the exclusion of all other news.

Significantly, the anchors on display were not the usual sports reporters or commentators. These were men and women who normally presented the channel's mainline political coverage. Prominent among them was the channel's executive editor Deepak Chaurasiya, usually seen only outside the offices of the BJP or the Congress. Their dressing up in the Indian team's colours was the equivalent of John Simpson of the BBC wearing the Union Jack and turning up in the news studio to cover an Ashes game between England and Australia. Café 20 was as clear a signal as possible that in an overcrowded satellite television market, Aaj Tak had hitched its fortunes to the aspirational nationalism of the Indian cricket fan. To drive the point home, the Aaj Tak logo was prominently displayed on the Team India jerseys the anchors were wearing, right next to the logo of Team India. The game itself did not begin until 5.30 p.m. India time but Aaj Tak's Café 20 began early in the morning and continued through the day. There was no pre-match analysis or reporting—simply news anchors in the Indian colours chatting informally about what they felt about the cricket team. One anchor held up a cricket bat as he showed the viewers his own take on the square cut, another demonstrated the intricacies of leg-spin bowling, while a third fondled his cricket pads.

When the match ended in an Indian victory after a nerve-wracking thriller that went down to the last over, the Aaj Tak camera cut once again to Café 20. This time the studio had not just the eight anchors who had begun the day's programming, it was overflowing with Aaj Tak's entire Delhi staff—all dancing in gay abandon to the tune of a dholak specially brought in for the occasion. Dancing with Aaj Tak was Kapil Dev, the first Indian captain to win a World Cup (in 1983), who had stayed in the studio through the day as a contracted expert. As other news channels went around the country showing instantaneous street celebrations, for 20 minutes, Aaj Tak's viewers saw only one sight: its entire staff doing a Punjabi bhangra in concert with Kapil Dev. It was yet another reaffirmation of television's allegiance to the tricolour: cricket, nationalism and television mixing in a seamless hue that more than anything else encapsulated how tightly India's satellite television revolution is inextricably entwined with cricket.

Aaj Tak was not an exception. Every other news channel—and India now has more than 50 24-hour satellite news networks (the equivalent of more than 50 Indian CNNs) in 11 languages—focused almost exclusively on cricket that day. An alien landing in India and watching Indian television that day would not have been wrong in assuming that cricket was the only news in the country that day. Yet it was a day when the ruling Congress announced the accession of Gandhi scion Rahul to a formal position as general secretary in the party's hierarchy and one of the Left parties supporting the Congress government targeted Prime Minister Manmohan Singh as 'immature and inexperienced' for pursuing India's nuclear deal with the United States. These barely featured as news. But news television's tunneled focus on cricket wasn't just a product of what is now a cliché: the fanatical Indian support for cricket. There was a clear economic dimension to the cricket coverage. According to one senior television news manager, his network had received more advertising for coverage of the Twenty-twenty World Cup, two months before the tournament even began, than the entire advertising it received for covering the Union Budget.[3] This, when the concerned channel was not even broadcasting the event—broadcast licensing rules allowed it only limited use of the actual match footage.[4] The economics of the private television business and the heavy advertiser interest in cricket meant that the news channel could not but focus its energies on the game.

Television coverage offers a useful prism to understand the contours of modern Indian identity; in a complex process of diffusion it subsumes both cause and effect. Television producers are cultural gatekeepers, mediators of what they understand to be an 'Indian' identity, as they try to appeal to it for economic profit. We have argued elsewhere that in a land divided at multifarious levels by factors like language, caste and custom the unrelenting drive to construct and capture a national market for maximizing profits led television producers and advertisers to turn to cricket as the lowest common dominator. Channels turned to cricket because of its indelible link with what might be termed 'Indian-ness'.[5] Their focus on cricket, in turn, further augmented its equation with notions of Indian identity. This is a process that unfolded through the 1990s and Aaj Tak's Café 20 was only the latest alliteration on this palimpsest. There is now a substantial literature tracking how cricket, from the colonial era, has always had a political dimension in India and much of this literature attributes the striking pre-eminence of cricket in the Indian imagination to a set of complex and contradictory processes that parallel the emergence of an 'Indian' nation.[6] As a crucial hinge of the modern Indian nation, cricket is also the easiest way to register on TV ratings.

But cricket is not the only game that Indians play, although it might seem so sometimes on television. Café 20 had a telling footnote. Less than a week after India's win in South Africa, news channels reported that four of India's hockey players, along with the assistant coach of the national team, were going on a hunger strike.[7] The protesters, all from Karnataka, would sit in a Gandhian protest outside the office of the chief minister of Karnataka to demand equal treatment with cricketers. The immediate trigger had been the state government's decision to reward cricket player Robin Uthappa and then national bowling coach Venkatesh Prasad with Rs 5 lakh each for their role in the T20 win. The protesting hockey players also attacked the Centre and the state governments of Jharkhand, which presented cricket captain Dhoni with a new luxury car, Haryana and Maharashtra for showering similar gifts on their cricketers while ignoring the hockey players. Justifying the strike, then national hockey coach Joaquim Carvalho pointed to the severe imbalance in the rewards for hockey players when they won the Asia Cup shortly before the T20 win. Speaking in a live interview on Times Now, his sense of hurt and pathos came through clearly:

> We are not jealous of the cricket players. We are not against them getting awards. We are also proud of them. We are simply saying that hockey is the national game. Why do governments and politicians not recognize our achievements? We just want the recognition we deserve.[8]

Carvalho's point was underscored even further by the cynical response of Karnataka Chief Minister H.D. Kumaraswamy: he declared that he would consider the hockey players for a reward only if they won the World Cup.[9] Once politicians would have been careful not to seem callous towards Indian hockey. Now there was not even a token statement of support for the hockey players' predicament. It was politically useful to be seen as supporting cricket, not hockey. It was unimaginable in the glory days of Indian hockey that a day would come when cricket would supplant the game to such an extent in the national imagination that hockey players would be driven to desperate measures.

In more ways than one, Aaj Tak's Café 20 and the subsequent hunger strike by the hockey players symbolized the vast gulf between the status of cricket vis-à-vis other games in modern India. There is no doubt that cricket rules but the question is, why cricket? Until the early 1980s, cricket was not the most pre-eminent Indian game. Cricket was popular but hockey was the 'national game' and soccer was equally popular in large parts of the country. Yet from the 1980s onwards cricket assumed centre-stage. Cricket's emergence as the new Indian 'national' game does not necessarily stem from some peculiar Indian affiliation for the game but is inextricably linked to the expansion of Indian television and a confluence of factors that came together: the creation of a large middle class, the economic reforms, the birth of the satellite television industry and a whole gamut of forces that fall under the broad rubric of globalization. This chapter will map the growth of Indian television to draw out these linkages and demonstrate the central role of television in making cricket integral to modern notions of Indian identity. This emergence also marks the sunset for the nation's Olympic sports, a condition likely to prevail in the Indian sporting landscape in the foreseeable future.

Cricket dominates television because its administrators adapted the best to the forces of television and globalization as they took shape in India. Hockey and soccer were left behind because their administrators refused to change and by the time they did, they had missed the bus. It would be foolhardy to attribute essentialist causal effects to television. Television does not explain everything but it is equally impossible to understand post-liberalization India without reference to satellite television. By 2007, India was home to as many as 300 indigenous satellite television networks[10] and television's embrace of cricket was the fuel that drove driven the rise of India as the financial centre of the global game. In a complete reversal of the earlier power order in the game, 80 per cent of the International Cricket Council's earnings are now estimated to come from India[11] and the Board of Control for Cricket in India (BCCI) is now the richest cricket body in the world.[12] India has always had the numbers but this new-found money power is a recent phenomenon deriving from the muscle of India's burgeoning private television industry. Between 1992 and 2006, the total number of Indian television households tripled to reach an estimated 112 million.[13] It made India the world's third largest television market, just behind China and the United States.[14] More than 60 per cent of these television sets are estimated to be connected to satellite dishes.[15] While numbers like these have attracted global media corporations, with both India and China gradually turning into new focal points of the global communication industry,[16] this industry has fundamentally changed the nature of cricket, nationally and globally. The power source of India's increased global clout in the organization of cricket is Indian television.

It is a measure of cricket's embrace of television, in direct opposition to other sports, that it has virtually defined the legal structure of India's satellite revolution. Historically, the story of Indian satellite television is the story of a private industry leapfrogging across stringent government regulations. In a country where the state monopolized television until the mid-1990s, the rise of the private satellite television networks is nothing short of a revolution. Till the time of writing, successive Indian governments had managed to pass only two legislations pertaining to the challenge of this new industry. As this chapter will show, since the early 1990s, the politics around the private television industry has been such that successive governments were forced to back off from virtually every controlling legislation that was mooted. The only two laws that managed enough support from Parliament came about because of cricket. Both these laws provide the legal superstructure of Indian television and in that sense, cricket has defined India's satellite television industry as much as television has defined it. The fact that they were passed by parliamentarians demonstrates the power of cricket in the Indian imagination and the wider significance of the game in Indian public culture.

The '6-second' Maharaja and the Jwalamukhi 'Million': Forgotten Histories of Indian Sport

There is no evidence to show that cricket was any bigger in India than other sports like hockey and soccer before the 1980s. During the colonial period, hockey, soccer and cricket—all three became important playing fields for the politics of identity and nationalist self-assertion.

Some of the greatest nationalist triumphs came not in cricket but in the other two games. Let us first consider soccer. The 1911 victory of the Calcutta-based Mohun Bagan Club over the British East York Regiment is seen by a number of historians as not just a sporting but also a nationalist milestone that spurred on the Swadeshi (indigenous) movement.[17] It was celebrated in vernacular popular culture as a fitting reply to the British discourse on Bengalis being effeminate and hence, in the ideology of the period, an inferior race. The victory on the soccer field had a resonance beyond the playing field precisely because it was seen as the Bengali answer to the charge of effeminacy that had become a leitmotif of the imperial discourse. This is why contemporary vernacular commentaries on the victory focused more on its social meaning than on the game itself. To cite one example, *Amrita Bazar Patrika* pointed out that mental and physical strength was 'an integral quality of Bengalees' and urged Europeans not to consider them 'non-martial' any more.[18] Similarly, *The Mussalman* commented: 'The victory of Mohun Bagan...has demonstrated that Indians are second to none in all manly games'.[19] No one caught the nationalist meaning of the 1911 victory for Bengali identity and self-assertion better than the *Nayak* which pointed out that the victory would fill 'every Indian with joy and pride to know that rice-eating, malaria-ridden bare-footed Bengalis have got the better of beef-eating, Herculean, booted John Bull in that peculiarly English sport'.[20]

A measure of the centrality of football in the Bengali consciousness is Swami Vivekanand's oft-quoted remark, 'playing football rather than reciting the Gita will take one near to God'.[21] By the 1930s, the noted literary figure Sajani Kanta Das had noted that three things personified Bengali colonial identity: Mohun Bagan, Subhash Chandra Bose and New Theatres.[22] Almost until independence, soccer had a legitimate claim to be among the most popular spectator sports in India. As sports historian Mihir Bose has noted:

> While the Indians were fighting the British for their independence, one of the most popular games in the country was football. Logically after independence, football should have become India's number one sport. It is cheaper, it certainly permeated more layers of Indian society—even down to the semi rural areas—than cricket and as in other parts of the world, could have been a metaphor for nationalism.[23]

This book is not the place to document the story of the decline of Indian soccer after independence. That has been well documented in studies elsewhere.[24] It must be pointed out though that in sharp contrast to India's abysmal position of 151 in the FIFA rankings at the time of writing, independent India began with a bang on the soccer field by winning the gold at the first Asiad in 1951. Its barefoot footballers beat the booted Iranians in the final. Similarly, in the 1956 Olympics, India became the first Asian nation to enter the semi-finals, eventually finishing fourth. Its last great international soccer victory came in the 1962 Jakarta Asiad when India won gold, followed by a bronze at the Bangkok Asiad of 1970. It has been pointed out that ever since, 'the unresolved dichotomy between the interest of the nation and club as well as the long-term failure of the AIFF/Sports ministry to appreciate the importance of professionalism and commercialism in Indian football'[25] have led to its terminal decline. The point, though, is that soccer always had a strong mass base in India, certainly not less so than cricket, before television arrived and changed everything.

Similarly, the astonishing success rate of Indian hockey in the late colonial and early post-colonial period, when it won six successive gold medals at the Olympics, between 1928 and 1956, turned that game into an icon for Indian nationalism. So much so that when the IOC toyed with the idea of dropping hockey as an event in the 1952 Helsinki Olympics, India even offered to host the hockey event separately in New Delhi.[26] The previous chapters have documented the rise and fall of Indian hockey in detail. The success of the Indian hockey teams in beating Western teams demonstrated to the nationalists that Indians could compete on equal terms with the West. The success of the Indian hockey teams was such that after independence the ministry of sport, not surprisingly, chose hockey as the official 'national game' of India.

It is significant that the Board of Control for Cricket in India was only founded as late as 1928, a full four years after the formation of Indian Hockey Federation. By this time, the hockey players had already won India its first Olympic gold. In fact, Anthony De Mello, one of the founders of the BCCI, has pointed out that it was the pride of the Olympic gold that first ignited the desire to create an Indian 'national' cricket team:

Railways and Sports
Complete concentration and perfect coordination are the primary requisites of all sports. The Railways also call for the utmost concentration from every one of their workers and perfect coordination between them. The Railways and sports both bring together thousands of people from various regions and states and both forge links of friendship and brotherhood between people. The Railways and sports both have built up age-old traditions and both have become deservedly popular. Both aim at building a strong and robust nation.

Tie of Kinship
The playground is a nursery of inter-stat fraternity. And it is h that a sense of kinsh springs up between the players and the spectators. Regional differences are no ba this emotional affinit is the Railway's huml but proud role to bri people together in fraternal association.

> Heightened by our hockey success at Amsterdam, our ambitions for Indian sport knew no bounds just then. We visualized our cricketers playing at the Oval, at Lord's...and straightway was born in those of us connected with the game in India the determination, that sooner or later, it should happen.[27]

It was hockey that had caught the national imagination and it led the way for cricket. Due to lack of popular support, 'cricket in India was far from being a flourishing national sport in the middle twenties.'[28] With the exception of Calcutta, Madras and Bombay, there were few facilities for cricket across the country. Compared to other sports, cricket was still dominated by the British, by the royalty or by the elites.[29]

This is not to say that cricket was not popular. Ramachandra Guha and Mihir Bose, among others, have demonstrated the role cricket played in galvanizing nationalist sentiment from the 1880s onwards.[30] Using the cricketing records of the army, it is even possible to speculate that playing, and defeating white soldiers, on an even playing field in cricket might have played a role in firming up the confidence of Indian sepoys for the Great Revolt of 1857.[31] In the early 20th century, the Bombay Pentangular tournament, for instance, was a huge commercial and popular success until it was shut down in the 1940s.[32] Yet, it was never the pre-eminent Indian sport. Cricket in the late 1920s was more of a 'healthy cheerful adult' than a fully grown adult.[33]

Even a pioneer of Indian cricket like Anthony De Mello saw the future of hockey as much brighter until well after independence. Writing in 1959, he saw an equally bright future for soccer as well, observing that, in contrast to cricket, they were both mass sports:

> Soccer in India, like hockey, is a poor man's game. It is a game which most boys around the country play at one time or another—at school or in the maidan...Thus there is a nationwide understanding of, and liking for, soccer, stronger than that for cricket, which has till now tended to be more a game for the rich man...[34]

Until well into the 1960s, all contemporary observers agreed that cricket certainly always had the 'glamour', due to its aristocratic roots, but its popular appeal in India was never more than that of soccer and hockey.[35]

A good illustration of this comes from the popular advertising of the era, which offers a prism to understand the popular culture of the time. From Air India to the Indian Railways, most public sector units until the 1960s used sporting metaphors to advertise themselves in print advertisements. Unlike the near-total saturation of cricket in sport-related advertising after the 1990s, the iconography of these advertisements of the 1960s largely focused on soccer, hockey or athletics. For instance, one Eastern Railways advertisement extolling its role in building 'ties of kinship' and 'fraternal association' across regional divides, drew parallels with how the playground is a 'nursery of inter-state fraternity'. Significantly, the designers of this particular advertisement chose to put the image of a footballer in the foreground, with a vast multitude forming the pictorial background.[36] Similarly, another Railways ad on its role in promoting sport, noted:

> The Railways and sports bring together thousands of people from various regions and states and forge links of friendship and brotherhood between people...Both (Railways and sport) aim to build a robust nation.[37]

Focusing on the Railways and its promotion of sport to weld the nation, the iconography of this particular advertisement gave as much space to soccer, hockey, tennis, athletics and boxing as it did to cricket.[38] Even the famous Air India maharajah that has symbolized the airline since its nationalization, featured in advertisements in the 1960s that showed him as an Olympic athlete, running the mile in 'six seconds'.[39] If that same ad were to be produced today it would be fair to guess that its copywriters would have no choice but to convert the six-second maharajah into a six-hitting Tendulkar. The fact that advertisers could use the imagery of non-cricket sports to sell popular products is a significant marker of how different sports were perceived in the popular imagination. If popular advertising is any indication, then cricket was never first among equals until television changed the very nature of Indian sport and nationalism.

Hidden amid the IOC archives at Lausanne is the intriguing story of an attempt to create an Indian equivalent of Olympia, in the town of Jwalamukhi. An Olympic torch is carried from Olympia to each venue of the Olympics every four years, and Indian sports administrators emulated this practice for the XIX National Games of 1960 from the Jogmaya temple in the holy town of Jwalamukhi near Hoshiarpur in

Punjab. The Greek ceremony got an Indian twist with high priests chanting Sanskrit shlokas and lighting the flame from the temple's sacrificial fire. This was a deliberate strategy by the organizers to build local interest. Such was the popular interest in the event that the IOA's chronicler noted:

> As the torch emerged from the temple, there was a tremendous ovation from the crowd of 10,000 that had collected outside the temple.[40]

About 1,500 torch-bearers carried the flame for the 350 km from Jwalamukhi to Delhi over ten days and it is significant that as many as a 'million people' turned up to see them en route. The Jogmaya connection seems to have given the Indian equivalent of the Olympic flame a kind of religious sanctity that fuelled the fervour. At Jullunder, for instance, the Town Hall, where the torch was kept for the night, became a 'virtual mandir' and thousands filed past the flame and 'made their offering.' At Ludhiana, on 18 February, as many as 50,000 lined up on both sides of the Grand Trunk Road as the torch-bearers made their way into the city. Such was the frenzy that policemen and soldiers 'found it difficult to control the rush of people who wanted to pay their homage to the flame.'[41] When the torch reached Patiala, the effusive chronicler noted:

> ...almost the entire population of Patiala came out to give an unprecedented reception to the torch on February 20. The main bazaars wore a festive appearance unknown in the recorded history of that city... at various corners in the city people distributed sweets. Milk, fruits and flowers were offered to the runners. Thousands of men and women filed past the torch at Yadavindra Stadium where it was kept for the night.[42]

Similarly, at Ambala city and Cantonment, 'all arrangements to control the crowds broke down' as the thousands gathered far exceeded the expectations of the organizers. From Panipat to Delhi, the Grand Trunk Road was lined with thousands as they came to get a glimpse of the holy torch that was to start the National Games.[43] Part of the fervour was certainly stoked by the sanctity attached to the Jogmaya Temple of Jwalamukhi but no one doubted the sporting nature of the event. The ritual of the Olympic flame relay had been Indianized and the breathtaking popular response was a measure of the support that the National Games and Olympic sport had at the time, at least in north India.

Cricket, Indian-ness and Television

It is possible to date the rise of cricket as the pre-eminent Indian game almost precisely to the date when television began expanding. Television became a mass medium in India only during the 1980s. The previous chapter has documented the centrality of the 1982 Asiad in its development. There were three intersecting factors: the creation of a national network of transmitters linked with satellite technology; Doordarshan's commercialization and resultant focus on entertainment; and economic reforms that made television sets cheaper.

Until the 1982 Asiad, Indians had never seen sporting events on television. The only way to follow any game had been to follow the commentary on radio. Now for the first time they could see their sporting heroes, in colour. That changed everything. India's dominance in hockey had declined since the late 1960s, but in the showpiece Delhi Asiad, the hockey team lost 7–1 to Pakistan in the finals. This was the first time most Indian viewers, not fortunate to be at the stadium, were seeing the hockey team in action and the camera was cruel. For instance, Mir Ranjan Negi, the hapless goalkeeper on that day, later complained that the inexperienced Doordarshan cameramen never showed how he charged at Pakistan's defenders. The camera would only cut to the empty goal after he had been beaten in his charge, with the effect that television viewers only saw an undefended goal post that seemed permanently open to Pakistan's roving forwards. Negi never played a game for India after that day and for years was hounded as a 'traitor', who had 'sold out'. Someone even cut the electricity at his wedding function, such was the popular anger he faced.[44] His story has since been picturized in the 2007 Bollywood blockbuster *Chak De India*. That loss to Pakistan on television, watched for the first time by a national Indian audience, did irreparable damage to the image of Indian hockey in the national imagination.

The tragedy of Indian hockey, as Shekhar Gupta points out, was that while television expanded, Indian hockey declined:

> Our last championship victory, the Kuala Lumpur World Cup in 1975, was telecast live but then all of India had no more than a thousand television sets, all black and white, and in the metros. Hardly anybody, therefore, would have seen the stirring image of Aslam Sher Khan, brought in as a

> desperate last-minute substitute to take a penalty corner, kissing his amulet before banging in the hit that took India into the final...
>
> A sporting 'product' was needed to sell those wares, to consume the sponsors' and the advertisers' money, and hockey did not make the grade.[45]

A detailed breakdown of Indian hockey performances bears out this analysis. India lost only two games in the first three hockey World Cups. Between 1986 and 1990, it won only one game. While it has performed consistently at the Asian Games, it has languished at the Olympics and in World Cup hockey.

Table 9.1
Indian Performance at Hockey World Cups, 1980–2006

Year	*Venue*	*Position*
1982	Mumbai	5
1986	London	12
1990	Lahore	10
1994	Sydney	5
1998	Utrecht	9
2002	Kuala Lumpur	10
2006	Mönchengladbach, Germany	11

Table 9.2
Indian Performance at Asian Games post-1982, 1980–2006

Year	*Venue*	*Position*
1982	Delhi	Silver
1986	Seoul	Bronze
1990	Beijing	Silver
1994	Hiroshima	Silver
1998	Bangkok	Gold
2002	Busan	Silver
2006	Doha	5th

Table 9.3
Indian Performance at Olympic hockey, 1980–2006

Year	*Venue*	*Position*
1980	Moscow	Gold
1984	Los Angeles	5th
1988	Seoul	6th
1992	Barcelona	7th
1996	Atlanta	8th
2000	Sydney	7th
2004	Athens	7th

The decline in hockey standards began to turn spectators away at a time when television was providing opportunities for building an entirely new support base. In this context, Ramachandra Guha has argued that interest in soccer too began to wane after the telecast of the 1982 World Cup.

> This was the first World Cup telecast live in India; alerted to the gap between their own local heroes and the great international stars, men in Calcutta began to turn away from their clubs. The slide continued; twenty years later, soccer ranks a poor second to cricket in the sporting passions of Bengal.[46]

What is significant from our point of view is that the creation of a national network for the Asian Games coincided with India's epochal Cricket World Cup win in 1983. This was not Indian cricket's first great win. The 1971 victory of Ajit Wadekar's team against England in England perhaps ranks higher in cricketing terms. Wadekar's team was welcomed back by huge street parades in Bombay but no one had actually seen them play. The 1983 World Cup was different. Unheralded, inexperienced in the one-day format, and led by a new young captain—Kapil Dev—'Kapil's Devils', as they became known, were seen by millions of Indians through their journey to winning the Cup. It is not surprising that this victory was followed by political felicitations that Wadekar's team and even the hockey players of an earlier era had never received.

The 1983 victory was followed by another victory in 1985 in the Benson and Hedges Champion of Champions Trophy in Australia.

Again, television was the conduit, as for the first time, Indians saw the Australian tournament live and in colour. In fact, it is possible to precisely map the rise of cricket with the increase in television penetration. From 1983, the expansion of the television network became a key governmental priority. Between July and October 1984, for instance, practically one TV transmitter a day was commissioned.[47] As Fig. 9.4 demonstrates, starting from just one transmitter in 1971, 18 had been set up by 1980. The graph leaps spectacularly in the early 1980s with the total number of transmitters going up to 172 in 1985 and 698 in 1995. This expansion was accompanied by a simultaneous increase in the sale of TV sets. In the first decade of television, the number of television sets increased from 41 to 24,838. It took another 12 years for this number to cross the 2 million mark. But from the mid-1980s, the graph suddenly rockets up and we see the makings of a mass medium. By 1986, 3 million TV sets were being produced in India, including 7 lakh colour sets [48] and by 1992 the figure had reached 34 million TV sets. 1992 was a watershed because that was the year when private satellite television first made its appearance. We examine its influence later in this chapter.

It is no coincidence that the cricketers of this era, while not necessarily more talented than those of earlier generations, became the first brand names among Indian sportsmen. As television advertising expanded, it looked for heroes, and found them in the national cricket team. Kapil Dev, Sunil Gavaskar, Ravi Shastri and Dilip Vengsarkar were hired to model a whole range of consumer products, from shaving cream and toothpaste to clothing and English language guides.

Advertising was first allowed on television in 1976 but it only grew in the 1980s with the creation of a national audience. The decision to allow advertising, the push to create a nationwide television network and the spread of colour television after 1982 all combined to create a new consumer spectacle. It has been suggested that the rise of commercial television formed the basis 'for a new notion of collectivity, expressed as "the middle class" and based on the "idea of the democratization of aspiration"'.[51] A number of scholars have focused attention on the intrinsic links between the 'exploding middle classes' of India in the 1980s and state-sponsored commercial

Figure 9.4 Growth of T.V. Transmitters[49]

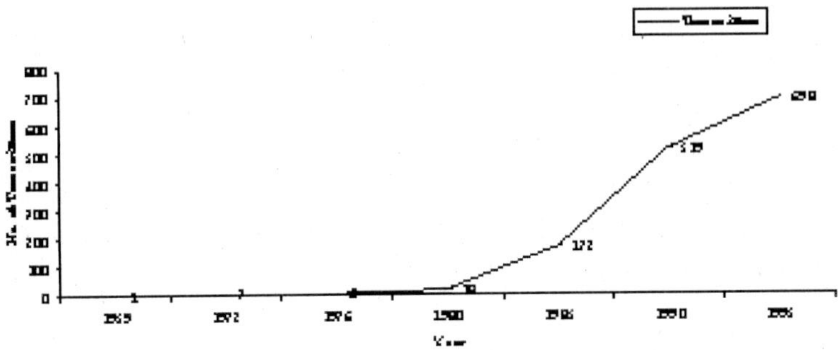

television through the 1980s.[52] Certainly, marketing and advertising professionals were in no doubt about what television meant for the new consumer economy. According to Ahmad Khan, head of Enterprise Nexus Lowe advertising:

> I think what television did was that it opened, for a few million people, *whole new worlds* which they never knew existed. And it made them want and need things which they never bought before. So from just saving money for the sake of saving money, I think for the first time people said, 'Oh, I make money so that I can do things with it.' And this is something which I think happened for the first time in our history. I think that's what television did.[53]

Television enabled the circulation of commodity images on a national scale in a way that simply wasn't possible before. Cricket and cricketers were key components of these commodity images. It is no accident that the historical lineage of the Indian middle class as a political

Fig. 9.5: TV Sets in India (1959–1992)[50]

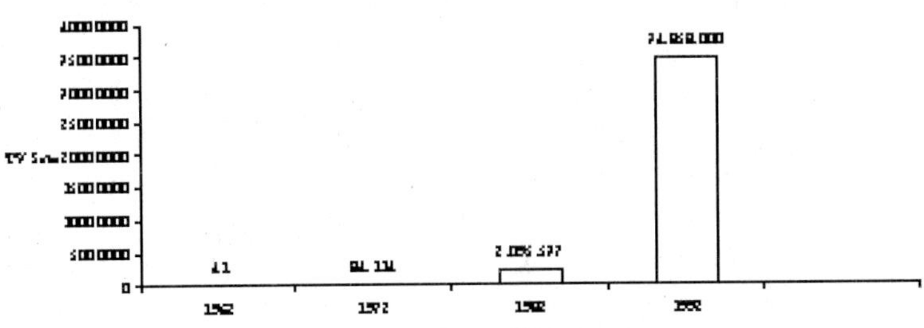

category can be traced to 1985. That was the year when Mani Shankar Aiyar, then a joint secretary in the prime minister's office, told the *Washington Post* that India contained a middle class of one hundred million and that this class looked up to Rajiv Gandhi.[54] It was the first political articulation of the middle class as a social category and this was only possible in the context of a newly created national television network with an overt middle class agenda, subsuming within it the state's lofty developmental objectives. This perception, in turn, fuelled television advertising and the focus on cricketers as the new heroes of the nation. By the 1986 Asian Games, cricket had become so popular that a reader of a national daily could write:

> The disgraceful performance of the 400-strong Asian contingent...is not surprising when the nation's main sport is following the cricket score on radio and television. The result is that city children take to breaking window panes and noses...Village children also have now taken to the Englishmen's game and dropped fast the Indian games...Unless cricket is banished from this country, the rest of the sports would not get any encouragement, people would not do honest work in their work places and youth would not get adequate exercise.[55]

As cricket embraced the new charms of television, hockey, with a combination of bad performances, lack of administrative foresight and short-sighted planning continued to languish until cricket supplanted it in the national imagination. As Harsha Bhogle points out:

> Television is the seed that breeds sponsorships, ignites passions and carries sport across boundaries. Formula One has shown that. A seemingly monotonous sport with invisible drivers thrives solely due to brilliant television. Hockey can do more, much more, if it chooses to.[56]

Globalization and the new economy were embraced by cricket while hockey administrators remained mired in old ways.[57] The few times that Indian hockey did well, like at the Bangkok Asiad, its success was followed by administrative wrangling and internal discord. Half the victorious team at Bangkok, for instance, was sacked soon after it won the gold because of differences between the players and the IHF. Hockey administrators have made belated attempts to embrace television like with the National Hockey League on ESPN-Star. However, as Rohit Brijnath put it, 'Cricket has settled on the mind and leaves little place and time for other pursuits. As a nation we are [now] guilty of a one-track mind.'[58]

'The Battering Ram': Satellite Television and the Centrality of Cricket

This book is not the place to detail the complex processes through which satellite television penetrated India. Suffice it to say that from 1991 onwards, satellite technology allowed private broadcasters to bypass the shackles of state control and break the state's monopoly over the medium. By 2007, India was home to as many as 300 indigenous satellite television networks. The initial spark was lit by the Hong-Kong based Star TV network that was soon bought over by Rupert Murdoch's News Corporation. Like elsewhere in the world, News Corporation banked on sport as a battering ram to capture the Indian television market. And given the events of the 1980s, by sport it meant cricket. Murdoch had first demonstrated the immense commercial power of sport when he turned around the ailing Sky TV's fortunes in the United Kingdom by buying telecast rights for the English Premier League in 1992.[59] News Corporation's various entities have consistently followed this strategy ever since—from buying television rights to Major League Baseball and American football to rugby league and rugby union rights in England. Murdoch has since branched out into buying sport clubs, a practice that other media players like Italy's Silvio Berlusconi have followed.[60] In a speech to shareholders, soon after News Corporation acquired Star TV, Murdoch outlined the importance of sport in his business plans for expanding into Asia:

> We have the long-term rights in most countries to major sporting events and we will be doing in Asia what we intend to do elsewhere in the world, using *sports as a battering ram* and a lead offering in all our pay-television operations. Sport absolutely overpowers film and everything else in the entertainment genre. [61]

Accordingly, News Corporation chose cricket as a lynchpin of its strategy in India and ESPN announced its entry into the Indian market in 1993 by acquiring the exclusive rights to telecast cricket in India for five years for $30 million.[62] This is a lesson that all major

Indian broadcasters have learnt as well and since the mid-1990s the exponential expansion of the Indian broadcast industry has been accompanied by vicious wars over cricket telecast rights. India's well-documented transformation into the 'spiritual and financial heart of world cricket'[63] during the same period is intrinsically linked to the infusion of television money.

Confusion and the Supreme Court: The Cricket Test

As the torch-bearer of satellite television, cricket has played a major role in the history of Indian broadcast reform and was the catalyst for the landmark Supreme Court judgement of 1995[64] that deprived the state of its legal monopoly over the airwaves. That judgement, in one stroke, gave a legal basis to the burgeoning new economy of satellite television. Since then, new stakeholders have arisen and in relative terms the once all-powerful ministry of information and broadcasting, the executive arm of the state in broadcasting matters, has found its power severely eroded. All of this stemmed from a dispute over cricket.

The state's monopoly over broadcasting accrued from the colonial Indian Telegraph Act of 1885 which gave the central government 'the exclusive privilege' of establishing, maintaining and working telegraphs as well as the right to grant licences.[65] The nationalist regime that succeeded the Raj continued to be guided by this 19th century legislation and an amendment to it in 1957 expanded the term 'telegraph' to mean any 'apparatus for the purpose of affording means of telegraphic communication'.[66] In 1991, foreign satellite television expanded in India like the American Wild West for two years before the state made its first serious intervention. Until then, satellite broadcasters found ingenious ways to get around the legal restrictions, often with help from 'pro-reform' sections of the state, but this dichotomy led to a serious crisis when the ministry of information and broadcasting first decided to enforce its legal monopoly in the dispute over cricket telecast rights between October 1993 and February 1995. Until 1993, Indian cricket had always been covered by Doordarshan and the crisis occurred when the Cricket Association of Bengal (CAB) sold the telecast rights of the five-nation Hero Cup[67] to the multinational television company TWI. Doordarshan, which had failed to match TWI's bid, refused to allow the foreign broadcaster to uplink from Indian soil.[68] Claiming an exclusive right to do so under the Telegraph Act of 1885, Doordarshan accused the Board of Control for Cricket in India (BCCI) and CAB of being 'anti-national' and the ensuing legal battle illustrated the complexity of economic liberalization.[69]

TWI and CAB signed the agreement for the Hero Cup in May 1993. Even though Doordarshan saw the grant of rights to anybody but itself as illegal, the ministry of home affairs, on 13 October, approved TWI's application to allow satellite up-linking. TWI even paid $29,640 to the government-owned Videsh Sanchar Nigam Limited (VSNL)[70] as up-link fees and the finance ministry allowed it to import its own broadcast equipment, waiving customs and additional duties.[71] Clearly, other ministries and departments did not have a problem with the TWI deal. In sharp contrast, the ministry of information and broadcasting condemned it as 'a diabolical move to violate the law of the land.'[72] As a pressure tactic, the ministry even forbade All India Radio from broadcasting ball-by-ball coverage of the tournament. Soon thereafter, customs authorities in Mumbai, under governmental instructions, confiscated TWI's broadcasting equipment.[73] This was the first serious muscle-flexing by the ministry and some media commentators immediately made the link with a larger crisis of the reform process itself:

> CAB will be bludgeoned into submission and somehow Doordarshan and the government will have their pound of flesh...the next time Mr. Narasimha Rao [then prime minister] and Mr. Jyoti Basu [then West Bengal chief minister] go round the world seeking investments and much else besides, they must expect to be asked some searching questions.[74]

With TWI's equipment in the custody of customs officials, CAB appealed to the Supreme Court of India. The court took the matter so seriously that a bench sat to consider it even though it was a government holiday. It has been observed that, 'Never before in the history of independent India did a Supreme Court Division bench sit in judgement on a government holiday at 11.30 pm'.[75] In an important ruling on 15 November 1993, the court overruled the government and allowed TWI to generate its own broadcasts.[76] The case was urgent because its significance extended far beyond the game of cricket: the crisis of the Hero Cup seemed to jeopardize the 1996 World Cup, which was to be co-hosted by India, Pakistan and Sri Lanka. The South Africa Cricket Board had threatened to withdraw South Africa's support for the subcontinent playing host to the tournament unless the wrangle over telecast rights was sorted out immediately. Following this, foreign broadcasting corporations were already demanding their money back from WorldTel, which held the World Cup telecast rights.[77] The issue of telecast rights threatened to take away foreign investment and was at the heart of economic liberalization itself.

The Supreme Court's 1993 ruling, however, was limited to the Hero Cup. It did not solve the basic dichotomy of satellite broadcasters challenging Doordarshan's legal monopoly. Consequently, Doordarshan and the BCCI locked horns again in 1994 when the BCCI granted ESPN the right to telecast India's series with West Indies as part of a $30 million deal which gave ESPN the exclusive right to telecast cricket in India for five years. Cricket was attracting foreign investors to India but the ministry of information and broadcasting was fighting tooth and nail to preserve its fiefdom. Once again, other government agencies opposed Doordarshan. For instance, VSNL,[78] which had granted up-link rights to ESPN, accused the ministry of deliberately obstructing its plans. VSNL was forced to return the advance it had received from ESPN[79] and VSNL officials were clearly unhappy at the financial loss:

> We do not need to put in any money for infrastructure because we already possess all the facilities but the Ministry of I&B will not let us do anything, even if it involves earning thousands of dollars for the country in foreign exchange...'[80]

Again, the BCCI appealed to the Supreme Court, which in an epochal judgement on 9 February 1995 ruled that the airwaves cannot be a state monopoly as they constitute public property. The court made it clear that it was the state's duty to see that airwaves were utilized to advance the fundamental right of free speech which could not be done in a monopoly. The broadcast media, the court said, 'should be under the control of the public as distinct from Government. This is the command implicit in Article 19(1)(a). It should be operated by a public statutory corporation or corporations...' The judges further added that the fundamental right to freedom of speech and expression includes the right to communicate effectively, including through the electronic media. Ruling that the Indian Telegraph Act of 1885 was totally inadequate, 'intended for an altogether different purpose when it was enacted', the judges ordered the government 'to take immediate steps to establish an autonomous public authority...to control and regulate the use of the airwaves'.[81] Thus ended the first Indian battle over broadcast reform. The state lost its monopoly and the ministry was ordered to evolve a new regulatory framework.

'National Interest': Cricket and the Last Broadcast Law

So central has cricket become to Indian television that it is also at the heart of the second broadcasting law that India has managed to pass. More than a decade after the Supreme Court's order, the Indian state has failed to evolve an overarching regulatory body to oversee broadcasting issues. Simultaneously, the ministry of information and broadcasting has periodically tried to fill the regulatory vacuum with draft legislation and summary executive directives, most of these designed to assert its control. Broadly speaking, it has consistently tried to put the genie of broadcasting back into the bottle at every step. Yet, almost every one of its measures has come up against serious challenges. At every step, the ministry's controlling instincts have had to contend with either the courts, or strong public opinion, or heavy corporate lobbying by the new broadcast capitalists. In every case, except for the 2007 law on mandatory sharing of sports feeds, the ministry has had to cede ground.

This last law is interesting because it is the only law pertaining to broadcasting that has managed to be passed in Parliament in over a decade. On at least eight occasions the ministry's controlling drive ran aground in the face of thick opposition but in cricket it found a populist catalyst that allowed it to build consensus. Its roots can be traced back to the 2004 India–Pakistan cricket series when the ministry first forced Ten Sports, which had the broadcast rights, to share its live telecast of matches with Doordarshan to benefit non-satellite watchers. This seemed like a popular cause to espouse but apart from acquiring these sports broadcasts, ostensibly in the 'public interest', Doordarshan also wanted to make money by selling advertising spots. This was a serious threat to Ten Sport's advertising revenues and its parent company Taj TV protested in a bitterly contested case in the

Supreme Court, where Prasar Bharati was forced to deposit Rs 500 million as damage guarantee against possible revenue damages. It was also forbidden to sell advertising and forced to carry the Ten Sports logo for the series broadcasts.[82] The ministry countered in late 2005 through new downlinking guidelines that made it mandatory for private sports channels to share feeds of all major sports events of 'national and international importance'[83] in the larger 'public interest'. These guidelines went to the heart of free market considerations and private sports broadcasters who had paid large sums of money to acquire broadcast rights repeatedly challenged their legal validity in various courts, through 2006 and early 2007. On at least three occasions, judicial rulings restrained the Central government from interfering with their rights. On 9 May 2006, for instance, the Supreme Court refused to force Ten Sports to share its coverage of India's cricket tour of the West Indies with the national broadcaster. A two-member bench of Justice Ashok Bhan and Justice L.K. Palta, went so far as to ask the government to 'bring a law' on the matter, saying, 'You can't act on guidelines.'[84] Similarly, in August 2006, the Supreme Court again ruled in favour of Ten Sports which contended that it would lose Rs 80 million a day in advertising—for the July tri-series involving Sri Lanka, India and South Africa—if it was forced to share its signals with Doordarshan.[85] ESPN-STAR, which had exclusive rights for India's tour of South Africa in late 2006, also received protection from the Supreme Court for refusing to share its signals.[86]

By early 2007, the dispute between private sports broadcasters and the ministry had reached boiling point. The immense confusion over legal structures meant that virtually every cricket series involving India was preceded by bitter court battles and tremendous uncertainty for viewers. In January 2007, Nimbus's initial refusal to share broadcasts with Prasar Bharati led to many cricket watchers missing the first few games of the India–West Indies series. Unlike ESPN-Star or Ten Sports, Nimbus's new sports channel, Neo Sports, was still not available in all parts of India. Even viewers with satellite connections were unable to see it and the Delhi High Court finally asked Nimbus to share its feed with Doordarshan after a seven-minute delay.[87] Apprehending the anger of the average cricket fan, the central government, on 3 February 2007, promulgated an ordinance that turned its mandatory fee-sharing guidelines into a law. This became the Sports Broadcasting Signals (Mandatory Sharing with Prasar Bharati) Bill that was passed by Parliament on 9 March. It stipulated a 75:25 revenue split between the rights holder and Doordarshan.[88] The Parliamentary debate over the bill reflected two things: the serious concern in the government over the legal challenges to its guidelines and the immense potential of cricket for building public and political opinion. Harnessing political support for an overall law on broadcasting was difficult but when it came to cricket, things were easier. When questioned about the infringement on the private market, Information and Broadcasting Minister Priya Ranjan Dasmunshi repeatedly pointed to the public's right to watch cricket, though the Bill itself was not cricket-specific:

> Cricket is a popular game of the masses...A long battle continued in court to get the terrestrial rights. Fifty million TV homes depend on terrestrial television in the villages, semi-urban areas, even in the rural areas to watch the matches...It was, therefore, a bounden duty of the Government to think something which can justify the cause of the people in the greater public interest. We had to bring the Ordinance keeping in view that the World Cup Cricket is coming up...one should also appreciate that out of the total fund generated through tickets in the whole world, more than 75 per cent is generated from the Indian market alone. But, the tragedy is that the Indian common viewers cannot see the match.[89]

The appeal to the rights of the cricket-watching public found favour with most Parliamentarians, cutting across party lines. The response of Dasmunshi's predecessor, the BJP's Ravishankar Prasad, was typical:

> Cricket, today, is not only a game, but it is almost a passion in India...We are one with you that the ordinary people of the country, who have got a simple antenna of the terrestrial [sic] should have the right to see the cricket matches because cricket, today, is not only an elitist game, but it has reached in rural areas also...If there are 4.5 crores of terrestrial homes in the country, the people must have the right to view the games...So, many litigations are going on. Therefore, in that way, our party appreciate[s] your concerns through this legislation. We are with you.[90]

The Bill raised serious issues that were worthy of debate: the myth of Prasar Bharati's autonomy and its commercial advantages through state patronage, deeper questions about the validity of the state's right to rule on what constituted a sporting event of 'national importance' and the rights of private operators who had paid large amounts of money for broadcast rights through open market bidding. Nimbus, for instance, claimed it would lose 12 per cent of the projected earnings from its $612 million contract to broadcast Indian cricket over the next four years.[91] But there was hardly a dissenting voice in the Parliamentary debate as speaker after speaker reiterated cricket's 'uniting' potential and the 'rights of the common man' to watch the game.[92] In 1995, cricket had been the catalyst for the Supreme Court's landmark judgement that freed the airwaves for private players. In 2007, the national passion for the game was again a catalyst for a major change in broadcast law, but this time it allowed the government to get back some measure of control.

Match ke Mujrim, *Munna Bhai* and Cricket as a Metaphor for Life

Cricket has clearly been central to the rise of Indian satellite television. In fact, the industry has appropriated the game to develop a unique programming model of its own.[93] The Indian television news industry, for instance, unlike in any other country in the world, has consciously ridden on cricket's shoulders to such an extent that by 2006, cricket-oriented programming, in terms of costs, had emerged as one of the most expensive news gathering activities (of all other news genres), if not the most expensive activity (on all news channels)'.[94] So dependent is news television on cricket, for revenues and for viewers; so prominent is cricket in news programming, that it would be fair to call this process the 'cricketization' of Indian television. The reasons for this cricketization lie within the economic structure of the industry and the inherent nature of capitalism itself. The unrelenting drive to construct and capture a national market for maximizing profits led television producers to turn to cricket as the lowest common dominator of what might be termed 'Indian-ness' but television's unrelenting focus, by its very nature, substantially redefined and reinforced these linkages. Given the narrow base of television ratings that increasingly define programming, cricket has emerged as an easy option for success. Cricket, along with Bollywood, has a pan-Indian appeal cutting across socio-economic and regional categories. News of a small-town crime in Mathura may not interest anybody in Kerala but news of the Indian cricket team interests people in every region of India. This is why when news editors want to lift the ratings of any show they look towards cricket. Star's India COO Uday Shankar draws a deep connection between cricket and national identity to explain its emergence as a prime attraction on television, even more so than Bollywood:

> I think as far as Indian identity is concerned, cricket overtakes even Bollywood. While Bollywood is a big source of entertainment, its conscious articulation as an Indian medium by the common people is not so pronounced.
>
> *But cricket is perhaps consciously the most nationalistic activity that Indians indulge in. So to that extent, there is no cricket minus India.* Every time that you watch cricket you are sub-consciously or consciously reminded of the Indian identity...Now in terms of importance, cricket has left Bollywood far behind. It is next only to big political stories and really big economic stories...And very often it overtakes political and economic stories as well.[95]

This is why cricket sells and is big on news television. Shankar's equation of cricket with Indian nationalism is revealing. Certainly this is a link that sociologists and historians have stressed, ever since C.L.R. James inaugurated the discipline of sport history with the statement: 'What do they know of cricket who only cricket know?' Presaging the rise of modern sport history and sociology, his classic *Beyond a Boundary* stressed how cricket either helped form or supplemented social practices based on the intersecting lines of colour and class in colonial and post-colonial societies.[96] It initiated the study of sport as a *relational idiom*, as a magnifying glass amplifying the values, symbols, fissures and tensions of a society. Indian cricket literature, in the past decade, has taken this line of enquiry and a great deal of scholarship has stressed its political dimension. There is no doubt that cricket's hegemony on television is tied to nationalism, and television, for its own purposes, has played a big role. As Arjun Appadurai has noted:

> ...television has now completely transformed cricket culture in India. As several commentators have pointed out, cricket is perfectly suited

> for television, with its many pauses, its spatial concentration of action, and its extended format. For audiences as well as advertisers it is the perfect television sport.[97]

Cricket's sheer length and complexity make it one of the most tele-friendly games on the planet. For instance, a TAM study in 2002 found that in comparison to soccer, cricket offered far greater and more effective opportunities for advertisers—in the stadium as well as on television.[98] This partly explains why in 2001 as many as 473 brands advertised on cricket-related programming, accounting for 16,400 advertising spots on television.[99] For television in general, cricket is a predictable news event, for which advertising can be bought and sold well in advance. This is why Indian television has been cricketized. Television focus on cricket as a spectacle has reinforced the link between cricket and what Appadurai calls the 'erotics of nationhood':

> ...cricket, through the enormous convergence of state, media, and private-sector interests, has come to be identified with 'India', with 'Indian' skill, 'Indian' guts, 'Indian' team spirit, and 'Indian' victories, the bodily pleasure that is at the core of the male viewing experience is simultaneously part of the erotics of nationhood. This erotics, particularly for working-class and lumpen male youth throughout India, is connected deeply to violence, not just because all agonistic sport taps the inclination to aggressiveness but because the divisive demands of class, ethnicity, language, and region in fact make the nation a profoundly contested community. The erotic pleasure of watching cricket for Indian male subjects is the *pleasure of agency* in an imagined community, which in many other arenas is violently contested.[100]

During Pakistan's tour to India in early 2005, Star News started a programme called *Match ke Mujrim* (Criminals of the Match). Set up like a court trial, the show was telecast on the evening of every match and featured a 'trial' of four Indian players who did not perform well on the day. It was performed in front of a live audience and featured a prosecution attorney, former Indian captain Bishen Singh Bedi, and another former cricketer as the defence lawyer. The two would present their case and ask viewers to vote on which Indian player was the villain of the day through SMS. Despite vehement criticism in the media, the show generated a tremendous response for Star News. On the day India lost the Bangalore test against Pakistan, it was staged live out of a public park in the city and more than 10,000 people turned up at the venue. This was in addition to the 20 million or so viewers Star News claimed to have access to. During its one-hour duration, when its phone lines were open for voting, Star News received 35,000 phone messages. This means that nearly 600 people were calling in every minute. The average SMS count for a typical episode, though, hovers between 5,000 and 10,000.[101] For the Star News CEO who initiated this programme, the justification was simple:

> For an average Indian cricket lover, *a player doing something that costs India the match is the closest thing that comes to treason on a daily basis ...*
>
> When people are let down then, unlike in the case of politicians, who still people feel they can fix when someday the guy comes to seek their votes ... With cricketers they have no such comforts... because cricketers in this country make so much money... people feel the guy can still get out to a very casual shot and there is nothing I can do about it ... We have channelized that popular anger in a very democratic forum... We felt it would be good idea to give people a forum to vent their anger and their point of view...
>
> The kind of interventions we make in other activities like politics, civic and municipal administration, economics... we have started doing that in cricket. In the same way that I would look at who's responsible for misery during Bombay floods... who is responsible for this goof-up in administration... Here we look at who is the culprit in the match.[102]

Indian news television is constantly searching for a national 'public' while attempting to create a national 'market'. *Match ke Mujrim* encapsulates this process. It extends the link between cricket and nationalism to a seemingly logical conclusion: players are gladiators for the nation; if they lose, they are traitors.

Entertainment channels have been cricketized as well. The first non-sport channel to get into cricket was Sony's India arm which in 2000 bought the telecast rights for all ICC-designated one-day cricket for seven years. Sony, which until then ran a single entertainment channel in India, launched a second channel, SET Max, specifically to broadcast cricket.[103] Having spent $255 million on the rights, Sony officials re-designed the network's entire branding around cricket. World Cup-winning former captain Kapil Dev was hired as brand ambassador, a series of cricket-related programmes were created around him and the network head made it clear that he expected Kapil to 'do for Sony Entertainment what Amitabh Bachchan did for Star'. A key aim of this strategy was to build programming that would draw in non-sport-watching viewers, with a special focus on families and women.[104] Sony hired women presenters for its 2003 World Cup coverage, who were specifically told to avoid cricket jargon and 'be the voice of the cricket-widows' by asking commentators basic question about the rules of cricket. Cricket magazines railed against what they called the 'invasion of the dumb belles' but by the end of the World Cup Sony's managers themselves were surprised by the ratings.[105] By the second week of the World Cup, 36.5 million women were estimated to have tuned in, nearly 46 per cent of the total viewership.[106]

The Sahara Group took the same route with the telecast of the 2006 India-England cricket series. With Sahara One, the group's flagship entertainment channel, doing badly on the ratings, Sahara bought the television rights for the series hoping cricket would induce non-Sahara viewers to sample it. The network built a synergy between its entertainment programming and cricket by getting the lead actors of all its soap operas to talk about the cricket series during their shows. As Sahara One's CEO explained:

> The ingredients of cricket are quite similar to that of a show on a general entertainment channel. There is drama, there is entertainment, anger and cheerfulness in cricket, which is there in all our soaps, too. Therefore, there is bound to be a great synergy.[107]

Sahara One's advertisement line, *Television ke begum aur cricket ke badshah ek hee channel pe* (The queens of television and the kings of cricket, all on one channel), summed up this philosophy. Kerry Packer's 1977 World Series had initiated the process of converting cricket into a television spectacle[108] but in India this process has evolved more than anywhere else with television networks turning cricket into a continuing soap opera, a spectacle far beyond the game itself.

A good way to examine cricket's rise as a central marker of popular culture is to examine the discourses in the idiom of Bollywood. Until the mid-1980s, cricket was only one of the sports that Bollywood characters engaged with. In the 1970s Hrishikesh Mukherjee film *Gol Maal*, Amol Palekar, as the hero, is forced to embark on a hilarious deception with his boss because he is caught watching a hockey game between India and Pakistan while skipping work. He is equally mad about soccer and in particular about Pele. When asked about his knowledge of soccer in a job interview, he waxes eloquently about the '30,000 *pagal* (madmen)' who went to the Calcutta airport to receive the legendary Pele when he first visited India. Similarly, films like the 1980s *Saahib* focused on a soccer goalkeeper's dedication to his sport. By the mid-1980s though, cricket, like in the wider national discourse, began to take over the portrayal of sport in Bollywood. There were exceptions like the Aamir Khan starrer *Joh Jeeta Woh Sikander*, which revolved around an inter-school cycle race, but increasingly films like *Awwal Number* and *Chamatkar* began to have plots centred around cricket.

At a deeper level, cricket began to seep into the everyday language of Bollywood. The 2006 Sanjay Dutt-starrer *Lage Raho Munna Bhai* was a striking film partly because it resurrects the Mahatma as a popular icon—not just as a distant nationalist figure, but as the personal Mahatma documented by Shahid Amin in his classic study on Chauri Chaura.[109] The second striking feature of the film, and one that reflects a wider trend in Bollywood, is the prominence of cricket terminology as a metaphor for life. The disputed house at the centre of the plot is called 'Second Innings House': the old men living in it are determined to play their 'second innings' in life on the 'front-foot', after having played the 'first innings on the back-foot'. When Gandhi asks the protagonist to follow the path of truth, he responds by articulating his doubts in the language of cricket: the truth would get him 'clean-bowled'. When Munna Bhai and his sidekick, Circuit, take on an astrologer at the end of the film, they try and dispel superstition with a cricketing analogy: 'If he was so good he should point out Indian cricketers whose horoscopes forecasted centuries and the team would never lose. It would always score 1,100 not out'.

Cricket itself is now so enmeshed in the social life of India that for the Indian it has ceased to be a game. It is a social practice that forms the background of everyday life. Indeed, it is a metaphor for life, and Bollywood cannot help but tap into this wider sociological trend. *Lage Raho Munna Bhai* is not the first film to do so. In *Kaante*, Mahesh Manjrekar's character spouts: '*Hindustani do cheez bardaasht nahi kar sakta. Kashmir mein* war *aur* cricket *mein haar*.' (An Indian cannot tolerate two things: war in Kashmir and a loss in cricket). In *Tathastu*, a film about the intensity of parenthood, the entire father-son relationship is built around watching cricket on television and grooming the son to be a cricketer. When the son is admitted to hospital with a severe illness, the father poignantly tells him: 'Get well soon so we can play cricket together'.

These films are unlike the cricket-oriented films that were made in the eighties and early nineties. What is happening now is different. *Lagaan* reflected the populism of cricket as an agent for nationalist agency but the game has now seeped into the everyday language of Bollywood. This Indianization of the imperial sport, of course, began in the colonial period itself but vernacularization of its terminology first began with All India Radio's commentary. In this respect, Arjun Appadurai has equated cricket's rise with the complex process of decolonization and the making of a new Indian identity:

> The general force of the media experience is thus powerfully synesthetic. Cricket is read, heard, and seen, and the force of daily life experiences of cricket, occasional glimpses of live cricket and stars, and the more predictable events of the cricket spectacle on television all conspire not just to vernacularize cricket but to inject the master terms and master tropes of cricket into the bodily practices and body-related fantasies of many young Indian males...cricket is simultaneously larger than life and close to life, because it has been rendered into lives, manuals, and news that are no longer English-mediated...the reception of cricket becomes a critical instrument of subjectivity and agency in the process of decolonization.[110]

The point is that cricket, in the Gramscian sense, is now a central pillar of the cultural superstructure of India. Bollywood is the second pillar of this superstructure and the two have now begun interfacing. Popular culture is a highly contested arena where the idea of India is constantly fought over. It is a relational idiom which reflects the ongoing conflicts, fissures and tensions of society. If one judges by the evidence of Bollywood, the verdict is clear: cricket is now central to the idea of India and Indian-ness and this cricket is very different from the gentlemanly imperial sport that the British had in mind when they first introduced it in India. India has appropriated and Indianized cricket. As Ashis Nandy said: 'Cricket is an Indian game, accidently discovered by the British'.[111]

Conclusion

This chapter began with Aaj Tak's aggressive identification with the Indian colours during the Twenty-twenty World Cup. It was the logical culmination of a process that began in the 1980s. Cricket's rise as the pre-eminent Indian game is intimately connected with Indian television. Television was consciously turned into a mass medium in the 1980s as a political/developmental strategy. This was accompanied by advertising, which augmented the creation of a 'new consumer class' and a new notion of collectivity expressed as 'the middle class'. The fact that these developments coincided with the 1983 World Cup win fundamentally changed the balance of power between cricket and other sports in India. Television created conditions for cricket to become a central component of new notions of national identity and consumer spectacle. The advent of satellite television pushed this linkage further. When television capitalists searched for 'national' publics in their quest to create a 'national' market, they ended up with cricket as the lowest denominator of Indian-ness.

Satellite television is a cultural arena where the idea of India is debated and fought for every day and its focus on cricket since the 1990s has reinforced the centrality of cricket as a pan-Indian marker of 'Indian-ness'. This is a two-way process and world cricket itself has been transformed by the massive infusion of capital from Indian television. The enormous money that television has generated for cricket has also transformed India into the spiritual and financial heart of the global cricket industry. In this process, however, hockey and other sports got left behind by the cold logic of capitalism and expanding markets. This is why Joaquim Carvalho, the hockey coach, was angry and threatened a hunger strike as perhaps the last resort for the nation's deprived hockey players after they weren't given due recognition following their spectacular 7–2 victory against South Korea in the Asia Cup final in 2007.

10

The Army, Indian-ness and Sport
The Nation in the Olympic Ideal

The Indian Army and its 'Mission Olympics'

A full four years after he had won the silver at the Athens Olympics in 2004, the face of Lt. Col. Rajyavardhan Singh Rathore remained one of the first images that struck the traveller as one drives into New Delhi from the city's international airport. India's lone medallist at the 2004 Games, Rathore remained a potent draw for the Army's recruitment planners, his visage decorating a huge, virtually permanent Army hoarding at the entry to Delhi Cantonment.[1] The photograph on the hoarding captured Rathore's face in a moment of pure ecstasy as he kissed his silver medal, with the ceremonial olive wreath on his head. A caption below the photograph informed the traveller: 'Join the Indian Army, Be a Winner for Life'. Rathore with his silver, only the fourth Olympic medal India has won since 1980, has been turned into a poster boy for the Indian Army's recruitment programme.[2]

This is understandable, given that he is a professional soldier in the Indian Army, which is currently suffering from a huge shortage of personnel.[3] What merits closer attention though is the discourse about the Army, the Olympics and Indian nationalism that followed India's failure to win more medals at Athens 2004. Speaking at a public function, President A.P.J. Abdul Kalam tapped into popular sentiment about the continuing Olympic failures when he asked the Army to come to the rescue: 'Why are we not winning Olympic medals is working on your mind. It is working on my mind also!... Some countries use armed forces. If our army decides to use one brigade only for sports, we will have arrived in the international sports scene'.[4] The Army responded by publicizing its commitment to a new programme called 'Mission Olympics'. This included recruiting young and talented sportsmen from around the country, giving them an Army rank without involving them in military work and training them for the 2008 Olympics. As far back as July 2001, after a similar debacle at Sydney, the Army had created a sports academy—the Army Sports Institute—at Pune with a funding of Rs 60 crore from the defence ministry's annual budget. The ministry's official website makes the aims of this project clear: 'To restore national pride in the hearts of our fellow countrymen and to project a winning image of the Army, the Chief of Army Staff has availed of the opportunity to meet the challenge of the Olympics'.[5]

These moves came at a time of great hand-wringing in the mainstream media about India's 'humiliation' at the Olympics. In a comment typical of the media discourse in 2004, Chandigarh's *Tribune* bemoaned the lack of sporting success, equating it with 'national' failure: 'A country of a billion people, but India is left to bite the dust even when facing competitions from countries like Moldova or Ethiopia at international arenas. Lack of proper training, infrastructure, planning and crass callousness of those at the helm have combined to ensure lacklustre performance by Indians in the competitions as competitive as Olympics [sic].'[6] Simultaneously, the Army's Mission Olympics was received by the press with virtually universal acclaim, praise that tapped into its credentials as a respected bulwark of the nation itself: 'If determination, dedication and discipline are the pre-requisite of success, the Indian Army has these in abundance. Besides, the Army has the advantage of accountability. So faith will not be misplaced if it is reposed in the Indian Army to win Olympic medals for the country'.[7] In other words, this discourse believed that India's Olympic efforts had failed because of poor sports management and only the Army was capable of turning things around. A typical view expressed at an online discussion group run by a news website on the topic illustrates this point: 'I do expect a lot from the Army. It will be all the more better if the Indian Olympic Association and its representatives are taken over by the Army. No one wants to see politicians involved in anything constructive'.[8]

The above discussion raises three issues about India's Olympic discourse over the past four years: the Olympics is clearly seen as a barometer of national pride and therefore viewed through a nationalist gaze; Olympic failures are blamed on sports management bodies which are seen as parochial and only interested in politics; the Indian Army, perceived as an apolitical edifice of the nation, is now seen by many as the last resort, capable of salvaging India's dream of winning Olympic medals. As such, India's engagement with Olympism is a useful entry point to understanding changing notions of Indian nationalism as well as the role of the Indian Army in a democratic Indian state.

What has been the Indian Army's role in India's Olympic movement and why has it become so central to it? The answer to these queries provide answers to other crucial issues: Why are the Olympics so important to Indian nationalism? To what extent are differences in internal regional identities responsible for India's Olympic failures and why have nationalist sentiments not overcome these? By fleshing out the history of the Indian Army's sporting engagement, this chapter sheds light on the development of notions of Indian-ness, the constant struggle with centrifugal regional identities, the politics of the Indian empire and the Army's transition from an imperial to a nationalist, apolitical force in independent India. At its core, Indian Olympism is a stage where competing Indian identities grapple with each other to impose their own hegemony. By focusing on the Army, this chapter provides new material that will feed into existing debates about the 'the idea of India' itself and indeed, questions about how many Indias exist within the Indian nation-state.

Sepoys on the Playing Field: 'The Principle Source of Sporting Inspiration'

Most sport historians of India acknowledge the British Indian Army's role in inculcating the practice of modern sport in the furthermost corners of the subcontinent. Writing in 1959, the pioneering sport administrator Anthony De Mello was unambiguous on this score:

> The principal source in the history of modern India is the British Army, whose members, for so long stationed in our country, had introduced most of the games we play...The inspiration for most of our sports came, as I have said, from the British Army.[9]

This claim was by no means an exaggeration. In the 19th century, at a time when virtually all Western sporting disciplines were being standardized into their present form, troops belonging first to the East India Company, and then the British Army carried these forms wherever they went. This is true of virtually all modern sports associated with Britain, with the exception of rugby (India's hard grounds precluding that possibility). Sport and what became known as the 'games ethic' was a way of life and its cultural dispersion was inevitable. The Army was its greatest conduit, simply by virtue of being the British organization with the greatest spread across the country. For instance, in the case of cricket, while most historians have traditionally attributed its organized rise in India to the Parsis of Bombay in the 1840s, there is now new evidence to show that the first Indians who took it up were sepoys of the East India Company. News reports published in the *Sporting Intelligence Magazine* brought out by the editor of the *Englishman* newspaper in 1833–50 document cricket matches played by Indian sepoys in places as far apart as Cuttack, Silchar, Barrackpore, Dum Dum, Agra, Cuttack, Midnapore and Sylhet.[10] These reports show that cricket was well established in the Indian heartland through the agency of the Army, well before Bombay's Parsi elites adopted it.

The early popularity of cricket among the sepoys was ascribed to the game's potential to bridge the differences between the European and the native. A report drew attention to this aspect of the sport, noting: 'Cricket is essential in improving one of the great defects, so often complained of, the distance of the Europeans in the intercourse with the native.' It goes on to suggest that European officers, from the senior to the junior, encouraged the game either as spectators or players. 'Were they not to do so…I fear the sepoys would not long continue to play.'[11] But once introduced, every cultural form assumes a life of its own. It is equally true that the sepoys in many cases were matching their English counterparts on the playing field. Contemporary descriptions of cricket in East India Army's maidans indicate that matches that pitted the native sepoys against European officers can also be seen as early historical prototypes of the fictional nationalist playing field depicted in the film *Lagaan*. As we have speculated elsewhere, 'It may be a mere coincidence that the cities and towns where sepoy cricket was fairly well developed were those which were prominent in the sepoy uprising of 1857'.[12]

Similarly, modern observers attribute the early spread of hockey to the British Army. While hockey, loosely defined, has historic antecedents going back to the stick games played by the ancient Greeks, it was invented in its modern form on the playing fields of imperial England. In his short account of the history of hockey, Chris Moore emphasizes that it was adopted in the empire:

> ...Mainly, it must be said because of the British Army which, in those imperial days, traveled widely in order to keep a watchful eye on all those red bits on the map. Wherever the army went they tended to take the British way of life with them. Including hockey. And that is how the game invented on the English cricket field came to be played the world over... At that time the British Army was everywhere, looking after the far flung domains of the Widow of Windsor. Notably, of course, in India.[13]

It is no accident that the great Dhyan Chand learnt all his hockey skills on regimental hockey fields. Both Chand and his brother Roop Singh, who also served India with distinction, were soldiers. Dhyan Chand's father, Subedar Sameshwar Dutt Singh, also played hockey in the Army and had grown up in a martial ambience where physical activity was valued. Dhyan Chand joined the First Brahmin Regiment in 1922, later transferring to the Punjab Regiment, and his real training began only after he put on the uniform. As he put it, 'I do not remember whether I played any hockey worth mentioning before I joined the Army.' His description of how he learnt the craft of the game illustrates the role of the Army in developing Indian sport:

> I shall tell you when I first started playing hockey. It was just an accident how it came about. When I joined the First Brahmin Regiment, we had a *Subedar-Major* by the name of Bale Tiwari who was a keen hockey enthusiast and a very fine player. He took a fancy to me.
>
> My regiment was well-known in hockey circles, and hockey was the only outdoor game to which the regiment devoted most of its sporting attention. Bale Tiwari initiated me into this game and gave me my first lessons. He was my guru. We had no fixed times at the Cantonment to play hockey. We indulged in it at all hours of the day.[14]

The indulgence in sport stemmed from two reasons. At one level, it was simply a consequence of British troops carrying their own culture with them. It is equally true, though, that the British Indian Army purposely adopted sport as a means of inculcating *esprit de corps* among its troops, native and European. In the case of hockey, one observer has noted tongue-in-cheek that doubtless part of its appeal was 'the wondrous chance it gave to privates and lance corporals to hit the colonel indiscriminately while pretending to aim the ball'.[15] Whether the colonels were hit or not, there is no doubt that team sports were seen by them as essential tools to develop bonds among men who were expected to fight shoulder to shoulder, besides serving the purpose of keeping them usefully occupied in peace time.

In a colonial force where notions of kinship and izzat (honour) were the key to inter-personal bonding,[16] sport was, in modern parlance, a useful management tool. In that sense, sport fulfilled a deeper social purpose specific to the martial traditions of the Army and we will return to this theme of the Army's special need for sporting activity later in the chapter. For now, it is enough to note that so pervasive was the Army's influence on hockey that the Army Sports Control Board virtually controlled Indian hockey affairs until at least 1928. As Dhyan Chand was to record:

> ...the IHF in those days was largely conducted by Army men; in fact the president of the IHF was Major Burn-Murdoch.
>
> There is a feeling in some ill-informed quarters that Englishmen did not do much for hockey in India. This is not quite true. For my hockey I am gratefully indebted to British Army Officers who not only took great interest in this game, but also played with us on all occasions forgetting their official rank and status.[17]

Dhyan Chand was not an exception as a successful soldier-sportsman in colonial India. It is no coincidence that Sansarpur, a tiny village on the outskirts of Jalandhar cantonment, produced as many great hockey players as it did. When the British Indian Army took over the entire agricultural land of the village for building the new Jalandhar cantonment, it was thought prudent to not only introduce hockey as a means of keeping village youth occupied but also to provide a source for fresh, physically fit recruits. Sansarpur emerged not only as a major breeding ground for the Army but also produced 14 Olympians and perhaps 'the world's highest per capita of Olympic medals'.[18] As late as 1996, when a *Sports Illustrated* reporter visited the village, he noted that the Army's legacy had deep roots. As a local told the magazine reporter, 'British Army brought hockey here at the turn of the century...The village's first Olympian was Colonel Singh in 1932'.[19] In fact, it would not be an exaggeration to say that the early rise of Punjab as the cradle of Indian hockey and the centrality of Punjabis in the Indian Army's recruitment after the 1857 Mutiny are not entirely unconnected. While the pre-eminence of hockey in colonial Punjab is also linked to the patronage of the house of Patiala and the complex interplay of princely politics, in a state where virtually every village boasted of serving or retired soldiers, social conditions enabled the game's players to acquire a pedigree and a skill set that was passed on from generation to generation in the early years.

The story of Indian football is also similar, with the Army leaving a deep imprint in the early years. While it is impossible to ascertain when the game was first played in India, it is reasonably clear that it came with the East India Company. Football's early pioneers were 'officers and men of Trading Farms and Regimental Battalions', besides naval officers who used to play at ports of call like Calcutta, Bombay, Madras and Karachi.[20] This is not to suggest that sport remained a preserve only of soldiers and men-in-arms. It is true though that the institutional foundation of football in India was laid by the defence services-led Dalhousie Club in 1878—acknowledged as the oldest football club in India.[21] There were no organized tournaments until the Dalhousie Club showed the way in 1889. The club raised subscriptions from commercial houses and started the Trades Cup in that year. For four years the tournament was the biggest event in the football calendar until the IFA Shield became the most prestigious tournament from 1893 onwards. A little later the Calcutta-based Indian Football Association (IFA) was affiliated to the English F.A. and it was only then that Indian football found another home.[22] Yet, a deeper analysis of the politics of Indian football until independence reveals that while the IFA was now the nodal body, the British-controlled Army Sports Control Board continued to hold the balance of power in the management of the sport.

Hamlet's Prince of Denmark: The Army and Football Politics in Colonial India

The Maharaja of Patiala and G.D. Sondhi succeeded Dorabji Tata and A.G. Noehren as president and secretary of the IOA in the late

1920s. These successions, it seems, marked the emergence of Indian Olympism as a new battleground for regional supremacy.[23] Evidence from elsewhere makes it clear that Indian sport in this period was racked by regional and princely tussles for hegemony. With Bombay taking the lead in cricket and Bengal doing the same in soccer, it was imperative for north India to take the lead in matters of Olympic sport.[24] Given this backdrop, the formation of the All India Football Federation (AIFA) in 1935 is a prime example of the ensuing turf wars, triggering off a bitter struggle for supremacy between Indian states—Bengal on the one hand and western and northern Indian states on the other, for assertion of supremacy over the control of the game.[25] As the Calcutta IFA—the country's oldest soccer association—and the AIFF locked horns over who really represented 'India' in football, the Bengali IFA repeatedly looked to the British Football Association as a source of legitimacy.

Joya Chatterji, among others, has argued that Muslim political ascendancy in 1930s Bengal led the Hindu bhadralok, patrons of sport, to look favourably upon British rule. Muslim political ascendancy led to the Bengali bhadralok reappraising their past and looking upon the British as liberators who had freed the Hindus of Bengal from Muslim rule.[26] Therefore, when faced with challenges from other Indian states over the control of soccer, they fell back on loyalist support of the British Football Association. This also explains why the bhadralok did not prevent the exclusively European Calcutta and Ballygunge Cricket Clubs from wielding power over Bengali cricket in the 1930s and 1940s.[27]

In such a backdrop, the struggle for control over soccer brought out in sharp relief the centrality of the British Indian Army in Indian affairs. Sport has always been a central component of military life but in an imperial context the Army's role became crucial.[28] Through the 1930s, as the conflict raged between different states, the Army Sports Control Board (ASCB) served as a neutral arbiter—the hinge on which the outcome depended. The Bengal IFA lobby, led by the Maharaja of Santosh, continually looked to British support.[29] Much like the rival factions of Indian hockey would look to the IHF for legitimacy in the 1970s, in this early battle over Indian football a great deal depended on recognition by the British Football Association. In colonial India, this, in turn, depended on patronage from the British Indian Army and its powerful Sports Control Board. In an emerging nation grappling with the politics of provincial identity in the sporting arena, the powerful institution of the Army emerged as a match referee.

To understand the role of the Army, we first need to take a brief look at the magnitude of the problems confronting Indian football, which lacked a truly national representative body until well into the 1930s. When the Maharaja of Santosh convened a conference of the provincial soccer associations of the country at Darbhanga in September 1935,[30] newspaper reports indicated that it would mark the formation of a new all-India governing body for the game. Things, however, did not go according to plan. Designated to chair the proceedings, the Maharaja found delegates from Delhi and Bombay unwilling to accept a Bengali chairperson.[31] He was also told that these delegates, and those from other states, were keen to keep Bengal out of the body and had already drafted the constitution of the all-India body. This is when the Maharaja decided to abandon the conference and return to Calcutta.[32] We must emphasize that it would be wrong to paint the non-Bengali delegates as the villains in this drama. The Maharaja and the Bengali lobby were perceived as overbearing by other states. The details of who was at fault are not as important as the fact that it ended with the Bengali delegation, thwarted in its bid for control, withdrawing. The Maharaja caught something of the real import of this failure, when he noted:

> I am going away from Darbhanga sorely disappointed over the question of the formation of an All India Federation. *I found the provinces of India hopelessly divided on this front. Internal suspicion and provincial jealousies retarded progress of the country in almost every department of public life.* I find that even the field of sport is unable to rise above these elements.[33]

Despite the lack of a national consensus on the question of representation and despite Bengal's non-cooperation, the All India Football Association was born at Darbhanga on 21 September 1935.[34] But it could not function smoothly for long. With Bengal opposed to the body, it was difficult for AIFA to raise necessary funds for its maintenance. Further, with the Maharaja of Santosh leading the opposition against it, other princes, allies of the Maharaja, refrained from according patronage to the newly formed body:[35] as the *Amrita Bazar Patrika* put it, an all-India body without Calcutta's premier IFA[36] was like 'the staging of Hamlet without the prince of Denmark'. As India's oldest football association, IFA's trump card was the fact that it had recognition from the British Football Assocation:[37]

> The Indian Football Federation was formed last year after the Darbhanga convention. But it has ever remained an isolated organization in which the IFA, the oldest and greatest corporate soccer body of India and the only Association which has been recognized by the FA of England, never joined. In fact the whole procedure can be compared to the staging of Hamlet without the prince of Denmark.[38]

If IFA was the prince of Denmark then the problem was that the prince of Denmark did not just want to be in *Hamlet*, he wanted to be Hamlet itself. Repeated efforts to find a compromise solution between AIFA and IFA failed over the Bengali insistence to retain total control. [39]

For all of IFA's jostling, the real prince of Denmark in the ensuing drama, it seems, was the Army Sports Control Board. The position of IFA vis-à-vis AIFA was strengthened when the Board decided to support IFA.[40] Accordingly, all local military sides were enlisted to take part in the Calcutta Football League to be conducted by IFA in June-July 1936.[41] It was also declared that the usual contingent of military teams would take part in the IFA shield competition.[42] The continued support of the Board was viewed in many quarters as the last nail in the coffin of AIFA. This support, it was argued, signalled the disintegration of the sovereignty of AIFA:[43]

> Though maintaining its legal position intact and unassailable, the AIFA had to admit de-facto defeat from Attock to Cape Comorin. The rout seemed almost to be complete, with the Army Sports Control Board holding the whip hand throughout.[44]

No other sports body had a national reach. The support of the Army Sports Control Board and its patronage encouraged IFA to once again issue a circular to the soccer associations of the country giving a fresh call to set up an all-India body under its banner.[45] IFA emphasized that it was ready and willing to enlarge its constitution by giving adequate representation on its council to all the provincial soccer associations.[46] It was also declared that the scheme had the sanction of the Football Association of England. To this end, IFA decided to organize a conference at Calcutta in December 1936 where this new body would finally come into existence.[47] The catch was that, emboldened by Army support, IFA was proposing nothing less than a recognition of itself as the national body, with token representation for others.

Not surprisingly, representatives from Delhi and Bombay reacted with suspicion to the new scheme. They immediately denounced it as one that sought direct dominance of IFA and Calcutta over all the other associations of the country.[48]

However, the UP association supported Bengal, suggesting that it was time to end the long drawn quarrel. The association was of the opinion that there was no denying Bengal's valuable service to the cause of football in India, whereby it was essential for Bengal to take the lead in forming the all-India body.[49] It also felt that a joint meeting attended by representatives of IFA, AIFA and the Army Sports Control Board was crucial to solve the impasse.[50] While representatives from Lucknow, Orissa, Jamshedpur, Ranchi, Patna, Jamalpur, Hazaribagh and UP had supported the Maharaja of Santosh and IFA, it was clearly the Army that was the real McCoy.[51] This is why, when the Maharaja wrote to thank the delegates for support, he emphasized that his hopes lay in the continued guidance of the Football Association of England and the potential co-operation of the Army in India.[52]

The conflict between Bengal and the other provinces did not abate and things again came to a head in December 1936.[53] The proposed conference at Calcutta proved a non-starter, and the fate of soccer in the country was left hanging by a thread. This was when the Army Sports Control Board put its foot down, solving the crisis that had plagued the fortunes of soccer in India for almost a decade. Its representative decided to strike a compromise between the two bodies by taking the initiative to form the new All India Football Federation, a body which would give considerable importance to IFA while not giving it the control it wanted.[54] With this in view, the Board invited all of India's soccer associations to usher in the new federation at a conference in Shimla in May 1937.[55] Bengal had so far fought tooth and nail against such a solution but it was the best result under the circumstances. Further, Bengal was in no position to alienate the Army Board, whose support was key to the survival of IFA. Though the IFA tried its best to postpone the formation of AIFF to September, the Army Board held firm.[56]

In a personal letter sent to the Maharaja of Santosh, the representative of the Board declared his intention to go ahead with the formation of AIFF at Shimla in May 1937. The Maharaja did try to stonewall by appearing reluctant to attend the conclave but now the Board used its clout, firmly putting him in his place:[57]

> I am sorry to say that it is quite impossible to accede to your request that the meeting, to be held next month at Simla and at which we hope to bring into being the All India Football Federation, should be postponed till July. As you know, the original date has already been put back one month to suit the IFA with considerable inconvenience to the other parties concerned, and any further postponement would, I know, cause great offence to them and upset all their arrangements. I regret that the present date is not very convenient for the IFA but I hope you will find it possible to send a suitable representative to the meeting.
>
> Your question regarding the number of representatives, which the IFA should send to the meeting is a little complicated...Until these rules have been approved, there can be no authority for the IFA to have more than one representative. I suggest therefore that the only possible solution is for the IFA to send one representative to the meeting; for the initial proceedings he will have only one vote; after the draft rules have been approved he will have two votes for all subsequent business.
>
> I agree that there is much to be said for accepting Calcutta as the headquarters of the AIFF for the first few years. Obviously, however, the decision cannot rest with me as the question will have to be decided by the forthcoming meeting. I also regret very much that you consider that the IFA has not been well treated. Since I became connected with this affair I have tried to be quite impartial and incidentally to ensure that sufficient weight was given to the prestige and traditions of the IFA. The alternative suggestion that the IFA should to all intents and purposes absorb thc AIFA was never of course a practical solution.[58]

The representative of the Board concluded the letter saying:

> I must confess that I find the last few lines of your letter rather perturbing as they imply that even at this late stage in the proceedings you may find it impossible to accept the AIFF or to co-operate loyally with such a body. I have, however, decided that if the meeting at Simla next month is unsuccessful and does not result in the formation of the AIFF to be loyally supported by all concerned, I shall be forced to refrain from any further

> participation in this football controversy. In such a contingency, I will be forced to forward to the FA in England a report on the happenings of the last few months and on the reasons for the breakdown of negotiations and thereafter events in India would have to follow their normal course.[59]

With the possibility of the Football Association of England turning its back on Bengal, the Maharaja of Santosh had no alternative but to support the formation of the AIFF. Faced with an ultimatum, the Bengal IFA backed down. The other associations too could not oppose it because it catered to their central demand, i.e., Bengal was no longer the sole arbiter of the fortunes of soccer in the country. Accordingly, a compromise AIFF come into existence in 1937, entirely due to the clout of the Indian Army. If Indian sport serves as a barometer for measuring political relations in the country, then this exchange points to the central role of the colonial Indian Army as the balancing fulcrum in regional rivalries.

Athletes in Olive Green: The Army and Sport in Independent India

After independence, the Army continued to play an important role in Indian sport although its position in a post-colonial setting had changed; it was now an apolitical institution. The Congress nationalist elite that came to power in 1947 had always been suspicious of the Army's steadfast loyalty to the British during the years of the independence movement and the Army was gradually weaned away from the pre-eminence it had hitherto enjoyed in the structures of power in New Delhi.[60] At one level, this was also a response to the multiple threats from Pakistan in the years following the 1948 war over Kashmir but the overall tenor of the time was to reduce the Army's perceived potential to intervene in politics.

As the Army was downgraded, the first three defence ministers—Baldev Singh, Gopalaswamy Ayyangar and Kailash Nath Katju—also tended to be comparatively less influential with Nehru as compared to other powerful Cabinet ministers like Maulana Azad and Govind Ballabh Pant. When Nehru's close confidante Krishna Menon was appointed defence minister in 1956, it did increase the ministry's profile, but for all the wrong reasons. The Army top brass was so upset with his disdain for them that General Thimayya resigned as Army chief.[61] It wasn't just about differences in perception and personal animosities. In real terms too, the Army found that Indian defence expenditure averaged a low 2 per cent of the GNP yearly, until the rude shock of the 1962 war with China.[62]

As its institutional clout declined, the Army could no longer act as a political force in sport in the manner that it had in the crisis over football in the 1930s. Be that as it may, sport continued to be central to day-to-day life in regimental maidans across the country. At least until the early 1970s, this ensured that the Army remained the dominant force in national competitions in most sporting disciplines. As it turned from being imperial arbiter to national protector, its sporting activities too became very much an extension of its new role as defender of the nation. While it was no longer to play a direct role in the politics of sport per se, the Indian sporting arena itself could not have survived without the Army's quiet lifeline of talent and expertise.

The Army's role in Indian Olympism after independence, therefore, provides valuable insights into imperial and post-imperial nationalistic assertion and denial. It also sheds light on the changing nature of the Indian Army and its place in democratic India. As this chapter will show, its dominance in sport declined from the 1970s as a direct function of its own changing profile and its growing entanglement in internal security duties.

So pre-eminent was the Army in Indian sport in the early years of independence that in 1962, a piece in the Indian Olympic Association's official journal could declare unambiguously:

> Little research is necessary to establish the fact that Services are today the backbone of the country's sporting endeavour. No fewer than nine of the major national championships in various branches of sport are held by Services teams or individuals today. Though still far from world standards the gap is gradually being narrowed.[63]

A roll call of the defence services' dominance in national sport in the first decade and a half of independence proves this point. At least until 1962, the Services held complete sway over national athletic competitions. Milkha Singh, the greatest male athlete India has ever known, began his career as a cook in the Army and it was from there that he rose to the heights of the Rome Olympics. From 1956–57 onwards, the Services dominated swimming as well. Services teams held the national basketball title for five consecutive years between 1957 and 1962 and the national boxing title between 1956–62.[64] In those early years, soldiers held the Gymnastics title seven times and featured on the honours roll of hockey four times.[65] They also achieved great success in golf,[66] squash, volleyball,[67] wrestling, football[68] and cycling,[69] winning a total of 56 national titles across all sports until 1962.

So dominant were soldiers in Indian sport that when the Sino-Indian war broke out in 1962, India was forced to withdraw from the Empire and Commonwealth Games at Perth that year. On its own, this was entirely understandable given the great shock and humiliation that the country was reeling from at the time. But there was another reason for the withdrawal. As the IOA noted:

> Two reasons that must have swayed the Government were the release of foreign exchange and the fact that a great number of Servicemen would be on 'sports duty'. *The composition of the team would have amounted to more than 50% of the contingent at Perth being athletes from the Services.*[70]

Simply put, without the soldiers, there was hardly a national team. This is the true measure of what the Services meant for Indian sport.

This is partly why in the national catharsis that followed the humiliation on the Chinese border, sportsmen from other professions were at the forefront of the effort to contribute to the emergency National Defence Fund created by the finance minister. Their efforts could not have matched those of the big business houses but carried great symbolism. Balbir Singh, the 1956 Olympic hockey captain, donated all three of his Olympic golds; K.D. Singh 'Babu' offered to donate his 1948 gold from the London Olympics; P.K. Bannerjee, India's 1960 Olympic football captain, gave away three of his gold medals from national competitions; Keshav Datt, who had played hockey for India at London and Helsinki, gave away his Olympic medals too; and S.K. Chatterjee, of the 1911 historic Mohun Bagan team which beat the East Yorkshire team to win the IFA Shield, gave away his gold medal from the club.[71]

The donations spree was not just restricted to Olympians. Sandhya Chandra, the national swimming champion, gave away her two national golds, Dilip Bose donated the Asian Tennis championship trophy[72] and Bengal's film stars organized a special cricket match for Indian cricketers to raise money for the war effort. The likes of Uttam Kumar and Mala Sinha rubbed shoulders with Lala Amarnath in Calcutta to add impetus to the fund-raising drive.[73] In addition, the pages of the IOA official journal were filled with fervent appeals for all sportsmen to invest in Defence Deposit Certificates—'Lend to Defend' was the catchline. The IOA appealed to all sports associations across the country to hold special events to collect money for the Defence Fund, arguing that sport was 'the most popular form of entertainment in the country' and urging its members to tap into its monetary potential by showcasing top stars in special events.[74] It is not known how much money was generated in this manner but there is no doubt that India's sporting community did its utmost to pay its debt to the Army at a time of national crisis. In the words of K.D. Singh 'Babu': 'Since I won this gold medal for the country, I think its best utilization would be none other than the cause of the country at a time when the enemy is knocking on our door'.[75]

'Army of Athletes': Sport, the Psychology of Soldiers and the Military Ideal

The Indian Army's evolution from a colonial force to the silent vanguard of the nationalist ideal in independent India is one reason for the stability of the modern Indian nation-state. Stephen Cohen, for instance, has shown that though the Army was never in any sense a major instrument for the liberation of the subcontinent, it nevertheless continues to have a profound influence on the polity.[76] More recently, Ramachandra Guha, among others, has identified the Army's steadfast professionalism—and its divorce from overt politics—as one of the reasons why Indian democracy endures, in sharp contrast to virtually every other post-colonial state.[77] The Army's cultural influence as a pan-Indian, disciplined, secular force has made it one of the staunchest pillars of modern India. In this context, its influence on Indian sport derives from the nature of the military force itself and the structures of governance that it has followed as a legacy of the colonial period. After independence, these traditions were re-labelled with the new aims of modern Indian nationalism. Yet the Army's imprint on the sporting arena has so far been a forgotten footnote in studies of the Army and, indeed, its wider role in the nation.

The Indian Army of post-colonial India continued the intense focus on sporting activity that it had inherited from the British. The Army's dominance in sport was not simply a function of its large numbers and facilities. The reasons for this are rooted in the sociological imperatives of creating a disciplined military force. Trained in the ways of dominant British culture, the Army's Indian officers continued after independence the British tradition of the 'Games Ethic' that saw sporting achievement as a form of character building and teamwork. There was something in the way of life of the Services that produced the kind of results that the Army's sportsmen delivered in the early years. In the 'gentlemanly' world of the Army's elite, sport was seen as a form of social mobility. It was a means of inculcating regimental bonding among men whose fighting potential was supposed to depend on such fraternal ties. As one IOA report noted:

> After a hard day's work (life can be tough in the Services) the men let off steam in some sporting activity. The big advantage is that officers in charge of sport in battalions and regiments have a solid technical background. This means that novices are taught on correct lines. A promising sportsman is encouraged to specialize and in a few months a new champion is in the making.[78]

Sport was so important that it often became a key barometer of a regiment's izzat, a tool for building fierce pride among soldiers and the competitive spirit that was seen as a tool to weld diverse groups of men into cohesive units. The playing field offered officers a useful arena to bond with the men they commanded and to build ties of kinship. Obedience flowed from respect, and what better way to build respect than by rubbing shoulders with subordinates as equals on the field? In a profession where following orders could sometimes mean certain death on the battlefield, astute commanders knew that the rigid bonds of Army discipline needed the glue of personal bonding. This was particularly important for young officers who were expected to lead soldiers directly in battle. As one senior former Army officer puts it:

> Men always look up to their commander. A hierarchy of kinship exists in the Army and this is strengthened in the sports field, especially if

> commanders play with the troops. It's the best place to get to know your men intimately. This is why there was always an emphasis on sports and particularly on youngsters. Your personality got built up on the sports field, in the eyes of the men and half your life as a youngster was spent on the playing grounds.[79]

Brig. Rakesh Mehta, who captained the Services cross-country team in the 1970s, remembers that when he was commissioned into the Army in 1970, the respect and esteem of a fighting unit in soldierly canteens and barracks depended on its sporting prowess. Commanding Officers saw the success of their regiments in sporting competitions as a way of raising their own profile and focused intensely on training athletes. In a martial world, 'manly' achievements on the playing field were highly valued and he remembers that in his regiment, virtually every officer, including the CO, played in some team or the other.[80] One of the key markers of regimental izzat was the laurels won in inter-regimental competitions. As another observer put it:

> Pride plays a big part in the fierce competitive spirit that exists in the Services. Regiments and divisions have gloriously old battle honours and this is an incentive for proud rivalry, which cannot be matched on the 'civvy street'.[81]

Ambitious young commanders never overlooked this aspect. In a fighting force where pride and tradition dictated identity, defeat on the sporting field was always looked upon as a slur on a regiment's reputation, linked to notions of honour and never to be tolerated.

In this context, it is instructive that in his foreword to Dhyan Chand's memoirs, Maj. Gen. A.A. Rudra chose to highlight what he meant for his regiment. His brief note on a career that was littered with breathtaking games for club and country, mentioned only one—played in defence of the regiment. Once, when playing in the final of the Punjab Indian Infantry tournament in Jhelum, Dhyan Chand's side was down by two goals to nil with only four minutes to go. This was when his commanding officer called out, '*Aage bado jawan, kuch toh karo Dhyan*' (Go forward soldier! Do something about it Dhyan!)' Dhyan Chand responded with three goals in four minutes to lead his team to victory. While the goals were a tribute to Dhyan Chand's own abilities, the incident also reveals the fierce competitive spirit of inter-regimental sport.[82] Dhyan Chand himself emphasized that annual tournaments were 'eagerly competed for' and that 'our officers felt very proud'.

Historians of the British Indian Army have documented that loyalty often accrued from personal ties in the feudal mode that were not necessarily based on the rank of the officer in question alone, but also his personal attributes. Respect had to be won and once given it was almost always unquestioned.[83] The independent Indian Army continued this tradition. In that sense, the use of the sporting field was more than just about the sport itself. It was a management tool. The Duke of Wellington, who attributed his victory at Waterloo to the 'playing fields of Eton' would have understood.

In a world before the evolution of the hi-tech battlefield, soldierly loyalties grew from elemental passions. A telling anecdote from an air defence regiment illustrates this beautifully. Out on a war game, the NCO asked a young major where to place the anti-aircraft gun. The major wanted to sit in the shade so he simply ordered for it to be placed under a tree, conveniently forgetting the sheer uselessness of such a position for a gun that was supposed to shoot into the sky. When the NCO objected for perfectly valid military reasons, the major, also a burly competitive wrestler, simply responded: 'Don't talk too much with me. If you don't like it, let's wrestle and he who wins will put the gun where he wants'. That was the end of the argument. The gun remained under the tree and the major, whose conduct could justifiably be termed unprofessional, became the toast of the soldier's barracks for his 'manliness'. On such talk are soldierly loyalties and ties of brotherhood sometimes built. [84]

The Indian Army is by no means unique in its focus on sport. It is well documented, for instance, that between 1917 and 1919, the US armed forces too made sports and athletics central components of military life. Millions of enlisted men participated in organized sport at domestic training camps and behind the frontlines in France. So intense was this focus that one writer observed: 'Uncle Sam has created not only an army of soldiers', but 'an army of athletes'.[85] In the American case, the linking of sport and the military was a new one, a reformist generation of officers after the Spanish–American war, using sport as a means to combat 'desertion, alcohol and the lure of prostitution'. As one officer put it, 'There is no better way to make a good sailor and at the same time a loyal and true man to ship and country, than [through] these athletics contests'.[86] According to one US military historian:

> Civilian military officials embraced sport and athletics as the most efficient means to cultivate national vitality, citizenship and the martial spirit. Military training, infused with a heavy dose of sports and athletics, would not only train American men in the 'soldierly values' of obedience, citizenship, and combat, but would also usefully repair class schisms and restore social order and patriotism to the nation.[87]

The Americans were learning what the Indian Army had always known. The success of military sport during WWI surpassed all expectations and 'accelerated the development of a national sports culture'[88] in the United States. Sport became an essential element of military training on the lines suggested by planners since the beginning of the 20th century. As early as 1906, one writer had suggested that 'Uncle Sam has not encouraged athletics for amusement', but for the way in which it produced *esprit de corps* among both officers and enlisted men, 'a rebuilding process which begins when the soldier puts on the blue or khakhi'.[89] This is precisely the planning principle that is at the heart of life in the Indian defence services.

'Scrape the Bottom of the Barrel': A Creaking Army and the Decline of Sport (1989–2008)

When the Air Defence Missile Regiment was raised in 1985, the first task its commanding officer Col. V.B. Mohan faced was to establish its reputation in a brigade full of illustrious old regiments. He responded by identifying good sportsmen among his new recruits and putting them into training. Within a year, these new sportsmen were winning inter-regimental tournaments, heralding 436's arrival in a pantheon of old regiments. In the words of one of Col. Mohan's battery commanders, the sportsmen became the 'pride of the regiment'. 'Sport was a way of projecting the CO and the Regiment's personality in the Army.'[90]

All this changed drastically in the late 1980s. From then on, the Indian Army has seen an unprecedented level of troop commitment. Up to four divisions were deployed in Sri Lanka from 1987 until their withdrawal in 1990. The north-eastern insurgencies required even greater troop deployment and so did Punjab until 1993 with Operation

Rakshak. But the greatest challenge came from the militancy in Kashmir from 1989 onwards.[91] By a rough estimate, some 4 lakh troops are currently actively deployed in Kashmir—on the Line of Control, in Siachen and in counter-insurgency operations. Then there are the 60,000 or so troops of the Rashtriya Rifles, the specialist counter-insurgency force raised in 1990 under the home ministry.[92] It was raised to reduce the internal policing burden on the Army but has ended up being composed predominantly of Army officers and soldiers on deputation. Since the mid-1990s, in order to ease the burden on infantry units, it has been mandatory for every young officer in the support services like the Army Supply Corps, Signals and Ordnance to serve a term in the Rashtriya Rifles. Further, 30,000–40,000 troops are actively involved in counter-insurgency operations in the north-eastern states.[93] Most observers agree that the heavy payload of internal security duties has meant that the 'Indian Army had to scrape the bottom of the barrel to meet this sudden rise in military commitments'.[94] As one former general sums up:

> The Army rose to the challenge magnificently in this period of turbulence. But, it did not remain unscathed. Prolonged operational deployments in the most adverse conditions took a heavy toll. Not merely in morale and well being of the Force, but also in its effort at modernization... There continued to be a clamour for more troops. Not only from the military commanders, but also from political leaders from the regions, who saw the Army as the first as well as the last resort when everything else seemed to fail.[95]

The extra burden has been compounded with other sociological and economic developments that have led to a severe officer shortage. The shortage went up from 17.31 per cent in 1986 to 30.11 per cent in 1999. In 2000, the Army said it was short of 12,883 officers, 28.18 per cent of the sanctioned strength, because young men did not see it as a lucrative career any more.[96] With the liberalization of the economy opening up lucrative options, the Army, which had always attracted 'gentlemanly elites' until well into the 1970s,[97] in 2008 saw its training institutes—the National Defence Academy (Khadakvasla) and the Indian Military Academy (Dehradun)—being under-subscribed.[98]

In an institution stretched to the limit by its professional demands, sport has had to take a backseat. An anecdote from 31 Armoured

Division tellingly illustrates this point. When Major General G.D. Singh took command, he issued orders for a new inter-regimental sporting competition within the division. This was a departure from the usual inter-brigade competitions at the division level. As part of his efforts to build fraternal ties across his command, even a ladies' sport meet for Army wives was organized in Jhansi. But the sting was in the tail. Orders were issued that regiments not taking part in the competition would have to pay a monetary fine that would go into the division's private discretionary fund. The order reflected the apprehension that regimental teams might simply not turn up. Where once sporting competition helped define regimental pride, now the threat of fines was needed to ensure participation. It is not that commanding officers did not want to participate. They simply did not have enough resources, time or men to spare for regular training. To give an example, regiments that had been operating with 50–60 officers each in the 1970s, were now operating with only 15–16. Where was the time for specialized sport? But orders had been passed, so some regiments simply scraped together a team as a formality.[99]

The professional landscape for the average Army officer has changed drastically. If Col. V.B. Mohan had raised an AD Missile Regiment in the 2000s, he would not have had the time or the personnel to focus on sporting glory.

The Army's changing orientation has had a drastic impact on its sporting achievements. In the 1960s and 1970s, teams like the Signals, ASC and the Guards were prominent contenders in national hockey, for instance. In recent years, however, Services teams have not been the dominant force they once were in national sport. The Army continues to play sport but the exigencies of its professional pressures mean that specialization and the competitive edge at the national level has gone down. Competitive sport demands time, dedication and specialized training. In a previous age, commanding officers could encourage and cajole their men to indulge in it. In peace-time, professional reputations, after all, were built on such men. Now, though the pride and the intent remain—witness the special celebrations in Col. Rajyavardhan Singh Rathore's unit when he won the Olympic silver—professional reputations increasingly depend on the battlefield. Hard-pressed and under-manned Commanding

Officers, having to choose between soldiers who fight and soldiers who play, increasingly are loath to let their men off for training. Budding Army sportsmen often have to make the difficult choice between a military career and sporting success.[100]

'This is What Army Officers are There For': Lt. Col. Rathore and Mission Olympics

When Lt. Col. (then Major) Rajyavardhan Singh Rathore won the silver in the double trap event at Athens, finishing behind the UAE's Sheikh Ahmed Al-Maktoum, his success brought home the silent role of the Army in India's sporting endeavours more than ever before. In a nation starved of Olympic success, Rathore, in his first triumphant comments, touched upon a theme that was to become the staple feature of the discourse around the Army and sport in days to come. 'That is what we army officers are there for,' he said, 'to make our country proud.'[101] Looking beyond the patriotic chest-thumping that followed, including the fervent appeal to the Army by President Kalam alluded to earlier, a closer analysis shows that Rathore is as much an example of what is right with the Army's sport as what is wrong with it.

Rathore, a graduate of the 77th NDA course,[102] passed out with a sword of honour from IMA before being commissioned into 9 Grenadiers. Military training gave him his first lessons in shooting and Rathore served with the Grenadiers in 1994–96 in the volatile Baramulla and Kupwara regions of Kashmir.[103] The exigencies of military service meant that he did not take up competitive shooting until 1998. In the selection trials for the Mavalankar competition, he participated in double trap, trap and skeet and won two gold medals and one silver medal. He was then advised to concentrate on double trap. 'Initially, there was no one to help him and he would watch seniors shoot and try to rectify his faults and mistakes.'[104] While honing his skills at the Army Marksman's Unit in Mhow,[105] Rathore asked for a posting to Delhi. His mother Manu Rathore hints at the difficult choice the young major had to make at that early stage of his shooting career:

> He chose to be posted at Delhi so that he could train without interruptions. *He did not even bother about his promotions*. All this while, Gayatri [his wife]

> has been with him, providing him support and comfort. She has been his pillar of strength, sharing his problems and calming him when the going got tough. She has been managing his schedule, booking his tickets and hotel rooms. In Italy, she would sit in the basement with the machine, pulling targets and assisting him.[106]

No sportsman can be a stranger to personal tales of sacrifice and hardship. But Rathore's tale holds a lesson in the strengths and the weaknesses of the Army's potential for creating world-class champions. The Army did support Rathore and its facilities provided him the bedrock for his early grooming. But to go beyond that, to compete with the best global sportsmen, you need wider exposure and the opportunity to train with the best. Rathore succeeded on the strength of his own drive but he was later to gently mention the kind of expert help that was sorely needed for Indian sportsmen in government service:

> ...there should be a set of people who should be entirely coordinating with these top few shooters where they want to train, how they want to train, with whom they want to train, which competitions they must shoot as training and which competitions they must shoot to win.
>
> If they are having problems at home those problems must be sorted out, because sportsmen, especially shooters, would not be able to concentrate if he has got a family problem. If there are any administrative problems, then the government can easily solve them.
>
> For example, it could be related to somebody's posting. An athlete may not be happy at the Railways; then move him to where he wants, because this is for a national cause. This is just giving an example of how the government can come forward and help.[107]

Consider this: long before he won the Olympic medal and became a national hero, Rathore had already won gold at the 2003 World Cup in Sydney. Yet, it took a full year even after Athens for Rathore to get the Army's permission to sign up for the endorsement contracts that were coming his way. In a world where sporting success is increasingly based on specialized training, the Army's seclusion from the wider global structures of sport is jarring. The best training facilities abroad cost money, money that could come in by way of endorsements. As advertisers lined up outside his door, Rathore had to wait for the defence ministry's approval.[108] He could have chosen to leave the Army but he did not, and when the permission came he chose to share his money with the Army:

> Fifty percent of my endorsement money goes to the Indian Army. It'll use it to promote sport. I have great regard for General Joginder Singh, who stood up to this changed environment, thought out of the box and has set a healthy precedent.[109]

Conditioned to working in splendid isolation, a tradition-bound Army moved slowly towards embracing the new global reality of sport as a commercial enterprise. Even though Rathore personally is all praise for the Army's support, the fact is that even a national hero like him had to wait his turn. Imagine the challenges faced by lesser sportsmen. Ever the gentleman, Rathore touches upon this gently:

> I have always stated that the entire Olympic movement in India is alive because of government support, and that stands true… a lot that I have achieved is courtesy to the funding provided by the government.
>
> Yet, a lot needs to be done to improve not only the sport of shooting, but other Olympic sports also. *The progress towards improvement is slow and at this speed it will take us ages to win the number of medals that India should actually be winning.* A lot of things need to be done, and need to be done faster. There are a lot of policies, a lot of directions, which are in place, but the execution is lacking.[110]

The permission for Rathore to cash in on his brand image came partly due to a realization in the ministry of defence that Rathore could be used to show the Indian Army in a 'positive light'. Therefore, he was to only take up endorsements that would project 'the image of the nation and image of the Army in good light'.[111] This explains the Army billboards of Rathore and his projection in the recruitment drive for officers.

Rathore's success came soon after the Army's widely publicized plan for creating Olympic champions was put into practice. In 2001, Army Chief Gen S. Padmanabhan, concerned about the lack of Olympic success, set up the Army Sport Institute (ASI) in Pune under Col. M.K. Naik, a former Asian Games gold medallist in rowing. Naik visited sport institutes across the country to study their shortcomings and set about creating a sporting academy of international standard. Key sports disciplines were identified and his officers then recruited budding youngsters from across the country who had excelled at the sub-junior and junior levels. Once selected, the boys were recruited in the rank of havaldar with a monthly income of Rs 6,000–8,000.

Their living costs—travel, clothes, food and other essentials— became the responsibility of the ASI, which was based upon a Rs 60 crore allocation from the defence ministry. According to Naik, the training had one aim: 'We want them to remember at all times that they are here to get India an Olympic medal'.[112]

By itself, such an academy is not novel. The Chinese have long had such training mechanisms aimed at Olympic glory, so have the Australians. What is unique about India is that here, it is the Indian Army that has taken the lead, in consonance with its wider objective of safeguarding national notions of pride and honour. The move was greeted with widespread media approval, one reporter calling it 'an emergency rescue act by the Army'.[113] By 2008, 115 sports cadets were under training at the ASI. According to the Army, 'The potential candidates are selected primarily based on performance in a structured selection process, without any reservation/quotas of any kind'.[114]

In some ways, the new Olympic mission of the Army was built upon a long-standing tradition sporting talent at various regimental training centres. For instance, Punjab Regiment, artillery and engineers had always followed a practice of hiring talented children from their recruiting bases under special Boys Companies with a view to building their own talent pool. They were later recruited as soldiers. In 2008, 952 sports cadets were being trained in 15 such Boys Companies across the country's regimental centres (See Table 10.1).[115]The ASI simply borrowed this template. The difference was that this time, the Olympics was the explicit goal, not just regimental glory.

Table 10.1
Boys Sports Companies

Ser . No	*Name and loc of BSC*	*Sports Disciplines*
1.	BSC, MEG & Centre, Bangalore	Boxing, Hockey, Swimming
2.	BSC, ASC Centre, Bangalore	Hockey, Football,
3.	BSC, DRC, Faizabad	Hockey, Handball, Volleyball
4.	BSC, RVC Centre, Meerut Cantt	Equestrian
5.	BSC, RRRC, Delhi Cantt	Athletics, Volley Ball, Basketball

6. BSC, 11 GRRC, Lucknow	Football, Boxing, Shooting
7. BSC, BEG & Centre, Roorkee	Athletics, Gymnastics, Kayaking & Rowing
8. BSC, ASI, Pune	Archery, Athletics, Boxing, Diving, Wrestling, Weight Lifting
9. BSC, 58 GTC, Shillong	Archery, Boxing, Football
10. BSC, 1 STC, Jabalpur	Boxing, Football, Athletics
11. BSC, BRC, Danapur	Football, Hockey, Archery
12. BSC, Arty Centre, Hyderabad	Boxing, Athletics, Basketball
13. BSC, BEG & Centre, Kirkee	Boxing, Rowing, Wrestling, Gym
14. BSC, MIRC, Ahmednagar	Shooting, Archery
15. BSC, RRC, Fatehgarh	Athletics, Basketball, Swimming

In a marked departure from the past, the ASI also brought in foreign coaches. By 2003, foreign specialists had been hired for boxing, sports medicine, archery and general theory.[116]This openness is a welcome departure from the hide-bound past and the Army's sports training is well spread across specialized centres across the nation. Tables 10.2-10.6 show the various centres, the key disciplines and the number of sportsmen being trained in February 2008.

Table 10.2
Army Sports Institute, Pune[117]

Ser No.	*Discipline*	*Sportsmen being trained (Army Pers)*	*Civ*	*Remarks*
1.	Archery	21	–	
2.	Athletics	27	–	
3.	Boxing	16	–	
4.	Diving	06	–	
5.	Wt Lifting	26	–	
6.	Wrestling	26	–	
7.	Fencing	–	–	Being introduced.

Table 10.3
Army Shooting Node, Mhow[118]

Ser No.	*Discipline*	*Sportsmen being trained (Army Pers)*	*Civ*	*Remarks*
1.	Shooting	288	03*	*Women

Table 10.4
Army Yachting Node, Mumbai[119]

Ser No.	*Discipline*	*Sportsmen being trained (Army Pers)*	*Civ*	*Remarks*
1.	Yachting	56	–	–

Table 10.5
Army Rowing Node, Pune[120]

Ser No.	*Discipline*	*Sportsmen being trained (Army Pers)*	*Civ*	*Remarks*
1.	Rowing	57	–	–

Table 10.6
Army Equestrian Node, Meerut[121]

Ser No.	*Discipline*	*Sportsmen being trained (Army Pers)*	*Civ*	*Remarks*
1.	Equestrian	23	–	–

The tables above also point to the weakness of the system. While the whole effort is admirable, the Army remains largely closed to outsiders. The lack of numbers in the civilian columns in the tables shows that these facilities are restricted to armymen and women alone. That begs the question: would it not make a big difference if civilian medal hopefuls like Anjali Bhagwat, Mansher Singh, Manavjit Singh and Abhinav Bindra were given the opportunity to use the facilities and the equipment at the Army's excellent shooting ranges? To give another example, in 2007, National Cadet Corps cadets stood second in the junior shooting national championship, second only to the Army, winning 34 medals in various categories.[122] Many of its young shooters beat Army marksmen but there is no institutionalized mechanism to adopt them for further training in either the armed forces, the paramilitary forces or the state police forces. Most of these NCC shooters currently come from low-income backgrounds and without institutional support their talent may well be lost to India.

When we first contacted the Army in 2005 for data on Mission Olympics, we thought it would be the easiest thing in the world. This, after all, was a showcase project of the Army and had been widely publicized already. We thought the Army's publicists would jump at the idea. Yet, we were first curtly informed by the spokesperson in Delhi that he was only authorized to give such information to journalists, not to writers. 'Call the Director General Military Training,' he said and hung up. When we found the military training department's numbers, the colonel there proved most courteous, but he too said he would need special clearance to release such data. When repeated written requests were stonewalled with the standard 'no clearance yet' response, we decided to use the time-tested method of New Delhi: influence. Through the good offices of family friends, we personally spoke to at least three senior generals in Army headquarters. Everyone was sympathetic, but nothing moved. In the end, a full year after our initial inquiries, a senior defence journalist, well respected in Army circles, helped us get the data. It was like we had been fishing for the Army's best-kept secrets, troop deployments and the like. The point of narrating this experience is that while the Army continues to be a bulwark of the nation, following its highest traditions in matters of sport, perhaps it could do with a refreshing air of openness. Until it breaks out of its splendid isolation and embraces the winds of change holistically, the task of winning Olympic medals will not get any easier.

11

Torchbearers of a Billion

India at the Games

For the record, India has won just 18 medals in its chequered Olympic history between 1928 and 2008. This is not counting the two medals won by the mysterious Norman Pritchard at the Paris Games of 1900.[1] For a nation that started participating in the Games in earnest in 1924, 18 medals in 24 Olympics hardly evoke a sense of fulfillment. Eleven of the 18 have come in hockey (eight gold, one silver and two bronze medals), two each in shooting and wrestling and one each in tennis, women's weight lifting and boxing. Clearly then, success stories have been few and far between. Accounts of failure far outnumber standout Indian performances. Stories of near-finishes have become even more poignant in this context, converting our Olympic journey into a tale of rued chances and laments of what could have been.

What would have happened had Henry Rebello's hamstring muscle not snapped during the finals of the triple jump event at London 1948? What would have happened had Milkha Singh not turned back for a quick side glance in the concluding moments of the 400 metres final at Rome in 1960? He could well have added an Olympic medal to his already impressive career record: four gold medals at the Asian Games, a gold in the Commonwealth Games in 1958, victory in 77 of the 80 races he ran in his career, and the 'Helms World trophy' in 1959, given by the United States Athletics Federation to the best 400 metres runner in the world. What would have happened had P.T. Usha thrust herself forward a millimetre, enough to nudge ahead of the Romanian Cristina Cojecaru, who caused national heartbreak after the results of the 400 metres hurdles were announced at Los Angeles in 1984? What would have happened had Abhinav Bindra not lost his nerve in the final at

Athens in 2004 after qualifying for the ultimate round in third place? Or, as his recently published autobiography reveals, had the floor not been loose under his feet during the final at Athens?

There are other heartrending stories of men and women who missed the grade narrowly and in so doing, lost their place in the country's sporting pantheon. Not many remember freestyle wrestler Sudesh Kumar, who in 1972 had come tantalizingly close to winning an Olympic gold medal. Again, few remember that the Indians played quality soccer when they got their first taste of international competition at the London Olympics of 1948. India matched a far superior French side, although it ultimately lost the game 1–2. The barefoot display of quality football impressed many in the West. In fact, India had also qualified for the World Cup in 1950 to be held in Brazil. Despite having a rich band of footballers, however, it could not take part in the only World Cup it qualified for. The most commonly ascribed reasons for this withdrawal are lack of foreign reserves, the barefoot style of play, the long sea journey and apprehensions about India's chances against the world's top teams. On the Asian circuit, India began with a bang. It clinched the gold medal in the first Asian Games soccer competition in 1951, beating a booted Iranian side in the final by a solitary goal. The pinnacle of India's soccer glory was the semi-final appearance as the first Asian nation at the Melbourne Olympic Games in 1956.[2]

India's Olympic encounter, this chapter will demonstrate, is as much a story of the men and women who have not been given their due. This is because a history of India at the Olympics cannot be complete without an evaluation of the athletes who have been pivotal to the nation's presence at the Olympics. When Leander Paes won a bronze at Atlanta in 1996 or Rajyavardhan Rathore punched his fists in the air after winning the silver medal at Athens, a billion people were rendered euphoric. Within minutes they became national icons at the pinnacle of sporting glory. Abhinav is even being considered for the Bharat Ratna, India's highest civilian honour. At the same time, when news trickled in that P.T. Usha had missed the bronze medal at Los Angeles, the country was thrust into a state of national mourning. In a nation where sporting legends are rare, news of such heartbreak often leaves a lasting impact. To put it bluntly, when such things happen, a billion-strong nationalist minds appear to crumble.

What is significant in this history of iconicity are the varying registers of stardom, especially so in the decades following the advancement of television and India's commercial revolution in the 1990s. Sports, by the 1980s, had become salve for a troubled nation. For example, K.D. Jadhav's bronze-medal winning effort in wrestling never found a first-page mention in leading newspapers in 1952. The celebrations were muted and were restricted to the sports pages, which were often inconsequential and insignificant.[3] Only the men from his native village, who escorted him with a cavalcade of over 150 cows, gave him a memorable reception. In contrast, Leander Paes' effort in 1996 was perceived as a 'national' triumph, one that was celebrated nationwide amidst all classes and vocations. In terms of significance, an Olympic medal in the 1990s appeared to matter much more than in the 1950s when sport was at an all-time low on the national list of priorities. This was yet another reason why athletes who failed to win medals rarely found a mention in India's nationalist history. Also, hockey had captured the nation's imagination in such a manner that other sports, team and individual, were not given due recognition.

To drive home the point, while there were a series of celebrations countrywide when the hockey team returned in triumph after the Helsinki Games in 1952, K.D. Jadhav's efforts were hardly given due acknowledgement. The political class, which celebrated hockey as a potent symbol of nationalism, did not treat Jadhav with similar respect even after he had won the first individual Olympic medal for independent India. This explains why Jadhav had to wait until 2001 to posthumously receive the Arjuna award for lifetime contribution to Indian sport and had to build a rather modest cottage by selling his wife's jewels in his lifetime.[4] Hockey's lasting nationalist significance since the 1920s, detailed in earlier chapters, was the principal reason behind such differential treatment. Politicians and sports administrators wanted to join the hockey bandwagon, just as people today are desirous of getting into the cash-rich Board of Control for Cricket in India.

This final chapter is also a personal tribute. It is a tribute to some exceptional people who have given India a voice in the biggest sporting realm of all. We remember watching Leander Paes play Andre Agassi at Atlanta in 1996 and the pride we felt each time Paes stunned the crowd with one of his fancy drop shots, too many of which may have ultimately cost him the match. Leander, then ranked 127 in the world, was an average tennis player who raised the bar a series of notches when he donned the national colours at the Olympics. In qualifying for the semi-finals, Leander upset four competitors ranked higher than him in the ATP rankings. This was a player who by sheer force of his passion and rage transcended 'his averageness when his nation's flag flew',[5] a rare non-cricketing hero who moved India like no other, a tennis player who was to be hailed as the 'spiritual leader' of a new movement of 'the art of the possible'.[6] We also remember the elation in the voice of the All India Radio newsreader when she revealed to the nation Karnam Malleswari's feat, finally getting Indian women into the Olympic medal winner's list. And we certainly remember watching with bated breath Rajyavardhan Rathore shoot his way to silver around 4 p.m. in the afternoon in India, becoming in the process the first Indian to win a silver medal in an individual event. Finally we remember Abhinav Bindra shooting a miraculous 10.7 in his final shot at Beijing giving India her first individual gold at the Games. At the same time, we remember as children the heart-wrenching gloom at school and in our localities when inexperience cost P.T. Usha the bronze at Los Angeles. Having won her semi-final, Usha, someone we had never seen or heard of before, was truly at the centre of our nationalist imagination in 1984. When the serious-looking DD newsreader on the black and white television set made the announcement, the sense of loss and sympathy extended far beyond the sporting realm—everyone, including our grandmothers, could empathize with the poor Indian girl who was believed to have been let down by the lack of modern training. If only she had bent her body forward as she crossed the finishing line, if only someone had told her—the conversations went on for days after the competition was over. In a country where sporting achievements were few and far between and where pathos is an enduring theme in popular culture, the misfortune of P.T. Usha struck a chord and turned her into a legend. Despite having failed to win a medal, Usha became a national icon and a symbol of women's empowerment at the same time.

Finally, the entire nation jumped with Anju Bobby George each time she started her run to the pit at Athens. Her jump of 6.83 metres may not have been good enough for a medal but it was enough to make her the poster girl of Indian athletics for some time. This is what the *Tribune* had to say about her on the eve of the Olympics: 'For a Syrian Christian girl from the remote village of Cheeranchira in Kottayam district of Kerala, an Olympic gold was farthest from her dream when she took to athletics at school, at the prodding of her businessman father K.T. Markose. She had the height, the stride and the stamina to become a long jumper of promise, but nobody told her that she was Olympic medal prospect, not even Markose'. It went on to suggest that 'Anju has shed gallons of tears and sweat to prepare for Athens Olympics 2004. She has been toiling with the one-pointed aim of striking gold at Athens'.[7] Coming from the great tradition of women's athletics in Kerala, Anju was the first Indian long-jumper to win gold at the Asiad, to land a Commonwealth bronze, and then the first Indian of any sex to win a World Championship bronze in 2003.[8] She could never replicate those efforts at the Olympics but her emergence was symbolic of a new resurgence, a sense that Indians could compete in the athletics track—in events that they had never competed in before.

The Early Heroes

Among the early heroes, barring the hockey gold-medal winning teams, was surely K.D. Jadhav, the first individual medal winner for India at the Games. At Helsinki in 1952, Jadhav started the competition in terrific form, winning all his early bouts. Such was his performance that he was assured of a medal even before he fought his last two fights on 22 July.[9] Whether or not complacency had crept in, history will never know. What is known is that had Jadhav not lost both of his last bouts, he would have managed a higher podium finish.

This is how the *Times of India* celebrated his achievement: 'History was created here today when India, who has been competing in the Olympic Games since 1924 gained a place in the individual honours list for the first time through K.D. Jadhav, the bantamweight wrestler, who won a bronze medal. Although Jadhav was today beaten by Russia's Roshind Mahmed Bekov (gold medal) and Japan's Shihii in a points decision (silver medal) he gained his place with a series of brilliant bouts during the last week'.[10] The newspaper went on to describe Jadhav's bout against the Russian in detail:

> Although Jadhav was aggressive and a good trier, able to equal the formidable Russian's skill he was unable to match his strength and this weighed the scales against him. The Russian won all three periods. In the first Jadhav jerked him down but was himself twisted over in falling and narrowly escaped a fall. Bekov had the Indian in difficulties after that but Jadhav always wriggled clear.[11]

What made Jadhav's performance all the more significant was that the rules at international contests were different from the rules followed in India. While Indian wrestlers were used to winning simply by putting their opponents flat on their backs, international rules specified that the opponent had to be pinned for two seconds on the canvas with their shoulders touching the mat before a fall verdict could be declared. Jadhav had learnt of this rule in London four years earlier when Reese Garder, the US lightweight champion, who had trained the Indian wrestlers for a week before the Games, coached him. In London, Jadhav had finished sixth in a field of 42.[12]

Jadhav is now a forgotten man in the annals of Indian sport but his story is one of true grit and resilience. The manner in which he made it to Helsinki is nothing short of thrilling. Gulu Ezekiel describes it thus:

> Jadhav's berth to Helsinki was sought to be sabotaged by officials who placed him second in the nationals at Madras. But Jadhav fought the system by writing a protest letter to the Maharaja of Patiala who intervened on his behalf.
>
> Back then, those representing the country in most sports had to fend for themselves and arrange their own funding. Friends and neigbhours helped out with the shopkeepers of Karad arranging to buy his kit. It was the remarkable sacrifice of the principal of Raja Ram College, Mr Khardekar who sold his house to get the funds needed for the trip, that finally saw Jadhav on his way to Helsinki.[13]

Another Indian wrestler who distinguished himself at Helsinki was K.D. Mangave, who eventually finished fourth in the featherweight category. Mangave bowed out of medal contention in the fifth round when Josiah Henson of the United States beat him. However, as the American had four bad marks and had gained another against Mangave, he too was eliminated from the medal race.[14]

While Jadhav had a medal to show for his performances, Henry Rebello was distinctly unlucky in the London Games of 1948. A young 19-year-old triple jumper, Rebello was a favourite to clinch gold, having shown exemplary promise in meets preceding the Games and consistently jumping over 50 metres, a distance covered by the eventual gold-medal winner at London.[15] Rated very high by experts, Rebello had qualified for the finals with ease with a jump of 49 feet, easily clearing the cut-off of 48 feet 6 inches. But as luck would have it, he tore a muscle during his first jump in the final and had to be carried off the field in pain in one of the worst tragedies in India's athletic history. This is how he later described his fate:

> We were huddled in our tracksuits and under blankets to keep ourselves warm. I was training with Ruhi Sarialp of Turkey when it was time for my turn. I was wondering how to approach the event. Should I go for a big jump in my first effort or keep it till the third or fourth attempt? I took off the track suit and was getting ready when an official suddenly stopped me as a prize distribution ceremony was about to commence near the jumping pit.[16]

When he was asked to commence his jump 15 minutes later, Rebello committed two follies that transformed his life:

> I was just 19-and-a-half and inexperienced. I should have insisted on some time for warming up. That was my first mistake—not to warm-up. My second was to go flat out on my first jump. We had a total of six and I should have taken things easy at the start...I approached the takeoff board at considerable speed. I got my takeoff foot on the board and started to take off for the first phase of the triple jump—the hop. Then, suddenly, I felt a sharp pain in my right hamstring muscle and heard a sort of 'thwack' like the snapping of a bowstring. My right hamstring muscle had ruptured. I was thrown off balance completely and landed with a tumble in the pit.[17]

Rebello, as Gulu Ezekiel has written, 'was carried off a on stretcher in agony. His hopes and dreams had been crushed'.[18]

Others who did well in the early years after independence were Lavy Pinto and Nilima Ghosh. They performed better than they had ever done at home at the Helsinki Games of 1952. Pinto ran his 200 metres in a time of 21.5 seconds, his best ever. Commenting on Pinto, the *Times of India* noted, 'India's ace sprinter Lavy Pinto, the fastest man in Asia after a slow beginning, finished with an electrifying burst of speed to nose out France's Bonino for second place in the eleventh heat of the 100 meters and so make the second round…'[19]

If Helsinki was an Olympiad where India's individual contestants fared well, Melbourne 1956 will forever be remembered as the finest hour for Indian soccer. This was the only time in its soccer history that India made the Olympic semi-final, defeating hosts Australia 4–2. Commenting on the performance, the *Hindu*, saw in it the start of a glorious Indian innings in the global game: 'Indian football made new history this afternoon when she scored a deserving 4–2 victory over Australia…N.D. Souza was in grand form to secure a hattrick… India richly deserved her victory. This should take her a long way in international football…'[20]

Even in the semi-final against Yugoslavia, which India lost 1–4 the team was not disgraced. The *Hindu*, in fact, hailed India's performance against the fancied Yugoslavs in glowing terms. 'The stock of Indian soccer shot high up today when India met Yugoslavia in the semi-final of the Olympic soccer tournament in spite of the fact that India lost four goals to one. After the conclusion of the match the President of the International Football Federation Mr J. McGuire accompanied by FIFA Secretary Kurt Gassman and Sir Stanley Rous came to the Indian dressing room and warmly congratulated the Indian team on its fine performance. Sir Stanley further conveyed the Duke of Edinburgh's congratulations who asked Sir Stanley to convey the Duke's felicitations to the Indian team. The Duke was an interested spectator throughout.'[21]

In the semi-final, the Indians had managed to hold the Yugoslavs at bay in the first half and had in fact taken the lead in the fifth minute of the second half. Also, had P.K. Banerjee not left the field, injured in the second half, the result may well have been different, something Banerjee talks about with passion. 'It was certainly our highest hour. We had a great tournament and I personally was in the best form of my life. Against Yugoslavia I had to leave the field and that's when things turned against us. Though we did not win a medal, I'll always remember with great fondness our performance at Melbourne.'[22]

Oh, Milkha! The First National Heartbreak

Even a week before the start of the Rome Olympics, Milkha Singh was considered to be the favourite for the 400 metres gold. Vince Reel, the American assistant coach to the Indian track team, was confident that Singh would win a medal, maybe even gold. Such hope was based on the fact that Milkha was in peak physical condition at Rome. His training was described by the *Hindu* in some detail: 'India's great hope has been devoting between an hour and an hour and a half to training every day since his arrival in Rome. He is cutting the distances to sprints of about 150 yards with the object of speeding up.' 'If he has not the stamina now, he will never have it', said Vince Reel, explaining the reason for reducing the distances.[23] What was expected to go in his favour in Rome was the tremendous heat which, Milkha Singh was confident, was sure to bother the others in the fray. Christopher Brasher, steeplechase winner at the Melbourne Games, also fancied Milkha Singh and suggested that he had a great chance of a podium finish for two reasons: his form and more importantly the schedule, which ensured that the semi-final and final were run on consecutive days and not on the same day as had been past practice. This was expected to help Milkha more than some of the other competitors.

Eventually, Milkha Singh finished fourth despite having broken the Olympic record in the process with a time of 45.6 seconds. This was a rare race where the first four finishers broke the existing world record. Hailed as the best ever, the race was captured in detail by the *Hindu* and the description deserves to be reproduced in detail:

> The quarter mile event for men was the best ever seen in the recent track meet with America's 28 year old Otis Davis cracking the world record by 3/10 of a second to claim the first place nosing out Germany's Kauffman at the tape. South Africa's Spence was third in 45.5 seconds and India's Milkha Singh was placed fourth in 45.6 seconds...There was nothing for the Indians to be upset by this result as Milkha Singh was caught among the top notchers of the world in peak form. The race was a feast to the eyes with all six setting terrific pace right from the start to finish. In fact, Milkha Singh ran the best ever in his life since his previous best was 45.8 seconds set up recently in Paris when he beat Abdul Seye of France...Milkha Singh drew his best lane and everything was in his

> favour to produce his best. The finalists took an excellent start and it was Milkha Singh and Kinder who led first. Nearing the finish Davis overtook all with Kauffman close on his heels. Milkha Singh was then lying fourth behind Spence. Between Milkha Singh and Spence there was hardly a foot difference and had Milkha Singh run a well judged race instead of bursting out from the start he might have clinched the bronze medal.[24]

Like P.T. Usha two and a half decades later, the agony of Milkha Singh was to turn into an enduring legend of Indian sport. The loss still rankles and he remembers each second of the race, one that he describes as the best and also the worst moment of his life:

> Going into the stadium for the final, I was relaxed and confident about my chances. But when I saw my competitors, tension within me mounted. And with each passing minute it increased. I drew lane five with South African Malcolm Spence to my left and the German Manfred Kinder on my right. As the race was a photofinish, the announcements were held up. The suspense was excruciating. I knew that I had made a fatal error. This may have been because I was all keyed up for the race and was extremely confident of winning a medal. After running furiously fast in lane five for the first 250 meters I slowed down a fraction. At that point I even looked back or maybe it was just a side-glance. But that fraction of a second decided my fate allowing others to overtake me. I could not cover the lost ground after that and that one mistake cost me the race and also the medal.[25]

'After the death of my parents, that is my worst memory,' says Singh, one of the most respected Indian athletes of all time. When pressed about his feelings after the race, he seemed to go back almost 50 years. 'I kept crying for days,' was his first reaction. A true sportsman, he had waited for the medal ceremony and congratulated Davis, Kaufmann and Spence. 'But to tell you honestly, I hated doing it. If I had my way I would have snatched the medals off their hands and run away.'[26] He was acutely distraught after the Games and had made up his mind to give up sport. It was after much persuasion that he began running again.

Milkha Singh had first established himself as an athlete of prowess in 1956 at the National Games in Patiala and two years later broke the 200 and 400 metres record in the national games at Cuttack. In the 1958 Tokyo Asiad, Singh continued to amaze, winning both the

200 and 400 metres. In the 1958 Cardiff Commonwealth Games, he won the 400 metres, beating South African sprinter Malcolm Spence. Spence, however, had the last laugh, beating Singh in Rome for the bronze medal.

There's little doubt that Singh is the greatest male athlete India has ever produced. Despite losing his parents in the bloody aftermath of Partition, Milkha went on to earn the title of 'The Flying Sikh'. His career was a fascinating prototype of P.T. Usha's later—he ruled the Asian tracks in his heyday while facing heartbreak at the Olympics. In 1947, Milkha Singh had been one of the millions of refugees of Partition, escaping to India by hanging from the footboard of a crowded train. Interestingly, when he went back to Pakistan later in his career, he was on many occasions mobbed by fans and admirers, a sign of the respect he had earned for himself across the subcontinent.

Stars Almost Forgotten

The other Sikh who almost made the Olympic stage his own was the 110-metre hurdler Gurbachan Singh Randhawa. He made it to the semi-final of his favourite event at Tokyo as the lucky loser and eventually finished a credible fifth in the final with a timing of 14.0 seconds. Bruce Kidd, who represented Canada in the same Olympics, remembers his interaction with Randhawa at Tokyo:

> He was a talented youngster. He was full of life and verve and when I congratulated him on entering the final, he was a little stunned. He had not expected a Canadian athlete to congratulate him for having made the final. In the final, he ran a good race and may well have made the podium had he done a few things better. In fact, had he started well he would surely have been in the first three. It was a standout performance for India had hardly ever produced an Olympic league sprinter.[27]

This is how Randhawa remembers the event:

> Tokyo in October had a fair amount of rain. We were praying for good weather as the track was of cinder. But despite the heavy downpour, it remained firm...Because of my lack of basic speed I was not good at starts. I took off rather slowly. But my hard training in different events had given me a lot of endurance and staying power. That came

> in handy. I covered a lot of ground between the fifth and eighth hurdles and almost caught up with the American Hayes Jones and Frenchman Marcel Duriez. I finished fourth in 14.3 seconds. But my painful wait was over when it was announced that I had qualified for the semi-finals as the fastest loser.[28]

In the semi-finals, Randhawa, Ezekiel writes, was pitted against the Unified Team of Germany's John Heinrich, Duriez, Anatoly Mikhailov (USSR), Giorgio Mazza (Italy), Lazaro Betancourt (Cuba), Davenport (US) and Valentine Chistyakov (USSR). Chistyakov had two false starts and was disqualified. As Randhawa remembers, 'It was a tough race. My joy knew no bounds when I looked at the giant scoreboard to see that I had finished second in a personal best of 14 seconds which was also the national record.'[29]

He thus described the final:

> Once off to the start, everything was forgotten. Again I had a slow start but I surged smoothly ahead of Duriez. Up front, the Italians Giorgio Mazza and Giovanni Cornacchia were struggling. Duriez tripped on the final hurdle and that gave me a slight advantage, allowing me to catch up with him at the tape...I had barely recovered from the effort when I saw the scoreboard. Light flashed on it, but soon they were put off. When they came on again, my name was at the fourth spot. But they went off again. When the lights returned I was in the fifth spot. The timing was 14 seconds...I have no regrets. Maybe I should have broken the 14 second barrier. I have had my share of bad luck in life. But I must tell you that I was lucky at Tokyo to get into the semis as the fastest loser.[30]

While Randhawa is still hailed as one of the best sprint hurdlers the country has produced, the men who are almost forgotten in India's sporting annals are the wrestlers Sudesh Kumar and Prem Nath. Both of them came close to winning medals in the freestyle competition of the tainted Munich Games in August 1972. In fact, on 31 August 1972, the *Times of India* had reported that India could hope for its first gold in Olympic wrestling if Kumar beat the Japanese Kiyomi Kato. Kumar had moved into contention by defeating Henrik Gal of Hungary in 3 minutes 17 seconds, using his pet hold of 'nikaal'. In the 52 kg class, six wrestlers remained in the fray for the three medals, giving Kumar a great chance for a podium finish. Sushil Jain in the *Times of India* described his bout against Gal in detail:

> In the opening second Hungarian Gal applied 'dhobi paat' to floor Sudesh but Sudesh was very swift to take a turn. Both wrestlers were on equal terms with two points each. In the second round Sudesh did not wait for Gal's attack. It soon was very difficult for Gal to counter Sudesh's hold. Sudesh gave no chance to Gal, lifted him and put him on the floor very neatly.[31]

And just like Rebello, fate was against Kumar in his bout against the Japanese. In this bout, which he eventually lost on points, a string of refereeing decisions went against him, decisively influencing the course of the contest. Sudesh was on level terms with his opponent in Round 1, with a point each. 'An undue warning to Sudesh and a point to Kiyomi turned the trend of the bout. Sudesh had to take the offensive, which gave ample chance to Kiyomi to play safe...Sudesh trailed behind by three points to one in the seventh minute. He tried a beautiful nikaal, which was countered and Kiyomi got another point.'[32]

In the dying minutes of the contest, Sudesh had almost floored Kiyomi, but time robbed him of victory. Soon after the bout, the secretary general of the Wrestling Federation of India, Dewan Pratapchand, raised an objection about bad refereeing but for some reason did not lodge a formal protest. Had India filed a formal complaint against the referee, it might have been a different story.[33]

Premnath, competing in the Olympics for the first time, had raised medal hopes by defeating the Argentine Naggiolio in the 57 kg class. He had applied the 'multani' on his opponent and had floored him in four minutes 17 seconds. Had he defeated Richard Sandero of the United States in Round Five, he would have been certain of either gold or silver. However, he failed to stand up to Sandero and was trailing 2–14 when he was finally floored. In his semi-final, which followed his defeat against Sandero, Premnath, a teenager of 17, was injured and carried off on a stretcher. Both Sudesh and Premnath finished fourth.

Sushil Jain ends his report on India's wrestling challenge at Munich with an interesting observation:

> This was the first time I saw an Indian visitor to the wrestling arena and he was Milkha Singh, who has been encouraging our wrestlers. Besides WFI officials none from the Indian camp including the Chef De Mission and the Government of India observers have ever cared to visit the wrestling matches.[34]

The third Singh who made an Olympic final after Milkha and Gurbachan was Sriram, who finished seventh in the final of the 800 metres at Montreal in 1976. A protégé of the dynamic Ilyas Babar, one of the best Indian athletics coaches of all time, Sriram moved to middle-distance running at Babar's insistence. He won silver at the Bangkok Asian Games of 1970 and followed it up with a gold at Tehran in 1974. However, Montreal was surely his finest hour, though he failed to win a medal.

That Sriram was a medal prospect was evident when he won a practice meet at Montreal days before the start of the Games.[35] Most leading runners had participated in this meet and Sriram gained valuable confidence from his performance. This was on show when, running in the first lane of the opening heat at Montreal, Sriram set a scorching pace to lead the field at the end of the first lap with a timing of 51.35 seconds. He continued with the good run for the next 300 metres before the American Richard Wohlhuntr, favourite to win gold at Montreal, overtook him. While the American finished first in this heat with a timing of 1 minute 45.7 seconds, Sriram with a career best of 1 minute 45.80 seconds finished second.[36]

He ran a strategically bad semi-final and was in fact very close to missing out on a final berth, allowing competitors from America, Britain and Cuba to stay ahead of him.

> Allowing himself to be boxed, which a front runner like him never relishes, Sriram had to stay content in the fourth position, but with only five meters for the finish, James Robinson from the United States put in a tremendous burst all but overtaking the Indian...Indian observers waited with bated breath for the result for to the naked eye it seemed the American, a world class runner, had just about made it but the wonderful world of electronics which leaves nothing to chance put the Indian a hundredth of a second or so ahead. There was a burst of cheering in the Indian camp when the result was flashed on the giant board. None looked more delighted than Sriram's mentor Ilyas Babar...[37]

In the final, as in the heat, Sriram set a blistering pace and led the field in the first 400 metres with an amazing time of 50.85 seconds, faster than the eventual gold medal winner Alberto Juantorena of Cuba. It was in the home stretch that he faded away and ultimately finished seventh with a timing of 1 minute 45.77 seconds. Juantorena, who won a gold medal with a world record timing of 1 minute 43.50 seconds, attributed his success to the pace set by Sriram Singh.

The First, *Chak De* Girls

Twenty-seven years before *Chak De India* was released, the first Indian women hockey players made it to the Olympics, and perhaps those early pioneers would empathize with the trials and tribulations of the fictional players in the film. When women's hockey was first introduced at the Moscow Olympiad in 1980 as a medal sport, India was one of the six teams that contested for honours. The other nations in the fray were Zimbabwe, USSR, Czechoslovakia, Poland and Austria. India began its campaign by defeating the Austrians 2–0 at the Young Pioneers stadium in Moscow. Despite the victory, coach Kartar Singh was dissatisfied. Speaking to the media, he declared, 'I would say what you saw was 50 per cent of the true capabilities of the team'.[38] Interestingly, the Indian girls began with the battle cry 'Sat sri akaal', as their male compatriots had done at Moscow. A fairly large contingent of Indian women, some of them Moscow residents, were seen in the stands supporting their team.

In their second match, the Indians beat the Poles 4–0. Yet again, their performance was below par, a fact attested to by their coach. 'Frankly, they played worse today than against Austria. They are not clicking the way they should, not combining well at all.'[39] Despite their unconvincing performances, they had won a large number of fans, evident from the following observation by K. Datta in the *Times of India*: 'The Indian girls' performance might not have satisfied the team officials or a few other critics. But it cannot be denied that their two wins so far have won them increasing respect of many a visitor to Moscow's hockey stadiums'.[40]

India's campaign was derailed in round three when, in an unexpected result, the Indians lost a close contest to Czechoslovakia 1–2. The defeat, more than the performance of the Czechs, was a result of some atrocious umpiring errors. The Indians were shocked at the two penalty corners awarded to the Czechs, one of which resulted in the winning goal nine minutes from finish. Antonina Tsetlina, a Soviet lady umpire, awarded the penalty corner. Kartar Singh went ballistic against this decision and suggested that an umpire from a country very much in the race for honours had been posted for the match although there were several umpires from 'neutral' countries available. However, in a show of sportsmanship, the Indians did not lodge a formal complaint with the organizers.[41]

Following this defeat, the Indians rallied brilliantly and put up a fighting performance against eventual winners Zimbabwe, drawing the contest 1–1. This left the Indians in second place, with just one match to be played. Despite some bad umpiring decisions yet again against Zimbabwe, the Indians, the *Times of India* reported, 'fought gallantly all the way against a very fit looking Zimbabwe side…It was a creditable performance under the added strain of unpredictable whistling'.[42]

In their last encounter against the Russians, the Indian girls frittered away all the good work done against Zimbabwe and the loss meant that they were out of medal contention. Eventually they finished fourth in the competition.

The Agony of P.T. Usha: The Second National Heartbreak

At Los Angeles, history of sorts was made when the Indian Olympic Association picked five women in a contingent of eight athletes. Of the five, P.T. Usha had impressed the most, having won the 400 metres hurdles in a pre-Olympic meet by defeating some of the world's best, including Debbie Flint of Australia and L. Mazie of USA. Her timing of 55.8 seconds may have been slightly higher than her best but it was certainly enough to make her a sure finalist at Los Angeles.[43]

Expectedly, Usha sailed through to the semi-finals without trouble, finishing second behind USA's Judy Brown. She ran a good race in the second lane, cleared the hurdles without trouble and finished off strongly to bring cheer to the faces of the Indians in stadium.[44]

The semi-finals saw Usha at her best. Running in the second semi-final, she won convincingly with a time of 55.54 seconds, beating Judy Brown, who finished second with a timing of 55.97 seconds. K. Datta reported in the *Times of India* that the afternoon timing of the semi-final suited Usha, who changed her tactics and preferred not to surge ahead from the start. It was only on the home stretch that Usha put in a last-ditch effort, leaving the others behind. Her timing was the third best among all the finalists and she had certainly emerged a strong medal prospect by the time of the final.[45]

The story of how P.T. Usha missed out on a bronze in the final is now part of Indian sporting folklore. The melodrama of her loss ushered India into a state of mourning and it is best to describe the race as it was then reported in the press:

> P T Usha came as close as one hundredth of a second to breaking India's medal drought in the Olympic Games. The finish had to be replayed again and again on the giant screen at the Los Angeles memorial Coliseum before the results were declared...For the third place Usha was beaten by the last desperate lunge by Romania's Cristina Cojecaru who was credited with a timing of 55.41 seconds. Usha's timing was officially shown as 55.42.[46]

In fact, to make sure nothing was left to chance, the Indians lodged a formal protest claiming third place for Usha. However, the jury, justly, did not agree. The medal ceremony was delayed to make sure every doubt had been cleared. After the event, Usha retreated to her room in the Olympic village without speaking a word to anyone. Her silence said it all. It was a tragedy that continues to haunt her even today. As she later recounted, for the first few minutes she didn't even realize that her dream had ended. It was only when reality dawned that she felt an emptiness that she had never felt in her life. Her Olympic dream had been shattered, as it appeared, due to her own inexperience.

There's little doubt, however, that P.T. Usha had done herself and her country proud. She was only the fourth Indian athlete and the first woman from the country to have figured in an Olympic track and field final. As one contemporary report noted:

> Coming to think of it, for all the disappointment of not winning a medal, it was a most creditable performance by a girl of her limited experience. Usha took up the event six months earlier and this was her first taste of international competition. Before taking the plane to Los Angeles she had competed in only two big hurdles races in India, the Bombay Open meet and the pre-Olympic trials. Her own state, Kerala, had objected to her entry when she first wished to try her hand at the event in the Inter-State meet in New Delhi...An Olympic medal would have been a great reward for a girl who has dominated Indian athletics for half a decade...When coach Nambiar introduced her to hurdling he

> had predicted a place in the final for her. Perhaps Usha herself had not expected to win a medal.[47]

She may not have won the Olympic medal but she inspired an extraordinary rise of women athletes from Kerala—Shiny Wilson, M.D. Valsamma, Molly Chacko and Mercy Kuttan. The trend coincided with a concentrated focus on athletics by the Kerala Sports Council during that period.[48]

No history of Indian sport can be complete without an elegy to the grit and determination of Leander Paes. In an age of instant stardom for even the worst performers in the national cricket team, Leander has soldiered on, relatively unsung. This chapter began by noting how his Olympic bronze in 1996 became the cause of nationalist celebration in sharp contrast to K.D. Jadhav's bronze in the 1952 which did not even merit a front page mention in the newspapers. Leander Paes has won Grand Slam after Grand Slam (in doubles), beating far higher ranked opponents while representing the country in the Asian Games, the Olympics and the Davis Cup. When he won his Olympic medal in 1996, he ended a 44-year individual medal drought for India.

Yet Paes continues to inspire, to amaze, to startle, and to top it all continues to win laurels for the nation with amazing regularity. At Atlanta, as a rank outsider and hardly a medal contender at the start of the tournament, he finished third because of his never-say-die attitude and unparalleled patriotism, which helped him psyche himself up and raise his game to a level he has never matched again. Rohit Brijnath, one of India's finest sport writers, beautifully captures the magic of the player:

> Everyone who has watched Leander Paes play has a story. Mine is corny. In 20 years of sports writing, no player has done what he did to me. On the day in Atlanta at the 1996 Olympics, as he battled stuttering form to win bronze, the strangest thing happened. I cried.
>
> It wasn't just because a nation of a billion had been tired of mediocrity, had been waiting so long, 44 years at that point, for one more individual Olympic medal, just to show we belonged, to feel briefly empowered.
>
> It was more than that. You cared because he cared. Because he was technically defective, and too short, and his game too high risk,

> but he'd fight every flaw, he'd front every challenge, he'd tilt wildly at windmills.
>
> This was not a great player by any stretch...But somehow he'd manage to transcend his averageness when his nation's flag flew.
>
> He'd move you because when he played for India he did that simplest of things. He tried.[49]

It has often been suggested that Leander is an average tennis player who reaches another level when he dons India colours. While on the one hand this is meant as praise—he continues to remain patriotic after 22 years of the professional grind—on the other, it dwarfs all his other achievements: 11 Grand Slam titles, which, to remind us all, have helped reinstate India on the world tennis map. If Andre Agassi could play the US Open all through his career as an American, play before his 'home' crowd and make them weep and dance at the same time, what makes us feel Leander only plays the Davis Cup or the Olympics for India and all other tournaments for himself?

For the record, it is almost impossible to follow men's doubles tennis action from India. All our sports channels are de facto cricket channels, for that's what sells in the country. Even if tennis is shown, it is generally the singles. The only way to keep tabs on Leander and Mahesh Bhupathi's exploits on the circuit therefore is to follow the live score on the internet. And if one downloads the point tracker onto one's desktop, it is a unique experience. You can hardly blink, for if you do, you run the risk of missing a point.

When Leander beat Fernando Melligeni of Brazil in the battle for third place at Atlanta, the country was at first too stunned to react. Finally, the medal drought had ended. But the true sportsman in Leander did not want to ride high on his achievements and come back to India to bask in Olympic glory. Rather, he stayed back in the US for a while to improve on his rankings, allowing the somewhat superficial euphoria to die down a little. His reaction after winning the bronze is yet another tribute to his sportsmanship. 'It's just amazing how things can happen with a little bit of effort. And that's really been my story at the Olympics. I've just been putting in effort match after match, point after point...Even on Saturday I was down a set. I was really nervous this morning. I guess the 44 years and 16 years that we have not won a medal was getting to me. It took a while to get over my nerves out there. The effort paid off in the end.'[50]

Interestingly, Paes, who had entered the Atlanta Olympics as a wildcard entry, praised the role played by his coach Jaideep Mukherjea and then doubles partner Mahesh in propelling him to Olympic glory. 'Bhupathi skipped one week of ATP tour play to stay with me and give me encouragement. I am very grateful for the gesture.'[51]

Table 11.1
Paes on His Way to the Bronze Medal

Ist Round—Beat Richie Reneberg who ultimately retired due to a hamstring injury.

2nd Round—Beat Nicolas Pereira of Venezuela 6–2, 6–3

3rd Round—Beat 3rd seed Thomas Enquist of Sweden 7–5, 7–6

Quarter final—Beat Renzo Furlan of Italy 6–1, 7–5

Semi-final—Lost to top seed Andre Agassi of the US 6–7, 3–6

Bronze medal play-off—Beat Fernando Meligeni of Brazil 3–6, 6–2, 6–4

Finally a Female Olympic Medallist

For Karnam Malleswari, the Sydney Olympic Games of 2000 will always be a reverie that came true. It was at Sydney that she re-wrote the history books, becoming in the process the first Indian woman to win an Olympic medal. For the record, Malleswari won a bronze medal in the 69 kg category. This was her first international meet in the 69 kg division after moving up from her usual 63 kg class. At Sydney, she lifted a total of 240 kg—110 kg in snatch and 130 kg in clean and jerk, to end up behind China's Lin Weining and Hungary's Erzsebet Markus who won gold and silver respectively. Soon after her victory, Prime Minister Atal Behari Vajpayee hailed her performance as 'a tribute to Indian womanhood'.

As is typical with Indian sport, her trip to Sydney was in jeopardy until the very last minute. The choice of the women's weightlifting team had been mired in controversy and Malleswari even ran the risk of missing out. On her return from Sydney, she made this stunning revelation in an interview:

> I was even blackmailed (on the eve of the Games). Coach Mr Sandhu told me if there was a choice between Malli or Kunjarani [Devi] then I would be the one who would be forced out of the team, because *Chanu* was an automatic choice. We were all tense till the last minute. We had no idea as to what might happen the next moment. I did not know that the choice was between Sonamacha and Kunjarani. I believed what I was told...I had won two world medals, but it did not seem to count for those who were involved in the selection process. I was hurt when someone came and told me that Sonamacha was better than me. Of course, the whole thing was being orchestrated. I felt bad about it. This misinformation campaign was being carried on by one of the coaches.[52]

Trained by the Belarussian, Leonid Taranenkohe, Malleswari was only the third individual Indian medal winner.

For a lifter moving up from the 63 kg to 69 kg class and taking part in her first competition in this weight category, Malleswari far exceeded expectations. Her effort was all the more commendable because a leading magazine had dismissed her chances of a medal on the eve of the Games on the ground that she was overweight, drank beer and ate 'too much' chicken and cheese.

While one hoped that her medal winning performance was enough to silence all her critics, what was written soon after draws attention to the politicized nature of modern Indian sport: 'Malleswari's bronze medal winning performance in the weightlifting event at the Sydney Olympic Games deserves praise, but minus the hyperbole and media generated hysteria. A bronze is a bronze and even high praise cannot turn it into a silver or a gold.'[53]

Rathore and the Silver

Rajyavardhan Singh Rathore's heroics at Athens have already been written about in the previous chapter. Suffice it to say here that the image of Rathore kissing his silver medal will forever remain a favourite picture postcard of the Indian sports fraternity across the country.

Happily for India, it is time to recognize that Rathore is only one of the most prominent of the many Indian shooters doing well now on the international circuit. With seven or more shooters in the top 20, India has transformed herself into a shooting powerhouse certainly in the Commonwealth, if not also in Asia.

However, as is always the story with Indian sports, Indian shooters found it hard to train for the Beijing Games, with the Sports Authority of India and the National Rifle Association locked in a war of words months before the Olympics. Each blamed the other for the lack of adequate ammunition for the shooters and the NRAI even went so far as to say that it was contemplating the drastic step of withdrawing India's shooting contingent from the Games.[54]

Sadly for India, shooters continue to be denied financial help by their state sporting associations and this became a serious impediment as they trained for London. Gagan Narang, who had a great Commonwealth Games and is among the best India has on current form along with Ranjan Sodhi came to the rescue of his fellow teammates by providing first rate facilities at his academy in Pune.[55]

Yet, in the run-up to London, many observers agree that the Indian shooters stand a realistic chance of winning medals at Beijing, as do Vikas Krishnan and Jai Bhagwan in Boxing.[56]

It would be foolish to make predictions but one thing is certain: with sports capturing the nation's imagination like nothing else, it is natural that the biggest sporting spectacle of all will enthrall the Indian sporting fraternity. This is because sport in India is no longer a vehicle for merely imagining the nation, but has become one by which to transcend the nation—to escape the troubled country and engage with the world on a level playing field.

12

Indian Sport on the Eve of London 2012

Will the turnaround finally happen?

The foundation was laid at the Commonwealth Games in Delhi in October 2010.[1] 101 medals, 38 of which were gold, second in the medals table displacing England for the first time ever in history, Indian Olympic sports and sports persons had made a statement to the world. Critics, however, had drawn attention to the relatively lower level of competition at the Commonwealth Games[2] and suggested that the real test was the Asian Games at Guangzhou in November 2010. And as India's shooters achieved modest success at the Asian Games,[3] the murmur was fast gathering strength. The CWG, the first week at Guangzhou had shown, was a false dawn. The national ritual celebrating failure was about to start and coupled with the CWG scams, which were, and still continues to be in focus, Indian sport was staring down the barrel.

But as with sport, conclusions should not be drawn till the last medal is actually won. India, which had one gold medal from Pankaj Advani in snooker to show at the end of the first week of competition at the Asian Games, suddenly came alive on 21 November 2010 to claim a further three. Ranjan Sodhi was on target in men's double trap and Preeja Sreedharan and Sudha Singh gave millions of Indian sports fans reasons to celebrate as they raced to gold in the 10,000 metres and 3000 metres steeplechase. Suddenly, the Doha 2006 haul of ten gold medals looked achievable and with the boxers putting up a stunning show, their best ever at the Asian Games, the CWG success did not look a distant dream.

Just as in the Commonwealth Games where Saina Nehwal's gold in badminton, India's 38th and last, was more than a medal, at Guangzhou Vijender Singh's gold, India's 14th, shone brighter than its colour. Achieved with a broken thumb in the 75 kilogram category in boxing, it propelled India to an unprecedented sixth place in the medal standings and summed up the story of India's athletes, fighting on despite administrative apathy and bureaucratic red tape at every step. London 2012, it is hoped, will allow these athletes to occupy centre stage and herald the start of a systemic overhaul in Indian sports that the nation is badly in need of and has been craving for years.

If the Asian Games was any indication, India, for the first time ever, can realistically expect 7 medals at London 2012,[4] more than double from what India had won at Beijing. For the first time the world media was forced to publish headlines such as 'China and India up, Japan down', in summing up Asian Games performances in November 2010.

Talking about a possible Indian sporting renaissance at London, Indian Olympic Association Secretary General and India's IOC member Randhir Singh suggests, 'It's a Catch-22 situation. You can't produce champions without money, and money doesn't come unless you have champions to flaunt.'[5] Fortunately for Randhir and India's moribund and deeply politicized sports bureaucracy, India now has a plethora of champions in multiple sporting disciplines to market and promote.

What should help in marketing these athletes is the fact that their achievements in Delhi and China were analysed for hours on television and turned them into national celebrities. That there is a perceptible change is evident from the coverage in the media, the harbingers of such change. In March-April 2009, leading lights of world badminton were in India to participate in the Indian Open tournament in Hyderabad. Around the same time, the Indian cricket team was playing New Zealand for a bilateral series in New Zealand. Even on the day of the Indian Open finals, coverage of the competition was relegated to the lower half of most sports pages across the country when items about India's preparation for the third Test of the series in New Zealand was given eight-column banner headlines.[6] This was startling because India now has a handful of players who have made it to the top twenty-five in world badminton. Saina Nehwal, India's best bet for a medal at the Olympics and ranked fifth in the world, trailed off with the following lament: 'A lot of cricket is happening ... nobody wants to take it (badminton) up professionally. It is not easy to be ranked number eight or nine. A lot of sacrifices have to be made and still not many are ready to do that. So maybe once in ten years we will have a Saina Nehwal.'[7]

In a glaring departure from the reality described above, every Indian achievement at Delhi and then at Guangzhou was a first-page headline while India's triumphs against Australia and New Zealand in cricket were relegated to the sports pages of the national dailies. A successful London 2012 and a sports culture will no longer be an illusion with India gradually starting to look beyond cricket and turning into a multi sporting nation.

Politics over the National Sports Bill: Red Tape Persists

After much deliberation and careful consideration the Indian sports ministry presented the national sports bill before the Union Cabinet on 30 August 2011. The bill, which had taken years in coming, provoked much outrage among several members of the Union Cabinet and wasn't allowed to be tabled before the members of Parliament. Sections of the bill were considered too radical and the sports minister was instructed to redraft the bill and place it once again at a subsequent date.[8] The leading opponent of the bill was the Union Agriculture Minister Sharad Pawar who is also the president of the International Cricket Council and a former president of the Board of Control for Cricket in India.

On losing the Board of Control for Cricket in India presidential election to Ranbir Singh Mahendra in September 2004 Pawar had famously said that he was helpless because 'the bowler, umpire and the third umpire was the same person'.[9] He was referring to his predecessor Jagmohan Dalmiya using the BCCI president's vote in levelling the poll count and subsequently using his casting vote to get Mahendra elected. It was, Pawar suggested, 'a classic case of conflict of interest'.[10] Sharad Pawar, as mentioned above, is now one of the principal detractors of the National Sports Bill. As president of the ICC, he is an interested party and as Union Agriculture minister and former BCCI chief, Pawar, in this case, is the bowler and umpire rolled into one. His opposition to the bill is also a classic case of conflict of interest.

Cases of conflict of interest over the bill don't end with Pawar. Farooq Abdulla, yet another senior member of the Union Cabinet and president of the Jammu and Kashmir Cricket Association, and Praful Patel, president of the All India Football Federation, are in the same league. It is natural that they would want to sink the bill for neither of them can debate it on merit as members of the Manmohan Singh Cabinet. While their opposition as sports czars is understandable, their challenging the bill from within the Union Cabinet is untenable.[11]

While there is little doubt that some of the concerns expressed on both sides, by the proponents and the detractors of the bill, were/are legitimate and tangible, far more problematic and far more significant, however, are the ego battles that were/are being fought around the bill. These games of one-upmanship are likely to have an adverse impact on the fortunes of Indian sport in the immediate future.

Unfortunately, the debates over the sports bill have hardly addressed the core concerns of transparency and accountability. The discussions are limited to the government trying to control the IOA and the Association doing its best to protect its autonomy. If there is one body that desperately needs to be made accountable it is the IOA. Its performance graph shows a consistent downward trend, natural in view of the gloom surrounding India's Olympic sports scene for the longest time after independence in 1947. While India has won just one individual gold medal in its 88 years of participation at the Olympics, it did not win a single medal at Seoul in 1988 and again at Barcelona in 1992. The controversies surrounding the Commonwealth Games have badly dented the IOA's image and its failure to organize the National Games in the last five years has had an adverse impact on Indian sport.

Moving on to specifics, despite a good number of shooters having achieved success at the international stage over the last few years India continues to rue the absence of a pistol coach, with the shooting federation and the IOA sidestepping such issues and focussing their attention on trying to protect their autonomy. That the Commonwealth

Games opportunity was partly lost was largely due to a dysfunctional IOA and an ineffective sports ministry. The Games, which could have been the gamechanger for India's Olympic sport, is remembered more for the associated scams and cases of malpractice.

Indian sport, to take advantage of the opportunities before it, needs to reform itself. Change is needed, both at the top and also at the grassroots, especially with London just days away. London 2012 can be a major turning point in India's quest to become a sporting nation, an opportunity that might be lost at the altar of ego battles over the national sports bill. Winning medals at London, it must be acknowledged, will provide a huge boost for the athletes and will also result in opening up the possibility of corporate investment in Olympic sport. But the politics over the sports bill has badly impacted preparations for the Games with administrators engaged in guarding their turf rather than concentrating on athletes training for London.

A FIRM 'NO' TO AN OLYMPIC BID

A survey of international media reports in the aftermath of CWG 2010 helped draw attention to one singular strand of argument—that India was finally ready to mount a strong Olympic bid. These arguments were based on assumptions that hosting the CWG was a stepping stone towards bidding for the 2020 Olympic Games.

Put bluntly, India is not ready to prepare a serious Olympic bid. The Commonwealth Games had come to India prematurely in 2003,[12] a decision that explains the problems in the lead-up to the Games and the clean-up act currently underway. Most top brass of the Games Organizing Committee are now in jail on charges of misappropriation of funds. An Olympic bid, which comes at a serious cost to a nation, will divert attention from the athletic achievement at CWG and Asian Games 2010, which for the first time ever in our sporting history has given us hope of achieving the objective of sport for all.

If the CWG experience is taken as evidence, an Indian bid will only be a waste of time, energy and money and will only result in huge money spent on non-sporting activities at the cost of our athletes with little returns on investment.

As Jacques Rogge had emphasized during his visit to Delhi in October 2010 when asked about an Indian Olympic bid, 'You have great athletes and you have one overriding sport, which is cricket. But we need more gold medals from the second-most populous country in the world before you make a pitch for hosting the Olympics.'[13]

The point the IOC president made is already a well-established paradigm in the West. Only after a country seriously invests in sport and improves its record by winning a handful of medals at the Games can it join the race for hosting the most prestigious global sports spectacle. A strong Olympic bid is premised on winning medals at the Olympic stage and unless India achieves the latter, the former is a non-starter. In the current context, an Olympic bid is a luxury in India, which its sportspersons can ill afford.

Lessons from Bhiwani: Demystifying the Revolution

The Bhiwani Boxing Club's iconic coach Jagdish Singh is fond of saying '*Geedar ka shikar karna ho to sher se ladna seekho.*' (If you want to hunt jackals, learn how to fight a lion.)[14] Surprisingly enough, till 2008, Bhiwani was a rather insignificant presence on the Indian sporting map. Despite giving the country multiple Asian Games gold medallists and a slew of medals in other international boxing competitions, the nation hadn't trained its eyes on Bhiwani before Beijing 2008. A few startling days at the Olympics changed all of this. As Akhil Kumar punched his way past Sergei Vodopyanov after four gruelling rounds in the 54 kg pre-quarterfinal and Vijender Singh matched up to Emilio Correa in the semifinals of the 75 kilogram category, media persons swarmed to make every inch of Bhiwani their own. Apathy soon gave way to unending television glare and Bhiwani, from being a shantytown, suddenly turned into the cynosure of all attention.

Bhiwani had its first tryst with international sporting success in the 1960s when Hawa Singh won gold at the 1966 Asian Games. He followed it up with another gold medal at the Bangkok Asian Games in 1970, giving rise to a boxing culture that has since flourished in this village on the Haryana–Rajasthan border. This is a well-established paradigm and one on which the Olympics are premised. Performance at the highest level has always served as the best inspiration for new participants wanting to embrace the sport. Despite such success at the international stage, no funding was directed towards developing a boxing culture. But that didn't dampen the gung-ho sporting spirit of the Bhiwani boxers, who continued to pursue their sporting dream. Things hardly looked up in the 1970s and '80s. Consequently, a section of the youth left Bhiwani for neighbouring states in search of work and livelihood. This was their way of showing discontentment over the Central government's prolonged apathy. Things reached a climax during the 1980s and early 1990s amidst a growing sense of frustration and uncertainty as unemployment prevailed. Thousands of Bhiwani youths were left with two options – either to take up sport or fall prey to unemployment.[15]

In a desperate act to protect young children from future unemployment, most parents encouraged their wards to embrace sports. To encourage this effort, the Sports Authority of India (SAI) started a training school, giving Bhiwani its first organized sports facility. They were encouraged to do so by the achievements of Raj Kumar Sangwan who won golds at two Asian-level meets—at Bangkok in 1991 and at Tehran in 1994. However, this solitary SAI facility did little to solve the problems of infrastructure. It was the Bhiwani Boxing Club, hardly a modern facility itself, which ultimately made a perceptible difference. The club, which is in a much better state today, was once described in the *Indian Express* thus:

> Tucked in a corner, almost hidden by fields, the yellow brick building is more a farm outhouse than a possible breeding centre of international sportspersons. If quaintness equalled success, the place would get top marks. And well, now it does ... The Bhiwani Boxing Club is just that, two rooms and a shed. A peepul tree and a Shiva idol stand to the left outside the gate, a sagging volleyball netting graces the right flank. Five punching bags hang next to the room, a huge mirror frames one wall, there is a basic weight-training machine on one side, and a new ring on the other.[16]

Problems of infrastructure were, however, more than counterbalanced by individual passion for boxing, as the turn of the century marked the arrival of a golden era of Bhiwani boxers in the national arena. Despite making a mark in almost every recognized competition, it was at Beijing 2008 that Bhiwani finally scripted an unparalleled success story. The nodal boxing body of Bhiwani – the Bhiwani Boxing Club – was established in 2002 by current coach Jagdish Singh. *Indian Express* reported it thus:

> Six years ago (in 2002), Singh, one of the many boxing coaches with the Sports Authority of India, decided the daily effort he was putting at the SAI centre in Bhiwani needed to be topped with something more. So, in a move that some would describe as whimsical, he got together his life's savings, took a bank loan, and set about realizing his dream of having his own boxing club. Singh has always had an eye for spotting talent and following an approach that focuses on dealing with the worst-case scenario, he trained a band of boxers who slowly began dominating the national scene.[17]

After almost seven years since its inception, the boxing club has finally spread its wings to the far-flung corners of the state through its policy of decentralization. In fact, Bhiwani's glittering track record (of producing as many as fifty sportspersons who have represented India in internationals competitions) can largely be attributed to the modus operandi of the nodal organization, which tried its best to promote a healthy sporting environment. Lack of exposure and absence of recruiters acted against Bhiwani's boxers, while mainstream Indian sport remained unaware of their maturing skills. At the turn of the millennium, a few self-made individuals training under the watchful eyes of Jagdish Singh finally broke all shackles to catapult Bhiwani to the national and subsequently international level. Akhil Kumar, for example, beat all odds to come out stronger from a career-threatening injury and made it to the Olympics quarterfinals.[18] Following his example, Olympic medallist Vijender Singh emerged as the biggest name in Indian boxing and is currently one of the most sought after sports celebrities in the country. Inspired by the simple logic that a good showing at the national level is the best bet to securing a government job, a vast array of talented youngsters have now taken to boxing in Bhiwani. In Jagdish Singh's words: 'Parents are keen to bring them here, knowing this is a future they can dream of. Now that they've seen the success stories, it's a reality they want to believe in.'[19]

THE PROBLEM: WE ARE LIKE THIS ONLY

While Bhiwani was/is at the centre of national attention, it is important to remember that only a sustained effort at building infrastructure could ensure that CWG 2010 and Gwangzhou aren't exceptions. Bhiwani continues to be a town which goes for days without electricity, where the rains have made it impossible to drive a car faster than 5 km/hour on most roads and where most people have to rely on inverters to watch the home boys win. In such a setting, sport has emerged as a way out for many.[20] The real success of Bhiwani lies in the rock-solid confidence of the new generation of athletes and a nascent public–private partnership which allowed them to transcend a system used to mediocrity. They have not been content to merely repeat the past; and this is the new Indian spirit that needs to be celebrated.

The picture is similar if we turn our gaze to shooting, India's favourite medal event since Bindra's gold at Beijing. While Gagan Narang, Bindra's compatriot in the 10-metre air rifle, has been in sizzling form since the Olympics and has even broken multiple world marks, his performances are once again the result of individual flair and brilliance. The fact that Narang could win four gold medals and two silvers at the Commonwealth Games and Asian Games respectively is testament to his skill and mental strength. While Narang's exploits give us ample hope before the London Games, in a shocking exposé it was brought to the nation's attention in April 2009 that the fifteen top coaches engaged in training India's shooters for the Commonwealth Games weren't paid between January and March 2009 when each of them was entitled to payments of up to Rs 30,000 per month as per the terms of their contract. Also, at the time of appointment, these coaches were promised advanced-level training abroad; but till April 2009, none had been sent. In an interview to Ajai Masand and Saurabh Duggal of the *Hindustan Times*, one of these coaches, engaged in training at the national camp in Pune, spilled the beans:

> All of us, barring national coach Sunny Thomas, have not received a paisa (penny) from the government for the work we have been putting in to prepare the 150-odd core group shooters ...[21]

At the time of writing with just months left for London, India still doesn't have a pistol coach and the nation's leading shooters are trying to circumnavigate the problem by making use of the facilities at compatriot Gagan Narang's academy in Pune.[22]

These discrepancies, born out of insurmountable administrative apathy at the highest levels of Indian sport, only add to the despondence of India's sportsmen and women. Blaming the media is the short cut sports administrators often resort to. However, that such a situation has been created in the first place speaks volumes of their efficiency. Unfortunately, in India, virtually every sporting body is controlled by a politician or a bureaucrat and, once entrenched, most manage to stay on for years, if not for decades, a point discussed at length in the Epilogue.

More alarming than politicians controlling sports is that these men have managed to stay on in power despite a high court ruling which decreed that guidelines on tenure of office bearers of the National Sports Federations are maintainable and enforceable. Suggesting that this is in no way a violation of the principles enshrined in the Olympic charter, Justice Geeta Mittal, sitting judge of the Delhi High Court, observed that even the International Olympic Committee had restrictions on the terms of its office bearers.[23] She went on to state:

> Firstly, I see no interference by the stipulation of the tenure condition as a condition for grant of recognition and assistance by the government. Secondly, the same does not enable the government to have any say of any kind in the affairs of running of the sports body ...A limited office tenure will have the impact of minimizing, if not eliminating, allegations, criticism and elements of nepotism, favouritism and bias of any kind.[24]

The court judgment, the *Hindu* noted, had serious ramifications on the tenure of office bearers and stipulated that an office bearer of a federation can have two terms of four years each at a stretch, the second one on a two-thirds majority. However, the same report went on to suggest that 'the IOA took the lead sometime in the mid-1980s to flout the guidelines by amending its constitution and almost all National Sports Federations followed suit'.[25]

Commenting on the impact of the ruling, the *Times of India* reported: 'Most of them do not believe in handing over the baton. Perched securely as heads of various sporting federations, sports bosses have been virtually unmovable. But maybe not for long. The ruling could lead to changes in the Indian Olympic Association as well as other sports bodies.'[26] What the court ruling highlights is that the International Olympic Committee needs to take into account local peculiarities while trying to push through its agenda of political independence of the NOCs. The ruling demonstrates that in cases like India you need the power of local legislation to force the IOA to get its act together. Unless global policies are mediated by local ground truths it might result in empowering the unworthy and it is important for the IOC to take note of these ground realities.

A More Proactive Sports Ministry?

Drawing strength from the high court ruling the sports ministry under the newly appointed minister Ajay Maken has now suggested in the National Sports Bill that no administrator can continue to head sports bodies past 70 years of age. Following the lead of the International Olympic Committee, which asks IOC members to retire at 70, the ministry is determined to ensure that Indian administrators give up their posts past this age. Again, this draws attention to the differing ground realities in particular local contexts. While the ministries' agenda may be perceived as interference by the IOC, the ministry is actually trying to implement a policy laid down by the IOC itself against opposition by the IOA, which, in turn, is drawing strength from the autonomy clause in the IOC charter.

Further continuing with its agenda of sports reform, the sports ministry, for the first time in years, sent out a circular to all sports federations, whose disciplines were in the 2010 Commonwealth Games, to send details of the past and recent performances of all 'core group' athletes. This directive came on the back of growing discord among sportspersons who felt that despite performing at their best they weren't being rewarded in the absence of proper laws and guidelines. Reacting against the groundswell of discontent, a ministry official emphasized that the directive was meant to weed out the non-performers and encourage sportsmen and women to excel in international competitions.

Carrying on with its objective of identifying talented sportspersons on the eve of the Delhi Games, the government, the *Telegraph* reported, endowed Rs 5 lakh for the Maulana Abul Kalam Azad Trophy, handed out to the best sporting university in India, to encourage talent at the collegiate level. It also identified Ladakh as a fertile ground for archery, ice hockey and figure skating.[27]

As Anirban Das Mahapatra reported:

> The government has upped financial incentives for successful sportspeople. Former medal winners at international events now have their pensions doubled. Financial assistance for medical treatment is now up a whopping 500 per cent to Rs 2 lakh (2800 GBP). The government has also released a grant of over Rs 6.5 crore (900000 GBP) for upgrading all four training centres of the Sports Authority of India, to provide state-of-the-art training facilities.[28]

It was in 2009 for the first time ever in India's sporting history that the government came forward with a grant of Rs 678 crore to enable our athletes to train abroad with the world's leading professionals. This was to ensure that they were exposed to the best of facilities before the 2010 Commonwealth Games and in the lead-up to London 2012.

While more money for sport is always welcome, the problem lies in the details and in how it is spent. One statistic is telling. Against an allocation of Rs 678 crore for the Commonwealth Games, the government had spent just over 35 per cent, only Rs 232.19 crores, by November 2009. If the idea of pumping in this money was to create champions for the Commonwealth Games, to use them as a springboard for greater sporting glory at London, clearly something went terribly wrong. Unless there is a serious organizational learning and a realization that London 2012 is India's last opportunity to become a sporting nation, it is impossible to expect radical change in the existing scenario. London 2012 is a potential gamechanger and this realization is crucial to heralding a fundamental transformation in the country's sporting scene.

The London Test

Talking about the possibility of a sporting resurgence, IOA Secretary General Randhir Singh suggested that individual prodigies aside, the connection between modern sport and commerce is undeniable. This is precisely why nascent private sector initiatives like the Mittal Champions Trust and Olympic Gold Quest, non-governmental organizations formed to stimulate sporting excellence, are much needed.

That Olympic Gold Quest is clearly focussed on the job at hand is evident from the following report published in *The Hindu*:

> With exactly a year to go for the London Olympics, Olympic Gold Quest (OGQ) announced that it was putting together the best possible package to help the athletes in their pursuit for the gold medals. Addressing a press conference, the Chief Executive Officer (CEO) of OGQ, Viren Rasquinha, said that five select athletes would get the support of 'performance and mental strength' coach, Abha Maryada Banerjee. Rasquinha mentioned that a personal masseur, Kassenova Kacehoba of Kazakhstan would help the shooters, who often complain of back and shoulder stiffness.[29]

Come August 2012 and the CWG legacy will be put to its sternest test. If India can double its medal count achieved at the 2008 Beijing Games, it will give an unprecedented fillip to Indian Olympic sport. A failed effort at London, on the other hand, organizationally and with regard to medals won, will mean that the lush promise of CWG and Asian Games 2010 will be confined to sports history books by the time of the next Olympics at Rio in 2016.

London, may well be a watershed event in the history of Indian sport. A successful Olympics will propel India to the forefront of Asian sport and may even translate into an Olympic bid a decade down the line. A failed Games experience on the other hand will mean Olympic sport taking a backward step and the country losing all momentum built at the Delhi CWG and the Asian Games at Guangzhou.

Epilogue

There are lies, damned lies and Indian sporting officials with their mouths open in front of microphone. They are the Caliphs of the Cliché, the Princes of Platitudes, the Viceroys of Vacillation. Personally though I prefer the Barons of Bullshit.

—Rohit Brijnath[1]

In 2000 the weekly magazine *Outlook* heralded the arrival of sting journalism in India with an operation that laid bare the dark secrets of match-fixing in cricket. It was an operation that nearly killed the BCCI's golden goose—sponsors for some time withdrew money from cricket like rats deserting a sinking ship[2]—a few players like Azharuddin, Ajay Jadeja and Nayan Mongia were banned and India saw the spectacle of World Cup winning captain Kapil Dev crying on national television to protest his innocence.[3] Indian cricket soon returned to normal; in a world where billions were riding on the consumer economy of the game, the dark spectre of match-fixing was quickly forgotten, relegated to the status of a bad dream. But the idea of the sting camera operation as a powerful new tool to uncover the darkest secrets of the republic remained like a ticking time bomb in India's newsrooms. The targets ranged from the noble to the ridiculous: BJP president Bangaru Laxman grubbily counting bundles of notes under the table; Jaya Jaitely discussing defence deals in Defence Minister George Fernandes's house; senior Army officers expressing willingness to fix defence deals for a bottle of scotch whiskey; the BJP's Dilip Singh Judeo raising bundles of notes to his head saying 'money is god'; MLAs in U.P. using their official cars for the smuggling of drugs; the Gujarat riot accused boasting of their crimes on camera; and actor Shakti Kapoor's embarrassing disclosures of the casting couch in Bollywood. At a time when television channels live and die by weekly ratings, the sting operation has not always been applied with the most honest of intentions and it has raised many ethical questions about privacy and the rules of journalism but there is no doubt that it symbolizes the intoxicating power of the new media like no other. So it was no surprise that when every other avenue to induce a transformation in the moth-eaten corridors of Indian hockey officialdom had failed it was the sting operation that unlocked the doors of change.

When the Indian men's hockey team failed to qualify for the Beijing Olympics, the failure unleashed a national witch-hunt and catharsis in the national media of the kind that in recent times has only been rivalled by India's humiliating first-round exit in the cricket World Cup of 2007. India's hockey teams had long ceased to be world beaters but as one article noted, not qualifying for the Olympics was the ultimate humiliation: 'This was like Brazil not qualifying for the World Cup Football. This is like West Indies not qualifying for World Cup Cricket.'[4] The festering wounds of Indian hockey, bleeding away for decades, had finally burst and could not be ignored any more. Following the 2–0 loss to Britain in the qualifiers that cost India a place at Beijing, anyone who was anyone in the system called for a complete overhaul of Indian hockey. It emerged, for instance, that administrators had hired Australian Ric Charlseworth as a consultant coach but he was not even given a ticket to accompany the national team to Santiago for the qualifiers. Former players blamed hockey administrators, fervently appealing for them to be sacked, former Sports Minister M.S. Gill made it clear that it was time for IHF chief K.P.S. Gill to bid goodbye and numerous media commentators asked the Sports Minister and the IOA to intervene. Yet K.P.S. Gill, the man who was given the sobriquet of 'super-cop' for his work in ending the Punjab insurgency in the early 1990s, and the czar of Indian hockey since 1994, refused to budge. As he said in an interview to NDTV:

> No other sport in the country has won as many titles (10) as hockey in all age-group tournaments in Asia, since I took over in 1994. Why has no newspaper or television channel bothered to highlight the achievements of the Indian hockey teams at the Asian level?[5]

Forget about taking moral responsibility, anyone who saw that interview on NDTV was left with no doubt that Gill actually believed he had done a good job. What infuriated many observers was the fact that the poor showing had not even induced a process of introspection among hockey mandarins, many of whom considered themselves indispensable. As IHF secretary general K. Jothikumaran announced: 'I want to know where our detractors were when India won the 2007 Asia Cup with a stylish performance. Was there a felicitation for us then? Our conscience is clear.'[6]

It was Jothikumaran's conscience, or lack of it, that Headlines Today/ Aaj Tak targeted in the aftermath of the Olympic disaster. When the channel's reporters approached him, posing as prospective organizers of an international hockey tournament, they secretly recorded the mustachioed apparatchik asking for a bribe to get a player included in the senior team and 'seed money' of Rs 5 lakh to initiate talks about the proposed tournament with the IHF's marketing company, Leisure Sports Management.[7] Headlines Today called the sting 'Operation Chak De'. It reported that the selection process in hockey was not 'always fair, the current administration is highly corrupt and that IHF President Gill is oblivious of the corrupt practices of his colleagues.'[8] It was claimed that after receiving a cash payment of Rs 2 lakh and taking a promise of another Rs 3 lakh to be given to his man in Delhi, Jothikumaran gave assurances about getting a certain player picked up for the senior national hockey team for the Azlan Shah hockey tournament in May.[9] The 'bribe money' was reportedly paid in a Delhi hotel on 10 and 11 April and when the tapes were released on television on 21 April, including telephone transcripts of conversations during which Jothikumaran allegedly made the deal about team selection, the IHF secretary general resigned within hours, but not without protesting his innocence:

> I was genuinely under the impression that a proposal for conducting a big tournament on the lines of Azlan Shah tournament was being debated with me by the reporters of 'Aaj Tak' and 'Headlines today'. At no point of time did I raise anything about selection... The money they allege that I had taken was in my opinion to meet the initial expenses for organizing the event in India on the same lines of Azlan Shah tournament.[10]

He may have been forced to quit but Jothikumaran went on to sue Aaj Tak for Rs 25 lakh for libel, arguing in the Madras High Court that the Aaj Tak tapes did not show any money-exchange for player selection.[11]

The denial notwithstanding, once the tapes were released on television, the reverberations were felt all the way down from the International Hockey Federation's headquarters in Lausanne to Delhi. Former Olympian Dhanraj Pillay went on to claim that Jothikumaran had similarly pushed Adam Sinclair in the 2004 Athens Olympic team using his clout: 'I can tell you that this boy did not know how to hit the ball but Jothikumaran got him in and the then coach Gerard Rach tutored him thrice a day to teach him the basics.'[12] This was an explosive disclosure but with the IHF digging its heels in—an adamant K.P.S. Gill told one TV editor that he had thrown Aaj Tak's reporters out thrice when they came to him with the same proposal as Jothikumaran, so why was not that shown on TV[13]—what ultimately tilted the scales against it was the explicit threat to withdraw funds by the Federation of International Hockey (FIH). In a terse letter to the IOA, FIH's secretary general noted the sting operation and asked for immediate action:

> The recent allegations in the Indian press concerning alleged improper conduct by the Hon. Secretary General of the Indian Hockey Confederation [sic] are a cause for very great concern. The FIH has invested very significant resources in the project 'Promoting Indian Hockey'. If the allegations are true, there would be negative impact on the project and the decision by the FIH to consider holding the men's World Cup in 2010 in Delhi, would be placed in serious jeopardy....
>
> The FIH believes that immediate and decisive action on the part of all authorities in India, especially the IOA, is required to ensure that the whole matter is investigated and appropriate action taken....
>
> Time is of essence, FIH urges IOA to intervene and ensure that appropriate action is taken to guarantee the administration of Indian Hockey Confederation [sic] and Indian hockey. FIH remains committed to the success of the project and supports you in your actions.[14]

The FIH could not have been more explicit. Facing the possible end of the FIH's showpiece project to rejuvenate Indian hockey as well as demise of plans for the 2010 World Cup in Delhi; hemmed in by the Union Sports Minister and angry Members of Parliament[15]—all demanding intervention—the IOA had little choice. In an emergency meeting of its executive body in Delhi, the IOA in a historic decision suspended the IHF, creating a five-member ad hoc body of former players to run Indian hockey.[16]

Not that this made much difference. The world cup was held in India as was the CWG. But Indian hockey continued to be plagued by internal dissensions and rifts. Things went to court and the sports ministry tried to get the two warring factions, IHF and Hockey India, to the table on multiple occasions to resolve the dispute. Things finally turned dire when the Champions Trophy was withdrawn from India and the Olympic qualifiers too were under threat. Though the qualifiers did take place the hockey scenario continues to be grim and faction ridden with the Competition Commission of India investigating disputes over World Series Hockey.

This intervention in 2009 was the second time the IOA had thus intervened in Indian hockey. The difference was that when the IOA similarly took over hockey in 1973, the FIH firmly opposed the move, siding with IHF administrators and ultimately forcing the IOA to back off. This time, though, the FIH chose to directly take on Indian hockey officials. It seemed worried, in strategic terms, about the possible dissolution of the world's largest hockey audience if Indian hockey was to plummet further. The big question, of course, is whether the IOA itself can do anything significantly better to improve Indian hockey. Its own record, after all, is not exactly glorious.

K.P.S. Gill's unceremonious ouster from the IHF was made possible because of the international threat to reign in the global purse strings. Irrespective of value judgments about the successes, or lack thereof, of his reign, the deeper issue here is of the longevity of his 14-year tenure and its meaning for Indian sport. If the hockey team had qualified for the Olympics, even if it had finished last in Beijing, it would have been well nigh impossible to press for his ouster. Gill's career as hockey chief is illustrative of a deeper trend in Indian sporting officialdom. Virtually every sporting body is controlled by a politician or a bureaucrat, and once entrenched most manage to stay on for years, if not for decades. The list is long: Congress MP Suresh Kalmadi, President of the Athletics Federation since 1989 continued to rule the IOA till he was finally jailed on charge of alleged misappropriation of CWG funds; BJP MP V.K. Malhotra, President of the Archery Federation since 1972 is now the IOA boss; Congress MP Priyaranjan Dasmunshi was President of the Football Federation since 1989 till the time he suffered a massive cardiac attack and former Congress MP K.P. Singh Deo is President of the Rowing Federation for 28 years.[17] In addition, BJP leader Yashwant Sinha has been running the Tennis Federation since 2000, V.K. Verma was in charge of badminton since 1998 before his arrest in connection with the CWG scams, the INLD's Ajay Chautala has been running table tennis since 2001 and Samata Party's Digvijay Singh has headed shooting since 2000 till his untimely demise in 2009.[18] Little wonder then that one of the forgotten initiatives of the late Sunil Dutt, as Sports Minister in 2004, had been to try and act against long-serving association heads. At the time, Congress leader Jagdish Tytler had been the chief of the Judo Federation for about 12 years and Himachal Congress chief Vidya Stokes had been heading the Indian Women's Hockey Federation for 12 years.[19] This is apart from the complete dominance of cricket bodies by politicians. To name just a few, at the time of writing, the NCP's Sharad Pawar is head of the ICC, the BJP's Arun Jaitely runs the Delhi Association, Chief Minister Narendra Modi heads the Gujarat Cricket Association and National Conference leader Farooq Abdullah is in charge of Jammu and Kashmir cricket. The RJD's Lalu Prasad Yadav used to head the now de-recognized Bihar cricket association. Cricket governance is no different from that of other Indian sports. It is just that despite sharing these features with other games, it has managed the new economy of television better and emerged as the pre-eminent Indian game (Chapter 9).

So why are politicians or bureaucrats attracted towards sport? This was the question raised at the 2008 Oxford Olympic legacies conference where we first presented our research on a public platform. Historian after sport historian in Oxford questioned why Indian sportsmen are largely absent from the firmament of sport administration. Is the preeminence of the politicians yet another example of Indian exceptionalism, deeply linked to the cultural forces that shape Indian society or is this a management system that has dangerously veered out of control, at variance with its avowed aims of sporting excellence? These are subliminal questions that lie at the heart of this book. What then, are the answers?

It must be emphasized that the pre-eminence of societal leaders in sporting bodies is not a uniquely Indian phenomenon. As was pointed out at Oxford, power politics at the top of domestic sporting bodies is a persistent feature of British sport as well, where most bodies are run by titled social elites.[20] The difference is that in India, these social elites have been replaced by that most pre-eminent of Indian societal figures: the politician. This suggests that Indian sporting structures, set up initially by the British, have largely followed the power patterns set by the Empire builders, except that the politicians who replaced the imperial officers have gradually replaced them in the sporting field as well.

Yet, by itself, this is too simplistic an explanation. For a more nuanced answer the clue lies in the early history of Indian Olympism and the attributes needed by sports administrators, as identified by Sir Dorabji Tata, the founder of the IOA. As Chaper 1 details, in 1927, when the IOC pressed Tata to recommend an Indian successor, he pushed for the Maharaja of Kapurthala, citing one major reason: that Kapurthala had the personal means and influence to visit Europe frequently. Tata's own commitment to Indian sport accrued directly out of a deep commitment to Indian nationalism. Yet, he argued in favour of a prince with the resources and the leisure to network with European society. This, in his view, was crucial to keep tabs on international developments and to coordinate with the IOC. Sir Dorabji Tata repeatedly emphasized that a regular presence in Europe was a necessary precondition.[21] Tata's arguments are revealing because they point to the fact that sporting structures were initially set up by political and moneyed elites. Only someone with the influence and power of a Tata or a prince in pre-independence India had the means to incur the expense required for running a national sporting body. India's emerging sporting structures were part of a fast-emerging global sporting network, and locked together as they were, in a relationship of power and patronage, only the elites could apply in the initial years.

After independence, as Nehruvian India grappled with the challenges of welding together a polyglot nation-state, many princes sought to integrate themselves even more with sports governance. Deprived of their kingdoms, the princes saw sport as one of the few arenas of power and social capital still open to them. While many princes became power-brokers or direct participants in the new game of democratic elections, many continued to see sport as a simultaneous site of social dominance. This, for instance, is why Patiala continued its pre-independence patronage of Olympism with an even greater vengeance and the house of Patiala has had an almost permanent presence in the higher structures of the IOA since 1947. The corollary to this argument is the fact that, at a time when sport was a low governmental priority, only the princes or a few handful of philanthropic Indian industrialists had the resources to devote themselves to sport. The middle class was still to emerge as a major social category and the post-libelarlization monetary avenues its emergence opened for popular games like cricket, for instance, were still in the distant future.

As the politician emerged as the pre-eminent dispenser of favours within the license-permit raj, his gaze shifted towards the sporting arena as yet another virgin territory of power and patronage. While India's experiment with democracy yielded new networks of power and created new social groups, it also threw up a new breed of sports administrators. In line with the changing equations of democratic India, powerful and ambitious politicians cutting across the spectrum gradually managed to usurp control over sporting bodies. Echoing Dorabji Tata's argument in favour of princes in 1927, V.K. Malhotra in 2004 was to argue for politicians citing precisely the same reasoning: means, power and influence. 'Being a politician helps in getting things done... It's easier to organize sponsors and get clearances from government since we are influential,' says Malhotra.[22] The argument was echoed by former hockey player Zafar Iqbal, 'The cost of running a federation is high. And players have to run to netas to get things done. Since they are influential and can get things done faster, politicians are preferred as federation heads.'[23] He did not, of course, mention that in the true traditions of the license-permit raj system, sporting control has also come to be seen as yet another avenue for the perks of office, influence, hogging the limelight and international travel. Summing up the arguments of many, Sharda Ugra wrote:

> Each sport becomes a fiefdom without tenure and comes with benefits. A gravy train of public funds to dip into and the chance to earn IOUs in exchange of overseas trips....On one hand there is power without responsibility, and on the other, responsibility without power.... If politics

> consists of major scams around stamp papers, cement and fodder, sports scams revolve around public money—yours and mine—being frittered away under the guise of awards and training expenses....
>
> Everything that stems from administration—forward planning, the quality of coaches, training, preparation, facilities—is at the mercy of the strongman of the national federation, whether it is the long-term secretary or the all-powerful president.[24]

In the popular perception it is this 'long-term secretary or the all-powerful president', more often than not a politician, who is at the crux of the problem of Indian sporting failure. So why are these 'strongmen' virtually permanent in their power and why is it difficult to dislodge them?

At its core, sport in any society is about the nature of power in that society and the patterns of control by politicians have followed the dominant patterns of Indian politics. A quick glance at the Indian political firmament confirms that the longevity of strongmen/women and their cliques is a feature shared by virtually every political party in every state of the union. The Nehru-Gandhis have controlled the Congress since independence, the firm of Advani and Vajpayee has held sway over the BJP since the mid-1970s, Farooq Abdullah's family has controlled the National Conference since its inception, the Chautalas' sway over Haryana's INLD remains unchallenged, Mayawati's iron-clad grip over the BSP is as solid as her mentor Kanshi Ram's, Chandrababu Naidu continues to define the TDP like his father-in-law N.T. Rama Rao, Mamata Bannerjee's Trinamool Congress is inseparable from her persona, the Left in West Bengal and Kerala has been defined as much by personality politics as other parties, Karunanidhi has controlled the DMK since at least the 1960s and Jayalalitha has successfully taken on the mantle of MGR in the AIADMK. Indian sport, in that sense, follows the political culture that mixes democratic processes with older forms of feudalism and organization. As early as 1970, Ashis Nandy had perceptively observed this fusion of culture and politics, arguing that:

> It is possible...to interpret the political process in India as a continuing attempt to reconcile older categories of thought and social character to the demands of nation-building and political culture as a complex of continuities in the style of response to the changing relationship between society and politics.[25]

At a deeper level, while India has undoubtedly grown more democratic with the growing empowerment of hitherto marginalized groups—OBCs, Dalits etc.[26]—the structures of political power even within these new groupings remain bound in tightly controlled immutable hierarchies.[27] To quote Nandy again:

> Authority in India was traditionally not so much a concentrated source of power and coercion, open to competition, pressures, and threats of dislodgment. It was a passive, apolitical, ascribed role which could not be contested by anyone from within the system. The pattern was validated by the absolute patriarchy of village and caste elders in group decision-making and by the history of distant arbitrary and political authorities who rarely interfered with the day to day living of their subjects. In present day Indian politics too, authority continues to have its 'natural, substantially hereditary seats' and cannot be dislodged without radically modifying the entire hierarchical structure within which it operates. This is expressed in the fear of and unconditional acceptance of established authority... (remember for example, the long history of collaboration with alien rulers...), the widespread faith in the supralogical intuition of accepted political leaders, and the manner in which individuals wield political charisma on the basis of their nonpolitical authority.[28]

Cultures are not fixed and it's important not to essentialize, but Nandy's explanation accounts for the continuance of feudal structures of power in most Indian political parties. It also explains the deeper social factors that drive the autocratic and closed political corridors of Indian sporting bodies. Seen in consonance with the rules governing such bodies, helps put it into perspective the political authoritarianism of individuals who seize control. For one, all sporting bodies are supposed to hold regular elections. Like political parties, these elections are mostly not held, or when held, they are largely a sham orchestrated by those in power. Once entrenched in power, it is virtually impossible for anyone to engineer the throw-out of a political satrap.

There is a crucial caveat though. While political parties are subject to five-yearly performance reviews by the electorate, which unleashes its own internal dynamics, there is no such mechanism to temper the behaviour of those who control sporting bodies. They operate in splendid isolation, as private bodies answerable only to the rules and strictures of the global bodies they are affiliated with. To illustrate this point further, the BCCI, responding to a PIL against its functioning, famously argued in court that it was a private body and did not represent India. It is impossible for the government to intervene — and its intervention may be worse than the problem — because all Olympic sporting bodies are governed by the Olympic charter, which militates against governmental intervention. This is why the IOA had to intervene in Indian hockey. Had the Government of India done so, Indian hockey could well have been disaffiliated from the global system. So, is change an impossibility? Are we condemned to a sporting system that will remain locked in place forever with no hope for change? Perhaps not. As the example of the hockey sting operation shows, the wider forces driving Indian society—in this case the media and the economic incentives of liberalization—do exert their own push and pull, so change, though not easy, is still possible. Sport, after all, is only a mirror in which to see the deeper imprint of a society.

As we gave seen, India's Olympic encounter has been a battleground where an emerging nation's internal dissensions were given full play: issues of national representation, colonial and post-colonial resistance, women's empowerment, the north-south divide, sports diffusion, the fight for the control of sporting organizations.

In the final analysis, the essence of Olympism does not reside in medals won, records broken or television rights sold as ends in themselves. The Olympics, and its relevant records and statistics, are important for the way in which they can affect societies surrounding them. Thus, when the Puerto Ricans march in the Olympic opening ceremony even when they don't have a representative in the United Nations, or when an unknown Anthony Nesty of Surinam wins gold by defeating the favourite Matt Biondi of the US, or when an Indian hockey team wins gold after defeating its former colonial masters in 1948, the significance of such acts stretches far beyond the narrow confines of sport.

Postscript
Sport Does Matter: Delhi and the 2008 Olympic Torch Relay

Seven security checkpoints, 21,000 security personnel, the heart of India's capital almost at a standstill, an attempt to storm the hotel Le Meridian—where the Olympic torch was kept since its arrival from Islamabad at 1.10 a.m. on the night of 16 April—and finally a series of peaceful, synchronized democratic protests by Tibetans and human rights groups from 8 a.m. in the morning across the country: the Indian leg of the Olympic torch relay was extraordinary in every sense. For the record, international legs of the Olympic torch relay have often been mired in controversy. While some say that the 2008 edition of the torch relay has witnessed unprecedented turmoil the world over, Olympic history demonstrates otherwise. The situation in Islamabad and Delhi was unusual in that the relays weren't open to the public and only invitees were allowed to attend, but this too was not without precedent.

The only other time that sections of the torch relay were completely closed to the public was during the flame-lighting ceremony at ancient Olympia for the 1984 Los Angeles Games. Armed Greek troops had closed off the sanctuary, refusing entry to the Greek public and to the hundreds of demonstrators who had vowed not to let the Americans have the flame. They were protesting the Los Angeles Olympic Organizing Committee's decision to sell the rights to be a torchbearer, a decision that many Greeks saw as an insult to Greek national sovereignty. The traditional public relay and key ceremonies in Greece, as John MacAloon points out, were cancelled. The Olympic priestess lit the flame in spite of death threats. The Americans took the flame out by helicopter to the Athens airport and left immediately for the safe haven of their own shores.[1]

Such protests lie at the very core of what is widely understood as 'Olympism'. As the popular saying goes in Olympic academic circles, 'Take sports out of the Olympics and you still have the movement to fall back on'. While this is certainly an exaggeration, it is time to accept that the Olympics and the torch relay are never only about sportspeople. The relay is not restricted to countries that win the most number of medals or those that have the best sports facilities for its athletes. Rather, it is meant as a mechanism to garner mass support in the poorest of countries, among men and women who will make it to an Olympic sports contest. That is why, traditionally, attendance at the Olympic torch relay is free. While Olympic competitions are prohibitively expensive, enthusiasts don't need tickets to attend the relay. For countries that can't even dream of hosting the games in view of the escalating costs, the torch relay remains the point of participation. It is this aspect of the Olympic movement that makes the world's biggest sports spectacle relevant for us in India. The flame, unlike the torch, can never be commercialized and is one of the most powerful symbols of peace in the modern world. The meanings attached to it belong neither to the IOC nor to local organizing committees. It has emerged as an enduring symbol of global harmony and mobilization, a fact evident on the streets of Delhi on 17 April 2008.

Before every summer games for the last 25 years, the Olympics have provided a forum for issues of international concern. While Seoul highlighted the Korea crisis, Barcelona brought to light ethnic differences within Spanish society. Atlanta drew world attention to the race issue in U.S.A. and Sydney highlighted the Aboriginal crisis Down Under. When Cathy Freeman lit the flame at the Sydney Games in 2000, it was much more than a sporting ritual. It symbolized the recognition of the tensions at the heart of modern Australian society, augmented further even when she later wrapped herself in the aboriginal flag in full view of the world's cameras. Similarly, when the Tibetans organized a parallel relay in Delhi in 17 April 2008, the Tibet crisis became the focus of international attention.

Prior to the Indian leg of the torch relay, there was considerable debate on whether New Delhi would allow Tibetan protesters to carry on with their demonstrations. With the West Bengal and Kerala governments, states ruled by communist parties, adopting a hardline approach towards such protests, the issue had assumed added significance. But in the final reckoning, the world's largest democracy could not be seen to be muffling dissent, even if this dissent was opposed by those who were advocating a closer strategic engagement with China. Also, it provided a subtle mechanism to the Indian government to call attention to the million square metres of Chinese occupation in Aksai Chin and China's reported illegal intrusions into Arunachal Pradesh and Sikkim. It was New Delhi's way of remonstrating against the Chinese decision to call the Indian Ambassador at 2 a.m. in the morning in Beijing, threatening her with dire consequences over India's failure to check alleged Tibetan attacks on the Chinese embassy in New Delhi. It was a delicate balancing act: allow the Tibetans their fundamental right to protest in full public view but guard against a diplomatic incident by ensuring that the torch relay itself, guarded by Chinese commandoes, was not disrupted. The price tag was the excessive security and the huge inconvenience caused to Delhi's residents on the day of the ritual.

A Mini-Tibet in Delhi: Following the Agitators

It was an incredible experience. Following the Tibetan protesters from Rajghat to Jantar Mantar in the scorching Delhi heat, trying to make sense of their slogans, was to go back into an older, idealistic world where agitations and public dissent of this kind still had meaning. It was to be reminded of the simple idealism of agitational politics, of the basic principles of civil action, where the participants were aware that they were marginal but found power and agency in simply making themselves heard.

For us, the experience of the relay had begun on the night of 16 April when we watched Tenzing Tsundue, a noted activist and leader of the Free Tibet movement, on *Times Now*. Soon after the show, Tenzing, we were later informed, was dropped off at a secret location since the police were desperate to detain him. The *Times Now* driver, Amjad, who ferried him to his hideout and who was with us the following day, took us there at the stroke of dawn. It was cloak-and-dagger stuff—a trip that led us to a hideout where 200 or more Tibetans were busy planning an assault on the flame. A group of senior Tibetan leaders were in attendance and were keen to ensure that 17 April 2008 turned into a day of international impact for their cause. Knowing full well that the police would outnumber them, they were planning guerilla attacks on the flame while it was on its way out of the Meridian on Janpath Road and travelling along India Gate. That such meticulous planning resulted in little tangible gain in the end is a different matter altogether. The police clampdown on central Delhi put paid to all their plans but to be to see the cold determination of the protestors—the steely look in their eyes, the idealism in their venture and the vociferous arguments over tactics—was enlightening. While these Tibetans were determined to make a mark and weren't averse to violence, others, who had already made Jantar Mantar their home, were single-minded in their determination to keep things peaceful. For them non-violent protest was the way to capture world attention and hence lifesize cut-outs of Mahatma Gandhi were juxtaposed with those of the Dalai Lama at the forefront of most of the protest rallies.

For these and thousands of other Tibetans who had arrived in Delhi the night before, things got underway in the early hours of the morning of 17 April with an assembly at Rajghat. This was a giant venture that needed planning and coordination on a national scale. When we reached at 7.30 a.m., we saw groups of men and women bracing themselves for the day's events by writing out posters or painting placards. Some were busy packing pouches of water and food, while others, who had travelled thousands of miles to be part of the movement, were catching up on a few hours of sleep. Young Tibetan girls and boys, mostly students from leading Delhi colleges, wrapped themselves in 'Free Tibet' flags and were busy distributing 'Free Tibet' T-shirts to anyone who wanted to join the assembly. Members of the Tibetan Parliament-in-Exile, key organizers of the rally, were busy putting final touches to preparations for the protest march. 'We wanted the Dalai Lama to be visible alongside Mahatma Gandhi for both are messiahs for global peace',[2] was their reasoned answer to our query on why most posters had the Tibetan leader sharing space with the father of the nation.

Just as the clock struck 10, there arrived at Rajghat a slew of Hindu, Muslim and Sikh religious preachers for joint prayers in solidarity with the Tibetans at Gandhi's Samadhi. It was truly surreal, a motley mix of preachers from varied religious backgrounds coming together to pray for a cause of global significance. It was good event management to be sure; but only the most cold-hearted cynic could remain unmoved by the solemnity of the occasion or fail to observe the fact that the global appeal of contemporary sport was what had made this possible. With the prayers over, the Tibetans lit their own parallel flame. This was different in shape to the Olympic torch and was more in the nature of a diya that was subsequently placed inside a round frame. They had been told that only a 'non-official' torch of this kind would pass official muster. As chants of 'Karuna ki jyoti amar rahe' and 'Shanti ki jyoti amar rahe', shattered the silence, the assembled leaders from all the major religious groups came together to carry the flame out of Rajghat. This was the point at which the huge police contingent, men and women who had been entirely co-operative until then, began to look tad jittery, until the rally leaders assured them that the march would be kept peaceful. So powerful was the group dynamic that some security men too were caught up in the emotionalism of the moment; a couple of those standing nearest to the protestors had tears in their eyes.

Once out of Rajghat, the rally began its 4 km long march to Jantar Mantar, the site which the Tibetans had made theirs for the day. Thousands of Tibetans from Varanasi, Mcleodgunj, Bangalore and Dharamshala had already assembled at Jantar Mantar the night before, carrying with them the bare minimum supplies. The location was not unsurprising. Jantar Mantar is the permanent protestors' corner in Delhi. For years it has been the site where people come to present their woes before the national media, hoping for greater visibility with the powers that be. And so the Tibetans came, jostling for space in this parliament of the oppressed, alongside stalls set up by the Bhopal gas victims, the Vishwa Dalit Parishad, the Foundation for Common Man, Justice for Nithari and even the Group 4-Securicor Mazdoor Union, asking for better wages.

But this was a day primarily for the Tibetans. As hundreds of specially deployed policemen watched from the sidelines and scores of reporters took notes, the entire panoply of anti-Chinese dissent was on display in a tent city that had come up virtually overnight on one of the side lanes leading up to Jantar Mantar. The centre-piece was a day-long funeral service for those who died at the hands of the Chinese, conducted by monks specially brought into Delhi for the occasion. As their chants and gongs filled the air, we could see a whole range of stalls—representatives of the banned Falung Gong, photographs of those dead and missing and pictures of torture and death at the hands of Chinese troops. This was where the bulk of the protest groups took up residence for most of the afternoon, once the 4 km distance from Rajghat had been covered, for a day-long ritual of songs, chants and slogans. With hundreds of local students joining hands, Jantar Mantar was turned into a mini-Tibet, the adjoining alleyways and streets leading up to Janpath Road and Connaught Place now chock-a-block with activists sporting 'Free Tibet' T-shirts and head bands. Their one-point demand: China must open its doors to envoys of the Dalai Lama.

By early afternoon, when the Tibetans resumed their peaceful march after a gap of almost three hours, the scene of action shifted to the stretch between Raisina Hill and India Gate, the venue for the official Olympic torch relay. This was when the cost of the protest to the ordinary commuter came home to us most forcefully. The five-minute drive from Jantar Mantar to India Gate turned into a 90 minute walk with the police having closed all access roads and all vehicular traffic. As we pleaded with the first police access point on Copernicus Road, we could hear the desperate pleas of a middle-aged man whose mother-in-law had suffered an accident at Safdarjang but who was stuck on this side of town with the police clampdown. 'What do I do?' he pleaded, 'how do I get there? Will you let me through?' The policemen were sympathetic but their orders were clear. These roads were off-limits. 'Try another route,' was the advice to the distraught man. As for us, we were by now late for the function, after having taken numerous diversions to reach the venue. Despite possessing all the necessary invites and IOA advisories, the policemen on duty had the same answer: 'Sorry, the road is now closed.' So we put on our most humble faces, protested about being academics writing on the torch relay and dropped a thousand names before the wall of resistance reluctantly melted. We could still hear the man with the injured mother-in-law arguing his case with another group of policemen as we entered. We were on foot; with his car, he had no chance. A policeman was explaining a long circuitous alternative route to him as we crossed the barricade.

Even on foot, only a handful of select invitees were allowed to line up along the relay route stretching for 2.7 km and manned by 3000 plus security personnel. As the sponsors' cheering groups performed their customary song and dance numbers without an audience, their act seemed superficial in comparison to the intensity of the protests in the morning. Declared Randhir Singh, Secretary General of the IOA:

> We have done everything possible to ensure the torch relay goes through peacefully. We did not intend it to be a closed one but there isn't much we could do. We would have loved the public to come and be part of this historic occasion in keeping with established Olympic tradition. But the situation is such that one blemish might lead to violence. Our national pride and international standing was at stake.[3]

And so it was. At exactly 4.40 p.m. Kunjarani Devi, India's legendary weightlifter, kickstarted the carefully orchestrated flame relay. As the official run began, the tension in the air was palpable. The IOA and the government were determined to get through the day's events as soon as possible. Within 50 minutes the flame had travelled the distance from Raisina Hill to India Gate, escorted by Chinese minders. Finally, when Leander Paes and Mahesh Bhupathi lit the cauldron, Suresh Kalmadi, President of the IOA, looked justly relieved.

As the troubled flame left Indian shores for Bangkok and then on to Canberra, Osaka and Seoul, we could not help but comment on the way in which the Olympic movement champions sport as a medium for inter-cultural communication and peaceful democratic exchange. In fact, it could be successfully argued following the Delhi leg of the international torch relay that the Olympic ideology promoted by the IOC since its creation is no longer founded on the unity of sport and culture alone, as extolled by De Coubertin at the beginning of the twentieth century: it has taken on a third dimension, of concern for human rights. This development is not only a sign of the times, but also a positive legacy of the modern Olympic Games.

Endnotes

Prologue

1. Works by Gulu Ezekiel and K. Arumugam in English and Chiranjeev in Bengali have done much to document achievements of Indian sportspersons at Olympic stage. Gulu has also helped at various stages of research and has a commitment to Olympic history that few have in this country. We are also indebted to Prof. Karl Lennartz, president of the Society of Olympic Historians for giving us access to his personal collection, perhaps the best individual collection on Olympism in the world.
2. Clifford Geertz, 'Deep Play': Notes on the Balinese Cockfight', in *The Interpretation of Cultures: Selected Essays*, (New York: Basic Books, 1973).
3. In recent times Indian supporters have far outnumbered supporters from other nations in international sports contests. At both the 2003 Cricket World Cup in South Africa and the 2007 World Cup in the Caribbean as also in the eight-nation hockey championship at Amstelveen in Holland in 2005, the Indians had great support, with the stadiums decked in the tricolour. Even when Sania Mirza had her dream US Open run in August 2005, Indians from all over the US flocked by the hundreds to Flushing Meadow, New York, to cheer their favourite tennis star.
4. Dipesh Chakrabarty, 'Introduction', in Boria Majumdar and J A Mangan (eds.), *Sport in South Asian Society: Past and Present*, (Routledge: London, 2005).
5. Ibid.

Chapter 1

1. Personal letter from Dorab J. Tata to the IOC president, Count Baillet Latour, 21 May 1929. Housed at the International Olympic Museum, Lausanne, ID Chemise 7334 CIO 3535 MBR-TATA-CORR, Correspondence de Dorabji Tata 1926–1930.

2. While campaigning for Tokyo's bid for the 1940 games, Count Soyeshima Michisima, Japan's delegate to the IOC, convinced Mussolini to withdraw Rome's candidature largely on the back of the claim that 1940 coincided with the 2,600th anniversary of the *Kigen*. Baron Yoriyasu saw Tokyo's victory in the Olympic race as affirmation not just of Japan's athletic progress but as proof that 'renascent Japan has advanced in worldly and grand terms'. Quoted in Sandra Collins, 'Conflicts of 1930s Japanese Olympic Diplomacy in Universalising the Olympic Movement', *The International Journal of the History of Sport*, Vol. 23, No. 7, Nov. 2006, pp. 1132–33.
3. Ibid., pp. 1128–51.
4. See for instance, Ramachandra Guha, *Corner of a Foreign Field: The Indian History of a British Sport* (New Delhi: Pan Macmillan, 2002), Richard Cashman, *Patrons, Players and the Crowd* (New Delhi, Orient Longman, 1979), Mihir Bose, *History of Indian Cricket* (London: Andre Deutsch, 1990).
5. It was the second oldest national Olympic Association in Asia after Japan, which was established in 1912.
6. For details see, Katharine Moore, 'The Warmth of Comradeship': The First British Empire Games and Imperial Solidarity', in *The International Journal of the History of Sport*, 6, (2), September 1989, pp. 243–51; Katharine Moore, 'A Divergence of Interests: Canada's Role in the Politics and Sport of the British Empire During the 1920's', in *The Canadian Journal of History of Sport*, 21 (1), 1990, pp. 21–29.
7. This was documented by Prof. Bruce Kidd at a course taught at the University of Toronto in May 2007 by him with Boria Majumdar titled 'The Politics of the Commonwealth Games'.
8. Ibid.
9. For instance, the Sir Dorabji Tata Trust provided the seed money to fund the setting up of one of India's premier scientific and engineering research institutions, the Indian Institute of Science, Bangalore.
10. Boria Majumdar, *Twenty Two Yards to Freedom: A Social History of Indian Cricket* (New Delhi: Penguin-Viking, 2004), pp. 93–94, Also see; P.N. Polishwala, *School and College Cricket in India* (Mumbai: 1921), p.11.
11. For details on the impact of the 'Games Ethic' on the colonies see, J.A. Mangan, *The Games Ethic and Imperialism* (London: Frank Cass, 2001); Brian Stoddart, 'Sport, Colonialism and Struggle: CLR James and Cricket', *Sport in Society*, 9 (5), 2006, pp.914–30.
12. See Cecil Headlam, *Ten Thousand Miles through India and Burma: An Account of the Oxford University Cricket Tour with Mr K. J. Kay in the Year of the Coronation Durbar* (London, 1903).
13. J.A. Mangan (ed.), *The Cultural Bond: Sport, Empire, Society* (London and Portland, OR: Frank Cass, 1992), p. 8.
14. Personal letter from Dorabji Tata to the IOC president, Count Baillet Latour, 21 May 1929. Housed at the International Olympic Museum,

Lausanne, ID Chemise 7334 CIO 3535 MBR-TATA-CORR, Correspondence de Dorabji Tata 1926–1930.

15. Ibid.
16. See the letters in ID Chemise 7334 CIO 3535 MBR-TATA-CORR, Correspondence de Dorabji Tata 1926–1930, International Olympic Museum, Lausanne.
17. Personal letter from Dorab J. Tata to the IOC president, Count Baillet Latour, 21 May 1929. Housed at the International Olympic Museum, Lausanne, ID Chemise 7334 CIO 3535 MBR-TATA-CORR, Correspondence de Dorabji Tata 1926–1930.
18. Ibid.
19. *The Statesman*, 3 June 1920, 'Indian Athletes at the Olympic Games: Team of Six from Bombay'.
20. Ibid.
21. *Amrita Bazar Patrika*, 30 August 1920.
22. Ibid.
23. Letter from A.G. Noehren to Dorabji J. Tata on 1 April 1924 housed at the International Olympic Museum, Lausanne. File OU MO 01 14 36, CIO CNO IND CORR, Olympic Studies Center, IOC Museum, Lausanne. This file deals primarily with correspondence exchanged between the Indian Olympic Association and the International Olympic Committee. Also, all documents sent from India to the IOC—letters, pamphlets, constitutions etc have been retained in this file. Also see IDD Chemise 9404 CIO CNO INDE CORR, Correspondence India 1924-1963.
24. Ibid.
25. Ibid.
26. *Amrita Bazar Patrika*, 18 January 1924.
27. Ibid., 13 February 1924.
28. Saradindu Sanyal, 'India and the Olympics', in *XVIII Olympiad Tokyo 1964: Official Souvenir of the Indian Olympic Association*: (Mumbai: Sportswriters Publishers, 1964), pp. 25–26.
29. Ibid.
30. Cesar Torres, 'The Latin American Olympic Explosion in the 1920s: Causes and Consequences', in Boria Majumdar and Sandra Collins (eds.), *Olympism: The Global Vision: From Nationalism to Internationalism*, Special Issue, *The International Journal of the History of Sport*, 23, (7), November 2006, pp. 1088–94.
31. Personal letter from Elswood S. Brown to Pierre De Coubertin, 3 February 1919, 'Young Men's Christian Associations. 1909–1927' (hereafter YMCA, 1909–1927), IOC Archives, Lausanne.
32. Personal letter from Elswood S. Brown to Pierre De Coubertin, 23 January 1929, (YMCA, 1909–1927), IOC Archives, Lausanne.
33. (YMCA, 1909–1927), IOC Archives, Lausanne.
34. Anthony S. De Mello, 'In the Ramayana and Mahabharata: Nehru's Favourite', in *Portrait of Indian Sport* (New Delhi: Macmillan 1959), p. 99.

35. Personal letter from Henry Gray to Count Baillet Latour, 28 December 1928. IOC Archives, ID Chemise 7334 CIO 3535 MBR-TATA-CORR, Correspondence de Dorabji Tata 1926–1930.
36. IOC Archives, ID Chemise 7334 CIO 3535 MBR-TATA-CORR, Correspondence de Dorabji Tata 1926–1930.
37. Personal letter from Dorabji J. Tata to the IOC president, Count Baillet Latour, 21 May 1929. Housed at the International Olympic Museum, Lausanne, ID Chemise 7334 CIO 3535 MBR-TATA-CORR, Correspondence de Dorabji Tata 1926–1930.
38. Personal letter from Dorabji J. Tata to the IOC president Count Baillet Latour, 21 Feb 1927. Housed at the International Olympic Museum, Lausanne, ID Chemise 7334 CIO 3535 MBR-TATA-CORR, Correspondence de Dorabji Tata 1926–1930.
39. For details on the stadium controversy see; Boria Majumdar, *Twenty Two Yards to Freedom: A Social History of Indian Cricket* (New Delhi: Penguin Viking, 2004), pp. 171–99.
40. IOC Archives, ID Chemise 7334 CIO 3535 MBR-TATA-CORR, Correspondence de Dorabji Tata 1926–1930.
41. Personal letter from IOC president to Sir Dorabji Tata, 22 April 1927. The IOC chief thanked Tata for his wonderful work in promoting the Olympic cause in India and indicated that the IOC was aware of the difficulties involved in replacing Sir Dorab with someone equally capable and equal to the task of assuming effective control of the Olympic movement in India. IOC Archives, ID Chemise 7334 CIO 3535 MBR-TATA-CORR, Correspondence de Dorabji Tata 1926–1930.
42. For details see; Boria Majumdar, *Twenty Two Yards to Freedom: A Social History of Indian Cricket* (New Delhi: Penguin Viking, 2004), Chapter 1.
43. Personal letter from IOC President to Sir Dorabji Tata, 22 April 1927. IOC Archives, ID Chemise 7334 CIO 3535 MBR-TATA-CORR, Correspondence de Dorabji Tata 1926–1930.
44. For details see Boria Majumdar and Kausik Bandyopadhyay, *Goalless: The Story of a Unique Footballing Nation* (New Delhi: Penguin Viking, 2006), Chapter 4.
45. For most of his letters see IOC Archives, ID Chemise 7334 CIO 3535 MBR-TATA-CORR, Correspondence de Dorabji Tata 1926–1930.
46. Personal letter from Sir Dorabji Tata to Count Baillet Latour, Geneva, 16 June 1927. IOC Archives, ID Chemise 7334 CIO 3535 MBR-TATA-CORR, Correspondence de Dorabji Tata 1926-1930. Also see; File OU MO 01 14 36, CIO CNO IND CORR, Olympic Studies Center, IOC Museum, Lausanne.
47. Ibid.
48. IOC Archives, ID Chemise 7334 CIO 3535 MBR-TATA-CORR, Correspondence de Dorabji Tata 1926-1930. Also see; File OU MO 01 14 36, CIO CNO IND CORR, Olympic Studies Center.

49. For details of the Ranji-Patiala proximity see; Boria Majumdar, *Twenty Two Yards to Freedom: A Social History of Indian Cricket*, (New Delhi: Penguin Viking, 2004), p. 62.
50. Personal letter from Sir Dorabji Tata to Count Baillet Latour on 13 September 1927. File OU MO 01 14 36, CIO CNO IND CORR, Olympic Studies Center.
51. Personal letter from Sir Dorabji Tata to Count Baillet Latour on 17 Jan. 1928. File OU MO 01 14 36, CIO CNO IND CORR, Olympic Studies Center.
52. Anthony S. De Mello, 'A Wardrobe of Coloured Blazers', in *Portrait of Indian Sport*, (New Delhi: Macmillan 1959), pp. 48–49.
53. Ibid.
54. Ibid.
55. Ibid.
56. File OU MO 01 14 36, CIO CNO IND CORR, Olympic Studies Center.
57. All quotes in this paragraph are from a personal letter from Henry Gray to Count Baillet Latour, 28 December 1928. IOC Archives, ID Chemise 7334 CIO 3535 MBR-TATA-CORR, Correspondence de Dorabji Tata 1926–1930.
58. IOC Archives, IDD Chemise 9404 CIO CNO INDE CORR, Correspondence India 1924–1963.
59. Personal letter from IOC President to Dorabji Tata on 11 May 1929. IOC Archives, ID Chemise 7334 CIO 3535 MBR-TATA-CORR, Correspondence de Dorabji Tata 1926–1930.
60. Personal letter from Sir Dorabji Tata to Count Baillet Latour, 21 May 1929 and letter from Sir Dorabji Tata to the Maharaja of Patiala on 6 May 1931. IOC Archives, ID Chemise 7334 CIO 3535 MBR-TATA-CORR, Correspondence de Dorabji Tata 1926-1930 and File OU MO 01 14 36, CIO CNO IND CORR, Olympic Studies Center.
61. IOC Archives, IDD Chemise 9404 CIO CNO INDE CORR, Correspondence India 1924–1963.
62. John J. Macaloon, 'Introduction', Revised and Updated edition of *This Great Symbol: Pierre De Coubertin and the Origins of the Modern Olympic Games,* Special Issue, *The International Journal of the History of Sport*, 23 (3–4), 2006, p. 344.
63. Rosalind O 'Hanlon, 'Issues of Masculinity in North Indian History: The Bangash Nawabs of Farrukhabad', in *Indian Journal of Gender Studies* 4 (1), (New Delhi: Sage, 1997).

Chapter 2

1. For details see Boria Majumdar and Kausik Bandyopadhyay, *Goalless: The Story of a Unique Footballing Nation* (New Delhi: Penguin Viking, 2006), Chapter 4.
2. Ibid.

3. The First Western Asiatic Games was held in New Delhi on 2–3 March 1934 under the patronage of the Indian Olympic Association.
4. Gupta, for example, was the secretary of the Bengal Hockey Association, represented the Indian Football Association at major meetings throughout the 1930s and was also a key power broker in the Cricket Association of Bengal and also the Board of Control for Cricket in India.
5. Letter from G.D. Sondhi to the IOC president, 30 March 1931. Housed at the International Olympic Museum, Lausanne. File OU MO 01 14 36, CIO CNO IND CORR, Olympic Studies Center, IOC Museum, Lausanne. This file deals primarily with correspondence exchanged between the Indian Olympic Association and the International Olympic Committee. Any document sent from India to the IOC—letters, pamphlets, constitutions etc—have been retained in this file. Also see IDD Chemise 9404 CIO CNO INDE CORR, Correspondence India 1924–1963.
6. Sondhi to De Coubertin, 17 January 1934. File OU MO 01 14 36, CIO CNO IND CORR, Olympic Studies Center.
7. Sondhi to De Coubertin, 14 March 1934. File OU MO 01 14 36, CIO CNO IND CORR, Olympic Studies Center.
8. Sondhi to De Coubertin, 31 May 1934. File OU MO 01 14 36, CIO CNO IND CORR, Olympic Studies Center.
9. Minutes of F.I.N.A. meeting 8–9 May 1935. This is also housed at the IOC Museum, Lausanne, is part of the India correspondence. IDD Chemise 9404 CIO CNO INDE CORR, Correspondence India 1924-1963.
10. Sondhi to Count Baillet Latour, 2 July 1935. File OU MO 01 14 36, CIO CNO IND CORR, Olympic Studies Center.
11. Ibid.
12. Sondhi to honorary secretary, FINA, 29 June, 1935. File OU MO 01 14 36, CIO CNO IND CORR, Olympic Studies Center.
13. Sondhi to Count Baillet Latour, 2 July 1935. File OU MO 01 14 36, CIO CNO IND CORR, Olympic Studies Center.
14. Ibid.
15. Ibid.
16. Letter from S.Y. Sircar, joint secretary of the National Swimming Association to Count Baillet Latour, 16 September 1935. File OU MO 01 14 36, CIO CNO IND CORR, Olympic Studies Center.
17. Ibid.
18. Letter from the Secretary of the Hatkhola Club to the Secretary of the International Olympic Committee, 28 March 1938. File OU MO 01 14 36, CIO CNO IND CORR, Olympic Studies Center.
19. Letter from the secretary of the Hatkhola Club to the secretary of the International Olympic Committee, 28 March 1938. File OU MO 01 14 36, CIO CNO IND CORR, Olympic Studies Center.
20. Letter from the secretary of the Hatkhola Club to the Secretary of the International Olympic Committee, 28 March 1938. File OU MO 01 14 36, CIO CNO IND CORR, Olympic Studies Center.

21. Ibid.
22. Ibid.
23. Letter from Pankaj Gupta to Count Baillet Latour, Date not found. File OU MO 01 14 36, CIO CNO IND CORR, Olympic Studies Center.
24. Ibid.
25. Sondhi to Pankaj Gupta, 16 June 1939. File OU MO 01 14 36, CIO CNO IND CORR, Olympic Studies Center.
26. Ibid.
27. Ibid.
28. Ibid.
29. Ibid.
30. Sondhi to Count Baillet Latour, 17 June 1939. File OU MO 01 14 36, CIO CNO IND CORR, Olympic Studies Center.
31. Ibid.
32. Tokyo and Helsinki had been awarded the 1940 and 1944 Olympiads respectively before the world war resulted in the cancellation of these games.
33. Sondhi to Count Baillet Latour, 17 June 1939. File OU MO 01 14 36, CIO CNO IND CORR, Olympic Studies Center.
34. Correspondence of Sohrab H. Bhoot with the IOC President Avery Brundage. IDD Chemise 9404 CIO CNO INDE CORR, Correspondence India 1924–1963.
35. Raja Bhalindra Singh, president, IOA, to Avery Brundage, president, IOC, 4 October 1958 CIO MBR SINGH CORR OU MO 01 4107 SINGH, Bhalindra Raja Correspondence 1947-1985.
36. Correspondence of Sohrab H. Bhoot with the IOC president, Avery Brundage. IDD Chemise 9404 CIO CNO INDE CORR, Correspondence India 1924–1963.
37. Raja Bhalindra Singh, president, IOA to Avery Brundage, president, IOC, 4 October 1958. CIO MBR SINGH CORR OU MO 01 4107 SINGH, Bhalindra Raja Correspondence 1947–1985
38. Correspondence of Sohrab H. Bhoot with the IOC president, Avery Brundage. IDD Chemise 9404 CIO CNO INDE CORR, Correspondence India 1924–1963.
39. For details see; 'Play the Game in the spirit of the Game: First Asian Games–New Delhi 1951', Anthony S. De Mello, *Portrait of Indian Sport*, (New Delhi: Macmillan, 1959).
40. http://www.cyclingfederationofindia.org/, accessed 10 August 2007.
41. Raja Bhalindra Singh, president, IOA, to Avery Brundage, president, IOC, 4 October 1958 CIO MBR SINGH CORR OU MO 01 4107 SINGH, Bhalindra Raja Correspondence 1947–1985
42. 'Sports News and Views of the Day by Leon', the *Times of India*, 25 September 1953, quoted in Ibid.

43. Raja Bhalindra Singh, president, IOA, to Avery Brundage, president, IOC, 4 October 1958. CIO MBR SINGH CORR OU MO 01 4107 SINGH, Bhalindra Raja Correspondence 1947–1985
44. Raja Bhalindra Singh, president, IOA to Avery Brundage, president, IOC, 4 October 1958. CIO MBR SINGH CORR OU MO 01 4107 SINGH, Bhalindra Raja Correspondence 1947–1985.
45. Raja Bhalindra Singh, president, IOA to Avery Brundage, president, IOC, 4 October 1958. CIO MBR SINGH CORR OU MO 01 4107 SINGH, Bhalindra Raja Correspondence 1947–1985
46. Letter to IOA from chairman, Warsaw–Berlin–Prague Road Race, 22 November 1955. Quoted in Ibid.
47. Raja Bhalindra Singh, president, IOA to Avery Brundage, president, IOC,4 October 1958. CIO MBR SINGH CORR OU MO 01 4107 SINGH, Bhalindra Raja Correspondence 1947–1985.
48. Raja Bhalindra Singh, president, IOA, to Avery Brundage, president, IOC,4 October 1958. CIO MBR SINGH CORR OU MO 01 4107 SINGH, Bhalindra Raja Correspondence 1947–1985
49. Ibid.
50. Letter from Sohrab H. Bhoot to the president and members of the IOC executive committee, 26 September 1956. IDD Chemise 9404 CIO CNO INDE CORR, Correspondence India 1924–1963.
51. Ibid.
52. Ibid.
53. Ibid.
54. Ibid.
55. http://www.cyclingfederationofindia.org/ accessed 10 August 2007.
56. Ibid.

Chapter 3

1. Review of the 1932 Olympic expedition by the president of the IHF, A.M. Hayman housed at the International Olympic Museum, Lausanne. File OU MO 01 14 36, CIO CNO IND CORR, Olympic Studies Center.
2. Rajdeep Sardesai, the *Sunday Times of India,* 1992
3. The magazines of the Presidency and St Xavier's Colleges in Calcutta between 1920 and 1940 are full of praise for the Indian hockey team's performance at the Olympics.
4. For details see; 'We Climb the Victory Stand: Hockey in *Excelsis*', in Anthony S. De Mello, *Portrait of Indian Sport*, (New Delhi: Macmillan, 1959).
5. Dhyan Chand, *Goal*, published in *Sport and Pastime*, 1952. The book has been digitized and is available in http://www.bharatiyahockey.org/granthalaya/goal/, accessed 10 September 2007.
6. For details see; 'We Climb the Victory Stand: Hockey in *Excelsis*', op. cit., p. 82.

7. Ibid.
8. Ibid., p. 83.
9. For details see C.D. Parthasarathy, 'Indian Hockey: Rise and Fall', in *Sport and Pastime*, 16 February 1963.
10. Dhyan Chand, *Goal*, op. cit. .
11. 'We Climb the Victory Stand...', op. cit., p. 85.
12. Ramachandra Guha, *India After Gandhi: The History of the World's Largest Democracy* (New Delhi: Picador, 2007), pp. 115–16
13. Subroto Sirkar, 'They came...they played...they conquered', *World Hockey*, 13 March 1995, p.8.
14. For details see Dhyan Chand, *Goal* op. cit. .
15. Notes from Jaipal's Singh's memoirs passed on to us by Amar Singh, Jaipal Singh's son, then secretary of the CC Morris Cricket Library, Pennsylvania in 2001. The memoirs were later edited by Rashmi Katyayan and published by Prabhat Khabar Publications, Ranchi, 2004.
16. Rashmi Katyayan (ed.), *Lo Bir Sendra* (Ranchi: Prabhat Khabar Publications, 2004), p. 35.
17. *Lo Bir Sendra*, op. cit., pp. 35–37.
18. Dhyan Chand, *Goal*, op. cit. .
19. The *Statesman*, 19 May 1928, p. 11.
20. Ibid.
21. The *Statesman*, 29 May 1928, p. 14.
22. Personal interview with Amar Singh, 2001, Jaipal Singh's life has quite a few unsolved mysteries. For example Jaipal's real name was Pramod Pahan. Later his name was changed to Jaipal and even he isn't sure why this happened. On Jaipal not playing in the final of the 1928 Olympiad Dhyan Chand writes in his memoirs, 'Jaipal Singh, I believe, used to fly from London to Amsterdam most of the time, returning after the match was over. It is still a mystery to me why Jaipal Singh, after ably captaining us in England, and in two of the three matches in the Olympic Games, suddenly left us. I have heard many stories, but so far I have not had the truth.' He later hints that 'communal and racial issues' might have been involved in Jaipal's sudden absence. According to Dhyan Chand, the only person who could clear the mystery was Jaipal himself. But Jaipal merely says in his autobiography that on his return to London from the Olympics, Lord Irwin, Viceroy of India, congratulated him personally.
23. The *Statesman*, 29 May 1928, p. 14.
24. Dhyan Chand, *Goal*, published in *Sport and Pastime*, 1952, Section on the 1928 Amsterdam Olympiad.
25. England did not participate in the hockey competition for the 1932 and 1936 games. The Games were not held thereafter till 1948, due to WWII.
26. A series of reports were published in the *Times of India* commenting on the significance of this victory against England in 1948. It was considered a great gift from the team for the people of the newly independent nation.

27. C.D. Parthasarathy, 'That Golden Age', in *Sport and Pastime*, 23 February 1963.
28. Quoted in C.D. Parthasarathy, 'Indian Hockey: Rise and Fall', in *Sport and Pastime*, 16 February 1963.
29. Rashmi Katyayan (ed.), *Lo Bir Sendra* (Ranchi: Prabhat Khabar Publications, 2004), p. 37.
30. For details see; Dhyan Chand, *Goal*, published in *Sport and Pastime*, 1952, Section on the 1928 Amsterdam Olympiad.
31. Rashmi Katyayan, op. cit. p. 38.
32. Ramachandra Guha, *India After Gandhi: The History of the World's Largest Democracy* (New Delhi: Picador, 2007), pp. 115–16.
33. Same as Reference 1.
34. Pankaj Gupta, 'India's Hockey Supremacy', in *Sport and Pastime*, 10 May 1958, pp. 37–38.
35. Ibid.
36. Ibid.
37. Quoted in the review mentioned in Reference 1.
38. Ibid.
39. Ibid.
40. Ibid.
41. Quoted in the *Statesman*, 2 August 1932, p. 11.
42. The *Statesman*, 9 August 1932, p. 11.
43. The *Statesman*, 4 August 1932, p. 11.
44. The *Statesman*, 6 August 1932, p. 12.
45. Mentioned in Hayman's review.
46. The *Statesman*, 13 August 1932, p. 9.
47. The *Statesman*, 14 August 1932, p. 12.
48. Ibid.
49. Same as Reference 1.
50. Ibid.
51. Ibid.
52. Ibid.
53. Ibid.
54. Ibid.
55. Ibid.
56. Ibid.
57. Ibid.
58. Quoted in C.D. Parthasarathy, 'That Golden Age', in *Sport and Pastime*, 23 February 1963. The original report is housed in the International Olympic Museum, Lausanne. File OU MO 01 14 36, CIO CNO IND CORR, Olympic Studies Center.
59. Quoted in, 'We Climb the Victory Stand: Hockey in *Excelsis*', in Anthony S. De Mello, *Portrait of Indian Sport* (New Delhi: McMillan 1959), pp. 93–95.

60. C.D. Parthasarathy, 'That Golden Age', in *Sport and Pastime*, 23 February 1963.
61. Same as Reference 1.
62. Ibid.
63. Boria Majumdar, *Twenty Two Yards to Freedom: A Social History of Indian Cricket*, (New Delhi: Penguin Viking, 2004), pp. 44.
64. Mihir Bose, *History of Indian Cricket* (London: Andre Deutsch, revised and updated 2002), p. 80.
65. The entire letter is published in Boria Majumdar, *The Illustrated History of Indian Cricket* (New Delhi: Roli Books, also published from London: Tempus, 2006), p. 84.
66. For details see Boria Majumdar and Kausik Bandyopadhyay, *Goalless: The Story of a Unique Footballing Nation* (New Delhi: Penguin Viking, 2006), Ch. 4.
67. For Indian cricket and the nationalist imagination, particularly in colonial India, see for instance, Ramachandra Guha, *Corner of a Foreign Field: The Indian History of a British Sport* (New Delhi: Pan Macmillan, 2002) and Boria Majumdar, *Twenty Two Yards to Freedom: A Social History of Indian Cricket* (New Delhi: Penguin, 2004).
68. See for instance, Kausik Bandopadhyaya, '1911 in Retrospect: A Revisionist Perspective on a Famous Indian Sporting Victory', pp. 27–47.
69. Boria Majumdar and Kausik Bandopadhyaya, Introduction to *A Social History of Indian Football: Striving to Score* (London: Routledge, 2006), p. 122.

CHAPTER 4

We have extensively used The *Statesman* reportage for this chapter because the memoirs/travel diaries of the Indian team members were published in this newspaper. Also, the paper documented in considerable detail India's gold medal winning tryst and thus served as a valuable contemporary source. Other papers like the *Times of India* were also consulted. However, with the match reports being of a similar nature we preferred the *Statesman* for this chapter.

Some facts mentioned in this chapter do not square up with the details in Dhyan Chand's autobiography. Where there is a dispute over facts, we have decided on balance to favour the considered evidence from other contemporary sources and press reportage on the Berlin Olympiad because Dhyan Chand's autobiography was only published a decade and a half later in 1952 and is likely that he may have forgotten some details.

1. Dhyan Chand, *Goal*, published in *Sport and Pastime*, 1952. Section on the 1936 Berlin Olympiad. The book has been digitized and is available in http://www.bharatiyahockey.org/granthalaya/goal/ accessed 29 September 2007.
2. For details see; Pankaj Gupta, 'India's Hockey Supremacy', in *Sport and Pastime*, 10 May 1958, pp. 37–38.

3. Dhyan Chand, *Goal*, op. cit.
4. Ibid.
5. For an account of Palwankar Baloo's fascinating story see Boria Majumdar, *Twenty Two Yards to Freedom: A Social History of Indian Cricket* (New Delhi: Penguin Viking, 2004) and Ramachandra Guha, *Corner of a Foreign Field: The Indian History of a British Sport* (New Delhi: Pan Macmillan, 2002).
6. Chris Bishop & David Jordan, *The Illustrated History of the Third Reich: Germany's Victories and Defeat 1939–1945* (Leicester: Silverdale), p. 12.
7. The IOC awarded the 1936 Olympics to Berlin, over Barcelona, in April 1931.
8. While Germany had secretly been repudiating the terms of the Treaty of Versailles since the early 1930s, Hitler asked Göring to openly announce the end of Germany's compliance with the Treaty in March, 1935 and reintroduced conscription. Chris Bishop & David Jordan, *The Illustrated History of the Third Reich: Germany's Victories and Defeat 1939–1945* (Leicester: Silverdale), p. 16.
9. See for instance, Gary Morris, 'Lonesome Leni: The Wonderful, Horrible Life of Leni Reifenstahl', *Bright Lights Film Journal*, 26, Nov. 1999. http://www.brightlights film.com/26/riefenstahl.html accessed 1 January 2008).
10. 'The Façade of Hospitality,' United States Holocaust Memorial Museum, http://www.ushmm.org/museum/exhibit/online/olympics/zcd060.htm, accessed 1 January 2008.
11. Figures from Frank C. Zarnowski, 'A Look at Olympic Costs', *Citius, Altius, Fortius* 1 (1), Summer 1992, pp. 16-32. Also see Arnd Kruger & W.J. Murray (eds.), *The Nazi Olympics: Sport, Politics and Appeasement in the 1930s* (University of Illinois Press, rev. ed., 2003).
12. The *Statesman*, 20 July 1936, p. 11.
13. Ibid.
14. Ibid.
15. Ibid.
16. Ibid.
17. For details on the journey see the *Statesman*, 22 July 1936, p. 11. The quote is from Dhyan Chand, *Goal*, published in *Sport and Pastime*, 1952. Section on the 1936 Berlin Olympiad. http://www.bharatiyahockey.org/granthalaya/goal/, accessed 29 September 2007.
18. The *Statesman*, 22 July 1936, p. 11.
19. Dhyan Chand, *Goal*, op. cit.
20. The *Statesman*, 22 July 1936, p. 11.
21. Ibid.
22. Dhyan Chand, *Goal*, op. cit.
23. Ibid.
24. The *Statesman*, 22 July 1936, p. 11.
25. Mentioned in Pankaj Gupta's reminiscences on the 1936 Olympiad published in the annual souvenir of the Bengal Hockey Association in 1939.

26. Dhyan Chand, *Goal*, op. cit., accessed 4 October 2007.
27. The *Statesman*, 23 July 1936, p.11.
28. The *Statesman*, 20 August 1936, p.13.
29. The *Statesman*, 28 July 1936, p.11.
30. The *Statesman*, 15 July 1936, p. 13.
31. The *Statesman*, 28 July 1936, p.12.
32. Ibid.
33. M.N. Masood, *The World's Hockey Champions 1936*, The book has been digitized and is available in http://www.bharatiyahockey.org/granthalaya/champions/, accessed 4 October 2007.
34. Ibid.
35. Dhyan Chand, *Goal*, op. cit., accessed 4 October 2007.
36. M.N. Masood, *The World's Hockey Champions 1936*, op. cit.
37. Ibid.
38. Ibid.
39. See for instance, http://www.ushmm.org/museum/exhibit/online/olympics/zcc028.htm, accessed 5 January 2008.
40. The *Statesman*, 2 August 1936, p.9.
41. The *Statesman*, 2 August 1936, p.9.
42. Jawaharlal Nehru quoted in T.A. Keenleyside, 'Prelude to Power: The Meaning of Non-Alignment Before Independence', *Pacific Affairs* Vol. 53, No. 3 (Autumn 1980) p. 467.
43. See Rajmohan Gandhi, *Mohandas: A True Story of a Man, His People and an Empire* (New Delhi: Penguin, 2006), pp. 443–46.
44. T.A. Keenleyside, 'Prelude to Power: The Meaning of Non-Alignment Before Independence', *Pacific Affairs* Vol. 53, No. 3 (Autumn 1980) p. 464.
45. The *Statesman*, 30 July 1936.
46. The *Statesman*, 31 July 1936, p.13.
47. The government required the Indian Broadcasting Company to collect licence fees and its share of import duties on radio equipment on its own. When the company collapsed, it was taken over by the government and renamed as the Indian State Broadcasting Service. The nomenclature of All India Radio was adopted in 1936. Until 1937, it functioned under the Department of Industries and Labour, whereupon it was transferred to the Department of Communication. The new Department of Information and Broadcasting assumed control over it in 1941 and upon independence in 1947, it became a new ministry. Chatterjee, *Broadcasting in India*, pp. 39–41.
48. The *Statesman*, 4 August 1936, p.11.
49. The *Statesman*, 13 August 1936, p.11.
50. Ibid.
51. Ibid.
52. The *Statesman*, 11 August 1936, p. 9.
53. For details on this visit see the *Statesman*, 10 July 1936, p.15.

54. The *Statesman*, 28 July 1936, p.12.
55. For a detailed match report see the *Statesman*, 7 August 1936, p.12.
56. Ibid.
57. Ibid.
58. The *Statesman*, 13 August 1936, p.11.
59. The *Statesman*, 22 August 1936, p.13.
60. The *Statesman*, 9 August 1936, p.14.
61. The *Statesman*, 20 August 1936, p.13.
62. Ibid.
63. The *Statesman*, 12 August 1936, p.11.
64. We are thankful to Isabella Fillon and Anne Jacquet from the Images Division at the IOC Museum, Lausanne, for showing us these videos.
65. The *Statesman*, 13 August 1936, p.11.
66. The *Statesman*, 14 August 1936, p.11.
67. The *Statesman*, 31 August 1936, p.11.
68. The *Statesman*, 16 August 1936, p.11.
69. Ibid.
70. The *Statesman*, 23 August 1936, p.17.
71. The *Statesman*, 19 August 1936, p.11.
72. Dhyan Chand, *Goal*, op. cit.
73. M.N. Masood, *The World's Hockey Champions 1936*, op. cit.
74. The *Statesman*, 20 August 1936, p. 13.
75. For details see Gulu Ezekiel and K. Arumugam, *Great Indian Olympians* (New Delhi: Thendral Thambi Publications, 2004).

CHAPTER 5

1. Brian Stoddart, 'Sport, Cultural Imperialism and Colonial Response in the British Empire: a Framework for Analysis', in *Comparative Studies in Society And History,* 14, no. 3 (Winter 1987), p. 673.
2. Balbir Singh, *The Golden Hattrick*, The book has been digitized and is available in http://www.bharatiyahockey.org/granthalaya/hattrick/, accessed 12 December 2007. Section on 1956 Melbourne Olympiad.
3. Dhyan Chand, *Goal*, published in *Sport and Pastime*, 1952. The book has been digitized and is available in http://www.bharatiyahockey.org/granthalaya/goal/, accessed 10 November 2007.
4. For Orwell's take on sport also see; 'The Sporting Spirit', in http://www.george-orwell.org/The_Sporting_Spirit/0.html.
5. Balbir Singh, *The Golden Hattrick*, op. cit.
6. For details see; Jeremy Black, *The British Seaborne Empire*, (New Haven: Yale University Press, 2004).
7. 'Indian Hockey Team in London', in the *Times of India*, 16 July 1948.
8. 'Another magnificent display by Babu', in the *Times of India*, 28 June1948.
9. Ibid., 2 July 1948.

10. Ibid., 3 July 1948.
11. Ibid., 20 July 1948.
12. Ibid., 12 July 1948.
13. Ibid., 20 July 1948.
14. The *Times of India* reported the protest at length. For details see edition of 22 July 1948.
15. Ibid., 28 July 1948.
16. For a detailed report on India's performance against Argentina, see the *Times of India*, 5 August 1948.
17. Ibid., 8 August 1948.
18. Ibid.
19. Ibid.
20. Ibid., 11 August 1948.
21. Ibid.
22. Ibid., 12 August 1948.
23. Balbir Singh, *The Golden Hattrick*, http://www.bharatiyahockey.org/granthalaya/hattrick/ Section on London 1948, accessed 12 December 2007.
24. The *Times of India*, 12 August 1948.
25. For details see 'We Climb the Victory Stand: Hockey in *Excelsis*', in Anthony S. De Mello, *Portrait of Indian Sport* (New Delhi: Macmillan, 1959).
26. The *Times of India*, 13 August 1948.
27. Balbir Singh, *The Golden Hattrick*, op. cit.
28. Ibid.
29. The *Times of India*, 19 June 1952.
30. Ibid.
31. Ibid.
32. Ibid.
33. Ibid., 22 July 1952.
34. Ibid., 18 July 1952.
35. Quoted in Balbir Singh, *The Golden Hattrick*, op. cit.
36. Ibid.
37. The *Times of India*, 22 July 1952.
38. Balbir Singh, *The Golden Hattrick*, op. cit.
39. Ibid.
40. For details see; Pankaj Gupta, 'India's Hockey Supremacy', in *Sport and Pastime*, 10 May 1958, pp. 37–38.
41. The *Hindu*, 27 November 1956.
42. Ibid.
43. For details of India's performance against the US, see the *Hindu* 29 November 1956.
44. The Hindu, 1 December 1956.
45. For details see Pankaj Gupta, 'India's Hockey Supremacy', in *Sport and Pastime*, 10 May 1958, pp. 37–38.
46. The *Hindu*, 4 December 1956.

47. Balbir Singh, *The Golden Hattrick*,
48. Ibid.
49. Pankaj Gupta, 'Past Matches Recalled', the *Hindu*, 26 August 1960.
50. (emphasis ours) For details see; Pankaj Gupta, 'India's Hockey Supremacy', in *Sport and Pastime*, 10 May 1958, pp. 37–38.
51. For details see the *Hindu* 28 August 1960.
52. Ibid., 6 September 1960.
53. Ibid., 31 August 1960.
54. Ibid., 8 September 1960.
55. Ibid., 10 September 1960.
56. S.M. Sait, 'Rome Debacle and Its Lessons', *Indian Olympic News* Vol. 1, no. 4, July 1962. The writer was honorary secretary, Indian Hockey Federation, NA
57. See for instance, S.M. Sait, 'Robust Hockey Vs. Skilful Hockey', *Indian Olympic News* Vol. 2, no. 2, May 1963 pp. 35–36.
58. S.M. Sait, 'Rome Debacle and Its Lessons', *Indian Olympic News* Vol 1, no. 4, July 1962., NA
59. Charanjit Rai, 'How to Regain World Hockey Title', *Indian Olympic News* Vol. 1, no. 4, July 1962, p. 35.
60. Ibid., pp. 35–36.
61. T.D. Parthasarathy, 'India's Chances in Hockey', the *Hindu*, 10 October 1964.
62. Ibid.
63. For details on this match see the *Hindu* 12 October 1964.
64. Ibid., 13 October 1964.
65. Ibid., 15 October 1964.
66. Ibid., 20 October 1964.
67. Ibid., 22 October 1964.
68. Rene G. Frank, 'Sayonara Tokyo—Au Revoir Tokyo: The Olympic Tournament in Retrospect', *FIH Official Bulletin*, No. 13, Dec. 1964, pp. 10–11.
69. Ibid.
70. For details on this match see the *Hindu*, 24 October 1964.
71. Ibid.
72. Ibid.
73. For details see the *Times of India*, 21 July 1980.
74. Ibid., 2 August 1980.
75. Ibid., 21 July 1980.
76. Ibid.
77. Ibid., 22 July 1980.
78. Ibid.
79. Ibid., 24 July 1980.
80. Ibid., 25 July 1980.
81. Ibid., 27 July 1980.
82. Ibid., 30 July 1980.

83. Ibid.
84. Ibid.
85. Ibid., 3 August 1980.
86. Ibid.
87. Ibid., 2 August 1980.

Chapter 6

1. Pankaj Gupta quoted in *IOA Annual Report*, 1962, p. 2 CIO CNO IND GENER OU MO 01 14 36 INDE Correspondance Generale 1950–1981
2. For details see; Steve Ruskin, 'Reign on the Wane', *Sports Illustrated*, 85 (4), 22 July 1996, pp. 170–74.
3. 'They Don't Give a Damn', Dhanraj Pillay interview with Shantanu Guha Ray,16 June 2007, http://www.tehelka.com/story_main31.asp? filename= hub160607They_dont.asp
4. Even college magazines like those of the Presidency and St Xavier's Colleges in Calcutta between 1920 and 1940 are full of praise for the Indian hockey team's performance at the Olympics.
5. 'Milestones Along the Olympic Road', See section 'The Fall of Rome', *World Hockey: The Magazine of the International Hockey Federation*, No. 26, June 1976, p. 6.
6. Even in the match for the seventh position, India got a lucky break against England, winning 2–1.
7. For details see; http://www.hindu.com/2007/09/10/stories/2007091055590100.htm, accessed 14 November 2007.
8. Laxmi Negi, 'Euphoria Over. Chak De's Soi Moi aka Nisha Nair is Back on Turf', 1 February 2008, the *Indian Express, Mumbai Newsline,* p. 1.
9. This is despite the fact that women's hockey has given India more laurels in recent times than men's hockey. As recently reported by the *Hindustan Times*, 'After 1982, international success (in women's hockey) was hard to come by. The nadir was hit in the 1998 world cup in The Netherlands when India finished 12th, losing 0–5 to China. They redeemed themselves somewhat in the Commonwealth Games in Malaysia, reaching the semi-finals before losing 1–3 to Australia. By year-end, though, the turnaround had begun with a silver medal in the Bangkok Asian Games. A runner up finish following a sudden death 2–3 loss to South Korea in the 1999 Asia Cup final showed that women's hockey was back on track. Then came the biggest high of all. India won the 2002 Commonwealth Games gold in Manchester despite there being stronger teams like Australia, New Zealand and England in the fray...Gold in the Afro-Asian Games and in a four nation meet in Singapore, where India thrashed South Korea 3-0 in the final in 2005, and a runner up finish in the Indira Gandhi Gold Cup the same year showed that it paid to reckon with India now.' *Hindustan Times*, 1 October 2007.

10. This is point made forcefully by Shekhar Gupta in 'The HMT Advantage', *The Indian Express*, Feb 15, 2003. Shekhar Gupta defines 'HMT' as 'Hindi-medium types' who are increasingly breaking the barriers of elitism in various sectors of the economy and also in Indian cricket.
11. 'Germany First Champions on Artificial Turf', *World Hockey*, October 1975, No 24, p. 8.
12. File OU MO01 14 36, CIO CNO IND CORR, Olympic Studies Centre, IOC Museum, Lausanne. This file deals primarily with correspondence exchanged between the Indian Olympic Association and the Indian Olympic Committee. Also, any document sent from India to the IOC—letters, pamphlets, constitutions etc have been retained in this file.
13. For details see; Pargat Singh, 'IHF destroying Indian Hockey', available online at http:// www.indianhockey.com/phpmodule/view, accessed 15 December 2005.
14. This was originally passed by Parliament in 1974 as a remedy for the nation's poor showing in international sports meets. There was severe protest by sports bodies soon after and eventually the ruling was disregarded, with the result that politicians have been at the helm of sporting federations for well over a decade.
15. Ramachandra Guha, *India After Gandhi: The History of the World's Largest Democracy* (New Delhi: Picador, 2007), p. 284.
16. See file OU MO01 14 36, CIO CNO IND CORR, Olympic Studies Centre, IOC Museum, Lausanne. The file contains details of the ongoing dispute between the two rival blocs, including original letters and other correspondence.
17. Ibid.
18. 'Hockey on an Artificial Pitch', *World Hockey*, October 1975, No. 24, p. 10.
19. Ibid.
20. Ibid.
21. Ibid.
22. For details see; Steve Ruskin, 'Reign on the Wane', *Sports Illustrated*, 85 (4), 22 July 1996, pp. 170-174.
23. Ibid.
24. See file OU MO01 14 36, CIO CNO IND CORR, Olympic Studies Centre, IOC Museum, Lausanne.
25. Rene Frank, president, FIH, to Lord Killanin, president, IOC, Feb 27, 1978, OU MO01 14 36, CIO CNO IND CORR 1977–78, Olympic Studies Centre,.
26. See File IDD CHEMISE 9404 CIO CNOINDE CORR, Olympic Studies Centre. Correspondence between the IOC and the Indian Olympic Association is chronologically arranged. This file mostly contains material on issues relating to Indian hockey.
27. Letter from Raja Bhalindra Singh to IOC President, 14 August 1974, OU MO01 14 36, CIO CNO IND CORR, Olympic Studies Centre.

28. Letter from Raja Bhalindra Singh to IOC president, 11 October 1974, ID Chemise 6826 CIO MBR SINGH CORR OU MO 01 41 07 SINGH, Bhalindra Raja Correspondence 1947–1985, Olympic Studies Centre.
29. Rene Frank, president, FIH, to Lord Killanin, president, IOC, 27 February 1978, OU MO01 14 36, CIO CNO IND CORR 1977–78, Olympic Studies Centre. Also see Raja Bhalindra Singh to Lord Killanin, March 10, 1978 ID Chemise 6826 CIO MBR SINGH CORR OU MO 01 41 07 SINGH, Bhalindra Raja Correspondence 1947–1985, Olympic Studies Centre.
30. For details see Balbir Singh, *The Golden Hat Trick: My Hockey Days*, (New Delhi: Vikas, 1977). The book contains fascinating material on how politicized Indian hockey was in the 1970s.
31. Balbir Singh, 'Kuala Lumpur Has Always Been Lucky', available online at http://www.indianhockey.com/mcol3/1.php, accessed 15 December 2005.
32. The release reported verbatim by UNI is available in OU MO01 14 36, CIO CNO IND CORR, Olympic Studies Centre.
33. This letter is available in file CIO FI FIH CORR OU MO 01 1433, Olympic Studies Centre.
34. Letter sent on 25 January 1976 by the Pakistan Olympic Association to Lord Killanin, available in file CIO FI FIH CORR OU MO 01 1433, Olympic Studies Centre, IOC Museum, Lausanne.
35. OU MO01 14 36, CIO CNO IND CORR, Olympic Studies Centre.
36. Extracts from the minutes of the IOA General Assembly Meeting held on 2 July 1977, OU MO01 14 36, CIO CNO IND CORR, Olympic Studies Centre.
37. Raja Bhalindra Singh to Lord Killanin, March 10, 1978 ID Chemise 6826 CIO MBR SINGH CORR OU MO 01 41 07 SINGH, Bhalindra Raja Correspondence 1947-1985, Olympic Studies Centre.
38. Extracts from the minutes of the IOA General Assembly Meeting held on 2 July 1977, OU MO01 14 36, CIO CNO IND CORR, Olympic Studies Centre.
39. OU MO01 14 36, CIO CNO IND CORR, Olympic Studies Centre.
40. Ibid.
41. Ibid.
42. The *Hindustan Times*, 10 January 1978.
43. Ibid., 14 January 1978.
44. Ibid., 2 December 1977.
45. Ibid.
46. Raja Bhalindra Singh, letter to Lord Killanin, 15 Jan. 1978, OU MO01 14 36, CIO CNO IND CORR, Olympic Studies Centre.
47. OU MO01 14 36, CIO CNO IND CORR, Olympic Studies Centre.
48. Injunction issued by the Madras Court on 18 Jan. 1978, OU MO01 14 36, CIO CNO IND CORR, Olympic Studies Centre.
49. Letter from Ramaswamy to Rene Frank, 21 Jan. 1978, OU MO01 14 36, CIO CNO IND CORR, Olympic Studies Centre.

50. Ibid.
51. OU MO01 14 36, CIO CNO IND CORR 1977–78, Olympic Studies Centre.
52. Ibid.
53. Ibid.
54. Ibid.
55. Letter from General Mehra to Rene Frank, 16 March 1978, OU MO01 14 36, CIO CNO IND CORR, Olympic Studies Centre.
56. The letter was published in the *Hindustan Times*, 9 June 1978.
57. The media were unanimous that Frank had overstepped his limits. Most reports expressed concern about the future of Indian hockey and lamented the gradual decline of a sport with a glorious tradition.
58. Bobby Talyarkhan, 'When Rene gets too Frank', OU MO01 14 36, CIO CNO IND CORR 1977–78, Olympic Studies Centre.
59. Air Chief Marshall O.P. Mehra, president, IOA, to Rene G. Frank, president, IHF, 24 June 1978. OU MO01 14 36, CIO CNO IND CORR 1977–78, Olympic Studies Centre.
60. Ibid.
61. OU MO01 14 36, CIO CNO IND CORR 1977–78, Olympic Studies Centre.
62. Ibid.
63. Lord Killanin, president, IOC to Rene Frank, president, IHF, OU MO01 14 36, CIO CNO IND CORR 1977–78, Olympic Studies Centre.
64. Boria and Kausik Bandyopadhyay, *Goalless: The Story of a Unique Footballing Nation*, (New Delhi: Penguin Viking, 2006), Chapter 4.
65. The letter is available in OU MO01 14 36, CIO CNO IND CORR 1977–78, Olympic Studies Centre.
66. Ibid.
67. Ibid.
68. OU MO01 14 36, CIO CNO IND CORR 1977–78, Olympic Studies Centre.
69. 'They Don't Give a Damn', Dhanraj Pillay interview with Shantanu Guha Ray, 16 June 2007, http://www.tehelka.com/story_main31.asp?filename= hub160607They_dont.asp

CHAPTER 7

1. Anthony De Mello, *Portrait of Indian Sport* (London: P.R. Macmillan, 1959), p. 291.
2. In December 2007 the UN had 192 member-states, the IOC 205 member states. See http://www.olympic.org/uk/organisation/noc/index_uk.asp, accessed 1 December 2007 and http://www.un.org/members/list.shtml, accessed 1 December 2007.
3. T.A. Keenleyside, 'Nationalist Indian Attitudes Towards Asia: A

Troublesome Legacy for Post-Independence Indian Foreign Policy', *Pacific Affairs*, Vol. 55, No. 2, Summer 1982, p. 210.

4. Tagore quoted in Ibid., p. 211. See Rabindranath Tagore, *Nationalism* (London: Macmillan, 1918), pp. 58–59, 67–68.
5. See for instance the writings of Okakura Kakuzo, in particular his *The Ideals of the East with Special Reference to the Art of Japan* (London: John Murray, 1903).
6. Birendra Prasad, *Indian Nationalism and Asia, 1900-1947* (Delhi: B.R. Publishing, 1979), pp. 41–47.
7. Jawaharlal Nehru in *The Discovery of India*, quoted by K.R. Narayanan, *Acceptance Speech by President of the Republic of India, at the Convocation Function at Tribhuvan University* (22 May 2000), http://72.14.235.104/search?q= cache:wmEKC_y8EaMJ: www.south-asia.com/Embassy-India/convocation.htm+asian+relations+conference+1947+delhi&hl= en&ct=clnk&cd=8&gl=in&client=firefox-a, accessed 12 November 2007).
8. T.A. Keenleyside, 'Nationalist Indian Attitudes Towards Asia: A Troublesome Legacy for Post-Independence Indian Foreign Policy', *Pacific Affairs*, Vol. 55, No. 2, Summer 1982, p. 216.
9. Ibid., p. 217.
10. Sen Gupta, mayor of Calcutta quoted in Ibid.
11. Sukarno in *GANEFO: Its Principles, Purposes and Organisation* (Jakarta: The Permanent Secretariat of the GANEFO Federation, 1965), p. 21. Quoted in Rusli Lutan and Fan Hong, 'The Politicization of Sport: GANEFO—A Case Study', Fan Hong (ed.), *Sport, Nationalism and Orientalism: The Asian Games* (London: Routledge, 2007), p. 31.
12. Sukarno's speech at opening of GANEFO Congress, 26 November 1963. Quoted in Rusli Lutan and Fan Hong, 'The Politicization of Sport: GANEFO—A Case Study', Fan Hong (ed.), *Sport, Nationalism and Orientalism: The Asian Games*, p. 27.
13. Fan Hong, 'Prologue: The Origins of the Asian Games: Power and Politics', Fan Hong (ed.), *Sport, Nationalism and Orientalism: The Asian Games*, p. xvii
14. Anthony De Mello, *Portrait of Indian Sport* (London: P.R. Macmillan, 1959), p. 295.
15. 'The Far Eastern Championship Games 1913–1934', Table 1, compiled by Huan Xiong in Fan Hong (ed.), *Sport, Nationalism and Orientalism: The Asian Games*, pp. 116–17.
16. The FECG were held in Manila (1913), Shanghai (1915), Tokyo (1917), Manila (1919), Shanghai (1921), Osaka (1923), Manila (1925), Shanghai (1927), Tokyo (1930) and Manila (1934). Anthony De Mello, *Portrait of Indian Sport* (London: P.R. Macmillan, 1959), pp. 295–98
17. Fan Hong, 'Prologue: The Origins of the Asian Games: Power and Politics', Fan Hong (ed.), *Sport, Nationalism and Orientalism: The Asian Games* , pp. xiii–xxiv.
18. Ibid., p. xiii.

19. Fan Hong, *Footbinding, Feminism and Freedom: The Liberation of Women's Bodies in Modern China* (London: Cass, 1997), p. 36.
20. Fan Hong, 'Prologue: The Origins of the Asian Games: Power and Politics', Fan Hong (ed.), *Sport, Nationalism and Orientalism: The Asian Games*, p. xvi
21. Andrew D. Morris, *Marrow of the Nation: A History of Sport and Physical Culture in Republican China* (Berkeley, CA: University of California Press, 2004), p. 23.
22. Fan Hong, op. cit., p. xvii.
23. Anthony De Mello, *Portrait of Indian Sport* (London: P.R. Macmillan, 1959), pp. 294–99.
24. Qing ji, quoted in Fan Hong, op. cit., pp. xx–xxi.
25. Ibid., pp. xxi–xxii
26. Anthony De Mello, *Portrait of Indian Sport* (London: P.R. Macmillan, 1959), pp. 299–300.
27. Constitution of the Westen Asiatic Games Federation, annexure to personal letter from G.D. Sondhi to Baron De Coubertin, 31 May 1934, International Olympic Museum, File CIO MBR SONDH CORR OU MO1 41 O7 Sondhi, Guru Dutt Correspondence 1929–67.
28. IOA Note to IOC, *History of Other Asian Games Organisations, n.d.* International Olympic Museum, File Correspondance du CNO de l'Inde (IND) 1924—1963.
29. G.D. Sondhi profile, International Olympic Museum, File CIO MBR SONDH CORR OU MO1 41 O7 Sondhi, Guru Dutt Correspondence 1929–67.
30. Mithlesh K. Sisodia, 'India and the Asian Games: From Infancy to Maturity', Fan Hong (ed.), *Sport, Nationalism and Orientalism: The Asian Games,* op. cit., p. 2.
31. Personal letter from G.D. Sondhi to Baron De Coubertin, 10 January 1934. International Olympic Museum, File CIO MBR SONDH CORR OU MO1 41 O7 Sondhi, Guru Dutt Correspondence 1929–67.
32. As late as January 1934, Sondhi was hoping for a yes from Persia to join his Federation, without much success. Ibid.
33. Personal letter from G.D. Sondhi to Baron De Coubertin, 11 March 1934. International Olympic Museum, File CIO MBR SONDH CORR OU MO1 41 O7 Sondhi, Guru Dutt Correspondence 1929–67.
34. Personal letter from G.D. Sondhi to Baron De Coubertin, 10 January 1934. International Olympic Museum, File CIO MBR SONDH CORR OU MO1 41 O7 Sondhi, Guru Dutt Correspondence 1929–67.
35. The athletics and hockey events took place on 23 March 1934 while the swimming and diving events were held in Patiala on March 25–26. Anthony De Mello, *Portrait of Indian Sport* (London: P.R. Macmillan, 1959), p. 294.
36. There is some confusion about the host city for the second WAG. While the IOA's official note to the IOC names Palestine, Sondhi wrote to De

Coubertin saying that Kabul had been chosen as the next venue. It seems Kabul was first chosen and the decision was changed later. Personal letter from G.D. Sondhi to Baron De Coubertin, 11 March 1934. International Olympic Museum, File CIO MBR SONDH CORR OU MO1 41 O7 Sondhi, Guru Dutt Correspondence 1929–67.

37. IOA Note to IOC, *History of Other Asian Games Organisations, n.d.* International Olympic Museum, File Correspondance du CNO de l'Inde (IND) 1924–1963
38. Emphasis is ours. Anthony De Mello, *Portrait of Indian Sport* (London: P.R. Macmillan, 1959), pp. 284-285.
39. Ibid., p. 287.
40. First Asian Relations Conference was held in Delhi in March–April, 1947. For details see Maurice T. Price, Review of *Asian Relations: Being Report of the Proceedings and Documentation of the First Asian Relations Conference, New Delhi, March–April, 1947,* in *Social Forces*, Vol. 28, No. 3 (March 1950), pp. 349–50.
41. As told by K.R. Narayanan, who later became India's first Dalit President, and had served with Nehru as an IFS officer. K.R. Narayanan, *Acceptance Speech by President of the Republic of India, at the Convocation Function at Tribhuvan University* (22 May 2000), http://72.14.235.104/search?q=cache:wmEKC_y8EaMJ:www.south-asia.com/Embassy-India/convocation.htm+asian+relations+conference+ 1947+delhi&hl=en&ct=clnk&cd=8&gl=in&client=firefox-a, accessed 12 November 2007.
42. Jawaharlal Nehru quoted in Ibid.
43. T.A. Keenleyside, 'Nationalist Indian Attitudes Towards Asia: A Troublesome Legacy for Post-Independence Indian Foreign Policy', *Pacific Affairs*, Vol. 55, No. 2, Summer 1982, p. 212.
44. IOA Note to IOC, *The First Asian Games Championships Will be Held in March 1951 at New Delhi,* n.d. International Olympic Museum, File Correspondance du CNO de l'Inde (IND) 1924–1963
45. Ibid.
46. T.A. Keenleyside, 'Nationalist Indian Attitudes Towards Asia: A Troublesome Legacy for Post-Independence Indian Foreign Policy', *Pacific Affairs*, Vol. 55, No. 2, Summer 1982, p. 224.
47. IOA Note to IOC, *The First Asian Games Championships Will be Held in March 1951 at New Delhi,* n.d. International Olympic Museum, File Correspondance du CNO de l'Inde (IND) 1924–1963.
48. Anthony De Mello, *Portrait of Indian Sport* (London: P.R. Macmillan, 1959), p. 300.
49. IOA Note to IOC, *The First Asian Games Championships Will be Held in March 1951 at New Delhi,* n.d. International Olympic Museum, File Correspondance du CNO de l'Inde (IND) 1924–1963.
50. Ibid.
51. Ibid.
52. Ibid.

53. Ibid.
54. Afghanistan, Burma, India, Pakistan and the Philippines became the first members of the AGF. The representatives of Ceylon, Nepal and Siam signed, subject to ratification by their respective National Sports Associations or their governments. Ibid.
55. Anthony De Mello, *Portrait of Indian Sport* (London: P.R. Macmillan, 1959), p. 304.
56. T.A. Keenleyside, 'Nationalist Indian Attitudes Towards Asia: A Troublesome Legacy for Post-Independence Indian Foreign Policy', *Pacific Affairs*, Vol. 55, No. 2, Summer 1982, pp. 228–29.
57. Ibid., p. 229.
58. Mohanlal Gautam, 'India's Foreign policy: The Congress View', *India Quarterly*, No. 7 (April–June 1951), p. 110.
59. T.A. Keenleyside, 'Nationalist Indian Attitudes Towards Asia: A Troublesome Legacy for Post-Independence Indian Foreign Policy', *Pacific Affairs*, Vol. 55, No. 2, Summer 1982, pp. 223–24.
60. Jawaharlal Nehru quoted in Ibid., p. 224.
61. Nehru's line was sent in a personal congratulatory message to the eventual chief organizer, Anthony De Mello, who adopted it as the Games motto. Anthony De Mello, *Portrait of Indian Sport* (London: P.R. Macmillan, 1989), p. 290.
62. Anthony De Mello, *Portrait of Indian Sport* (London: P.R. Macmillan, 1959), p. 306.
63. The Government of India agreed to pay Pakistan its share on the third day of Gandhi's protest march on 15 January 1948.
64. Anthony De Mello, *Portrait of Indian Sport* (London: P.R. Macmillan, 1959) Ibid., pp. 287, 306.
65. Ibid., p. 306.
66. Ibid., p. 307
67. Ibid., p. 311.
68. Boria Majumdar, *Twenty Two Yards to Freedom* (New Delhi: Penguin Viking, 2004), p. 97.
69. Anthony De Mello, *Portrait of Indian Sport* (London: P.R. Macmillan, 1959), p. 308.
70. Mithlesh K. Sisodia, 'India and the Asian Games: From Infancy to Maturity', Fan Hong (ed.), *Sport, Nationalism and Orientalism: The Asian Games,* pp. 3–5.
71. Anthony De Mello, *Portrait of Indian Sport*, p. 307.
72. Ibid., p. 309.
73. Ibid., p. 313.
74. G.D. Sondhi, 'Athletic Development of Asia', Paper Read at Symposium conducted by the Philippines Amateur Athletic Federation, on the occasion of its Golden Jubilee Celebrations, 1–3 December 1961. International Olympic Museum, IDD Chemise 9404 CIO CNO INDE CORR, Correspondence India 1924–1963.

75. Emphasis is ours. De Mello's note to Nehru quoted in Anthony De Mello, *Portrait of Indian Sport* (London: P.R. Macmillan, 1959), p. 291.
76. Ibid., p.312.
77. Ibid., p. 306.
78. Ibid., p. 307.
79. Ibid., pp. 307–08
80. 'Our Playfields-II: National Stadium', *Indian Olympic Association Bulletin*, Vol. 2, January–March 1960, p. 34.
81. Anthony De Mello, *Portrait of Indian Sport*, p. 308.
82. Ibid., p. 291.
83. Ibid., p. 312.
84. 'Our Playfields-II: National Stadium', *Indian Olympic Association Bulletin*, Vol. 2, January-March 1960, p. 34.
85. Ibid.
86. Ibid.
87. Anthony De Mello, *Portrait of Indian Sport*, pp. 285–86.
88. Quoted in Mithlesh K. Sisodia, 'India and the Asian Games: From Infancy to Maturity', Fan Hong (ed.), *Sport, Nationalism and Orientalism: The Asian Games* (London: Routledge, 2007), p. 4. i
89. Anthony De Mello, *Portrait of Indian Sport* (London: P.R. Macmillan, 1959), p. 291.
90. David Levinson and Karen Chrstensen (eds.), *Encyclopedia of World Sports from Ancient Times to the Present* (Santa Barbara, CA, ABC-CLIO), Vol. I, pp. 56–59 .
91. Anthony De Mello, *Portrait of Indian Sport*, p. 289.
92. Ibid., pp. 291–92.
93. Ibid., p. 286.
94. Hugh Sweeney, 'A Peep in to the Past', *Indian Olympic News*, Vol. 1, No. 5, 15 August 1962.
95. Anthony De Mello, *Portrait of Indian Sport*, p. 290.
96. Werner Levi, *Free India in Asia* (Minneapolis: University of Minnesota Press, 1952), p. 39.
97. Quoted in the *Statesman*, 17 June 1950.
98. Anthony De Mello, *Portrait of Indian Sport*, p. 289
99. *The IX Asian Games Delhi 1982, Official Report, Vol. 1* (New Delhi: Thompson Press, 1982), p. 202.
100. Anthony De Mello, *Portrait of Indian Sport*, p. 313
101. This certainly is the view of K.R. Narayanan, who served with Nehru as an IFS officer. Narayanan, *Acceptance Speech by President of the Republic of India, at the Convocation Function at Tribhuvan University* (May 22, 2000), http://72.14.235.104/search?q=cache:wmEKC_y8EaMJ:www.south-asia.com Embassy-India/convocation.htm+asian+relations+conference+1947+ delhi&hl= en&ct=clnk&cd=8&gl=in&client=firefox-a, accessed 12 November 2007.

102. Rusli Lutan, 'Indonesia and the Asian Games: Sport, Nationalism and the 'New Order', Fan Hong (ed.), *Sport, Nationalism and Orientalism: The Asian Games*, p. 12.
103. Ibid., p. 13.
104. Ibid., p. 16.
105. Ibid., p. 17.
106. S.M. Mainual Haq, Report submitted to IOA on AGF meet in Jakarta on Aug 22, 1962, published as 'Our Delegate, Mr. S.M. Mainual Haq's Report, on A.G.F. Conference at Djakarta', *Indian Olympic News*, Vol. 1, No. 8, November 1962, p. 19.
107. Ibid., p. 20.
108. Ibid.
109. Ibid., p. 21.
110. Ibid.
111. Ibid., p. 22.
112. Speech by Maladi, Chief of Staff of President for GANEFO Affairs at Committee I–IV Meeting, July 19, 1963. Quoted in Rusli Latan & Fan Hong, 'The Politicization of Sport: GANEFO—A Case Study', Fan Hong (ed.), *Sport, Nationalism and Orientalism: The Asian Games*, p. 28.
113. S.M. Mainual Haq, *Report submitted to IOA on AGF meet in Jakarta on Aug 22, 1962*, published as 'Our Delegate, Mr. S.M. Mainual Haq's Report, on A.G.F. Conference at Djakarta', *Indian Olympic News*, Vol. 1, No. 8, November 1962, p. 22.
114. Ibid.
115. Ibid.
116. Rusli Latan & Fan Hong, 'The Politicization of Sport: GANEFO—A Case Study', Fan Hong (ed.), *Sport, Nationalism and Orientalism: The Asian Games*, pp. 27–28.
117. Emphasis is Sondhi's. G.D. Sondhi letter to Avery Brundage, president, IOC, 26 December 1962. International Olympic Museum, File CIO MBR SONDH CORR OU MO1 41 O7 Sondhi, Guru Dutt Correspondence 1929–67.
118. Rusli Latan & Fan Hong, op. cit., p.24.
119. Ibid., pp. 25–26.
120. 'Sport Improves the Spirit', *Indian Olympic News*,Vol. 1, No. 10, January 1963.
121. 'Congress of the International Amateur Athletic Federation Held at Belgrade, Official Report of Shri P.K. Mathur, our Representative', published in *Indian Olympic News*, Vol. 1, No. 8, November 1962.
122. Dr. Soebandrio, 1963. Quoted in Rusli Latan & Fan Hong, 'The Politicization of Sport: GANEFO—A Case Study', Fan Hong (ed.), *Sport, Nationalism and Orientalism: The Asian Games* , p.29.
123. Ibid., pp. 28–29, 31.
124. Raja Bhalindra Singh, president, IOA to Otto Mayer, chancellor, IOC, 26 August 1963 and 17 August 1963. International Olympic Museum,

ID Chemise 6826 CIO MBR SINGH CORR OU MO 01 41 07 SINGH, Bhalindra Raja Correspondence 1947–1985. Also see G.D. Sondhi to Otto Mayer, 27 April 1963. International Olympic Museum, File CIO MBR SONDH CORR OU MO1 41 O7 Sondhi, Guru Dutt Correspondence 1929–67.

125. 'More at the Games than Sport', *Indian Olympic News*, Vol. 1, No. 6, September 1962.
126. Rusli Latan & Fan Hong, 'The Politicization of Sport: GANEFO—A Case Study', Fan Hong (ed.), *Sport, Nationalism and Orientalism: The Asian Games*, pp. 32–33.
127. Ibid.

CHAPTER 8

1. Rajiv Gandhi, then prime minister of India, in 'Foreword', *IX Asian Games Delhi 1982, Official Report Vol. 1* (New Delhi: IX Asian Games Special Organising Committee, 1985). Page number unlisted.
2. Buta Singh, chairman, Special Organising Committee IX Asian Games, in 'Sport Loses its Greatest Patron', *IX Asian Games Delhi 1982, Official Report Vol. 1* (New Delhi: IX Asian Games Special Organising Committee, 1985).
3. Boria Majumdar, 'A Legacy Deeply Mired in Contradiction: World Cup 2007 in Retrospect', in Nalin Mehta, Dominic Malcolm, Jon Gemmell (eds.), *Cricket and the New Dawn: Race, Nations and Identity,* forthcoming special issue of *Sport in Society*.
4. See for instance, 'House Prices Go for Gold in Olympic Host Cities', http://209.85.175.104/search?q=cache:0wY9s11OI_AJ:www.hbosplc.com/economy/includes/18-10-4Olympichostcities.doc+sydney+olympic+property+prices& hl=en&ct=clnk&cd=1&gl=in&client=firefox-a accessed 18 September 2007.
5. Sumit Mitra, Anita Kaul, 'The Tedium is the Message', *India Today*, 31 May 1982, p. 16.
6. See Nalin Mehta, *India on Television: How TV News Changed the Ways We Think and Act* (New Delhi: HarperCollins, 2008, forthcoming).
7. Robin Jeffrey, 'The Mahatma Didn't Like Movies and Why it Matters: Indian Broadcasting Policy, 1920s–90s', *Global Media and Communication*, Vol. 2, No. 2 (August 2006), pp. 204–24.
8. See for instance, Arvind Rajagopal, *Politics After Television: Religious Nationalism and the Reshaping of the Indian Public* (Cambridge: Cambridge University Press, 2001); Purnima Mankekar, *Screening Culture, Viewing Politics: An Ethnography of Television, Womanhood, and Nation in Postcolonial India* (Durham: Duke University Press, 1999); G.C. Awasthy, *Broadcasting in India* (Bombay, Allied, 1965); Christiane Brosius & Melissa Butcher (eds.) *Image Journeys: Audio-Visual Media and Cultural Change in India* (New Delhi: Sage, 1999); Monroe E. Price & Stefaan G. Verhulst (eds.),

Broadcasting Reform in India: Media Law from a Global Perspective (New Delhi: Oxford University Press, 1998).

9. Sevanti Ninan, *Through the Magic Window: Television and Change in India* (New Delhi: Penguin, 1995), pp. 20–21.
10. William Mazzarella, *Shoveling Smoke: Advertising and Globalization in Contemporary India* (Durham: Duke University Press, 2003), pp. 73, 98.
11. In this context, see Robin Jeffrey, 'Monitoring Newspapers and Understanding the Indian State', *Asian Survey*, Vol. 34, No. 8 (August 1994), pp. 71–75 .
12. These estimates are based on capitalized billings of more than 100 major advertising agencies. Helen Anchan, 'Advertising Scene: 1965–90', *Press and Advertisers Yearbook, 1989-90*, p. 77.
13. Nalin Mehta, 'Indianising Television: News, Politics and Globalisation', Ph.D thesis, La Trobe University, Melbourne, pp. 1–2, 33.
14. Buta Singh, chairman, Special Organising Committee IX Asian Games, 'Sport Loses its Greatest Patron', in *IX Asian Games Delhi 1982, Official Report Vol. 1* (New Delhi: IX Asian Games Special Organising Committee, 1985).
15. Buta Singh at the time of his appointment as chairman of the Special Organising Committee of the IX Asian Games was minister of state for shipping and transport. *IX Asian Games Delhi 1982, Official Report Vol. 1* (New Delhi: IX Asian Games Special Organising Committee, 1985), p. 203.
16. Indira Gandhi quoted in Ramachandra Guha, *India After Gandhi: The History of the World's Largest Democracy* (Picador India: 2007), p. 550.
17. Ibid., pp. 550–51.
18. Ibid., pp. 549–50.
19. Raja Bhalindra Singh to Juan Antonio Samaranch, 15 September 1981, No. IOA/48/16, International Olympic Museum, Lausanne, CIO MBR Singh CORR OU MO 01 4107 SINGH, Bhalindra Singh Correspondence 1947–85.
20. See International Olympic Museum, Lausanne,CIO CNO IND BUREX OU MO O1 14 36 INE BUREAU EXECUTIF 1975-1984 and CNO D'INDE BUREAU EXECUTIF 1985–1988
21. *IX Asian Games Delhi 1982, Official Report Vol. 1* (New Delhi: IX Asian Games Special Organising Committee, 1985), pp. 287.
22. Ramachandra Guha, *India After Gandhi: The History of the World's Largest Democracy* (Picador India: 2007), pp. 519–21.
23. Juan Antonio Samaranch quoted in *IX Asian Games Delhi 1982, Official Report Vol. 1* (New Delhi: IX Asian Games Special Organising Committee, 1985), pp. 287–88.
24. Government of India, Ministry of Education and Social Welfare (Dept of Education), Confidential Circular No. F 11-4/74YS1 (2), Sub: Improvement of the Standard of Sports and Games in Country—Conditions for Financial and Other Assistance to National Sports Federations/Associations etc.

Issued to the Indian Olympic Association, National Sports Federations on 9 April, 1974. Attached as annexure to personal letter from S. Kimalal, C.C. Mivashunti, H. Mubutu, A..C. Kituzi, M.V. Matoves and B. Ddreme to Lord Killanin, president, IOC, 20 January 1976. See International Olympic Museum, Lausanne, International Olympic Museum, CIO CNO IND GENER OU MO 01 14 36 INDE Correspondance Generale 1950–1981.

25. Indira Gandhi, message by prime minister, 27 June 1976, published in *Indian Tracks to Success: ITDC Souvenir for IOA, 1976 Montreal Games* (New Delhi: ITDC, 1976).
26. Personal letter from Ashwini Kumar, secretary-general, IX Asian Games Committee, to Lord Killanin, president IOC, 19 April 1980. International Olympic Museum, Lausanne, CIO MBR KUMAR CORR OU MO 01 41 07 KUMAR, Ashwini Correspondence 1973-1983.
27. Personal Letter from Ashwini Kumar, DG BSF and Secretary, IOA to Lord Killanin, president, IOC, Sep. 15, 1975, International Olympic Museum, Lausanne, CIO MBR KUMAR CORR OU MO 01 41 07 KUMAR, Ashwini Correspondence 1973–1983.
28. Personal letter from Ashwini Kumar, DG BSF and secretary, IOA to Lord Killanin, president, IOC, 15 September 1975, International Olympic Museum, Lausanne, CIO MBR KUMAR CORR OU MO 01 41 07 KUMAR, Ashwini Correspondence 1973–1983.
29. Emphasis in original. Personal letter from S. Kimalal, C.C. Mivashunti, H. Mubutu, A.C. Kituzi, M.V. Matoves and B. Ddreme to Lord Killanin, president, IOC, 20 January 1976, International Olympic Museum, CIO CNO IND GENER OU MO 01 14 36 INDE Correspondance Generale 1950–1981
30. Anonymous letter from Lahore to Lord Killanin, president, IOC, 25 January 1976, International Olympic Museum, CIO CNO IND GENER OU MO 01 14 36 INDE Correspondance Generale 1950–1981.
31. Anonymous letter from Lahore to Lord Killanin, president, IOC, 25 January 1976, International Olympic Museum, CIO CNO IND GENER OU MO 01 14 36 INDE Correspondance Generale 1950–1981.
32. Personal Letter from Ashwini Kumar, secretary-general, IX Asian Games Committee, to Lord Killanin, president, IOC, 19 April 1980. International Olympic Museum, Lausanne, CIO MBR KUMAR CORR OU MO 01 41 07 KUMAR, Ashwini Correspondence 1973–1983.
33. Personal letter from Ashwini Kumar, secretary-general, IX Asian Games Committee, to Lord Killanin, president, IOC, 19 April 1980. International Olympic Museum, Lausanne, CIO MBR KUMAR CORR OU MO 01 41 07 KUMAR, Ashwini Correspondence 1973-1983.
34. Buta Singh, 'Report on the Functions of the Chief Coordinators Office, Before and During the IX Asian Games', *IX Asian Games Delhi 1982, Official Report Vol. II* (New Delhi: IX Asian Games Special Organising Committee, 1985), p. 7.

35. *IX Asian Games Delhi 1982, Official Report Vol. 1,* op. cit. p. 23.
36. Ibid., pp. 200–13.
37. See Ramachandra Guha, *India After Gandhi: The History of the World's Largest Democracy* (Picador India: 2007), p. 549.
38. Buta Singh, 'Ever Onward', in Melville De Mellow (ed.), *IX Asian Games Delhi 1982, Official Report Vol. 1,* op. cit.
39. Vidyacharan Shukla, president, IOA to Juan Antonio Samaranch, president, IOC, 12 April 1985. International Olympic Museum, Lausanne, CIO CNO IND CORR O MO 01 14 36 INDE Correspondance 1983–86.
40. This was the version of one senior IOA official who was privy to the discussions between Rajiv Gandhi and V.C. Shukla on the 1992 Olympic bid. He was speaking on condition of anonymity. Personal conversation in Lausanne, March 2006.
41. *IX Asian Games Delhi 1982, Official Report Vol. 1,* op. cit., p. 27.
42. Ibid., unlisted page number.
43. Ibid., p. 60.
44. Ibid., p. 55.
45. Ibid.
46. *IX Asian Games Delhi 1982, Official Report Vol. II* (New Delhi: IX Asian Games Special Organising Committee, 1985), p. 16.
47. *IX Asian Games Delhi 1982, Official Report Vol. 1* (New Delhi: IX Asian Games Special Organising Committee, 1985), p. 55.
48. *IX Asian Games Delhi 1982, Official Report Vol. II* (New Delhi: IX Asian Games Special Organising Committee, 1985), p. 16.
49. Ibid., p.19. Also see *IX Asian Games Delhi 1982, Official Report Vol. 1* (New Delhi: IX Asian Games Special Organising Committee, 1985), p. 55.
50. *IX Asian Games Delhi 1982, Official Report Vol. 1* (New Delhi: IX Asian Games Special Organising Committee, 1985), p. 55.
51. Buta Singh, 'Report on the Functions of the Chief Coordinators Office, Before and During the IX Asian Games', *IX Asian Games Delhi 1982, Official Report Vol. II* (New Delhi: IX Asian Games Special Organising Committee, 1985), p. 9.
52. *IX Asian Games Delhi 1982, Official Report Vol. II* (New Delhi: IX Asian Games Special Organising Committee, 1985), pp. 17–1 8.
53. Ibid., p. 18
54. Ibid., pp. 161–62.
55. Ibid., p. 157.
56. Ibid., p. 348.
57. Ibid., p. 26.
58. *IX Asian Games Delhi 1982, Official Report Vol. 1* (New Delhi: IX Asian Games Special Organising Committee, 1985), p. 33.
59. As told to authors by a senior NCC official.
60. Ibid., pp. 67–68.
61. Ibid., p. 27.

62. *IX Asian Games Delhi 1982, Official Report Vol. II* (New Delhi: IX Asian Games Special Organising Committee, 1985), p. 48.
63. Sumit Mitra, Anita Kaul, 'The Tedium is the Message', *India Today*, 31 May 1982, p. 16.
64. Ibid., pp. 16–17.
65. G.C. Awasthy, *Broadcasting in India* (Bombay, Allied, 1965), p. 11.
66. Sevanti Ninan, *Through the Magic Window: Television and Change in India* (New Delhi: Penguin, 1995), pp. 18–19.
67. Ibid.
68. Bhaskar Ghose, *Doordarshan Days* (New Delhi: Penguin Viking, 2005), p. 22.
69. S.R. Joshi, *Asia Speaks Out: The Indian Television Landscape*, Report No. SRG-96-047 (Ahmedabad: Development and Educational Communication Unit, Indian Space Research Organisation, April 1996), p. 2.
70. Bhaskar Ghose, *Doordarshan Days* (New Delhi: Penguin Viking, 2005), p. 22.
71. Doordarshan figures quoted in S.C. Bhatt, *Satellite Invasion of India* (New Delhi: Gyan Publishing, 1994), Appendix VII, p. 281.
72. Jawaharlal Nehru, *The Discovery of India* (Calcutta: Signet, 1948, first published 1945), p. 469.
73. David Page & William Crawley, *Satellites Over South Asia: Broadcasting, Culture and the Public Interest* (New Delhi: Sage, 2001), pp. 53–56 .
74. Figures from National Sample Survey, Fourteenth Round: July 1958-June 1959, No. 109, Tables with Notes on Indian Villages (New Delhi: Cabinet Secretariat, 1966), p. 16. Quoted in Jeffrey, 'The Mahatma Didn't Like Movies and Why it Matters', pp. 209–10.
75. *Radio and Television: Report of the Committee on Broadcasting and Information Media* (New Delhi: Ministry of Information and Broadcasting, 1966), p. 199.
76. P.C. Chatterjee, *Broadcasting in India* (New Delhi: Sage, 1991, 2nd ed.) pp. 52–53 .
77. David Page & William Crawley, *Satellites Over South Asia: Broadcasting, Culture and the Public Interest* (New Delhi: Sage, 2001), pp. 54–56.
78. Sevanti Ninan, *Through the Magic Window: Television and Change in India* (New Delhi: Penguin, 1995), p. 20.
79. With the Satellite Instructional Television Experiment (SITE) in 1975–76, India became the first country in the world to use a direct broadcast satellite to reach remote villages directly with educational information. Under SITE, an American satellite was used to transmit four hours of educational programming a day to 2,338 villages spread across six Indian states—Rajasthan, Bihar, Orissa, Madhya Pradesh, Karnataka and Andhra Pradesh. The primary objective was to help family planning, improve agricultural practices and contribute towards national integration. A NASA satellite was used for transmission. ISRO handled all hardware ground systems for transmission/reception of signals and All India Radio

had primary responsibility for production of all the TV programmes. Bella Mody, 'Programming for SITE', *Journal of Communication*, Vol. 29, No. 4 (1979), pp. 91–92.

80. K.S. Duggal, *What Ails Indian Broadcasting* (New Delhi: Marwah Publications, 1980), p. 126.
81. Amartya Sen, for instance, has noted the narrow instrumentalities of the Mahalanobis model, its exclusion of alternative choices and the political rationale behind investment decisions. Quoted in Sunil Khilnani, *The Idea of India* (New York: Farrar, Straus & Giroux, 1997, first published 1997), p. 86. In this context, Vivek Chibber has convincingly noted that it was not the idea of state-led intervention that was flawed—it worked in Korea—but the strategy of import-substitution industrialization, as opposed to export-led industrialization. See Vivek Chibber, *Locked in Place: State-Building and Late Industrialization in India* (Princeton: Princeton University Press, 2003). Lord Meghnad Desai has argued that the Indian model was under-developed state capitalism, not socialism. But he praises the Nehru era policies, arguing that these served their purpose and should have been re-assessed, not frozen in stone by the Indira Gandhi regime. Lord Meghnad Desai, 'Capitalism, Socialism and the Indian Economy' in Kalyan Bannerji & Tarjani Vakil (eds.), *India: Joining the World Economy* (New Delhi: Tata McGraw-Hill, 1995), pp. 183–200.
82. The traditional Soviet method of controlling media relied on centralization, Communist Party control of outlets and saturation. Ellen Mickiewicz, *Changing Channels: Television and the Struggle for Power in Russia* (New York: Oxford University Press, 1997), pp. 25–29.
83. This draws on the hermeneutic tradition to emphasize that individuals are not passive recipients of media messages but interpret them in their own ways. John B. Thompson summed up this argument to develop his notion of mediated communication. See John B. Thompson, *The Media and Modernity: A Social Theory of the Media* (Cambridge: Polity Press, 1995), pp. 25–42.
84. David Page & William Crawley, *Satellites Over South Asia: Broadcasting, Culture and the Public Interest* (New Delhi: Sage, 2001), pp. 54–66 .
85. Sevanti Ninan, *Through the Magic Window: Television and Change in India* (New Delhi: Penguin, 1995), pp. 28–29.
86. Bhaskar Ghose, *Doordarshan Days* (New Delhi: Penguin Viking, 2005), p. 28.
87. Emphasis is mine. *IX Asian Games Delhi 1982, Official Report Vol. II* (New Delhi: IX Asian Games Special Organising Committee, 1985), p. 187.
88. *IX Asian Games Delhi 1982,* p. 285.
89. Ibid.
90. Ibid., p. 301.
91. Bhaskar Ghose, *Doordarshan Days* (New Delhi: Penguin Viking, 2005), p. 28.

92. Ibid., p. 29.
93. Textual and audience studies since the early 1980s have shown that different audience respond to the same television product in multiple ways, based on local cultural and social factors, and that responses are often different from those intended by producers. See for instance, Iean Ang, *Watching Dallas: Soap Opera and the Melodramatic Imagination* (London: Methuen, 1985).
94. Bhaskar Ghose, *Doordarshan Days* (New Delhi: Penguin Viking, 2005), pp. 28–30.
95. Sumit Mitra, Anita Kaul, 'The Tedium is the Message', *India Today*, May 31, 1982, p. 16.
96. Sevanti Ninan, *Through the Magic Window: Television and Change in India* (New Delhi: Penguin, 1995), p. 30.
97. Audience Research Unit, Directorate General Doordarshan, Cited in Joshi, *Asia Speaks Out*, pp. 5–8.
98. David Page and William Crawley, *Satellites Over South Asia*: *Broadcasting, Culture and the Public Interest* (New Delhi: Sage, 2001). p. 56.
99. Audience Research Unit, Directorate General Doordarshan, Cited in Joshi, *Asia Speaks Out*, pp. 5–8; NRS 2006.
100. Atul Kohli, 'Politics of Economic Liberalization in India', *World Development*, Vol. 17, No. 3 (1989), p. 308.
101. Ibid., p. 312.
102. Nikhil Sinha, 'Doordarshan, Public Service Broadcasting and the Impact of Globalization: A Short History', in Price and Verhulst (eds.), *Broadcasting Reform in India*, p. 35.
103. Ibid., pp. 63–64.
104. Ibid., p. 35.
105. Doordarshan, http://www.ddindia.gov.in/About+DD/Commercial+Service accessed 10 July 2005.
106. Mohammad Khan, head of Enterprise Nexus Lowe advertising, quoted in William Mazzarella, *Shoveling Smoke: Advertising and Globalization in Contemporary India* (Durham: Duke University Press, 2003), p. 74.
107. Mohammad Khan interviewed by Tara Sehgal, 'In London, I Felt a Fool. In the US, I Felt so Superior', *Tehelka,* Vol. 5, Issue 4, 2 February 2008.
108. See for instance, Government of India, *An Indian Personality for Television: Report of the Working Group on Software for Doordarshan,* 2 vols. (New Delhi: Publications Division, Ministry of Information and Broadcasting, 1985.)
109. Purnima Mankekar, 'National Texts and Gendered Lives: An Ethnography of Television Viewers in a North Indian City', *American Ethnologist,* Vol. 20, No. 3 (August 1993), p. 547.
110. Quoted in Victoria L. Farmer, 'What a TV Epic did to India', the *Hindu* (17 November 1996)
111. Lavina Melwani, 'Ramanand Sagar's Ramayana Serial Re-Ignites Epic's Values', *India Worldwide*, February, 1988, pp. 56–57. Quoted in Philip

Lutgendorf, 'All in the (Raghu) Family: A Video Epic in Cultural Context' in Lawrence A. Babb and Susan S. Wadley (eds.) *Media and the Transformation of Religion in South Asia* (Philadelphia: University of Pennsylvania Press, 1995), p. 224.

112. Arvind Rajagopal, *Politics After Television,* p. 15.
113. Robin Jeffrey, 'An Unbottled Genie: Television in Asia, An Introduction' in Nalin Mehta, Robin Jeffrey (eds.), 'Television in Asia' section, *Biblio: A Review of Books,* Vol. XI, Nos. 9 & 10, (New Delhi: September–October 2006, p. 13).
114. Marshall McLuhan in 'Playboy interview' reproduced in Eric McLuhan & Frank Zingrone (eds.), *Essential McLuhan* (London: Routledge, 1997, first published 1995), p. 239.
115. See Marshall McLuhan, *Understanding Media: The Extensions of Man* (London: Routledge, K. Paul, 1964) and Marshall McLuhan, *The Gutenberg Galaxy: The Makings of Typographic Man* (New York: Mentor, 1969, first published 1962).
116. McLuhan quoted in William Kuhns, 'A McLuhan Sourcebook' in McLuhan & Zingrone (eds.), *Essential McLuhan*, p. 272.
117. Ibid., p. 273.
118. Rajiv Gandhi, then prime minister of India, in 'Foreword', *IX Asian Games Delhi 1982, Official Report Vol. 1* (New Delhi: IX Asian Games Special Organising Committee, 1985). Page number not listed.

CHAPTER 9

1. Shekhar Gupta, 'Hockey Isn't just Cricket', the *Indian Express*, 7 September 2002.
2. Sundeep Misra, 'Don't Compare Hockey with Cricket', reproduced on www.indianhockey.com/html3/sundeep20.php accessed 2 November 2007.
3. The manager and the channel cannot be named for obvious reasons. However, I have permission to quote the conversation, without identifying the source.
4. ESPN-Star had the T20 World Cup broadcast rights for India.
5. Nalin Mehta, 'The Great Indian Willow Trick: Cricket, Nationalism and India's TV News Revolution, 1998-2005', *The International Journal of the History of Sport*, Vol. 24, No. 9 (September 2007), pp. 1187–99.
6. Arjun Appadurai, *Modernity at Large: Cultural Dimensions of Globalization* (Minneapolis: University of Minnesota Press, 1996), p. 90. For Indian cricket and the nationalist imagination, see for instance, Ramachandra Guha, *Corner of a Foreign Field: The Indian History of a British Sport* (New Delhi: Pan Macmillan, 2002); Boria Majumdar, *Twenty Two Yards to Freedom: A Social History of Indian Cricket* (New Delhi: Penguin, 2004); Ashis Nandy, *Tao of Cricket: On Games of Destiny and the Destiny of the Games* (New York: Viking, 1989).

7. The players were S.V. Sunil, Vickram Kanth, Ignace Turkey and V. Raghunath. They were accompanied by Ramesh Parameshwaram, assistant coach of the national team and R.K. Shetty, Karnataka State Hockey Association President. Report telecast on Times Now, 26 September 2007.
8. Live phone interview with Nalin Mehta on Times Now, 26 September 2007. The Indian Hockey Federation acted fast to nip the hunger strike but the point had been made.
9. Quoted in T.N. Raghu, 'Starved Hockey Ready to Fast', the *Asian Age*, 27 September 2007.
10. The union ministry of information and broadcasting has a master list of 290 channels: 207 of these are licensed Indian private channels, 54 are foreign-owned and 27 are run by the state-controlled Doordarshan. http://mib.nic.in/informationb/CODES/frames.htm (5 November 2005; 11 November 2006), accessed 30 November 2006 and Ministry of Information and Broadcasting, *Answer to Lok Sabha Unstarred Question No. 2056* (9 March 2006), http://164.100.24.208/lsq14/quest.asp? qref=26637, accessed 29 May 2006, [hereafter MIB + date].
    The actual numbers of channels is much higher because a large number of foreign and local channels are not covered by official data. A good example is the Delhi High Court order of 17 June 2006 that restrained 92 cable operators in 11 states from telecasting the FIFA World Cup through free-to-air satellite channels like TV5, Cambodia TV, CC5 Channel, CCTV1, Super Sports, Multi-choice and Dream Satellite because none of them were registered with the MIB. 'Delhi High Court Restrains 92 Cable Operators From Unauthorized Telecast of the FIFA World Cup', 17 June 2006, http://www.indiantelevision.com/headlines/y2k6/june/june240.htm, accessed 21 June 2006.
11. Interview with Lalit Modi, vice-president, BCCI, 12 October 2006, http://content-usa.cricinfo.com/ci/content/story/262512.html, accessed 13 October 2006.
12. Samyabrata Ray Goswami 'Man U Model for BCCI', the *Telegraph,* 28 December 2005, http://www.telegraphindia.com/1051228/asp/nation/story_ 5652982.asp, accessed 6 January 2006.
13. India had 34,858,000 TV sets in 1992. Joshi, Trivedi, *Mass Media and Cross-Cultural Communication*, p. 16. The National Readership Studies Council 2006 survey estimated a total of 112 million television sets in India. *NRS 2006 Press Release—Key Findings,* p. 4.
14. PricewaterhouseCoopers, Federation of Indian Chambers of Commerce and Industry [hereafter PwC-FICCI], *The Indian Entertainment Industry*, p 36.
15. NRS 2006 estimated 68 million satellite and cable households, *NRS 2006 Press Release—Key Findings*, p. 4.
16. India and China are not very big revenue earners for global corporations yet. For instance, Rupert Murdoch's pan-Asian network, Star, contributed

less than 2% of News Corporation's total revenues until early 2005 but in strategic terms, the pure numbers of China and India mean that these two countries are key focus areas for the corporation over the next decade. Interview with Peter Mukerjea, chief executive, Star India, 1999–2006, Mumbai: 12 January 2005. For Chinese television, see for instance, Zhenzi Wang, Zhi-Qiang Liu & Steve Fore, 'Facing the Challenge: Chinese Television in the New Media Era', *Media International Australia Incorporating Culture and Policy*, 'Copyright, Media and Innovation', No. 114 (February 2005), pp. 135–46; Michael Curtin, *Playing to the World's Biggest Audience: The Globalization of Chinese Film and TV* (Berkeley: University of California Press, 2007).

17. See for instance, Kausik Bandopadhyaya, '1911 in Retrospect: A Revisionist Perspective on a Famous Indian Sporting Victory' in Boria Majumdar, J.A. Mangan (eds.), *Sport in South Asian Society: Past and Present* (London: Routledge, 2005), pp. 27–47.
18. *Amrit Bazar Patrika*, 31 July 1911.
19. Quoted in *Mohun Bagan Platinum Jubilee Souvenir* , (Calcutta: Mohun Bagan Club, 1964), p. 25
20. *Nayak*, 4 August 1911.
21. Swami Vivekanand, quoted in Boria Majumdar, Kausik Bandopadhyaya, 'From Recreation to Competition: Early History of Indian Football', in 'A Social History of Indian Football: Striving to Score', *Soccer & Society*, Special Issue, Vol. 6, No. 2/3, June–September 2005, p. 135
22. Boria Majumdar, Kausik Bandopadhyaya, Introduction to 'A Social History of Indian Football: Striving to Score', *Soccer & Society*, Vol. 6, No. 2/3, June/September 2005, p. 122.
23. Mihir Bose, *A History of Indian Cricket* (London: Andre Deutsch Ltd., 1990), pp. 16–17.
24. For details see Boria Majumdar and Kausik Bandopadhyaya, *Goalless: The Story of a Unique Footballing Nation* (New Delhi: Penguin Viking, 2006).
25. Boria Majumdar, Kausik Bandopadhyay, Introduction to 'A Social History of Indian Football: Striving to Score', *Soccer & Society*, Vol. 6, No. 2/3, June/ September 2005, p. 288.
26. Alarm bells rang in India when Helsinki, in 1949, expressed its unwillingness to host all hockey teams for 1952 because of lack of accommodation. The Indian Hockey Federation immediately proposed to the IOC to host the hockey event separately in Delhi. Eventually Helsinki did host the event but the Indian offer was indicative of how important hockey was to Indian sport. Letter from Dr. A.C. Chatterji, honorary secretary, Indian Hockey Federation to Demaurex, honorary secretary, Switzerland Hockey Federation, May 10, 1949, CIO FI FIH PROGR OU MO 0114 33 FIH-Hockey Programme 1946–1949.
27. Anthony De Mello, *Portrait of Indian Sport* (London: P.R. Macmillan, 1959), p. 3.
28. Ibid.

29. Ibid.
30. See Ramachandra Guha, *Corner of a Foreign Field: The Indian History of a British Sport* (New Delhi: Pan Macmillan, 2002). Mihir Bose, *History of Indian Cricket* (London: Andre Deutsch, 2002).
31. Boria Majumdar, 'When the Sepoys Batted: 1830–50 on the Playing Field', in Boria Majumdar & Sharmishtha Gooptu, *Revisiting 1857: Myth, Memory, History* (New Delhi: Roli, 2007), pp. 73–91.
32. See Boria Majumdar, *Twenty Two Yards to Freedom: A Social History of Indian Cricket* (New Delhi: Penguin, 2004).
33. Anthony De Mello, *Portrait of Indian Sport* (London: P.R. Macmillan, 1959), p. 9.
34. Ibid, pp. 9–10.
35. Ashwini Kumar, 'Whither Indian Hockey-I?', *Indian Olympic Association Official Bulletin*, Vol. 1, No. 2, January–March 1960.
36. Eastern Railways advertisement, published in *Indian Olympic News*, Vol. 1, No. 3, June 1962.
37. South Eastern Railways advertisement, published in *Indian Olympic News*, Vol. 1, No. 2, May 1962.
38. Ibid.
39. Air India advertisement, published in *Indian Olympic News*, Vol. 1, No. 4, July 1962.
40. J. Butalia, Jwalamukhi— the Olympia of India, *Indian Olympic Association Official Bulletin*, Vol. 2, January–March 1960, p. 35.
41. Ibid, pp. 36–37.
42. Ibid, p. 38.
43. Ibid.
44. Mir Ranjan Negi's Interview with Shekhar Gupta, the *Indian Express*, 17 September 2007.
45. Shekhar Gupta, 'Hockey Just Isn't Cricket', the *Indian Express*, 7 September 2002.
46. Ramachandra Guha, *India After Gandhi: The History of the World's Largest Democracy* (India: 2007), pp. 736–37.
47. Sevanti Ninan, *Through the Magic Window: Television and Change in India* (New Delhi: Penguin, 1995), p. 30.
48. David Page and William Crawley, *Satellites Over South Asia*: *Broadcasting, Culture and the Public Interest* (New Delhi: Sage, 2001). p. 56.
49. Audience Research Unit, Directorate General Doordarshan, Cited in Joshi, *Asia Speaks Out*, pp. 5–8; NRS 2006.
50. Audience Research Unit, Directorate General Doordarshan, 1995.Cited in Joshi & Trivedi, *Mass Media and Cross-Cultural Communication*, p. 16.
51. William Mazzarella, *Shoveling Smoke: Advertising and Globalization in Contemporary India* (Durham: Duke University Press, 2003), p. 98.
52. See for instance Purnima Mankekar, *Screening Culture, Viewing Politics: An Ethnography of Television, Womanhood, and Nation in Postcolonial India* (Durham: Duke University Press, 1999); Arvind Rajagopal, *Politics*

After Television: Religious Nationalism and the Reshaping of the Indian Public (Cambridge: Cambridge University Press, 2001).

53. Quoted in William Mazzarella, *Shoveling Smoke: Advertising and Globalization in Contemporary India* (Durham: Duke University Press, 2003), pp. 74–75.
54. Vir Sanghvi, 'A New Middle Class Fidelity?' the *Hindustan Times,* New Delhi, 20 May 2006, http://www.hindustantimes.com/news/181_1702508, 00300001. htm, accessed 21 May 2006.
55. Shalimar Mary, letter to editor, the *Indian Express*, 5 October 1986. Quoted in Nandy, *The Tao of Cricket*, pp. 1–2.
56. Harsha Bhogle, 'India Needs to Rediscover Another Sport', the *Week*, 27 July 2003.
57. Ibid.
58. Rohit Brijnath, 'The Lopsidedness in Indian Sports', *Sportstar*, 5–11 June, 2004.
59. Rupert Murdoch's News Corporation bought a controlling stake in Sky in 1983 and re-launched as Sky Television in 1989 but it made heavy losses until 1992 when BSkyB (Sky and BSB merged in 1990) acquired the rights to broadcast Premier League Soccer games for $465 million. Almost a million subscribers signed up immediately and by 1993 it reached financial stability. Bharat Anand & Kate Attea, 'News Corporation', Harvard Business School Case No. 9-702-425 (Boston: Harvard Business School Publishing, rev. 27 June 2003), p. 8. For a concise history of Sky Television and News Corporation's television operations see also, Pankaj Ghemawat, 'British Satellite Broadcasting Versus Sky Television,' Harvard Business School Case No. 9-794-031 (Boston: Harvard Business School Publishing, rev. ed. 22 August 1994).
60. In 1999, for instance, News Corporation owned the Los Angeles Dodgers baseball club and had shares in the New York Knicks and Los Angeles Lakers basketball clubs, and the New York Rangers. In September 1998, BSkyB launched a takeover bid for Manchester United, the world's richest football club, which was blocked by the British Mergers and Monopolies Commission on grounds that it was 'anti-competitive' in broadcasting. David Rowe, 'To Serve and To Sell: Media Sport and Cultural Citizenship', Paper at How you Play the Game: First International Conference on Sports and Human Rights, Sydney, 1–3 September 1999, p. 186, http://www. ausport. gov.au/fulltext/1999/nsw/p182-191.pdf, accessed 27 August 2006.
61. Emphasis is mine. Rupert Murdoch to his shareholders in Adelaide, 15 October 1996. Quoted in S. Millar, 'Courtship Ends as Soccer and TV are United', the *Guardian,* 7 September 1998.
62. Boria Majumdar, *Twenty Two Yards to Freedom*, p. 176. ESPN is part of ESPN-Star, which is jointly owned by News Corporation and Walt Disney.
63. Boria Majumdar, *The Illustrated History of Indian Cricket,*(New Delhi: Roli, 2006), p. 198.
64. Supreme Court Case 161 before Justices, P.B. Sawant, S Mohan and B.P. Jeevan Reddy, Civil Appeals Nos. 1429-30 of 1995, The Secretary

Information & Broadcasting, Government of India & Others vs. Cricket Association of Bengal & Others, with Writ Petition (Civil) No. 836 of 1993, Cricket Association of Bengal vs. Union of India and Others (decided on 9 February 1995).

65. *The Indian Telegraph Act*, Act XIII of 1885, pt. II.
66. Section 7 of Act 47 of 1957, an amendment to the 1885 Act. There were five amendments to this Act from 1957 to 1974. Sevanti Ninan, 'History of Indian Broadcasting Reform', in Monroe Price & Stefaan G. Verhulst (eds.) *Broadcasting Reform in India: Media Law from a Global Perspective* (New Delhi: Oxford University Press, 1998), pp. 1–2.
67. The five nations that eventually participated in the Hero Cup were India, South Africa, West Indies, Sri Lanka and Zimbabwe.
68. Doordarshan put in a bid of Rs 10 million (roughly $3,18,471 at 1993 exchange rates), as against TWI's vastly superior minimum guarantee of $5,50,000. It was specified that if TWI received any sum in excess of the guaranteed sum, it would be split in a 70:30 ratio in favour of CAB. Supreme Court Case 161 before Justices, P.B. Sawant, S Mohan and B.P. Jeevan Reddy, Civil Appeals Nos. 1429-30 of 1995.
69. Boria Majumdar, 'Cricket, Television, Globalization: Defining India in the 1990s', paper presented at the 'Television in Asia' conference, La Trobe University, Melbourne, 14 December 2005, p. 2.
70. VSNL was created as a public sector undertaking in 1986. The Government of India first disinvested some stake in 1999 but remained a majority stakeholder till 2002. It is now managed by the Tatas.
71. Supreme Court Case 161 before Justices, P.B. Sawant, S Mohan and B.P. Jeevan Reddy, Civil Appeals Nos. 1429–30 of 1995.
72. A senior ministry official quoted in Boria Majumdar, 'Cricket, Television, Globalization: Defining India in the 1990s', paper presented at the 'Television in Asia' conference, La Trobe University, Melbourne, 14 December 2005, p. 7.
73. Supreme Court Case 161 before Justices, P.B. Sawant, S Mohan and B.P. Jeevan Reddy, Civil Appeals Nos. 1429–30 of 1995.
74. C.R. Irani, 'Someone is Remembering Sanjay Gandhi', the *Statesman,* 13 November 1993.
75. Boria Majumdar, 'Cricket, Television, Globalization: Defining India in the 1990s', paper presented at the 'Television in Asia' conference, La Trobe University, Melbourne, 14 December 2005, p. 8.
76. Supreme Court Case 161 before Justices, P.B. Sawant, S Mohan and B.P. Jeevan Reddy, Civil Appeals Nos. 1429–30 of 1995.
77. Boria Majumdar, 'Cricket, Television, Globalization: Defining India in the 1990s', paper presented at the 'Television in Asia' conference, La Trobe University, Melbourne, 14 December 2005, pp. 9–10.
78. See Reference 70.
79. Supreme Court Case 161 before Justices, P.B. Sawant, S Mohan and B.P. Jeevan Reddy, Civil Appeals Nos. 1429–30 of 1995.

80. Meenal Baghel, 'Doordarshan Jams VSNL Plans to Uplink', the *Asian Age,* 19 September 1994.
81. B.P.J. Reddy concurring, Supreme Court Case 161 before Justices, P.B. Sawant, S Mohan and B.P. Jeevan Reddy, Civil Appeals Nos. 1429–30 of 1995.
82. Ten Sports estimated its initial damages to be worth Rs 2.8 billion. 'DD to get Ten Sports feed for all Matches', the *Hindu BusinessLine,* 18 March 2004.
83. Ministry of Information and Broadcasting, Policy Guidelines for Downlinking of Television Channels, 11 November 2005.
84. 'Supreme Court Restrains DD from Interfering with Rights of Ten Sports', the *Hindu,* 10 May 2006.
85. 'Don't Interfere with Ten Sports' Rights: Court', the *Hindu,* 5 August 2006.
86. UNI, 'SC allows ESPN-STAR to Approach it if coerced by the Centre', 8 January 2007, http://www.indlawnews.com/2C829C337F2DBD858EAC 77A542 63988C, accessed 8 January 2007.
87. PTI, 'Telecast India-WI Series with Delay: HC', 23 January 2007, http://timesofindia.indiatimes.com/articleshow/1403569.cms, accessed 23 January 2007.
88. The government contended that about 9–10% of Doordarshan's 25% share would pay for its expenditure in the broadcast while the remaining revenue would be ploughed back into national sports. Rajya Sabha, Synopsis of Debates (Proceedings other than Questions and Answers), Statutory Resolution Seeking Disapproval of the Sports Broadcasting Signals (Mandatory Sharing with Prasar Bharati) Ordinance, 2007 and the Sports Broadcasting Signals (Mandatory Sharing with Prasar Bharati) Bill, 2007 (9 March 2007), http://www.rajyasabha.nic.in/rsdebate/synopsis/210/09032007.htm, accessed 11 March 2007.
89. Ibid.
90. Ibid.
91. The BCCI agreed to share half of the losses. PTI, 'BCCI to Share Nimbus Losses', 23 March 2007, http://www.indianexpress.com/story/26365.html, accessed 23 March 2007.
92. In the Rajya Sabha, for instance, only two speakers dissented. http://www.rajyasabha.nic.in/rsdebate/synopsis/210/09032007.htm, accessed 11 March 2007.
93. See Nalin Mehta, *India on Television: How TV News Changed the Ways We Think and Act* (New Delhi: HarperCollins, 2008).
94. Interview with Uday Shankar, CEO and editor, Star News, 2003–04, Shanghai, 22 August 2005.
95. Emphasis is Shankar's. Interview with Uday Shankar, ibid.
96. C.L.R. James, *Beyond a Boundary* (London: Hutchinson, 1963).
97. Appadurai, *Modernity at Large*, p. 101.
98. Atul Phadnis, 'New TAM-ADEX Analysis: Greater Opportunities for In-Program or On-Ground Promotions During Cricket than Soccer!'

(Mumbai: TAM ADEX, 24 January 2002, http://www.indiantelevision.com /tamadex/y2k3/tamadex.htmm, accessed 29 August 2006.
99. 'Cricket—Who is Riding it?: An exchange4media Analysis of 2001', http://www.exchange4media.com/e4m/others/cricket_ad.asp, accessed 24 August 2006.
100. Appadurai, *Modernity at Large*, p. 111.
101. Interview with Uday Shankar, CEO and editor, Star News, 2003–07, Shanghai, 22 August 2005.
102. Ibid.
103. SET Max would revert to regular entertainment programming when cricket was not on.
104. Kunal Dasgupta, CEO, Sony Entertainment Television, interview on http://www.indiantelevision.com/interviews/y2k2/executive/kunal.htm, 3 June 2002, accessed 1 August 2006.
105. Sheela Reddy, 'Hooked,' *Outlook,* 24 March 2003, http://www.outlookindia.com/archivecontents.asp?fnt=20030324, accessed 1 August 2006.
106. Atul Phadnis, 'Adex World Cup Barometer: 2nd Week of Cricket World Cup Rakes in 36.5 Million Female Viewers,' TAM India Report, 3 March 2003, http://www.indiantelevision.com/tamadex/y2k3/mar/cricbra5.htm, accessed 31 July 2006.
107. Purnendu Bose, COO, SaharaOne, quoted in Latha Venkatraman, Ajita Shashidhar, 'Taking Refuge in Cricket', *BusinessLine,* 9 March 2006.
108. When Kerry Packer's Channel 9 failed to win the broadcast rights to Australian cricket, he set up World Series Cricket as an independent cricket attraction. Channel 9's WSC signed up the world's top international players and introduced day-night one-day games, coloured clothing and aggressive marketing tactics to re-invent cricket as a television game. For details see Gideon Haigh, *The Cricket War: The Inside Story of Kerry Packer's World Series Cricket* (Melbourne: Text, 1993).
109. See Shahid Amin, 'Gandhi as Mahatma: Gorakhpur District, Eastern UP, 1921–2' in Ranajit Guha (ed.), *Subaltern Studies III: Writings on South Asian History and Society* (Delhi, 1984), pp. 1–55.
110. See Arjun Appadurai, 'Modernity at Large: Cultural Dimensions of Globalization', (Minneapolis: University of Minnesota Press, 1996). The same article was reproduced in Carol A Breckenridge (ed.), *Consuming Modernity: Public culture in a South Asian World*, (Minneapolis, University of Minnesota Press, 1995), pp. 23–48.
111. Ashis Nandy, *The Tao of Cricket: On Games of Destiny and the Destiny of the Games* (New York: Viking, 1989), p. 1.

CHAPTER 10

Much of the data used in this chapter is also the product of ethnography that was part of a growing up experience in Army cantonments across the country.

1. Rathore won the silver medal in men's double trap shooting at Athens 2004. The billboard bearing his photograph was first seen by the author in January 2005 and then in January 2008.
2. India's other Olympic medals have been gold in hockey, 1980; bronze in tennis (Leander Paes), 1996; bronze in women's weightlifting (Karnam Malleswari), 2000.
3. The Indian Army's officer shortage went up from 17.31% in 1986 to 30.11% in 1999. In 2000 the Army said it was short of 12,883 officers, 28.18% of the sanctioned strength because young men did not see it as a lucrative career any more. In a clear reflection of the Army's social base, 60% of the officers commissioned in 2001–04 came from families with an income of less than Rs 10,000 a month. The figures are from Indian Military Academy, Dehradun. News reports compiled by the author for New Delhi Television. Broadcast on 17/12/200 and 14/6/2004 respectively.
4. Sanjay Sharma, 'President APJ Abdul Kalam Looks to Indian Army & Govt Support to Produce Indian Olympic Medallists', 15 September 2004. www.indian olympic.com/story/2004/9/15/205540/587, accessed 15 August 2005.
5. http://mod.nic.in/rec&training/body.htm, accessed 15 August, 2005. Also see *Ministry of Defence Annual Report*, 2001–2002, p. 32.
6. Gopal Sharma, 'Army Out to Salvage Pride in Olympics', the *Tribune*, 14 August 2004.
7. Ibid.
8. Krishna Bobji, 3 February 2005. http://mboard.rediff.com/board/board.php?action=m&boardid=sports2003sep04spec&messageid=1598131597#1598131597
9. Anthony De Mello, *Portrait of Indian Sport* (London: P.R. Macmillan, 1959), pp. 3, 8.
10. The entire collection of this magazine is available in the Rare Section of the Regenstein Library, University of Chicago.
11. *Sporting Intelligence* magazine, March 1845, p. 450.
12. Boria Majumdar, 'When the Sepoys Batted: 1830–1850 on the Playing Field', in Sharmistha Gooptu and Boria Majumdar (eds.), *Revisiting 1857: Myth, Memory, History*, (New Delhi: Roli Books, 2007), p. 77.
13. Chris Moore, 'A History of Hockey', *6th FIH World Hockey Cup for Men: National Hockey Centre, London, England, 4th–19th October, 1986, Official Souvenir Programme* (London: World Hockey Cup), pp. 33–34.
14. Dhyan Chand, *Goal*, published in *Sport and Pastime*, 1952. http://www.bharatiyahockey.org/granthalaya/goal/, accessed 29 September 2007.
15. Chris Moore, 'A History of Hockey', *6th FIH World Hockey Cup for Men: National Hockey Centre, London, England, 4th–19th October, 1986, Official Souvenir Programme* (London: World Hockey Cup), p. 34.
16. See for instance, Jeffrey Greenhut, 'Sahib and Sepoy: An Inquiry into the Relationship Between the British Officers and Native Soldiers of the British Indian Army', *Military Affairs*, Vol. 48, No. 1, Jan. 1984.

17. Dhyan Chand, *Goal*, published in *Sport and Pastime*, 1952. http://www.bharatiya hockey.org/granthalaya/goal/, accessed 29 September 2007.
18. 'Olympians Dot Sansarpur Plains', the *Tribune*, 8 November 2003
19. Steve Ruskin, 'Reign on the Wane', *Sports Illustrated*, 85 (4), 22 July 1996, p. 172.
20. Boria Majumdar and Kausik Bandyopadhyay, *Striving to Score: A Social History of Indian Football*, (London: Routledge, 2006), p. 124.
21. The Calcutta Football Club (1872) devoted to playing rugby football initially, predated the Dalhousie Club by over a decade and is technically the oldest Indian football club. Boria Majumdar and Kausik Bandyopadhyay, Striving to Score: A Social History of Indian Football, p. 124.
22. 'Services Lead the Way', *Indian Olympic News*, July 1962, Vol. 1, No. 4, p. 5.
23. Indian Olympic Association. http://nocindia.nic.in/history.html, accessed 15 August 2005.
24. For a detailed analysis of cricket and the politics surrounding it see Ramachandra Guha, *A Corner of a Foreign Field: The Indian History of a British Sport* and Boria Majumdar, *22 Yards to Freedom: A Social History of Indian Cricket.*
25. *Amrita Bazar Patrika*, 20 September (1936). This entire episode in Indian football history is narrated in great detail in Boria Majumdar, Kausik Bandopadhyay, 'Contesting Neighbours: The Years of Turmoil', in Striving to Score: A Social History of Indian Football, pp.171–84.
26. Joya Chatterjee, *Bengal Divided: Hindu Communalism and Partition 1932–1947*, (Cambridge: Cambridge University Press, 1995), p. 16
27. Pankaj Gupta, A Brief History of the Association in *Cricket Association of Bengal Silver Jubilee Souvenir*, (Calcutta: 1954–55), pp. 37–45; In a meeting held on 3 February 1928, presided over by the president of the Calcutta Cricket Club, it was agreed by the clubs present that the Cricket Association of Bengal and Assam should be formed with the president and secretary of the Calcutta Cricket Club serving as the president and secretary of the association. The working committee, it was agreed, would consist of 9 members, of which 3 were to be Europeans, 2 Hindus, with a member each from among the Parsis, Mohammedans, Anglo-Indians and Assam. As the president and secretary of the CCC were president and secretary of the CAB, the Europeans had two additional seats on the working committee, giving them a numerical superiority in matters of dispute and those which called for voting. This framework continued till the beginning of the 1940s.
28. For a good analysis of sports in military life see Steven W. Pope, 'An Army of Athletes: Playing Fields, Battlefields, and the American Military Sporting Experience, 1890–1920', *Journal of Military History*, Vol. 59, No. 3.
29. *The Orient Illustrated Weekly*, 11 October 1936.
30. *Amrita Bazar Patrika*, 15 September 1935.
31. *Amrita Bazar Patrika*, 22 September 1935.

32. *Forward*, 22 September 1935.
33. Emphasis is ours. Ibid.
34. *Amrita Bazar Patrika*, 22 September 1935.
35. *Advance*, 28 September 1935.
36. *Amrita Bazar Patrika*, 14 March 1936.
37. Ibid.
38. Ibid.
39. The *Statesman*, 13 April 1936.
40. Ibid.
41. Ibid.
42. Ibid.
43. *Amrita Bazar Patrika*, 10 September 1936.
44. Ibid.
45. Ibid.
46. Ibid.
47. Ibid.
48. The *Statesman*, 12 September 1936.
49. *Amrita Bazar Patrika*, 14 September 1936.
50. Ibid.
51. The *Statesman*, 15 September 1936.
52. Ibid.
53. Despite the efforts of the IFA to go ahead with the proposed conference at Calcutta in December the hostile reaction of the other provinces eventually resulted in the abandonment of the plan. The IFA, infuriated at such actions, had become determined not to accede to any demand advanced by the AIFA.
54. Private papers of the maharaja of Santosh, Nehru Memorial Museum and Library, New Delhi.
55. Ibid.
56. Ibid.
57. Ibid.
58. Ibid.
59. Ibid.
60. See for instance, Stephen Cohen, *The Indian Army: Its Contribution to the Development of a Nation* (Berkeley: University of California Press, 1971).
61. Raju G.C. Thomas, 'The Armed Forces and the Indian Defence Budget', *Asian Survey*, Vol. XX, No. 3, March 1980, pp. 280–81.
62. Ibid, pp. 281–82.
63. 'Services Lead the Way', *Indian Olympic News*, July 1962, Vol. 1, No. 4, p. 5.
64. Ibid, p. 6.
65. Ibid; 'Punjabis Pioneers in Organised Gymnastics', *Indian Olympic News*, Aug 1963, Vol 2, No. 5, p. 6–7.
66. Capt. G.C. Sethi won the golf championship twice in three years. 'Services Lead the Way', *Indian Olympic News*, July 1962, Vol. 1, No. 4, p. 6

67. Services won volleyball twice, including in 1959–60. Ibid.
68. Services first won football in the 1960–61 season, Ibid.
69. Services won the cycling championship in 1962, Ibid.
70. 'Sportsmen Come Forward', editorial in *Indian Olympic News*, Nov. 1962, Vol. 1, No, 8, p. 3.
71. 'To the National Defence Fund', *Indian Olympic News*, Dec. 1962, Vol. 1, No. 9, p. 37.
72. Others who donated were Behala Athletics Sports Association, Rs 151 (as a first installment); Obaid Al, retired cricketer of Mohammedan Sporting Club, one gold ring; Fani Mitra, one time well known footballer and boxer, three gold medals and a gold souvenir; Bimal Mukherjee, for his father the late Moni Mukherjee, member of the 1911 Mohun Bagan team, one gold medal. Ibid, pp. 37–38.
73. The volumes of *Indian Olympic News* for late 1962 carry lovely pictures of film stars holding cricket bats as they gather for the game.
74. 'Sportsmen Come Forward', editorial in *Indian Olympic News*, November 1962, Vol. 1, No, 8, p. 3.
75. Quoted in 'To the National Defence Fund', *Indian Olympic News*, December 1962, Vol. 1, No. 9, p. 37.
76. See Stephen Cohen, *The Indian Army: Its Contribution to the Development of a Nation* (Berkeley: University of California Press, 1971).
77. Ramachandra Guha, *India After Gandhi: The History of the World's Largest Democracy* (New Delhi: Picador, 2007).
78. 'Services Lead the Way', *Indian Olympic News*, July 1962, Vol. 1, No. 4, pp. 6–7.
79. Interview with Brig (retd.) Rakesh Mehta, former commander, Territorial Army, Western Command; former DDG Training and Logistics, National Cadet Corps, 25 January 2008.
80. Ibid. The unit in question is 144 Air Defence Regiment.
81. 'Services Lead the Way', *Indian Olympic News*, July 1962, Vol. 1, No. 4, p. 7.
82. Major General A.A. Rudra in the foreword of Dhyan Chand's biography, *Goal*, published in *Sport and Pastime*, 1952. The book has been digitized and is available in http://www.bharatiyahockey.org/granthalaya/goal/, accessed 29 September 2007.
83. See Jeffrey Greenhut, 'Sahib and Sepoy: An Inquiry into the Relationship Between the British Officers and Native Soldiers of the British Indian Army', *Military Affairs*, Vol. 48, No. 1, Jan. 1984.
84. See Reference No. 79.
85. Steven W. Pope, 'An Army of Athletes: Playing Fields, Battlefields, and the American Military Sporting Experience, 1890–1920', *Journal of Military History*, Vol. 59, No. 3., July 1995, p. 435.
86. Ibid, p. 436.
87. Ibid.
88. Ibid.

89. Dan Allen Willey, 'The Spirit of Sport in the Army', *Harper's Weekly*, 50, 1906, pp. 1,100–01.
90. See Ref. No. 79.
91. Maj. Gen. (Retd) D. Bannerjee, 'Manpower Reduction in the Army', Article No.53, Jan 27, 1998, Institute of Peace and Conflict Studies. http://www.ipcs.org/printArticle.jsp? kValue=53, accessed 30 January 2008.
92. 'Rashtriya Rifles', www.globalsecurity.org/military/world/india/rashtriya-rifles.htm, accessed 30 January 2008.
93. The exact figures of troops deployments are not available for security reasons. But this is a reasonable estimate agreed upon by most specialists. I am grateful to Srinjoy Chowdhary, senior editor, Times Now, who has covered the defence ministry for over a decade, for providing these estimates.
94. Maj. Gen. (retd) D. Bannerjee, 'Manpower Reduction in the Army', Article No.53, 27 January 1998, Institute of Peace and Conflict Studies. http://www.ipcs.org/printArticle.jsp?kValue=53, accessed 30 January 2008.
95. Ibid. In this context also see Lt Gen. Vijay Oberoi, *Army 2020* (New Delhi: Knowledge World, 2005).
96. In a clear reflection of the Army's social base, 60% of the officers commissioned from 2001–2 004 came from families with an income of less than Rs 10,000 a month. The figures are from Indian Military Academy, Dehradun. News reports compiled by the author for New Delhi Television. Broadcast on 17/12/200 and 14/6/2004 respectively.
97. See for instance, P.E. Razzell, 'Social Origins of Officers in the Indian and British Home Army: 1758–1962', *The British Journal of Sociology*, Vol. 14, No. 3 (September 1963), pp. 248–60.
98. Just 86 officer recruits turned up for NDA's January 2008 course, out of total vacancies for 250. AFP, 'Indian Army Faces Dire Shortage of Officers', 16 January 2008.
99. The information on 31 Armoured Division is gleaned from a senior officer who was serving in the division at the time but does not want to be named for obvious reasons.
100. The conclusions in this paragraph are based on conversations with several senior serving Army officers who do not want to be named.
101. AFP, 'Olympic history for India, UAE', 18 August 2004, http://www.abc.net.au/sport/contcnt/200408/s1178859.htm
102. He was the cadet sergeant major of the Echo squadron at the NDA. Vibhay Sharma, 'A Sure Shot', the *Tribune*, 21 August 2004, http://www.tribuneindia. com/2004/20040821/saturday/main1.htm
103. AFP, 'Olympic history for India, UAE', 18 August 2004, http://www.abc.net.au/sport/content/200408/s1178859.htm
104. 'A Sure Shot', the *Tribune*, 21 August 2004, http://www.tribuneindia.com/2004/20040821/saturday/main1.htm
105. Prabhjot Singh, 'At Last a Silver Lining', the *Tribune*, 21 August 2004, http://www.tribuneindia.com/2004/20040821/saturday/main1.htm.

106. Emphasis is ours. Quoted in 'A Sure Shot', the *Tribune*, 21 August 2004, http://www.tribuneindia.com/2004/20040821/saturday/main1.htm.
107. Rathore interview with Harish Kotian, 25 August 2005, http://www.rediff.com/sports/2005/aug/26sinter.htm.
108. Rajesh Mishra, 'Officer and a Gentleman', *Swagat*, October 2005, pp. 88–89.
109. Rajyavardhan Singh Rathore, quoted in Rajesh Mishra, 'Officer and a Gentleman', *Swagat*, Oct. 2005, pp. 88–89.
110. Emphasis is ours. Rathore interview with Harish Kotian, 25 August 2005, http://www.rediff.com/sports/2005/aug/26sinter.htm.
111. Rajesh Mishra, 'Officer and a Gentleman', *Swagat*, October 2005, pp. 89.
112. Faisal Sharif, 'Indian Army Launches Operation Olympic Medal', 4 September 2003, http://www.rediff.com/sports/2003/sep/04spec.htm.
113. Faisal Sharif, 'Indian Army Launches Operation Olympic Medal', 4 September 2003, http://www.rediff.com/sports/2003/sep/04spec.htm.
114. Col. Ajay Das, SC, Dir ALC, ADGPI. Email correspondence on 21 February 2008. We are thankful for Srinjoy Chowdhary for facilitating this data from the Army.
115. Figures from Col. Ajay Das, SC, Dir ALC, ADGPI. Email correspondence on 21 February 2008. We are thankful for Srinjoy Chowdhary for facilitating this data from the Army.
116. Faisal Sharif, 'Indian Army Launches Operation Olympic Medal', 4 September 2003, http://www.rediff.com/sports/2003/sep/04spec.htm.
117. Figures from Col Ajay Das, SC, Dir ALC, ADGPI. Email correspondence on 21 February 2008. We are thankful for Srinjoy Chowdhary for facilitating this data from the Army.
118. Ibid.
119. Ibid.
120. Ibid.
121. Ibid.
122. Figures from directorate general, NCC, ministry of defence.

CHAPTER 11

1. There is considerable debate over Pritchard's identity. Whether Pritchard represented British India or whether he considered himself a representative of British India is still unresolved. Hence Pritchard remains a liminal figure in India's Olympic story and we thought it best to leave out his medals from India's tally. The IOC archives and contemporary records that we could access do not shed light on his antecedents—whether he was an Anglo Indian (in the sense of being of mixed race) or an Anglo-Indian (in the sense of a Britisher who simply lived in India). Norman Gilbert Pritchard was born in Alipore, near Calcutta, on 23 June 1875, to George Peterson Pritchard and Helen Maynard Pritchard. He won the Bengal province 100-yards title from 1894 to 1900 and in July 1900,

took part in the British Amateur Athletics Association Championships. He went to the 1900 Paris Olympics with the British team and took part in 60 metres, 100 metres and 200 metres sprints and 110 metres and 200 metres hurdles. The programme listed him variously as representing either England or British India. He won the 200 metres sprint silver with a time of 22.5 seconds behind the American Walter Tewkesbury, and second silver behind the American Alvin Kraenzlein in 200 metres hurdles. After competing in the Paris Games, he returned to India and became secretary of the Indian Football Association. Later, he emigrated to America and became a silent movie actor, appearing alongside stars such as Gary Cooper, Clara Bow and Ronald Colman. His most famous film was Beau Geste, in 1926.

2. For a detailed history of Indian soccer see Boria Majumdar and Kausik Bandyopadhyay, *Goalless: The Story of a Unique Footballing Nation* (New Delhi: Penguin-Viking, 2006).
3. We have consulted most of the leading newspapers of the time for this book and not one carried a major story on Jadhav's achievement on Page 1.
4. Jadhav, despite his achievements, always led a life sans luxury or well being because of the neglect meted out to him by the Indian sports authorities.
5. Rohit Brijnath, 'Leander—leading the way', 23 April 2006 http://news.bbc.co.uk/2/hi/south_asia/4929784.stm, accessed 10 February 2008.
6. Rohit Brijnath, 'He Doesn't Surrender', *Sportstar*, Vol 28, No. 20, 14–20 May 2005, http://www.hinduonnet.com/tss/tss2820/stories/20050514005800900.htm
7. 'Saturday Extra' in the *Tribune*, 19 June 2004.
8. Rohit Brijnath, 'India's Queen of the Runway', 26 July 2004, http://news.bbc.co.uk/2/hi/south_asia/3925857.stm
9. The *Times of India*, 23 July 1952.
10. Ibid.
11. Ibid.
12. Statistical indexes of all Indian athletes who have participated at the Olympic Games have been compiled at the end of the book as an Appendix. We are grateful to Charles Davis for providing us with these statistics. Without his help, it was impossible to give this huge corpus of data a manageable shape.
13. Gulu Ezekiel, 'K D Jadhav- A man of bronze' in http://sify.com/sports/olympics/fullstory.php?id=13538760&page=2, accessed 12 January 2008.
14. The *Times of India*, 24 July 1952.
15. The gold medal-winning jump at London measured 50 ft 6 inches.
16. For details see, Gulu Ezekiel, 'Oh Henry', *Sportstar*, 17–23 December 2005.
17. Ibid
18. Ibid.

19. For details on Pinto's performance see the *Times of India*, 21 July 1952.
20. The *Hindu*, 2 December 1956.
21. Ibid., 5 December 1956.
22. Interview with P.K. Banerjee, 10 January 2007.
23. The *Hindu*, 30 August 1960.
24. Ibid., 7 September 1960.
25. Interview with Milkha Singh, 28 November 2007.
26. Ibid.
27. Interview with Bruce Kidd at the University of Toronto, 25 May 2007.
28. For details see Gulu Ezekiel, 'Gurbachan Randhawa—A rare Breed' in *The Sportstar*, 8 April 2006.
29. Ibid.
30. Ibid.
31. The *Times of India*, 31 August 1972.
32. Ibid., 1 September 1972.
33. Ibid.
34. Ibid.
35. He won this race with a timing of 1.48.9 seconds. For details on this race see the *Times of India*, 16 July 1976.
36. Ibid., 25 July 1976.
37. Ibid., 26 July 1976.
38. *Ibid.,* 26 July 1980.
39. Ibid., 28 July 1980.
40. Ibid.
41. For details see The *Times of India*, 29 July 1980.
42. Ibid., 2 August 1980.
43. Ibid., 29 July 1984.
44. Ibid., 6 August 1984.
45. Ibid., 8 August 1984.
46. Ibid, 10 August 1984.
47. Ibid.
48. Usha Sujit Nair, 'Government and Sport in Kerala, India',*Journal of Sport Management*, September 1993, Vol. 7, No. 3, pp. 256–62.
49. Rohit Brijnath, 'Leander—leading the way', 23 April 2006 http://news.bbc.co.uk/2/hi/south_asia/4929784.stm, accessed 10 February 2008.
50. The *Times of India*, 5 August 1996.
51. Ibid.
52. Karnam Malleswari interview published in www.rediff.com, http://202.54.124.133/sports/2000/oct/05malles.htm, accessed 10 February 2007.
53. The *Tribune*, editorial, 21 September 2000.
54. The *Times of India*, 14 February 2008.
55. Gagan Narang interview in the *Deccan Herald*, 30 January 2008.
56. Akhil Kumar qualified for the Olympics in the bantamweight class at the Asian Qualifying event in February 2008. He won gold, defeating the

Olympic silver medallist Worapoj Pitchkoom of Thailand and was also awarded the best boxer trophy in the competition.

CHAPTER 12

1. The Commonwealth Games was held in New Delhi between 3–14 October 2010.
2. In the absence of many star athletes who had withdrawn from the Delhi games the standard of competition in some events was modest to say the least. World stars like Usain Bolt or Yohan Blake did not make it to Delhi nor did Chris Hoy or Andy Murray or US Open Champion Samantha Stosur.
3. Contrary to expectations India just won a solitary shooting gold at the Guangzhou Asian Games.
4. India can expect medals in shooting, tennis, boxing, archery, badminton and wrestling.
5. Personal interview with Randhir Singh, 10 November 2010. He said the exact same things to the *Telegraph* reporter Anirban Das Mahapatra on 1 February 2009.
6. This discrepancy was noticeable across the media. I have looked at ten leading national newspapers and not a single one had the Indian Open as its first headline.
7. Quoted in *The Telegraph*, 1 April 2009.
8. For details see; *The Times of India*, 31 August 2011. First Page.
9. Quoted in *The Times of India*, Oped, 5 September 2011.
10. Ibid.
11. Patel even went on to suggest that had the bill been implemented it will mean a Joint Secretary running the affairs of a NSF. Quoted in *The Times of India*, 2 September 2011.
12. India beat Hamilton to win the hosting rights for the 2010 Commonwealth Games at Montego Bay in Jamaica in November 2003.
13. Personal interview with Jacques Rogge in New Delhi, 2 October 2010.
14. Personal interview with Jagdish Singh, 6 September 2008.
15. Personal interview with Raj Kumar Sangwan, 8 September 2008.
16. 'Inside India's Fight Club', *The Indian Express*, 24 August 2008.
17. Ibid.
18. His rustic yet pleasant statements to the media have endeared him to the nation's sports fraternity. When Majumdar asked him a question in English after his win against the Russian world number one on his way to the Olympic quarterfinals, his candid confession was startling. 'If I could speak English that well, I'd be doing what you are,' he had retorted in jest.
19. Personal interview with Jagdish Singh, 6 April 2009.
20. There is a telling television commercial which shows village folk sitting huddled together in front of a television set operating on battery watching their local lad in action. This inverter advertisement is a pithy comment on the realities of Bhiwani.

21. *The Hindustan Times*, 10 April 2009.
22. Several pistol shooters suggested this way out to us on condition of anonymity. The only person who came on record was Samresh Jung, one of India's veteran pistol shooters and one who had won the best athlete award at the Melbourne Commonwealth Games in 2006.
23. For details, see *The Hindu*, 7 March 2009, also see *The Times of India*, 7 March 2009.
24. *The Hindu*, 7 March 2009.
25. Ibid.
26. *The Times of India*, 7 March 2009.
27. *The Telegraph*, 1 February 2009.
28. Ibid.
29. *The Hindu*, 28 July 2011.

EPILOGUE

1. Rohit Brijnath, ''The bitter half of the story', Oct 27, 2000, http://www.rediff.com/sports/2000/oct/27rohit.htm, accessed Fab 24, 2008.
2. Conversation with Jagmohan Dalmiya, President of BCCI when the sting operation occurred (Kolkata: Dec. 1, 2007).
3. Kapil Dev's name arose as of those players alleged to be involved in match-fixing, charges he denied vehemently in a cathartic interview with Karan Thapar on BBC World.
4. Bharatiya Hockey Monthly Bulletin, April 2008, http://www. bharatiya hockey.org/calendar/calbulletins.asp?year=2008&mon=apr&bkmark=Photo, accessed May 1, 2008.
5. Quoted in Ibid.
6. Ibid
7. 'Operation Chak De: Hockey's Hall of Fame', video posted on www.indiatoday.com, accessed May 2, 2008.
8. Aaj Tak press release quoted in Press Trust of India, 'Operation Chak De impact: Jothikumaran resigns' (New Delhi: April 21, 2008).
9. Ibid.
10. Ibid.
11. *The Hindu*, 'TV Channel Sued', (New Delhi: April 22, 2008).
12. Press Trust of India, 'Operation Chak De impact: Jothikumaran resigns' (New Delhi: April 21, 2008).
13. Conversation with a senior editor with CNN-IBN (New Delhi: May 1, 2008).
14. FIH Secretary General letter quoted in *The Hindu*, 'Indian Olympic Association Acts tough: Suspends IHF', (New Delhi: April 29, 2008).
15. ITGD Bureau, 'Operation Chak de impact: Furore in Lok Sabha'(New Delhi, April 22, 2008), posted on www.indiatoday.com, accessed April 30, 2008.
16. In addition, a selection committee was formed consisting of former

Olympians, Aslam Sher Khan, Ashok Kumar, Ajit Pal Singh, Zafar Iqbal and Dhanraj Pillay.

17. Sharda Ugra, 'Track Record of Shame' *India Today* June 21, 2004
18. Ayaz Memon, 'KPS Gill is not the only exception', *DNA* (Mumbai: March 12, 2008).
19. Vineeta Pandey, 'Why a political head for sports?', *The Times of India*, July 24, 2004
20. This issue repeatedly came up for discussion at the Olympic Legacies Conference at Oxford on 29–30 March 2008.
21. For most of his letters see; IOC Archives, ID Chemise 7334 CIO 3535 MBR-TATA-CORR, Correspondence de Dorabji Tata 1926–1930.
22. Vineeta Pandey, 'Why a political head for sports?', *The Times of India*, July 24, 2004
23. Ibid
24. Sharda Ugra, 'Track Record of Shame' *India Today* June 21, 2004
25. Ashis Nandy, 'The Culture of Indian Politics: A Stock-Taking', *The Journal of Asian Studies*, Vol 30, No. 1 (Nov. 1970) p. 58.
26. This for instance is the conclusion of Ashutosh Varshney in 'Is India Becoming More Democratic', *The Journal of Asian Studies*, Vol 59, No. 1, Feb 2000, pp. 3–25
27. See for instance, MN Srinivas, *Caste in Modern India.*
28. Ashis Nandy, 'The Culture of Indian Politics: A Stock-Taking', *The Journal of Asian Studies*, Vol 30, No. 1 (Nov. 1970) p. 70

POSTSCRIPT

1. John MaAaloon, *Flame Relays and the Struggle for the Olympic Movement*, Routledge, Forthcoming.
2. Personal interview at Rajghat on 17 April 2008.
3. Interview with Randhir Singh, 17 April 2008.
4. Interview with Jim Yardley, 27 April 2008.
5. Rohit Mahajan, 'Ah The Human Race', in *Outlook*, 28 April 2008.
6. Quoted in MacAloon, *Flame Relays and the Struggle for the Olympic Movement.*
7. Jim Yardley, 'China Says It Is Ready to Meet Dalai Lama Envoys', in *New York Times, 26 April 2008.*

Index

Note on the Appendix

The appendix is the most exhaustive database on India's Olympic History. It includes details of all athletes who have represented the country, their results, timings, dates of birth, events and other relevant information. In compiling the Appendix we have relied on all available Olympic databases and the records of the IOC. In doing so we have kept the format and spellings used by international Olympic databases intact. Accordingly, the database spells Khashaba Jadhav as Kha Shaba Jadhav (highlighted).

Also, Olympic databases list athletes on the basis of surnames. And if an athlete has changed surnames with marriage or otherwise he or she can be listed in multiple places. They are not repeat listings though. We have retained this practice through the appendix in case researchers wish to use it for future work. Accordingly, Shiny Wilson is listed in three different places, all of which are highlighted.

Some of the IOC databases list Norman Pritchard as an Indian athlete. We have already explained why we haven't considered Pritchard as part of our story. Here, we have listed him for reasons of consistency but once again his performances are highlighted.

For some athletes the IOC lists multiple dates of birth. We have listed both dates in cases of dispute.

Finally, for athletes with the same name, Ashok Kumar for example, the Olympic databases often list them on occasions with their first name (mistakenly assuming its the surname) and then go on to list others with the same name differently. We have kept it the same and hence Ashok Kumar's are listed in the Appendix in different places. Again, there are no repeat listings.

To round off, the Indian participants at Beijing are listed in Appendix 2 separately.

Appendix 1

Men/ Women	*Year*	*Event*	*Name*	*DoB*	*Event*	*Stage*	*Race #*	*Rnk*	*Score-Result/Opponent/ Opposition*	*Misc*	*Misc*	*Misc*	*Medal*	*Other Sport*
Men	1948	Football	Aao, Talimeran					2rd						
Women	**1984**	**Athletics**	**Abraham, Shiny K**	**8-May-1965**	**4x400m**	**final**		**7**	**3m32.49**					
Women	**1984**	**Athletics**	**Abraham, Shiny K**	**8-May-1965**	**4x400m**	**heat**		**4**	**3m33.85**					
Women	**1984**	**Athletics**	**Abraham, Shiny K**	**8-May-1965**	**800m**	**heat**		**4**	**2m04.69**					
Women	**1984**	**Athletics**	**Abraham, Shiny K**	**8-May-1965**	**800m**	**semi**		**8**	**2m05.42**					
Men	1992	Weightlifting	Adisekar, Badathala	14-Apr-1966	fly			10	97.5+125=222.5					
Men	1996	Weightlifting	Adisekar, Badathala	14-Apr-1966	54			18	230/ sn - 105	cj - 125				
Men	1996	Judo	Aga, Najib		65kg	2nd Round			lost to /HUN/ Csak, Jozsef	Ippon				
Men	1996	Judo	Aga, Najib		65kg	Repechage			lost to /RSA/ Mackin-non, Duncan	Ippon				
Men	1948	Water polo	Ahir, J.		2nd rnd				2 games					
Men	1980	Equestrian	Ahluwalia, J.	9-May-1955	3day/indiv	final		el.	Shiwalik					
Men	1980	Equestrian	Ahluwalia, J.	9-May-1955	3day/team	final		el.	Shiwalik					
Men	1956	Football	Ahmed, A.Husein	y1932				4 pl.	1 game					
Men	1992	Hockey	Ahmed, Shaqeel	2-Nov-1970				7 pl.	7 games					

Men/ Women	*Year*	*Event*	*Name*	*DoB*	*Event*	*Stage*	*Race #*	*Rnk*	*Score-Result/Opponent/ Opposition*	*Misc*	*Misc*	*Misc*	*Medal*	*Other Sport*
Men	1992	Hockey	Ajit, Lakra	9-Jan-1966				7 pl.	5 games					
Men	1964	Athletics	Akotkar, Balkrishan	1-Jul-1937	marathon	final		33	2h29m27.4					
Women	1988	Athletics	Alapurackal, Mercy Kuttan Math	28-May-1960	400m	heat		5	53.41					
Women	1988	Athletics	Alapurackal, Mercy Kuttan Math	28-May-1960	4x400m	heat		7	3m33.46					
Women	1988	Athletics	Alapurackal, Mercy Kuttan Math	28-May-1960	400m	Round 2		8	53.93					
Men	1996	Hockey	Alexander, Anil					8th	Group A 3rd (2W, 1L, 2D)					
Men	1988	Tennis	Ali Syed, Zeeshan	1-Jan-1970	singles	1/16rd			lost to/ Hlasek, J. (Sui) 4:6, 5:7, 5:7					
Men	1988	Tennis	Ali Syed, Zeeshan	1-Jan-1970	singles	1/32rd			defeated/ Caballero, V. (Par) 6:3, 6:2, 6:4					
Men	1976	Hockey	Ali, Syed	21-Aug-1956				7 pl.	6 games					
Men	1980	Hockey	Allan, Schofield	26-Jan-1957				1 pl.	1 game				Gold	
Men	1928	Hockey	Allen, Richard James	4-Jun-1902				1 pl.	5 games				Gold	
Men	1932	Hockey	Allen, Richard James	4-Jun-1902				dns						
Men	1936	Hockey	Allen, Richard James	4-Jun-1902				1 pl.	4 games				Gold	
Women	2004	Athletics	Aloysius, Bobby	22-Jun-1974	High	Qualif.	A	13	1.85		1.75 o, 1.8 o, 1.85 xo, 1.89 xxx			
Men	1948	Cycling	Amin, J.		4000m pursuit/ team	final		1rd.						

Men/ Women	*Year*	*Event*	*Name*	*DoB*	*Event*	*Stage*	*Race #*	*Rnk*	*Score-Result/Opponent/ Opposition*	*Misc*	*Misc*	*Misc*	*Medal*	*Other Sport*
Men	1988	Tennis	Amrit Raj, Anand	20-Mar-1952	doubles	1/16rd			defeated/ Yoo, Jin-Sun/ Kim, Bong-Soo (Kor) 6:3, 7:6, 6:2	wilh Amrit Raj, V.				
Men	1988	Tennis	Amrit Raj, Anand	20-Mar-1952	doubles	1/8rd			lost to/ Mecir, M./ Srejber, M.(Tch) 6:4, 4:6, 6:4, 4:6, 2:6	wilh Amrit Raj, V.				
Men	1988	Tennis	Amrit Raj, Vijay	14-Dec-1953	doubles	1/16rd			defeated/ Yoo, Jin-Sun/ Kim, Bong-Soo (Kor) 6:3, 7:6, 6:2	with Amrit Raj, A.				
Men	1988	Tennis	Amrit Raj, Vijay	14-Dec-1953	singles	1/32rd			lost to/ Leconte, H.(Fra)6:4, 4:6, 4:6, 6:3, 3:6					
Men	1988	Tennis	Amrit Raj, Vijay	14-Dec-1953	doubles	1/8rd			lost to/Mecir, M./ Srejber, M.(Tch) 6:4, 4:6, 6:4, 4:6, 2:6	with Amrit Raj, A.				
Men	1956	Gymnastics	Anant, Ram	y1932	indiv.	final		63	65.55					
Men	1964	Wrestling	Andalkar, Ganpat	15-Apr-1935	F/heavy	1rd			defeated/ McNamara, D. (Gbr) 1:3					
Men	1964	Wrestling	Andalkar, Ganpat	15-Apr-1935	GR/middle	1rd			lost to/ Baughman,R. (USA)3:1					
Men	1964	Wrestling	Andalkar, Ganpat	15-Apr-1935	F/heavy	2rd			lost to/ Stingu, S. (Rom) 4:0 (8.47)					
Men	1964	Wrestling	Andalkar, Ganpat	15-Apr-1935	F/heavy	3rd			lost to/ Kubat, B. (Tch) 4:0 (4.58)					
Mixed	2000	Equestrian	Anees, Imtiaz	25-Dec-1970	Individual 3-Day	Dressage		32	61.00		Spring Invader			
Mixed	2000	Equestrian	Anees, Imtiaz	25-Dec-1970	Individual 3-Day	Cross Country		25	0-0.00-0-165.60/ 226.60.		Spring Invader			

Men/ Women	Year	Event	Name	DoB	Event	Stage	Race #	Rnk	Score-Result/Opponent/ Opposition	Misc	Misc	Misc	Medal	Other Sport
Mixed	2000	Equestrian	Anees, Imtiaz	25-Dec-1970	Individual 3-Day	Final		23	236.60/ 61.00,165.60,10.00		Spring Invader			
Men	1992	Hockey	Anjaparavanda Bopaiah, Subbaiah	8-Aug-1970				dns						
Men	1996	Hockey	Anjararavanda, Subbaiah					8th	Group A 3rd (2W, 1L, 2D)					
Men	1984	Athletics	Annavi, Nellaswamy	12-May-1965	high			dns						
Men	1952	Football	Anthony, Berland	y1923				1rd						
Men	1952	Football	Anthony, Joseph	y1925				1rd						
Men	1960	Hockey	Antic, Joseph	13-Mar-1931				2 pl.	2 games				Silver	
Women	2004	Athletics	Antil, Seema	27-Jul-1983	Discus Throw	Qualif.	B	7	60.64		59.93	60.64 58.41		
Men	2004	Wrestling	Anuj Kumar, NA	15-Aug-1980	84kg Freestyle	Prelim.	Pool 1	2	6/ Classif.: 1+1	Tech: 1+5				
Men	1936	Wrestling	Anwar, Rashid	12-Apr-1910	F/welter	1rd			lost to/Schleimer, J. (Can) 3:0 (2.52)					
Men	1936	Wrestling	Anwar, Rashid	12-Apr-1910	F/welter	2rd			lost to/Beke,J. (Bel)3:0(7.43)					
Men	1936	Wrestling	Asanare, Hari		F/light	dns								
Men	**1988**	**Hockey**	**Ashok, Kumar**	**8-Apr-1966**				**6 pl.**	**6 games**					
Men	**1980**	**Wrestling**	**Ashok, Kumar**	**28-Oct-1959**	**F/fly**	**1rd**			**defeated/ Jang, DokRyong (PRK) 1:3**					
Men	**1980**	**Wrestling**	**Ashok, Kumar**	**28-Oct-1959**	**F/fly**	**2rd**			**lost to/ Selimov, N. (Bul) 4:0 (2.25)**					
Men	**1980**	**Wrestling**	**Ashok, Kumar**	**28-Oct-1959**	**F/fly**	**3rd**			**lost to/ Stecyk, W. (Pol) 4:0**					

Men/ Women	*Year*	*Event*	*Name*	*DoB*	*Event*	*Stage*	*Race #*	*Rnk*	*Score-Result/Opponent/ Opposition*	*Misc*	*Misc*	*Misc*	*Medal*	*Other Sport*
Men	1932	Hockey	Aslam, Sirdar Mohammad					dns						
Men	1952	Football	Azizuddin, Syed Khaja (Aziz, Syed Khaja A.)	12-Jul-1929				1rd						
Men	1992	Table Tennis	Baboor, Chetan Panduranga (Baboor Panduranga, Chetan)	22-Apr-1974	singles	Prelim.		4 pl.						
Men	1992	Table Tennis	Baboor, Chetan Panduranga (Baboor Panduranga, Chetan)	22-Apr-1974	singles	Prelim.			lost to/ Prean, C. (Gbr) 0:2 (-11, -12					
Men	1992	Table Tennis	Baboor, Chetan Panduranga (Baboor Panduranga, Chetan)	22-Apr-1974	singles	Prelim.			lost to/ Choi, Gyong Sob (PRK) 0:2 (-14, -16)					
Men	1992	Table Tennis	Baboor, Chetan Panduranga (Baboor Panduranga, Chetan)	22-Apr-1974	singles	Prelim.			lost to/ Casares, R. (Esp) 1:2 (20, -8, -2I)					
Men	1996	Table tennis	Baboor, Chetan Panduranga (Baboor Panduranga, Chetan)	22-Apr-1974	Singles	Group P		lost to	Kreanga, Kalin (GRE)/ 22-20 21-9					
Men	1996	Table tennis	Baboor, Chetan Panduranga (Baboor Panduranga, Chetan)	22-Apr-1974	Singles	Group P		lost to	Chila, Patrick (FRA)/ 21-15 16-21 21-18					
Men	1996	Table tennis	Baboor, Chetan Panduranga (Baboor Panduranga, Chetan)	22-Apr-1974	Singles	Group P		lost to	Toriola, Segun (NGR)/ 21-12 11-21 21-16					
Men	2000	Table Tennis	Baboor, Chetan Panduranga (Baboor Panduranga, Chetan)	22-Apr-1974	Doubles	1st round			lost to/Heister, Danny/ Keen, Trinko (NED)/ 21-17, 21-14	Subra-manian, Raman				

Men/ Women	Year	Event	Name	DoB	Event	Stage	Race #	Rnk	Score-Result/Opponent/ Opposition	Misc	Misc	Misc	Medal	Other Sport
Men	2000	Table Tennis	Baboor, Chetan Panduranga (Baboor Panduranga, Chetan)	22-Apr-1974	Doubles	1st round			lost to/Heister, Danny/ Keen, Trinko (NED)/ 21-17, 21-14	Subra-manian, Raman				
Men	2000	Table Tennis	Baboor, Chetan Panduranga (Baboor Panduranga, Chetan)	22-Apr-1974	Doubles	1st round			lost to/Kazeem, Nosiru/Toriola, Segun (NGR)/ 26-24, 17-21, 21-18	Subra-manian, Raman				
Men	2000	Table Tennis	Baboor, Chetan Panduranga (Baboor Panduranga, Chetan)	22-Apr-1974	Singles	1st round			lost to/Korbel, Petr (CZE)/ 13-21, 21-17, 21-16, 21-14					
Men	2000	Table Tennis	Baboor, Chetan Panduranga (Baboor Panduranga, Chetan)	22-Apr-1974	Singles	1st round			def. /Jackson, Peter (NZL)/ 25-23, 21-18, 23-21					
Men	1972	Athletics	Babu, Suresh	10-Feb-1953	high	qu			1.90					
Women	1980	Hockey	Bagli, Hutoxi	26-Jul-1961				res.						
Men	1984	Sailing	Bahl, Anil	9-Jan-1948	470			dns						
Men	1956	Swimming	Bajaj, Sri Chand	y1934	100m freestyle	heat		7	61.6					
Men	1956	Wrestling	Bakhshish Singh	y1925	F/middle	1rd			defeated/ Davies, W. (Aus) 0:3					
Men	1956	Wrestling	Bakhshish Singh	y1925	F/middle	2rd			lost to/ van Zyl, H. (SAF) 3:0					
Men	1956	Wrestling	Bakhshish Singh	y1925	F/middle	3rd			lost to/ Lindblad, B. (Swe) 3.55					
Men	1956	Hockey	Bakshi, Amit Singh	y1936				1 pl.	1 game				Gold	
Men	1956	Hockey	Bakshish Singh, Sandhu	14-Jun-1929				1 pl.	3 games				Gold	

Men/ Women	*Year*	*Event*	*Name*	*DoB*	*Event*	*Stage*	*Race #*	*Rnk*	*Score-Result/Opponent/ Opposition*	*Misc*	*Misc*	*Misc*	*Medal*	*Other Sport*
Men	2000	Athletics	Bala Krishnan, Rajeev	31-Mar-1971	4x100m	Round 1	1	7	40.23					
Men	1988	Hockey	Baladakalaiash, Subramani	24-Apr-1962				6 pl.	7 games/ 1 goal					
Men	1956	Football	Balaram, Tulsidas B. (Balaraman, Tulsidas B.)	30-Nov-1936				4 pl.	1 game					
Men	1960	Football	Balaram, Tulsidas B. (Balaraman, Tulsidas B.)	30-Nov-1936				ER	3 games, 2 goals					
Men	1980	Basketball	Baldev, Singh	3-Jan-1951				12 pl.	7 games, 30 pts.					
Men	1956	Hockey	Balkishan Singh, Grewal	10-Mar-1933				1 pl.	2 games				Gold	
Men	1992	Hockey	Ballal, Ashish Kumar	8-Oct-1970				7 pl.	7 games					
Men	1988	Hockey	Balwinder, Singh	24-Sep-1965				6 pl.	6 games/ 1 goal					
Women	2004	Archery	Banerjee, Dola	2-Jun-1980	Indiv.	Round of 64			lost to/ Lewis, Kirstin Jean (RSA)	131-141				
Women	2004	Archery	Banerjee, Dola	2-Jun-1980	Team	Ranking		5	1900					
Women	2004	Archery	Banerjee, Dola	2-Jun-1980	Team	Round of 16			def./ GBR	230-228				
Women	2004	Archery	Banerjee, Dola	2-Jun-1980	Team	Quarter			lost to/ FRA	227-228				
Men	1952	Shooting	Banerjee, Harihar (Banerjee, Hari Har)	y1922	free rifle			24	994					
Men	1952	Shooting	Banerjee, Harihar (Banerjee, Hari Har)	y1922	small bore rifle			29	394					
Men	1952	Shooting	Banerjee, Harihar (Banerjee, Hari Har)	y1922	small bore rifle/3 pos.			36	1095					

Men/ Women	*Year*	*Event*	*Name*	*DoB*	*Event*	*Stage*	*Race #*	*Rnk*	*Score-Result/Opponent/ Opposition*	*Misc*	*Misc*	*Misc*	*Medal*	*Other Sport*
Men	1956	Shooting	Banerjee, Harihar (Banerjee, Hari Har)	y1922	small bore rifle/3 pos.			35	1111					
Men	1956	Football	Banerjee, Pradip Kumar	15-Oct-1936				4 pl.	2 games					
Men	1960	Football	Banerjee, Pradip Kumar	15-Oct-1936				ER	3 games, 1 goal					
Men	1956	Football	Banerjee, Samar	y1932				4 pl.	1 game					
Men	1920	Athletics	Bannerjee, Purna C.		100m	heat		5						
Men	1920	Athletics	Bannerjee, Purna C.		400m	heat		4	53.10					
Men	2000	Hockey	Barla, Lajrus	4-Nov-1979				7th	Group B 3rd (2W, 1L, 2D)					
Men	1952	Swimming	Barman, Bijoy Kumar	1-Dec-1928	100m backstroke	heat		5	1m27.3					
Men	1952	Water polo	Barman, Bijoy Kumar	1-Dec-1928	Prelim.				1 game					
Men	1952	Water polo	Basak, Birendra Nath	1-Feb-1912	Prelim.				1 game					
Men	1948	Football	Basheer, A.S.					2rd						
Men	1972	Sailing	Basith, Ahmed Abdul	9-Jan-1942	Flying Dutchman			29	201/ (29-28-29-25-dnf-27-dnf)					
Men	1976	Hockey	Baskaran, Vasudevan	17-Aug-1950				7 pl.	4 games					
Men	1980	Hockey	Baskaran, Vasudevan	17-Aug-1950				1 pl.	6 games/ 5 goals				Gold	
Men	1960	Athletics	Bastian, Erman R.	8-Sep-1934	hammer			dns						

Men/ Women	*Year*	*Event*	*Name*	*DoB*	*Event*	*Stage*	*Race #*	*Rnk*	*Score-Result/Opponent/ Opposition*	*Misc*	*Misc*	*Misc*	*Medal*	*Other Sport*
Women	1996	Athletics	Beenamol, K. Mathews (K.M. Beena Mol) (Mathew, Beenamol K.)	15-Aug-1975	4x400m	Round 1	1	6	3m35.91					
Women	2000	Athletics	Beenamol, K. Mathews (K.M. Beena Mol) (Mathew, Beenamol K.)	15-Aug-1975	400m	Round 1	7	1	51.51					
Women	2000	Athletics	Beenamol, K. Mathews (K.M. Beena Mol) (Mathew, Beenamol K.)	15-Aug-1975	400m	Round 2	3	4	51.81					
Women	2000	Athletics	Beenamol, K. Mathews (K.M. Beena Mol) (Mathew, Beenamol K.)	15-Aug-1975	400m	Semi	2	8	52.04					
Women	2000	Athletics	Beenamol, K. Mathews (K.M. Beena Mol) (Mathew, Beenamol K.)	15-Aug-1975	4x400m	Round 1	2	5	03m31.46					
Women	2004	Athletics	Beenamol, K. Mathews (K.M. Beena Mol) (Mathew, Beenamol K)	15-Aug-1975	4 x 400m	Final		7	3m28.48/ 27		51.52 (4) # 1:44.43 (6) #	Runner # 2		

Men/ Women	*Year*	*Event*	*Name*	*DoB*	*Event*	*Stage*	*Race #*	*Rnk*	*Score-Result/Opponent/ Opposition*	*Misc*	*Misc*	*Misc*	*Medal*	*Other Sport*
Women	2004	Athletics	Beenamol, K. Mathews (K.M. Beena Mol) (Mathew, Beenamol K.)	15-Aug-1975	4 x 400m	Round 1	Heat 2	3	3m26.92/ Q	NR	52.67 (5) # 1:44.53 (2) #	Runner # 2		
Men	1964	Boxing	Bahadur Mall, Padam		light	dns								
Women	2004	Shooting	Bhagwat, Anjali	12-May-1969	Air Rifle	Qualifica-tion		20	393					
Women	2004	Shooting	Bhagwat, Anjali	12-May-1969	50m Rifle 3 Pos.	Qualifica-tion		13	575					
Men	1936	Athletics	Bhalla, Gyan Prakash Bhalla	22-Jul-1910	400m	heat		5	52.40					
Men	1936	Athletics	Bhalla, Gyan Prakash Bhalla	22-Jul-1910	800m	heat		8						
Men	1984	Sailing	Bhandari, Dhruv (Bhandari, Dhruv)	28-Dec-1959	470			17	129 /(15-20-12-18-11-dnf-17)					
Women	1980	Hockey	Bhandari, Gangotri	13-Aug-1956				4 pl.	5 games					
Men	1948	Wrestling	Bhargava, A.		F/welter	1rd			lost to/ Dogu, Y. (Tur) fall 2.58					
Men	1948	Wrestling	Bhargava, A.		F/welter	2rd			defeated/ Qjeda, E. (Mex)					
Men	1948	Wrestling	Bhargava, A.		F/welter	3rd			lost to/ Garrard, R. (Aus) fall 2.20					
Men	1952	Swimming	Bharucha, A.		200m breast-stroke	dns								

Men/ Women	*Year*	*Event*	*Name*	*DoB*	*Event*	*Stage*	*Race #*	*Rnk*	*Score-Result/Opponent/ Opposition*	*Misc*	*Misc*	*Misc*	*Medal*	*Other Sport*
Women	1980	Hockey	Bhatia, Balwinder Kaur	19-Dec-1958				4 pl.	2 games					
Men	1960	Athletics	Bhatia, Ranjit	27-May-1936	marathon	final		60	2h57m6.2					
Men	1960	Athletics	Bhatia, Ranjit	27-May-1936	5000m	heat		11	15m06.6					
Men	1948	Boxing	Bhatta, Robin.		fly	1/8 round			lost to/ Sodano, F. (USA) (ko.1rd.-only USA rep.)					
Men	1992	Badminton	Bhattacharya, Deepankar	1-Feb-1972	double	1rd			lost to/ Sidek, J./Sidek, R. (Mas) 6:15, 3:15	with Kumar.V.				
Men	1992	Badminton	Bhattacharya, Deepankar	1-Feb-1972	single	1rd			defeated/ Ivanov, I. (Bul) 15:4, 15:1					
Men	1992	Badminton	Bhattacharya, Deepankar	1-Feb-1972	single	2rd			defeated/ Fuchs, H. (Aut) 8:15, 15:11, 15:11					
Men	1992	Badminton	Bhattacharya, Deepankar	1-Feb-1972	single	3rd			lost to/ Zhao, Jianhua (Chn) 4:15, 12:15					
Men	1996	Badminton	Bhattacharya, Deepankar		Singles	2nd Round			lost to Heryanto Arbi (INDONESIA)/ 15-5 15-4					
Men	1976	Shooting	Bhimsingh, Maharao	14-Sep-1909	skeet			67	161					
Men	1956	Hockey	Bhola, Raghbir Singh	18-Aug-1927				1 pl.	4 games				Gold	
Men	1960	Hockey	Bhola, Raghbir Singh	18-Aug-1927				2 pl.	6 games/ 6 goals				Silver	
Men	1964	Gymnastics	Bhosle, Bandu	10-Oct-1945	indiv.	final		122	87.75					

Men/ Women	*Year*	*Event*	*Name*	*DoB*	*Event*	*Stage*	*Race #*	*Rnk*	*Score-Result/Opponent/ Opposition*	*Misc*	*Misc*	*Misc*	*Medal*	*Other Sport*
Men	1964	Gymnastics	Bhosle, Bandu	10-Oct-1945	team	final		18	428.35					
Men	1996	Tennis	Bhupathi, Mahesh	7-Jun-1974	Doubles	1st Round		def.	Pan, Bing/ Xia, Jia-Ping (CHN)/ 4-6 6-4 6-4	Paes, Leander				
Men	1996	Tennis	Bhupathi, Mahesh	7-Jun-1974	Doubles	2nd Round		lost to	Woodbridge, Todd/ Woodforde, Mark (AUS)/ 6-4 2-6 2-6	Paes, Leander				
Men	2000	Tennis	Bhupathi, Mahesh	7-Jun-1974	doubles	1st round		def.	Pavel, Andrei/ Trifu, Gabriel (ROM)/ 6-3, 6-4	Paes, Leander				
Men	2000	Tennis	Bhupathi, Mahesh	7-Jun-1974	doubles	1st round		def.	Pavel, Andrei/ Trifu, Gabriel (ROM)/ 6-3, 6-4	Paes, Leander				
Men	2000	Tennis	Bhupathi, Mahesh	7-Jun-1974	doubles	2nd round		lost to	Woodbridge, Todd/ Woodforde, Mark (AUS)/ 6-3, 7-6 (1)	Paes, Leander				
Men	2004	Tennis	Bhupathi, Mahesh	7-Jun-1974	doubles	Quarter		def.	Black, Wayne/Ullyett, Kevin/ ZIM	(2-0) : (6-4, 6-4)	Paes, Leander			
Men	2004	Tennis	Bhupathi, Mahesh	7-Jun-1974	doubles	Round 2		def.	Allegro, Yves/Federer, Roger/ SUI	(2-0) : (6-2, 7-6(9-7))	Paes, Leander			
Men	2004	Tennis	Bhupathi, Mahesh	7-Jun-1974	doubles	Round 1		def.	Fish, Mardy/Roddick, Andy/ USA	(2-0) : (7-6(7-5), 6-3)	Paes, Leander			
Men	2004	Tennis	Bhupathi, Mahesh	7-Jun-1974	doubles	Bronze		lost to	Ancic, Mario/Ljubicic, Ivan/ CRO	(2-1) : (7-6(7-5), 4-6, 16-14)	Paes, Leander			
Men	2004	Tennis	Bhupathi, Mahesh	7-Jun-1974	doubles	Semi		lost to	Kiefer, Nicolas/ Schuettler, Rainer/ GER	(2-0) : (6-2, 6-3)	Paes, Leander			

Men/ Women	Year	Event	Name	DoB	Event	Stage	Race #	Rnk	Score-Result/Opponent/ Opposition	Misc	Misc	Misc	Medal	Other Sport
Men	1972	Hockey	Billimogaputtaswamy, Govinda (Govinda, Bilimogga)	4-Sep-1951				3 pl.	8 games/ 3 goals				Bronze	
Men	1976	Hockey	Billimogaputtaswamy, Govinda (Govinda, Bilimogga)	4-Sep-1951				7 pl.	1 game					
Men	1988	Judo	Billimoria, Cawas	25-Oct-1962	halfheavy	dns			dns					
Men	1992	Judo	Billimoria, Cawas	25-Oct-1962	heavy	ER			lost to/ Muller, I. (Lux) 0.56					
Men	1964	Cycling	Billing, Amar Singh	10-Jan-1944	4000m pursuit/ team	final		1rd.	dsq					
Men	1964	Cycling	Billing, Amar Singh	10-Jan-1944	road/team	final		ret.						
Men	2000	Shooting	Binder, Aranka	19-Jun-1966	10m Air Rifle	Qual.		12	590					
Men	2004	Shooting	Binder, Aranka	28-Sep-1982	Air Rifle	Qualifica-tion		3	597/Q					
Men	2004	Shooting	Binder, Aranka	28-Sep-1982	Air Rifle	Final		7	97.6	Total= 694.6				
Men	2004	Athletics	Binu, K. Mathews	20-Dec-1980	400m	Round 1	Heat 5	3	45.48	NR	0.225			
Men	2004	Athletics	Binu, K. Mathews	20-Dec-1980	400m	Semi	2	6	45.97		0.254			
Men	1988	Boxing	Birajdar, Shahuraj	19-Jul-1963	bantam	1/16 round			defeated/ Akomatsri, A. (Tog)5:0					
Men	1988	Boxing	Birajdar, Shahuraj	19-Jul-1963	bantam	1/8 round			lost to/ McKinney, K. (USA) w.o.					

Men/ Women	Year	Event	Name	DoB	Event	Stage	Race #	Rnk	Score-Result/Opponent/ Opposition	Misc	Misc	Misc	Medal	Other Sport
Men	1972	Wrestling	Birajdarhar, Sh Chander		F/super-heavy	dns								
Men	1964	Wrestling	Bishambhar (Singh, Bishamber)	10-Oct-1940	F/bantam	1rd			defeated/ Leibovich, R. (Arg) 0:4 (2.16)					
Men	1964	Wrestling	Bishambhar (Singh, Bishamber)	10-Oct-1940	GR/ bantam	1rd			defeated/ Lopez Ruiz, M. (Mex) 1:3					
Men	1964	Wrestling	Bishambhar (Singh, Bishamber)	10-Oct-1940	F/ bantam	2rd			defeated/ Bazar, S. (Mgl) 1:3					
Men	1964	Wrestling	Bishambhar (Singh, Bishamber)	10-Oct-1940	GR/ bantam	2rd			lost to/ Trostiansky, V. (URS) 3:1					
Men	1964	Wrestling	Bishambhar (Singh, Bishamber)	10-Oct-1940	F/ bantam	3rd			defeated/ Lopez Ruiz, M. (Mex) 1:3					
Men	1964	Wrestling	Bishambhar (Singh, Bishamber)	10-Oct-1940	GR/ bantam	3rd			lost to/ Basergil, U. (Tur) 3:1					
Men	1964	Wrestling	Bishambhar (Singh, Bishamber)	10-Oct-1940	F/ bantam	4rd			lost to/ Auble, D. (USA) 3:1					
Men	1964	Wrestling	Bishambhar (Singh, Bishamber)	10-Oct-1940	F/ bantam	5rd			lost to/ Akbas, H. (Tur) 3:1					
Men	1964	Wrestling	Bishambhar (Singh, Bishamber)	10-Oct-1940	F/ bantam			6 place						
Men	1968	Wrestling	Bishambhar (Singh, Bishamber)	10-Oct-1940	F/ bantam	1rd			bye					
Men	1968	Wrestling	Bishambhar (Singh, Bishamber)	10-Oct-1940	F/ bantam	2rd			defeated/ Singerman, H. (Can) 0.5:3.5					
Men	1968	Wrestling	Bishambhar (Singh, Bishamber)	10-Oct-1940	F/ bantam	3rd			defeated/ Sevnic, H. (Tur) 1:3					
Men	1968	Wrestling	Bishambhar (Singh, Bishamber)	10-Oct-1940	F/ bantam	4rd			lost to/ Behm, D. (DSA) 3.5:0.5					

Men/ Women	*Year*	*Event*	*Name*	*DoB*	*Event*	*Stage*	*Race #*	*Rnk*	*Score-Result/Opponent/ Opposition*	*Misc*	*Misc*	*Misc*	*Medal*	*Other Sport*
Men	1968	Wrestling	Bishambhar (Singh, Bishamber)	10-Oct-1940	F/ bantam	5rd			lost to/ Uetake, Y. (Jpn) 3.5:0.5					
Men	2000	Athletics	Bishnoi, Jagdish	20-May-1972	Javelin	qu	1	15	70.86					
Women	1992	Badminton	Bisht, Madhumita	5-Oct-1964	single	1rd			defeated/ Nielsen, E. (Isl) 11:4, 11:2					
Women	1992	Badminton	Bisht, Madhumita	5-Oct-1964	single	2rd			lost to/ Muggeridge, J. (Gbr) 7:11, 8:11					
Men	1992	Boxing	Bisth, Narendar Singh	1-Apr-1966	feather	1/16 round			lost to/ Gerena Allende, C. (Pur) 11:20					
Women	2000	Athletics	Biswas, Soma	16-May-1978	Heptathlon	Final		25	5481/ 200: 915, 800: 812	100H: 947, SP: 604	JV: 591, LJ: 837, HJ: 842			
Women	2004	Athletics	Biswas, Soma	16-May-1978	Heptathlon			24	5965/ 100H 13.86/ 998 (), LJ 5.92/ 825 (23), SP 12.01/ 662 (27), 200m 24.5/ 933 (9), HJ 1.7/ 855 (22)	JT 44.84/ 760 (13), 800m 2m12.27/ 932 (3)				
Women	2004	Athletics	Bobby George, Anju	19-Apr-1977	Long Jump	Qualif.	A	5	6.69/Q		6.69			
Women	2004	Athletics	Bobby George, Anju	19-Apr-1977	Long Jump	Final		6	6.83	NR	6.83	6.75 x 6.68 6.61 x		
Men	1932	Hockey	Bokhari, S. Lal Shah					1 pl.	2 games				Gold	
Men	1960	Athletics	Bondada, Sathynarayana (Bondada, Venkata S.)	9-May-1935	long	qu			7.08					

Men/ Women	Year	Event	Name	DoB	Event	Stage	Race #	Rnk	Score-Result/Opponent/ Opposition	Misc	Misc	Misc	– Medal	Other Sport
Men	1964	Athletics	Bondada, Sathynarayana (Bondada, Venkata S.)	9-May-1935	long	qu			6.76					
Men	1984	Athletics	Borromeo, Charles	1-Dec-1958	800m	heat		5	1m51.52					
Men	1948	Boxing	Bose, Benoy Kumar	25-Nov-1929	feather	1/16 round			lost to/ Nunez, F. (Arg)					
Men	1952	Boxing	Bose, Benoy Kumar	25-Nov-1929	feather	1/16 round			lost to/ Brown, E. (USA) 0:3					
Men	1948	Wrestling	Bose, N.		F/bantam	1rd			lost to/ Leeman, G. (USA) fall 7.35					
Men	1948	Wrestling	Bose, N.		F/bantam	2rd			lost to/ Johnsson, E. (Fin)					
Men	1952	Cycling	Bose, Pradip Kumar		road/ind	final		ret.						
Men	1932	Hockey	Brewin, Frank Gerald	21-Oct-1909				dns						
Men	1928	Athletics	Burns, R.		100m	heat		6						
Men	1928	Athletics	Burns, R.		200m	heat		4						
Men	1928	Athletics	Burns, R.		4x400m	heat								
Men	1988	Judo	Byala, Sandeep	23-Nov-1967	halflight	dns			dns					
Men	1992	Judo	Byala, Sandeep	23-Nov-1967	halflight	ER			defeated/ Al Soraihi, M. (Yem) 0.35					
Men	1992	Judo	Byala, Sandeep	23-Nov-1967	halflight	ER			lost to/ Cantin, J. (Can) 5.00					
Men	1952	Cycling	Bysack, Netai Chand	21-Mar-1921	4000m pursuit/ team	final		1rd.						

Men/ Women	Year	Event	Name	DoB	Event	Stage	Race #	Rnk	Score-Result/Opponent/ Opposition	Misc	Misc	Misc	Medal	Other Sport
Men	1952	Cycling	Bysack, Netai Chand	21-Mar-1921	sprint	final result		1rd.						
Men	1992	Sailing	Cama, Cyprus	6-Nov-1971	470			23	147/ (failed start-18-13-13-21-22-24)					
Men	1932	Athletics	Carr, Richard John		4x100m	heat		5						AT/ HO
Men	1932	Hockey	Carr, Richard John					1 pl.	2 games				Gold	HO/ AT
Men	1984	Hockey	Carvaho, Joaquim Martin	16-Aug-1959				5 pl.	7 games/ 2 goals					
Men	1952	Cycling	Chakravarty, Suprovat	28-Nov-1931	4000m pursuit/ team	final		1rd.						
Men	1952	Cycling	Chakravarty, Suprovat	28-Nov-1931	road/ind	final		ret.						
Men	1952	Cycling	Chakravarty, Suprovat	28-Nov-1931	Time Trial	final		27	1m26.0					
Men	1928	Hockey	Chand Bais, Dhyan	28-Aug-1905				1 pl.	5 games				Gold	
Men	1932	Hockey	Chand Bais, Dhyan	28-Aug-1905				1 pl.	2 games				Gold	
Men	1936	Hockey	Chand Bais, Dhyan	28-Aug-1905				1 pl.	5 games				Gold	
Men	1980	Shooting	Chand, Gian		small bore rifle			38	590					
Men	1972	Wrestling	Chandgi, Ram	15-Mar-1938	F/light-heavy	1rd			lost to/ Saunders, G. (Can) 4:0 (1.59)					
Men	1972	Wrestling	Chandgi, Ram	15-Mar-1938	F/light-heavy	2rd			lost to/ Strakhov, G. (URS) 4:0 (2.45)					

Men/ Women	*Year*	*Event*	*Name*	*DoB*	*Event*	*Stage*	*Race #*	*Rnk*	*Score-Result/Opponent/ Opposition*	*Misc*	*Misc*	*Misc*	*Medal*	*Other Sport*
Men	1952	Water polo	Chandnani, Ran Shor	y1930	Prelim.				1 game					
Men	1960	Football	Chandrasekhar, Menon	10-Jul-1936				ER	3 games					
Men	1988	Weightlifting	Chandrasekhara, Raghavan (Chanderasekaran, Raghavan)	9-Jun-1970	fly			19	92.5+115=207.5					
Men	1996	Weightlifting	Chandrasekhara, Raghavan (Chanderasekaran, Raghavan)	9-Jun-1970	59			11	252.5/ sn - 112.5	cj - 140				
Men	1972	Hockey	Charles, Cornelius	27-Oct-1945				3 pl.	2 games				Bronze	
Men	1948	Water polo	Chaterjee, S.		2nd rnd				3 games					
Men	1972	Shooting	Chatterjee, Prithipal K.	19-Oct-1943	small bore rifle			95	572					
Men	1948	Water polo	Chatterjee, S.N.		2nd rnd				1 game					
Men	1976	Hockey	Chattri, Birbahadur	7-Sep-1955				7 pl.	5 games					
Men	1980	Hockey	Chattri, Birbahadur	7-Sep-1955				1 pl.	6 games				Gold	
Women	1980	Hockey	Chaudhry, Sudha	1-Jul-1961				4 pl.	5 games					
Men	1920	Athletics	Chaugle, Phadeppa F.		marathon	final		19	2h50m45.4					
Men	1920	Athletics	Chaugle, Phadeppa F.		10000m	heat		dnf						
Men	1980	Athletics	Chauhan, Bahadur Singh	8-Feb-1946	Shot Put	qu			17.5					

Men/ Women	*Year*	*Event*	*Name*	*DoB*	*Event*	*Stage*	*Race #*	*Rnk*	*Score-Result/Opponent/ Opposition*	*Misc*	*Misc*	*Misc*	*Medal*	*Other Sport*
Men	2000	Hockey	Chauhan, Devesh (Chauhan, Devesh Singh)	11-Dec-1981				7th	Group B 3rd(2W,1L,2D)					
Men	2004	Hockey	Chauhan, Devesh (Chauhan, Devesh Singh)	11-Dec-1981		Prelim.	B	7	Prelim. 4th (W1, L3, D1)/ Classification 7-8 def. KOR 5 - 2			GK		
Men	1928	Athletics	Chavan, D.B.		10000m	heat		ret.						
Men	2004	Wrestling	Cheema, Palwinder Singh	11-Nov-1982	120kg Freestyle	Prelim.	Pool 1	1	4/ Classif.: 0+1	Tech: 0+4				
Men	1960	Shooting	Cheema, Paul Singh	26-Sep-1920	rapid fire pistol			57	434					
Men	1996	Archery	Chhangte, Lalremsanga		Indiv.	Prelim.		32	650					
Men	1996	Archery	Chhangte, Lalremsanga		Indiv.	elim1/16		lost to	FRANGILLI, Michele/ ITA					
Men	1996	Archery	Chhangte, Lalremsanga		Team	Prelim.		14	650/ 1928		Elim.			
Men	1980	Basketball	Chopra, Ajmer Singh	12-Dec-1953				12 pl.	7 games, 149 pts.					
Men	1972	Shooting	Choudhary, S.K. Roy (Choudhary, Chaudhri)	21-Jan-1946	small bore rifle			99	567					
Men	1980	Shooting	Choudhary, S.K. Roy (Choudhary, Chaudhri)	21-Jan-1946	small bore rifle			44	588					
Men	1952	Shooting	Chowdhury, Souren	25-Jul-1918	small bore rifle			39	391					
Men	1964	Hockey	Christy, Rajendra Absolem	1-Jul-1938				dns						

Men/ Women	*Year*	*Event*	*Name*	*DoB*	*Event*	*Stage*	*Race #*	*Rnk*	*Score-Result/Opponent/ Opposition*	*Misc*	*Misc*	*Misc*	*Medal*	*Other Sport*
Men	1968	Hockey	Christy, Rajendra Absolem	1-Jul-1938				3 pl.	2 games				Bronze	
Men	1948	Swimming	Chundra, Bimal		1500m freestyle	heat		6	22m52.9					
Men	1948	Swimming	Chundra, Bimal		400m freestyle	heat		7	5m38.6					
Men	1948	Hockey	Claudius, Leslie Walter	27-Mar-1927				1 pl.	1 game				Gold	
Men	1952	Hockey	Claudius, Leslie Walter	27-Mar-1927				1 pl.	2 games				Gold	
Men	1956	Hockey	Claudius, Leslie Walter	27-Mar-1927				1 pl.	5 games				Gold	
Men	1960	Hockey	Claudius, Leslie Walter	27-Mar-1927				2 pl.	6 games				Silver	
Men	1972	Sailing	Contractor, Sohrab Janshed	27-Jul-1938	Flying Dutchman			29	201/ (29-28-29-25-dnf-27-dnf)					
Men	1964	Athletics	Coutinho, Anthony Francis	25-Aug-1940	4x100m	heat		5	40.6					
Men	1964	Athletics	Coutinho, Anthony Francis	25-Aug-1940	4x100m	semi		7	40.5					
Men	1948	Boxing	Cranston, R.		welter	1/16 round			lost to/ Diaz Cadabeda, A. (Esp)					
Men	2000	Hockey	Dad, Sameer	25-Nov-1978				7th	Group B 3rd(2W,1L,2D)		2			
Men	1992	Wrestling	Dahiya, Dharanvir Singh	12-Jul-1969	F/feather	1rd			lost to/ Moustopoiilos, G. (Gre) 1:3					
Men	1992	Wrestling	Dahiya, Dharanvir Singh	12-Jul-1969	F/feather	2rd			lost to/ Mueller, M. (Sui) 1:3					

Men/ Women	Year	Event	Name	DoB	Event	Stage	Race #	Rnk	Score-Result/Opponent/ Opposition	Misc	Misc	Misc	Medal	Other Sport
Men	1984	Wrestling	Dahiya, Rohtas Singh	2-Jul-1960	F/bantam	1rd			defeated/ Nkondog, S. (Cmr) 4:0 (1.03)					
Men	1984	Wrestling	Dahiya, Rohtas Singh	2-Jul-1960	F/bantam	2rd			defeated/ Leslie, S. (Pan) 4:0 (2.23)					
Men	1984	Wrestling	Dahiya, Rohtas Singh	2-Jul-1960	F/bantam	3rd			bye.					
Men	1984	Wrestling	Dahiya, Rohtas Singh	2-Jul-1960	F/bantam	4rd			lost to/ Tomiyania, H. (Jpn) 0:4 (2.19)					
Men	1984	Wrestling	Dahiya, Rohtas Singh	2-Jul-1960	F/bantam	5/6 place			defeated/ Sorov, Z. (Yug) 3:1					
Men	1984	Wrestling	Dahiya, Rohtas Singh	2-Jul-1960	F/bantam	group final-2rd			lost to/ Caceres, O. (Pur) 0.5:3.5					
Men	1984	Wrestling	Dahiya, Rohtas Singh	2-Jul-1960	F/bantam			5 place						
Men	1952	Hockey	Daluz, Meldric St-Clair	1-Apr-1921				1 pl.	1 game				Gold	
Men	1992	Archery	Damor, Dhulchand	8-Aug-1964	team	final		13		final				
Men	1992	Archery	Damor, Dhulchand	8-Aug-1964	ind	pr.		66	1212					
Men	1992	Archery	Damor, Dhulchand	8-Aug-1964	team	pr.		15	3761					
Men	1948	Weightlifting	Dandamudi, R.G. (Rajagopal, Dandumudi)	y1916	heavy			16	92.5+90+122.5=305					
Men	1956	Weightlifting	Dandamudi, R.G. (Rajagopal, Dandumudi)	y1916	heavy			9	122.5+105+132.5= 360					
Men	1948	Weightlifting	Daniel, Pon Mony	12-Aug-1921	feather			16	85+85+110=280					
Men	1952	Weightlifting	Daniel, Pon Mony	12-Aug-1921	feather			12	95+90+115=300					

Men/ Women	Year	Event	Name	DoB	Event	Stage	Race #	Rnk	Score-Result/Opponent/ Opposition	Misc	Misc	Misc	Medal	Other Sport
Men	1936	Hockey	Dara, Iqtidar Ali Shah	1-Apr-1915				1 pl.	2 games				Gold	
Men	1964	Weightlifting	Das, A.K.	6-Sep-1935	bantam			dns						
Men	1948	Water polo	Das, D.		2nd rnd				3 games					
Men	1960	Weightlifting	Das, Lazmi Kanta	1-Nov-1939	feather			12	90+95+130=315					
Men	1964	Weightlifting	Das, Lazmi Kanta	1-Nov-1939	feather			13	100+100+132.5= 332.5					
Women	2004	Table tennis	Das, Mouma	24-Feb-1984	singles	Round 1		lost to	Komwong, Nanthana (THA)/ (4-0) 11-6, 11-7, 11-3, 12-10			51 seed		
Men	1952	Wrestling	Das, Niranjan	y1931	F/fly	1rd			lost to/ Mollaghassemi, M. (Irn) 4:0 (6.32)					
Men	1952	Wrestling	Das, Niranjan	y1931	F/fly	2rd			lost to/ Weber, H. (Ger) 4:0 (3.15)					
Men	1948	Football	Das, Robi					2rd						
Men	1980	Boxing	Dass, Amala		fly	1/16 round			lost to/ Yo, Ryon Sik (PRK) 0:5					
Men	1948	Water polo	Dass, J.		2nd rnd				1 game					
Men	1920	Athletics	Datar, Sadashir V.		marathon	final		dnf						
Men	1948	Hockey	Datt, Keshava (Datt, Keshav C.)	29-Dec-1925				1 pl.	5 games				Gold	
Men	1952	Hockey	Datt, Keshava (Datt, Keshav C.)	29-Dec-1925				1 pl.	3 games				Gold	
Women	1960	Athletics	Davenport, Elizabeth	1-Oct-1938	javelin			dns						
Men	2000	Athletics	David Thottan, Lijo	1-Jun-1974	4x400m	Round 1	2	4	03m08.38					
Men	1956	Wrestling	Daware, Baban Dharamaji	y1931	F/fly	1rd			lost to/ Asai, J. (Jpn) 2.00					

Men/ Women	*Year*	*Event*	*Name*	*DoB*	*Event*	*Stage*	*Race #*	*Rnk*	*Score-Result/Opponent/ Opposition*	*Misc*	*Misc*	*Misc*	*Medal*	*Other Sport*
Men	1956	Wrestling	Daware, Baban Dharamaji	y1931	F/fly	2rd			defeated/ Lee, J.K. (Kor) 0:3					
Men	1956	Wrestling	Daware, Baban Dharamaji	y1931	F/fly	3rd			lost to/ Tsalka-lamanidze, N. (URS) 8.50					
Men	1948	Hockey	de Souza, Walter					1 pl.	1 game				Gold	
Men	1996	Boxing	Debendra, Thapa		48	elim1/16		lost to	MAKEPULA, Masi-bulele/ RSA		14			
Women	2004	Shooting	Deshpande, Deepali	3-Aug-1969	50m Rifle 3 Pos.	Qualifica-tion		19	572					
Men	1952	Hockey	Desmuthu, Chinadorai (Deshmuthu, Chinadorai)	26-Oct-1932				1 pl.	1 game				Gold	
Men	1960	Hockey	Desmuthu, Chinadorai (Deshmuthu, Chinadorai)	26-Oct-1932				res.						
Men	1960	Football	Devdas, Mundiyath	12-Mar-1935				res.						
Men	1956	Wrestling	Devi Singh	y1926	F/welter	1rd			lost to/ Sorouri, N. (Irn) 9.29					
Men	1956	Wrestling	Devi Singh	y1926	F/welter	2rd			lost to/ Ikeda, M. (Jpn) 9.50					
Women	2000	Judo	Devi, Lourembam Brojeshori	1-Jan-1981	48-52kg	Round 5	table A Match 2	def.	Jaha, Arijana (BSH)/ Ippon 04m08					
Women	2000	Judo	Devi, Lourembam Brojeshori	1-Jan-1981	48-52kg	Round 4	table A Match 1	def.	Kaiser, Ulrike (LIE)/ Hansokumake 01m30					

Men/ Women	*Year*	*Event*	*Name*	*DoB*	*Event*	*Stage*	*Race #*	*Rnk*	*Score-Result/Opponent/ Opposition*	*Misc*	*Misc*	*Misc*	*Medal*	*Other Sport*
Women	2000	Judo	Devi, Lourembam Brojeshori	1-Jan-1981	48-52kg	Round 3	table A Match 1	lost to	Liu, Yuxiang (CHN)/ Ippon 01m30					
Women	2000	Judo	Devi, Lourembam Brojeshori	1-Jan-1981	48-52kg	Round 3	table A Repe-chage 1	lost to	Dinea, Ioana Maria (ROM)/ Ippon 12m19					
Men	1964	Shooting	Devi, Singh	10-Aug-1932	clay pigeon			49	168					
Women	2000	Athletics	Dey, Saraswati	23-Nov-1979	4x100m	Round 1	3	6	45.2					
Men	1992	Judo	Dhanger, Rajinder Kumar	4-Oct-1961	middle	ER			lost to/ Okada, H. (Jpn) 0.22					
Men	1952	Athletics	Dhanoa, Sohan Singh	15-Feb-1930	800m	heat		2	1m52.0					
Men	1952	Athletics	Dhanoa, Sohan Singh	15-Feb-1930	800m	semi		6	1m54.9					
Men	1992	Hockey	Dhanraj Pillay, Pillay	16-Jul-1968				7 pl.	6 games					
Men	1932	Athletics	Dhawan, Mehar Chand		triple	final		14	13.66					
Men	1932	Athletics	Dhawan, Mehar Chand		4x100m	heat		5						
Women	1992	Shooting	Dhillan, Abha	28-Dec-1953	air pistol	prelim.		45	366					
Men	1992	Hockey	Didar, Singh	2-Apr-1964				7 pl.	5 games					
Men	1980	Basketball	Diniar, Parvez Irani	7-Mar-1954				12 pl.	7 games, 24 pts.					
Men	1976	Hockey	Diwan, Ashok	9-Aug-1954				7 pl.	3 games					
Men	1996	Archery	Dorje, Skalzang		Indiv.	Prelim.		55	634					
Men	1996	Archery	Dorje, Skalzang		Indiv.	elim1/32		lost to	BISIANI, Matteo/ ITA					
Men	1996	Archery	Dorje, Skalzang		Team	Prelim.		14	634/ 1928		Elim.			

Men/ Women	*Year*	*Event*	*Name*	*DoB*	*Event*	*Stage*	*Race #*	*Rnk*	*Score-Result/Opponent/ Opposition*	*Misc*	*Misc*	*Misc*	*Medal*	*Other Sport*
Men	1948	Hockey	Dosanjh, Balbir Singh	19-Oct-1924				1 pl.	1 game				Gold	
Men	1952	Hockey	Dosanjh, Balbir Singh	19-Oct-1924				1 pl.	3 games				Gold	
Men	1956	Hockey	Dosanjh, Balbir Singh	19-Oct-1924				1 pl.	3 games				Gold	
Women	1980	Hockey	D'Silva, Selma	24-Jul-1960				4 pl.	5 games					
Men	2004	Hockey	D'Souza, Adrian	24-Mar-1984		Prelim.	B	7	Prelim. 4th (W1, L3, D1)/ Classification 7-8 def. KOR 5 - 2			GK		
Men	1992	Hockey	D'Souza, Darryl Aloysious	21-Jun-1966				7 pl.	6 games					
Women	1952	Athletics	D'Souza, Mary Emily	18-Jul-1931	100m	heat		5	13.1					
Women	1952	Athletics	D'Souza, Mary Emily	18-Jul-1931	200m	heat		7	26.3					
Men	1956	Football	D'Souza, Neville Stephen J.	y1932				4 pl.	3 games					
Women	1960	Athletics	D'Souza, Stephi	26-Dec-1936	200m			dns						
Women	1960	Athletics	D'Souza, Stephi	26-Dec-1936	800m			dns						
Women	1964	Athletics	D'Souza, Stephi	26-Dec-1936	400m	heat		6	58.00					
Men	2000	Athletics	Durai, C Thirugnana	1-May-1974	4x100m	Round 1	1	7	40.23					
Men	2004	Wrestling	Dutt, Yogeshwar	2-Nov-1982	55kg Freestyle	Prelim.	Pool 4	2	5/ Classif.: 1+1	Tech: 3+2				
Women	1984	Shooting	Dutta, Soma	25-Dec-1967	air rifle			22	376					

Men/ Women	*Year*	*Event*	*Name*	*DoB*	*Event*	*Stage*	*Race #*	*Rnk*	*Score-Result/Opponent/ Opposition*	*Misc*	*Misc*	*Misc*	*Medal*	*Other Sport*
Women	1984	Shooting	Dutta, Soma	25-Dec-1967	small bore rifle/3 pos.			17	562					
Women	1988	Shooting	Dutta, Soma	25-Dec-1967	air rifle			30	385					
Women	1988	Shooting	Dutta, Soma	25-Dec-1967	small bore rifle/3 pos.			23	575					
Women	1992	Shooting	Dutta, Soma	25-Dec-1967	air rifle	prelim.		35	383					
Women	1992	Shooting	Dutta, Soma	25-Dec-1967	small bore rifle/3 pos.	prelim.		22	572					
Men	1996	Hockey	Edwards, Alloysuis					8th Ov.	Group A 3rd (2W, 1L, 2D)					
Men	1980	Weightlifting	Ekambaram, Karunagaran	6-Jun-1954	fly			el.	90+0					
Men	1936	Hockey	Emmett, Lionel C.	8-Jan-1913				1 pl.	1 game				Gold	
Men	1948	Hockey	Fernandes, Lawrie					1 pl.	4 games				Gold	
Women	1980	Hockey	Fernandes, Lorraine	24-Dec-1954				4 pl.	5 games/ 1 goal					
Men	1936	Hockey	Fernandes, Peter Paul	15-Sep-1916				1 pl.	2 games				Gold	
Men	1980	Hockey	Fernandis, Mervyn	12-Apr-1959				1 pl.	6 games/ 2 goals				Gold	
Men	1984	Hockey	Fernandis, Mervyn	12-Apr-1959				5 pl.	7 games/ 6 goals					
Men	1988	Hockey	Fernandis, Mervyn	12-Apr-1959				6 pl.	7 games/ 3 goals					
Men	1996	Hockey	Ferreira, Gavin					8th Ov.	Group A 3rd (2W, 1L, 2D)					

Men/ Women	*Year*	*Event*	*Name*	*DoB*	*Event*	*Stage*	*Race #*	*Rnk*	*Score-Result/Opponent/ Opposition*	*Misc*	*Misc*	*Misc*	*Medal*	*Other Sport*
Men	1988	Boxing	Francis, John William	24-Apr-1965	feather	1/16 round			lost to/ Uu, Dong (Chn) 2:3					
Men	1948	Hockey	Francis, Ranganathan	15-Mar-1920				1 pl.	2 games				Gold	
Men	1952	Hockey	Francis, Ranganathan	15-Mar-1920				1 pl.	2 games				Gold	
Men	1956	Hockey	Francis, Ranganathan	15-Mar-1920				1 pl.	1 game				Gold	
Men	1960	Football	Franco, Fortunate	2-May-1939				res.						
Men	1924	Tennis	Fyzee, Ashok	y1883	singles	1rd			defeated/ Langaard. C. (Nor) 6:2, 6:2, 6:3					
Men	1924	Tennis	Fyzee, Ashok	y1883	singles	2rd			lost to/ Zerlantis, A. (Gre) 3:6, 6:1, 6:3, 3:6, 4:6					
Men	1936	Hockey	Galibardy, Joseph Deville Thomas	10-Jan-1915				1 pl.	5 games				Gold	
Men	1928	Hockey	Gateley, Maurice A.					1 pl.	3 games				Gold	
Women	2004	Athletics	Geetha, Satti	5-Jul-1983	4 x 400m	Final		7	3m28.48/ 27		52.91 (8) #	Runner # 1		
Men	1948	Hockey	Gentle, Randhir Singh	22-Sep-1922				1 pl.	3 games				Gold	
Men	1952	Hockey	Gentle, Randhir Singh	22-Sep-1922				1 pl.	3 games				Gold	
Men	1956	Hockey	Gentle, Randhir Singh	22-Sep-1922				1 pl.	5 games				Gold	
Women	2000	Table Tennis	Ghatak, Poulomi	3-Jan-1983	Singles	1st round		lost to	Pavlovich, Veronika (BLR)/ 21-14, 21-17, 21-16					

Men/ Women	Year	Event	Name	DoB	Event	Stage	Race #	Rnk	Score-Result/Opponent/ Opposition	Misc	Misc	Misc	Medal	Other Sport
Women	2000	Table Tennis	Ghatak, Poulomi	3-Jan-1983	Singles	1st round		lost to	Boileau, Anne (FRA)/ 21-12, 21-9, 21-9					
Men	1988	Table Tennis	Ghorpade, Sujayyashwant	10-Jan-1965	singles	1rd		7 pl.						
Men	1988	Table Tennis	Ghorpade, Sujayyashwant	10-Jan-1965	singles	1rd			lost to/ Miyazaki, Y. (Jpn) 0:3					
Men	1988	Table Tennis	Ghorpade, Sujayyashwant	10-Jan-1965	singles	1rd			lost to/ Grubba, A. (Pol) 0:3					
Men	1988	Table Tennis	Ghorpade, Sujayyashwant	10-Jan-1965	singles	1rd			lost to/ Musa, A. (Ngr) 1:3					
Men	1988	Table Tennis	Ghorpade, Sujayyashwant	10-Jan-1965	singles	1rd			lost to/ Rosskopf (Frg) 0:3					
Men	1988	Table Tennis	Ghorpade, Sujayyashwant	10-Jan-1965	singles	1rd			defeated/ Lopez, F. (Ven) 3:2					
Men	1988	Table Tennis	Ghorpade, Sujayyashwant	10-Jan-1965	singles	1rd			lost to/ Haberl, G. (Aus) 2:3					
Men	1988	Table Tennis	Ghorpade, Sujayyashwant	10-Jan-1965	singles	1rd			lost to/ Primorac, Z. (Yug) 0:3					
Men	1988	Table Tennis	Ghorpade, Sujayyashwant	10-Jan-1965	doubles	Prelim.		6 pl.		with Mehta, K.				
Men	1988	Table Tennis	Ghorpade, Sujayyashwant	10-Jan-1965	doubles	Prelim.			lost to/ Lindh, H./Persson, J. (Swe) 0:2	with Mehta, K.				
Men	1988	Table Tennis	Ghorpade, Sujayyashwant	10-Jan-1965	doubles	Prelim.			lost to/ Chen, Longcan/Wei, Qingguang (Chn) 0:2	with Mehta, K.				
Men	1988	Table Tennis	Ghorpade, Sujayyashwant	10-Jan-1965	doubles	Prelim.			lost to/ Prean, C./ Cooke, A. (Gbr) 0:2	with Mehta, K.				
Men	1988	Table Tennis	Ghorpade, Sujayyashwant	10-Jan-1965	doubles	Prelim.			lost to/ Ono, S./Miyazaki, Y. (Jpn) 0:2	with Mehta, K.				

Men/ Women	*Year*	*Event*	*Name*	*DoB*	*Event*	*Stage*	*Race #*	*Rnk*	*Score-Result/Opponent/ Opposition*	*Misc*	*Misc*	*Misc*	*Medal*	*Other Sport*
Men	1988	Table Tennis	Ghorpade, Sujayyashwant	10-Jan-1965	doubles	Prelim.			defeated/ Ben Taiof, S./ Sta, N. (Tun) 2:0	with Mehta, K.				
Men	1988	Table Tennis	Ghorpade, Sujayyashwant	10-Jan-1965	doubles	Prelim.			defeated/ Chan, Chi Ming/Liu, Fuk Man (Hkg) 2:0	with Mehta, K.				
Men	1988	Table Tennis	Ghorpade, Sujayyashwant	10-Jan-1965	doubles	Prelim.			lost to/ Klampar, T./ Kriston, Z. (Hun) 1:2	with Mehta, K.				
Men	1992	Table Tennis	Ghorpade, Sujayyashwant	10-Jan-1965	doubles	Prelim.		4 pl.		with Mehta, K.				
Men	1992	Table Tennis	Ghorpade, Sujayyashwant	10-Jan-1965	doubles	Prelim.			lost to/ Appelgren, M./ Waldner, J. (Swe) 0:2 (-19, -16)	with Mehta, K.				
Men	1992	Table Tennis	Ghorpade, Sujayyashwant	10-Jan-1965	doubles	Prelim.			lost to/ Grujic, S./ Lupulesku, I.IOP)0:2 (-17, -14	with Mehta, K.				
Men	1992	Table Tennis	Ghorpade, Sujayyashwant	10-Jan-1965	doubles	Prelim.			lost to/ Nakamura, K, Avatanabe, T. (Jpn) 0:2 (-16, -16)	with Mehta, K.				
Women	1952	Athletics	Ghose, Nilima	15-Jun-1935	100m	heat		5	13.6					
Women	1952	Athletics	Ghose, Nilima	15-Jun-1935	80m/h	heat		5	12.9					
Men	1964	Weightlifting	Ghosh, Mohon Lal	15-Jul-1944	bantam			14	87.5+95+130=312.5					
Men	1968	Weightlifting	Ghosh, Mohon Lal	15-Jul-1944	feather			15	100+107.5+135= 342.5					
Men	1960	Wrestling	Gian, Parkash	19-Jun-1937	F/light	1rd			lost to/ Wilson, S. (USA) 3:1					
Men	1960	Wrestling	Gian, Parkash	19-Jun-1937	F/light	2rd			defeated/ Yanez, J. (Cub) 1:3					
Men	1960	Wrestling	Gian, Parkash	19-Jun-1937	F/light	3rd			lost to/ Peltoniemi, M. (Fin) 3:1					

Men/ Women	Year	Event	Name	DoB	Event	Stage	Race #	Rnk	Score-Result/Opponent/ Opposition	Misc	Misc	Misc	Medal	Other Sport
Men	1964	Cycling	Gill, Dalbir Singh	25-Nov-1936	4000m pursuit/ team	final								
Men	1964	Cycling	Gill, Dalbir Singh	25-Nov-1936	4000m pursuit/ team	final		1rd.	dsq					
Men	1964	Cycling	Gill, Dalbir Singh	25-Nov-1936	road/team	final		ret.						
Men	1964	Cycling	Gill, Dalbir Singh	25-Nov-1936	Time Trial	final		26	1m21.62					
Men	1964	Cycling	Gill, Dalbir Singh	25-Nov-1936	Time Trial	final		26	1m21.62					
Women	1980	Hockey	Gill, Harpreet	28-Oct-1958				4 pl.	1 game					
Men	1928	Hockey	Gill, K.S.					dns						
Men	2000	Hockey	Gill, Sukhbir Singh	14-Dec-1975				7th	Group B 3rd(2W,1L,2D)		1			
Men	1948	Hockey	Glacken, Gerry (Glacken, Gerald)					1 pl.	1 game				Gold	
Men	1972	Badminton (Demo.)	Goel, Suresh											
Men	1992	Boxing	Gollen, Sandeep Kumar	27-May-1972	light-welter	1/16 round			lost to/ Bouneb, L. (Alg) 4:11					
Men	1984	Hockey	Gomes, Marcellus Mark	16-Jan-1961				5 pl.	3 games					
Men	1936	Hockey	Goodsir-Cullen, Earnest John	15-Jul-1912				1 pl.	5 games				Gold	
Men	1928	Hockey	Goodsir-Cullen, William John					1 pl.	3 games				Gold	

Men/ Women	Year	Event	Name	DoB	Event	Stage	Race #	Rnk	Score-Result/Opponent/ Opposition	Misc	Misc	Misc	Medal	Other Sport
Men	1960	Football	Gosh, Arun (Ghosh, Arun)	7-Jul-1941				res.						
Men	1960	Football	Goswami, Subimal	15-Jan-1938				ER	3games					
Men	1984	Weightlifting	Govindasami, Deven	5-May-1963	bantam			10	105+130=235					
Men	2004	Athletics	Gowda, Vikas Shive	5-Jul-1983	Discus Throw	Qualif.	B	7	61.39		61.35	61.39 59.87		
Men	1960	Athletics	Grewal, Balkrishan	10-Mar-1933	3000m/st			dns						
Men	1936	Hockey	Grewal, Guroharan Singh	4-May-1911				1 pl.	1 game				Gold	
Men	1984	Hockey	Grewal, Iqbaljit	4-Nov-1959				5 pl.	3 games					
Men	2000	Hockey	Grewal, Ramandeep Singh	8-Aug-1971				7th	Group B 3rd(2W,1L,2D)					
Women	2000	Athletics	Gudandda Ganapathy, Pramila	8-May-1977	Heptathlon	Final		24	5548/ 200: 766, 800: 914	100H: 826, SP: 765	JV: 715, LJ: 720, HJ: 879			
Men	1988	Hockey	Gundeep, Kumar	15-May-1965				6 pl.	7 games					
Men	2004	Badminton	Gupta, Abhinn Shyam	22-Oct-1979	Singles	Round of 32	Un-seeded	lost to	Park, Tae Sang (KOR)/ Unseeded	15-12 15-0 (51')				
Men	1976	Shooting	Gurbirsingh, Sandhu	20-Feb-1951	skeet			56	176					
Men	1948	Athletics	Gurnam Singh, S.		high	final		18	1.8					
Men	1980	Basketball	Gurumurthy, Dilip	18-Sep-1956				12 pl.	5 games, 0 pts.					
Men	2000	Swimming	Habibulla, Hakimuddin Shabbir	25-Sep-1979	200m Freestyle	Prelims	1	4	01m58.35	split 56.90				

Men/ Women	*Year*	*Event*	*Name*	*DoB*	*Event*	*Stage*	*Race #*	*Rnk*	*Score-Result/Opponent/ Opposition*	*Misc*	*Misc*	*Misc*	*Medal*	*Other Sport*
Men	1924	Tennis	Hadi, Subimal M.	y1901	doubles	1/8rd			defeated/ Sabbadini, R./Colombo, C. (Ita) w.o.	with Rutnam, D.				
Men	1924	Tennis	Hadi, Subimal M.	y1901	doubles	2rd			defeated/ Nielsen, J./ Langaard, C. (Nor) 6:2, 6:3, 6:0	with Rutnam, D.				
Men	1924	Tennis	Hadi, Subimal M.	y1901	singles	2rd			lost to/ Williams, R. (USA) 0:6, 2:6, 1-6					
Men	1924	Tennis	Hadi, Subimal M.	y1901	doubles	quarter			lost to/ Borona, J./ Lacoste, J. (Fra) 2:6, 2:6, 3:6	with Rutnam, D.				
Men	1960	Football	Hakim Syed, Shahid	25-Jun-1939				res.						
Men	2004	Hockey	Halappa, Arjun	17-Feb-1980		Prelim.	B	7	Prelim. 4th (W1, L3, D1)/ Classification 7-8 def. KOR 5 - 2		7games, 1goal			
Men	1924	Athletics	Hall, James S. (Hall, J.J.)	y1902	4x400m	final		dns						
Men	1924	Athletics	Hall, James S. (Hall, J.J.)	y1902	100m	heat		3						
Men	1924	Athletics	Hall, James S. (Hall, J.J.)	y1902	200m	heat		4						
Men	1928	Athletics	Hall, James S. (Hall, J.J.)	y1902	200m	heat		4						
Men	1928	Athletics	Hall, James S.(Hall, J.J.)	y1902	400m	heat		2						
Men	1928	Athletics	Hall, James S. (Hall, J.J.)	y1902	4x400m	heat								
Men	1928	Athletics	Hall, James S. (Hall, J.J.)	y1902	400m	Round 2		5						

Men/ Women	*Year*	*Event*	*Name*	*DoB*	*Event*	*Stage*	*Race #*	*Rnk*	*Score-Result/Opponent/ Opposition*	*Misc*	*Misc*	*Misc*	*Medal*	*Other Sport*
Men	1928	Athletics	Hamid, Abdul		110m/h	heat		4						
Men	1928	Athletics	Hamid, Abdul		400m/h	heat		6						
Men	1928	Athletics	Hamid, Abdul		4x400m	heat								
Men	1960	Football	Hamid, Habibul Hasan	11-Mar-1942				res.						
Men	1928	Hockey	Hammond, Leslie Charles					1 pl.	3 games				Gold	
Men	1932	Hockey	Hammond, Leslie Charles					1 pl.	2 games				Gold	
Men	1964	Athletics	Harbanslal, Harbanslal	11-Apr-1938	marathon	final		43	2h37m5.8					
Men	1980	Basketball	Harbhajan, Singh	12-Apr-1950				12 pl.	6 games, 0 pts.					
Men	1964	Hockey	Harbinder, Singh (Singh, Harbinder)	8-Jul-1943				1 pl.	8 games/ 5 goals				Gold	
Men	1968	Hockey	Harbinder, Singh (Singh, Harbinder)	8-Jul-1943				3 pl.	9 games/ 5 goals				Bronze	
Men	1972	Hockey	Harbinder, Singh (Singh, Harbinder)	8-Jul-1943				3 pl.	9 games				Bronze	
Men	1956	Hockey	Hari Pal Chand, Kaushik (Kaushik, Haripal)	2-Feb-1934				1 pl.	1 game				Gold	
Men	1960	Hockey	Hari Pal Chand, Kaushik (Kaushik, Haripal)	2-Feb-1934				res.						
Men	1964	Hockey	Hari Pal Chand, Kaushik (Kaushik, Haripal)	2-Feb-1934				1 pl.	9 games/ 1 goal				Gold	

Men/ Women	*Year*	*Event*	*Name*	*DoB*	*Event*	*Stage*	*Race #*	*Rnk*	*Score-Result/Opponent/ Opposition*	*Misc*	*Misc*	*Misc*	*Medal*	*Other Sport*
Men	1976	Athletics	Harichand, Hari	1-Apr-1953	10000m	heat		8	28m48.72					
Men	1980	Athletics	Harichand, Hari	1-Apr-1953	marathon	final		31	2h22m8.0					
Men	1980	Athletics	Harichand, Hari	1-Apr-1953	10000m	heat		10	29m45.8					
Men	1972	Wrestling	Harishchandra		F/middle	1rd			lost to/ Aspin, D. (Nzl) 4:4 (7.08)					
Men	1972	Wrestling	Harishchandra		F/middle	2rd			lost to/ Sasaki, T. (Jpn) 4:0 (8.55)					
Men	1948	Cycling	Havaldar, M.		road/ind	final		dnf						
Men	1948	Cycling	Havewalla, A.		4000m pursuit/ team	final		1rd.						
Men	1924	Athletics	Heathcote, J.C.		4x400m	final		dns						
Men	1936	Hockey	Henderson, E.					res.						
Men	1964	Cycling	Heri, Chetan Singh	14-Sep-1936	4000m pursuit/ team	final		1rd.	dsq					
Men	1964	Cycling	Heri, Chetan Singh	14-Sep-1936	road/team	final		ret.						
Men	1924	Athletics	Hildreth, Wilfred E. (Hildreth, W.R.)	y1896	4x400m	final		dns						
Men	1932	Hockey	Hind, Arthur Charles					1 pl.	2 games				Gold	
Men	1924	Athletics	Hinge, M.R.	y1888	10000m	final		notclas-sified						
Men	1924	Athletics	Hinge, M.R.	y1888	marathon	final		29	3h37m36.0					
Men	1948	Hockey	Husain, Akhtar (Hussain, Akhtar) (Akhtar, Husain)	23-Aug-1926				1 pl.	1 game				Gold	

Men/ Women	Year	Event	Name	DoB	Event	Stage	Race #	Rnk	Score-Result/Opponent/ Opposition	Misc	Misc	Misc	Medal	Other Sport
Men	1936	Hockey	Husain, Sayed Mohomed	1-Oct-1911				1 pl.	4 games				Gold	
Men	1984	Hockey	Iqbal, Zafar (Zafar, Iqubal)	12-Jun-1956				5 pl.	7 games/ 1 goal					
Men	1952	Athletics	Jacob, Ivan	1-Jan-1928	400m	heat		6	51.30					
Men	1924	Tennis	Jacob, Samuel M.	y1879	mixed	1/8rd			lost to/ Wallis, M./ McCrea, E. (Irl) 7:9, 6:4, 7:9	with Polley, V.				
Men	1924	Tennis	Jacob, Samuel M.	y1879	singles	1/8rd			defeated/ Washburn, W. (USA) 6:1, 6:4, 8:10, 6:2					
Men	1924	Tennis	Jacob, Samuel M.	y1879	doubles	1rd			lost to/ Tegner, E./ Ulrich, E. (Den) 3:6, 4:6, 6:4, 4:6	with Sleeni, M.				
Men	1924	Tennis	Jacob, Samuel M.	y1879	singles	1rd			defeated/ Morales Manques, R. (Esp) 6:2, 6:4, 6:4					
Men	1924	Tennis	Jacob, Samuel M.	y1879	singles	2rd			defeated/ Ferrier, M. (Sui) 5:7, 6:3, 6:1, 6:1					
Men	1924	Tennis	Jacob, Samuel M.	y1879	singles	3rd			defeated/ Willard, A. (Aus) 6:1, 6:2, 3:6, 2:6, 6:3					
Men	1924	Tennis	Jacob, Samuel M.	y1879	singles	quarter			lost to/ Borotra, J. (Fra) 6:4, 4:6, 5:7, 3:6					
Men	1948	Wrestling	Jadhav, Kha Shaba Digvijai	y1926	F/fly	1rd			defeated/ Hams, B. (Aus)					
Men	1948	Wrestling	Jadhav, Kha Shaba Digvijai	y1926	F/fly	2rd			defeated/ Jernigan, B. (USA)					

Men/ Women	*Year*	*Event*	*Name*	*DoB*	*Event*	*Stage*	*Race #*	*Rnk*	*Score-Result/Opponent/ Opposition*	*Misc*	*Misc*	*Misc*	*Medal*	*Other Sport*
Men	1948	Wrestling	Jadhav, Kha Shaba Digvijai	y1926	F/fly	3rd			lost to/ Raissi, M. (Irn) fall 5.31					
Men	1948	Wrestling	Jadhav, Kha Shaba Digvijai	y1926	F/fly			6 place						
Men	1952	Wrestling	Jadhav, Kha Shaba Digvijai	y1926	F/bantam	1rd			defeated/ Poliquin, A. (Can) 0:4 (14.25)					
Men	1952	Wrestling	Jadhav, Kha Shaba Digvijai	y1926	F/bantam	2rd			defeated/ Basurto, P. (Mex) 0:4 (5.20)					
Men	1952	Wrestling	Jadhav, Kha Shaba Digvijai	y1926	F/bantam	3rd			defeated/ Schmitz, F. (Ger) 1:2					
Men	1952	Wrestling	Jadhav, Kha Shaba Digvijai	y1926	F/bantam	4rd			bye					
Men	1952	Wrestling	Jadhav, Kha Shaba Digvijai	y1926	F/bantam	5rd			lost to/ Mamedbekov, R. (URS) 3:0					
Men	1952	Wrestling	Jadhav, Kha Shaba Digvijai	y1926	F/bantam	6rd			lost to/ Ishii, S. (Jpn) 3:0					
Men	1952	Wrestling	Jadhav, Kha Shaba Digvijai	y1926	F/bantam			3 place					Bronze	
Men	1952	Wrestling	Jadav, Shrirang Vithoba	15-Nov-1927	F/light-heavy	1rd			lost to/ Theron, J. (SAF) 2:1					
Men	1952	Wrestling	Jadav, Shrirang Vithoba	15-Nov-1927	F/light-heavy	2rd			lost to/ Englas, A. (URS) 4:0 (0.58)					
Men	1988	Hockey	Jagbir, Sing	20-Feb-1965				6 pl.	6 games					
Men	1992	Hockey	Jagbir, Singh	20-Feb-1965				7 pl.	6 games/ 1 goal					
Men	1980	Wrestling	Jagmander, Singh (Singh Balayan, Jagmander)	1-Mar-1956	F/light	1rd			lost to/ Oidov, Z. (Mgl) 3:1					

Men/ Women	*Year*	*Event*	*Name*	*DoB*	*Event*	*Stage*	*Race #*	*Rnk*	*Score-Result/Opponent/ Opposition*	*Misc*	*Misc*	*Misc*	*Medal*	*Other Sport*
Men	1980	Wrestling	Jagmander, Singh (Singh Balayan, Jagmander)	1-Mar-1956	F/light	2rd			defeated/ Nguyen, Dinh Chi (Vie) 0:4 (2.17)					
Men	1980	Wrestling	Jagmander, Singh (Singh Balayan, Jagmander)	1-Mar-1956	F/light	3rd			defeated/ Kocsis, J. (Hun) 0:4					
Men	1980	Wrestling	Jagmander, Singh (Singh Balayan, Jagmander)	1-Mar-1956	F/light	4rd			defeated/ Faris, A. (Irq) 0:4					
Men	1980	Wrestling	Jagmander, Singh (Singh Balayan, Jagmander)	1-Mar-1956	F/light	5rd			lost to/ Yankov, I. (Bul) 3:1					
Men	1980	Wrestling	Jagmander, Singh (Singh Balayan, Jagmander)	1-Mar-1956	F/light			4 place						
Men	1984	Wrestling	Jagmander, Singh (Singh Balayan, Jagmander)	1-Mar-1956	F/light	1rd			defeated/ Manzur Aguilar, G. (Esa) 4:0 (1.24)					
Men	1984	Wrestling	Jagmander, Singh (Singh Balayan, Jagmander)	1-Mar-1956	F/light	2rd			lost to/ You, In Tak (Kor) 0:4 (4.39)					
Men	1984	Wrestling	Jagmander, Singh (Singh Balayan, Jagmander)	1-Mar-1956	F/light	3rd			defeated/ Brulon, E. (Fra) 3:1					
Men	1984	Wrestling	Jagmander, Singh (Singh Balayan, Jagmander)	1-Mar-1956	F/light	4rd			lost to/ Seker, F. (Tur) 0:4 (2.32)					
Men	1972	Wrestling	Jagrup, Singh	15-Sep-1942	F/light	1rd			lost to/ Natsagdorj, T. (Mgl) 3:1					

Men/ Women	*Year*	*Event*	*Name*	*DoB*	*Event*	*Stage*	*Race #*	*Rnk*	*Score-Result/Opponent/ Opposition*	*Misc*	*Misc*	*Misc*	*Medal*	*Other Sport*
Men	1972	Wrestling	Jagrup, Singh	15-Sep-1942	F/light	2rd			lost to/ Hallin, I. (Isr) 3:1					
Men	1984	Hockey	James, Romeo	15-Sep-1958				5 pl.	4 games					
Men	1948	Hockey	Jansen, Patrick					1 pl.	5 games				Gold	
Men	1960	Football	Jarnail Singh, Dhillon	20-Feb-1936				ER	3 games					
Men	1948	Boxing	Joachim, M.		light-heavy	1/16 round			lost to/ Szymura, F. (Pol)					
Men	1980	Basketball	Jorawar, Singh	7-Jul-1951				12 pl.	7 games, 10 pts.					
Men	1960	Athletics	Joshi Tilak Raj	1-Sep-1936	100m	heat		7	11.30					
Men	1988	Hockey	Jude Felix, Sebastian	26-Jan-1965				6 pl.	7 games/ 3 goals					
Men	1996	Weightlifting	Kabeer, Samsudeen		70			23	275/ sn - 125	cj - 150				
Men	2004	Table tennis	Kamal Achanta, Sharath	12-Jul-1982	singles	Round 1		def.	Boudjadja, Mohamed (ALG)/ (4-1) 11-4, 12-10, 11-6, 11-13, 11-7			49 seed		
Men	2004	Table tennis	Kamal Achanta, Sharath	12-Jul-1982	singles	Round 2		lost to	Ko Lai Chak(HKG)/ (4-0) 11-9, 11-5, 11-9, 11-6			49 seed		
Men	1960	Shooting	Kami Singh (Kami, Singh D.R.)	21-Aug-1924	clay pigeon	Elim. Rnd.		17	89					
Men	1960	Shooting	Kami Singh (Kami, Singh D.R.)	21-Aug-1924	clay pigeon	final		8	183					
Men	1964	Shooting	Kami Singh (Kami, Singh D.R.)	21-Aug-1924	clay pigeon			26	186					
Men	1968	Shooting	Kami Singh (Kami, Singh D.R.)	21-Aug-1924	skeet			28	187					

Men/ Women	*Year*	*Event*	*Name*	*DoB*	*Event*	*Stage*	*Race #*	*Rnk*	*Score-Result/Opponent/ Opposition*	*Misc*	*Misc*	*Misc*	*Medal*	*Other Sport*
Men	1968	Shooting	Kami Singh (Kami, Singh D.R.)	21-Aug-1924	Trap			10	194					
Men	1972	Shooting	Kami Singh (Kami, Singh D.R.)	21-Aug-1924	skeet			36	186					
Men	1972	Shooting	Kami Singh (Kami, Singh D.R.)	21-Aug-1924	Trap			34	180					
Men	1980	Shooting	Kami Singh (Kami, Singh D.R.)	21-Aug-1924	trap			14	188					
Men	1952	Weightlifting	Kamineni, Eswararao (Eswararao, Kamineni)	y1926	middle-heavy			ret.	107.5+105+0					
Men	1956	Weightlifting	Kamineni, Eswararao (Eswararao, Kamineni)	y1926	middle-heavy			11	122.5+110+147.5 =380					
Men	1936	Wrestling	Kane, Shripad		F/welter	dns								
Men	2004	Badminton	Kanetkar, Nikhil	13-May-1979	Singles	Round of 16	Seed 6	lost to	Gade, Peter (DEN). Unseeded	15-10 15-6 (43')				
Men	2004	Badminton	Kanetkar, Nikhil	13-May-1979	Singles	Round of 32	Un-seeded	lost to	Llopis, Sergio (ESP)/ Seed 6	15-7 13-15 15-13 (66')				
Men	1984	Wrestling	Kangar, Jai Prakash	1-Jan-1958	F/light-heavy	1rd			defeated/ Rahman, A. (Irq) 3:1					
Men	1984	Wrestling	Kangar, Jai Prakash	1-Jan-1958	F/light-heavy	2rd			lost to/ Azzola, M. (Ita) 0:4 (0.47)					
Men	1960	Football	Kannan, Dharmalingam	8-Jul-1936				ER	1game					
Men	1984	Weightlifting	Kannan, Mahendran	5-Mar-1964	fly			10	100+115=215					
Men	1956	Football	Kannayan, Muhamed K.	y1932				4 pl.	2 games					

Men/ Women	*Year*	*Event*	*Name*	*DoB*	*Event*	*Stage*	*Race #*	*Rnk*	*Score-Result/Opponent/ Opposition*	*Misc*	*Misc*	*Misc*	*Medal*	*Other Sport*
Men	1964	Gymnastics	Karande, Vithal	12-Mar-1940	indiv.	final		123	86.2					
Men	1964	Gymnastics	Karande, Vithal	12-Mar-1940	team	final		18	428.35					
Men	1980	Wrestling	Kartar Singh (Dhillon, Kartar Singh) (Singh, Kartar)	7-Oct-1953	F/light-heavy	1rd			lost to/ Ghinov, I. (Bul) 4:0 (7.55)					
Men	1980	Wrestling	Kartar Singh (Dhillon, Kartar Singh) (Singh, Kartar)	7-Oct-1953	F/light-heavy	2rd			lost to/ Pikos, M. (Aus) 4:0 (1.00)					
Men	1984	Wrestling	Kartar Singh (Dhillon, Kartar Singh) (Singh, Kartar)	7-Oct-1953	F/heavy	1rd			defeated/ Gustavs.son, K. (Swe) 4:0 (5.08)					
Men	1984	Wrestling	Kartar Singh (Dhillon, Kartar Singh) (Singh, Kartar)	7-Oct-1953	F/heavy	2rd			lost to/ Atiyeh, J. (Syr) 0:4 (0.33)					
Men	1984	Wrestling	Kartar Singh (Dhillon, Kartar Singh) (Singh, Kartar)	7-Oct-1953	F/heavy	3rd			lost to/ Puscasu, V. (Rom) 1:3					
Men	1984	Wrestling	Kartar Singh (Dhillon, Kartar Singh) (Singh, Kartar)	7-Oct-1953	F/heavy			7 place						

Men/ Women	Year	Event	Name	DoB	Event	Stage	Race #	Rnk	Score-Result/Opponent/ Opposition	Misc	Misc	Misc	Medal	Other Sport
Men	1988	Wrestling	Kartar Singh (Dhillon, Kartar Singh) (Singh, Kartar)	7-Oct-1953	F/heavy	1rd			defeated/ Honda, T. (Jpn) 3:1					
Men	1988	Wrestling	Kartar Singh (Dhillon, Kartar Singh) (Singh, Kartar)	7-Oct-1953	F/heavy	2rd			lost to/ Javhlantugs, B. (Mgl) 0:3					
Men	1988	Wrestling	Kartar Singh (Dhillon, Kartar Singh) (Singh, Kartar)	7-Oct-1953	F/heavy	3rd			lost to/ Joe, Byung-Eun (Kor) 0:4 (4.29)					
Women	2000	Athletics	Kaur, Gurmeet	20-Jun-1970	Javelin	qu	1	17	52.78					
Women	2004	Athletics	Kaur, Harwant	5-Jul-1980	Discus Throw	Qualif.	A	7	60.82		60.82	59.2 59.95		
Women	2004	Athletics	Kaur, Manjeet	4-Apr-1982	4 x 400m	Round 1	Heat 2	3	3m26.92/Q	NR	49.85 (1) #	Runner # 4		
Women	2000	Athletics	Kaur, Paramjit	2-Apr-1976	4x400m	Round 1	2	5	03m31.46					
Women	2004	Athletics	Kaur, Rajwinder	24-Jan-1980	4 x 400m	Final		7	3m28.48/ 27		51.53 (7) #	Runner # 4		
Women	2004	Athletics	Kaur, Rajwinder	24-Jan-1980	4 x 400m	Round 1	Heat 2	3	3m26.92/ Q	NR	51.86 (3) #	Runner # 1		
Men	1980	Hockey	Kaushik, Maharaj Krishon	2-May-1955				1 pl.	5 games/ 3 goals				Gold	
Men	1956	Football	Kempiah, Muhamed K.	10-Feb-1933				4 pl.	3games					
Men	1960	Football	Kempiah, Muhamed K.	10-Feb-1933				ER	3games					

Men/ Women	*Year*	*Event*	*Name*	*DoB*	*Event*	*Stage*	*Race #*	*Rnk*	*Score-Result/Opponent/ Opposition*	*Misc*	*Misc*	*Misc*	*Medal*	*Other Sport*
Men	1960	Shooting	Keshav, Sen	21-Sep-1923	clay pigeon	Elim. Rnd.		el.						
Men	1948	Football	Khan, Ahmed Muhammed (Ahmed, Khan Mohamed)	24-Dec-1926				2rd						
Men	1952	Football	Khan, Ahmed Muhammed (Ahmed, Khan Mohamed)	24-Dec-1926				1rd						
Men	1936	Hockey	Khan, Ahsan Mohomed	7-Apr-1916				1 pl.	1 game				Gold	
Men	1972	Hockey	Khan, Aslamsher (Khan, Aslam)	15-Aug-1953				dns						
Men	1976	Hockey	Khan, Aslamsher (Khan, Aslam)	15-Aug-1953				7 pl.	5 games/ 2 goals					
Men	1980	Equestrian	Khan, Hussain	10-Sep-1944	3day/indiv	final		ret.	Rajdoot					
Men	1980	Equestrian	Khan, Hussain	10-Sep-1944	3day/team	final		el.	Rajdoot					
Men	2000	Rowing	Khan, Kasam	1-Jan-1974	coxless pairs	Preliminary	1	5	7m09.94/ Q	Inderpal Singh				
Men	2000	Rowing	Khan, Kasam	1-Jan-1974	coxless pairs	Repechage		6	7m16.10	Inderpal Singh				
Men	1980	Equestrian	Khan, Mohammed	4-Sep-1943	3day/indiv	final		el.	I-Am-It					
Men	1980	Equestrian	Khan, Mohammed	4-Sep-1943	3day/team	final		el.	I-Am-It					
Men	1956	Swimming	Khan, Shamsher	y1931	200m breast-stroke	heat		5	3m17.0					
Men	1956	Swimming	Khan, Shamsher	y1931	200m but-terfly	heat		6	3m06.3					

Men/ Women	Year	Event	Name	DoB	Event	Stage	Race #	Rnk	Score-Result/Opponent/ Opposition	Misc	Misc	Misc	Medal	Other Sport
Men	1960	Football	Khan, Yousif	5-Aug-1937				ER	3games					
Men	1984	Shooting	Kharab, Baljit Singh	10-Jul-1956	free pistol			31	539					
Men	2004	Wrestling	Khatri, Mukesh	8-Oct-1982	55kg Greco-Roman	Prelim.	Pool 6	0	0/ Classif.: 0+0	Tech: 0+0				
Men	1956	Football	Kittu, Krishna Swamy	y1932				4 pl.	3games					
Women	1996	Judo	Kohli, Shah		+72kg	1st Round		lost to	CUB/ Rodriguez, Estela	Ippon				
Women	1996	Judo	Kohli, Shah		+72kg	Repechage		lost to	KOR/ Shon, Hyun-Me	Ippon				
Men	1968	Hockey	Krishnamurthy, Perumal (Perumal, Krishna Murtay)	26-Sep-1947				3 pl.	1 game				Bronze	
Men	1972	Hockey	Krishnamurthy, Perumal (Perumal, Krishna Murtay)	26-Sep-1947				3 pl.	8 games				Bronze	
Men	1992	Tennis	Krishnan, Ramesh	5-Jun-1961	doubles	1rd			defeated/ Bozic, I./ Trupej, B. (Slo) 6:3. 6:2, 6:2	with Paes, L.				
Men	1992	Tennis	Krishnan, Ramesh	5-Jun-1961	singles	1rd			defeated/ 4 Courier, J. (USA) 2:6, 6:4, 1:6, 4:6					
Men	1992	Tennis	Krishnan, Ramesh	5-Jun-1961	doubles	2rd			defeated/ Fitzgerald, J./ Woodbridge, T. (Aus) 6:4, 7:5, 4:6, 6:1	with Paes, L.				
Men	1992	Tennis	Krishnan, Ramesh	5-Jun-1961	doubles	quarter			lost to/ Ivanisevic, G./ Prpic, G. (Cro) 6:7, 7:5, 4:6, 3:6	with Paes, L.				
Men	1932	Hockey	Kullar, Gurmit Singh					1 pl.	2 games				Gold	

Men/ Women	*Year*	*Event*	*Name*	*DoB*	*Event*	*Stage*	*Race #*	*Rnk*	*Score-Result/Opponent/ Opposition*	*Misc*	*Misc*	*Misc*	*Medal*	*Other Sport*
Men	2004	Boxing	Kumar, Akhil	27-Mar-1981	48-51kg	Round of 32		lost to	Thomas, Jerome/ FRA	(37-16)				
Men	1948	Hockey	Kumar, Amir Chand	10-Aug-1923				1 pl.	4 games				Gold	
Men	1956	Hockey	Kumar, Amir Chand	10-Aug-1923				1 pl.	4 games				Gold	
Men	1992	Wrestling	Kumar, Anil	27-Oct-1971	F/fly	1rd			lost to/ Orel, A. (Tur) 0:4 (3.46)					
Men	1992	Wrestling	Kumar, Anil	27-Oct-1971	F/fly	2rd			lost to/ Torkan, M. (Iri) 0:4 (4.08)					
Men	2000	Athletics	Kumar, Anil (Kumar P, Anil)	20-Jun-1975	4x100m	Round 1	1	7	40.23					
Men	2004	Athletics	Kumar, Anil (Kumar P, Anil)	20-Jun-1975	Discus Throw	Qualif.	A	NM	NM		x	x -		
Men	**1972**	**Hockey**	**Kumar, Ashok**	**1-Jun-1950**				**3 pl.**	**9 games/ 3 goals**				**Bronze**	
Men	**1992**	**Wrestling**	**Kumar, Ashok**	**7-Jul-1969**	**F/bantam**	**1rd**			**lost to/ Mallahi, O. (Iri) 1:3**					
Men	**1992**	**Wrestling**	**Kumar, Ashok**	**7-Jul-1969**	**F/bantam**	**2rd**			**lost to/ Musaoglu, R. (Tur) 0:3**					
Men	1980	Hockey	Kumar, Charanjit	11-Apr-1956				1 pl.	1 game				Gold	
Men	1984	Hockey	Kumar, Charanjit	11-Apr-1956				5 pl.	7 games/ 1 goal					
Men	2000	Boxing	Kumar, Jitender	4-Sep-1977	71-75kg	1/16 Final Match 11		def.	Orr, Donald Grant/ CAN	Head-blow-3				
Men	2000	Boxing	Kumar, Jitender	4-Sep-1977	71-75kg	1/8 Final Match 6		lost to	Diaconu, Adrian/ ROM	12-3.				

Men/ Women	*Year*	*Event*	*Name*	*DoB*	*Event*	*Stage*	*Race #*	*Rnk*	*Score-Result/Opponent/ Opposition*	*Misc*	*Misc*	*Misc*	*Medal*	*Other Sport*
Men	2004	Boxing	Kumar, Jitender	4-Sep-1977	75-81kg	Round of 32			lost to/ Fedchuk, Andriy/ UKR	TKO	Stopped by referee, round 2)			
Men	1988	Wrestling	Kumar, Naresh	17-Nov-1965	F/welter	1rd			defeated/ Diallo, M. (Gui) 3:0 (5.07)					
Men	1988	Wrestling	Kumar, Naresh	17-Nov-1965	F/welter	2rd			lost to/ Westendorf, U. (GDR) 1:3					
Men	1988	Wrestling	Kumar, Naresh	17-Nov-1965	F/welter	3rd			lost to/ Vagozari, A. (Irn) 0:4 (5.51)					
Men	1968	Athletics	Kumar, Praveen	6-Dec-1946	hammer	qu			60.84					
Men	1972	Athletics	Kumar, Praveen	6-Dec-1946	discus	qu			53.12					
Men	1984	Athletics	Kumar, Raj	2-Mar-1962	5000m			dns						
Men	1988	Wrestling	Kumar, Rajesh	15-Sep-1969	F/light-fly	1rd			defeated/ Liang, Dejin (Chn) 3:1					
Men	1988	Wrestling	Kumar, Rajesh	15-Sep-1969	F/light-fly	2rd			defeated/ Suhbatar, T. (Ind) 3:1 (6.37)					
Men	1988	Wrestling	Kumar, Rajesh	15-Sep-1969	F/light-fly	3rd			lost to/ Heugabel, R. (Frg) 0:3.5					
Men	1988	Wrestling	Kumar, Rajesh	15-Sep-1969	F/light-fly	4rd			lost to/ Tzonov, I. (Bul) 1:3					
Men	1996	Weightlifting	Kumar, Sandeep		64			33	252.5/ sn - 110	cj - 142.5				
Men	1996	Hockey	Kumar, Sanjeev					8th Ov.	Group A 3rd (2W, 1L, 2D)					
Men	1980	Athletics	Kumar, Sant	24-Jul-1959	1500m	heat		8	3m55.6					
Men	1968	Wrestling	Kumar, Sudesh	10-Mar-1950	F/fly	1rd			defeated/ Dimouski, B. (Yug) 0.5:3.5					

Men/ Women	*Year*	*Event*	*Name*	*DoB*	*Event*	*Stage*	*Race #*	*Rnk*	*Score-Result/Opponent/ Opposition*	*Misc*	*Misc*	*Misc*	*Medal*	*Other Sport*
Men	1968	Wrestling	Kumar, Sudesh	10-Mar-1950	GR/fly	1rd			Kanrious,M.(Mar)2:2					
Men	1968	Wrestling	Kumar, Sudesh	10-Mar-1950	F/fly	2rd			defeated/ Ramirez, G. (Gua) 0:4 (5.32)					
Men	1968	Wrestling	Kumar, Sudesh	10-Mar-1950	GR/fly	2rd			lost to/ Aiker, I. (Hun) 4:0 (2.57)					
Men	1968	Wrestling	Kumar, Sudesh	10-Mar-1950	F/fly	3rd			lost to/ Castillo, W. (Pan) 3:1					
Men	1968	Wrestling	Kumar, Sudesh	10-Mar-1950	F/fly	4rd			bye					
Men	1968	Wrestling	Kumar, Sudesh	10-Mar-1950	F/fly	5rd			lost to/ Sanders, R. (USA) 4:0 (1.34)					
Men	1968	Wrestling	Kumar, Sudesh	10-Mar-1950	F/fly			6 pl.						
Men	1972	Wrestling	Kumar, Sudesh	10-Mar-1950	F/fly	1rd			defeated/ Ali, R. (Tur) 1:3					
Men	1972	Wrestling	Kumar, Sudesh	10-Mar-1950	F/fly	2rd			defeated/ Kim, Young-Yun (Kor) 0:4 (4.01)					
Men	1972	Wrestling	Kumar, Sudesh	10-Mar-1950	F/fly	3rd			defeated/ Martinez, F. (Mex) 0:4 (7.07)					
Men	1972	Wrestling	Kumar, Sudesh	10-Mar-1950	F/fly	4rd			defeated/ Gal, H. (Hun) 0:4 (3.17)					
Men	1972	Wrestling	Kumar, Sudesh	10-Mar-1950	F/fly	5rd			lost to/ Kato, K. (Jpn) 3:1					
Men	1972	Wrestling	Kumar, Sudesh	10-Mar-1950	F/fly	6rd			lost to/ Alakhverdiev, A. (URS) 3:1					
Men	1992	Badminton	Kumar, Vimal	19-Nov-1962	double	1rd			lost to/ Sidek, J./Sidek, R. (Mas) 6:15, 3:15	with Bhatta-charya, D.				

Men/ Women	Year	Event	Name	DoB	Event	Stage	Race #	Rnk	Score-Result/Opponent/ Opposition	Misc	Misc	Misc	Medal	Other Sport
Men	1992	Badminton	Kumar, Vimal	19-Nov-1962	single	1rd			lost to/ Laiiridsen, T.S. (Den) 6:15, 6:15					
Men	1988	Wrestling	Kumar, Vinod	15-Aug-1965	F/bantam	1rd			lost to/ Nagy, B. (Hun) 0:4 (0.39)					
Men	1988	Wrestling	Kumar, Vinod	15-Aug-1965	F/bantam	2rd			defeated/ Holmes, L. (Can) 3:1					
Men	1988	Wrestling	Kumar, Vinod	15-Aug-1965	F/bantam	3rd			lost to/ Beloglazov, S. (URS) 0:4 (1.44)					
Women	2004	Archery	Kumari, Reena	15-Jan-1984	Indiv.	Ranking		43	620					
Women	2004	Archery	Kumari, Reena	15-Jan-1984	Indiv.	Round of 64			def./ Esebua, Kristine (GEO)	153-149				
Women	2004	Archery	Kumari, Reena	15-Jan-1984	Indiv.	Round of 32			lost to/ Chhoden, Tshering (BHU)	134-134				
Women	2004	Archery	Kumari, Reena	15-Jan-1984	Indiv.	Round of 16			lost to/ Yuan Shu Chi (TPE)	148-166				
Women	2004	Archery	Kumari, Reena	15-Jan-1984	Team	Ranking		5	1900					
Women	2004	Archery	Kumari, Reena	15-Jan-1984	Team	Round of 16			def./ GBR	230-228				
Women	2004	Archery	Kumari, Reena	15-Jan-1984	Team	Quarter			lost to/ FRA	227-228				
Women	2004	Weightlifting	Kunjarani, Namecrakpam	1-Mar-1968	48kg	Final		4	190/ Snatch 82.5 (82.5x, 82.5, 85.0x)	Clean & Jerk 107.5 (102.5, 107.5, 112.5x)	Body Wt 48 kg			
Women	**1988**	**Athletics**	**Kurisingal, Abraham Shiny**	**8-May-1965**	**4x400m**	**heat**		**7**	**3m33.46**					
Women	**1988**	**Athletics**	**Kurisingal, Abraham Shiny**	**8-May-1965**	**800m**	**heat**		**6**	**2m03.26**					

Men/ Women	*Year*	*Event*	*Name*	*DoB*	*Event*	*Stage*	*Race #*	*Rnk*	*Score-Result/Opponent/ Opposition*	*Misc*	*Misc*	*Misc*	*Medal*	*Other Sport*
Women	1996	Athletics	Kutty, Rosa	3-Jan-1964	4x400m	Round 1	1	6	3m35.91					
Women	2000	Athletics	Kutty, Rosa	3-Jan-1964	4x400m	Round 1	2	5	03m31.46					
Men	1960	Football	Lahiri Malay, Kumar	20-Sep-1934				res.						
Women	1996	Badminton	Lakshimi, P.V.V.		Singles	1st Round		def.	Anne Gibson (GBR)/ 11-6 11-6					
Women	1996	Badminton	Lakshimi, P.V.V.		Singles	2nd Round			lost to / Katarzyna Krasowska (POL)/ 11-5 11-6					
Men	1924	Athletics	Lakshmanan, K. (Lakshmanan, G.K. or C.K.)		4x400m	final		dns						
Men	1924	Athletics	Lakshmanan, K. (Lakshmanan, G.K. or C.K.)		110m/h	heat		5						
Men	1972	Sailing	Lal Verma, Brij	12-Mar-1926	res.									
Men	1948	Hockey	Lal, Kishan	2-Feb-1917				1 pl.	5 games				Gold	
Men	1960	Hockey	Lal, Mohendera (Lal, Mohinder) (Mohinder, Lal)	1-Jun-1936				2 pl.	5 games				Silver	
Men	1964	Hockey	Lal, Mohendera (Lal, Mohinder) (Mohinder, Lal)	1-Jun-1936				1 pl.	7 games/ 3 goals				Gold	
Men	1980	Shooting	Lal, Mohinder	24-Feb-1947	rapid fire pistol			dns						
Men	1984	Shooting	Lal, Mohinder	24-Feb-1947	rapid fire pistol			34	577					

Men/ Women	Year	Event	Name	DoB	Event	Stage	Race #	Rnk	Score-Result/Opponent/ Opposition	Misc	Misc	Misc	Medal	Other Sport
Men	1948	Boxing	Lall, Babu		bantam	1/16 round			defeated/ Monterio, A. (Pak) rsc. 1rd.					
Men	1948	Boxing	Lall, Babu		bantam	1/8 round			defeated/ Venegas, J. (Pur)					
Men	1952	Hockey	Lall, Sharma Raghbir (Lal, Raghivir)	15-Nov-1929				1 pl.	3 games				Gold	
Men	1956	Hockey	Lall, Sharma Raghbir (Lal, Raghivir)	15-Nov-1929				1 pl.	2 games				Gold	
Men	1992	Archery	Lalremsanga, Chhangte	28-Dec-1973	team	final		13		final				
Men	1992	Archery	Lalremsanga, Chhangte	28-Dec-1973	ind	pr.		53	1243					
Men	1992	Archery	Lalremsanga, Chhangte	28-Dec-1973	team	pr.		15	3761					
Men	1952	Football	Latif, Abdul (Lateef, Shaikh Abdul L.)	8-May-1934				2rd						
Men	1956	Football	Latif, Abdul (Lateef, Shaikh Abdul L.)	8-May-1934				4 pl.	2 games					
Men	1960	Football	Latif, Abdul (Lateef, Shaikh Abdul L.)	8-May-1934				ER	3 games					
Men	1960	Hockey	Laxman, Shankar	1-Jul-1933				2 pl.	6 games				Silver	
Men	1964	Hockey	Laxman, Shankar	1-Jul-1933				1 pl.	9 games				Gold	
Men	1956	Hockey	Laxman, Shankar Pillay	4-Jul-1927				1 pl.	4 games				Gold	
Men	1996	Archery	Limba, Ram (Ram, Limba)	30-Jan-1972	Indiv.	Prelim.		44	644					
Men	1996	Archery	Limba, Ram (Ram, Limba)	30-Jan-1972	Indiv.	elim1/32			lost to/VERMEIREN, Paul/ BEL					

Men/ Women	*Year*	*Event*	*Name*	*DoB*	*Event*	*Stage*	*Race #*	*Rnk*	*Score-Result/Opponent/ Opposition*	*Misc*	*Misc*	*Misc*	*Medal*	*Other Sport*
Men	1996	Archery	Limba, Ram (Ram, Limba)	30-Jan-1972	Team	Prelim.		14	644/ 1928		Elim.			
Men	1988	Archery	Limba, Ram (Ram, Limba)	30-Jan-1972	ind			39	1232	final				
Men	1988	Archery	Limba, Ram (Ram, Limba)	30-Jan-1972	team			20	3615	final				
Men	1992	Archery	Limba, Ram (Ram, Limba)	30-Jan-1972	ind	final		23		final				
Men	1992	Archery	Limba, Ram (Ram, Limba)	30-Jan-1972	team	final		13		final				
Men	1992	Archery	Limba, Ram (Ram, Limba)	30-Jan-1972	ind	pr.		11	1306					
Men	1992	Archery	Limba, Ram (Ram, Limba)	30-Jan-1972	team	pr.		15	3761					
Men	1992	Wrestling	M.R.Patil	20-Jan-1968	GR/feather	1rd			lost to/ Pazaj, A. (Iri) 1:3					
Men	1992	Wrestling	M.R.Patil	20-Jan-1968	GR/feather	2rd			defeated/ Dietsche, H. (Sui) 0:3					
Men	2004	Wrestling	Maan, Sujeet	15-Dec-1978	74kg Freestyle	Prelim.	Pool 1	0	0/ Classif.: 0+0	Tech: 0+0				
Men	1976	Boxing	Machiach, Chand C.		light-welter	1/32 round			lost to/ Beyer, U. (GDR) 0:5					
Men	1960	Wrestling	Madho Singh (Singh Madho)	7-Jul-1929	F/middle	1rd			defeated/ Bults, A. (Gbr) 0:4 (4.03)					
Men	1960	Wrestling	Madho Singh (Singh Madho)	7-Jul-1929	F/middle	2rd			defeated/ Caraffini, G. (Ita) 0:4 (9.55)					
Men	1960	Wrestling	Madho Singh (Singh Madho)	7-Jul-1929	F/middle	3rd			lost to/ Antonsson, H. (Swe) 3:1					

Men/ Women	*Year*	*Event*	*Name*	*DoB*	*Event*	*Stage*	*Race #*	*Rnk*	*Score-Result/Opponent/ Opposition*	*Misc*	*Misc*	*Misc*	*Medal*	*Other Sport*
Men	1960	Wrestling	Madho Singh (Singh Madho)	7-Jul-1929	F/middle	4rd			lost to/ Skhirtladze, G. (URS) 3:1					
Men	1960	Wrestling	Madho Singh (Singh Madho)	7-Jul-1929	F/middle			5 pl.						
Men	1964	Wrestling	Madho Singh (Singh Madho)	7-Jul-1929	F/welter	1rd			defeated/ Graifigna, J. (Arg) 1:3					
Men	1964	Wrestling	Madho Singh (Singh Madho)	7-Jul-1929	F/welter	2rd			lost to/ Ogan, I. (Tur) 3:1					
Men	1964	Wrestling	Madho Singh (Singh Madho)	7-Jul-1929	F/welter	3rd			defeated/ Allen, R. (Gbr) 1:3					
Men	1964	Wrestling	Madho Singh (Singh Madho)	7-Jul-1929	F/welter	4rd			lost to/ Sagaradze, G. (URS) 3:1					
Men	1984	Tennis	Madhusudan Nair, Gopinath		singles	1/16rd			lost to/ Bale, S. (Gbr) 2:6, 1:6					
Women	1980	Hockey	Madraswalla, Nazleen	6-Sep-1962				4 pl.	4 games					
Men	1948	Football	Mahomed, Taj					2rd						
Women	2000	Tennis	Malhotra, Manisha	19-Sep-1976	doubles	1st round			lost to/Dokic, Jelena/ Stubbs, Rennae (AUS)/ 6-0,6-0	Vaidyana-than, Nirupama				
Men	1932	Swimming	Malik, Nalin Chandra		1500m freestyle	heat		4	23m52.4					
Men	1932	Swimming	Malik, Nalin Chandra		400m freestyle	heat		4	5m59.0					
Men	1984	Weightlifting	Malla Venkata, Manikyalu	13-May-1958	fly			0	0+el.					
Women	2000	Weightlifting	Malleswari, Karnam	1-Jun-1975	69	Final		3	240		sn: 110, c&j: 130	Bodywt: 67.9	Bronze	

Men/ Women	Year	Event	Name	DoB	Event	Stage	Race #	Rnk	Score-Result/Opponent/ Opposition	Misc	Misc	Misc	Medal	Other Sport
Women	2004	Weightlifting	Malleswari, Karnam	1-Jun-1975	63kg	Final		9	NR		Body Wt 63 kg			
Men	1964	Wrestling	Malva, Singh	14-Mar-1940	F/fly	1rd			defeated/ Neff, P. (Ger) 1:3					
Men	1964	Wrestling	Malva, Singh	14-Mar-1940	GR/fly	1rd			Kerezov,A.(Bul)2:2					
Men	1964	Wrestling	Malva, Singh	14-Mar-1940	F/fly	2rd			defeated/ Fernando, E. (Cey) 0:4 (default)					
Men	1964	Wrestling	Malva, Singh	14-Mar-1940	F/fly	3rd			lost to/ Simons, E. (USA) 3:1					
Men	1964	Wrestling	Malva, Singh	14-Mar-1940	F/fly	4rd			lost to/ Aliev, A. (URS) 4:0 (2.00)					
Men	1964	Wrestling	Mane, Manuti	10-Aug-1938	F/light-heavy	1rd			lost to/ Jutzeler, P. (Sui) 3:1					
Men	1964	Wrestling	Mane, Manuti	10-Aug-1938	GR/light-heavy	1rd			lost to/ Kiss, F. (Hun) 4:0 (1.59)					
Men	1964	Wrestling	Mane, Manuti	10-Aug-1938	F/light-heavy	2rd			defeated/ Kiehl, H. (Ger) 1:3					
Men	1964	Wrestling	Mane, Manuti	10-Aug-1938	F/light-heavy	3rd			lost to/ Vigh, I. (Hun) 3:1					
Men	1980	Hockey	Maneypanda, Somaya Muttana (Maney-pandemuttana, Somaya Muttana)	8-May-1959				1 pl.	5 games				Gold	
Men	1984	Hockey	Maneypanda, Somaya Muttana (Maney-pandemuttana, Somaya Muttana)	8-May-1959				5 pl.	7 games					

Men/ Women	*Year*	*Event*	*Name*	*DoB*	*Event*	*Stage*	*Race #*	*Rnk*	*Score-Result/Opponent/ Opposition*	*Misc*	*Misc*	*Misc*	*Medal*	*Other Sport*
Men	1988	Hockey	Maneypanda, Somaya Muttana (Maney-pandemuttana, Somaya Muttana)	8-May-1959				6 pl.	7 games					
Men	1952	Wrestling	Mangave, Keshav D.	10-Jun-1926	F/feather	1rd			bye					
Men	1952	Wrestling	Mangave, Keshav D.	10-Jun-1926	F/feather	2rd			defeated/ Lugo, I. (Ven) dna					
Men	1952	Wrestling	Mangave, Keshav D.	10-Jun-1926	F/feather	3rd			lost to/ Guivehlchi, N. (Irn) 3:0					
Men	1952	Wrestling	Mangave, Keshav D.	10-Jun-1926	F/feather	4rd			defeated/ Bernard, A. (Can) 0:4 (14.05)					
Men	1952	Wrestling	Mangave, Keshav D.	10-Jun-1926	F/feather	5rd			lost to/Henson, J. (USA) 3:0					
Men	1952	Wrestling	Mangave, Keshav D.	10-Jun-1926	F/feather			4 place						
Men	1952	Athletics	Mann, Gulzara Singh	4-Jul-1924	3000m	heat		12	9m48.6					
Men	1948	Football	Manna, Sailen	20-Sep-1924				2rd						
Men	1952	Football	Manna, Sailen	20-Sep-1924				1rd						
Men	1980	Boxing	Manoharan, Ganapathy		bantam	1/16 round			defeated/Diallo, S. (Gui) 4:1					
Men	1980	Boxing	Manoharan, Ganapathy		bantam	1/8 round			lost to/Issaick, G. (Tan) rsc. 2rd. (2.38)					
Men	1948	Swimming	Mansoor, Isaac (Monsoor, Isaac)	30-May-1929	100m freestyle	heat		7	1m06.4					
Men	1952	Swimming	Mansoor, Isaac (Monsoor, Isaac)	30-May-1929	100m freestyle	heat		7	1m10.8					

Men/ Women	Year	Event	Name	DoB	Event	Stage	Race #	Rnk	Score-Result/Opponent/ Opposition	Misc	Misc	Misc	Medal	Other Sport
Men	1948	Water polo	Mansoor, Isaac (Monsoor, Isaac)	30-May-1929	2nd rnd				3 games					
Men	1952	Water polo	Mansoor, Isaac (Monsoor, Isaac)	30-May-1929	Prelim.				2 games					
Men	1972	Hockey	Manuel, Frederick	20-Oct-1948				3 pl.	8 games				Bronze	
Men	1988	Hockey	Markphilip, Patterson	26-May-1969				6 pl.	1 game					
Men	1928	Hockey	Marthins, George E.					1 pl.	5 games				Gold	
Men	1972	Wrestling	Maruti, Adkar	15-Feb-1950	F/light-fly	1rd			lost to/Dmitriev, R. (URS) 4:0 (8.14)					
Men	1972	Wrestling	Maruti, Adkar	15-Feb-1950	F/light-fly	2rd			lost to/Jang Dog, Ryong (PRK) 3:1					
Men	1960	Hockey	Mascarenhas, John	24-Jun-1935				res.						
Men	1936	Hockey	Masood, Mirza Nasir-ud-Din	23-Nov-1908				1 pl.	1 game				Gold	
Men	1952	Athletics	Mathur, Surat Singh	22-Aug-1930	marathon	final		52	2h58m9.2					
Men	1952	Boxing	Mazumdar, Sakti M.	13-Nov-1931	fly	1/16 round			defeated/Nguyen Van, C. (Vie) ret.					
Men	1952	Boxing	Mazumdar, Sakti M.	13-Nov-1931	fly	1/8 round			lost to/Han, S. (Kor) 0:3					
Men	1988	Archery	Meena, Shyam Lal	4-Mar-1965	ind			71	1150	final				
Men	1988	Archery	Meena, Shyam Lal	4-Mar-1965	team			20	3615	final				
Men	1948	Cycling	Mehrah, Raj Kumar	16-Apr-1918	road/ind	final		dnf						

Men/ Women	*Year*	*Event*	*Name*	*DoB*	*Event*	*Stage*	*Race #*	*Rnk*	*Score-Result/Opponent/ Opposition*	*Misc*	*Misc*	*Misc*	*Medal*	*Other Sport*
Men	1952	Cycling	Mehrah, Raj Kumar	16-Apr-1918	4000m pursuit/ team	final		1rd.						
Men	1952	Cycling	Mehrah, Raj Kumar	16-Apr-1918	road/ind	final		ret.						
Men	1988	Table Tennis	Mehta, Kamlesh	1-May-1960	singles	1rd		4 pl.						
Men	1988	Table Tennis	Mehta, Kamlesh	1-May-1960	singles	1rd			defeated/Loukov, M. (Bul) 3:1					
Men	1988	Table Tennis	Mehta, Kamlesh	1-May-1960	singles	1rd			lost to/Kim, Ki Taik (Kor) 0:3					
Men	1988	Table Tennis	Mehta, Kamlesh	1-May-1960	singles	1rd			defeated/Gambra, J. (Chi) 3:0					
Men	1988	Table Tennis	Mehta, Kamlesh	1-May-1960	singles	1rd			lost to/Persson, J. (Swe) 1:3					
Men	1988	Table Tennis	Mehta, Kamlesh	1-May-1960	singles	1rd			lost to/Saito, K. (Jpn) 0:3					
Men	1988	Table Tennis	Mehta, Kamlesh	1-May-1960	singles	1rd			defeated/Elsaket, S. (Egy) 3:1					
Men	1988	Table Tennis	Mehta, Kamlesh	1-May-1960	singles	1rd			defeated/Molenda, P. (Pol) 3:1					
Men	1988	Table Tennis	Mehta, Kamlesh	1-May-1960	doubles	Prelim.		6 pl.		with Ghorpade, S.				
Men	1988	Table Tennis	Mehta, Kamlesh	1-May-1960	doubles	Prelim.			lost to/Lindh, E./ Persson, J. (Swe) 0:2	with Ghorpade, S.				

Men/ Women	Year	Event	Name	DoB	Event	Stage	Race #	Rnk	Score-Result/Opponent/ Opposition	Misc	Misc	Misc	Medal	Other Sport
Men	1988	Table Tennis	Mehta, Kamlesh	1-May-1960	doubles	Prelim.			lost to/Chen, Longcan/Wei, Qingguang (Chn) 0:2	with Ghorpade, S.				
Men	1988	Table Tennis	Mehta, Kamlesh	1-May-1960	doubles	Prelim.			lost to/Prean, C./ Cooke, A. (Gbr) 0:2	with Ghorpade, S.				
Men	1988	Table Tennis	Mehta, Kamlesh	1-May-1960	doubles	Prelim.			lost to/Ono, S./ Miyazaki, Y. (Jpn) 0:2	with Ghorpade, S.				
Men	1988	Table Tennis	Mehta, Kamlesh	1-May-1960	doubles	Prelim.			defeated/Ben Taiof, S./ Sta, N. (Tun) 2:0	with Ghorpade, S.				
Men	1988	Table Tennis	Mehta, Kamlesh	1-May-1960	doubles	Prelim.			defeated/Chan, Chi Ming/Liu, Fuk Man (Hkg) 2:0	with Ghorpade, S.				
Men	1988	Table Tennis	Mehta, Kamlesh	1-May-1960	doubles	Prelim.			lost to/Klampar, T./ Kriston, Z. (Hun) 1:2	with Ghorpade, S.				
Men	1992	Table Tennis	Mehta, Kamlesh	1-May-1960	doubles	Prelim.		4 pl.		with Ghorpade, S.				
Men	1992	Table Tennis	Mehta, Kamlesh	1-May-1960	doubles	Prelim.			lost to/Appelgren, M, AValdner, J. (Swe) 0:2 (-19, -16)	with Ghorpade, S.				
Men	1992	Table Tennis	Mehta, Kamlesh	1-May-1960	doubles	Prelim.			lost to/Grujic, S./ Lupulesku, I. IOP) 0:2 (-17, -14)	with Ghorpade, S.				
Men	1992	Table Tennis	Mehta, Kamlesh	1-May-1960	doubles	Prelim.			lost to/Hakamura, K./ Watanabe, T. (Jpn) 0:2 (-16, -16)	with Ghorpade, S.				

Men/ Women	*Year*	*Event*	*Name*	*DoB*	*Event*	*Stage*	*Race #*	*Rnk*	*Score-Result/Opponent/ Opposition*	*Misc*	*Misc*	*Misc*	*Medal*	*Other Sport*
Men	1992	Table Tennis	Mehta, Kamlesh	1-May-1960	singles	Prelim.		2 pl.						
Men	1992	Table Tennis	Mehta, Kamlesh	1-May-1960	singles	Prelim.			defeated/Lu, Lin (Chn) 2:0 (18, 16)					
Men	1992	Table Tennis	Mehta, Kamlesh	1-May-1960	singles	Prelim.			lost to/ Kim, Taek (Kor) 1:2 (-13, 18, -13)					
Men	1992	Table Tennis	Mehta, Kamlesh	1-May-1960	singles	Prelim.			defeated/Legdali, A. (Mar) 2:1 (-17, 20, 13)					
Women	1992	Judo	Mehta, Sangita	9-Sep-1966	heavy	ER			defeated/Yompakdee, S. (Tha) 3.35					
Men	1972	Boxing	Mehtabs Singh, Nghlwa	11-Nov-1948	light-heavy	1/16 round			lost to/Oliveira, V. (Bra) 0:5					
Men	2000	Hockey	Menezes, Jude	5-Aug-1971				7th	Group B 3rd(2W,1L,2D)					
Men	1948	Football	Mewalall, S.					2rd						
Men	1972	Hockey	Michael, Kindo	20-Jun-1947				3 pl.	9 games/3 goals				Bronze	
Men	1936	Hockey	Michie, Cyril James	28-Aug-1900				1 pl.	1 game				Gold	
Women	2000	Swimming	Millet, Nisha	20-Mar-1982	200m Freestyle	Prelims	1	1	02m08.89	split 2m08.89				
Men	1932	Hockey	Minhas, Masude Ali Khan					1 pl.	2 games				Gold	
Men	1948	Cycling	Mistry, E.		road/ind	final		dnf						
Women	2000	Athletics	Mistry, Rachita	4-Mar-1974	4x100m	Round 1	3	6	45.2					
Men	1948	Swimming	Mitra, Dilip		100m freestyle	heat		8	1m06.9					
Men	1948	Swimming	Mitra, Pratip		100m backstroke	heat		7	1m24.5					

Men/ Women	Year	Event	Name	DoB	Event	Stage	Race #	Rnk	Score-Result/Opponent/ Opposition	Misc	Misc	Misc	Medal	Other Sport
Men	1972	Sailing	Mogul, Tehmasp Rustom	19-Feb-1938	Finn			34	230/(31-34-30-dnf-30-dnf-34)					
Men	1980	Hockey	Mohamed, Shahid (Mohammad, Shahid)	14-Apr-1960				1 pl.	6 games/4 goals				Gold	
Men	1984	Hockey	Mohamed, Shahid (Mohammad, Shahid)	14-Apr-1960				5 pl.	7 games/3 goals					
Men	1988	Hockey	Mohamed, Shahid (Mohammad, Shahid)	14-Apr-1960				6 pl.	6 games/1 goal					
Men	2000	Hockey	Mohammed, Riaz Nabi (Riaz, Mohamed)	5-Jun-1972				7th	Group B 3rd (2W, 1L, 2D)					
Men	1988	Hockey	Mohinderpalsingh	16-Oct-1962				6 pl.	7 games/5 goals					
Men	1952	Football	Moinuddin, Syed Khaja	y1924				1rd						
Men	1972	Hockey	Mollerapoovayya, Ganesi	8-Jul-1948				3 pl.	9 games/1 goal				Bronze	
Men	1964	Gymnastics	Mondal, Darshan	7-Jun-1940	indiv.	final		128	54.7					
Men	1964	Gymnastics	Mondal, Darshan	7-Jun-1940	team	final		18	428.35					
Men	1972	Weightlifting	Mondal, Yanil Kumar (Mondal, Anil)	4-Aug-1951	fly			11	95+85+117.5=297.5					
Men	1976	Weightlifting	Mondal, Yanil Kumar (Mondal, Anil)	4-Aug-1951	fly			dsq	0+0					
Men	1956	Weightlifting	Mookan, Valli Asari	y1931	bantam			12	80+80+112.5=272.5					
Men	1964	Gymnastics	More, Yagmal	10-Sep-1944	indiv.	final		125	77.8					

Men/ Women	Year	Event	Name	DoB	Event	Stage	Race #	Rnk	Score-Result/Opponent/ Opposition	Misc	Misc	Misc	Medal	Other Sport
Men	1964	Gymnastics	More, Yagmal	10-Sep-1944	team	final		18	428.35					
Men	1928	Swimming	Mulji, D.D.		100m freestyle	dns								
Men	1928	Swimming	Mulji, D.D.		1500m freestyle	dns								
Men	1928	Swimming	Mulji, D.D.		400m freestyle	dns								
Men	1948	Cycling	Mullafiroze, R.		sprint	final result		1rd.						
Men	1948	Swimming	Mullick, P.		200m breast-stroke	heat		8	3m14.9					
Women	1980	Hockey	Mundphan, Rekha	3-Mar-1956				4 pl.	5 games					
Men	1980	Weightlifting	Muniswamy, Tamil Selvan	3-Feb-1955	bantam			el.	100+0					
Men	1948	Water polo	Murarji, D.		2nd rnd				1 game					
Men	1928	Athletics	Murphy, J.		4x400m	heat								
Men	1928	Athletics	Murphy, J.		800m	heat		7						
Men	2000	Weightlifting	Muthu, Thandava Murthy	21-Jan-1975	56	Final		16	245		sn: 110, c&j: 135	Bodywt: 55.9		
Men	1988	Weightlifting	Muthuswamy, Gurunathan	21-Jul-1963	fly			11	102.5+125=227.5					
Women	1960	Athletics	Mystri, Siloo	11-Aug-1935	100m	heat		dns						
Women	2004	Weightlifting	N Pratima Kumari	30-Jan-1976	63kg	Final		11	NR		Body Wt 63 kg			
Men	1992	Weightlifting	Naalamuthu Pillai, Sivaraj	25-Apr-1968	feather			22	115+140=255					

Men/ Women	*Year*	*Event*	*Name*	*DoB*	*Event*	*Stage*	*Race #*	*Rnk*	*Score-Result/Opponent/ Opposition*	*Misc*	*Misc*	*Misc*	*Medal*	*Other Sport*
Men	1952	Water polo	Naegamwalla, Jehangir J.		Prelim.				2 games					
Men	1948	Swimming	Nag, Sachindra N. (Nag, Sachin)	5-Jul-1920	100m freestyle	heat		6	1m03.8					
Men	1948	Water polo	Nag, Sachindra N. (Nag, Sachin)	5-Jul-1920	2nd rnd				3 games					
Men	1952	Water polo	Nag, Sachindra N. (Nag, Sachin)	5-Jul-1920	Prelim.				1 game					
Men	1980	Basketball	Nagarajan, Amarnath	2-Apr-1954				12 pl.	7 games, 36 pts.					
Men	1992	Hockey	Nandanoori, Mukesh KUB	16-Apr-1970				7 pl.	7 games/3 goals					
Men	2000	Hockey	Nandnoori, Mukesh Kumar(Nandonoori, Mukesh Kumar)	16-Apr-1970				7th	Group B 3rd(2W,1L,2D)		2			
Men	1996	Hockey	Nandonoori, Mukesh Kumar					8th Ov.	Group A 3rd (2W, 1L, 2D)					
Men	2004	Shooting	Narang, Gagan	6-May-1983	Air Rifle	Qualification		12	593					
Men	1956	Football	Narayan, Subramaniam Sankar	12-Nov-1934				4 pl.	2 games					
Men	1960	Football	Narayan, Subramaniam Sankar	12-Nov-1934				res.						
Men	1972	Boxing	Narayanan, Chander Hav	18-Aug-1947	fly	1/16 round			lost to/Blazynski, L. (Pol) 2:3					
Men	1960	Athletics	Nat, Jagmohan	1-Apr-1932	110m/h	heat		5	15.2					
Men	1920	Wrestling	Navale, Kumar		F/middle	2rd			lost to/Johnson, C. (USA) 6.47					

Men/ Women	Year	Event	Name	DoB	Event	Stage	Race #	Rnk	Score-Result/Opponent/ Opposition	Misc	Misc	Misc	Medal	Other Sport
Men	2000	Hockey	Nayak, Dinesh	17-May-1975				7th	Group B 3rd(2W,1L,2D)					
Men	1992	Hockey	Nayakar, Ravi	22-May-1971				7 pl.	5 games					
Women	1952	Swimming	Nazir, Dolly Rustom		100m freestyle	heat		7	1m24.6					
Women	1952	Swimming	Nazir, Dolly Rustom		200m breast-stroke	heat		7	3m37.9					
Women	1980	Hockey	Nelson, Eliza	27-Sep-1956				4 pl.	5 games					
Men	1960	Athletics	Nil Lal, Chand	19-Jul-1928	marathon	final		40	2h32m13.0					
Men	1936	Hockey	Nimal, Baboo Narsoo	15-Mar-1908				1 pl.	3 games				Gold	
Men	1948	Cycling	Noble, R.		4000m pursuit/ team	final		1rd.						
Men	1948	Cycling	Noble, R.		Time Trial	final		19	1m22.9					
Men	1956	Football	Noor, N. Muhamed	y1925				4 pl.	3 games					
Men	1928	Hockey	Norris, Rey A. (Norris, Rex A.)					1 pl.	5 games				Gold	
Men	1952	Boxing	Norris, Ron	10-Sep-1932	welter	1/8 round			defeated/Butula, J. (Can) tko. 3rd.					
Men	1952	Boxing	Norris, Ron	10-Sep-1932	welter	quarter			lost to/Jorgensen, V. (Den) 0:3					
Men	1956	Football	Nundu, Nikhil Kumar	y1932				4 pl.	2games					
Men	1948	Boxing	Nuttall, J.		middle	1/8 round			lost to/Fontana, I. (Ita)					

Men/ Women	Year	Event	Name	DoB	Event	Stage	Race #	Rnk	Score-Result/Opponent/ Opposition	Misc	Misc	Misc	Medal	Other Sport
Men	1984	Wrestling	Dutt, Sunil	9-Dec-1967	F/light-fly	1rd			lost to/Son, Gab Do (Kor) 0:4 (1.48)					
Men	1984	Wrestling	Dutt, Sunil	9-Dec-1967	F/light-fly	2rd			lost to/Andersson, K. (Swe) 1:3					
Men	1992	Tennis	Paes, Leander	17-Jun-1973	doubles	1rd			defeated/Bozic, I./ Trupej, B. (Slo) 6:3, 6:2, 6:2	with Krish-nan, R.				
Men	1992	Tennis	Paes, Leander	17-Jun-1973	singles	1rd			lost to/Yzaga, J. (Per) 6:1, 6:7, 0:6, 0:6					
Men	1992	Tennis	Paes, Leander	17-Jun-1973	doubles	2rd			defeated/Fitzgerald, J./ Woodbridge, T. (Aus) 6:4, 7:5, 4:6, 6:1	with Krish-nan, R.				
Men	1992	Tennis	Paes, Leander	17-Jun-1973	doubles	quarter			lost to/ Ivanisevic, G./ Prpic, G. (Cro) 6:7, 7:5, 4:6, 3:6	with K rishnan, R.				
Men	1996	Tennis	Paes, Leander	17-Jun-1973	Singles	1st Round		def.	Reneberg, Richey (USA)/ 6-7 (2-7) 7-6 (9-7) 1-0, ret.					
Men	1996	Tennis	Paes, Leander	17-Jun-1973	Singles	2nd Round		def.	Pereira, Nicolas (VEN)/ 6-2 6-3					
Men	1996	Tennis	Paes, Leander	17-Jun-1973	Singles	Quarter		def.	Furlan, Renzo (ITA)/ 6-1 7-5					
Men	1996	Tennis	Paes, Leander	17-Jun-1973	Singles	Bronze		def.	Meligeni, Fernando (BRA)/3-6 6-2 6-4				Bronze	
Men	1996	Tennis	Paes, Leander	17-Jun-1973	Singles	Third Round			lost to/Enqvist, Thomas (SWE)/ 5-7 6-7 (37)					
Men	1996	Tennis	Paes, Leander	17-Jun-1973	Singles	Semi			lost to/Agassi, Andre (USA)/ 6-7 (5-7) 3-6					

Men/ Women	Year	Event	Name	DoB	Event	Stage	Race #	Rnk	Score-Result/Opponent/ Opposition	Misc	Misc	Misc	Medal	Other Sport
Men	1996	Tennis	Paes, Leander	17-Jun-1973	Doubles	1st Round		def.	Pan, Bing/ Xia, Jia-Ping (CHN)/4-6 6-4 6-4	Bhupathi, Mahesh				
Men	1996	Tennis	Paes, Leander	17-Jun-1973	Doubles	2nd Round			lost to/Woodbridge, Todd/ Woodforde, Mark (AUS)/ 6-4 2-6 2-6	Bhupathi, Mahesh				
Men	2000	Tennis	Paes, Leander	17-Jun-1973	doubles	1st round		def.	Pavel, Andrei/ Trifu, Gabriel (ROM)/6-3, 6-4	Bhupathi, Mahesh				
Men	2000	Tennis	Paes, Leander	17-Jun-1973	doubles	1st round		def.	Pavel, Andrei/ Trifu, Gabriel (ROM)/ 6-3, 6-4	Bhupathi, Mahesh				
Men	2000	Tennis	Paes, Leander	17-Jun-1973	doubles	2nd round			lost to/Woodbridge, Todd/ Woodforde, Mark (AUS)/ 6-3, 7-6(1)	Bhupathi, Mahesh				
Men	2000	Tennis	Paes, Leander	17-Jun-1973	singles	1st round			lost to/Tillstrom, Mikael (SWE)/ 6-2, 6-4					
Men	2004	Tennis	Paes, Leander	17-Jun-1973	doubles	Quarter		def.	Black, Wayne/Ullyett, Kevin/ZIM	(2-0) : (6-4, 6-4)	Bhupathi, Mahesh			
Men	2004	Tennis	Paes, Leander	17-Jun-1973	doubles	2nd round		def.	Allegro, Yves/Federer, Roger/SUI	(2-0) : (6-2, 7-6(9-7))	Bhupathi, Mahesh			
Men	2004	Tennis	Paes, Leander	17-Jun-1973	doubles	1st round		def.	Fish, Mardy/Roddick, Andy/USA	(2-0) : (7-6(7-5), 6-3)	Bhupathi, Mahesh			
Men	2004	Tennis	Paes, Leander	17-Jun-1973	doubles	Bronze			lost to/Ancic, Mario/ Ljubicic, Ivan/CRO	(2-1) : (7-6(7-5), 4-6, 16-14)	Bhupathi, Mahesh			

Men/ Women	Year	Event	Name	DoB	Event	Stage	Race #	Rnk	Score-Result/Opponent/ Opposition	Misc	Misc	Misc	Medal	Other Sport
Men	2004	Tennis	Paes, Leander	17-Jun-1973	doubles	Semi			lost to/Kiefer, Nicolas/ Schuettler, Rainer/GER	(2-0) : (6-2, 6-3)	Bhu-pathi, Mahesh			
Men	1980	Hockey	Pal Singh, Ravinder (Singh, Ravinder Pal)	6-Sep-1960				1 pl.	6 games				Gold	
Men	1984	Hockey	Pal Singh, Ravinder (Singh, Ravinder Pal)	6-Sep-1960				5 pl.	2 games					
Men	1964	Athletics	Pal, Amrit	5-Jun-1939	400m/h	heat		7	53.3					
Men	1964	Athletics	Pal, Amrit	5-Jun-1939	4x400m	heat		4	3m08.8					
Men	1956	Football	Pal, Krishna Chandra	y1934				4 pl.	1 game					
Men	2004	Rowing	Pandari Kunnel, Paulose	21-May-1977	Single Sculls	Heats	Heat 3	5	8m0.12/bow	1m49.38	3m48.96	5m 56.57		
Men	2004	Rowing	Pandari Kunnel, Paulose	21-May-1977	Single Sculls	Heats	Repe-chage 1	4	7m29.45/bow	1m42.55	3m35.82	5m 35.83		
Men	2004	Rowing	Pandari Kunnel, Paulose	21-May-1977	Single Sculls	final D/E/F - Race 2		5	7m48.37/bow	1m48.51	3m40.83	5m 42.48		
Men	2004	Rowing	Pandari Kunnel, Paulose	21-May-1977	Single Sculls	Final E		3	7m22.62/bow	1m43.33	3m33.14	5m 29.61		
Men	1956	Wrestling	Pandey, Lakshmi Kant	y1936	F/light	1rd			lost to/Nizzola, G. (Ita) 9.30					
Men	1956	Wrestling	Pandey, Lakshmi Kant	y1936	F/light	2rd			lost to/Guengoer, R. (Tur) 3:0					
Men	1956	Wrestling	Pandey, Tarakeshwar	y1936	F/bantam	1rd			lost to/Kammerer, F. (Ger) 3:0					
Men	1956	Wrestling	Pandey, Tarakeshwar	y1936	F/bantam	2rd			defeated/Vercauteren, O. (Bel) 0:3					
Men	1956	Wrestling	Pandey, Tarakeshwar	y1936	F/bantam	3rd			lost to/Yaghoubi, M. (Irn) 2.36					

Men/ Women	*Year*	*Event*	*Name*	*DoB*	*Event*	*Stage*	*Race #*	*Rnk*	*Score-Result/Opponent/ Opposition*	*Misc*	*Misc*	*Misc*	*Medal*	*Other Sport*
Women	1988	Athletics	Pandurang Shanbagh, Vandana	19-Sep-1963	4x400m	heat		7	3m33.46					
Men	1948	Football	Parab, R.B.					2rd						
Men	1980	Basketball	Paramdip, Singh	31-Oct-1952				12 pl.	7 games, 17 pts.					
Men	1980	Basketball	Paramjit, Singh	30-Dec-1952				12 pl.	7 games, 63 pts.					
Men	1988	Hockey	Pargat, Singh	5-Mar-1965				6 pl.	7 games					
Mixed	2004	Sailing	Patel, Sumeet	19-Oct-1969	Open Double-handed Dinghy-49er	Overall		19	253/292	17,(19),18, 15,18,19,1 8,19,19,19, 18,19,(20), 19,17,18	C	Shroff, Malav		
Men	1960	Hockey	Patil, Bandhu(Patil, Bandu)	1-Jan-1936				res.						
Men	1964	Hockey	Patil, Bandhu(Patil, Bandu)	1-Jan-1936				1 pl.	2 games				Gold	
Men	1964	Wrestling	Patil, Bandu	16-Sep-1942	F/feather	1rd			Jaskari,T.(Fin)2:2					
Men	1964	Wrestling	Patil, Bandu	16-Sep-1942	GR/feather	1rd			lost to/Mewis, J. (Bel) 4:0 (1.10)					
Men	1964	Wrestling	Patil, Bandu	16-Sep-1942	F/feather	2rd			lost to/Douglas, B. (USA) 4:0 (8.07)					
Men	1964	Wrestling	Patil, Bandu	16-Sep-1942	GR/feather	2rd			lost to/Macioch, K. (Pol) 4:0 (default)					
Men	1948	Cycling	Pavri.H.		road/ind	final		dnf						
Men	1952	Hockey	Perumal, Govind	y1928				1 pl.	3 games				Gold	
Men	1956	Hockey	Perumal, Govind	y1928				1 pl.	4 games				Gold	

Men/ Women	*Year*	*Event*	*Name*	*DoB*	*Event*	*Stage*	*Race #*	*Rnk*	*Score-Result/Opponent/ Opposition*	*Misc*	*Misc*	*Misc*	*Medal*	*Other Sport*
Men	1980	Athletics	Perumal, Subramanian	12-Aug-1955	200m	heat		5	22.39					
Men	1960	Hockey	Peter, John Victor	19-Jun-1937				2 pl.	6 games/2 goals				Silver	
Men	1964	Hockey	Peter, John Victor	19-Jun-1937				1 pl.	6 games/1 goal				Gold	
Men	1968	Hockey	Peter, John Victor	19-Jun-1937				3 pl.	8 games				Bronze	
Women	2000	Athletics	Phillip, Jincy	12-Apr-1977	4x400m	Round 1	2	5	03m31.46					
Men	1948	Athletics	Phillips, E. (Phillips, Rajamicka)	y1925	100m	heat		2	11					
Men	1948	Athletics	Phillips, E. (Phillips, Rajamicka)	y1925	200m	heat		5						
Men	1948	Athletics	Phillips, E. (Phillips, Rajamicka)	y1925	100m	Round 2		6						
Men	1936	Hockey	Phillips, Joseph	24-Mar-1911				1 pl.	1 game				Gold	
Men	1972	Hockey	Phillips, V.J.	1-Sep-1949				dns						
Men	1976	Hockey	Phillips, Vaduvelu	1-Sep-1950				7 pl.	7 games/3 goals					
Men	1964	Athletics	Pichaya, Rajasekaran	3-Jan-1941	4x100m	heat		5	40.60					
Men	1964	Athletics	Pichaya, Rajasekaran	3-Jan-1941	4x100m	semi		7	40.50					
Men	1996	Hockey	Pillay, Dhanraj (Pillai, Dhanraj)	16-Jul-1968				8th Ov.	Group A 3rd (2W, 1L, 2D)					
Men	2000	Hockey	Pillay, Dhanraj (Pillai, Dhanraj)	16-Jul-1968				7th	Group B 3rd(2W,1L,2D)					
Men	2004	Hockey	Pillay, Dhanraj (Pillai, Dhanraj)	16-Jul-1968		Prelim.	B	7	Prelim. 4th (W1, L3, D1)/ Classification 7-8 def. KOR 5-2		7 games, 2 goals			

Men/ Women	*Year*	*Event*	*Name*	*DoB*	*Event*	*Stage*	*Race #*	*Rnk*	*Score-Result/Opponent/ Opposition*	*Misc*	*Misc*	*Misc*	*Medal*	*Other Sport*
Men	2004	Hockey	Pillay, Vikram	27-Nov-1981		Prelim.	B	7	Prelim. 4th (W1, L3, D1)/ Classification 7-8 def. KOR 5-2		7 games, 1 goal			
Men	1988	Boxing	Pingale, Manoj	22-Oct-1967	fly	1/16 round			defeated/Chongo, J. (Zam) 5:0					
Men	1988	Boxing	Pingale, Manoj	22-Oct-1967	fly	1/8 round			lost to/Gonzalez, M. (Mex) 1:4					
Men	1928	Hockey	Pinniger, Broome Eric (Pinninger, Broome Eric)	28-Dec-1902				1 pl.	5 games				Gold	
Men	1932	Hockey	Pinniger, Broome Eric (Pinninger, Broome Eric)	28-Dec-1902				1 pl.	2 games				Gold	
Men	1936	Hockey	Pinniger, Broome Eric (Pinninger, Broome Eric)	28-Dec-1902				res.						
Men	1952	Athletics	Pinto, Lavy Thomas	23-Oct-1929	100m	heat		2	10.9					
Men	1952	Athletics	Pinto, Lavy Thomas	23-Oct-1929	200m	heat		1	21.6					
Men	1952	Athletics	Pinto, Lavy Thomas	23-Oct-1929	100m	Round 2		3	10.7					
Men	1952	Athletics	Pinto, Lavy Thomas	23-Oct-1929	200m	Round 2		2	21.6					
Men	1952	Athletics	Pinto, Lavy Thomas	23-Oct-1929	100m	semi		4	10.7					
Men	1952	Athletics	Pinto, Lavy Thomas	23-Oct-1929	200m	semi		5	21.7					
Men	1948	Hockey	Pinto, Leo					1 pl.	3 games				Gold	

Men/ Women	*Year*	*Event*	*Name*	*DoB*	*Event*	*Stage*	*Race #*	*Rnk*	*Score-Result/Opponent/ Opposition*	*Misc*	*Misc*	*Misc*	*Medal*	*Other Sport*
Men	1924	Athletics	Pitt, Terence K. (Pitt, J.K.)	y1903	4x400m	final		dns						
Men	1924	Athletics	Pitt, Terence K. (Pitt, J.K.)	y1903	100m	heat		3						
Men	1924	Athletics	Pitt, Terence K. (Pitt, J.K.)	y1903	200m	heat		3						
Men	1924	Athletics	Pitt, Terence K. (Pitt, J.K.)	y1903	400m	heat		1	49.80					
Men	1924	Athletics	Pitt, Terence K. (Pitt, J.K.)	y1903	400m	Round 2		4	51.5					
Women	1924	Tennis	Polley, V.	y1893	mixed	1/8rd			lost to/Wallis, M./ McCrea, E. (Irl) 7:9, 6:4, 7:9	with Jacob, S.				
Women	1924	Tennis	Polley, V.	y1893	singles	1/8rd			lost to/Alvarez, E. (Esp) 0:6, 3:6					
Women	1924	Tennis	Polley, V.	y1893	singles	2rd			defeated/Valaoriti Scaramanga, L. (Gre) 1:6, 6:3, 6:2					
Men	1992	Hockey	Poonacha, Cheppudira Subbaih	18-Aug-1965				7 pl.	4 games					
Women	2000	Badminton	Popat, Aparna	18-Jan-1978	Singles	Round of 64			lost to/Morgan, Kelly (GBR)/11-5 7-11 2-11					
Women	2004	Badminton	Popat, Aparna	18-Jan-1978	Singles	Round of 32	Un-seeded	def.	Edwards, Michelle (RSA)/ Seed 4	11-6 11-3 (23')				
Women	2004	Badminton	Popat, Aparna	18-Jan-1978	Singles	Round of 16	Seed 4		lost to/Audina, Mia (ED)/ Unseeded	9-11 11-1 11-3 (43')				
Men	1992	Hockey	Powar, Pargat Singh	5-Mar-1965				7 pl.	7 games/2 goals					

Men/ Women	*Year*	*Event*	*Name*	*DoB*	*Event*	*Stage*	*Race #*	*Rnk*	*Score-Result/Opponent/ Opposition*	*Misc*	*Misc*	*Misc*	*Medal*	*Other Sport*
Men	1996	Hockey	Powar, Pargat Singh	5-Mar-1965				8th Ov.	Group A 3rd (2W, 1L, 2D)					
Men	1964	Athletics	Powell, Kenneth Lawrence	20-Apr-1940	100m	heat		4	10.7					
Men	1964	Athletics	Powell, Kenneth Lawrence	20-Apr-1940	200m	heat		6	21.9					
Men	1964	Athletics	Powell, Kenneth Lawrence	20-Apr-1940	4x100m	heat		5	40.6					
Men	1964	Athletics	Powell, Kenneth Lawrence	20-Apr-1940	4x100m	semi		7	40.5					
Men	1984	Boxing	Pradhan, Jaslal	24-Apr-1957	light-welter	1/32 round			lost to/Umponmaha, D. (Tha) 0:5					
Men	1964	Diving	Prasad, Ansuya	17-Aug-1936	3m Spring-board	final		25	69.04					
Men	1992	Athletics	Prasad, Bahadur	1-Sep-1965	5000m	heat		8	13m50.71					
Men	1996	Athletics	Prasad, Bahadur	1-Sep-1965	1500m	Round 1	5	8	3m46.16					
Men	2004	Boxing	Prasad, Diwakar	6-Sep-1984	51-54kg	Round of 16			lost to /Bolum, Nestor/ NIG	TKO	Stopped by referee due to superior-ity, round 3)			
Men	2004	Boxing	Prasad, Diwakar	6-Sep-1984	51-54kg	Round of 32			def./Ait Bighrade, Hamid/MAR	(25-17)				
Men	1948	Football	Prasad, M.					2rd						
Men	1992	Boxing	Prasad, Rajendra	17-Nov-1972	light-fly	1/16 round			defeated/ Rzany, A. (Pol) 12:6					
Men	1992	Boxing	Prasad, Rajendra	17-Nov-1972	light-fly	1/8 round			lost to/ Velasco, R. (Phi) 6:15					

Men/ Women	*Year*	*Event*	*Name*	*DoB*	*Event*	*Stage*	*Race #*	*Rnk*	*Score-Result/Opponent/ Opposition*	*Misc*	*Misc*	*Misc*	*Medal*	*Other Sport*
Men	2004	Archery	Prasad, Satyadev	19-Sep-1979	Indiv.	Ranking		48	634					
Men	2004	Archery	Prasad, Satyadev	19-Sep-1979	Indiv.	Round of 64			def./Hamano, Yuji (JPN)	155-150				
Men	2004	Archery	Prasad, Satyadev	19-Sep-1979	Indiv.	Round of 32			def./Van Der Hoff, Ron (NED)	158-155				
Men	2004	Archery	Prasad, Satyadev	19-Sep-1979	Indiv.	Round of 16			lost to/Im Dong Hyun (KOR)	165-167				
Men	2004	Archery	Prasad, Satyadev	19-Sep-1979	Team	Ranking		10	1938					
Men	2004	Archery	Prasad, Satyadev	19-Sep-1979	Team	Round of 16			lost to/AUS	236-248				
Men	1972	Wrestling	Premnath, Prem	9-Jul-1955	F/ bantam	1rd			defeated/Barry, R. (Aus) 0:4 (8.37)					
Men	1972	Wrestling	Premnath, Prem	9-Jul-1955	F/ bantam	2rd			defeated/Fuentes Gonzalez, L. (Gua) 1:3					
Men	1972	Wrestling	Premnath, Prem	9-Jul-1955	F/ bantam	3rd			defeated/Sideer, G. (Afg) 0:4 (6.39)					
Men	1972	Wrestling	Premnath, Prem	9-Jul-1955	F/ bantam	4rd			defeated/Maggiolo, E. (Arg) 0:4 (4.33)					
Men	1972	Wrestling	Premnath, Prem	9-Jul-1955	F/ bantam	5rd			lost to/Sanders, R. (USA) 4:0 (6.47)					
Men	1972	Wrestling	Premnath, Prem	9-Jul-1955	F/ bantam	6rd			bye					
Men	1972	Wrestling	Premnath, Prem	9-Jul-1955	F/ bantam	7rd			lost to/Yanagida, H. (Jpn) 4:0 (5.10)					
Men	1972	Wrestling	Premnath, Prem	9-Jul-1955	F/ bantam			4 pl.						

Men/ Women	*Year*	*Event*	*Name*	*DoB*	*Event*	*Stage*	*Race #*	*Rnk*	*Score-Result/Opponent/ Opposition*	*Misc*	*Misc*	*Misc*	*Medal*	*Other Sport*
Men	1956	Gymnastics	Pritam Singh	y1924	indiv.	final		61	77.35					
Men	**1900**	**Athletics**	**Pritchard, Norman D.**		**110m/h**	**final**		**5**						
Men	**1900**	**Athletics**	**Pritchard, Norman D.**		**200m**	**final**		**2**					**Silver**	
Men	**1900**	**Athletics**	**Pritchard, Norman D.**		**200m/h**	**final**		**2**					**Silver**	
Men	**1900**	**Athletics**	**Pritchard, Norman D.**		**60m**	**final**		**4**	**7.2**					
Men	**1900**	**Athletics**	**Pritchard, Norman D.**		**100m**	**heat**		**1**	**11.4**					
Men	**1900**	**Athletics**	**Pritchard, Norman D.**		**110m/h**	**heat**		**1**	**16.60**					
Men	**1900**	**Athletics**	**Pritchard, Norman D.**		**200m/h**	**heat**		**1**	**26.2**					
Men	**1900**	**Athletics**	**Pritchard, Norman D.**		**100m**	**repe.**		**2**						
Men	**1900**	**Athletics**	**Pritchard, Norman D.**		**100m**	**Round 2**		**3**						
Men	2000	Badminton	Pullela, Gopi Chand	16-Nov-1973	Singles	Round of 16			lost to /Hendrawan (INA)/9-15 4-15					
Men	2000	Badminton	Pullela, Gopi Chand	16-Nov-1973	Singles	Round of 32		def.	Druzhchenko, Vladyslav (UKR)/15-3 10-15 15-7					
Men	1988	Swimming	Punja, Ranjoy	19-Oct-1966	100m backstroke	heat		dns						
Women	1996	Swimming	Puri, Sangeeta	14-Dec-1979	50M Freestyle	Heat	1	2	28.02					

Men/ Women	*Year*	*Event*	*Name*	*DoB*	*Event*	*Stage*	*Race #*	*Rnk*	*Score-Result/Opponent/ Opposition*	*Misc*	*Misc*	*Misc*	*Medal*	*Other Sport*
Men	1980	Basketball	Radhey, Shyam	1-May-1953				12 pl.	7 games, 107 pts.					
Women	1996	Table tennis	Radhika, Ambika		Singles	Group N			lost to/Vriesekoop, Huberta (NED)/21-8 21-6					
Women	1996	Table tennis	Radhika, Ambika		Singles	Group N			lost to/Badescu, Otilia (ROM)/ 21-17 21-3					
Women	1996	Table tennis	Radhika, Ambika		Singles	Group N			lost to/Garkauskaite, Ruta (LTU)/21-13 21-13					
Men	1960	Athletics	Ragho, Jagmal	20-Mar-1923	marathon	final		45	2h35m1.2					
Men	1956	Football	Rahaman, T. Abdul	y1934				4 pl.	2 games					
Men	1992	Hockey	Rai, Jagdev Singh	8-Jul-1969				7 pl.	1 game					
Men	2000	Athletics	Rai, Sanjay K	1-May-1979	Long	qu	A	-	NM					
Men	1996	Weightlifting	Rai, Satheesha		76			15	317.5/sn - 140	cj - 177.5				
Men	1976	Boxing	Rai, Sen K.		feather	1/16 round			lost to/Herrera, A. (Cub) ko. 1rd. (1.43)					
Men	1976	Boxing	Rai, Sen K.		feather	1/32 round			defeated/Andeh, D. (Ngr) w.o.					
Men	2004	Archery	Rai, Tarundeep	22-Feb-1984	Indiv.	Ranking		32	647					
Men	2004	Archery	Rai, Tarundeep	22-Feb-1984	Indiv.	Round of 64			lost to/Karageorgiou, Alexandros (GRE)	143-147				
Men	2004	Archery	Rai, Tarundeep	22-Feb-1984	Team	Ranking		10	1938					

Men/ Women	Year	Event	Name	DoB	Event	Stage	Race #	Rnk	Score-Result/Opponent/ Opposition	Misc	Misc	Misc	Medal	Other Sport
Men	2004	Archery	Rai, Tarundeep	22-Feb-1984	Team	Round of 16			lost to/AUS	236-248				
Men	1952	Hockey	Rajagopal, Muniswamy	31-Mar-1925				1 pl.	3 games				Gold	
Men	1980	Wrestling	Rajender Singh (Singh Rajender)	1-Aug-1954	F/welter	1rd			defeated/Steingraber, R. (GDR) 1:3					
Men	1980	Wrestling	Rajender Singh (Singh Rajender)	1-Aug-1954	F/welter	2rd			defeated/Fawaz, B. (Syr) 0:4 (0.55)					
Men	1980	Wrestling	Rajender Singh (Singh Rajender)	1-Aug-1954	F/welter	3rd			lost to/Niccolini, R. (Ita) 3:1					
Men	1980	Wrestling	Rajender Singh (Singh Rajender)	1-Aug-1954	F/welter	4rd			lost to/Raitchev, V. (Bul) 3:1					
Men	1980	Wrestling	Rajender Singh (Singh Rajender)	1-Aug-1954	F/welter			6 pl.						
Men	1984	Wrestling	Rajender Singh (Singh Rajender)	1-Aug-1954	F/welter	1rd			defeated/Higuchi, N. (Jpn) 3:1					
Men	1984	Wrestling	Rajender Singh (Singh Rajender)	1-Aug-1954	F/welter	2rd			defeated/Zayar, M. (Irq) 3:1					
Men	1984	Wrestling	Rajender Singh (Singh Rajender)	1-Aug-1954	F/welter	3/4 place			lost to/Sejdi, S. (Yug) 1:3					
Men	1984	Wrestling	Rajender Singh (Singh Rajender)	1-Aug-1954	F/welter	3rd			defeated/Olawale, S. (Ngr) 3:1					
Men	1984	Wrestling	Rajender Singh (Singh Rajender)	1-Aug-1954	F/welter	4rd			lost to/Knosp, M. (Frg) 0:4 (1.31)					
Men	1984	Wrestling	Rajender Singh (Singh Rajender)	1-Aug-1954	F/welter	5rd			defeated/Mongeon, M. (Can) 3.5:0					
Men	1984	Wrestling	Rajender Singh (Singh Rajender)	1-Aug-1954	F/welter			4 pl.						

Men/ Women	*Year*	*Event*	*Name*	*DoB*	*Event*	*Stage*	*Race #*	*Rnk*	*Score-Result/Opponent/ Opposition*	*Misc*	*Misc*	*Misc*	*Medal*	*Other Sport*
Men	1988	Hockey	Rajinder Singh, Rawat	30-Jan-1964				6 pl.	6 games					
Men	1948	Hockey	Rajput, Jaswant					1 pl.	1 game				Gold	
Men	1956	Athletics	Ram Mehar, N.	y1934	long	final		dnq						
Men	1964	Gymnastics	Ram, Anant	21-Oct-1932	indiv.	final		126	66.5					
Men	1964	Gymnastics	Ram, Anant	21-Oct-1932	team	final		18	428.35					
Men	1960	Football	Ram, Bahadur Chhettri	15-Feb-1937				ER	2 games					
Men	1984	Athletics	Ram, Chand	26-Jan-1958	20000 walk	final		22	1h30m6					
Men	1952	Gymnastics	Ram, Khushi	15-Jan-1916	indiv.	final		185	29.75					
Men	1956	Wrestling	Ram, Lila		F/heavy	1rd			lost to/Richmond, K. (Gbr) 3:0					
Men	1956	Wrestling	Ram, Lila		F/heavy	2rd			lost to/Kaplan, H. (Tur) 14.45					
Men	1960	Hockey	Ram, Shanta	1-May-1931				res.						
Men	2000	Athletics	Ramachandran, P	20-May-1971	4x400m	Round 1	2	4	03m08.38					
Men	1948	Football	Raman, S. (Raman, Dhanraj)					2rd						
Men	2004	Wrestling	Ramesh Kumar, NA (Ramesh Kumar)	15-Nov-1981	66kg Freestyle	Prelim.	Pool 3	4	11/Classif.: 1+3	Tech: 8+3				
Men	1996	Shooting	Rana, Jaspal		10M Air Pistol	Prelims.		34	574					

Men/ Women	*Year*	*Event*	*Name*	*DoB*	*Event*	*Stage*	*Race #*	*Rnk*	*Score-Result/Opponent/ Opposition*	*Misc*	*Misc*	*Misc*	*Medal*	*Other Sport*
Men	1996	Shooting	Rana, Jaspal		50M Free Pistol	Prelims.		45	534					
Men	1960	Athletics	Randhava, Gurbachan Singh	6-Jun-1939	decathlon	final		ret.	4106.0					
Men	1960	Athletics	Randhava, Gurbachan Singh	6-Jun-1939	high	qu			1.9					
Men	1964	Athletics	Randhava, Gurbachan Singh	6-Jun-1939	110m/h	final		5	14					
Men	1964	Athletics	Randhava, Gurbachan Singh	6-Jun-1939	110m/h	heat		4	14.3					
Men	1964	Athletics	Randhava, Gurbachan Singh	6-Jun-1939	110m/h	semi		2	14.0					
Men	1964	Shooting	Randhir, Singh	18-Oct-1946	clay pigeon			dns						
Men	1968	Shooting	Randhir, Singh	18-Oct-1946	Trap			17	192					
Men	1972	Shooting	Randhir, Singh	18-Oct-1946	Trap			44	173					
Men	1976	Shooting	Randhir, Singh	18-Oct-1946	Trap			21	175					
Men	1980	Shooting	Randhir, Singh	18-Oct-1946	Trap			21	186					
Men	1984	Shooting	Randhir, Singh	18-Oct-1946	Trap			35	176					
Men	1992	Weightlifting	Rangaswamy, Ponnuswamy	13-Aug-1964	bantam			18	102.5+127.5=230					
Men	1980	Athletics	Ranjit, Singh	25-Nov-1957	20000 walk	final		18	1h38m27.2					

Men/ Women	*Year*	*Event*	*Name*	*DoB*	*Event*	*Stage*	*Race #*	*Rnk*	*Score-Result/Opponent/ Opposition*	*Misc*	*Misc*	*Misc*	*Medal*	*Other Sport*
Men	1988	Sailing	Rao, Kelly Subbanand	17-Jan-1963	470			17	170.7/(19-20-19-6-ret.-20-15)					
Men	1992	Sailing	Rao, Kelly Subbanand	17-Jan-1963	dns									
Women	1956	Athletics	Rao, Mary Leela	y1940	100m	heat		dns						
Women	1956	Athletics	Rao, Mary Leela	y1940	100m			dnf						
Women	1984	Athletics	Rao, Vandana	21-Apr-1963	4x400m	final		7	3m32.49					
Women	1984	Athletics	Rao, Vandana	21-Apr-1963	4x400m	heat		4	3m33.85					
Women	1988	Athletics	Rao, Vandana	21-Apr-1963	4x400m	heat		7	3m33.46					
Men	2004	Hockey	Rasquinha, Viren	13-Sep-1980		Prelim.	B	7	Prelim. 4th (W1, L3, D1)/ Classification 7-8 def. KOR 5-2					
Men	1936	Wrestling	Rasul, Karam Kashmiri	17-May-1911	F/middle	1rd			defeated/Rihetzky, J. (Hun) 3:1					
Men	1936	Wrestling	Rasul, Karam Kashmiri	17-May-1911	F/middle	2rd			lost to/ Voliva, R. (USA) 3:1					
Men	1980	Basketball	Rathore Han, Uman Singh	16-Dec-1950				12 pl.	5 games, 10 pts.					
Men	2004	Shooting	Rathore, Rajyavardhan S.	29-Jan-1970	Double Trap	Qualification		4	135/Q					
Men	2004	Shooting	Rathore, Rajyavardhan S.	29-Jan-1970	Double Trap	Final		2	44	Total= 179			Silver	
Women	1984	Athletics	Rawat, Suman	6-Mar-1961	1500m	heat		dns						
Men	1948	Boxing	Raymond, G.		light	1/16 round			lost to/Wad, S. (Den)					
Men	1948	Athletics	Rebello, Henry		triple	final		0						

Men/ Women	*Year*	*Event*	*Name*	*DoB*	*Event*	*Stage*	*Race #*	*Rnk*	*Score-Result/Opponent/ Opposition*	*Misc*	*Misc*	*Misc*	*Medal*	*Other Sport*
Men	1948	Athletics	Rebello, Henry		triple	qu			14.65					
Men	1968	Hockey	Rehman, Inamur	23-Nov-1943				3 pl.	2 games				Bronze	
Men	1948	Hockey	Rehman, Latifur	1-Jan-1929				1 pl.	1 game				Gold	
Men	1996	Hockey	Riaz, Mohamed					8th Ov.	Group A 3rd (2W, 1L, 2D)					
Women	1980	Athletics	Rilavulakandi, T. Usha (Pilavulakandi, T. Usha)	20-May-1964	100m	heat		6	12.27					
Women	1980	Athletics	Rilavulakandi, T. Usha (Pilavulakandi, T. Usha)	20-May-1964	200m	heat		7	25.16					
Women	1984	Athletics	Rilavulakandi, T. Usha (Pilavulakandi, T. Usha)	20-May-1964	400m/h	final		4	55.42					
Women	1984	Athletics	Rilavulakandi, T. Usha (Pilavulakandi, T. Usha)	20-May-1964	4x400m	final		7	3m32.49					
Women	1984	Athletics	Rilavulakandi, T. Usha (Pilavulakandi, T. Usha)	20-May-1964	400m/h	heat		2	56.81					
Women	1984	Athletics	Rilavulakandi, T. Usha(Pilavulakandi, T. Usha)	20-May-1964	4x400m	heat		4	3m33.85					
Women	1984	Athletics	Rilavulakandi, T. Usha (Pilavulakandi, T. Usha)	20-May-1964	400m/h	semi		1	55.54					

Men/ Women	*Year*	*Event*	*Name*	*DoB*	*Event*	*Stage*	*Race #*	*Rnk*	*Score-Result/Opponent/ Opposition*	*Misc*	*Misc*	*Misc*	*Medal*	*Other Sport*
Women	1988	Athletics	Rilavulakandi, T. Usha (Pilavulakandi, T. Usha)	20-May-1964	400m/h	heat		7	59.55					
Men	1928	Hockey	Rocque, Michael E.					1 pl.	5 games				Gold	
Men	1948	Hockey	Rodrigues, Reginald					1 pl.	1 game				Gold	
Women	1988	Table Tennis	Roy Shah, Niyati C.	30-Sep-1965	singles	1rd		6 pl.						
Women	1988	Table Tennis	Roy Shah, Niyati C.	30-Sep-1965	singles	1rd			lost to/Boulatova, F. (URS) 0:3					
Women	1988	Table Tennis	Roy Shah, Niyati C.	30-Sep-1965	singles	1rd			lost to/Bogaerts, K. (Bel) 0:3					
Women	1988	Table Tennis	Roy Shah, Niyati C.	30-Sep-1965	singles	1rd			lost to/Hrachova, M. (Tch) 0:3					
Women	1988	Table Tennis	Roy Shah, Niyati C.	30-Sep-1965	singles	1rd			lost to/Leong, Mee Wan (Mal) 0:3					
Women	1988	Table Tennis	Roy Shah, Niyati C.	30-Sep-1965	singles	1rd			lost to/Chang, Hsiu-Yu (Tpe) 0:3					
Women	1992	Table Tennis	Roy Shah, Niyati C.	30-Sep-1965	singles	Prelim.		3 pl.						
Women	1992	Table Tennis	Roy Shah, Niyati C.	30-Sep-1965	singles	Prelim.			lost to/Badescu, O. (Rom) 0:2 (-10, -14)					
Women	1992	Table Tennis	Roy Shah, Niyati C.	30-Sep-1965	singles	Prelim.			lost to/Fazlic, J. (IOP) 0:2 (-12, -16)					
Women	1992	Table Tennis	Roy Shah, Niyati C.	30-Sep-1965	singles	Prelim.			defeated/Ramirez, M. (Cub) 2:0 (13, 12)					
Men	1948	Wrestling	Roy, K.P.		F/middle	1rd			lost to/Vachon, M. (Can) fall 0.54					

Men/ Women	*Year*	*Event*	*Name*	*DoB*	*Event*	*Stage*	*Race #*	*Rnk*	*Score-Result/Opponent/ Opposition*	*Misc*	*Misc*	*Misc*	*Medal*	*Other Sport*
Men	1948	Wrestling	Roy, K.P.		F/middle	2rd			lost to/Arthur, R. (Aus) fall 40.15					
Men	1924	Tennis	Rutnam, David	y1901	doubles	1/8rd			defeated/Sabbadini, R./ Colombo, C. (Ita) w.o.	with Hadi, S.				
Men	1924	Tennis	Rutnam, David	y1901	doubles	2rd			defeated/ Nielsen, J./ Langaard, C. (Nor) 6:2, 6:3, 6:0	with Hadi, S.				
Men	1924	Tennis	Rutnam, David	y1901	doubles	quarter			lost to/ Borotra, J./ Lacosle, J. (Fra) 2:6, 2:6, 3:6	with Hadi, S.				
Women	1952	Swimming	Saha, Arati		200m breast-stroke	heat		6	3m40.8					
Men	1952	Water polo	Saha, Sambhu	1-Nov-1925	Prelim.				2 games					
Women	2004	Athletics	Saha, Saraswati	23-Jan-1979	200m	Round 1	Heat 3	5	23.43					
Men	1980	Athletics	Saini, Gopal	18-Apr-1954	5000m	heat		9	14m06.6					
Women	1980	Hockey	Saini, Rup Kumari	2-Sep-1954				4 pl.	5 games/4 goals					
Men	1968	Hockey	Sait, Munir	27-May-1940				3 pl.	7 games				Bronze	
Men	1960	Wrestling	Sajjan, Singh	24-Apr-1932	F/light-heavy	1rd			defeated/Marcucci, A. (Ita) 1:3					
Men	1960	Wrestling	Sajjan, Singh	24-Apr-1932	F/light-heavy	2rd			defeated/Rauchbach, D. (Ger) 0:4 (3.45)					
Men	1960	Wrestling	Sajjan, Singh	24-Apr-1932	F/light-heavy	3rd			lost to/Gurics, G. (Hun) 4:0 (3.37)					
Men	1960	Wrestling	Sajjan, Singh	24-Apr-1932	F/light-heavy	4rd			lost to/Palm, V. (Swe) 3:1					

Men/ Women	*Year*	*Event*	*Name*	*DoB*	*Event*	*Stage*	*Race #*	*Rnk*	*Score-Result/Opponent/ Opposition*	*Misc*	*Misc*	*Misc*	*Medal*	*Other Sport*
Men	1956	Football	Salam, Muhamed Abdus(Salaam, Muhamed Abdus)	y1931				4 pl.	2 games					
Men	1984	Shooting	Samai, Bhagirath	11-Aug-1957	air rifle			39	562					
Men	1984	Shooting	Samai, Bhagirath	11-Aug-1957	small bore rifle			45	583					
Women	2000	Weightlifting	Sanamacha Chanu, Thingbaijam (Chanu, Thing Baijan Sanamacha)	2-Oct-1978	53	Final		6	195		sn: 85, c&j: 110	Bodywt: 52.16		
Women	2004	Weightlifting	Sanamacha Chanu, Thingbaijam (Chanu, Thing Baijan Sanamacha)	2-Oct-1978	53kg	Final		8	DSQ		Body Wt 53 kg			
Men	1984	Shooting	Sandhu, Harisimransingh	4-Jan-1950	skeet			64	166					
Women	1972	Athletics	Sandhu, Kamaljit	20-Aug-1948	400m	heat		8	57.74					
Men	2004	Shooting	Sandhu, Manavjit Singh	3-Nov-1976	Trap	Qualifica-tion		19	116					
Men	1984	Weightlifting	Santra, Kamalakanta	1-Jul-1960	bantam			15	95+130=225					
Women	1980	Hockey	Sareen, Geeta	16-Feb-1953				res.						
Men	1948	Cycling	Sarkari, P.		4000m pursuit/ team	final		1rd.						
Men	1956	Wrestling	Sarup, Ram		F/feather	1rd			lost to/Mewis, J. (Bel)					
Men	1956	Wrestling	Sarup, Ram		F/feather	2rd			bye					

Men/ Women	*Year*	*Event*	*Name*	*DoB*	*Event*	*Stage*	*Race #*	*Rnk*	*Score-Result/Opponent/ Opposition*	*Misc*	*Misc*	*Misc*	*Medal*	*Other Sport*
Men	1956	Wrestling	Sarup, Ram		F/feather	3rd			lost to/Salimoulline, L. (URS) 3:0					
Men	1980	Wrestling	Satpal, Singh	1-Feb-1955	F/heavy	1rd			lost to/Strnisko, J. (Tch) 4:0 (4.28)					
Men	1980	Wrestling	Satpal, Singh	1-Feb-1955	F/heavy	2rd			lost to/Busse, T. (Pol) 4:0					
Men	1972	Wrestling	Satpalsingh, Sat Pal	1-Jul-1956	F/feather	1rd			defeated/Stolarski, Z. (Poi) 1:3					
Men	1972	Wrestling	Satpalsingh, Sat Pal	1-Jul-1956	F/feather	2rd			lost to/Akdag, V. (Tur) 4:0 (7.26)					
Men	1972	Wrestling	Satpalsingh, Sat Pal	1-Jul-1956	F/feather	3rd			lost to/Burge House, J. (Gua) 3:1					
Men	1952	Football	Sattar, Madar Abdus	y1925				1rd						
Men	1988	Wrestling	Satyawan	25-Nov-1964	F/light	1rd			lost to/Leipold, A. (Frg) 1:3					
Men	1988	Wrestling	Satyawan	25-Nov-1964	F/light	2rd			lost to/Amara, H. (Mgl) 1:3					
Men	2004	Archery	Sawaiyan, Majhi	23-Dec-1981	Indiv.	Ranking		22	657					
Men	2004	Archery	Sawaiyan, Majhi	23-Dec-1981	Indiv.	Round of 64			lost to/Wunderle, Vic (USA)	128-145				
Men	2004	Archery	Sawaiyan, Majhi	23-Dec-1981	Team	Ranking		10	1938					
Men	2004	Archery	Sawaiyan, Majhi	23-Dec-1981	Team	Round of 16			lost to/AUS	236-248				
Men	1960	Hockey	Sawant, Govind	28-Nov-1933				2 pl.	1 game				Silver	
Men	1964	Hockey	Sayeed, Ali	10-Jul-1942				1 pl.	1 game				Gold	

Men/ Women	*Year*	*Event*	*Name*	*DoB*	*Event*	*Stage*	*Race #*	*Rnk*	*Score-Result/Opponent/ Opposition*	*Misc*	*Misc*	*Misc*	*Medal*	*Other Sport*
Men	1948	Water polo	Seal, G.		2nd rnd				3 games					
Men	1928	Hockey	Seaman, Federic S.					1 pl.	5 games				Gold	
Men	1992	Hockey	Sebastian, Jude Felix	26-Jan-1965				7 pl.	6 games/1 goal					
Men	1984	Wrestling	Sehrawat, Gian Singh	2-Jul-1959	F/feather	1rd			lost to/Brown, C. (Aus) 1:3					
Men	1984	Wrestling	Sehrawat, Gian Singh	2-Jul-1959	F/feather	2rd			defeated/Dunbar, M. (Gbr) 3:1					
Men	1984	Wrestling	Sehrawat, Gian Singh	2-Jul-1959	F/feather	3rd			lost to/Lewis, R. (USA) 0:4 (1.53)					
Men	2000	Hockey	Selvaraj Thirumal Valavan	27-Nov-1970				7th	Group B 3rd(2W,1L,2D)					
Women	1996	Badminton	Sentoso, Yuliani		Singles	3rd Round			lost to/Yan Yao (CHN)/11-6 11-5					
Men	1972	Athletics	Sequeira, Edward	6-Feb-1942	5000m	heat		11	14m01.4					
Men	1952	Cycling	Sett, Tarit Kumar	y1931	4000m pursuit/ team	final		1rd.						
Men	1936	Hockey	Shabban, S. Shahab-ud-Din	8-Nov-1909				1 pl.	4 games				Gold	
Men	2004	Judo	Shah, Akram	27-Jul-1978	under 60kg	Round of 32			lost to/Tsagaanbaatar, Khashbaatar/MGL	Ippon 0:44				
Men	1948	Swimming	Shah, Kantilall	13-Oct-1929	100m backstroke	heat		7	1m19.9					
Men	1952	Swimming	Shah, Kantilall	13-Oct-1929	100m backstroke	heat		7	1m18.3					
Men	1952	Water polo	Shah, Kantilall	13-Oct-1929	Prelim.				1 game					

Men/ Women	*Year*	*Event*	*Name*	*DoB*	*Event*	*Stage*	*Race #*	*Rnk*	*Score-Result/Opponent/ Opposition*	*Misc*	*Misc*	*Misc*	*Medal*	*Other Sport*
Men	1952	Water polo	Shah, Kedar Nath	23-Mar-1923	Prelim.				2 games					
Men	1956	Gymnastics	Sham Lal	y1938	indiv.	final		62	77.1					
Men	2000	Athletics	Shankar, Jata	20-Jun-1972	4x400m	Round 1	2	4	03m08.38					
Men	1960	Hockey	Sharma, Jaman Lal	6-Feb-1934				2 pl.	6 games				Silver	
Women	1980	Hockey	Sharma, Nisha	1-Jun-1959				4 pl.	3 games/2 goals					
Women	2004	Archery	Sharma, Sumangala	30-Dec-1986	Indiv.	Ranking		20	638					
Women	2004	Archery	Sharma, Sumangala	30-Dec-1986	Indiv.	Round of 64			def./Chen Li Ju (TPE)	142-133				
Women	2004	Archery	Sharma, Sumangala	30-Dec-1986	Indiv.	Round of 32			lost to/Lewis, Kirstin Jean (RSA)	153-157				
Women	2004	Archery	Sharma, Sumangala	30-Dec-1986	Team	Ranking		5	1900					
Women	2004	Archery	Sharma, Sumangala	30-Dec-1986	Team	Round of 16			def./GBR	230-228				
Women	2004	Archery	Sharma, Sumangala	30-Dec-1986	Team	Quarter			lost to/FRA	227-228				
Men	1984	Hockey	Sharma, Vineet Kumar	6-Jan-1959				5 pl.	7 games/6 goals					
Men	1928	Hockey	Shaukat, Ali	06-10-1897				1 pl.	3 games				Gold	
Men	1956	Shooting	Shaw, Hari Charan	y1922	small bore rifle/3 pos.			38	1102					
Men	1936	Hockey	Sher, Ahmed Sher Khan	1-Nov-1912				1 pl.	1 game				Gold	
Men	1960	Wrestling	Shiam, Sunder	5-Jul-1930	F/feather	1rd			lost to/Mewis, J. (Bel) 4:0 (4.52)					

Men/ Women	Year	Event	Name	DoB	Event	Stage	Race #	Rnk	Score-Result/Opponent/ Opposition	Misc	Misc	Misc	Medal	Other Sport
Men	1960	Wrestling	Shiam, Sunder	5-Jul-1930	F/feather	2rd			defeated/not present at 'weight in'					
Men	1920	Wrestling	Shinde, D.Randhir		F/feather	3/4 place			lost to/Bernard, P.W. (Gbr) 0.19					
Men	1920	Wrestling	Shinde, D.Randhir		F/feather	quarter			defeated/Inman (Gbr)					
Men	1920	Wrestling	Shinde, D.Randhir		F/feather	semi			lost to/Gerson, S. (USA)					
Men	1920	Wrestling	Shinde, D.Randhir		F/feather			4 pl.						
Women	2004	Shooting	Shirur, Suma	10-May-1974	Air Rifle	Qualifica-tion		6	396/Q					
Women	2004	Shooting	Shirur, Suma	10-May-1974	Air Rifle	Final		8	101.2	Total= 497.2				
Women	2004	Athletics	Shobha, J J	14-Jan-1978	Heptathlon			11	6172/100H 13.53/1046 (), LJ 6.36/962 (4), SP 12.52/696 (20), 200m 23.41/1038 (4), HJ 1.67/ 818 (31)	JT 44.36/ 751 (16), 800m 2m17.28/ 861 (16)				
Mixed	2004	Sailing	Shroff, Malav	1-May-1974	Open Dou-ble-handed Dinghy-49er	Overall		19	253/292	17,(19),18, 15,18,19,1 8,19,19,19, 18,19,(20), 19,17,18	S	Patel, Sumeet		
Men	1952	Football	Shunmugham, Thulukhanam	19-Jun-1924				1rd						
Men	1952	Athletics	Sidhu, Mengha Singh	15-Aug-1922	high	qu			1.7					
Women	1996	Athletics	Sikdar, Jyotirmoyee	11-Dec-1969	4x400m	Round 1	1	6	3m35.91					

Men/ Women	*Year*	*Event*	*Name*	*DoB*	*Event*	*Stage*	*Race #*	*Rnk*	*Score-Result/Opponent/ Opposition*	*Misc*	*Misc*	*Misc*	*Medal*	*Other Sport*
Men	2004	Hockey	Sinclair, Adam	29-Feb-1984		Prelim.	B	7	Prelim. 4th (W1, L3, D1)/Classification 7-8 def. KOR 5-2		6 games, 1 goal			
Men	1956	Hockey	Singh Garchey, Hardyal	28-Nov-1928				1 pl.	2 games				Gold	
Men	1972	Athletics	Singh Gill, Mohinder	12-Apr-1947	long	qu			7.30					
Men	1972	Athletics	Singh Gill, Mohinder	12-Apr-1947	triple	qu			0.00					
Men	1956	Hockey	Singh Kullar, Gurdev	12-Aug-1933				1 pl.	5 games				Gold	
Men	1952	Hockey	Singh Kullar, Udham (Singh Kullar, Udhum)	4-Aug-1928				1 pl.	2 games				Gold	
Men	1956	Hockey	Singh Kullar, Udham (Singh Kullar, Udhum)	4-Aug-1928				1 pl.	5 games				Gold	
Men	1960	Hockey	Singh Kullar, Udham (Singh Kullar, Udhum)	4-Aug-1928				2 pl.	6 games/1 goal				Silver	
Men	1964	Hockey	Singh Kullar, Udham (Singh Kullar, Udhum)	4-Aug-1928				1 pl.	1 game				Gold	
Men	1952	Football	Singh Ravat, Chandan	26-Jul-1926				1rd						
Men	2000	Athletics	Singh, Ajay Raj	1-May-1978	4x100m	Round 1	1	7	40.23					
Men	1956	Athletics	Singh, Ajit	y1931	high	final		14	1.96					
Men	1956	Athletics	Singh, Ajit	y1931	high	qu			1.92					

Men/ Women	*Year*	*Event*	*Name*	*DoB*	*Event*	*Stage*	*Race #*	*Rnk*	*Score-Result/Opponent/ Opposition*	*Misc*	*Misc*	*Misc*	*Medal*	*Other Sport*
Men	1960	Athletics	Singh, Ajit	25-Nov-1936	20000 walk	final		ret.						
Men	1960	Athletics	Singh, Ajit	25-Nov-1936	50000 walk	final		15	4h47m28.4					
Men	1972	Hockey	Singh, Ajit	2-Mar-1952				dns						
Men	1976	Hockey	Singh, Ajit	2-Mar-1952				7 pl.	8 games/3 goals					
Men	1968	Hockey	Singh, Ajitpal	1-Apr-1947				3 pl.	8 games/1 goal				Bronze	
Men	1972	Hockey	Singh, Ajitpal	1-Apr-1947				3 pl.	9 games				Bronze	
Men	1976	Hockey	Singh, Ajitpal	1-Apr-1947				7 pl.	6 games/1 goal					
Men	1964	Athletics	Singh, Ajmer	1-Feb-1940	4x400m	heat		4	3m08.8					
Men	1984	Athletics	Singh, Ajmer	10-Sep-1958	discus			dns						
Men	1980	Hockey	Singh, Amarjit Rana	3-Feb-1960				1 pl.	3 games/2 goals				Gold	
Men	1976	Hockey	Singh, Ashok	1-Jun-1950				7 pl.	8 games/2 goals					
Men	2000	Athletics	Singh, Bahadur	7-May-1973	Shot Put	qu	2	13	18.7					
Men	2004	Athletics	Singh, Bahadur	7-May-1973	Shot Put	Qualif.	A	NM	NM		x	x x		
Men	1968	Hockey	Singh, Balbir	8-Aug-1942				3 pl.	1 game				Bronze	
Men	1968	Hockey	Singh, Balbir	5-Apr-1945				3 pl.	9 games/3 goals				Bronze	
Men	1968	Hockey	Singh, Balbir	21-Sep-1945				3 pl.	9 games/1 goal				Bronze	
Men	1948	Athletics	Singh, Baldev		decathlon	final		ret.	4205.00					
Men	1948	Athletics	Singh, Baldev		long	final		0						
Men	1976	Hockey	Singh, Baldev	23-Aug-1951				7 pl.	6 games					

Men/ Women	Year	Event	Name	DoB	Event	Stage	Race #	Rnk	Score-Result/Opponent/ Opposition	Misc	Misc	Misc	Medal	Other Sport
Men	1996	Hockey	Singh, Baljeet (Singh, Baljit Dhillon)	18-Jun-1973				8th Ov.	Group A 3rd (2W, 1L, 2D)					
Men	1996	Hockey	Singh, Baljeet (Singh, Baljit Dhillon)	18-Jun-1973				8th Ov.	Group A 3rd (2W, 1L, 2D)					
Men	2000	Hockey	Singh, Baljeet (Singh, Baljit Dhillon)	18-Jun-1973				7th	Group B 3rd (2W, 1L, 2D)		3			
Men	2000	Hockey	Singh, Baljeet (Singh, Baljit Dhillon)	18-Jun-1973				7th	Group B 3rd (2W, 1L,2D)		3			
Men	2004	Hockey	Singh, Baljeet (Singh, Baljit Dhillon)	18-Jun-1973		Prelim.	B	7	Prelim. 4th (W1, L3, D1)/Classification 7-8 def. KOR 5-2		7 games, 1 goal			
Men	1984	Athletics	Singh, Balwinder	5-Dec-1959	Shot Put			dns						
Men	1948	Wrestling	Singh, Banta		F/light	1rd			lost to/Hassan, M. (Egy)					
Men	1948	Wrestling	Singh, Banta		F/light	2rd			lost to/Atik, C. (Tur) fall 5.08					
Men	1968	Athletics	Singh, Bhim	y1946	high	qu			2.09					
Men	1980	Equestrian	Singh, Bishal	4-Jan-1943	3day			dns						
Men	1976	Hockey	Singh, Chand	25-Mar-1949				7 pl.	6 games/1 goal					
Men	1960	Hockey	Singh, Charanjit	22-Feb-1931				2 pl.	4 games				Silver	
Men	1964	Hockey	Singh, Charanjit	22-Feb-1931				1 pl.	9 games				Gold	
Men	1972	Athletics	Singh, Chauhan Vijay	21-Jan-1949	decathlon	final		17	7378.00					
Men	1948	Athletics	Singh, Chota		marathon	final		dnf						
Men	1924	Athletics	Singh, Dalip	y1898	4x400m	final		dns						

Men/ Women	*Year*	*Event*	*Name*	*DoB*	*Event*	*Stage*	*Race #*	*Rnk*	*Score-Result/Opponent/ Opposition*	*Misc*	*Misc*	*Misc*	*Medal*	*Other Sport*
Men	1924	Athletics	Singh, Dalip	y1898	long	qu			6.35					
Men	1928	Athletics	Singh, Dalip	y1898	long	qu			6.45					
Men	1964	Hockey	Singh, Darshan	15-Apr-1938				1 pl.	9 games/2 goals				Gold	
Men	1980	Equestrian	Singh, Darya	5-Sep-1947	3day/ indiv	final		el.	Bobby					
Men	1980	Equestrian	Singh, Darya	5-Sep-1947	3day/team	final		el.	Bobby					
Men	1980	Hockey	Singh, Deavinder	7-Dec-1952				1 pl.	6 games/8 goals				Gold	
Men	1964	Hockey	Singh, Dharam	19-Jan-1919				1 pl.	9 games				Gold	
Men	1952	Hockey	Singh, Dharam	19-Jan-1919				1 pl.	3 games				Gold	
Men	2000	Hockey	Singh, Gagan Ajit	9-Dec-1980				7th	Group B 3rd(2W,1L,2D)					
Men	2004	Hockey	Singh, Gagan Ajit	9-Dec-1980		Prelim.	B	7	Prelim. 4th (W1, L3, D1)/ Classification 7-8 def. KOR 5-2		7games, 7goals			
Men	1948	Hockey	Singh, Grahanandan Nandy	19-Feb-1926				1 pl.	2 games				Gold	
Men	1952	Hockey	Singh, Grahanandan Nandy	19-Feb-1926				1 pl.	1 game				Gold	
Men	1928	Athletics	Singh, Gurbachan		1500m	heat								
Men	1928	Athletics	Singh, Gurbachan		5000m	heat								
Men	2000	Wrestling	Singh, Gurbinder	6-Jun-1977	Greco-Rom. 58-63kg	Elim.	Group E / 4		def. /Djakrir, Yassine	ALG	3 to 0 OT 06m08 Passivity.			
Men	2000	Wrestling	Singh, Gurbinder	6-Jun-1977	Greco-Rom. 58-63kg	Elim.	Group E / 1		lost to/Maren, Juan Luis	CUB	8 to 0 Passivity.			

Men/ Women	*Year*	*Event*	*Name*	*DoB*	*Event*	*Stage*	*Race #*	*Rnk*	*Score-Result/Opponent/ Opposition*	*Misc*	*Misc*	*Misc*	*Medal*	*Other Sport*
Men	2000	Wrestling	Singh, Gurbinder	6-Jun-1977	Greco-Rom. 58-63kg	Elim.	Group E / 6		lost to/Manukyan, Mkkhitar	KAZ	8 to 3.			
Men	1964	Hockey	Singh, Gurbux	11-Feb-1935				1 pl.	9 games				Gold	
Men	1968	Hockey	Singh, Gurbux	11-Feb-1935				3 pl.	8 games				Bronze	
Men	1996	Boxing	Singh, Gurcharan (Singh, Gurcham)	10-Apr-1977	81	elim1/16			lost to/FLORES, Enrique/PUR		4			
Men	2000	Boxing	Singh, Gurcharan (Singh, Gurcham)	10-Apr-1977	75-81kg	1/16 Final Match 7		def.	Choi, Ki-Soo/KOR	11-9.				
Men	2000	Boxing	Singh, Gurcharan (Singh, Gurcham)	10-Apr-1977	75-81kg	1/8 Final Match 4		def.	Venter, Danie/RSA	Head-blow-4				
Men	2000	Boxing	Singh, Gurcharan (Singh, Gurcham)	10-Apr-1977	75-81kg	Quarter Match 2			lost to/Fedtchouk, Andri/UKR	12-12 (60-42).				
Men	1980	Hockey	Singh, Gurmail	10-Dec-1959				1 pl.	1 game				Gold	
Men	1984	Athletics	Singh, Gurtej	15-Oct-1959	javelin	qu			70.1					
Men	1972	Hockey	Singh, Harcharan	15-Jan-1950				3 pl.	3 games				Bronze	
Men	1976	Hockey	Singh, Harcharan	15-Jan-1950				7 pl.	7 games					
Men	1984	Hockey	Singh, Hardeep	5-Oct-1960				5 pl.	7 games/1 goal					
Men	1968	Hockey	Singh, Harmik	10-Jun-1947				3 pl.	8 games				Bronze	
Men	1972	Hockey	Singh, Harmik	10-Jun-1947				3 pl.	9 games/4 goals				Bronze	

Men/ Women	*Year*	*Event*	*Name*	*DoB*	*Event*	*Stage*	*Race #*	*Rnk*	*Score-Result/Opponent/ Opposition*	*Misc*	*Misc*	*Misc*	*Medal*	*Other Sport*
Men	2004	Hockey	Singh, Harpal	11-Oct-1983		Prelim.	B	7	Prelim. 4th (W1, L3, D1)/ Classification 7-8 def. KOR 5-2					
Men	1992	Hockey	Singh, Harpreet	25-Feb-1973				7 pl.	7 games					
Men	1996	Hockey	Singh, Harpreet	25-Feb-1973				8th Ov.	Group A 3rd (2W, 1L, 2D)					
Men	1968	Hockey	Singh, Inder	25-Feb-1944				3 pl.	8 games/1 goal				Bronze	
Men	2000	Rowing	Singh, Inderpal	2-Mar-1975	coxless pairs	Preliminary	1	5	7m09.94/Q	Kasam Khan				
Men	2000	Rowing	Singh, Inderpal	2-Mar-1975	coxless pairs	Repechage		6	7m16.10	Kasam Khan				
Men	1956	Athletics	Singh, Jagdev	y1931	400m/h	heat		5	55.2					
Men	1964	Hockey	Singh, Jagjit	1-Jan-1944				1 pl.	2 games				Gold	
Men	1968	Hockey	Singh, Jagjit	1-Jan-1944				3 pl.	1 game				Bronze	
Men	1972	Athletics	Singh, Jagraj		Shot Put	qu			17.15					
Men	1928	Hockey	Singh, Jaipal					1 pl.	2 games				Gold	
Men	1960	Hockey	Singh, Jaswant	10-Aug-1931				2 pl.	6 games/3 goals				Silver	
Men	1964	Wrestling	Singh, Jit	13-Jan-1937	F/middle	1rd			lost to/Kobelt, R. (Sui) 4:0 (0.41)					
Men	1964	Wrestling	Singh, Jit	13-Jan-1937	F/middle	2rd			lost to/Gardjev, P. (Bul) 4:0 (5.54)					
Men	1920	Wrestling	Singh, Jit, snr	13-01-1887	F/feather	1rd			lost to/Barathon (Fra) forfeit					
Men	1960	Hockey	Singh, Joginder	13-Aug-1940				2 pl.	6 games				Silver	

Men/ Women	*Year*	*Event*	*Name*	*DoB*	*Event*	*Stage*	*Race #*	*Rnk*	*Score-Result/Opponent/ Opposition*	*Misc*	*Misc*	*Misc*	*Medal*	*Other Sport*
Men	1964	Hockey	Singh, Joginder	13-Aug-1940				1 pl.	9 games				Gold	
Men	1984	Boxing	Singh, Kaur (Singh, Kaliq)	9-Aug-1950	heavy	1/16 round			defeated/Ajjoub, N. (Syr) 5:0					
Men	1984	Boxing	Singh, Kaur (Singh, Kaliq)	9-Aug-1950	heavy	1/8 round			lost to/Tillman, H. (USA) rsch. 1rd. (1.46)					
Men	1968	Athletics	Singh, Kirpal	y1947	10000m	final		dns						
Men	1988	Wrestling	Singh, Kuldeep	5-Feb-1966	F/fly	1rd			defeated/Nguyen Kim, Huong (Vie) 4:0 (5.35)					
Men	1988	Wrestling	Singh, Kuldeep	5-Feb-1966	F/fly	2rd			lost to/Biro, L. (Hun) 1:3					
Men	1988	Wrestling	Singh, Kuldeep	5-Feb-1966	F/fly	3rd			defeated/ Munoz Ech-everry, O. (Col) 3:1					
Men	1988	Wrestling	Singh, Kuldeep	5-Feb-1966	F/fly	4rd			lost to/Enebayar, T. (Mgl) 1:3					
Men	1972	Hockey	Singh, Kulwant	18-Dec-1948				3 pl.	7 games/ 4 goals				Bronze	
Men	1948	Hockey	Singh, Kunwar Digvijai	28-Feb-1922				1 pl.	5 games				Gold	
Men	1952	Hockey	Singh, Kunwar Digvijai	28-Feb-1922				1 pl.	3 games				Gold	
Men	1964	Athletics	Singh, Labh	y1941	triple	qu			14.95					
Men	1968	Athletics	Singh, Labh	y1941	triple			dns						
Men	1996	Boxing	Singh, Lakha		91	elim1/16			lost to/BARTNIK, Woiciech/POL		13			
Men	1980	Wrestling	Singh, Mahavir (Singh, Mahabir)	1-Sep-1964	F/light-fly	1rd			defeated/Rasovan, G. (Rom) 1:3					

Men/ Women	Year	Event	Name	DoB	Event	Stage	Race #	Rnk	Score-Result/Opponent/ Opposition	Misc	Misc	Misc	Medal	Other Sport
Men	1980	Wrestling	Singh, Mahavir (Singh, Mahabir)	1-Sep-1964	F/light-fly	2rd			defeated/Nguyen, Van Cong (Vie) 0:4 (3.56)					
Men	1980	Wrestling	Singh, Mahavir (Singh, Mahabir)	1-Sep-1964	F/light-fly	3rd			defeated/Pollio, C. (Ita) 0.5:3.5					
Men	1980	Wrestling	Singh, Mahavir (Singh, Mahabir)	1-Sep-1964	F/light-fly	4rd			lost to/Falandys, J. (Pol) 3.5:0.5					
Men	1980	Wrestling	Singh, Mahavir (Singh, Mahabir)	1-Sep-1964	F/light-fly	5rd			lost to/Kornilaev, S. (URS) 4:0					
Men	1980	Wrestling	Singh, Mahavir (Singh, Mahabir)	1-Sep-1964	F/light-fly			5 pl.						
Men	1984	Wrestling	Singh, Mahavir (Singh, Mahabir)	1-Sep-1964	F/fly	1rd			defeated/Olvera, B. (Mex) 4:0 (2.39)					
Men	1984	Wrestling	Singh, Mahavir (Singh, Mahabir)	1-Sep-1964	F/fly	2rd			defeated/Diaw, J. (Sen) 4:0 (5.09)					
Men	1984	Wrestling	Singh, Mahavir (Singh, Mahabir)	1-Sep-1964	F/fly	2rd			lost to/Takada, Y. (Jpn) 0:4 (2.51)					
Men	1984	Wrestling	Singh, Mahavir (Singh, Mahabir)	1-Sep-1964	F/fly	3rd			defeated/Gonzales, J. (USA) 4:0 (0.58)					
Men	1984	Wrestling	Singh, Mahavir (Singh, Mahabir)	1-Sep-1964	F/fly	3rd			lost to/Trstena, S. (Yug) 0:4 (1.13)					
Men	1984	Wrestling	Singh, Mahavir (Singh, Mahabir)	1-Sep-1964	F/fly	5/6 place			lost to/Seyhanli, A. (Tur) 0.5:3.5					
Men	1984	Wrestling	Singh, Mahavir (Singh, Mahabir)	1-Sep-1964	F/fly	group final-1rd			bye					
Men	1984	Wrestling	Singh, Mahavir (Singh, Mahabir)	1-Sep-1964	F/fly			6 pl.						
Men	1964	Athletics	Singh, Makhan	28-Oct-1938	4x100m	heat		5	40.60					

Men/ Women	Year	Event	Name	DoB	Event	Stage	Race #	Rnk	Score-Result/Opponent/ Opposition	Misc	Misc	Misc	Medal	Other Sport
Men	1964	Athletics	Singh, Makhan	28-Oct-1938	4x400m	heat		4	3m08.8					
Men	1964	Athletics	Singh, Makhan	28-Oct-1938	4x100m	semi		7	40.50					
Men	1984	Shooting	Singh, Mansher	1-Dec-1965	Trap			35	176					
Men	1996	Shooting	Singh, Mansher	1-Dec-1965	Trap	Prelims.		35	118					
Men	2004	Shooting	Singh, Mansher	1-Dec-1965	Trap	Qualification		21	115					
Men	1956	Athletics	Singh, Milkha	20-Nov-1935	200m	heat		4	22.30					
Men	1956	Athletics	Singh, Milkha	20-Nov-1935	400m	heat		4	48.9					
Men	1960	Athletics	Singh, Milkha	20-Nov-1935	400m	final		4	45.60					
Men	1960	Athletics	Singh, Milkha	20-Nov-1935	400m	heat		2	47.60					
Men	1960	Athletics	Singh, Milkha	20-Nov-1935	400m	Round 2		2	46.50					
Men	1960	Athletics	Singh, Milkha	20-Nov-1935	400m	semi		2	45.90					
Men	1964	Athletics	Singh, Milkha	20-Nov-1935	4x400m	heat		4	3m08.8					
Men	1976	Hockey	Singh, Mohinder	3-Apr-1953				7 pl.	8 games/1 goal					
Men	1956	Athletics	Singh, Mohinder N.	y1934	triple	final		15	15.20					
Men	1956	Athletics	Singh, Mohinder N.	y1934	triple	qu			14.93					
Men	1972	Hockey	Singh, Mukhbain	12-Dec-1944				3 pl.	9 games/9 goals				Bronze	

Men/ Women	Year	Event	Name	DoB	Event	Stage	Race #	Rnk	Score-Result/Opponent/ Opposition	Misc	Misc	Misc	Medal	Other Sport
Men	1968	Wrestling	Singh, Mukhtiar (Mukhtiar, Singh)	25-Oct-1943	F/welter	1rd			lost to/Shakhmuradov, Y. (URS) 4:0 (0.37)					
Men	1968	Wrestling	Singh, Mukhtiar (Mukhtiar, Singh)	25-Oct-1943	F/welter	2rd			lost to/Sasaki, T. (Jpn) 4:0 (10.10)					
Men	1972	Wrestling	Singh, Mukhtiar (Mukhtiar, Singh)	25-Oct-1943	F/welter	1rd			defeated/Akers, B. (Aus) 1:3					
Men	1972	Wrestling	Singh, Mukhtiar (Mukhtiar, Singh)	25-Oct-1943	F/welter	2rd			lost to/Robin, D. (Fra) 4:0 (2.24)					
Men	1972	Wrestling	Singh, Mukhtiar (Mukhtiar, Singh)	25-Oct-1943	F/welter	3rd			lost to/Ambrus, L. (Rom) 4:0 (2.27)					
Men	1992	Judo	Singh, Narinder	23-May-1968	extra light	El.			defeated/sayed, A. (Egy) 5.00					
Men	1992	Judo	Singh, Narinder	23-May-1968	extra light	ER			lost to					
Men	1996	Judo	Singh, Narinder	23-May-1968	60kg	1st Round		def.	IRL/Sullivan, Sean	Ippon				
Men	1996	Judo	Singh, Narinder	23-May-1968	60kg	2nd Round			lost to/BLR/Bagirov, Natik	Yuko				
Women	2000	Athletics	Singh, Neelam Jaswant	8-Jan-1971	Discus	qu	2	14	55.26					
Women	2004	Athletics	Singh, Neelam Jaswant	8-Jan-1971	Discus Throw	Qualif.	B	9	60.26		60.26	57.25 60.1		
Men	2000	Boxing	Singh, Ngangom Dingko	1-Jan-1979	51-54kg	1/8 Final Match 2			lost to/Danylchenko, Sergiy/UKR	14-5.				
Men	1984	Hockey	Singh, Nila Komol	1-Jun-1963				5 pl.	3 games					
Men	1924	Athletics	Singh, Pala	y1902	10000m	final		notclas-sified						
Men	1924	Athletics	Singh, Pala	y1902	4x400m	final		dns						

Men/ Women	*Year*	*Event*	*Name*	*DoB*	*Event*	*Stage*	*Race #*	*Rnk*	*Score-Result/Opponent/ Opposition*	*Misc*	*Misc*	*Misc*	*Medal*	*Other Sport*
Men	1924	Athletics	Singh, Pala	y1902	1500m	heat		6						
Men	1924	Athletics	Singh, Pala	y1902	5000m	heat		9						
Men	2000	Athletics	Singh, Paramjit	22-Aug-1971	400m	Round 1	6	6	46.64					
Men	2000	Athletics	Singh, Paramjit	22-Aug-1971	4x400m	Round 1	2	4	03m08.38					
Men	2004	Hockey	Singh, Prabhjot	14-Aug-1980		Prelim.	B	7	Prelim. 4th (W1, L3, D1)/ Classification 7-8 def. KOR 5-2		7 games, 1 goal			
Men	1960	Hockey	Singh, Prithipal (Singh, Prithi Pal)	28-Jan-1932				2 pl.	6 games/5 goals				Silver	
Men	1964	Hockey	Singh, Prithipal (Singh, Prithi Pal)	28-Jan-1932				1 pl.	9 games/10 goals				Gold	
Men	1968	Hockey	Singh, Prithipal (Singh, Prithi Pal)	28-Jan-1932				3 pl.	9 games/7 goals				Bronze	
Men	1996	Hockey	Singh, Rahul					8th Ov.	Group A 3rd (2W, 1L, 2D)					
Men	1964	Hockey	Singh, Rajinder	14-Jun-1935				dns						
Men	1980	Hockey	Singh, Rajinder	7-Jan-1958				1 pl.	1 game/1 goal				Gold	
Men	1984	Hockey	Singh, Rajinder	13-May-1959				5 pl.	6 games					
Men	1996	Hockey	Singh, Ramandeep					8th Ov.	Group A 3rd (2W, 1L, 2D)					
Men	1936	Athletics	Singh, Raunak Singh (Singh, Gill)	20-Feb-1910	10000m	final		ret.						
Men	1936	Athletics	Singh, Raunak Singh (Singh, Gill)	20-Feb-1910	5000m	heat		15						

Men/ Women	*Year*	*Event*	*Name*	*DoB*	*Event*	*Stage*	*Race #*	*Rnk*	*Score-Result/Opponent/ Opposition*	*Misc*	*Misc*	*Misc*	*Medal*	*Other Sport*
Men	1932	Hockey	Singh, Roop (Bais, Roopsingh)	8-Sep-1910				1 pl.	2 games				Gold	
Men	1936	Hockey	Singh, Roop (Bais, Roopsingh)	8-Sep-1910				1 pl.	5 games				Gold	
Men	2004	Hockey	Singh, Sandeep	27-Feb-1986		Prelim.	B	7	Prelim. 4th (W1, L3, D1)/Classification 7-8 def. KOR 5-2					
Men	1988	Archery	Singh, Sanjeeva	18-Nov-1963	ind			36	1233	final				
Men	1988	Archery	Singh, Sanjeeva	18-Nov-1963	team			20	3615	final				
Men	1996	Athletics	Singh, Shakti	14-May-1968	Discus	Round 1	B	13	56.58					
Men	2000	Athletics	Singh, Shakti	14-May-1968	Shot Put	qu	1	17	18.4					
Men	1976	Athletics	Singh, Shivnath	11-Jul-1946	marathon	final		11	2h16m22.0					
Men	1980	Athletics	Singh, Shivnath	11-Jul-1946	marathon	final			abandon					
Men	1976	Athletics	Singh, Shriram	18-Feb-1948	800m			dns						
Men	1956	Athletics	Singh, Sohan	y1932	800m	heat		4	1m52.4					
Men	2000	Boxing	Singh, Soubam Suresh	1-Mar-1980	48kg	1/16 Final Match 9			lost to/Kim, Ki-Suk/ KOR	9-5.				
Men	1972	Athletics	Singh, Sriram	21-Jun-1950	800m	heat		4	1m47.7					
Men	1976	Athletics	Singh, Sriram	21-Jun-1950	800m	final		7	1m45.77					
Men	1976	Athletics	Singh, Sriram	21-Jun-1950	800m	heat		2	1m45.86					
Men	1976	Athletics	Singh, Sriram	21-Jun-1950	800m	semi		4	1m46.42					
Men	1980	Athletics	Singh, Sriram	21-Jun-1950	800m	heat		4	1m49.8					

Men/ Women	*Year*	*Event*	*Name*	*DoB*	*Event*	*Stage*	*Race #*	*Rnk*	*Score-Result/Opponent/ Opposition*	*Misc*	*Misc*	*Misc*	*Medal*	*Other Sport*
Men	1980	Athletics	Singh, Sriram	21-Jun-1950	800m	semi		8	1m49.0					
Men	1992	Hockey	Singh, Sukhjit	13-Nov-1969				7 pl.	7 games					
Men	1980	Hockey	Singh, Surinder	22-Jun-1959				1 pl.	6 games/15 goals				Gold	
Men	1976	Hockey	Singh, Surjit	8-Oct-1951				7 pl.	8 games/4 goals					
Men	1968	Hockey	Singh, Tarsem	9-Dec-1946				3 pl.	8 games				Bronze	
Men	1948	Hockey	Singh, Trilochan					1 pl.	5 games				Gold	
Men	1964	Gymnastics	Singh, Trilok	13-Jun-1933	indiv.	final		124	79.6					
Men	1964	Gymnastics	Singh, Trilok	13-Jun-1933	team	final		18	428.35					
Men	1972	Sailing	Singh, Viajaishwar Pratap	1-Oct-1944	res.									
Men	1972	Hockey	Singh, Virinder (Singh, Varinder)	16-May-1947				3 pl.	1 game				Bronze	
Men	1976	Hockey	Singh, Virinder (Singh, Varinder)	16-May-1947				7 pl.	8 games					
Men	1960	Athletics	Singh, Virsa	16-Apr-1933	long	qu			6.7					
Men	1960	Athletics	Singh, Zora	15-Jun-1929	20000 walk	final		20	1h43m19.8					
Men	1960	Athletics	Singh, Zora	15-Jun-1929	50000 walk	final		8	4h37m44.6					
Men	1964	Diving	Singh,Sohan	15-Sep-1936	10m Platform	final		30	74.18					
Men	1964	Cycling	Singh,Suchha	21-Jul-1933	sprint	final result		1rd.						
Men	1948	Athletics	Singha, S.		50000 walk	final		dnf						

Men/ Women	*Year*	*Event*	*Name*	*DoB*	*Event*	*Stage*	*Race #*	*Rnk*	*Score-Result/Opponent/ Opposition*	*Misc*	*Misc*	*Misc*	*Medal*	*Other Sport*
Men	1948	Athletics	Singha, S.		10000 walk	heat		place un-known						
Men	1956	Athletics	Siri Chand Ram	y1934	110m/h	heat		6	15.20					
Men	1924	Tennis	Sleem, M.	y1892	mixed	1/8rd			lost to/Alvarez, E./ Flaquer, E. (Esp) w.o.	with Tata.M.				
Men	1924	Tennis	Sleem, M.	y1892	doubles	1rd			lost to/ Tegner, E./ Ulrich, E. (Den) 3:6, 4:6, 6:4 4:6	with Jacob.S.				
Men	1924	Tennis	Sleem, M.	y1892	singles	2rd			defeated/ Van der Feen, M. (Hol) 6:4, 6:1, 6:4					
Men	1924	Tennis	Sleem, M.	y1892	singles	3rd			lost to/ Richard, V. (USA) 6:8, 6:2, 4:6, 6:4, 2:6					
Men	1964	Cycling	Sokhi, Amar Singh	2-Jul-1935	4000m pursuit/ ind	final		1rd.						
Men	1964	Cycling	Sokhi, Amar Singh	2-Jul-1935	4000m pursuit/ team	final		1rd.	dsq					
Men	1964	Cycling	Sokhi, Amar Singh	2-Jul-1935	road/team	final		ret.						
Women	2004	Athletics	Soman, Chitra K	10-Sep-1983	4 x 400m	Final		7	3m28.48/27		52.55 (6) # 2:36.98 (7) #	Runner # 3		
Women	2004	Athletics	Soman, Chitra K	10-Sep-1983	4 x 400m	Round 1	Heat 2	3	3m26.92/Q	NR	52.51 (5) # 2:37.04 (4) #	Runner # 3		
Men	1948	Athletics	Somnath, S.		hammer	final		dnq						

Men/ Women	Year	Event	Name	DoB	Event	Stage	Race #	Rnk	Score-Result/Opponent/ Opposition	Misc	Misc	Misc	Medal	Other Sport
Women	1980	Hockey	Soni, Varsha	12-Mar-1957				4 pl.	5 games					
Women	1980	Hockey	Sonir, Prem Maya	14-Jul-1961				4 pl.	5 games/2 goals					
Men	2000	Hockey	Sonkhla, Deepak Thakur (Sonkhla, Deepak)	28-Dec-1980				7th	Group B 3rd(2W,1L,2D)					
Men	2004	Hockey	Sonkhla, Deepak Thakur (Sonkhla, Deepak)	28-Dec-1980		Prelim.	B	7	Prelim. 4th (W1, L3, D1)/ Classification 7-8 def. KOR 5-2		4games, 1goal			
Men	1952	Water polo	Sopher, David M.	1-Feb-1929	Prelim.				1game					
Men	1956	Hockey	Stephen, Charles	7-May-1930				1 pl.	4 games				Gold	
Men	2000	Table Tennis	Subramanyan, Raman (Subramanian, Raman)	23-Jun-1969	Doubles	1st round			lost to/Heister, Danny/Keen, Trinko (NED)/21-17, 21-14	Baboor Panduran-ga, Chetan				
Men	2000	Table Tennis	Subramanyan, Raman (Subramanian, Raman)	23-Jun-1969	Doubles	1st round			lost to/Heister, Danny/Keen, Trinko (NED)/21-17, 21-14	Baboor Panduran-ga, Chetan				
Men	2000	Table Tennis	Subramanyan, Raman (Subramanian, Raman)	23-Jun-1969	Doubles	1st round			lost to/Kazeem, Nosiru/Toriola, Segun (NGR)/26-24, 17-21, 21-18	Baboor Panduran-ga, Chetan				
Men	1988	Hockey	Sujit Kumar	26-Oct-1962				6 pl.	3 games					
Men	1932	Hockey	Sullivan, William Patrick					dns						
Men	2000	Shooting	Sultan, Anwer	19-Jul-1962	Trap	Qual.		27	108					

Men/ Women	*Year*	*Event*	*Name*	*DoB*	*Event*	*Stage*	*Race #*	*Rnk*	*Score-Result/Opponent/ Opposition*	*Misc*	*Misc*	*Misc*	*Medal*	*Other Sport*
Men	1980	Athletics	Sumariwalla, Adille (Sumarwalla, Adile)	6-Aug-1958	100m	heat		7	11.04					
Men	1984	Athletics	Sumariwalla, Adille (Sumarwalla, Adile)	6-Aug-1958	100m			dns						
Men	1948	Wrestling	Suryavanshi, S.B.		F/feather	1rd			lost to/Parsons, A. (GBR)					
Men	1948	Wrestling	Suryavanshi, S.B.		F/feather	2rd			lost to/Muller, A. (Sui) fall 6.32					
Women	1996	Badminton	Susanti, Susi (Susanti Haditono, Susy)	11-Feb-1971	Singles	3rd Round		def.	Katarzyna Krasowska (POL)/11-4 11-0					
Men	2004	Wrestling	Sushil Kumar, NA (Sushil Kumar)	26-May-1983	60kg Freestyle	Prelim.	Pool 3	3	9/Classif.: 0+3	Tech: 0+9				
Men	1932	Athletics	Sutton, Mervyn		100m	heat		4						
Men	1932	Athletics	Sutton, Mervyn		110m/h	heat		3						
Men	1932	Athletics	Sutton, Mervyn		4x100m	heat		5						
Men	1932	Athletics	Sutton, Mervyn		110m/h	semi		4						
Men	1936	Athletics	Swami, C.S. Arul Swami	18-Dec-1913	marathon	final		37	3h10m44.0					
Men	1960	Football	Swamidas, Simon Sunder Raj	9-Nov-1937				ER	3 games					
Men	1964	Boxing	Swamy, Denis		feather	dns								
Men	1984	Hockey	Syed, Jalaludin	10-Jan-1958				5 pl.	2 games					
Men	1932	Hockey	Syed, Mohd Jafar	y1911				1 pl.	2 games				Gold	
Men	1936	Hockey	Syed, Mohd Jafar	y1911				1 pl.	5 games				Gold	
Men	1980	Hockey	Sylvanus, Dung Dung	27-Jan-1949				1 pl.	5 games				Gold	
Women	2004	Swimming	Tandon, Shikha	20-Jan-1985	50f	Heat	6	6	27.08	0.73				

Men/ Women	Year	Event	Name	DoB	Event	Stage	Race #	Rnk	Score-Result/Opponent/ Opposition	Misc	Misc	Misc	Medal	Other Sport
Women	2004	Swimming	Tandon, Shikha	20-Jan-1985	100f	Heat	2	7	59.7	(7) 28.31 2.32				
Men	1932	Hockey	Tapsell, Carlyle Carrel (Tapsell, Carrol)	24-Jul-1909				1 pl.	2 games				Gold	
Men	1936	Hockey	Tapsell, Carlyle Carrel (Tapsell, Carrol)	24-Jul-1909				1 pl.	4 games				Gold	
Men	1984	Sailing	Tarapore, Farokh	3-Aug-1960	470			17	129/(15-20-12-18-11-dnf-17)					
Men	1988	Sailing	Tarapore, Farokh	3-Aug-1960	470			17	170.7/(19-20-19-6-ret.-20-15)					
Men	1992	Sailing	Tarapore, Farokh	3-Aug-1960	470			23	147/(failed start-18-13-13-21-22-24)					
Men	1980	Basketball	Tarlok, Singh Sandhu	1-Jan-1955				12 pl.	7 games, 12 pts.					
Women	1924	Tennis	Tata, M.	y1879	mixed	1/8rd			lost to/Alvarez, E./ Flaquer, E. (Esp) w.o.	with Sleem, M.				
Men	2004	Archery	Team		Team	Ranking		10	1938					
Men	2004	Archery	Team		Team	Round of 16			lost to/AUS	236-248				
Women	2004	Archery	Team		Team	Ranking		5	1900					
Women	2004	Archery	Team		Team	Round of 16			def./GBR	230-228				
Women	2004	Archery	Team		Team	Quarter			lost to/FRA	227-228				
Men	1980	Basketball	team			Prelim. round			URS65:121					
Men	1980	Basketball	team			Prelim. round			Tch65:133					

Men/ Women	Year	Event	Name	DoB	Event	Stage	Race #	Rnk	Score-Result/Opponent/ Opposition	Misc	Misc	Misc	Medal	Other Sport
Men	1980	Basketball	team			Prelim. round			Bra64:137(4pl.)					
Men	1980	Basketball	team			semi round			Pol67:113					
Men	1980	Basketball	team			semi round			Sen59:81					
Men	1980	Basketball	team			semi round			Swe63:119					
Men	1980	Basketball	team			semi round			Aus75:93					
Men	1980	Basketball	team					12 pl.						
Men	1948	Football	team			2rd			Fra 1:2					
Men	1952	Football	team			1rd			Yug1:10					
Men	1956	Football	team			2rd			Aus 4:2					
Men	1956	Football	team			3/4place			Bul 0:3					
Men	1956	Football	team			3/4place			4pl.					
Men	1956	Football	team			semi			Yug 1:4					
Men	1960	Football	team			ER			Hun 1:2					
Men	1960	Football	team			ER			Fra 1:1					
Men	1960	Football	team			ER			Per 1:3					
Men	1960	Football	team			ER			4pl.					
Men	1928	Hockey	team			final		1 pl.					Gold	
Men	1928	Hockey	team			final			Hol3:0					
Men	1928	Hockey	team			PR		1 pl.						
Men	1928	Hockey	team			PR			Sui6:0					
Men	1928	Hockey	team			PR			Bel9:0					
Men	1928	Hockey	team			PR			Aut6:0					
Men	1928	Hockey	team			PR			Den5:0					
Men	1932	Hockey	team			RR		1 pl.						

Men/ Women	*Year*	*Event*	*Name*	*DoB*	*Event*	*Stage*	*Race #*	*Rnk*	*Score-Result/Opponent/ Opposition*	*Misc*	*Misc*	*Misc*	*Medal*	*Other Sport*
Men	1932	Hockey	team			RR			Jpn11:1					
Men	1932	Hockey	team			RR			USA24:1					
Men	1936	Hockey	team			final		1 pl.					Gold	
Men	1936	Hockey	team			final			Ger8:1					
Men	1936	Hockey	team			PR		1 pl.						
Men	1936	Hockey	team			PR			Hun4:0					
Men	1936	Hockey	team			PR			USA7:0					
Men	1936	Hockey	team			PR			Jpn9:0					
Men	1936	Hockey	team			semi			Fra10:0					
Men	1948	Hockey	team			final		1 pl.					Gold	
Men	1948	Hockey	team			final			GBR4:0					
Men	1948	Hockey	team			PR		1 pl.						
Men	1948	Hockey	team			PR			Aut8:0					
Men	1948	Hockey	team			PR			Arg9:1					
Men	1948	Hockey	team			PR			Esp2:0					
Men	1948	Hockey	team			semi			Hol2:1					
Men	1952	Hockey	team			final		1 pl.					Gold	
Men	1952	Hockey	team			final			Hol6:1					
Men	1952	Hockey	team			quarter			Aut4:0					
Men	1952	Hockey	team			semi			GBR3:1					
Men	1956	Hockey	team			final		1 pl.					Gold	
Men	1956	Hockey	team			final			Pak1:0					
Men	1956	Hockey	team			PR		1 pl.						
Men	1956	Hockey	team			PR			Afg14:0					
Men	1956	Hockey	team			PR			USA16:0					

Men/ Women	*Year*	*Event*	*Name*	*DoB*	*Event*	*Stage*	*Race #*	*Rnk*	*Score-Result/Opponent/ Opposition*	*Misc*	*Misc*	*Misc*	*Medal*	*Other Sport*
Men	1956	Hockey	team			PR			Sin6:0					
Men	1956	Hockey	team			semi			Ger1:0					
Men	1960	Hockey	team			Elim.		1 pl.						
Men	1960	Hockey	team			Elim.			Den10:0					
Men	1960	Hockey	team			Elim.			Hol4:1					
Men	1960	Hockey	team			Elim.			Nzl3:0					
Men	1960	Hockey	team			final		2 pl.					Silver	
Men	1960	Hockey	team			final			Pak0:1					
Men	1960	Hockey	team			quarter			Aus1:0					
Men	1960	Hockey	team			semi			Gbr1:0					
Men	1964	Hockey	team			final		1 pl.					Gold	
Men	1964	Hockey	team			final			Pak1:0					
Men	1964	Hockey	team			PR		1 pl.						
Men	1964	Hockey	team			PR			Bel2:0					
Men	1964	Hockey	team			PR			Ger1:1					
Men	1964	Hockey	team			PR			Esp1:1					
Men	1964	Hockey	team			PR			Hkg6:0					
Men	1964	Hockey	team			PR			Mal3:1					
Men	1964	Hockey	team			PR			Can3:0					
Men	1964	Hockey	team			PR			Ho12:1					
Men	1964	Hockey	team			semi			Aus3:1					
Men	1968	Hockey	team			Bronze		3 pl.					Bronze	
Men	1968	Hockey	team			Bronze			Ger2:1					
Men	1968	Hockey	team			PR		1 pl.						
Men	1968	Hockey	team			PR			Nzl1:2					

Men/ Women	*Year*	*Event*	*Name*	*DoB*	*Event*	*Stage*	*Race #*	*Rnk*	*Score-Result/Opponent/ Opposition*	*Misc*	*Misc*	*Misc*	*Medal*	*Other Sport*
Men	1968	Hockey	team			PR			Ger2:1					
Men	1968	Hockey	team			PR			Mex8:0					
Men	1968	Hockey	team			PR			Esp1:0					
Men	1968	Hockey	team			PR			Bel2:1					
Men	1968	Hockey	team			PR			Jpn5:0(forfeit)					
Men	1968	Hockey	team			PR			GDR1:0					
Men	1968	Hockey	team			semi			Aus1:2					
Men	1972	Hockey	team			Bronze		3 pl.					Bronze	
Men	1972	Hockey	team			Bronze			Hol2:1					
Men	1972	Hockey	team			PR		1 pl.						
Men	1972	Hockey	team			PR			Hol1:1					
Men	1972	Hockey	team			PR			Gbr5:0					
Men	1972	Hockey	team			PR			Aus3:1					
Men	1972	Hockey	team			PR			Pol2:2					
Men	1972	Hockey	team			PR			Ken3:2					
Men	1972	Hockey	team			PR			Mex8:0					
Men	1972	Hockey	team			PR			Nzl3:2					
Men	1972	Hockey	team			semi			Pak0:2					
Men	1976	Hockey	team			5/8place			Ger2:3					
Men	1976	Hockey	team			7/8place		7 pl.						
Men	1976	Hockey	team			7/8place			Mal2:0					
Men	1976	Hockey	team			PR		3 pl.						
Men	1976	Hockey	team			PR			re play-Aus1:1(4:5)					
Men	1976	Hockey	team			PR			Arg4:0					
Men	1976	Hockey	team			PR			Hol1:3					

Men/ Women	Year	Event	Name	DoB	Event	Stage	Race #	Rnk	Score-Result/Opponent/ Opposition	Misc	Misc	Misc	Medal	Other Sport
Men	1976	Hockey	team			PR			Aus1:6					
Men	1976	Hockey	team			PR			Can3:0					
Men	1976	Hockey	team			PR			Mal3:0					
Men	1980	Hockey	team			final		1 pl.					Gold	
Men	1980	Hockey	team			final			Esp4:3					
Men	1980	Hockey	team			PR			Tan18:0					
Men	1980	Hockey	team			PR			Pol2:2					
Men	1980	Hockey	team			PR			Esp2:2					
Men	1980	Hockey	team			PR			Cub13:0					
Men	1980	Hockey	team			PR			URS4:2					
Women	1980	Hockey	team			RR		4 pl.						
Women	1980	Hockey	team			RR			Aut2:0					
Women	1980	Hockey	team			RR			Pol4:0					
Women	1980	Hockey	team			RR			Tch1:2					
Women	1980	Hockey	team			RR			Zim1:1					
Women	1980	Hockey	team			RR			URS1:3					
Men	1984	Hockey	team			5/6place		5 pl.						
Men	1984	Hockey	team			5/6place			Hol5:2					
Men	1984	Hockey	team			5/8place			Nzl1:0					
Men	1984	Hockey	team			PR		3 pl.						
Men	1984	Hockey	team			PR			USA5:1					
Men	1984	Hockey	team			PR			Mal3:1					
Men	1984	Hockey	team			PR			Esp4:3					
Men	1984	Hockey	team			PR			Aus2:4					
Men	1984	Hockey	team			PR			FRG0:0					

Men/ Women	Year	Event	Name	DoB	Event	Stage	Race #	Rnk	Score-Result/Opponent/ Opposition	Misc	Misc	Misc	Medal	Other Sport
Men	1988	Hockey	team			5/6place		6 pl.						
Men	1988	Hockey	team			5/6place			Pak1:2					
Men	1988	Hockey	team			5/8place			Arg6:6(4:3)					
Men	1988	Hockey	team			PR		3 pl.						
Men	1988	Hockey	team			PR			URS0:1					
Men	1988	Hockey	team			PR			FRG1:1					
Men	1988	Hockey	team			PR			Kor3:1					
Men	1988	Hockey	team			PR			Can5:1					
Men	1988	Hockey	team			PR			Gbr0:3					
Men	1992	Hockey	team			5/8place			Esp0:2					
Men	1992	Hockey	team			7/8place		7 pl.						
Men	1992	Hockey	team			7/8place			Nzl3:2					
Men	1992	Hockey	team			PR		4 pl.						
Men	1992	Hockey	team			PR			Ger0:3					
Men	1992	Hockey	team			PR			Arg1:0					
Men	1992	Hockey	team			PR			Gbr1:3					
Men	1992	Hockey	team			PR			Aus0:1					
Men	1992	Hockey	team			PR			Egy2:1					
Men	1996	Hockey	Team			Group	A	3rd (2W, 1L, 2D)	lost to ARG 0-1					
Men	1996	Hockey	Team			Group	A	3rd (2W, 1L, 2D)	def. SUR 4-0					

Men/ Women	*Year*	*Event*	*Name*	*DoB*	*Event*	*Stage*	*Race #*	*Rnk*	*Score-Result/Opponent/ Opposition*	*Misc*	*Misc*	*Misc*	*Medal*	*Other Sport*
Men	1996	Hockey	Team			Group	A	3rd (2W, 1L, 2D)	drew PAK 0-0					
Men	1996	Hockey	Team			Group	A	3rd (2W, 1L, 2D)	def. ESP 3-1					
Men	1996	Hockey	Team			Group	A	3rd (2W, 1L, 2D)	drew GER 1-1					
Men	1996	Hockey	Team			Classifica-tion			def. KOR 3-3 (5-3 OT)					
Men	1996	Hockey	Team			7th-8th		8	lost to GBR 3-4					
Men	2000	Hockey	Team			Group	B	3rd (2W, 1L ,2D)						
Men	2000	Hockey	Team			Group	B		def. ARG 3-0					
Men	2000	Hockey	Team			Group	B		def. ESP 3-2					
Men	2000	Hockey	Team			7th-8th		7	def. ARG 3-1					
Men	2000	Hockey	Team			Group	B		drew AUS 2-2					
Men	2000	Hockey	Team			Group	B		lost to KOR 0-2					
Men	2000	Hockey	Team			Group	B		drew POL 1-1					
Men	2000	Hockey	Team			Classifica-tion			lost to GBR 1-2					
Men	2004	Hockey	Team			Prelim.			drew ARG 2-2/ (1-0, 2-2)					

Men/ Women	Year	Event	Name	DoB	Event	Stage	Race #	Rnk	Score-Result/Opponent/ Opposition	Misc	Misc	Misc	Medal	Other Sport
Men	2004	Hockey	Team			Prelim.			lost to NZL 1-2/(0-0, 1-2)					
Men	2004	Hockey	Team			Classification 7-8		7	def. KOR 5-2/(0-4, 2-5)					
Men	2004	Hockey	Team			Classification 5-8 2			lost to PAK 0-3/(0-0, 3-0)					
Men	2004	Hockey	Team			Prelim.			lost to AUS 3-4/(1-1, 4-3)					
Men	2004	Hockey	Team			Prelim.			def. RSA 4-2/(2-1, 2-4)					
Men	2004	Hockey	Team			Prelim.			lost to NED 1-3/(1-0, 3-1)					
Men	2004	Hockey	Team			Prelim.	B	4th (W1, L3, D1)						
Men	1952	Diving	Thakker, K.P.		3m Springboard	dns								
Women	1996	Judo	Thakur, Sunith		52kg	2nd Round			lost to/JPN/Sugawara, Noriko	Ippon				
Men	1956	Football	Thangaraj, Peter Ramaswamy	24-Dec-1935				4 pl.	1 game					
Men	1960	Football	Thangaraj, Peter Ramaswamy	24-Dec-1935				ER	3 games					
Men	1980	Boxing	Thapa, Birender Singh	10-Feb-1953	light-fly	1/16 round			lost to/Geilich, D. (GDR) 2:3					
Men	1988	Hockey	Thoiba Singh	1-Dec-1955				6 pl.	7 games/2 goals					
Men	1936	Wrestling	Thorat, Shankarrao Ramrao	12-Dec-1909	F/bantam	1rd			lost to/Gaudard, C. (Sui) 3:0 (6.43)					

Men/ Women	Year	Event	Name	DoB	Event	Stage	Race #	Rnk	Score-Result/Opponent/ Opposition	Misc	Misc	Misc	Medal	Other Sport
Men	1936	Wrestling	Thorat, Shankarrao Ramrao	12-Dec-1909	F/bantam	2rd			lost to/Flood, R. (USA) 3:0 (4.50)					
Men	1996	Hockey	Tirkey, Dilip (Tirkey, Dilip Kumar)	25-Nov-1977				8th Ov.	Group A 3rd (2W, 1L, 2D)					
Men	2000	Hockey	Tirkey, Dilip (Tirkey, Dilip Kumar)	25-Nov-1977				7th	Group B 3rd (2W, 1L, 2D)		3			
Men	2004	Hockey	Tirkey, Dilip(Tirkey, Dilip Kumar)	25-Nov-1977		Prelim.	B	7	Prelim. 4th (W1, L3, D1)/Classification 7-8 def. KOR 5-2		7 games, 1goal	C		
Men	2004	Hockey	Tirkey, Ignace	10-May-1981		Prelim.	B	7	Prelim. 4th (W1, L3, D1)/ Classification 7-8 def. KOR 5-2					
Men	1988	Swimming	Tokas, Khazansingh		200m butterfly	heat		5	2m03.95					
Men	1984	Hockey	Topno, Manohar	25-Jun-1958				5 pl.	6 games					
Women	1980	Hockey	Toscano, Margaret	9-Aug-1956				4 pl.	5 games					
Women	2000	Athletics	Tripathi, Vinita	15-Oct-1980	4x100m	Round 1	3	6	45.2					
Men	1972	Sailing	Uberoi, Satish	19-May-1939	res.									
Men	1960	Wrestling	Udey, Chand (Chand, Udey)	24-Jul-1937	F/welter	1rd			defeated/Feeney, J. (Irl) 1:3					
Men	1960	Wrestling	Udey, Chand (Chand, Udey)	24-Jul-1937	F/welter	2rd			lost to/Balavadze, N. (URS) 3:1					
Men	1960	Wrestling	Udey, Chand (Chand, Udey)	24-Jul-1937	F/welter	3rd			lost to/Ogan, I. (Tur) 4:0 (4.11)					
Men	1964	Wrestling	Udey, Chand (Chand, Udey)	24-Jul-1937	F/light	1rd			defeated/Savolainen, A. (Fin) 1:3					

Men/ Women	*Year*	*Event*	*Name*	*DoB*	*Event*	*Stage*	*Race #*	*Rnk*	*Score-Result/Opponent/ Opposition*	*Misc*	*Misc*	*Misc*	*Medal*	*Other Sport*
Men	1964	Wrestling	Udey, Chand (Chand, Udey)	24-Jul-1937	F/light	2rd			lost to/Dimov, E. (Bul) 4:0 (4.09)					
Men	1964	Wrestling	Udey, Chand (Chand, Udey)	24-Jul-1937	F/light	3rd			lost to/Beriashvili, Z. (URS) 3:1					
Men	1968	Wrestling	Udey, Chand (Chand, Udey)	24-Jul-1937	F/light	1rd			defeated/Aldama, M. (Gua) 0:4 (1.55)					
Men	1968	Wrestling	Udey, Chand (Chand, Udey)	24-Jul-1937	F/light	2rd			lost to/Rost, K. (Ger) 3:1					
Men	1968	Wrestling	Udey, Chand (Chand, Udey)	24-Jul-1937	F/light	3rd			defeated/Till, D. (Gbr) 0:4 (2.07)					
Men	1968	Wrestling	Udey, Chand (Chand, Udey)	24-Jul-1937	F/light	4rd			defeated/Lebequer, O. (Cub) 0:4 (6.49)					
Men	1968	Wrestling	Udey, Chand (Chand, Udey)	24-Jul-1937	F/light	5rd			lost to/Movahed, C. (trn) 3:1					
Men	1968	Wrestling	Udey, Chand (Chand, Udey)	24-Jul-1937	F/light			6 pl.						
Women	2000	Athletics	V, Jayalakshmi	5-Aug-1971	4x100m	Round 1	3	6	45.2					
Women	2000	Tennis	Vaidyanathan, Nirupama	NA	doubles	1st round			lost to/Dokic, Jelena/Stubbs, Rennae (AUS)/6-0,6-0	Malhotra, Manisha				
Women	1984	Athletics	Valsamma, M.D.	20-Oct-1960	4x400m	final		7	3m32.49					
Women	1984	Athletics	Valsamma, M.D.	20-Oct-1960	400m/h	heat		5	60.03					
Women	1984	Athletics	Valsamma, M.D.	20-Oct-1960	4x400m	heat		4	3m33.85					
Men	1952	Football	Vankatesh, Padamttom	y1926				1rd						

Men/ Women	*Year*	*Event*	*Name*	*DoB*	*Event*	*Stage*	*Race #*	*Rnk*	*Score-Result/Opponent/ Opposition*	*Misc*	*Misc*	*Misc*	*Medal*	*Other Sport*
Men	1948	Football	Varadaraj, K.					2rd						
Men	1996	Hockey	Varkey, Sabu					8th Ov.	Group A 3rd (2W, 1L, 2D)					
Men	1948	Hockey	Vaz, Maxie					1 pl.	4 games				Gold	
Men	1972	Hockey	Vece, Paes	30-Apr-1945				3pl					Bronze	
Women	**2000**	**Shooting**	**Vedpathak, Anjali Ramakanta**	5-Dec-1969	**10m Air Rifle**	**Qual.**		7	**394/Q**					
Women	**2000**	**Shooting**	**Vedpathak, Anjali Ramakanta**	5-Dec-1969	**10m Air Rifle**	**Final**		**8**	**99.1/8**					
Women	**2000**	**Shooting**	**Vedpathak, Anjali Ramakanta**	5-Dec-1969	**Carbine Standard, 3 position**	**Qual.**		**33**	**566**					
Men	1924	Athletics	Venkataramana-swamy, V.N.		4x400m	final		dns						
Men	1992	Boxing	Venkatesan, Devarajan	22-Jul-1973	bantam	1/16 round			lost to/Casamayor Jhonson, J. (Cub) 7:13					
Men	1972	Boxing	Venu, Muniswamy Hav	20-Apr-1946	light	1/16 round			defeated/Cole, N. (Gbr) rsc. 3rd. (0.51)					
Men	1972	Boxing	Venu, Muniswamy Hav	20-Apr-1946	light	1/8 round			lost to/Mbugua, S. (Ken) 0:5					
Men	1988	Wrestling	Verma, Subhash	15-Jul-1960	F/light-heavy	1rd			lost to/Toth, G. (Hun) 1;3					
Men	1988	Wrestling	Verma, Subhash	15-Jul-1960	F/light-heavy	2rd			defeated/Cox, C. (Can) 4:0 (2.41)					
Men	1988	Wrestling	Verma, Subhash	15-Jul-1960	F/light-heavy	3rd			lost to/Scherr, J. (USA) 1:3					

Men/ Women	*Year*	*Event*	*Name*	*DoB*	*Event*	*Stage*	*Race #*	*Rnk*	*Score-Result/Opponent/ Opposition*	*Misc*	*Misc*	*Misc*	*Medal*	*Other Sport*
Men	1992	Wrestling	Verma, Subhash	15-Jul-1960	F/heavy	1rd			defeated/Bourdoulis, P. (Gre) 3:0					
Men	1992	Wrestling	Verma, Subhash	15-Jul-1960	F/heavy	2rd			defeated/Aavik, A. (Est) 3:0					
Men	1992	Wrestling	Verma, Subhash	15-Jul-1960	F/heavy	3rd			defeated/Gholami, K. (Iri) 3:1					
Men	1992	Wrestling	Verma, Subhash	15-Jul-1960	F/heavy	4rd			lost to/Coleman, M. (USA) 1:3					
Men	1992	Wrestling	Verma, Subhash	15-Jul-1960	F/heavy	5/6 place			lost to/Radomski, A. (Pol) 0:3					
Men	1992	Wrestling	Verma, Subhash	15-Jul-1960	F/heavy	5rd			lost to/Kim, Tae (Kor) 1:3					
Men	1992	Wrestling	Verma, Subhash	15-Jul-1960	F/heavy			6 pl.						
Men	1932	Athletics	Vernieux, Ronald Alfred		100m	heat		4						
Men	1932	Athletics	Vernieux, Ronald Alfred		200m	heat		4						
Men	1932	Athletics	Vernieux, Ronald Alfred		4x100m	heat		5						
Men	1948	Athletics	Vickers, John		110m/h	heat		1	14.7					
Men	1948	Athletics	Vickers, John		110m/h	semi		4	14.7					
Men	1984	Shooting	Vij, Rajinderkumar	15-Jul-1939	rapid fire pistol			32	578					
Men	2004	Boxing	Vijender	29-Oct-1985	60-64kg	Round of 32			lost to/Karagollu, Mustafa/TUR	(25-20)				
Men	1988	Hockey	Vivek Singh	1-Aug-1967				6 pl.	7 games					
Men	1952	Boxing	Ward, Oscar Alfred	15-Oct-1927	light-heavy	1/16 round			lost to/Kistner, K. (Ger) ko. 2rd.					

Men/ Women	*Year*	*Event*	*Name*	*DoB*	*Event*	*Stage*	*Race #*	*Rnk*	*Score-Result/Opponent/ Opposition*	*Misc*	*Misc*	*Misc*	*Medal*	*Other Sport*
Men	1936	Weightlifting	Weik, Zaw	7-Mar-1911	middle			15	87.5+100+122.5=310					
Men	1936	Hockey	Wells, Franc					res.						
Men	1936	Athletics	Whiteside, Eric Stanley	25-Oct-1910	100m	heat		5						
Men	1936	Athletics	Whiteside, Eric Stanley	25-Oct-1910	200m	heat		4						
Women	**1992**	**Athletics**	**Wilson, Shiny**	**8-May-1965**	**800m**	**heat**		**4**	**2m01.90**					
Women	**1996**	**Athletics**	**Wilson, Shiny**	**8-May-1965**	**4x400m**	**Round 1**	**1**	**6**	**3m35.91**					
Men	2004	Hockey	Xalco, William	14-Jun-1984		Prelim.	B	7	Prelim. 4th (W1, L3, D1)/ Classification 7-8 def. KOR 5-2					
Men	1984	Boxing	Xavier, Mariaprakashm	23-Apr-1960	light	dns								
Men	1996	Swimming	Xavier, Sebastian	10-Feb-1970	50M Freestyle	Heat	4	6	24.15					
Men	1992	Boxing	Yadav, Dharmendra	29-Dec-1972	fly	1/16 round			lost to/Kovacs, I. (Hun) 5:21					
Men	1992	Wrestling	Yadav, Pappu	25-Feb-1974	GR/light-fly	1rd			defeated/Farago, J. (Hun) 4:0 (3.34)					
Men	1992	Wrestling	Yadav, Pappu	25-Feb-1974	GR/light-fly	2rd			defeated/Hassoun, M. (Syr) 3:1					
Men	1992	Wrestling	Yadav, Pappu	25-Feb-1974	GR/light-fly	3rd			defeated/Simkhah, R. (Iri) 1:3					
Men	1992	Wrestling	Yadav, Pappu	25-Feb-1974	GR/light-fly	4rd			lost to/Maenza, V. (Ita) 0:4 (2.47)					

Men/ Women	*Year*	*Event*	*Name*	*DoB*	*Event*	*Stage*	*Race #*	*Rnk*	*Score-Result/Opponent/ Opposition*	*Misc*	*Misc*	*Misc*	*Medal*	*Other Sport*
Men	1992	Wrestling	Yadav, Pappu	25-Feb-1974	GR/light-fly	7/8 place			defeated/Ronningen, L. (Nor) 0:0					
Men	1992	Wrestling	Yadav, Pappu	25-Feb-1974	GR/light-fly			8 pl.						
Men	1996	Wrestling	Yadav, Pappu	25-Feb-1974	Greco-Roman 52kg	1st round		elim.	0					
Men	1984	Athletics	Yadav, Suresh	13-Sep-1959	1500m			dns						
Men	1976	Athletics	Yohannan, Tc.	19-May-1947	long	qu			7.67					
Men	1928	Hockey	Yusuf, Sayed Mohomed	y1895				1 pl.	4 games				Gold	
Men	1956	Football	Zulfaikar, M.Z.					res.						
Women	1980	Athletics	Zutshi, Gita	20-Dec-1956	800m	heat		6	2m06.6					
Women	1984	Athletics	Zutshi, Gita	20-Dec-1956	3000m	heat		8	9m40.63					

Appendix 2: Indian Contingent for Beijing 2008

	Year	*Sport*	*Country*	*Name*	*DoB*	*Event*	*Medals*
ARCHERY							
Women	2008	Archery	IND	Banerjee, Dola	02.06.1980	Team	
Women	2008	Archery	IND	Vardhineni, Pranitha	17.11.1990	Team	
Women	2008	Archery	IND	Laishram, Bombayala Devi	22.02.1985	Team	
Men	2008	Archery	IND	Champia, Mangal Singh	09.11.1983	Individual	
ATHLETICS							
Women	2008	Athletics	IND	Bobby George, Anju	19.04.1977	Long Jump	
Women	2008	Athletics	IND	Poonia, Krishna	05.05.1982	Discus Throw	
Women	2008	Athletics	IND	Kaur, Harwant	05.07.1980	Discus Throw	
Women	2008	Athletics	IND	Sreedharan, Preeja	13.03.1982	10000m	
Women	2008	Athletics	IND	Kaur, Manjeet	04.04.1982	400m	
Women	2008	Athletics	IND	Soman, Chitra K.	10.07.1983	4x400 Relay	
Women	2008	Athletics	IND	Jose, Sini	25.05.1987	4x400 Relay	
Women	2008	Athletics	IND	Poovamma, Machettira Raju	05.05.1990	4x400 Relay	
Women	2008	Athletics	IND	Kaur, Mandeep	19.04.1988	4x400 Relay	
Women	2008	Athletics	IND	Geeta, Satti	05.07.1983	4x400 Relay	
Women	2008	Athletics	IND	Shobha, J.J.	14.01.1978	Heptathlon	
Women	2008	Athletics	IND	Roy, Susmita Singha	26.03.1984	Heptathlon	
Women	2008	Athletics	IND	Ganapathy, G. Pramila	08.03.1977	Heptathlon	
Men	2008	Athletics	IND	Gowda, Vikas	05.07.1983	Discus Throw	

	Year	Sport	Country	Name	DoB	Event	Medals
Men	2008	Athletics	IND	Maheswary, Renjith	30.01.1986	Triple jump	
Men	2008	Athletics	IND	Singh, Surendra	01.10.1978	10000m	
BADMINTON							
Men	2008	Badminton	IND	Sridhar, Anup	11.04.1983	Singles	
Women	2008	Badminton	IND	Nehwal, Sania	17.03.1990	Singles	
BOXING							
Men	2008	Boxing	IND	Kumar, Jitendra	18.07.1988	51 kg.	
Men	2008	Boxing	IND	Kumar, Anil	27.03.1981	54 kg.	
Men	2008	Boxing	IND	Singh, Vijender	29.10.1985	75 kg.	**BRONZE**
Men	2008	Boxing	IND	Lakra, Anthresh Lalit	22.10.1983	57 kg.	
Men	2008	Boxing	IND	Kumar, Dinesh	25.08.1988	81 kg.	
JUDO							
Women	2008	Judo	IND	Devi, Khumujam Tombi	01.01.1982	48 kg.	
Women	2008	Judo	IND	Divya	01.08.1984	78 kg.	
ROWING							
Men	2008	Rowing	IND	Takhar, Bajrang Lal	05.01.1981	Single (M1x)	
Men	2008	Rowing	IND	Khandwal, Devender Kumar	10.07.1986	Light Wt. Double cull (LM2X)	
Men	2008	Rowing	IND	Singh, Manjeet	10.10.1988	Light Wt. Double cull (LM2X)	
SHOOTING							
Men	2008	Shooting	IND	Rathore, Rajyavardhan Singh	29.01.1970	Clay Pigeon Double Trap	

	Year	*Sport*	*Country*	*Name*	*DoB*	*Event*	*Medals*
Men	2008	Shooting	IND	Sandhu, Manavjit Singh	03.11.1976	Clay Pigeon Trap	
Men	2008	Shooting	IND	Singh, Mansher	01.12.1965	Clay Pigeon Trap	
Men	2008	Shooting	IND	Narang, Gagan	06.05.1983	10m Air Rifle 50m Rifle 3p & 50m rifle prone	
Men	2008	Shooting	IND	Bindra, Abhinav	28.09.1982	10m Air Rifle	**GOLD**
Women	2008	Shooting	IND	Sidhu, Avneet Kaur	11.12.1981	Air Rifle 10m/ 50m Rifle 3p	
Men	2008	Shooting	IND	Rajput, Sanjeev	05.01.1981	50m Rifle 3p 50m Rifle prone	
Men	2008	Shooting	IND	Jung, Samaresh	19.05.1970	Air pistol 10m/ 50m pistol	
Women	2008	Shooting	IND	Bhagwat, Anjali	05.12.1969	50m rifle 3p/ 10m air rifle	
SWIMMING							
Men	2008	Swimming	IND	Poncha, Rehan	03.08.1986	200m Butterfly	
Men	2008	Swimming	IND	Khade, Virddawal	29.08.1991	50m 100m 200 m (FS)	
Men	2008	Swimming	IND	Poseria, Ankur	16.03.1987	100m Butterfly	
Men	2008	Swimming	IND	Sejwal, Sandeep	23.01.1989	100m 200m (BS)	
TABLE TENNIS							
Men	2008	T.T.	IND	Kamal, Achanta Sharath	12.07.1982	Singles	
Women	2008	T.T.	IND	Aggarwal, Neha	11.01.1990	Singles	

	Year	*Sport*	*Country*	*Name*	*DoB*	*Event*	*Medals*
TENNIS							
Men	2008	Tennis	IND	Paes, Leander	17.06.1973	Doubles	
Men	2008	Tennis	IND	Bhupati, Mahesh	07.06.1974	Doubles	
Women	2008	Tennis	IND	Mirza, Sania	15.11.1986	Singles, Doubles	
Women	2008	Tennis	IND	Rao, Sunitha	27.10.1985	Doubles	
WRESTLING							
Men	2008	Wrestling	IND	Kumar, Sushil	26.05.1983	66 kg. free style	**BRONZE**
Men	2008	Wrestling	IND	Dutt, Yogeshwar	02.11.1982	60 kg. free style	
Men	2008	Wrestling	IND	Tomar, Rajeev	31.12.1980	120 kg. free style	
YATCHING							
Men	2008	Yatching	IND	Johal, N.S.	15.07.1979	Yatching/ Heavy wt. Dinghy (Finn) Open events	